W9-BMY-560

OUR WORLD

A GLOBAL STUDIES TEXT

Andrew Peiser
Michael Serber

Dedicated to serving

AMSCO

our nation's youth

When ordering this book, please specify
either **R 618 S** or OUR WORLD: A GLOBAL STUDIES TEXT, Softbound

AMSCO SCHOOL PUBLICATIONS, INC.
315 Hudson Street / New York, N.Y. 10013

About the Authors

Dr. Andrew Peiser is department chair of social studies at Sheepshead Bay High School in New York City. He received a doctorate from New York University and has taught on both the high school and college levels. He is a coauthor of *U.S. History and Government*.

Michael Serber is department chair of social studies at Forest Hills High School in New York City. Prior to that, he was director of the social studies department at William Howard Taft High School, also in New York City. He is a coauthor of *U.S. History and Government*.

Andrew Peiser dedicates this book to his wife, Barbara, for her support and assistance; and to his children, Richard, Jacqueline, and Brett; and to his mother, Marianne, for their care and concern.

Michael Serber dedicates this book to his wife, Adele; and to his children, Richard, Ellen, and Jeff, for their patience, support, and understanding; and to his parents, Faye and Otto.

ISBN 0-87720-888-3

Copyright © 1995 by Amsco School Publications, Inc.
No part of this book may be reproduced in any form without written permission of the publisher.

Printed in the United States of America

1   2   3   4   5   6   7   8   9   10   00   99   98   97   96   95   94

PREFACE

You are one person in a billion. In fact, it is more accurate to say that you are one person in five and a half billion. That is roughly the current population of our world; and the number keeps rising. More than ever before in world history, every person's life affects and is affected by other people of the globe. What are the cultures, or ways of life, of people living on the plains of Africa, the rain forests of South America, the river valleys of South Asia, the mountainous islands of Japan, and other distant places?

You will find answers to such questions in this book, OUR WORLD: A GLOBAL STUDIES TEXT. It describes the cultures, geography, and history of major world regions: Africa, the Middle East, Latin America, South Asia, Southeast Asia, East Asia, Western Europe, and Russia and Eastern Europe. In addition, the text discusses the current issues and problems that confront each region in our fast-changing world.

We, the authors of this text, have taught global studies for many years. We know that a global studies course can seem overwhelming to students because it covers such a broad subject—the geography, history, and cultures of the entire world. To make this subject more manageable and meaningful, we have written a relatively brief text—one that you can easily read and understand. The following special features of the text were created to help you do well in a challenging and important course:

MAIN IDEAS: Some facts and ideas are more important than others. To help you focus on the most important ideas about a region, we have listed them for you at the beginning of each chapter. (See, for example, the "Main Ideas" for the chapter on Africa, pages 38–39.) To derive the most benefit from this feature, we suggest that you study the list of ideas *before* reading a chapter. Then, *after* reading the chapter, look at the Main Ideas a second time.

MAP FEATURE: THE REGION AT A GLANCE: In a global studies course, it is crucial to know: (1) what nations are included in a region; (2) where the major mountains, deserts, and rivers are located; and (3) how a region's geography has influenced its history. For each chapter, all three types of information are presented "at a glance" on a large map. Numbered captions corresponding to the circled numbers on the map explain the importance of a certain river valley, a mountain range, and some other geographic features. Notice, for example, how the map feature on Africa on pages 40–41 shows how the Sahara Desert and the Nile River have affected Africa's history.

In addition to The Region at a Glance feature, you will find in the text many other maps (as well as graphs, photographs, and political cartoons) that illustrate important aspects of a region's geography, history, and culture.

IN REVIEW: To help you review key terms, facts, and ideas, we have provided a set of questions at the end of every major section of a chapter. The last question challenges you to think critically about what you have read.

MULTIPLE-CHOICE QUESTIONS: To help you review a chapter's most important facts and ideas, each chapter concludes with at least 30 multiple-choice questions. The questions are arranged according to their difficulty. The first set of questions (called "Level 1") are slightly more challenging than the second set of questions ("Level 2").

ESSAY QUESTIONS: Essay questions test your ability to organize and write about the information that you have learned. The essay questions at the end of each chapter will give you practice in this important skill. "Level 1" essay questions are more challenging than the "Level 2" questions. To guide you in your efforts, see the special feature, "Tips on Answering an Essay Question," pages 35–37.

BOXED FEATURES: Reading an excerpt from a historical document can bring a distant time and place into sharper focus in your mind. Throughout this text, you will find a number of boxed features labeled "Documents." One such document, for example, is a speech by the South African leader, Nelson Mandela (pages 71–72). Another type of boxed feature focuses on the skills of interpreting information as presented in graphs and maps. Finally, some boxed features extend the chapter narrative by describing a topic in depth: for example, the British parliamentary system of government (page 344) and the organization of the United Nations (pages 383–384).

SPECIAL CHAPTER ON STUDYING FOR A FINAL EXAM: A global studies course includes a lot of information about almost every part of the world. How do you prepare for a final exam in such a course? A special chapter in the Appendix provides a plan of study that will enable you to review, for each region, the most important terms, facts, and ideas—the ones that are most likely to be emphasized on the exam.

KEY TERMS: Throughout the text, key terms such as *nationalism* and *cultural diffusion* are printed in italics and defined. A Glossary in the back of the book lists these terms in alphabetical order. If you have forgotten what an important term means, it is always a good idea to look it up in the Glossary.

As teachers, we know that students can become discouraged if presented with too much information on too many topics. That is why we have concentrated on creating a global studies text that describes each region of the world concisely, yet fully. We hope that it provides you with the knowledge you will need to better understand the cultures and nations that make up our world.

Andrew Peiser
Michael Serber

CONTENTS

FEATURES

MAPS

OUR
WORLD
A GLOBAL STUDIES TEXT

CHAPTER 1

How the World

Main Ideas

1. **CULTURE:** Social scientists use the term "culture" to refer to all the customs, practices, and beliefs of a group of people.

2. **TRADITIONAL SOCIETIES:** A traditional society is one that follows a way of life from an earlier period of its history.

3. **CULTURAL DIFFUSION:** As different societies have come in contact with one another through trade, travel, or migration, they have often adopted aspects of one another's cultures. This important cause of change is known as cultural diffusion.

4. **IMPACT OF MODERN TECHNOLOGIES:** Modern technologies, such as air travel and electronic communication, have increased both the speed and the extent of cultural diffusion.

5. **GEOGRAPHIC ISOLATION:** Certain geographic features, such as deserts, mountains, and oceans, have acted as barriers to human movement and cultural diffusion.

6. **REGIONS:** A region is an area that is tied together by one or more characteristics. (For example, the region may be

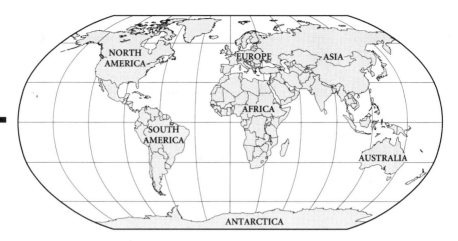

Changes

distinguished by a shared religion, geographic feature, or political history.)

7. **WORLD REGIONS:** Major world regions include Africa, the Middle East, Latin America, Canada and the United States, South Asia, Southeast Asia, East Asia, Western Europe, and Russia and Eastern Europe.

8. **INDUSTRIALIZATION:** In modern times, a major cause of change has been the economic process of industrialization (shifting of a nation's resources from agriculture to manufacturing).

9. **NATIONALISM:** Another major cause of change in modern times is nationalism (a people's desire to either expand their nation or break away from foreign rule to establish a new nation).

10. **INTERDEPENDENCE:** More than ever, nations today interact through trade and depend upon one another for essential products and services. This condition is known as global interdependence.

Our world is a complicated place, to say the least. And it is getting more complicated each day. In every part of the globe, human societies are changing at a faster pace than at any other time in history. High-speed communication and transportation systems put all societies in direct touch with one another. What happens in one part of the globe soon affects all other parts. We are living, in other words, in a global society. How can we, as Americans, understand the complicated forces that continue to change our world?

We should look to the past as a way to understand the present. Although the pace of change is now faster, the forces producing global change are much the same as they were in the past. One such force, geography, is as important to the development of modern Egypt as it had been to the ancient civilization that built the pyramids there. Other forces of change include the timeless efforts of people everywhere to achieve economic progress, political power, and social status. This chapter identifies a number of such major forces of change. Later chapters will show how these forces have shaped both the past and the present in major regions of the world.

Let us begin with geography. We will look briefly at the way different landforms, bodies of water, and climates affect human life.

I. How Geography Influences Culture

Geography, the study of the earth's physical features and their effect on humans, has two major branches. Those scientists who study physical geography are concerned chiefly with the earth's landforms, bodies of water, climates, and natural resources. Those who study human geography (or cultural geography) examine the impact of an area's land, water, climate, and resources on the people who live there.

A. MAJOR LANDFORMS

The seven continents of the world are made up of four basic landforms: mountains, deserts, plains, and plateaus.

Mountains Not all mountain ranges are alike. Some, like the Himalayas in South Asia, rise to heights of 29,000 feet. In contrast, the highest point in the Ural Mountains in Eastern Europe is some 6,000 feet above sea level.

Some regions are far more mountainous than others. Much of the land in Western Europe, for example, is mountainous. Africa, though several times larger than Europe in area, has fewer mountains.

Until recent times, mountains posed a major obstacle to the movement of people and ideas from one area to another. For example, there was relatively little contact between ancient civilizations in China and

India because the towering Himalayas stood between them. Also, throughout history mountains have served as a natural defense against attack and invasion. In our times, however, airplanes and satellite communications have reduced the significance of mountains as a barrier to transportation and communication.

Deserts   As dry places where little rain falls, deserts are found in most major regions of the world. They range in size from the enormous Sahara in North Africa to the much smaller Atacama Desert in South America. Like mountains, deserts have served as barriers to travel and communication. Some peoples, though, have survived within deserts by living as *nomads*. They move from place to place seeking water and vegetation for their grazing animals. Others live more permanently in deserts at *oases* (green areas within deserts that have sources of water).

Today, deserts can easily be crossed by flying over them. But deserts as dry and barren as the Sahara still prevent people from settling there in large numbers. As you might expect, the world's deserts have a very low *population density* (number of people per square mile).

Plains   As broad, flat stretches of land, plains are usually of two main types: interior plains and coastal plains. An *interior plain* usually has

OASIS IN A DESERT: In an oasis in the Sahara, there is just enough underground water for palm trees to grow. If deserts are among the least habitable areas on earth, what are the most habitable areas and why?

a river or a river system flowing through it. Because rivers sometimes flood the plains, these plains are good for agriculture. As the floods retreat, they leave the soil enriched with minerals.

All along a continent's coastline are lowland areas known as *coastal plains*. Such areas usually receive a lot of rain and are generally good for farming. Furthermore, bays and inlets on the coast make good harbors for ships. In such places, cities often develop as centers of trade. For good reason, both the coastal plains and the interior river valleys have always been the most densely populated areas in the world.

Among the major plains of the world are the: Great European Plain, which stretches across France, Germany, and Poland into Russia; Great Plains of the central United States; and broad river valleys watered by the Indus and Ganges rivers in South Asia.

The flatness of plains makes them good places for people to settle on or to travel across for trade. At the same time, however, this same feature makes it easier for invading armies to enter and take over an area. Thus, the people inhabiting plains are vulnerable to being conquered by newcomers coming from other places.

Plateaus Elevated plains are called *plateaus*. Because of their elevation, they have cooler temperatures than do lowlands. Often they are drier, too. Because there are fewer rivers running through plateaus, the soil there is less rich than in lowland plains. Less land is cultivated on plateaus than in the lowlands. Instead, the grazing of livestock is a more common agricultural activity on the plateaus. Major plateaus include the highlands of Kenya in Africa and the Deccan Plateau in India.

B. BODIES OF WATER

Major bodies of water include oceans, seas, lakes, and rivers.

Oceans The world's four oceans are the Pacific, the Atlantic, the Indian, and the Arctic. Both the Pacific and Atlantic oceans are much larger than any continent. At one time, because of their huge size, these oceans were barriers to the movement of people, ideas, and products. Since the late 1400s, however, improvements in shipbuilding and navigation have helped make the oceans highways for travel, trade, and communication.

Seas Large bodies of water that are (*1*) smaller than oceans and (*2*) partly or wholly enclosed by land are called seas. Because of their smaller size relative to oceans, seas were easier for people to travel across. Often, cities located near seas became important trading centers. Constantinople (now Istanbul, Turkey) became a major center of trade, for example, primarily because of its location on a *strait* (narrow water passage) between the Mediterranean and Black seas. Other major world seas include the Caribbean Sea, South China Sea, and Red Sea.

Lakes   In contrast to seas, lakes are smaller bodies of water and are always surrounded on all sides by land. Usually, only the largest lakes have played a major role in the history of a country. In North America, the Great Lakes are connected to each other and to the Atlantic Ocean by waterways. They therefore helped in the settlement of the interior of both the United States and Canada. In East Africa, people from several countries have long traveled across Lake Victoria and other large lakes to trade with one another.

Rivers   Most of the world's earliest civilizations developed along rivers. These bodies of water have provided fertile soil to the valleys surrounding them and have served as important transportation routes. As a result, river valleys have generally been heavily populated. Early river civilizations arose along the Yangtze and Yellow rivers in China, the Indus River in India, the Tigris and Euphrates rivers in the Middle East, and the Nile River in Africa.

COMPARING MAP PROJECTIONS

A map is a flat surface that is used to represent the exact shapes, sizes, and locations of land and water areas. Maps that show small areas of the globe can be drawn with some accuracy. Maps of the entire globe, however, are always distorted in some way. That is because the true shape of the earth is a globe, or sphere. Its roundness cannot be shown on a flat surface without distorting either the shape, the relative size, or the relative location of the continents and oceans.

When representing either the whole globe or *hemisphere* (half of the globe), mapmakers can choose from among various methods. Each method, known as a *map projection*, has both advantages and disadvantages. Consider the four maps shown on the following pages.

Map A is an example of a *Mercator projection*. This type of world map fairly accurately shows Africa, South America, Europe, and the southern sections of Asia and North America. Its chief disadvantage is that it greatly distorts land and water areas near the North and South poles. Notice how the map makes the island of Greenland appear to be as large as Africa. In fact, this island is less than one-twelfth Africa's size.

Map B, a *Mollweide projection*, shows the sizes of all continents (except Antarctica) in the correct proportion to one another. To

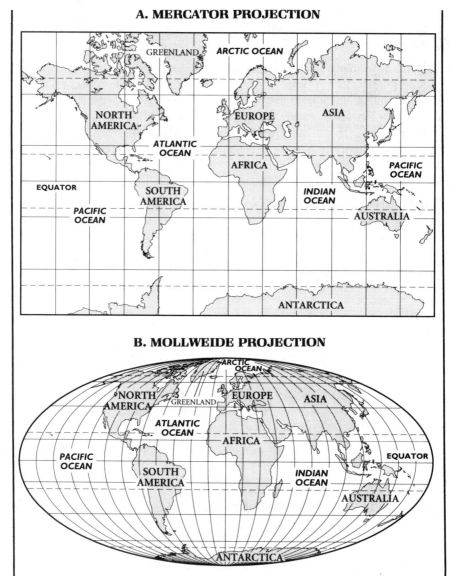

A. MERCATOR PROJECTION

B. MOLLWEIDE PROJECTION

achieve this accuracy, however, the map must distort the shapes of the continents and oceans. Compare, for example, the shape of South America in Map B with the shape of that continent in Map A. The shape of South America in Map A is more accurate.

Map C, a *broken projection*, is drawn as if the globe were the skin of a peeled orange that has been flattened along the lines of the cuts. Both the shapes and relative sizes of major land areas are fairly accurate as shown. The oceans and Antarctica, however, are pulled apart.

C. BROKEN PROJECTION

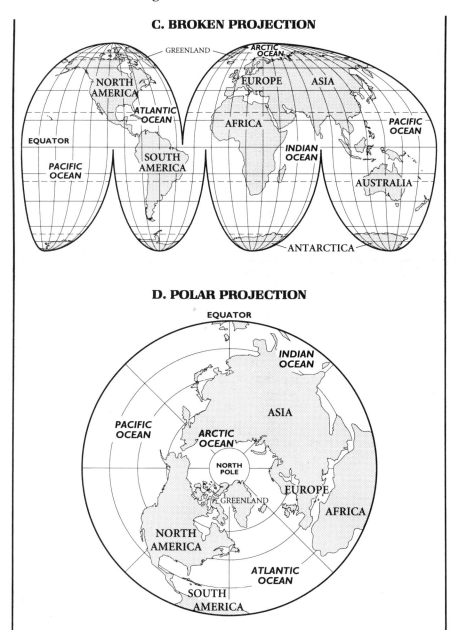

D. POLAR PROJECTION

Map D, a *polar projection*, shows only one hemisphere (in this case, the Northern Hemisphere). Instead of the polar area being distorted (as in other map projections), lands close to the North Pole have the correct size and shape. Airplane pilots traveling between North American cities and Asian cities often use this type of map to determine the shortest air routes.

Questions for Discussion

1. Why do you think that maps A, B, and C distort the continent of Antarctica more than the continent of Europe?
2. Which of the maps shown would be *most useful* to a ship captain traveling across the Atlantic Ocean between the United States and Africa? Why? Which map would be *least useful*? Why?
3. Why would airplane pilots flying from Asia to North America prefer to use a polar projection to guide them?

C. CLIMATE

Climate is the pattern of weather in a place over a long time. It helps determine where people settle and how they live. Three major climate zones in the world are the (1) tropical, (2) temperate, and (3) subarctic and polar zones.

Tropical zone   Located on and near the equator, the *tropical zone* is characterized by high temperatures, heavy rainfall, and rain forests. This zone includes the rain forests of Central America and equatorial Africa. Tropical rain forests are lightly populated because of their hot, humid climate and dense vegetation. Groups of people, however, have introduced farming to these areas using traditional methods. With the *slash-and-burn technique*, for example, they cut down trees and other vegetation and burn them to clear an area for farming.

Temperate zones   The *temperate zones* are located north and south of the tropical zone. Their climate is noted for moderate temperatures, moderate amounts of rainfall, and seasonal changes. These conditions have helped to produce fertile soil, thereby aiding crop production. As a result, most of the world's population lives in the two temperate zones.

Subarctic and polar zones   The *polar regions* near the North and South poles are characterized by extremely low temperatures. Their landforms and bodies of water are covered by snow and ice for much of the year. Because of these severe conditions, few people live in the polar regions. An example of a *subarctic zone* is the frozen *tundra* of Russia. It stretches across the northern part of that country, lacks trees, has permanently frozen subsoil, and supports only a small population.

Factors affecting climate   The climate is not the same everywhere within a climate zone. Climate can be moderated in areas that are near oceans and mountains.

Oceans generally moderate the temperatures of nearby lands. This process happens because bodies of water heat up and cool down slower than do nearby land areas. Thus, lands nearest oceans are usually cooler in summer and warmer in winter than areas further inland. Ocean currents can also bring to nearby land areas either warm or cold air, depending upon whether the currents themselves are warm or cold. The warm Japan Current, for example, brings warm air to the islands of Japan. In contrast, the cold Labrador Current brings cold air to Labrador and Newfoundland, in Canada.

Mountains affect climate by influencing temperature and rainfall. The higher up a mountain one goes, the lower the temperature. Thus, people living at high altitudes can have a cool climate even if they are near the equator. As clouds rise over mountains, they lose their moisture as rain or snow. But as the clouds start down the other side of mountains, they stop releasing moisture. Thus, one side of a mountain or mountain range tends to be wet, while the other side tends to be dry. Deserts are often found on the "dry" side of mountain ranges.

D. NATURAL RESOURCES

A major feature of the global environment is its variety of natural resources. Mineral and agricultural resources play especially important roles in the global economy.

Mineral resources   Valuable mineral resources are found in all world regions. The Middle East's plentiful supply of oil enriches that region and helps supply the energy needs of people in all regions. The large deposits of coal and iron found in Western Europe have helped that region develop its industrial strength. Other minerals that have

HOW MOUNTAINS AFFECT RAINFALL

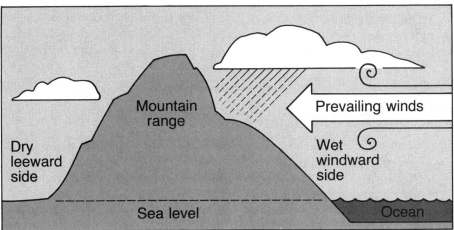

become important in world trade and industrialization include the gold and diamonds found in Africa and the tin and copper found in South America.

Agricultural resources Important world agricultural resources include the wheat grown in Europe, Asia, and North and South America; the rice grown in Asia; and the cotton grown in North America, Africa, and Asia. Each region also raises farm animals, such as cattle, sheep, pigs, and chickens. Like mineral resources, agricultural products are traded in world markets.

In Review

The following questions refer to Section I: How Geography Influences Culture.

1. *Key terms:* Define each of the following:

    nomad   plain   climate
    population density   plateau   tundra

2. Give the characteristics of each of the following climate zones: (*a*) tropical, (*b*) temperate, and (*c*) subarctic.

3. Give *three* examples of how the physical geography of an area either aids or hinders the movement of people.

4. *Critical thinking:* "In the modern world, geography no longer presents a barrier to travel and communication." Do you agree or disagree with this statement? Explain your answer.

II. Cultural Traditions and Cultural Diffusion

The term *culture* refers to a group of people's whole way of life. It includes that group's religion, values, language, customs, art, music, literature, technology, economic system, and political system. The scientific study of human cultures—both past and present—is called *anthropology*. Those who study anthropology are called *anthropologists*.

A. STUDYING CULTURES OF THE PAST

What evidence do scholars look at when studying various cultures? Books, newspapers, and other written records help them to draw conclusions about *historic cultures* (those with a written record). But how can scholars learn about people of the distant past who had not yet invented a system of writing? *Prehistoric cultures* are those cultures of the past whose people did not leave any written record. Fortunately, however, prehistoric peoples left behind *artifacts* (objects) of their culture that can be examined and interpreted. The social science that is most directly concerned with such evidence of past cultures is called *archeology*, a branch of anthropology.

Sometimes *archeologists*, those who study ancient artifacts, can directly view stone monuments or other structures that are still standing. More often, they must dig in the ground to find the remains of buildings, burial sites, and campsites. Each artifact that they find can become a clue to finding the way that a prehistoric people lived.

Archeologists can determine the approximate age of bones and other artifacts in a burial site by a process called *radiocarbon dating*. Their instruments measure the amount of radioactive carbon that is present in an object. Since radioactive carbon slowly decays at a constant rate, the amount of it that remains in an artifact tells archeologists approximately how old it is.

Another important clue to the prehistoric past is provided by *oral traditions*. In some societies that did not develop writing systems,

ARTIFACTS: The objects above were created by a prehistoric people in Europe more than 10,000 years ago. Can you identify the uses for any of these artifacts?

knowledge of the past has been transmitted by word of mouth. Thus, the stories, folktales, songs, and poems of a people are often of ancient origin and provide significant clues to the way their early ancestors lived. In many societies, traditional folktales and songs continue to have importance because they help maintain cultural identity.

Prehistoric societies From their study of artifacts and oral traditions, archeologists believe that they understand how prehistoric societies were organized. These societies consisted of small groups of people who migrated from one campsite to the next in search of food. The earliest human groups had an economy based on fishing, hunting of wild animals, and gathering of wild fruits, nuts, and grains. Their tools (including knives, needles, arrows, spears, and harpoons) were made of stone, wood, and bone. Tools of metal—copper, bronze, and iron—were the artifacts of more advanced societies of later ages.

Although the cultures of prehistoric peoples are important, this book will concentrate on describing later cultures—those that have engaged in agriculture, built cities, fashioned metal tools, and developed a written language.

B. ELEMENTS OF CULTURE

While all cultures share parts of the same global environment, they differ in how they relate to that environment.

Religion and values Many different religions have come about through the ages. The dominant religion of a people often influences their values. For example, a basic belief of Hinduism, the major religion of India, is *reincarnation*. This is the belief that one's soul does not die when the body dies. Instead, the soul reappears after death in another living form, such as in another person or in an animal. Because of this belief, Hinduism teaches respect for all forms of human and animal life. Consequently, many Hindus do not eat meat.

Language In today's world, some 3,000 languages are spoken. But only 19 of these languages, including English and Spanish, are considered "major" (spoken by at least 50 million people). Some languages originated very early in a culture's history. Some were imposed on a culture through military conquest. Spanish, for example, became the dominant language in Central and South America after Spain had conquered and colonized much of that region in the 1500s. Other languages were adopted from another culture in more peaceful circumstances, such as when a group migrates and settles near people of a different culture.

Social organization In all cultures of the past and present, the basic unit of social organization has been the family. The most common family unit of past societies was the *extended family*. In such a family, several generations—grandparents, parents, aunts, uncles, and children—lived together in the same household. Villages in traditional societies often consisted of family members who were descended from the same ancestral couple. Such a social unit is called a *clan*. Extended families and clans still exist. But today, especially in urban areas, nuclear and single-parent families are more common. In a *nuclear family*, two parents and their children live in the same household. In a single-parent family, just one parent and her or his children live together.

Traditionally, the teaching of a culture's values was chiefly the responsibility of the adult members of the family. Children tended to adopt the cultural values of their parents and to marry according to their elders' wishes. Today, families in modern cultures still teach values. But their influence on children is shared with schools, places of worship, governments, and the *media* (television, radio, recorded music, newspapers, books, and magazines).

Economic systems   An *economic system* is the way that a society chooses to produce and distribute its goods and services. The three major systems are generally described as traditional, market, and command. A fourth system, known as a mixed economy, reflects aspects of both the market and command economies.

A *traditional economy* is one in which old ways of producing goods are continued without change for generations. In traditional economies, children tend to follow the occupational roles of their parents. In parts of Africa, Latin America, and Asia, for example, people in villages still plant and harvest food on their own land.

A *market economy* is one in which many businesses compete to sell their goods and services to potential buyers. Consumers are free to decide which of the competing goods and services offered for sale they will buy and which they will reject. Consumers thus have the last word in determining what goods and services will be produced. A leading example of a market economy is the one we have in the United States.

The United States and other countries with a market economy have *free enterprise*. That is, private businesses compete freely with one another in their quest for profits. Governments regulate this competition to protect consumers. Free enterprise is one of the basic principles of *capitalism*, another term for a market economy.

A *command economy* is one in which key economic decisions are made by the government, and all major industries are under government control. The leading example of such a system was the economy of the Soviet Union. When the Communist party governed this nation, all means of production were owned and operated by the Soviet government, including factories, farms, mines, railroads, and retail shops.

Another term for a command economy is *socialism*, an economic system in which the means of production (factories, farms) are

SHOPPING IN TOKYO: Japan is a leading example of a capitalist, or free enterprise, system. In such a system, how do both buyers and sellers determine what goods shall be produced?

publicly owned. A socialist government may make decisions on what to produce, whom to hire, and what prices and wages should be. An extreme form of socialism is *communism*, which combines the socialist economic system with a dictatorship. According to Communist theory, the dictatorship (and all other forms of government) will eventually disappear. In fact, however, no Communist society has ever achieved such a stage of development.

In some forms of socialism, certain industries may be owned privately while others are owned and operated by the government. Examples of such economies include India and Sweden. (The latter two nations have also been called *welfare states* because the government of each provides citizens with extensive social services, such as health care.)

Political systems   The way in which people are governed is called a *political system*. In the 16th century, for example, some monarchs in Europe and Asia governed with absolute power. They believed that all political power rested in their hands. They did not want to share this power with anyone else (such as with religious leaders or nobles). We call this type of political system an *absolute monarchy*. Saudi Arabia provides a present-day example of this political system, which is not very common today.

In the 18th century, certain European philosophers challenged the idea of absolute rule. They insisted that laws had to have the consent of elected representatives of the people. Another of their ideas was that governments must protect the basic rights, or liberties, of all people. These ideas became the basis for *democracy*, the system of government upon which the U.S. government is based. Today, democracy is popular in many regions of the world.

Still another form of political system is the dictatorship. In a *dictatorship*, the ruler (dictator, emperor) has total control over his or her nation's political system. All government officials take orders from the dictator. The dictatorship is similar to the absolute monarchy except for the fact that a dictator usually does not inherit power from a parent. Instead, the dictator usually comes to office by seizing power. Fidel Castro of Cuba provides an example of a modern-day dictator.

Some dictators (and some absolute monarchs) have ruled *totalitarian* governments. The word "totalitarian" comes from the word "total." Under a totalitarian government, the state aims for total control over all activities of the people—their religions, social organizations, art— even over what they read, write, and say. Such regimes demand total loyalty of their subjects. Nazi Germany under Adolf Hitler, the Soviet Union under Joseph Stalin, and China under Mao Zedong all had totalitarian governments.

C. CULTURAL DIFFUSION

Once again, we may ask why and how cultures change over time. Historic changes would probably occur more slowly, if at all, if it were not for one simple fact: People move about from one place to another. They travel; they trade; and they migrate. As they do so, they come into contact with cultures different from their own. Contact with ideas that are different tends to produce a strong reaction. It challenges traditional ways of doing things. People then must decide whether to accept or reject the unfamiliar religions, customs, and technologies that they encounter in a foreign culture. If they accept them, then *cultural diffusion* takes place. This is the process by which ideas and practices from one area spread to another.

History provides many examples of cultural diffusion. One is the spread of the religion Buddhism from India to other parts of Asia. Another example is the spread of Islam from the Arabian Peninsula throughout the rest of the Middle East and elsewhere.

Today, cultural diffusion is less dependent upon the movement of peoples. Now ideas and ways of doing things can easily travel via television, the mails, and computer networks and through the export of films and recorded music. Young people in Russia, for example, now dance to rock music that originated in the United States and Western Europe.

D. ETHNOCENTRISM

Contact between cultures can have a negative effect if, as often happens, one culture rejects another. Dislike, and even hatred, can develop, for example, as one people migrates into an area that has long been settled by another. Under such circumstances, it is common for a feeling of *ethnocentrism* to develop. This is the belief that one's own culture is superior to all other cultures. Throughout history, enthnocentrism has been a powerful force, one that underlies the outbreak of many wars.

History has provided many examples of the destructive effects of ethnic pride. In ancient times, both the Romans in Europe and the Chinese in Asia viewed foreigners as barbarians. Chinese rulers tried to limit the contact of their people with foreigners. In modern times, the German dictator Adolf Hitler argued that the Germans belonged to a superior race whose duty was to destroy "lesser races." Acting on this ethnocentric idea, Hitler first ordered the persecution of Jews, Gypsies, Slavs, and other groups. Then during World War II (1939–1945), he launched a campaign to round up and kill all Jews and many others whom he considered to be of "inferior races."

ETHNOCENTRISM: In the 1930s, Adolf Hitler (standing in the car) came to power in Germany by arousing Germans' feelings of racial or national pride. What examples of ethnocentrism do we find in the 1990s?

Today, ethnocentrism is still strong. In Eastern Europe in the 1990s, Serbs, Croatians, and Muslims fought bitterly over control of land in the tiny state of Bosnia. Serbs adopted a policy of *ethnic cleansing*, forcing thousands of Muslims to leave their homes and towns. (This subject is discussed further in Chapter 8.)

In Review

The following questions refer to Section II: Cultural Traditions and Cultural Diffusion.

1. *Key terms:* Define each of the following:

culture	archeologist	cultural diffusion
artifact	totalitarian	ethnocentrism

2. Give the characteristics of each of the following economic systems: (*a*) traditional economy, (*b*) market economy, and (*c*) command economy.

3. State how a democratic form of government differs from both (*a*) an absolute monarchy and (*b*) a totalitarian system.

4. *Critical thinking:* "In our times, cultural diffusion is occurring at a faster rate then ever before." Do you agree with this statement? What evidence could you give to either support or refute the statement?

III. Innovation and Leadership

Human societies need to cope successfully with a variety of problems. Here are some examples:

- An economic problem: How can a society assure its members of an adequate food supply?
- A military problem: How can a society defend itself from attack by a neighboring society?
- A social problem: How can a society prevent conflicts and quarrels among individuals from interfering with the general welfare and order of the group?

In response to these and other problems, human beings are often challenged to seek solutions. To solve the economic problem, an agricultural society may invent a better system for irrigating the land. To solve the military problem, a society may seek to invent a superior weapon. To solve the social problem, a society may develop a religion that stresses a strong moral code. If the idea for solving a problem succeeds, a society may well adopt it permanently as the new way of doing things. Thus, in response to a problem, significant change can come about.

A. TECHNOLOGICAL INNOVATION

Change in the way things are made is known as *technological innovation*. We use the term *technology* to refer to a culture's methods and tools for making things. *Innovation* is any newly invented process.

From earliest times to our own, technological innovation has been important to every culture's development. One such innovation of about 5,500 years ago significantly helped the Sumerian people in the Middle East create one of the world's first civilizations. As you will read in Chapter 3, the Sumerians lived in Mesopotamia (modern-day Iraq). They depended upon water from the Tigris and Euphrates rivers to grow crops on nearby land. But they had a problem: How could they keep their crops growing through the hot, dry summers? The Sumerians came up with the idea of digging long channels, or ditches, that led from the rivers to their fields. This technology is called *irrigation*. They also invented a plan for measuring the land, dividing it into sections, and carefully distributing the water to each section as needed. To make this plan work, the Sumerians had to change their society from one of small farming villages into a more complex society with an elaborate government. A complex society is one way to define *civilization*.

History is full of examples of technological innovations and their impact on societies. The invention of a system of writing in ancient China had a profound effect on Chinese art and literature. The invention of a printing press using movable type in Western Europe around 1450 would make the written word available to millions. In modern times, the invention of new methods of communication (telegraph, telephone, radio, television, and so on) has radically altered the cultures and economies of most societies.

For every innovation mentioned on the pages of this book, there have been thousands (perhaps millions) of others. Each has made a difference in the way people live.

B. INDIVIDUAL GENIUS AND LEADERSHIP

Political and religious leaders have also played a role in changing their societies. Every culture in the world can point to leaders whose courage and vision have shaped events. This book will describe the impact of some of these leaders. You will be learning about the religious teachings of Siddhartha Gautama (Buddha) in India; of Confucius in China; and of Moses, Jesus, and Mohammed in the Middle East. You will also read about the impact on their societies—for better or for worse—of such figures as Genghis Khan of Mongolia, Peter the Great of Russia, Queen Elizabeth I of England, Napoleon Bonaparte of France, Simón Bolívar of Colombia, Mohandas Gandhi of India, Mao Zedong of China, Nelson Mandela of South Africa, Corazon Aquino of the Philippines, and dozens of other leaders.

IV. The Dynamics of Change

At times in the history of the world, changes occur slowly. One ... two ... even three generations may pass without people's noticing any real changes in their culture's pattern of life. At other times, the pace of change speeds up. Cultures that once existed in relative isolation suddenly come into direct contact with others. At such times, the process of change throughout the world becomes *dynamic*. There is a constant and forceful interaction between one region and another. For example, the conquests of Alexander the Great in the 4th century B.C. spread knowledge of Greek culture over a vast area from Egypt all the way to northern India. During the Hellenistic Age that followed, art, religion, and science in the Middle East showed signs of Greek influence. At the same time, the Greeks adopted some aspects of Middle Eastern culture (the ancient religious cults of Egypt and Persia, for example). During this age of change, economic and cultural influences rippled outward, back and forth, and in all directions.

A. THE AGE OF EXPLORATION

Change has proceeded in an especially dynamic fashion ever since the late 1400s, when the Age of Exploration began. After Christopher Columbus's voyages across the Atlantic in the 1490s, Europeans explored and colonized parts of North and South America. They also expanded trade with Africa and Asia. As a result, for the first time in history, people in all these continents were in continuous contact with one another. The world's two largest oceans, the Atlantic and the Pacific, no longer prevented cultures in one part of the globe from influencing cultures in other parts.

In this text, you will often encounter the phrase "dynamics of change." It usually refers to the time since the late 1400s when change everywhere in the world has speeded up. Change accelerated in Europe partly because of the new wealth and nutritious foods added to that region by contact with the Americas. Change also accelerated in North and South America when European conquerors introduced their religions, languages, and technologies there. Civilizations in Africa, the Middle East, and Asia also have undergone change and stress since the late 1400s.

B. REVOLUTIONS OF MODERN TIMES

The increased pace of change has sometimes led to violent social and political upheavals. Such events, known as *revolutions*, have resulted in the overthrow of governments. One reason for revolutions has been that governments sometimes fail to meet the changing needs of society.

Revolutions for national independence   The first major revolution of modern times was the American Revolution. Beginning in 1776, the 13 colonies on the East Coast of North America fought for and won independence from Great Britain. The United States came into being as a new nation. The American Revolution—followed soon afterward by revolutions in France and Haiti—inspired revolutionary thinking throughout Latin America. People living in the Spanish colony of Mexico, for instance, felt pride in being Mexicans. They increasingly resented the rule of administrators sent from Spain. In 1825, their revolution led to Mexico's independence from Spain. Similar revolutions created other new nations throughout Latin America in the 19th century and in Asia and Africa in the 20th century.

In all of these revolutions, *nationalism* (loyalty to one's own country and/or cultural heritage) became a powerful force for change. You will be reading about nationalism and revolutions for independence in every chapter of this text. Every world region has been affected by them.

Social revolutions   Another type of violent change in modern times has been the *social revolution*. In such a revolution, one social group within a country gains power at the expense of another. In the French Revolution (1789–1799), a privileged class of nobles lost power to French people of the middle and lower classes. In the Bolshevik (Communist) Revolution of 1917 in Russia, again a wealthy and privileged class lost power. The victorious Russian revolutionaries then ruled in the name of industrial workers and peasants. (You will be reading more about these two revolutions and the worldwide impact of each in Chapters 7 and 8.)

The Industrial Revolution   One revolution of modern times—perhaps the most important of all—was economic in nature. Known as the *Industrial Revolution*, it involved sweeping changes in the way people produced goods. Instead of working with hand tools in home workshops, Europeans in the late 1700s began to mass-produce goods in factories using complex machinery. Eventually, this new system of factory production would spread to societies around the world.

V. Interdependence in Our Times

All the forces of geography and history—and all the dynamics of change of past eras—have created the world of the 1990s. One word seems to characterize today's world better than any other. That word is *interdependence*. It means simply that all societies and nations depend upon one another for their economic existence.

An interdependent world is not entirely new. Societies of the past

ERAS IN WORLD HISTORY

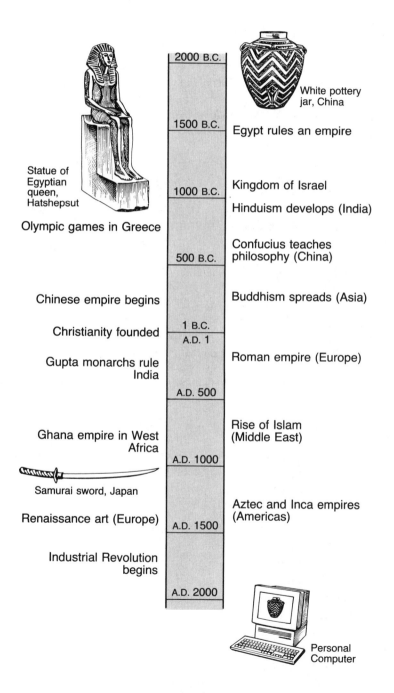

Statue of Egyptian queen, Hatshepsut

Olympic games in Greece

Chinese empire begins

Christianity founded

Gupta monarchs rule India

Ghana empire in West Africa

Samurai sword, Japan

Renaissance art (Europe)

Industrial Revolution begins

White pottery jar, China

Egypt rules an empire

Kingdom of Israel

Hinduism develops (India)

Confucius teaches philosophy (China)

Buddhism spreads (Asia)

Roman empire (Europe)

Rise of Islam (Middle East)

Aztec and Inca empires (Americas)

Personal Computer

2000 B.C.
1500 B.C.
1000 B.C.
500 B.C.
1 B.C.
A.D. 1
A.D. 500
A.D. 1000
A.D. 1500
A.D. 2000

also depended upon one another to some extent. The ancient Romans, for example, obtained jewelry from the Middle East and silks and spices from China. The West African empire of Mali traded its gold for salt from people in North Africa. Today because of improved transportation networks, world trade is faster and more extensive than in the past. And because of electronic communications, global banking and other financial transactions can take place instantly.

Interdependence creates problems as well as opportunities. Several such problems—global pollution, worldwide terrorism, and others—will be examined in the concluding chapter.

VI. Major Regions of the World

So far, this chapter has spoken of *regions* without defining what they are. Geographers define the term as any area of any size that is different in some way from neighboring areas. An example of a small region is a part of a city where most shops and office buildings are located. This downtown, or commercial, region is clearly different from the residential parts of town where most houses are located. Nations, too, may be divided into various kinds of regions. Using physical characteristics as a guide, you could divide a nation like ours into a mountainous region (the Rocky Mountain states), a plains region (the Great Plains states), and coastal regions (such as the Atlantic seaboard). Using cultural characteristics, you could divide the same nation into a Southern region, a New England region, a Middle Western region, and a Western region.

A. DEFINING THE WORLD'S REGIONS

When considering the world as a whole, many geographers find it convenient to divide it into major regions. Each is defined by at least one of several characteristics: political history, physical geography, and culture. The regions include:

- *Africa*, the only region that includes no more and no less than one continent
- *The Middle East*, a region that includes parts of three continents (Africa, Asia, and Europe)
- *Latin America*, a region that includes all of South America, Central America, and Mexico
- *South Asia*, the part of Asia that includes India and Pakistan
- *Southeast Asia*, the part of Asia that includes Vietnam, Indonesia, and the Philippines
- *East Asia*, the part of Asia that includes China, Japan, and Korea

- *Western Europe*, the part of Europe that includes such nations as Spain, France, Germany, Italy, and Great Britain
- *Eastern Europe and Russia*, a region that combines the eastern half of Europe with all the lands once included in the Soviet Union
- *Canada and the United States*, a region consisting of just two nations of North America. (Note, since the United States is treated in depth in U.S. history courses, this region receives less attention in this book than do the other regions.)

Most of the above regions are treated by themselves, with their own chapter. For each region (except the last one), the book describes its geography, early history, dynamics of change (modern period up to about World War II), and contemporary society (including foreign policy).

B. SUBREGIONS

Every large region, such as Africa, is made up of many smaller regions—or *subregions*. North Africa, for example, is a subregion. Being mostly arid, it is different physically from the rest of Africa. And so too is its culture different. Most of the people in North Africa are Muslims, while most of the people in the rest of Africa follow other religions.

Sometimes, a single subregion can be included in more than one region. To see how this can happen, compare the map of Africa on page 40 with the map of the Middle East on pages 88–89. Notice that North Africa is included as a part of each region. That is partly because North Africa has an Islamic heritage that links it with the Middle East. In terms of its physical location, however, North Africa is part of the African continent. In that sense, it belongs to the region of Africa.

The West   Just as regions can be broken down into subregions, they can also be combined to form superregions. In television news reports, for example, you may have heard a speaker refer to "the West." If the subject is international news, then the speaker does *not* mean the western subregion of the United States. Instead, "the West" refers to nations on three continents that share a common cultural tradition. Included in this superregion are Western Europe, the United States and Canada, and Latin America.

These three regions are all "Western" in several ways. First, Western Europe is obviously west of other European lands (Poland, Russia, and so on). Second, the Western Hemisphere (North and South America) is by definition the western half of the world. Third, the majority of people living in regions of the West have a common cultural heritage going back to ancient Greece and Rome. The majority of the people in the West are Christians. In a broad sense, their general outlook and cultural biases have been labeled "Western" to distinguish them from other cultures—those of Asia, Africa, and the Middle East.

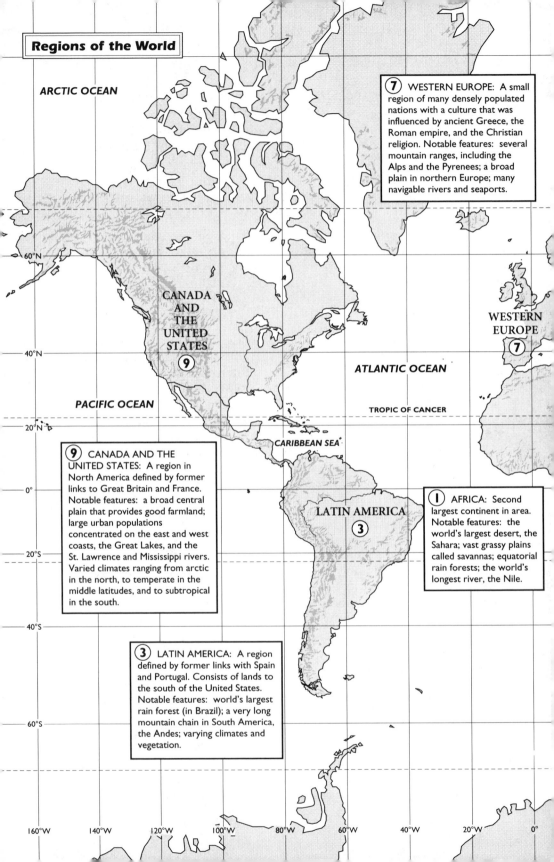

Regions of the World

ARCTIC OCEAN

⑦ WESTERN EUROPE: A small region of many densely populated nations with a culture that was influenced by ancient Greece, the Roman empire, and the Christian religion. Notable features: several mountain ranges, including the Alps and the Pyrenees; a broad plain in northern Europe; many navigable rivers and seaports.

60°N

CANADA
AND
THE
UNITED
STATES
⑨

WESTERN EUROPE ⑦

40°N

ATLANTIC OCEAN

PACIFIC OCEAN

TROPIC OF CANCER

20°N

CARIBBEAN SEA

⑨ CANADA AND THE UNITED STATES: A region in North America defined by former links to Great Britain and France. Notable features: a broad central plain that provides good farmland; large urban populations concentrated on the east and west coasts, the Great Lakes, and the St. Lawrence and Mississippi rivers. Varied climates ranging from arctic in the north, to temperate in the middle latitudes, and to subtropical in the south.

0°

LATIN AMERICA ③

① AFRICA: Second largest continent in area. Notable features: the world's largest desert, the Sahara; vast grassy plains called savannas; equatorial rain forests; the world's longest river, the Nile.

20°S

40°S

③ LATIN AMERICA: A region defined by former links with Spain and Portugal. Consists of lands to the south of the United States. Notable features: world's largest rain forest (in Brazil); a very long mountain chain in South America, the Andes; varying climates and vegetation.

60°S

160°W 140°W 120°W 100°W 80°W 60°W 40°W 20°W 0°

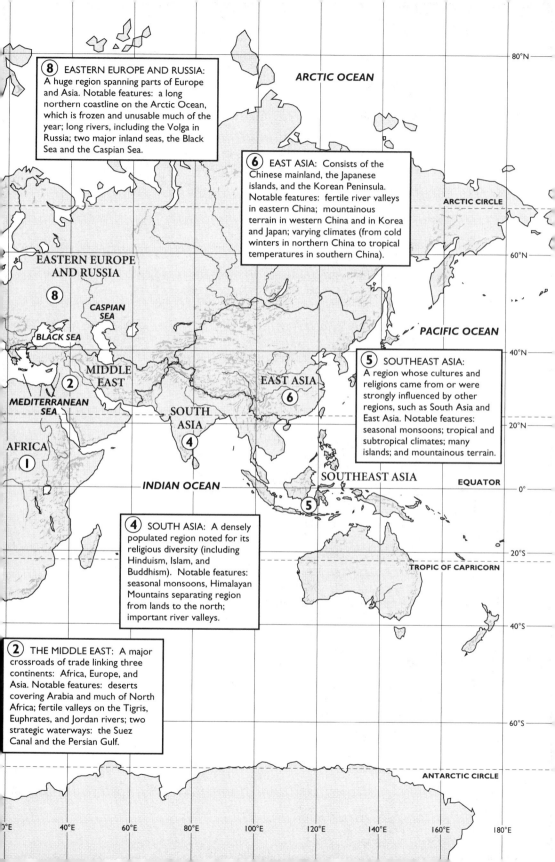

8 EASTERN EUROPE AND RUSSIA: A huge region spanning parts of Europe and Asia. Notable features: a long northern coastline on the Arctic Ocean, which is frozen and unusable much of the year; long rivers, including the Volga in Russia; two major inland seas, the Black Sea and the Caspian Sea.

6 EAST ASIA: Consists of the Chinese mainland, the Japanese islands, and the Korean Peninsula. Notable features: fertile river valleys in eastern China; mountainous terrain in western China and in Korea and Japan; varying climates (from cold winters in northern China to tropical temperatures in southern China).

5 SOUTHEAST ASIA: A region whose cultures and religions came from or were strongly influenced by other regions, such as South Asia and East Asia. Notable features: seasonal monsoons; tropical and subtropical climates; many islands; and mountainous terrain.

4 SOUTH ASIA: A densely populated region noted for its religious diversity (including Hinduism, Islam, and Buddhism). Notable features: seasonal monsoons, Himalayan Mountains separating region from lands to the north; important river valleys.

2 THE MIDDLE EAST: A major crossroads of trade linking three continents: Africa, Europe, and Asia. Notable features: deserts covering Arabia and much of North Africa; fertile valleys on the Tigris, Euphrates, and Jordan rivers; two strategic waterways: the Suez Canal and the Persian Gulf.

ARCTIC OCEAN

ARCTIC CIRCLE

EASTERN EUROPE AND RUSSIA

8

CASPIAN SEA

BLACK SEA

PACIFIC OCEAN

MIDDLE EAST

2

MEDITERRANEAN SEA

SOUTH ASIA

4

EAST ASIA

6

AFRICA

1

INDIAN OCEAN

EQUATOR

SOUTHEAST ASIA

5

TROPIC OF CAPRICORN

ANTARCTIC CIRCLE

80°N
60°N
40°N
20°N
0°
20°S
40°S
60°S

0°E   40°E   60°E   80°E   100°E   120°E   140°E   160°E   180°E

In Review

The following questions refer to the topics discussed on pages 19–27.

1. *Key terms:* Define or identify each of the following:

   technology   revolution   Industrial Revolution
   civilization   nationalism   interdependence

2. Give an example of how a technological innovation can bring about major changes in society.

3. Identify the characteristics of a   (a) political revolution and (b) social revolution.

4. List *eight* major regions of the world. For each region, give   (a) one characteristic of its culture or   (b) one characteristic of its physical geography.

5. *Critical thinking:* Which do you think would have the greater effect on the history of the 21st century: (a) improvements in computer technology or   (b) political revolutions in Asia and Africa? Explain your answer.

A STRATEGY FOR UNDERSTANDING GLOBAL STUDIES

As we've said, our world is a complicated place. How do you begin to understand that world, its geography, history, and current problems? For studying a subject as big as the whole world, you need a strategy, or plan. Here's a simple, three-part strategy for studying each of the remaining chapters of this book:

1. Before reading a chapter. Get an overview of it by looking at two of the chapter's special features. Each chapter begins by presenting a list of "Main Ideas." By studying this list, you will quickly gain an idea of how a region developed over time. The details that you encounter in the chapter (names of important people and places) will then fit into your overall impression of the region. Next, look at the large map of the region included at the beginning of each chapter. Preview, for example, the map of Africa on page 40. Notice the numbered captions on the next page. Each refers to a major geographic feature of the region. Each explains in a few words how a particular place or geographic feature has influenced the region's history. By studying this map, you will form a mental picture of the region's unique geography.

2. As you read the body of a chapter. Try to make connections in your mind between two things: (*a*) facts or ideas that are already familiar to you, and (*b*) facts or ideas that are unfamiliar, or new. In other words, you should always try to link "new knowledge" (what is new to you) with "old knowledge" (what you have learned before). For example, you are now familiar with the term "cultural diffusion." You will encounter this phrase in every chapter. Build upon your "old knowledge" by collecting new examples of cultural diffusion. Sometimes, a chapter will call attention to the term by stating: "This event is an example of cultural diffusion." Other times, the chapter leaves it to you—the active and alert reader—to notice when cultural diffusion is taking place. When you read about one culture borrowing from another, the thought will occur to you: "Aha! Cultural diffusion again."

Another way to build upon old knowledge is to observe what familiar words mean in a new context. For example, Muslims' religious beliefs are presented in most detail in the chapter on the Middle East. Chapters on other regions also refer to Muslims and the religion of Islam. As you come upon the terms "Muslim" and "Islam," quiz yourself. What do you remember about the religion? If your memory is fuzzy, go back and reread the paragraphs about the half-remembered terms.

3. After reading the chapter. Use the multiple-choice questions at the chapter's end to help you review and remember. When you answer a question correctly, pat yourself on the back for having learned something. When you answer a question incorrectly, take the opportunity to review the topic. In this way, you can plug another gap in your learning.

The essay questions at the end of each chapter are more challenging than the multiple-choice questions. To answer them, you must not only remember key concepts and facts but also organize that information in written form. Writing effectively is a crucial skill for success in the modern world. The essay questions give you practice in developing that skill.

What do you remember about the main ideas of this chapter? How well can you write about them in essay form? Test yourself by answering the questions that follow. Then, by applying the strategies just discussed to later chapters, you will steadily build your knowledge of the major regions of the world.

TEST YOURSELF

NOTE: Some of the multiple-choice and essay questions in each chapter are more challenging than others. Those listed under the heading "Level 1" are generally more difficult than those labeled "Level 2." If you are preparing to take a challenging comprehensive exam in global studies, you would do well to answer (a) all multiple-choice questions (Level 1 and Level 2), and (b) the Level 1 essay question or questions.

Multiple-Choice Questions

On a separate sheet of paper, write the number of the word or expression that, of those given, best completes each statement or answers each question.

Level 1

1. Mountains have generally served as   (1) home to nomadic groups   (2) barriers to the movement of people   (3) sources of abundant crops   (4) grazing land for cattle.

Base your answer to Question 2 on the graph below and on your knowledge of social studies.

WEATHER AND CLIMATE

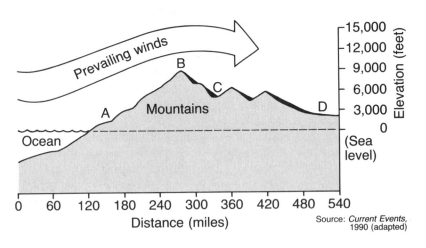

Source: *Current Events,*
1990 (adapted)

2. Which area, as illustrated in the drawing, would be the warmest and driest?   (1) A   (2) B   (3) C   (4) D.

3. Archeology, oral traditions, and radiocarbon dating are all used mainly to   (1) predict future developments in a nation's economy   (2) investigate human rights violations   (3) analyze current political issues   (4) discover and interpret a society's past.

4. Which was true of food-gathering societies in prehistoric times? (1) Society was highly industrialized. (2) The population tended to be small. (3) The concept of private property was important. (4) There was a system of mass production.

5. The geographic isolation of a people frequently reinforces (1) a traditional way of life (2) the development of scientific investigation (3) the need for higher education (4) a process of cultural diffusion.

6. Which is a characteristic of most traditional societies? (1) Cultural diffusion leads to a strong sense of nationalism. (2) Change is quickly accepted at all levels of society. (3) Families in rural areas tend to be smaller than those in urban areas. (4) Religious beliefs and long-established customs govern the way people live.

7. Which generalization is characteristic of traditional economic systems? (1) People move from city to city seeking new jobs. (2) Sons learn the same trades that their fathers had. (3) A high degree of social mobility exists. (4) All people have the same economic opportunities.

8. "Hindus and Muslims both live in India. While Hindus refuse to eat beef, Muslims do eat it." This statement reflects (1) cultural diffusion (2) ethnocentrism (3) cultural differences (4) economic exploitation.

9. Cultural diffusion occurs most rapidly in societies that (1) adhere to traditional social values (2) have extended families (3) come into frequent contact with other groups (4) have a strong oral history.

10. Modern technology has affected global society by (1) increasing the speed and extent of cultural diffusion (2) reducing the effects of social change (3) reinforcing traditional values and customs (4) preventing the spread of democratic principles to developing nations.

11. The spread of Islam throughout the African continent is an example of (1) national security (2) socialism (3) cultural diffusion (4) self-determination.

12. Which is the best evidence that culture may extend beyond many politically drawn boundaries? (1) The same language is spoken in many countries. (2) Neighboring countries often have different religions. (3) Independent nations have their own currency. (4) Countries near each other are often historic enemies.

13. Which generalization about democracy is most valid? (1) Democratic political systems require a highly industrialized society. (2) Absolute monarchies are among the most democratic forms of government. (3) Democratic governments prevent their citizens from traveling abroad. (4) Democratic governments protect the basic rights of their people.

14. "A group of planners makes all economic decisions. The group assigns natural, human, and capital resources to the production of those goods and services that it wants. The group decides how to

produce them and to whom to distribute them." This description best applies to a   (1) democracy   (2) capitalist country   (3) command economy   (4) monarchy.

15. Nationalism is best defined as   (1) the achievement of world peace and global understanding   (2) the desire to take over other societies by force   (3) a method of solving basic economic problems of the society   (4) the loyalty of a people to their values, traditions, and a geographic region.

16. Which quotation best reflects a feeling of nationalism?   (1) "An eye for an eye, and a tooth for a tooth."   (2) "A person's greatest social obligation is loyalty to the family."   (3) "For God, King, and Country."   (4) "Opposition to evil is as much a duty as is cooperation with good."

17. "Zionists Demand a Homeland"
"Croatians Call for Self-Determination of Croatia"
"German Unification Completed"

These headlines reflect the concept of   (1) nationalism   (2) militarism   (3) Marxism   (4) isolationism.

18. A study of revolutions would most likely lead to the conclusion that governments that are about to be overthrown   (1) are more concerned about human rights than are the governments that replace them   (2) refuse to modernize their armed forces with advanced technology   (3) attempt to bring about the separation of government from religion   (4) fail to meet the political and economic needs of their people.

19. A study of the causes of the American, French, and Russian revolutions indicates that revolutions usually occur because   (1) a society has become dependent on commerce and trade   (2) a society has a lower standard of living than the societies around it   (3) an existing government has been resistant to change   (4) the lower classes have strong leaders.

20. Russian grain purchases from the United States, sales of Japanese cars in Latin America, and Western European reliance on Middle Eastern oil are all examples of   (1) the creation of free-trade areas   (2) increased economic interdependence   (3) economically self-sufficient nations   (4) a worldwide spirit of imperialism.

Level 2

21. Early civilizations developed mainly in   (1) areas with abundant mineral resources   (2) valleys near rivers   (3) areas with climatic diversity   (4) mountainous areas.

22. The study of culture primarily involves   (1) observing the physical environment of people   (2) learning why various peoples live as they do   (3) understanding the technology of modern machinery   (4) analyzing the personalities of children of the same family.

23. In most traditional societies, the teaching of values was mainly the responsibility of the   (1) judicial system   (2) government   (3) educational system   (4) family.

24. In many societies, traditional folktales and songs continue to have importance mainly because they   (1) help to maintain cultural identity   (2) make use of contemporary rhythms and instruments   (3) discourage contacts with other societies   (4) illustrate the need to keep written records.

25. Which statement cites an example of cultural diffusion?   (1) Venezuela has large reserves of oil.   (2) Young people dance to rock music in Russia.   (3) Students in China learn calligraphy in school.   (4) The caste system is an important part of life in India.

26. Both the ancient Romans and the ancient Chinese viewed foreigners as barbarians. This is an example of   (1) cultural diffusion   (2) materialism   (3) imperialism   (4) ethnocentrism.

27. Which factor is necessary for the development of democratic institutions?   (1) strong military forces   (2) respect for individual rights   (3) a one-party system   (4) an agricultural economy.

28. Nationalism is most likely to develop in an area that has   (1) land suited to agriculture   (2) adequate industry to supply consumer demands   (3) a moderate climate with rivers for irrigation   (4) common customs, language, and history.

29. In France, a person drinks coffee imported from Brazil, works at a computer made in Japan, and drives a German automobile. This situation illustrates the concept of   (1) empathy   (2) scarcity   (3) interdependence   (4) world citizenship.

30. Latin America and Eastern Europe are examples of   (1) Spanish-speaking parts of the world   (2) continents   (3) subregions   (4) regions.

Essay Questions

Level 1

Geographic factors have influenced the development of many nations and regions of the world.

   Geographic Factors
   Climate
   Deserts
   Mountains
   Natural resources
   River systems

Select *three* of the geographic factors listed. For each factor, discuss how it has affected the development of a nation or region.

Level 2

People in various parts of the world have been influenced by many factors.

Factors
Cultural diffusion
Ethnocentrism
Nationalism
Technological innovation
Interdependence

A. Select *three* of the factors listed and give an example of each.

B. Base your answer to Part B on your answer to Part A. However, additional information may be included. Write an essay in which you discuss examples of the factors listed above. Begin your essay with this topic sentence:

> There are many factors that have influenced people in various parts of the world.

NOTE: Study the model answer to this question on page 36. Then create an answer of your own. Try to make it similar in form to the model. But be sure to use different examples in parts A and B than those that are provided in the model examples.

TIPS ON ANSWERING AN ESSAY QUESTION

The essay questions at the end of each chapter of this text—both Level 1 and Level 2—are complex. Each consists of: (1) a general statement, (2) a list of topics related to the statement, and (3) instructions for using the given topics in an essay. How do you make sure that the essay you write fully answers such a complex question? Here are some suggestions that should help you.

Writing a Level-1 essay The key to success in writing a complex essay is to *think and plan* before you write. First, make sure you understand what the question is asking. Take as an example the Level-1 essay question on page 33. The statement reads: "Geographic factors have influenced the development of many nations and regions of the world." You can easily turn this statement into a question: How have geographic factors influenced the development of nations and regions?

What geographic factors should you include in your essay? They are listed for you right under the statement: climate, deserts, etc. But notice that the third part of the question—the sentence of instruction—tells you to select only *three* of the five items listed. Put checkmarks next to the three geographic factors that you think you understand the best. (If you include more than the three required, you will not receive additional credit.)

What are you going to say about the items you select? On a scrap piece of paper, jot down relevant facts or ideas for each item. You might write, for example:

Influence of climate: The amount of rainfall determines where crops will grow. Southeast Asia is densely populated partly because of that region's hot and rainy climate.

Influence of deserts: The Sahara in Africa poses a barrier to settlement and travel. The area to the south of the desert (sub-Saharan Africa) therefore developed differently than the area to the north.

Influence of mountains: Ancient China was isolated from contact with ancient India by the Himalayas. Hence, these civilizations developed along different lines.

Now you are ready to write your essay. Referring to your notes, write three brief paragraphs. The first should comment on the influence of climate on Southeast Asia (first paragraph); the second, on the influence of deserts on Africa (second paragraph); and the third, on the influence of mountains on China and India. Start each paragraph with a topic sentence that shows you are answering the question. For example, "The hot and rainy climate of Southeast Asia demonstrates the role that climate plays in a region's development."

Writing a Level-2 essay   There is one main difference between writing a Level-1 essay and writing a Level-2 essay. A good Level-1 essay is a composition of fully developed paragraphs. You receive no credit for your notes ("Influence of climate," etc.), even though these will serve as a major help to you. A Level-2 essay, in contrast, consists of two parts. The first part asks simply for a list of factual notes. Your teacher will give you credit for these notes if they present accurate information. The second part of the question asks you to turn your notes into a short essay.

Study this model answer to the Level-2 question on page 34.

Question: People in various parts of the world have been influenced by many factors.

   Factors
   Cultural diffusion
   Ethnocentrism
   Nationalism
   Technological innovation
   Interdependence

A.   Select *three* of the factors listed and give an example of each.

Model answer:

   An example of nationalism: the desire of the American people in the 1770s to win independence from British rule.

   An example of technological innovation: the invention of the personal computer.

   An example of interdependence: Japanese depend on Middle Eastern oil, while Middle Easterners drive Japanese (and other imported) cars.

Question:

B.   Base your answer to Part B on your answer to Part A. However, additional information may be included. Write an essay in which you discuss examples of the factors listed above.

Model answer:

There are many factors that have influenced people in various parts of the world. One factor, nationalism, has played a major role in the history of modern nations. For example, the nationalism of the American people in the 1770s was one cause of their revolution against British rule.

A second factor, technological innovation, has also been a cause of major historical changes. In modern times, for example, the invention of the personal computer has changed the way people keep records, do research, conduct business, and enjoy their leisure hours.

A third factor, interdependence, is especially important in the modern world. The Japanese economy, for example, could not operate without oil from the Middle East. Neither could nations of the Middle East do without cars and other products imported from Japan and other industrial nations.

CHAPTER 2

Africa

Main Ideas

1. **DIVERSITY:** Africa's varied climates and terrains have promoted cultural diversity. Africans belong to more than 2,000 culturally distinct societies and speak more than 1,000 languages.

2. **TRADITION:** Traditional religious beliefs affect nearly every aspect of African life, including art and music.

3. **PAST CIVILIZATIONS:** Africa was home to a number of great ancient civilizations, including ancient Egypt, Kush, Axum, Ghana, Mali, Songhai, and Zimbabwe.

4. **SLAVE TRADE:** The Atlantic slave trade (about 1500 to 1850) caused widespread social upheaval and was history's largest forced migration.

5. **IMPERIALISM:** The colonial powers of Europe drew national boundaries in Africa that cut across historical, ethnic, and cultural lines.

6. **MODERNIZATION:** The colonial era in Africa led to economic development, greater social mobility, and rapid industrialization.

7. **AGRICULTURAL CHANGE:** Europeans forced Africans to produce crops, such as cotton, that could be sold for cash on world markets. As a result, many Africans became dependent on world trade for their livelihood.

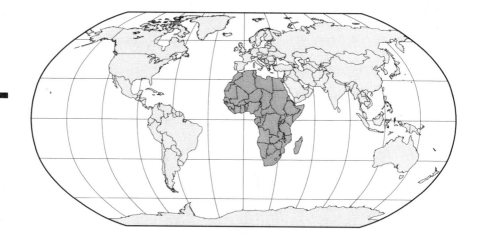

8. **NATIONAL INDEPENDENCE:** After World War II, African nationalism led to the independence of dozens of new nations.

9. **APARTHEID:** In the 20th century in South Africa, white rule and apartheid laws divided population groups along racial lines.

10. **SOCIAL CHANGE:** New technologies and urbanization are bringing changes in African ways and causing new attitudes, which clash with traditional ideas.

11. **COLD WAR TENSIONS:** During the cold war, the United States and the Soviet Union each tried to win as many allies in Africa as they could. In the process, they sometimes took sides in African wars.

12. **ECONOMIC DEPENDENCE:** Africa remains deeply dependent on the industrialized nations of the West for trade, capital, and food.

13. **DESERTIFICATION:** Population pressures and drought have caused millions of acres of African grasslands to turn into deserts.

14. **ARTS:** Most works created by African artists and musicians had a religious purpose. Africa's artistic traditions have influenced contemporary art and music in Africa as well as in other world regions.

Africa: The Region at a Glance

ASIA

ATLANTIC OCEAN

EUROPE

50°N

40°N

MEDITERRANEAN SEA

Tunis

Algiers · TUNISIA

Rabat
Casablanca

MOROCCO

Atlas Mts.

Tripoli

Alexandria

SUEZ CANAL

30°N

Cairo

①

WESTERN SAHARA

ALGERIA

LIBYA

EGYPT

⑦

RED SEA

②

Nile R.

TROPIC OF CANCER

Sahara Desert

ERITREA
Asmara

20°N

MALI

DJIBOUT
Djibouti

SENEGAL
Dakar

Nouakchott

BURKINA FASO
Ouagadougou

NIGER

CHAD

SUDAN

Khartoum

MAURITANIA

GAMBIA
Banjul

Bamako

Niamey

③

Blue Nile

Gulf of Aden

Lake Chad

Ethiopian
Highlands

10°N

NIGERIA

N'Djamena

White Nile

GHANA

Abuja

Addis
Ababa

ETHIOPIA

GUINEA
Conakry

Accra

Lagos

④

CENTRAL AFRICAN
REPUBLIC

Niger R.

CAMEROON

SOMALIA

GUINEA-
BISSAU
Bissau

SIERRA
LEONE
Freetown

CÔTE
D'IVOIRE
Abidjan

BENIN
Porto Novo

Yaoundé

Bangui

Zaire R.

ZAIRE

UGANDA

KENYA

Mogadishu

EQUATOR

LIBERIA
Monrovia

TOGO
Lomé

EQUATORIAL
GUINEA
Malabo

Libreville

GABON

Kampala

Nairobi

0°

RWANDA
Kigali

Lake
Victoria

CONGO
Brazzaville

Kinshasa

BURUNDI
Bujumbura

⑥

**INDIAN
OCEAN**

Great Rift Valley

Luanda

*Lake
Tanganyika*

Dar es Salaam

TANZANIA

10°S

**ATLANTIC
OCEAN**

ANGOLA

ZAMBIA
Lusaka

*Lake
Malawi*

MALAWI
Lilongwe

NAMIBIA

Zambezi R.

Harare

ZIMBABWE

MOZAMBIQUE

20°S

Antananarivo

MADAGASCAR

BOTSWANA

TROPIC OF CAPRICORN

Windhoek

Gaborone

Pretoria

Maputo

**Kalahari
Desert**

Johannesburg

SWAZILAND
Mbabane

30°S

⑤

SOUTH
AFRICA

LESOTHO
Maseru

Cape Town

N
W E
S

40°S

| 0 | | 1000 Kilometers |
| 0 | | 1000 Miles |

50°S

① NORTH AFRICA: From early times, this subregion on the Mediterranean Sea was strongly influenced by regular contacts with Europe and the Middle East. The Atlas Mountains intercept currents of moist air, causing rain to fall over coastal areas and preventing it from falling over the desert to the south. Thus, farming is limited to the narrow coastal plain on the Mediterranean.

② THE SAHARA: Throughout Africa's history, this huge desert has presented a barrier to travel and communication between the Mediterranean coast and the rest of Africa. Because of this barrier, lands to the south—sub-Saharan Africa—had little contact with Europe until the age of imperialism in the 19th century.

③ WEST AFRICA SAVANNA: For centuries, diverse ethnic groups in this area have grazed herds of cattle on the grasslands (savannas) watered by the Niger River. In the Middle Ages, a number of powerful monarchs established empires in the region: Ghana, Mali, and Songhai. In the 20th century, droughts, overpopulation, and overgrazing have caused some of the grasslands to turn into a desert.

④ EQUATORIAL RAIN FOREST: A tropical climate (high temperatures and much rain throughout the year) has produced this densely forested environment. For the various ethnic groups that live here, tributaries of the Zaire River still provide the best means of transportation. Roads through such terrain are difficult to build and maintain. Soils are poor for farming—one reason for the widespread poverty in Zaire.

⑤ SOUTH AFRICA: The discovery of rich deposits of gold and diamonds in this region led to a war (1899–1902) between British and Dutch (or Boer) settlers. Mining is still the basis of South Africa's modern economy. For years, the country's black majority suffered from the racist policies of the white minority. Now South Africans are in the process of forming a democratic, multiracial society.

⑥ GREAT RIFT VALLEY: Most of eastern and central Africa is a plateau. Cutting across that plateau in a north-south direction is a deep canyon or trough, hundreds of miles long. This Great Rift Valley has separated African cultures on the east coast from those in the interior.

⑦ EGYPT AND THE NILE: In ancient times, the regular flooding of the Nile River in Egypt gave rise to one of the earliest civilizations. Even today, the Egyptian people rely completely on the Nile for the water that irrigates their farms. The rest of the country is a desert.

I. Geography

Africa is a huge continent—the second largest in the world (after Asia). To give you a better idea of its size, think of it as three times the area of the United States.

A. LOCATION

The African continent is surrounded by major bodies of water: the Mediterranean Sea to the north, the Atlantic Ocean to the west, and the Red Sea and Indian Ocean to the east. Despite its long coastline, Africa has few good bays or inlets for harbors.

The oceans and seas that surround Africa have both isolated it from and opened it to contact with other regions. Until the 1400s, the rough water and vast size of the Atlantic Ocean served as a formidable barrier to ships. In contrast, the smaller and relatively calm Mediterranean Sea has acted since ancient times as a highway for trade with both Europe and the Middle East. The Indian Ocean also has served as more of a pathway than a barrier to trade. Ships from Arabia and China traded at East African ports hundreds of years before European ships arrived.

B. CLIMATE

Much of Africa has a hot, tropical climate because of the continent's location on the equator. The direct sunlight falling on lands just north and south of the equator accounts for the high average temperatures there in all seasons of the year. Be aware, however, that not all of Africa is tropical. People living on the coasts of North Africa and South Africa, for example, experience moderate temperatures that vary with the seasons.

C. VARIED TOPOGRAPHY

If you were to travel across the vast expanse of the African continent, you would observe a great diversity of landscapes and geographic features.

Savannas   More than two-fifths of the African continent consists of broad and open plains where wild grasses and scattered trees grow. These *savannas*, or grasslands, support herds of grazing wild animals, such as zebras, elephants, gazelles, and giraffes. Large numbers of Africans have made their homes on the savannas as farmers and herders. Each year, their livelihood comes to depend upon whether sufficient rain falls. They need water to grow crops and to sustain the grasses on which cattle graze. In any given year, the level of rainfall on the savannas could be heavy or light.

AFRICAN TEA PLANTATION: The tea plant flourishes in tropical and subtropical climates at elevations of between 3,000 to 7,000 feet. What parts of Africa would be suitable for growing tea? Where in Africa could it *not* be grown?

Deserts The largest desert in the world, the Sahara, spans most of North Africa. In size, it is almost as large as the United States. The Sahara is an extremely hot and largely barren environment of rock, gravel, and sand. Years may go by without a single drop of rain falling over some parts of the desert. To a certain extent, the Sahara poses a barrier to trade and communication between Africa's Mediterranean coast and *sub-Saharan Africa* (the part of Africa south of the Sahara). But although the journey is difficult and hazardous, camel caravans have crossed the Sahara for centuries.

Far to the south, a second desert—the Kalahari—covers an area about the size of Texas. Today, part of the Kalahari in Botswana serves as a game preserve.

Rain forests The densely forested area near the equator makes up a relatively small part of Africa (less than 10 percent). It is called a *rain forest* because of the large amount of rainfall it receives. Although a good habitat for thousands of species of birds and animals, the rain forest poses unusual difficulties for the Africans who live there. It is infested with disease-carrying insects that prey on humans and their domesticated animals. In addition, heavy rains have *leached* (washed away) minerals from the soil. Thus, even if the forests were cleared, the land would be generally unsuitable for farming. The plants of the rain forests help to maintain an ecological balance and provide the basis for many important medicines.

Plateaus   Much of the African continent consists of a plateau that slopes gradually downward from a high point in East Africa to a low point in West Africa. A deep and dramatic division, or crack, in the plateau rock extends for 4,000 miles through the interior of East Africa. This *Great Rift Valley*, as it is called, contains rich deposits of volcanic soil, which provide fertile farmland. At the same time, however, the valley's steep cliff walls are barriers to transportation.

Mountains   Three African nations are known for their mountainous terrain—Morocco, Algeria, and Ethiopia. The Atlas Mountains stretch for hundreds of miles through Morocco and Algeria in North Africa. Mountains in Ethiopia rise out of the East African Plateau and reach heights of more than 15,000 feet above sea level. Africa's two highest peaks are in Tanzania and Kenya.

Rivers   The world's longest river, the Nile, flows in a northerly direction from the East African Plateau through the Sudan and Egypt until it finally empties into the Mediterranean Sea. In ancient times, the fertile soil annually deposited by the flooding Nile gave rise to Egyptian civilization. Other major African rivers—the Niger in West Africa, the Zaire in Central Africa, and the Zambezi in East Africa—have only limited value as means of water transportation. Waterfalls and rapids on the Zambezi, for example, provide major obstacles to boats.

Lakes   Africa's largest and most important lakes—Lake Victoria and Lake Tanganyika—are located within the Great Rift Valley. For centuries, Africans have used the lakes to transport goods across them. The lakes are also important sources of salt and soda ash (material used for the manufacture of glass and other products).

The Suez Canal   Another major body of water in Africa is little more than a hundred years old. Built in the late 19th century, the Suez Canal connects the Mediterranean and Red seas. It provides a shortcut for ships traveling between Europe and Asia. Before this major waterway was built, ships had to go almost all the way around Africa's long coastline.

D. THE LAND'S IMPACT ON AFRICANS

Africa's geographic diversity is the chief reason for its remarkable cultural diversity. In earliest times, as different groups of Africans migrated across the continent, they adapted to the various types of lands (deserts, mountains, rain forests, and so on). Eventually, hundreds of different ethnic groups emerged, each with its own language, social customs, and religious beliefs. In modern times, especially in rural areas, traditions of the past and membership in individual ethnic groups and clans still shape Africans' identities.

Population patterns Much of Africa is a harsh environment in which it is very difficult for humans to live. Large parts of the deserts and rain forests have virtually no people living in them. Therefore, the great majority of Africans must support themselves on those parts of the continent that are habitable: the savannas, the river valleys, the narrow coastal strips, and the fertile farmlands of the East African Plateau.

Desertification Currently, the amount of grazing and farming land in Africa is dwindling at an alarming rate. By a process known as *desertification* (land becoming desert-like), millions of acres of savanna grass have died out. The problem has two basic causes. First, Africa's population on the savannas is growing. Increasing numbers of nomadic herders are grazing their cattle on the savanna's parched and thinning grass cover. The land cannot stand the pressure of too little rain and too much grazing. Eventually, the grass dies and shrivels to nothing. Winds take the dry topsoil and shift it from place to place. The savanna soil becomes too hard for plants to grow in. The land that once supported African nomads and their cattle turns into desert.

The second cause of desertification involves periodic shifts in climate. Thousands of years ago, the Sahara was covered with forests and grasslands. Rainfall then was so plentiful that the area supported many lakes and rivers. For reasons scientists are not sure of, the area gradually became drier. Perhaps the present changes are part of this long-term pattern.

FAMINE IN ETHIOPIA: A famine in the 1980s drove this family and thousands of others to abandon their villages and seek relief in refugee camps. What are the causes of such famines?

Desertification is a terrible problem in the *Sahel*, the vegetation zone located along the southern edge of the Sahara. The Sahel is used for both farming and cattle grazing. As the grasslands turn to desert, people living there and their herds must either move away or starve. Some abandon their way of life and move to the cities. Others move their cattle into areas where plant life still grows. But, of course, this migration only puts pressure on other lands. Sooner or later, they too may become desert.

Disease   Just as lack of water slows economic development in parts of Africa, so does the existence of diseases spread by insects. Particularly troublesome is the tsetse fly, which preys on both cattle and people. It transmits a fatal disease known as sleeping sickness. Horses and oxen are particularly susceptible to the disease. For this reason, much of sub-Saharan Africa cannot use these animals for plowing fields and pulling loads. The mosquito is another disease-causing insect of Africa. The millions of mosquitos that swarm through the rain forests carry yellow fever and malaria.

E. MINERAL RESOURCES

In one way, at least, geography has been generous to Africans. The African continent is richly endowed with mineral resources of many kinds. South Africa, for example, has the world's largest deposits of gold. From the diamond mines of Zaire and South Africa come about four-fifths of the world's diamond supply. A "copper belt" stretching from Zaire to Zambia produces about one-fourth of the world's copper. Nigeria and Libya are major producers of oil.

Scientists suspect that there may be huge sources of mineral wealth in Africa waiting to be found and developed. But it takes large sums of money to explore for minerals. Unfortunately, most African nations lack the *capital* (financing) to open up new mines. The most likely sources of the needed capital are foreign banks and businesses.

In Review

The following questions refer to Section I: Geography.

1.   *Key terms:* Define or identify each of the following:

     savanna   Sahel   desertification
     sub-Sahara   Great Rift Valley

2.   List several of Africa's geographic advantages and several of its disadvantages in regard to human settlement.

3.   Explain why desertification has become a major problem in Africa.

4. Explain the connection between Africa's geographic diversity and its cultural diversity.

5. *Critical thinking:* In which pair of nations would you expect cultures to be most similar? (a) Ethiopia and Zaire (b) Egypt and Nigeria (c) Mali and Chad (d) South Africa and Angola. (Refer to maps on pages 40, 48, and 49.) Explain your answer.

COMPARING MAPS

What would happen if a mapmaker tried to include every kind of geographic information about Africa on a single map? The result would be extremely confusing. Various dots, lines, shadings, and labels would be piled on top of one another. Nobody would be able to read such a complicated map. That is why *atlases* (books of maps) present a number of different kinds of maps dealing with the same continent or region. Each kind focuses on a different aspect of geography.

On the following pages, for example, we see four maps of Africa. The key, or legend, in each map's left-hand corner identifies what the map is about. Notice that the maps give the boundaries of African nations without identifying them by name. Another type of map, known as a *political map*, gives the names of nations—and usually the names of cities as well.

A *topographic map* shows the way a region might appear if viewed from a satellite circling the earth. It shows the region's major natural features: its mountains, plateaus, deserts, rivers, and lakes. The map of Africa on page 40 has both topographic and political information. Refer to that map as well as to the four maps on the following pages to answer these questions.

Questions for Discussion

1. Name five African nations that are largely covered by savanna vegetation.
2. Name three African countries that have high population densities (areas of more than 150 people per square mile).
3. Name one African nation that has these characteristics: areas of high population density, rich mineral resources, and a climate that is partly warm and rainy.
4. There is often a connection between a region's climate and its population density. In the North African nations of Morocco and Algeria, how would you describe this connection?

48

A. MAJOR CLIMATE REGIONS

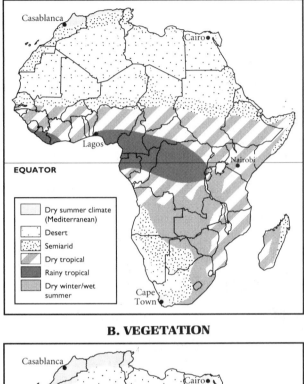

Casablanca

Cairo

Lagos

Nairobi

EQUATOR

Dry summer climate
(Mediterranean)

Desert

Semiarid

Dry tropical

Rainy tropical

Dry winter/wet
summer

Cape
Town

B. VEGETATION

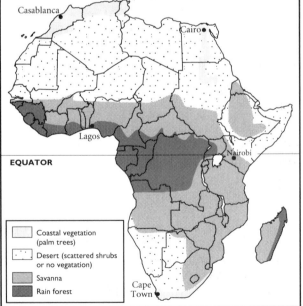

Casablanca

Cairo

Lagos

Nairobi

EQUATOR

Coastal vegetation
(palm trees)

Desert (scattered shrubs
or no vegetation)

Savanna

Rain forest

Cape
Town

C. POPULATION DENSITY

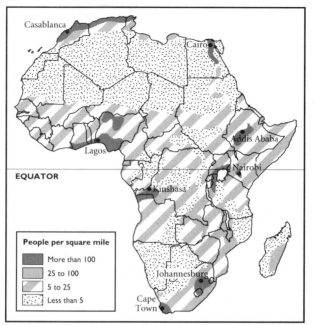

D. MINING AND MANUFACTURING CENTERS

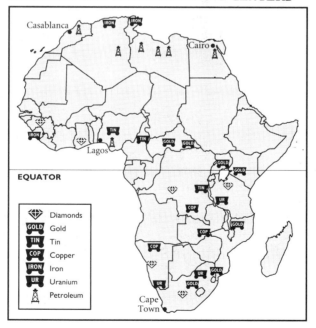

II. Early History

Human life probably originated in Africa. This theory is based, in part, on the work of two archeologists, Mary and Louis Leakey. They explored East Africa's Great Rift Valley and found fossil remains of skeletons and footprints that resemble those of humans. The Leakeys concluded that hunting bands of near-humans lived in East Africa as early as four million years ago. They also claimed that the first true humans lived in present-day Ethiopia, Kenya, and Tanzania about two million years ago. Many archeologists maintain that these prehistoric people of East Africa are the earliest ancestors of everyone who has ever lived.

If human life did originate in East Africa, then we may suppose that, over the course of many centuries, early peoples migrated in various directions. Some went north along the Nile River Valley. Others went west to the Niger River. Still others moved south as far as the tip of the African continent. Gradually, as each small hunting band adapted to different climates and terrains, hundreds of culturally distinct societies came into being.

So long as people moved over the land as hunters of wild game and gatherers of wild plants, their societies remained small. Gradually, however, certain prehistoric groups on the Nile River developed a more settled way of life and an economy based on agriculture. Nomadic hunters turned into crop-raising farmers. This revolutionary change gave rise to one of history's earliest civilizations, ancient Egypt.

A. EGYPT

The fertile soil deposited regularly by the Nile River encouraged the development of agriculture in Egypt as early as 7,000 years ago. Through the introduction of irrigation and the plow, Egyptian farmers gradually improved their crop yields until they produced *surpluses* (more than they needed for themselves and their families). As farmers produced crop surpluses, some workers were free to engage in other economic tasks, such as making pottery and weaving cloth.

Rival villages and clans fought for control of the Nile Valley. Around 3000 B.C., the leader of one such clan—a ruler known as a *pharaoh*— overcame rival forces and brought under his control a long stretch of fertile land and villages along the Nile. For hundreds of years thereafter, pharaohs ruled a united Egypt. They presided over a civilization characterized by cities, massive building projects (including the pyramids), artistic achievements, and scientific and mathematical knowledge.

Religious beliefs   Egyptians worshipped many gods, a form of religion known as *polytheism*. They regarded their pharaoh as a godlike being whose soul never died. On a pharaoh's orders, they erected gigantic pyramids in the desert. When a pharaoh died, the pyramid became the tomb of his or her *mummy* (carefully preserved dead body). Also placed in the pyramid for the dead pharaoh's use in the afterlife were food, wine, and jewelry. On the walls of the burial chamber, artists made paintings that illustrated the pharaoh's good deeds.

Writing A major hallmark of Egyptian civilization was the creation of a written language. Ancient Egyptians used picture symbols to represent words, sounds, and objects. Modern scholars are now able to read Egyptian *hieroglyphics*, as their writing is called. Because of this knowledge, we know much about the history of ancient Egypt.

Science and technology The priests and government officials of Egypt found that they needed a precise system for measuring the passage of time. By observing the shifting position of the sun in the sky, ancient Egyptians were able to invent a calendar of 365 days. They also devised an ingenious system for measuring land area—part of a field of mathematics that we call geometry.

Another major step forward for Egypt was the discovery of a way to extract copper from rock. After this discovery, metal tools began to

GRAPE HARVEST IN ANCIENT EGYPT: This scene was painted on an inside wall of an Egyptian noble's tomb. Why did Egyptian pharaohs and nobles arrange for their tombs to be decorated with images of grapes, other foods, and scenes from daily life?

replace stone ones. A later technological advance was the use of bronze, a metal manufactured by mixing heated copper and tin. (Bronze was first discovered in Sumer, a civilization in western Asia.) Weapons made of bronze were harder and more durable than copper ones. Use of bronze weapons gave the Egyptians a military advantage over neighboring peoples. So important was the invention of bronze to Egypt and other civilizations that its use defines an era. The *Bronze Age* (beginning between 4000 and 3000 B.C.) refers to the time when people began using bronze tools and weapons.

Trade   Traveling up the Nile by boat, Egyptians carried on a regular trade with people to the south, the Nubians. They exchanged such items as gold jewelry and *papyrus sheets* (paper) for Nubian leopard skins, copper, ivory, and spices. Egyptian boats also sailed on the Mediterranean and Red seas. As a result of peaceful contacts with neighboring peoples, Egypt's influence gradually spread outward to areas beyond the Nile.

Decline   Starting about 1100 B.C., Egyptian civilization went into a slow decline. Various groups within Egypt struggled for power. Later, Egypt was conquered by foreigners. Alexander the Great's armies came in 332 B.C.; and the Romans, in 31 B.C.

B. KUSH AND AXUM

The Kushites, a people living to the south of Egypt, developed a civilization similar in some ways to that of their powerful neighbors. About 750 B.C., a Kushite king led a successful military expedition against Egypt. For a brief time, the Egyptians lived under Kushite rule. The Kushites went a step further than the Egyptians in developing their metal technologies. They learned the technique for separating iron from iron ore. Iron is a much harder metal than either copper or bronze. For hundreds of years, the kingdom of Kush carried on an extensive trade in iron and ivory with kingdoms and empires of the Middle East and South Asia.

The capital of Kush was conquered in A.D. 330 by armies marching down from the high plateau of what is today Ethiopia. The conquerors called their land the kingdom of Axum. Like Kush, Axum prospered by trading with merchants from the Middle East and Asia. Axum's King Ezana adopted the religious beliefs and rituals of Christianity. This early form of Christianity, known as the Coptic Church, is still the dominant religion in Ethiopia.

C. EMPIRES OF WEST AFRICA

Larger than a kingdom, an empire usually consisted of several different kingdoms brought under the control of one central government.

Near the upper Niger River in West Africa, three great empires arose. Each successive empire was larger and more powerful than the one it replaced. The economies of all three empires were similar. Each was based on agriculture, mining, and trade.

Ghana The first of the West African empires, Ghana, began its rise to power about A.D. 500 and dominated the region for 600 years. The emperor of Ghana based his power on the gold mines that he alone controlled. His wealth enabled him to maintain a large army and a lavish court. A military attack from the north finally caused the empire to break apart.

Mali Not long after the fall of Ghana, another African people on the Niger River established political dominance over a wide area. The empire of Mali flourished for about a hundred years (from the middle of

EARLY CIVILIZATIONS OF AFRICA

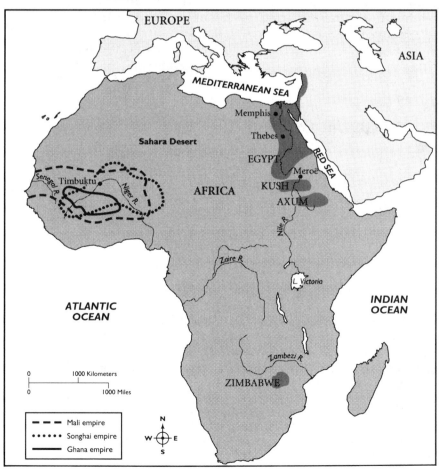

the 1200s to the middle of the 1300s). Its most famous monarch was Mansa (Emperor) Musa. Before his reign, the religion of Islam had spread from the Middle East into North and West Africa. As a believer in Islam, Mansa Musa made a pilgrimage to the Arabian city of Mecca, a place that *Muslims* (followers of Islam) regard as holy. Mali's great monarch journeyed eastward with thousands of attendants. His long procession of camels was laden down with huge quantities of gold.

Through its highly organized and efficient government, Mali controlled the trade in gold and salt that was so vital to West Africa's economy. Gold from Mali's mines was regularly traded for salt from the Sahara—salt that was in short supply on the West African savanna.

Songhai   The third and largest of the West African empires was Songhai. It controlled a vast region from the Niger River to the Atlantic Coast (roughly comprising present-day Senegal). The most powerful Songhai ruler, Askia the Great, used his powers to convert much of West Africa to Islam. Under Askia's rule (1493–1528), the city of Timbuktu became a center of Islamic culture. A major university in Timbuktu attracted Islamic scholars from far and wide. The Songhai empire lasted from the time of its founding in 1464 to the time of its collapse in 1591. In the latter year, an invading army from the North African kingdom of Morocco overran Timbuktu and brought the empire to an end.

D. KINGDOM OF ZIMBABWE

In the southern part of Africa, a legendary leader of the Bantu people, Mbire, used his control of gold mines to build a powerful state. Established around 1300, the kingdom of Zimbabwe was noted for its immense stone buildings. The Bantu word *zimbabwe* means "great stone house." Some of the buildings of that early kingdom still stand in the present-day nation of the same name—Zimbabwe.

E. RELIGIONS OF AFRICA

From one part of Africa to another, the various ethnic groups and tribes of early Africa developed different, complex religious beliefs and rituals. The spirits and gods worshipped by the Bantu of Zimbabwe, for example, differed from the spirits and gods worshipped by various peoples of West Africa. In general terms, however, the earliest African religions had much in common. They were examples of a type of religion known as *animism*.

Animism   Animists believe that spirits inhabit both living and non-living things. They believe that such spirits are responsible for the general welfare of the group. The spirits may cause a person to become sick or healthy, determine whether a crop grows or withers, and decide whether a hunt succeeds or fails. Among the spirits that influence events for good or evil are the spirits of a family's dead ancestors.

In animist societies, there is always someone whose role is to understand and interact with the spirits. This person is made the group's religious leader. By performing an elaborate ritual, the leader tries to communicate with the spirits and protect society from evil forces. The leader also advises those individuals who have violated the group's moral code on ways to appease the spirits and win forgiveness.

In Africa today, approximately a tenth of the population still practice animism. Although most widely practiced in southern and central Africa, these traditional religions of Africa also have some influence elsewhere on the continent. The prevailing religion in a certain area may be Islam or Christianity. But many African Muslims and Christians have not completely discarded their belief in animist spirits.

Islam   The Islamic religion is based upon the teachings of a Middle Eastern prophet, Mohammed. (For a discussion of Islam, see Chapter 3.) Islam first entered Africa in the 7th century when Muslim armies from Arabia conquered Egypt and much of the rest of North Africa. Trade, as well as conquest, would play a role in the spread of Islam even further. Beginning in the 8th century, Muslims of North Africa carried on an extensive trade with West African groups. Also, Arab traders traveled regularly to and from cities along the East African coast. African converts to Islam freely blended their new faith with traditional beliefs of animism.

The holy book of Islam—the *Koran*—sets forth a large number of laws for regulating daily life. Therefore, in parts of Africa where Islam was adopted, Africans of diverse cultures began to observe a common moral and legal code.

Christianity   The Christian religion is based upon the teachings of Jesus. His followers believe that Jesus is the son of God and savior of humankind. (The religion is discussed in more detail in Chapters 3 and 7.)

Christian missionaries introduced Christianity to the kingdom of Axum during the 4th century. More than a thousand years later, Portuguese explorers and slave traders converted some of the tribal chiefs of Central Africa to Christianity. The religion spread dramatically through Africa in the 19th century, a time when Christian missionaries were arriving in Africa in large numbers. Many Africans became Christians, and some adapted Christian practices to their own traditions. Later, groups of African Christians broke away from the churches set up by the European missionaries; they established new churches that better expressed their own traditions.

F. TRADITIONAL AFRICAN ARTS

Long before the coming of Islam and Christianity, African tribes and clans had developed unique forms of art and music. African artists and musicians had a religious purpose behind almost everything that they created. They carved their remarkable wooden sculptures, masks, and ornaments as mediums for communicating with the spirits. Masks used in a religious ceremony were meant to protect against evil forces or bring about some social benefit, such as a good harvest, fertility, or success in the hunt. The images and forms chosen by African artists had deep symbolic meanings. They expressed Africans' ideas about the nature of the universe. Complex, rhythmic forms of music and dance were also used in religious ceremonies. In addition to its religious functions, African music helped to transmit traditions and oral history from one generation to the next.

Art serves to give every society a unique identity. The artistic style developed by each African society was different from any other's style. It helped set that society apart from its neighbors.

In the 19th and 20th centuries, European and other Western artists became aware of Africans' approach to artistic expression. Painters and sculptors like Spain's Pablo Picasso began to experiment with

AFRICAN ART AND MODERN ART: Compare the traditional African mask on the left with the 20th-century painting by a French artist on the right. What similarities do you observe?

images closely resembling African masks. Admiration of African art helped Picasso and others to revolutionize their approach to their own art. Thus, what we call "modern art" in the West was influenced by artistic traditions of Africa.

Musicians in the United States and Europe were also influenced by Africa's rich cultural traditions. Jazz, rock and roll, and modern dance trace their origins to African music.

In Review

The following questions refer to Section II: Early History.

1. *Key terms:* Define or identify each of the following:

   pharaoh   hieroglyphics   animism
   polytheism   Muslim   the Koran

2. Why do many archeologists believe that human life originated in Africa?

3. Describe the location of *each* of the following African civilizations: (*a*) ancient Egypt, (*b*) Kush, (*c*) ancient Zimbabwe, (*d*) ancient Mali, and (*e*) Songhai.

4. State *two* examples that show how African art forms have influenced other regions of the world.

5. *Critical thinking:* Compare the civilization of ancient Egypt (about 1500 B.C.) with the civilization of Songhai (about A.D. 1500). (*a*) In what ways were they similar? (*b*) In what ways were they different?

III. The Dynamics of Change

Since the dawn of recorded history, North Africans have been in contact with other lands that border the Mediterranean—lands both in Europe and in the Middle East. In ancient times, however, people in sub-Saharan Africa had almost no contact with other regions. Then in the 8th and 9th centuries, Berbers in North Africa began crossing the Sahara to trade salt for Ghana's gold. In a later period, Arab merchants regularly crossed the Red Sea and Indian Ocean to trade for African wares in the cities of East Africa. The cargo carried away in Arab boats included human captives, or slaves.

The societies of sub-Saharan Africa were severely damaged by foreigners. First Arabs and later Europeans and Americans forcibly took millions of people from Africa.

A. SLAVERY AND THE SLAVE TRADE IN AFRICA

Slavery was an ancient institution that had been practiced in all parts of the world, not just in Africa. The ancient Greeks and Romans made slaves of people they captured in wars. Only for the past 100 to 150 years has slavery been abolished by law in countries around the world. Historians distinguish between two kinds of slavery in Africa— internal and external slavery.

Internal slavery   The kings and emperors of sub-Saharan Africa acquired slaves as part of the spoils of intertribal warfare. Usually, a person held as a slave could eventually look forward to being released from that condition at some time in his or her life. Slaves could purchase their freedom if they earned enough working for pay during their free time. Within African societies, an enslaved person could appeal for protection to the laws of the community. Slavery of this kind that was limited to just Africa can be labeled *internal slavery*.

External slavery   A harsher kind of slavery developed when foreigners came to Africa to trade their goods for slaves. This *external slavery* was "external" in the sense that non-Africans were involved, including Arabs, Europeans, and Americans. African rulers, too, participated in the slave trade. They arranged for large numbers of captives to be traded to foreigners in exchange for weapons and barrels of rum.

The external slave trade began in the 11th century when Arab conquerors of North Africa acquired slaves from African kingdoms to the south. Those held as slaves were kept in bondage for life and denied all legal rights.

The worst effects of the slave trade did not occur until the 1700s— the final years of the European "Age of Exploration." By this time, the Portuguese, Spaniards, French, and English had each established colonies in the Americas. Colonists found that they needed a large labor force to toil in mines and on plantations. To supply the needed labor, they came to depend upon the cruel business of importing enslaved persons from Africa. In the British colonies of North America, the first African slaves arrived in the early 1600s. African captives were forced onto ships that carried them from their homeland to a strange and, for them, frightening and hostile world across the ocean. Unlike the kind of slavery practiced in Africa, slavery in the Americas had a racial character. White masters treated black Africans as inferior beings—a form of property without any rights before the law.

Impact of the Atlantic slave trade   Yearly in the 1600s, Africans were shipped across the seas by the thousands, and in the 1700s, by the hundreds of thousands. This immensely destructive trade in human beings did not end until the 1800s, when various governments in Europe and the Americas finally decided to outlaw both slavery and the slave trade. Slavery continued in parts of Africa into the 20th century.

While it lasted (and for generations afterward), the overseas slave trade had devastating effects on African society. Some of the negative consequences were:

- Loss of life: Millions of Africans lost their lives as a result of the brutal treatment they suffered on the overland trek to the African coast and on the long ocean voyage to the Americas.

- Decline in population: The removal of generations of young Africans from their native villages and tribes badly weakened the societies' ability to carry on. Many parts of West Africa suffered drastic losses in population.

- Increased warfare: Africans warred among themselves with increasing frequency in order to capture prisoners to sell to foreign slave merchants. The incessant warfare was a further drain on African economic and political life.

- Loss of stability: The former stability of African kingdoms was destroyed.

- Loss of heritage: Those taken to the Americas as enslaved people eventually lost touch with much of their African heritage.

ATLANTIC SLAVE TRADE

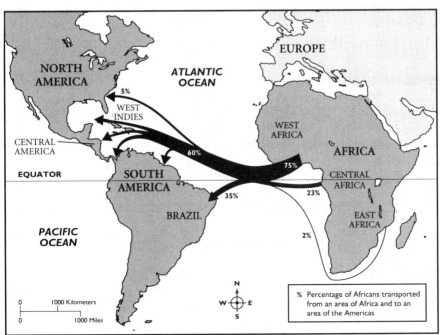

In short, the forced migration of Africans left a bitter legacy. It greatly set back the political, economic, and social development of sub-Saharan Africa.

One unintended consequence of the slave trade was cultural diffusion. As slaves arrived in the Americas, African culture began to influence American culture. Art, sculpture, music, and dance from Africa would have important influences on the various cultures of the peoples of North and South America.

B. EUROPEAN EXPLORATION AND EXPLOITATION

Before the 19th century, European traders and missionaries had been active primarily in coastal areas of Africa. They had set up a series of trading posts on Africa's west, east, and south coasts. In the mid-1800s, just as the slave trade was coming to an end, European adventurers and missionaries became interested in going into Africa's interior. From the European point of view, Africa seemed a "dark" (unknown) continent. The explorations of Dr. David Livingstone, Henry Stanley, and others soon led to a competition among Europeans to carve all of Africa into colonies. As we will see, their ambitions produced revolutionary changes throughout the entire African continent.

European nations were acquiring new colonies not only in Africa, but also in other world regions, especially in Southeast Asia and islands of the Pacific Ocean. Their campaign to build an overseas empire is often labeled *imperialism*. (An imperialist policy is one in which a strong country tries to gain economic, social, and political control over a weaker one.)

Reasons for imperialism   Western Europeans were able to take over much of Africa because of their advanced military technology. Their rifles and cannons overwhelmed those African societies that had not yet discovered the use of gunpowder. The major powers of Western Europe (especially Great Britain, France, and Germany) scrambled to acquire African colonies for three main reasons:

1. Economic reasons. By the late 1800s, Western Europe was rapidly industrializing. Factories needed increased supplies of mineral ores and other raw materials. Europeans who explored Africa discovered that it was rich in mineral wealth. Under the rain forests of Central Africa lay immense deposits of copper ore. Within the hills of South Africa were some of the world's richest sources of gold and diamonds. Besides competing to control these resources, Europe's industrial powers were seeking new markets for their manufactured goods. They thought Africans would buy some of these goods. Moreover, Europeans saw Africa as a good place to invest money.

To expand international trade, Western Europeans wanted to open up a better sea route between Europe and Asia. Sailing around Africa took too long. Thus, in 1869, a French company completed building the Suez Canal in Egypt. It connected the Mediterranean and Red seas, enabling ships to go between Europe and Asia much more quickly. Six years after the canal was opened, the British purchased partial ownership of the Canal Company. British and French control of this waterway would become crucial to the economic life of Europe in the early 20th century.

2. Political reasons. Strengthening the economic motives for imperialism was the political force known as nationalism. In the late 1800s, the British, French, Germans, and others expressed growing pride in their own countries and jealousy and fear of neighboring countries.

IMPERIALISM IN AFRICA

They thought that a nation's prestige in the world depended in part upon the colonies that it controlled. Thus, the French competed with the British for control of Egypt. While the British prevailed in that struggle (and in many others), the French succeeded in colonizing Morocco, Algeria, and much of West Africa. This imperialist "scramble for Africa" eventually resulted in dozens of colonies being created. In Africa, only Liberia and Ethiopia managed to remain independent of European control.

3. *Social reasons.* Europeans in the 19th and early 20th centuries regarded their civilization as superior to all others. Many Christians there believed that they had a duty to win converts to their faith. Europeans also assumed that African societies could only benefit from being introduced to Western science, medicine, and industrial technology. British poet Rudyard Kipling maintained that colonizing Africa and other parts of the world was "the white man's burden." Cultural imperialists like Kipling thought that Europeans had a noble mission to uplift people everywhere.

C. EFFECTS OF EUROPEAN RULE ON AFRICA

Both for better and for worse, European imperialism made dramatic changes in all aspects of African life.

Positive effects   Supporters of imperialism pointed to the following benefits of colonial rule:

- Medicine and health: Europeans practiced a scientific approach to medicine that proved effective in treating many African diseases. As a result of European medicine, most African societies experienced a drop in the rate of infant deaths and a rise in *life expectancy* (number of years a newly born infant is expected to live.)

- Agriculture: European colonists introduced scientific methods of farming, which greatly increased the production of crops. (Note, however, that crops such as cotton and coffee were grown for export and did nothing to increase Africans' food supply.)

- Transportation and communication: Europeans built networks of railroads and telegraph lines that linked together formerly remote and isolated parts of Africa. Modern transportation made possible a more efficient use of the continent's natural resources.

- Education: The schools built by Europeans taught a small percentage of Africans the basic skills of reading, writing, and calculating. Some of the privileged few who attended such schools would rise to positions of leadership when African nations became independent in the 20th century.

Negative effects Africans today look back upon the era of imperialism with deep resentment. They generally blame the European colonizers for weakening the traditional values and institutions of their societies. The negative effects of imperialism were:

- The downgrading of African cultures: European schools in Africa disregarded African culture and offered instruction only in the history and languages of Europe.

- Forced labor: Colonial governments often forced Africans to work without pay in plantations, factories, and mines. In some colonies, Africans suffered from brutal mistreatment. For example, the Congo (present-day Zaire) fell under the control of Belgium's King Leopold II in the 1880s. To gain as much wealth as possible from the rain forest's resources (rubber and copper, for example), Leopold's colonial overseers would force Africans to work hard for long hours. As a result, many workers died of exhaustion and abuse.

- The weakening of group ties: Traditionally, members of an African village would hold their land in common. In contrast, European colonizers introduced a radically different system in which individual farmers owned separate plots of land. The change from one system to the other tended to weaken the social bonds that were at the heart of African society.

- A change to a money economy: Before the Europeans came, money in the form of coins and paper notes was largely unknown in sub-Saharan Africa. The money system that Europeans imposed on their African colonies badly disrupted Africans' traditional way of making a living.

- A change from *subsistence farming*: Traditionally, African farmers had grown just enough food to meet the subsistence needs of their own village. (*Subsistence* is the minimum needed by humans to support life.) But under colonial rule, Africans were required to farm for other purposes. Instead of subsistence farming, many Africans had to grow commercial crops for export. Profits from the sale of the crops went mainly to European colonists. Moreover, many Africans now became economically dependent on Europeans.

- Artificial political boundaries: The colonial boundaries drawn by Europeans failed to take account of Africans' traditional loyalties. Within each European colony, several rival ethnic groups coexisted. Later, after each colony declared itself to be independent, true national unity was difficult to achieve. Civil wars broke out in many new nations of Africa, partly because of the unnatural boundaries inherited from the colonial past.

D. AFRICAN NATIONALISM

After World War II ended in 1945, African nationalists demanded that Europeans surrender control of the colonies and grant independence. Why did African nationalism emerge in the postwar period as a major force for change?

Sources of nationalism   First of all, the bombings and other destruction of World War II had left much of Europe in ruins. The chief colonial powers, Great Britain and France, no longer had the economic strength or military will to keep up their colonial empires. Moreover, European leaders had already learned that governing distant colonies was costly and not always profitable.

Second, the few Africans who attended universities in Europe and America learned about Western ideas of democracy and nationalism. They insisted that Europeans live up to their own values by granting democracy and self-rule to the various peoples of Africa.

Third, during World War II, the United Nations was founded. The charter of this international organization listed a number of idealistic purposes. Among these were: (1) the protection of everyone's *human rights* (basic rights that all people should enjoy) and (2) *self-determination* (the right of national groups under the rule of others to declare independence).

Fourth, Africans' struggles for national independence were part of a global revolt against colonialism. The Vietnamese in Southeast Asia and the Indians and Pakistanis in South Asia fought for and attained independence from colonial rule in the 1940s and early 1950s. The successes of these revolts inspired African nationalists.

Fifth, many Africans had fought for the Allies in World War II. They helped turn the tide against the Germans and Italians. Thus, they felt that they were owed independence.

Movements for independence   Africans employed both violent and nonviolent methods for gaining their independence. In the Gold Coast, a British colony in West Africa, nationalist leader Kwame Nkrumah used generally peaceful methods of protest against foreign rule. Nkrumah was jailed more than once for the part he played in organizing strikes and boycotts. In 1957, Great Britain gave in to the nationalists' demands by granting the Gold Coast its independence. The new nation—the first black African colony to win independence—adopted the name Ghana.

The struggle in the British colony of Kenya was more violent. Here a militant nationalist named Jomo Kenyatta joined with others in armed attacks against white settlers. "Mau Mau," as the nationalists called their movement, was one of the forces that eventually caused Britain to grant Kenya its independence. In 1963, Kenyatta became the new nation's first prime minister.

AFRICAN NATIONALISM: In 1963, Jomo Kenyatta (center) campaigned for election to be the leader of Kenya, a nation that he had helped to create. What were (a) the causes and (b) the consequences of African nationalism?

One by one, other African colonies also became independent. By 1977, there were more than 40 newly independent nations of Africa. In 1990, a colony first ruled by Germany (and later by South Africa) finally won its independence as the new nation of Namibia. This event marked the final passing of colonial rule from the continent of Africa.

Political problems after independence Making the transition from colony to nation was a difficult process. Recall that the Europeans had set up colonial boundaries that usually made no sense culturally or politically. A single colony such as the Gold Coast (Ghana) had contained dozens of ethnic groups with differing cultural and political traditions. People's attachment to their own cultural group was often far stronger than any loyalty toward a central, national government. Typically, when an African colony gained its independence, a civil war would erupt among rival groups. The strongest group would eventually achieve political control and elect their leader as the country's president. The leader would often rule with an iron hand as a military dictator.

A civil war in Nigeria provided just one example of the political troubles experienced by many African nations. The conflict began in

1967, seven years after Nigeria had gained independence from British rule. One ethnic group in Nigeria, the Ibos, revolted against the more powerful Hausas, who controlled Nigeria's government. The Ibos fought to establish an independent Ibo nation, to be called Biafra. In 1970, however, the rebellion was crushed, and the Ibos were forced to accept Hausa rule.

Uganda offers an example of an African nation whose government became both authoritarian and corrupt. In 1971, a Uganda army leader, Idi Amin, overthrew the elected government and established a military dictatorship. He then gave government jobs to members of his own family and his own ethnic group. These officials used their position of power to amass large fortunes for themselves. Against his political enemies, Idi Amin used brutal methods. Opponents were killed by the hundreds of thousands. After eight years of misrule, Idi Amin was finally overthrown and forced to flee the country.

In the 1980s, most African governments were one-party dictatorships. While not all dictators were as ruthless as Idi Amin, many yielded to the temptations of misusing their power to enrich themselves and their families.

Multiparty democracies   In the late 1980s and early 1990s, Africans in many nations expressed growing dissatisfaction with one-party dictatorships. From Nigeria in West Africa to Kenya in East Africa, people demanded elections in which several political parties could compete freely. Bowing to popular pressure, one African dictator after another promised to permit multiparty elections. Some dictators, such as Kenneth Kaunda of Zambia, carried through on their promises and permitted free elections. In 1991, Kaunda went down to defeat after having ruled Zambia for 27 years. Other dictators, such as President Mobutu Sese Seko of Zaire, promised multiparty elections but invented excuses for delaying or canceling them.

Despite setbacks, the movement for multiparty democracies in Africa is a significant force for change in the 1990s.

Pan-Africanism   What happens in one part of Africa is usually of great interest to people throughout the region. This has been true for many decades. As early as the 1920s, Jomo Kenyatta and other young African nationalists believed in the idea of *Pan-Africanism* (the unity and cooperation of all African peoples). They thought that Africans everywhere should support one another in their common plan to achieve nationhood. In 1945, Kenyatta helped organize a Pan-African Congress, which was attended by Africans from many parts of the continent. Delegates to the Congress announced their common purpose to end colonialism throughout Africa.

In 1963, a number of African nations formed the Organization of African Unity (OAU). It aimed to create a sense of unity among Africans.

It also sought areas in which African nations could work cooperatively to solve common problems. For years, representatives from OAU's member nations have met periodically to discus Pan-African issues. They have sought to increase the influence of Africa in world affairs, especially in the United Nations. For 30 years, the OAU campaigned to persuade the world that the rule of a white minority in South Africa was racist and illegitimate.

Origins of apartheid in South Africa   Beginning in 1948, the Republic of South Africa became the center of controversy when its government imposed strict rules of racial separation. The government's policy of *apartheid*—keeping the races apart—was a product of South Africa's colonial past.

The first Europeans to settle in South Africa were the Dutch in the 1600s. In 1815, Holland agreed to give up control of its South African colony to the British. Unwilling to be governed by foreigners, though, Dutch farmers in South Africa moved away from British-controlled areas near the coast. They set up two republics in the interior. The white, Dutch-speaking citizens of these republics called themselves *Afrikaners* (or *Boers*). Eager to control the gold mines of interior South Africa, the British went to war against the Afrikaners. British victory in this Boer War (1899–1902) was followed by the formation of a self-governing dominion, the Union of South Africa. It became fully independent in 1931. But the black population of the country was excluded from participating in the all-white government. Outnumbering the British, the Dutch-speaking Afrikaners organized a political party that won control of the government in 1948.

One of the first acts of the Afrikaner-controlled government was to adopt apartheid. This policy separated the people of South Africa into four racial groups: whites, blacks, Asians, and "coloreds" (people of mixed ancestry). (Many Asians, mainly from India, had migrated to South Africa to work on tea plantations.) Less than 20 percent of the population were white. The overwhelming majority—more than 70 percent—were black. The government's purposes in adopting apartheid were to (1) maintain white rule, (2) keep the races from associating with one another, and (3) maintain white control over the economic wealth of South Africa.

Apartheid applied to all aspects of life. Socially, blacks had to live apart from the other races, travel in separate buses and trains, and attend separate schools. Politically, blacks could not vote or run for public office. Economically, they could work only in certain low-paying occupations. They had to carry identification passes and could enter white areas only for limited times. South Africa's all-white government set aside certain parts of the country for the exclusive use of blacks. These "tribal homelands" were located far from the coastal

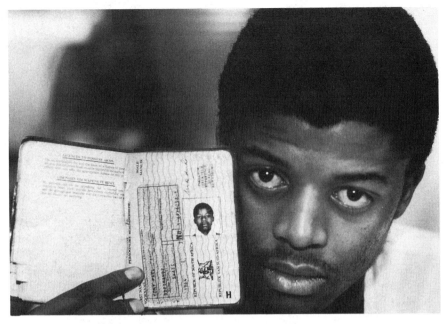

PASS BOOK: Apartheid laws of South Africa required blacks (but not whites) to carry a pass book for identification. In what other ways were black South Africans discriminated against?

cities. Most of those forced to move to these areas had never lived there before, even though the lands were referred to as "homelands."

Black African opposition to apartheid   Although they were subject to being jailed for challenging apartheid, many black South Africans joined or supported an anti-apartheid organization called the African National Congress (ANC). South Africa's all-white government outlawed the ANC in 1960 and made it a crime to participate in ANC activities. Also in 1960, the police shot and killed more than 60 protesters in Sharpeville, a township near Johannesburg. Blacks throughout Africa reacted angrily to news of the "Sharpeville massacre," as it was labeled. Despite its illegal status, the ANC continued to mobilize black resistance to apartheid and white rule. One of its leaders, Nelson Mandela, was captured and sentenced in 1964 to prison for life.

In Review

The following questions refer to Section III: The Dynamics of Change.

1. *Key terms:* Define each of the following:

internal slavery	imperialism	apartheid
external slavery	human rights	self-determination

2. Give *four* reasons for the development of African nationalism after World War II.

3. State *two* types of political problems that often arose in newly independent African nations.

4. *Critical thinking:* "European influences on Africa were far more negative than positive." Explain why you either agree or disagree with this statement.

IV. Contemporary Nations (1970 to the Present)

Since 1970, the nations of Africa have struggled to overcome major obstacles to economic and political progress. Chief among these obstacles are the problems of civil wars, overpopulation, droughts, urban poverty, and mounting burdens of financial debt.

A. ENDING APARTHEID IN SOUTH AFRICA

Black Africans achieved a notable victory in the early 1990s by finally prevailing upon the white government of South Africa to abandon apartheid. How did this victory come about?

Dedicated leadership Leaders of South African blacks played a major role in winning the support of the international community. For his nonviolent struggle against apartheid, Zulu Chief Albert Luthuli received the Nobel Peace Prize in 1960. For similar efforts on behalf of South Africans' human rights, Anglican Bishop Desmond Tutu received that prize in 1984. The award gave Bishop Tutu worldwide recognition. In trips to many countries, he called for support of a boycott against South African products and an embargo on all goods shipped to South Africa.

Nelson Mandela, the ANC leader, spent more than 27 years in prison for advocating an end to white minority rule. In 1990, he finally gained his freedom. Famous for his heroic struggles, Mandela visited many nations and urged governments around the world to stop trading with South Africa until that country abandoned apartheid.

Strikes and protest demonstrations During the 1980s, labor unions of South African, black workers organized a series of strikes against railroads and mines. They were protesting against oppressive labor laws and apartheid. In June 1988, almost two million workers participated in a nationwide strike. These strikes hurt the nation's economy and rallied millions of people to the anti-apartheid cause.

International sanctions Outside South Africa, people of many nations became angry over the racist policies of South Africa's government. On university campuses around the world, millions of students participated in anti-apartheid demonstrations and rallies. Various international organizations, such as the United Nations and the OAU, urged member nations to adopt economic and cultural sanctions against South Africa's all-white regime. Many nations carried out the requested sanctions, which included:

- cutting off trade with South Africa
- refusing to invest in South Africa's industries and businesses
- excluding South Africa from membership in the UN General Assembly
- barring South Africa's athletes from competing in the Olympics.

Toward a new constitution   International pressure on South Africa's government had its intended effect. In the late 1980s and early 1990s, the government began to repeal its apartheid laws and move toward a political system open to all South Africans.

The first significant change was the government's decision to abolish the *pass laws*. No longer would blacks have to carry passbooks. (*Passbooks* indicated where a person could live, work, or travel.)

In 1989, white South Africans elected a new president, Frederik W. de Klerk. This leader recognized that international sanctions had labeled South Africa as a kind of outlaw among nations. At the same time, there was the growing danger of civil strife and open revolt against the white regime. De Klerk decided that the time had come for fundamental reforms. He persuaded the legislature to do away with (1) laws that segregated public places, (2) laws that banned marriages between people of different races, and (3) laws that required all South Africans to be classified by race. In 1990, de Klerk ordered ANC leader Nelson Mandela released from jail. He also restored the ANC as a legal organization.

The ANC was not the only political party to speak for black South Africans. Challenging the ANC was the Inkatha Freedom party, which represented the Zulu ethnic group. Hostility between these rival parties led to armed clashes and mob attacks.

Hoping to avoid civil war, de Klerk and Mandela negotiated an agreement between the South African government and the ANC. De Klerk urged white voters of South Africa to support a new constitution that would allow blacks equal voting rights. A crucial *referendum* (vote on a public issue by the people) was held in March 1992. White voters were asked whether or not there should be a new constitution and nationwide elections open to people of all races. An overwhelming majority voted yes.

In September 1993, South Africa's legislature voted to hold in 1994 an election in which all races could participate. Having achieved one of his major goals, Mandela called for an end to all economic sanctions against South Africa. The appeal was quickly heeded, as governments and institutions around the world lifted their trade and investment sanctions. The first all-race election in South Africa's history went ahead as planned in April 1994. Black South Africans celebrated an overwhelming political victory. The ANC won a majority of seats in the legislature, and its longtime leader, Nelson Mandela, became South Africa's first black president.

For their efforts in dismantling apartheid, Mandela and de Klerk were jointly awarded the Nobel Peace Prize in 1993. The Nobel Committee cited their "personal integrity and great political courage" and said that their actions point "the way to the peaceful resolution of similar deep-rooted conflicts elsewhere in the world."

DOCUMENT: MANDELA ARGUES AGAINST APARTHEID

Born in South Africa in 1918, Nelson Mandela spent much of his life fighting against racism. He was expelled from a South African college for joining in a student strike. Later, he earned a law degree from another university and became a lawyer. In 1952, he received a nine-month prison sentence for organizing opposition to apartheid. In 1964, he was sentenced to life imprisonment on a charge of conspiring to overthrow the South African government. At his trial, he presented the following arguments against apartheid.

Africans want to be paid a living wage. Africans want to perform work which they are capable of doing, and not work which the Government declares them to be capable of. Africans want to be allowed to live where they obtain work, and not be endorsed out of [excluded from] an area because they were not born there. Africans want to be allowed to own land in places where they work, and not be obliged to live in rented houses which they can never call their own. Africans want to be part of the general population, and not confined to living in their own ghettos. African men want to have their wives and children to live with them where they work, and not be forced into an unnatural existence in men's hostels. African women want to be with their menfolk and not be left permanently widowed in the reserves. Africans want to be allowed out after 11 o'clock at night and not be confined to their rooms like little children. Africans want to be allowed to travel in their own country and to seek work where they want to and not where the Labour Bureau tells them to. . . .

Nelson Mandela at the United Nations, 1990

Above all, we want equal political rights, because without them our disabilities will be permanent. I know this sounds revolutionary to the Whites in this country, because the majority of voters will be Africans. This makes the White man fear democracy.

Think About It

Consider each of the "wants" that Mandela presents. Do you think each "want" is also a basic right of all people everywhere? Or would you argue that some of the "wants" are rights, while others are not? How might Mandela's views, as expressed here, apply to the way that Mandela serves as South Africa's president, beginning in 1994?

Source: *Nelson R. Mandela, "Statement during the Rivonia Trial" (April 20, 1964). Reprinted in* The Human Rights *Reader, edited by Walter Laqueur and Barry Rubin. New York: New American Library, 1989.*

B. AFRICAN LIFE IN TRANSITION

In every African country today, similar forces are at work to bring about rapid change. Even though all of Africa's nations have won their independence from colonial rule, the impact of Western culture and technology remains strong.

Tensions between the new and the old   As in other parts of the world, the forces of *modernization* (the process of adopting new customs and technologies) are often in conflict with the forces of *tradition* (observing old customs). Rural areas of Africa tend to retain traditional values and practices. For example, a household in rural villages commonly includes grandparents, aunts, uncles, and other relatives as well as parents and their children. These extended families differ from the nuclear families and single-parent families that one tends to find in urban areas.

Traditional marriage customs are still widely practiced in many parts of Africa, especially in the rural villages. Following a custom known as *polygamy*, a man may have two or more wives at one time. It is also common for marriages to be arranged by the parents, and for the bride's family to receive a payment in return for their agreement to the marriage. This "bride's money" is given to compensate the bride's family for the loss of the young woman's labor.

In Africa's growing cities, however, marriage customs tend to follow a modern pattern. Women in cities marry by choice and insist that their husbands be *monogamous* (married to just one spouse). Compared with women in rural areas, urban women are more likely to be educated and to pursue business or professional careers.

Africans living in cities acquire attitudes that clash with traditional values and practices. Many accept ideas derived from the West such as the ideas that property should be privately owned and that government should be based on majority rule. The desire to acquire the latest imported consumer goods is fostered by modern forms of communication, including radio, television, films, magazines, and newspapers.

Economic problems   The nations of Africa remain dependent on industrialized nations for trade, technical help, and capital. In order to industrialize, Africa's developing nations must import Western and Japanese technology. To purchase this costly technology, they must borrow money from international lending agencies, such as the World Bank and the International Monetary Fund (IMF). They also seek loans from Western banks and Western governments. African nations import more than they export. Almost every year, they end up with an *unfavorable balance of trade* (value of imports exceeds value of exports). Thus, they find themselves deeper in debt to the World Bank and to other lending institutions.

Most African nations also have the problem of relying on foreign sources of oil to sustain their industrial development. When oil prices rise, African nations are forced to go deeper into debt to finance their purchases of this necessary source of energy.

Adding to African nations' problems are the consumer demands of Africa's middle class. Many of the consumer goods bought by this group, such as cars and television sets, are produced in Japan, Europe, and North America. Only a small percentage of high-priced consumer goods are produced in Africa. As Africans purchase more Western and Japanese goods, their nations' balance of trade becomes even more unfavorable.

Natural disasters have also contributed to Africans' economic woes. Lack of rainfall in East Africa produced devastating droughts in the 1970s and 1980s and caused mass starvation in Ethiopia, Somalia, and Sudan. Relief efforts by charities and the United Nations were not enough to make up for food shortages. African nations affected by the droughts were forced to rely even more heavily on imported food from the West.

Population problems   African societies also suffer from the problem of *overpopulation* (having too many people competing for scarce resources). In the 40 years from 1950 to 1990, Africa's population almost tripled. Its nearly 700 million people represent 15 percent of the world's total population.

Why is Africa's population growing so rapidly? The chief reason is the impact of modern medicine. Because of improved health care in the 20th century, death rates among African nations have dropped. But birth rates remain as high as ever. In order to close the gap between many births and fewer deaths, the birth rate would have to be reduced. But traditional beliefs and attitudes encourage just the opposite. Why is this? In African villages of the past, a fairly high percentage of children would die before reaching maturity. Women were encouraged to give birth to many children because this ensured the community's survival. Circumstances are now different, but traditional practices and beliefs are slow to change. Another factor is that African governments lack the funds to provide adequate family planning services in rural villages.

Overpopulation is a major cause of widespread poverty and hunger in Africa. Every year, there are more people to be fed and not enough resources to meet the growing need for food. Various factors contribute to the problem of food shortages and *malnutrition* (having not enough or the wrong kinds of food). These factors include (1) the high costs of modern equipment and fertilizers, (2) desertification, (3) destruction from civil wars, and (4) frequent droughts.

Proposed solutions   What can African nations do about the related problems of water shortages and food shortages? Irrigation might be one solution to the water problem. It has been difficult, however, to increase the amount of land irrigated because of the need to train more workers and the high costs of buying irrigation equipment.

Breakthroughs in agricultural sciences also hold out hope for increasing Africa's crop yields. Through *genetic engineering* (altering the genes of plants and animals), scientists have developed new strains of wheat and other grains that are perfectly suited to African soils and climates. Since the 1960s, farmers in Africa (and in other regions as well) have dramatically increased crop yields by using scientifically developed seeds. Efforts to increase worldwide food supply have been dramatic enough to be called the *Green Revolution*. Unfortunately in the case of Africa, crop yields have not increased fast enough to keep pace with the growing population.

Urbanization   A large majority of Africans still live in *rural* (country) areas—but this fact is rapidly changing. In recent decades, African societies have been undergoing *urbanization* (a shift in population from rural areas to cities). One reason for this trend has been the series of droughts (and accompanying food shortages) in the savannas. Other

URBANIZATION IN KENYA: The population of Kenya's capital, Nairobi, has increased five times since 1960. It is now 1.1 million—and growing. What are the social and economic causes of urbanization in African nations?

reasons are the economic and educational opportunities in urban areas. There are more jobs in the cities than in rural areas. But the number of people who migrate to the cities each year far exceeds the number of new job openings.

The influx of so many people into the cities has led to widespread urban poverty. Overwhelmed by the masses of poor, African governments have found it difficult to provide the essential city services of sanitation, education, public health, and police protection.

Another problem with urbanization is that newcomers tend to become alienated from their villages. They are less likely to live in extended families in the cities, and, thus, they lose the social support that large families can provide. Some may break their cultural ties to the village in which they formerly lived. Their loyalty to the national government may increase, while their loyalty to their ethnic group may decrease.

C. AFRICA IN THE GLOBAL CONTEXT

Since winning their independence, African nations have sought economic aid from the United States and other developed countries. At the same time, most African leaders have tried to avoid forming strong ties with any outside power. Two policies have typically guided their approach to foreign affairs: (1) membership in international organizations and (2) nonalignment.

Membership in international organizations   African nations have found that they can increase their leverage and influence in world affairs by making maximum use of the United Nations and other international organizations.

1. *Africans in the United Nations.* The more than 50 African nations belonging to the United Nations represent that organization's largest regional bloc. Because of their numbers, African countries can exert considerable influence on decisions of the General Assembly. Here small and large nations alike cast just one vote each. On many issues, African nations tend to vote as a bloc (along with many nations of Latin America and Asia).

On a number of occasions, the United Nations has voted to send peacekeeping forces to end civil wars in Africa. During the 1960s, UN troops helped stop a civil war in the Congo (present-day Zaire). In the early 1990s, UN peacekeeping forces were active in four African nations at once: Angola, Western Sahara, Somalia, and Mozambique.

For help in dealing with financial problems, African nations have turned to two specialized UN agencies, the World Bank and the International Monetary Fund (IMF). The World Bank provides loans and technical assistance for major economic projects. The IMF seeks to stabilize currencies and solve other short-term problems of member nations.

2. Africans in the Commonwealth of Nations. Another source of economic help comes from those European nations that once colonized Africa. Nations such as Ghana, Kenya, Nigeria, and Tanzania had once been colonies of Great Britain. Now these nations enjoy special trading privileges as members of the Commonwealth of Nations (formerly called the British Commonwealth). For members of this organization, tariffs are lower and markets are subject to fewer restrictions than for nonmembers.

3. Africans in OPEC. Four African nations—Algeria, Gabon, Libya, and Nigeria—have rich deposits of oil. To maximize their economic gains from the sale of oil, these nations have joined the Organization of Petroleum Exporting Countries (OPEC). The purpose of this worldwide organization is to boost world oil prices. It tries to do this by limiting the production of oil by member nations. With less oil available worldwide, the demand for the oil that is available will increase. If demand increases, then the price of oil will tend to rise.

4. Africans in the OAU. One organization is open only to African nations. The Organization of African Unity (OAU) attempts to promote cooperation among its more than 50 members. It has settled boundary disputes, helped member nations fund energy projects, and led an international movement to end apartheid in South Africa.

Nonalignment   Beginning in the 1960s, the United States and the Soviet Union competed with each other to influence the politics of African nations. While the Soviet government would back one side in a war (or civil war), the U.S. government would back the other side. In the 1980s, for example, the United States supplied arms to Somalia in its war with the Soviet-backed government of Ethiopia. In another example, a Communist government in Angola received military support from both the Soviet Union and Cuba. Meanwhile, the United States supplied arms to a rebel group that was fighting to overthrow Angola's government.

The U.S.–Soviet competition in Africa was part of the *cold war* (ongoing conflict between two countries that stops short of actual fighting by them). By supplying economic and military aid, the two *superpowers* (extremely powerful nations) each tried to win as many allies in Africa as they could. But most African nations remained *nonaligned* (not allied to any power) in this cold war competition. In other words, they refused to side with either the Soviet Union or the United States. Instead, they accepted military and economic aid from both powers, provided that this aid came with "no strings attached."

After the cold war   The cold war ended in 1991 when the Soviet Union broke apart and became Russia and other, smaller states. The end of the cold war marked a turning point in African nations' relations with the rest of the world. No longer can African governments count on receiving the levels of economic and military aid that they

UN TROOPS IN SOMALIA: UN forces (including the Nigerian soldiers in the armored car) originally entered Somalia to bring food supplies to starving people. What political complications made their job difficult?

had received during the cold war. Russia does not have the financial resources to provide much aid. Faced with economic problems of its own, the United States has scaled back on its aid programs to African nations. Africans are worried that their countries' problems will be ignored by the industrialized nations of the world.

Somalia provides an illustration of this point. A civil war there in the early 1990s left the country with no effective government. Somali warlords fought each other for control of various parts of the country. As a result of the fighting, food distribution networks broke down, and Somali farmers found it difficult to grow food. At the same time, a drought hit the country and further diminished food supplies. World-wide televised reports of famine in Somalia alerted people in other countries to the situation. Finally in 1992, the United States and other nations sent troops to Somalia. Acting under United Nations command, the troops worked to restore order and improve food distribution. But the UN troops ended up fighting various Somali warlords and their supporters. After some U.S. troops were killed there, Americans began calling for the withdrawal of U.S. forces from Somalia. The last U.S. troops left Somalia in 1994.

Africans are having to rely more on their own resources. At meetings of the OAU, for example, delegates have called for the formation of an all-African peacekeeping force to solve military conflicts on the continent. Some African leaders see regional cooperation as the answer.

In fact, a regional force was created in 1990 to try to stop a civil war in Liberia. A group of West African nations sent a multinational force into that country to try to keep order and set up a stable government. If this mission succeeds, we may see still other examples of regional or all-African cooperation.

In Review

The following questions refer to Section IV: Contemporary Nations (1970 to the Present).

1. *Key terms:* Define or identify each of the following:

   pass law   Green Revolution   cold war
   modernization   urbanization   nonalignment

2. Explain the role of each of the following in bringing apartheid to an end: (*a*) Nelson Mandela, (*b*) Frederik W. de Klerk, and (*c*) the United Nations.

3. State three examples of the conflict between modernization and tradition in Africa.

4. *Critical thinking:* Which of Africa's problems do you think is probably the most difficult to solve? Give reasons for your answer.

TEST YOURSELF

Multiple-Choice Questions

Level 1

On a separate sheet of paper, write the number of the word or expression that, of those given, best completes each statement or answers each question.

1. Which statement is a valid generalization about the geography of Africa? (1) The continent of Africa has diverse resources and topography. (2) Most African nations have vast oil reserves. (3) The nations of North Africa are dominated by rain forests. (4) The irregular coastline of Africa provides many excellent harbors.

2. In Africa, an effect of topography and climate has been to (1) encourage rapid industrialization of the interior (2) prevent the development of kingdoms (3) promote large-scale trade between Africa and Asia (4) promote the growth of diverse societies.

3. One similarity between Axum and Kush was that they were both (1) military leaders in the Neolithic Age (2) rivers along which early trade developed (3) writers of epic poems about Greek cities (4) early civilizations in Africa.

4. Which statement best describes the effects of the geography of Africa? (1) Geography has encouraged physical mobility throughout Africa. (2) Certain features of African geography hindered economic development. (3) The geography of Africa has stimulated political and cultural unity. (4) The geography of Africa has resulted in most African countries having similar economic and social systems.

5. The basic characteristic of subsistence agriculture is that farmers (1) produce mostly staple crops to sell (2) sell large portions of their crops at the market price (3) produce crops mainly for their own immediate use (4) produce crops according to government orders.

6. Which is often a characteristic of traditional African art? (1) African art forms reflect society's desire to become industrialized. (2) African works of art are an important part of religious life. (3) African art forms generally support government-approved objectives. (4) African works of art primarily commemorate important battles and victories.

7. Which is a major characteristic of traditional African art? (1) African art contains a great deal of symbolism. (2) The human form is represented very realistically in African art. (3) Painting is the primary medium for African art. (4) African art reflects a highly urban culture.

8. Which statement is most accurate about the African slave trade from the 15th through the 19th centuries? (1) The slave trade was limited to East Africa. (2) The slave traders brought ivory and timber to Africa. (3) The slave trade involved African, Arab, and European slave traders. (4) Most slaves were transported from Africa to Europe.

9. The influence of African culture on some areas of Latin America was largely a result of the (1) American Revolution (2) building of the Panama Canal (3) success of Communist revolutions (4) Atlantic slave trade.

10. The major factor that enabled Western Europe to dominate large parts of Africa in the 19th and early 20th centuries was the (1) technological and military superiority of European nations (2) acceptance of Christianity by many Africans (3) desire of Africans for European raw materials (4) refusal of Africans to fight against European imperialism.

11. European imperialism promoted the development of nationalism in African countries by (1) unintentionally uniting people to oppose foreign domination (2) promoting free-trade associations among the colonies (3) establishing Christianity as the common religion (4) discouraging patriotic feelings toward the mother country.

12. Which is an accurate statement about the partitioning of Africa by European imperialist nations during the 1800s? (1) New nations were based on old tribal boundaries. (2) The cultural and ethnic diversity of the African people was disregarded. (3) The continent was divided equally among the colonial powers. (4) African unity was encouraged.

13. Which statement best describes the political situation in Africa after World War II? (1) Increased nationalism led to independence for many African nations. (2) France and West Germany sought to establish colonies in Africa. (3) European nations increased their control over their African colonies. (4) The United Nations opposed the idea of self-determination for African nations.

14. Which statement best expresses a major idea of Pan-Africanism? (1) African doctors should be trained in Western schools. (2) European nations should reestablish economic relationships with their former African colonies. (3) African nations should work together to solve their problems. (4) African nations should send peacekeeping forces to settle disputes in other areas of the world.

15. The apartheid system in the Republic of South Africa (1) reflected democratic ideals (2) promoted discrimination (3) encouraged social mobility (4) provided economic equality.

16. In the 1980s, global concern for blacks in the Republic of South Africa led many nations to (1) impose economic sanctions on South Africa (2) demand that whites return to their European homelands (3) send troops to South Africa (4) support policies of apartheid.

17. Which statement best describes the significance of awarding the 1984 Nobel Peace Prize to Bishop Desmond Tutu of South Africa? (1) The world community was endorsing the apartheid practices of the government of South Africa. (2) The European policy of remaining neutral in regard to human rights issues was reaffirmed. (3) The separation of church and state was promoted as a universal concept. (4) Nonviolence was recognized as a way to bring about change in South Africa.

Base your answer to question 18 on the cartoon below and on your knowledge of social studies.

18. What did the cartoon illustrate about the Republic of South Africa? (1) The white minority was continuing to gain power. (2) Racial equality in employment and education had been achieved. (3) The black majority was forcing concessions from the white minority. (4) The British government still had control over internal affairs.

Steve Kelley, Copley News Service

19. A major factor in the development of 20th-century nationalist movements throughout Africa was a common (1) language throughout most of Africa (2) goal to end European rule in Africa (3) ethnic bond among the people of Africa (4) religion throughout most of Africa.

20. Since the 1960s, a major improvement in African agriculture has been (1) a greater emphasis on subsistence farming (2) an increased dependence on a one-crop economy in many countries (3) a decreased reliance on irrigation systems (4) an increased use of scientific farming techniques.

21. During the 1980s, a major problem in many economically developing countries in Africa was the (1) fear of competition with industrialized countries (2) decreasing numbers of potential employees in these countries (3) increasing foreign debt in these countries (4) shortage of markets in industrialized nations.

22. A major cause for the high birth rates in many developing nations in Africa has been (1) the need for a large urban work force (2) a desire to counteract an increasing death rate (3) a need to replace people killed during civil wars (4) traditional beliefs and the economic need to have large families.

23. Which conclusion is valid concerning the food shortages in some nations of Africa during the 1970s and 1980s? (1) Overuse of the land has led to desertification of a vast area. (2) Too few people in Africa are involved in food production. (3) Acid rain has been the major cause of crop failures. (4) European nations stopped shipping food to Africa.

24. During the cold war, most African nations attempted to (1) side with the Communist bloc (2) follow the guidance of their former colonial ruler (3) pursue their idea of national self-interest (4) support the United States.

25. During the cold war era, many African nations followed a policy of nonalignment because they (1) had the same goals and needs as the Soviet Union (2) needed the natural resources of Western European nations (3) wished to receive aid from both the Soviet Union and the United States (4) were afraid of losing their vote in the United Nations.

Level 2

Base your answers to questions 26 and 27 on the diagrams on the next page and on your knowledge of social studies.

26. The Fulani people are most likely (1) hunters and gatherers (2) commercial farmers (3) merchants (4) nomadic herders.

27. The life-style of the Fulani people is most directly the result of (1) desertification and deforestation (2) sharp differences between the great basins and high plateaus (3) changes in growing seasons and available food sources (4) abundant jungle resources.

MOVEMENT OF THE FULANI PEOPLE

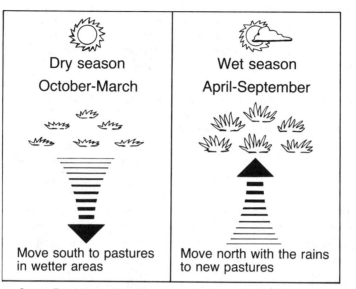

Source: *Population and Food Resources in the Developing World* (adapted)

28. Discoveries by the Leakeys and other archeologists have provided evidence that (1) humans have existed for only 1,000 years (2) early humans lived in eastern Africa (3) early humans failed to invent tools (4) river valleys hindered cultural development.

29. A major result of the development of civilization in ancient Egypt was the (1) conquest and settlement of Western Europe by the Egyptian empire (2) establishment of a democratic system of government in Egypt (3) establishment of trade routes between Egypt and other kingdoms (4) decline of agriculture as an important occupation in Egypt.

30. Ancient African kingdoms such as Ghana and Mali based their economic systems primarily on (1) oil exports (2) agriculture and trade (3) commercial fishing (4) hunting and gathering.

31. The influence of traditional African cultures is best seen today in Western (1) technological advances (2) art forms (3) family patterns (4) political ideas.

32. During the 19th century, the African continent was affected most by (1) the Commercial Revolution (2) the introduction of socialism (3) the Crusades (4) European imperialism.

33. Between 1880 and 1914, which nations were most involved in colonizing Africa? (1) industrialized Western European nations (2) Eastern European nations controlled by Russia (3) East Asian nations seeking to establish new markets (4) oil-rich Middle Eastern nations.

34. After 1880, European nations sought colonies in Africa primarily because the Europeans were   (1) in need of land for their surplus populations   (2) competing for raw materials and markets   (3) determined to bring Christianity to the Muslim world   (4) interested in completing their geographic knowledge of the world.

35. Which was a major effect of European imperialism on Africa? (1) Trade between Europe and Africa declined.   (2) Africans and Europeans developed a respect for each other's cultures.   (3) Africans became economically dependent on European nations.   (4) Most Africans voluntarily gave up their cultures.

36. Jomo Kenyatta and Kwame Nkrumah were African leaders opposed to   (1) militarism   (2) socialism   (3) nationalism   (4) colonialism.

37. Many modern-day African nations have had difficulty uniting their people because the people   (1) have strong ethnic ties   (2) are still loyal to the former colonial power   (3) do not wish to remain in Africa   (4) are unwilling to accept authority figures.

38. Which statement is accurate concerning the policy of apartheid in the Republic of South Africa?   (1) It was encouraged by other nations. (2) It was an attempt to improve living conditions for blacks.   (3) It was based on racial segregation.   (4) It resulted in equal treatment for whites and blacks.

39. In most societies, urbanization has   (1) weakened traditional values and life patterns   (2) strengthened the influence of the extended family system   (3) discouraged economic growth   (4) promoted population growth.

40. In Africa, people have moved from rural villages to urban areas primarily to   (1) avoid the high cost of living in rural areas   (2) escape the poor climates in rural areas   (3) find job opportunities in the cities   (4) live among people of different ethnic backgrounds in the cities.

Essay Questions

Level 1

1. The developing nations of Africa have been affected by problems caused by the factors listed below.

Factors
Urbanization
Industrialization
Droughts
Population growth

Select *three* of the factors listed. For each factor chosen, describe a problem that has been caused by that factor.

2. The relationships among colonialism, imperialism, and nationalism have formed an important part of Africa's history.

   A. Discuss specific reasons that European nations colonized most of Africa.

   B. Discuss two effects that European colonization had on the people of Africa.

   C. Describe how nationalism within Africa contributed to the movements for independence from European nations.

Level 2

3. Africa has a great diversity of geographic features.

Geographic Features
Deserts
Savannas
Regular coastline
Rivers
Lakes

   A. Select *three* of the geographic features listed. For each feature chosen, explain how it affected the development of Africa.

   B. Base your answer to Part B on your answer to Part A. However, additional information may be included. Write an essay discussing the effects of the selected geographic features on the development of Africa. Begin your essay with this topic sentence:

   > Many geographic features have influenced the development of Africa.

4. Many events in Africa have had important results.

Events
Islam spreads to West Africa (8th and 9th centuries)
Atlantic slave trade develops (16th to 19th centuries)
European nations conquer most of Africa (19th century)
Afrikaners win control of South African government (1948)
Nelson Mandela freed from prison (1990)

   A. Select *three* of the events listed. For each event, state one result.

   B. Base your answer to Part B on your answer to Part A. However, additional information may be included. Write an essay explaining how each of the events selected from the list had important results. Begin your essay with this topic sentence:

   > Many events in Africa have had important results.

CHAPTER 3

The Middle East

Main Ideas

1. **CROSSROADS OF TRADE:** Because of its central location, the Middle East has served as an economic and cultural crossroads connecting Africa, Asia, and Europe.

2. **MUCH OIL, LITTLE WATER:** The Middle East is rich in oil but poor in other vital resources, particularly water.

3. **MONOTHEISM:** Advocating monotheism (worship of a single god), the religion of Judaism marked a significant change from earlier religions.

4. **JUDAISM AND CHRISTIANITY:** After originating in the Middle East, Judaism and Christianity spread to Europe, where each profoundly influenced Western values, ideals, and culture.

5. **ISLAM:** After its founding in Arabia in the early 600s, the religion of Islam spread to all parts of the Middle East, where it greatly influenced the history and culture of the region.

6. **CULTURAL CONTRIBUTIONS:** In the Middle Ages, the Islamic world preserved the classic texts of Greece and Rome and also laid the foundations for modern sciences and mathematics.

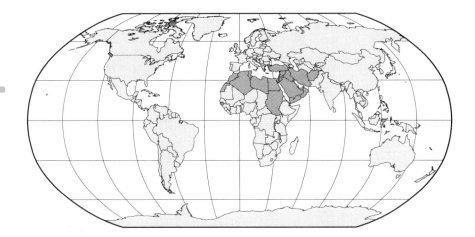

7. **TOLERATION:** Islamic rulers were known for their religious toleration and acceptance of cultural diversity.

8. **NATIONALISM:** Nationalism in the Middle East developed slowly in the early part of the 20th century. Since World War II, it has been a strong agent for change.

9. **ISRAEL AND THE PALESTINIANS:** In recent times, a major world conflict has been the clash between Arab Palestinians' demand for nationhood and Israel's need for security.

10. **FUNDAMENTALISM:** Muslim fundamentalists view the forces of modernization and industrialization as posing a threat to Islam's traditional customs and beliefs.

11. **CONTROL OF OIL:** The oil-rich nations of the Middle East have attempted to increase their political power and income by controlling oil production and prices.

12. **STATUS OF WOMEN:** In most of the region, women generally are not granted equal rights.

The Middle East: The Region at a Glance

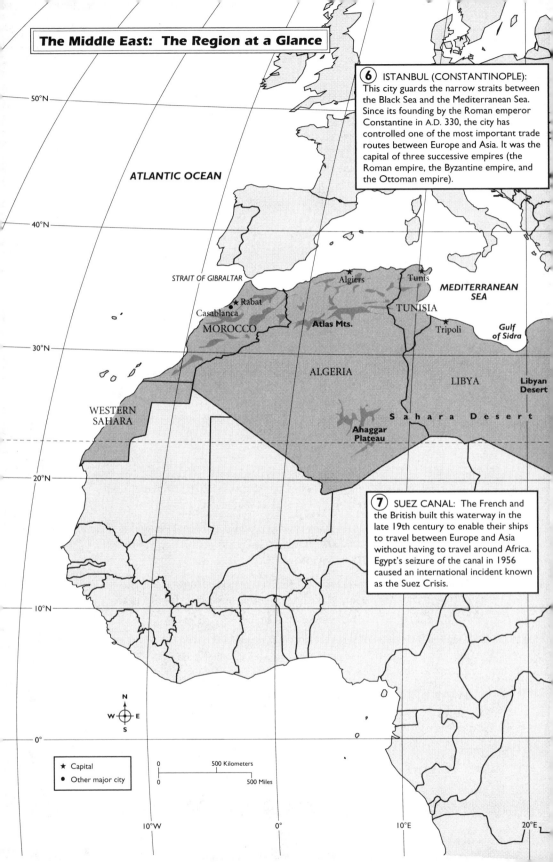

ATLANTIC OCEAN

6 ISTANBUL (CONSTANTINOPLE): This city guards the narrow straits between the Black Sea and the Mediterranean Sea. Since its founding by the Roman emperor Constantine in A.D. 330, the city has controlled one of the most important trade routes between Europe and Asia. It was the capital of three successive empires (the Roman empire, the Byzantine empire, and the Ottoman empire).

STRAIT OF GIBRALTAR

★ Rabat

Casablanca•

MOROCCO

Algiers ★

Tunis ★

TUNISIA

MEDITERRANEAN SEA

Tripoli ★

Gulf of Sidra

Atlas Mts.

ALGERIA

LIBYA

Libyan Desert

WESTERN SAHARA

S a h a r a   D e s e r t

Ahaggar Plateau

7 SUEZ CANAL: The French and the British built this waterway in the late 19th century to enable their ships to travel between Europe and Asia without having to travel around Africa. Egypt's seizure of the canal in 1956 caused an international incident known as the Suez Crisis.

50°N
40°N
30°N
20°N
10°N
0°

10°W
0°
10°E
20°E

N
W ⊕ E
S

★ Capital
• Other major city

0   500 Kilometers
0   500 Miles

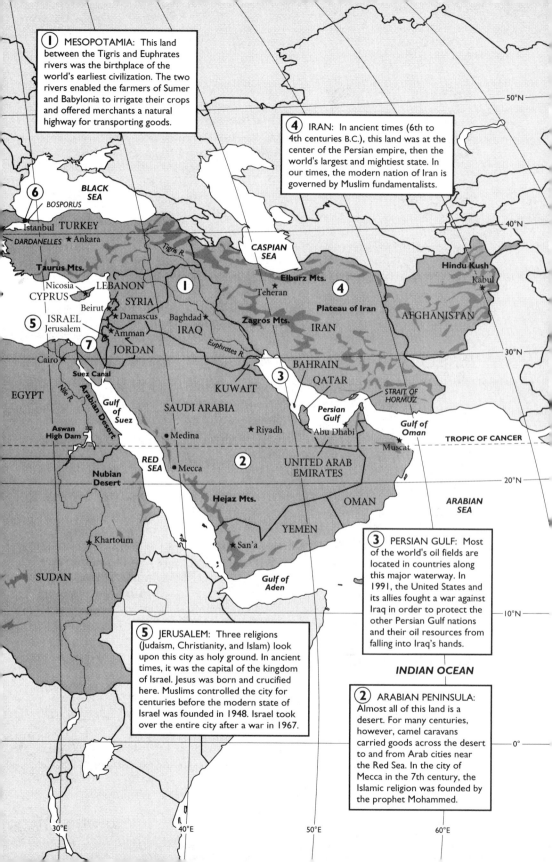

① MESOPOTAMIA: This land between the Tigris and Euphrates rivers was the birthplace of the world's earliest civilization. The two rivers enabled the farmers of Sumer and Babylonia to irrigate their crops and offered merchants a natural highway for transporting goods.

④ IRAN: In ancient times (6th to 4th centuries B.C.), this land was at the center of the Persian empire, then the world's largest and mightiest state. In our times, the modern nation of Iran is governed by Muslim fundamentalists.

③ PERSIAN GULF: Most of the world's oil fields are located in countries along this major waterway. In 1991, the United States and its allies fought a war against Iraq in order to protect the other Persian Gulf nations and their oil resources from falling into Iraq's hands.

⑤ JERUSALEM: Three religions (Judaism, Christianity, and Islam) look upon this city as holy ground. In ancient times, it was the capital of the kingdom of Israel. Jesus was born and crucified here. Muslims controlled the city for centuries before the modern state of Israel was founded in 1948. Israel took over the entire city after a war in 1967.

② ARABIAN PENINSULA: Almost all of this land is a desert. For many centuries, however, camel caravans carried goods across the desert to and from Arab cities near the Red Sea. In the city of Mecca in the 7th century, the Islamic religion was founded by the prophet Mohammed.

BLACK SEA

BOSPORUS

⑥

Istanbul TURKEY

DARDANELLES ★ Ankara

CASPIAN SEA

Taurus Mts.

Hindu Kush

Kabul

Nicosia LEBANON

CYPRUS

Beirut

★ Damascus

⑤ ISRAEL

Jerusalem

Elburz Mts.

Teheran

④

Plateau of Iran

AFGHANISTAN

SYRIA

Baghdad ★

①

Tigris R.

Zagros Mts.

IRAN

IRAQ

★ Amman

Euphrates R.

JORDAN

⑦

Cairo ★

Suez Canal

BAHRAIN

QATAR

③

STRAIT OF HORMUZ

EGYPT

Arabian Desert

Gulf of Suez

KUWAIT

SAUDI ARABIA

Persian Gulf

Abu Dhabi ★

Gulf of Oman

Muscat ★

TROPIC OF CANCER

Nile R.

Aswan High Dam

★ Riyadh

UNITED ARAB EMIRATES

Nubian Desert

RED SEA

● Medina

● Mecca

②

Hejaz Mts.

OMAN

ARABIAN SEA

Khartoum ★

YEMEN

★ San'a

SUDAN

Gulf of Aden

INDIAN OCEAN

50°N

40°N

30°N

20°N

10°N

0°

30°E   40°E   50°E   60°E

I. Geography

The Middle East straddles major portions of two continents, Africa and Asia. It even includes a small section of a third continent, Europe. The Asian part of the region stretches from Afghanistan in the east all the way to Turkey in the west. The region then extends across all of Northern Africa, from Egypt to Morocco. The European piece of the region is the little corner of Turkey that lies nearest to Greece (see the map).

Why have we included North Africa in two regions, both Africa and the Middle East? Geographically, it lies within the African continent. But North Africa is sometimes also considered part of the Middle East. The nations of North Africa are all Islamic, as are most of the nations in the rest of the Middle East. Moreover, Arabic—the main language in North Africa—is also the main language of most other Middle Eastern countries.

A. LOCATION: ECONOMIC AND CULTURAL CROSSROADS

As the central link connecting three continents—Africa, Asia, and Europe—the Middle East has acted throughout history as an economic and cultural crossroads. Traveling by camel caravans across the deserts and by ships across the Mediterranean, Red, and Arabian seas, the various peoples of the Middle East have transmitted their religions and transported articles of trade across an immense area.

B. CLIMATE

The climate of the Middle East is both unusually hot and unusually *arid* (dry). Because little rain falls over the region, much of the land area is a barren desert. Less than 15 percent of the land of the Middle East is suitable for farming. The scarcity of water is a major problem in most Middle Eastern countries. It limits economic development and the production of food.

C. RESOURCES

While it is poor in water, the region is rich in oil. In the 20th century, much of the world has come to depend on the oil wells of the Middle East. Large deposits of oil, however, are found only in a few nations of the region—especially in Saudi Arabia, Kuwait, Iraq, Iran, and the United Arab Emirates. Today, those nations that happen to be oil-rich are many times more wealthy than those nations in the region that have little or no oil.

IRRIGATION ON THE JORDAN: This Israeli farmer relies upon water from the Jordan River to irrigate crops. Why is irrigation so important to farmers in every country of the Middle East?

D. TOPOGRAPHY

Stretching over millions of acres of land, much of the Middle East consists of plateaus and deserts. The region is less mountainous than some other world regions.

Plateaus   The Asian part of the Middle East is made up of three immense plateaus. In the north, the Anatolian Plateau forms much of Turkey. In the east, the Iranian Plateau makes up almost all of Iran. In the south, the vast Arabian Peninsula is both a plateau and a desert. Of these three huge areas, the Anatolian Plateau receives the most rainfall, and thus is the area best suited for raising crops.

Deserts   Two vast deserts cover more than half of the land area of the Middle East.

- Almost all of the Arabian Peninsula is a desert.
- Spanning almost the whole of North Africa from Egypt to the Atlantic Ocean is the world's largest desert—the Sahara. (This desert is discussed in Chapter 2.)

Rivers   Because water is so scarce in the Middle East, most people have settled close to the region's four major rivers. Here water is available and irrigation is possible.

- Two rivers, the Tigris and the Euphrates, originate in eastern Turkey and flow through Syria and Iraq. Before emptying into the Persian Gulf, they meet in southern Iraq to form a single channel, the Shatt-al-Arab. The largely fertile land between the Tigris and Euphrates rivers forms a distinct and important subregion called *Mesopotamia*.

- In Chapter 2, you read about another river, the Nile. It has long played a central role in the life of Egypt.

- A fourth river, the Jordan, is smaller than the other three. But it is no less important to the millions of people of Jordan, Syria, and Israel who depend upon it. The Jordan empties into a saltwater lake, the Dead Sea, which is the world's saltiest body of water.

The fertile region between the Tigris and Euphrates rivers extends in a wide arc to connect with the fertile strip of land along the Jordan River. This arc of well-watered land was commonly known as the *Fertile Crescent*. Here the civilizations of southwest Asia had their beginnings.

Rivers of the Middle East are vitally important for three major reasons. First, they provide the water for irrigating crops. Second, their regular flooding enriches the soil. Third, they serve as natural waterways for transporting people and goods.

Strategic waterways   Nations outside the Middle East look upon the region as a crossroads for trade and a vital source of oil. Thus, industrial nations like the United States, Great Britain, and Japan are concerned about protecting their sea routes leading to and through the Middle East. Several waterways are important to outside powers.

One is the Suez Canal, located in northeastern Egypt. This canal allows merchant ships to go directly from the Mediterranean to the Red Sea, and then out into the open waters of the Indian Ocean. Of course, ships can also go in the opposite direction: from the Indian Ocean into the Red Sea, and then on to the Mediterranean.

A second vitally important waterway is the Persian Gulf. This body of water, 500 miles long, is nearly surrounded by major oil-producing nations of the Middle East. Included among these "Gulf States" are Iran, Iraq, Kuwait, and Saudi Arabia. The Strait of Hormuz, the narrow body of water at the eastern end of the Persian Gulf, serves as a gateway controlling access to the Gulf. Oil tankers from around the world daily pass through this strait. Because they provide a transportation route to the world's richest oil fields, the Persian Gulf and the Strait of

MESOPOTAMIA AND THE FERTILE CRESCENT

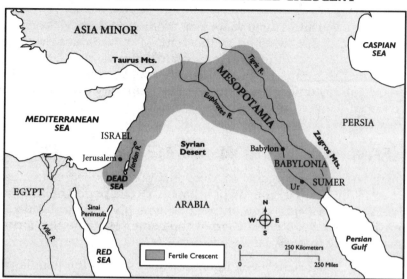

Hormuz have great strategic value. If any one nation ever gained total military control of these waterways, it could control much of the world's oil supply.

Two other straits in the Middle East control the movement of ships between the Black Sea and the Mediterranean Sea. These strategic waterways, the Bosporus and the Dardanelles, are located in western Turkey. In the 19th century, Russia's ambition to control these straits led to war (discussed on pages 425–426).

In Review

The following questions refer to Section I: Geography.

1. *Key terms:* Define or identify each of the following:

   arid   Tigris   Mesopotamia
   Sahara   Euphrates   Fertile Crescent

2. Explain how the Middle East's location has made it   (a) an economic and cultural crossroads and   (b) an area with strategic importance to nations outside the region.

3. List *five* characteristics of Middle Eastern geography.

4. *Critical thinking:* Referring to the map on pages 88–89, analyze the location of major Middle Eastern cities. What relation do you observe   (a) between cities and bodies of water and   (b) between cities and the desert?

II. Early History

Between 5,000 and 10,000 years ago, prehistoric peoples learned to grow crops on lands watered by the Tigris and Euphrates rivers. The development of agriculture in Mesopotamia made it possible for people to establish permanent settlements there. In most other parts of the world at this time, people still lived in temporary camps and wandered from place to place as nomadic hunters of wild animals and gatherers of wild plants.

A. EARLY CIVILIZATIONS OF MESOPOTAMIA

Small farming settlements in Mesopotamia produced a surplus of food and supported a growing population. Over a period of hundreds of years, some villages grew into cities, which were surrounded by defensive walls. Such cities were at the center of a complex form of human society that we call civilization.

Sumerians   Historians give the name Sumerians to the people who built the first cities of Mesopotamia. It is believed that the first cities of Sumer developed about 5,500 years ago, several hundred years before ancient Egypt's first cities. Sumer's early cities were governed by priests and kings. In city marketplaces, merchants traded a variety of goods. The highest urban structures were temples, each a multilevel tower.

In order to record information needed to carry on trade and government, Sumerian priests and officials invented wedge-like symbols that represented words and ideas. This form of writing is called *cuneiform*. Other Sumerian inventions included wheeled vehicles for transporting goods, irrigation systems for watering crops, and arches for supporting heavy structures over doorways.

Babylonians   Frequent wars among Sumerian city-states led to the downfall of Mesopotamia's first major civilization. Later, other groups in the region created civilizations. Like Sumer, the Babylonians also built walled cities, including its beautiful capital—Babylon—located on the Euphrates.

The Babylonians made important contributions in mathematics. To help make calculations in geometry, they divided the circle into 360 degrees. To help keep track of time, they invented an hour that was divided into 60 minutes. They also invented a calendar that had a 12-month year, a 7-day week, and a 24-hour day.

Around 1750 B.C., a Babylonian king named Hammurabi ordered a fundamental change in the kingdom's laws. Before Hammurabi's time, laws had varied from place to place, and they were often not written down. Hammurabi ordered a code of laws be written. This code improved the system of justice by making it predictable and consistent throughout the kingdom. The *Code of Hammurabi* ensured an orderly way for settling disputes and punishing crimes.

The Code of Hammurabi was a product of its time. It included the concept of an eye for an eye: "If a man destroy the eye of another man, they shall destroy his eye." It also attempted to give some manner of justice to women and slaves. For example, it gave women the right to buy and sell property. Male slaves had the right to own property and to marry free women.

B. ORIGINS OF THREE RELIGIONS

The Middle East was the birthplace of three major religions: Judaism, Christianity, and Islam. All three express a belief that there is just one God in the universe.

Judaism   The oldest religion of the three is *Judaism*. It originated as the religion of a nomadic people living in the western part of the Fertile Crescent. The Hebrew people (ancestors of modern Jews) believed that there was only one God. *Monotheism* (belief in one God) was a unique idea in the world when it originated some 3,500 years ago. Everyone else in the Middle East then worshipped many gods—a form of religion called polytheism.

A second fundamental belief of Judaism was that God required all people to obey certain moral laws. For the Hebrews, the most

PRAYING IN JERUSALEM: In Jerusalem, the 40-foot-high Wailing Wall (also known as the Western Wall) is regarded by Jews as a holy shrine—a symbol of their survival as a people.

important of these laws were the *Ten Commandments*. Three such commandments, for example, forbade killing, stealing, and committing adultery. Another commandment called for honoring one's mother and father.

A third unique aspect of Judaism was the belief that God's ways were revealed to human beings through holy writings or scriptures. The Hebrews believed that those scriptures contained moral lessons that God wanted to teach people. The sacred books of the Jews were written in ancient times over a period of hundreds of years. Today, Christians refer to this collection of sacred books as the *Old Testament* of the Bible.

Christianity   A second major religion, Christianity, derived many of its fundamental teachings from Judaism. It, too, is monotheistic and teaches obedience to moral laws. The founder of the religion, Jesus, was born into a Jewish family in Palestine, which was then part of the Roman empire. Jesus urged his followers to banish sin from their lives. If they truly believed in his teachings, he promised, they would be admitted after death into the "Kingdom of Heaven." Jesus's teachings challenged the authority of Roman officials. Thus, the Romans took him prisoner and condemned him to suffer the painful death of *crucifixion*—being nailed to a cross. (For a history of the Roman empire, see Chapter 7.)

After the crucifixion, followers of Jesus believed that he had risen from the dead. They spread the Christian religion, teaching that Jesus was the son of God and would return as a savior. To the older sacred writings of the Jews (the Old Testament), Christians added other sacred books about Jesus. These books are collectively called the *New Testament*.

The spread of Judaism and Christianity   In the century following the death of Jesus—the first century of the Christian calendar—Jews and Christians moved to other parts of the world. The Jews were forced to flee Palestine after their revolts against Roman rule, starting in A.D. 66, had been ruthlessly crushed. They still believed, however, that the city of Jerusalem—once the capital of the Hebrew kingdom of Israel—was their spiritual home. They further believed that the land surrounding Jerusalem was their "promised land" (promised to them by God). The migration of Jews to Turkey, Greece, and other parts of the world is known as the *diaspora* (scattering or dispersion).

Christianity spread slowly to various parts of the Roman empire. At first, it was strongest in the empire's eastern part, which included almost all of the Middle East. Roman emperors at first opposed Christianity and persecuted Christians for practicing their religion. In the year 313, a Roman emperor named Constantine I officially allowed

CARRYING THE CROSS IN JERUSALEM. In remembrance of "Good Friday," the day that Jesus was crucified by Roman soldiers, Christians annually carry a heavy cross through Jerusalem.

Christianity to be practiced. He also placed the religion under government protection. Soon thereafter, Christianity became the dominant religion in the Roman empire. (What happened to Christianity after the breakup of the Roman empire is treated in Chapter 7.)

Origins of Islam In the early 600s, a third monotheistic religion was founded in the Middle East, on the Arabian Peninsula. This religion, Islam, represented the teachings of Mohammed. He had been familiar with both Judaism and Christianity. In fact, Mohammed taught his followers to consider Abraham, Moses, Jesus, and other Jewish and Christian religious figures as prophets. Muslims, however, consider **Mohammed** to be the major prophet and often use the phrase "the Prophet" when referring to him.

Mohammed's new religion included many of the key principles of Judaism and Christianity. Islam taught that there was only one God, whom the Arabs called Allah. The teachings of Islam were contained in a holy book, the Koran. This book stressed the idea that Allah would reward believers who strictly obeyed the moral laws of the Islamic faith.

The spread of Islam During Mohammed's lifetime (570–632), various Arab clans adopted his religious teachings. By the time of his death, almost all of the Arabian Peninsula had come under the military control of Mohammed's thousands of followers. For the next hundred years, Arab armies faithful to Islam carried their new religion into all parts of the Middle East. By the year 750, their conquests extended westward across all of North Africa and into Spain. Eventually, Islamic conquerors would spread the religion eastward into India. And Muslim traders would introduce Islam as far east as Indonesia.

Why were believers in Islam so successful in spreading their religion over such a vast territory? One reason was the intense religious zeal of Muslim soldiers. They fought for Islam, believing that if they died in battle, their souls would automatically win entrance into heaven. Another reason for Islam's success was that Muslim merchants traveled far and wide to trade with the peoples of Africa, Asia, and Europe. Whether fighting or trading, Muslims daily worshipped Allah and regularly won converts to Islam. As the influence of Islam spread, a huge area became culturally united. From the rain forests of Indonesia to the deserts of Morocco, people acquired a common religion, Islam. Many, but not all, of these Muslim nations also acquired a common language, Arabic.

Muslim beliefs and practices   The teachings of Islam are the same today as they were in Mohammed's time. The Koran serves as Muslims' guide for daily living. The faithful Muslim is obligated to carry out five practices known as the *Five Pillars of Wisdom*. They are: (1) reciting a statement of faith, "There is no God but Allah, and Mohammed is his prophet."; (2) praying five times a day while facing toward Mecca, a Saudi Arabian city that Muslims regard as sacred; (3) regularly giving *alms* (charity) to the poor; (4) fasting daily from sunrise to sunset during the Muslim month of Ramadan; and (5) taking a pilgrimage to Mecca at least once in one's lifetime. Beyond these five duties, Muslims must try to obey rules for daily living. Thus, Muslims' religious beliefs regulate all their activities.

Like Jews and Christians, Muslims believe that God rewards those who faithfully abide by the teachings of their religion.

Divisions within Islam   After Mohammed's death, his followers debated over who should be named his successor. One group, the *Shiites*, argued that Mohammed's son-in-law, Ali, was the legitimate successor. A second group, the *Sunnis*, argued that succession was not based on heredity but could be passed to any Muslim leader who was willing and able to defend Islam. The conflict between these two groups has continued into modern times. For example, most people in Saudi Arabia are Sunni Muslims, while most Iranians adhere to the Shiite branch of the religion. Saudi Arabia's relations with Iran have often been tense, in part because of the religious differences.

The Shiites and Sunnis were sometimes intolerant toward each other. In their attitude toward Jews and Christians, however, many

THE SPREAD OF ISLAM, 634–1250

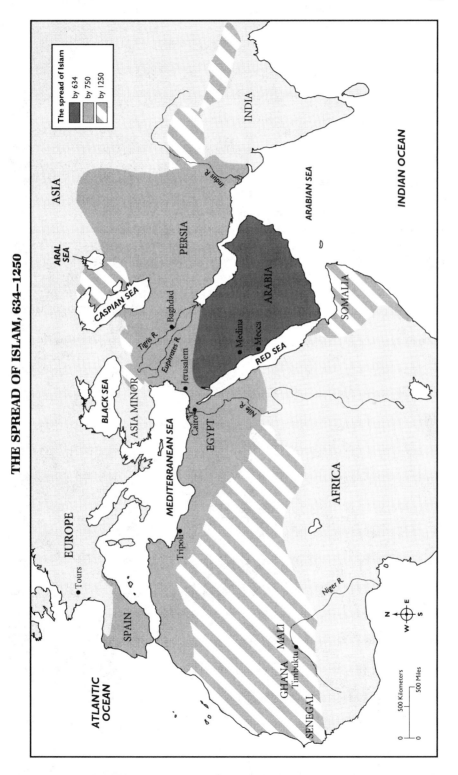

Muslim societies were known for their high degree of religious tolerance. They did not persecute people of different faiths.

C. THE "GOLDEN AGE" OF MUSLIM CULTURE

Muslim civilization in the Middle East flourished between the 9th and 14th centuries. This historic period was the Muslims' "Golden Age." (A *golden age* is a time of unusually great achievements in the arts and sciences.) A high level of trade during this period provided the foundation for Muslim achievements. Trade led to the growth of cities and the founding of many excellent schools, universities, and libraries.

Literacy in the Middle East during this era was much higher than in Europe. Children would attend an elementary school connected to a *mosque* (Muslim place of worship). At various universities, Muslim scholars studied and debated the writings of ancient Greeks, Romans, Hindus, and Persians. They also wrote important works of their own in the fields of history, science, math, geography, and philosophy. Writing in Arabic or Persian, Muslim poets and storytellers created a refined and imaginative literature.

Muslims made original discoveries in medicine. One doctor, for example, found a treatment for both smallpox and measles. Other Muslim doctors were the first in history to perform operations using strips of animal intestines to sew up patients.

MUSLIM ARCHITECTURE: This courtyard of the Alhambra, a 13th-century palace in Granada, Spain, is a fine example of Muslim architecture during the Muslims' Golden Age. Where else would you expect to find examples of Muslim architecture?

Cultural diffusion   From the Muslims' "Golden Age" come many examples of cultural diffusion. Muslims learned from the Hindus of India about the concept of zero and about the number symbols 1 through 9. This numerical system was eventually passed on to Europeans, who called the numbers "Arabic numerals."

Europeans learned of Muslim culture through contacts with Arab traders. They also learned about it as a result of a series of wars known as the *Crusades*. (These Christian campaigns against Islamic forces for control of Palestine are discussed in Chapter 7.) At the same time as the Crusades, during the 1100s and 1200s, some European scholars visited Muslim libraries in Spain. There they came across classical texts from the days of ancient Greece and Rome. Their discovery of these texts stimulated a revival of classical learning in Europe—a revival known as the *Renaissance* (also discussed in Chapter 7).

D. THE OTTOMAN EMPIRE

The Turks were once a nomadic and warlike people whose original homeland was Central Asia, north of Iran. After converting to Islam, two successive groups of Turks won control of much of the Middle East. The Seljuk Turks ruled from Baghdad (the current capital of Iraq). As their power weakened, their empire fell under the control of another group, the Ottoman Turks, in 1301. Armies of the Ottoman empire marched into Eastern Europe and defeated the Serbs at the battle of Kosovo in 1389. By this victory, the Turks added to their empire most of the Balkan Peninsula. The Ottoman empire became a major world power in 1453 by conquering Constantinople, the capital and last stronghold of the once mighty Byzantine empire (discussed in Chapter 8).

The Ottoman empire's greatest *sultan* (ruler) was Suleiman I (1520–1566). He was named "The Lawgiver" because of his reforms of the empire's legal system. He gathered around himself leading architects, who designed a number of aqueducts, bridges, fortresses, mosques, and other structures.

The Ottoman empire was best known for its extensive trading network and its well-run system of government. Within the empire, people of different religions and ethnic groups were generally treated with tolerance.

At the height of its power, in the 1600s, the Ottoman empire stretched over a vast territory. It included much of the Balkans, Turkey, North Africa, and the Fertile Crescent. In the 1700s, however, the empire began to decline. Tensions among the many ethnic groups within the empire were a constant source of unrest. While the empire weakened militarily, several of its neighbors (including Russia and Austria) became stronger. By 1900, the Ottoman empire was on the verge of collapse.

OTTOMAN EMPIRE AT ITS HEIGHT

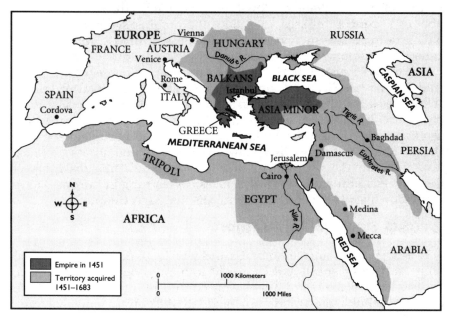

In Review

The following questions refer to Section II: Early History.

1. *Key terms:* Define or identify each of the following:

    cuneiform   Ten Commandments   Five Pillars of Wisdom
    monotheism   diaspora   Ottoman empire

2. Name *two* accomplishments of the Babylonians.

3. Describe how Judaism, Christianity, and Islam each originated in the Middle East and how each spread to other regions.

4. *Critical thinking:* "The religions of Judaism, Christianity, and Islam have some similarities." Explain why you either agree or disagree with this statement.

III. The Dynamics of Change (1800–1950)

In the 19th and early 20th centuries, the politics of the Middle East were transformed by the same external forces that were changing Africa and other regions. These forces were (1) European imperialism and (2) nationalism.

A. THE IMPACT OF EUROPEAN IMPERIALISM

In the mid-1800s, it became obvious to European observers that the government of the Ottoman empire was corrupt and weak. They commonly referred to this once-great empire as the "sick man of Europe." (Actually, only a small part of this empire extended into southeastern Europe. The remainder was in western Asia and North Africa.)

Russian ambitions   Russia was particularly eager to take advantage of the weakening empire on its southwestern border. For centuries, it had wanted to take control of the two straits—the Bosporus and the Dardanelles—that connected the Black Sea and the Mediterranean. In 1853, a dispute between Russia and the Ottoman empire led to war between the two powers. Europeans referred to the conflict as the "Crimean War," named for the Crimean Peninsula in southern Russia where the major battles took place.

Opposing Russia in the war, both Great Britain and France sent troops to the aid of the Ottoman government. French and British leaders were afraid of what might happen if a rival power, Russia, were allowed to seize territory in Europe. Britain in particular was committed to preserving a *balance of power*. (A balance of power is an international situation whereby two equally strong powers or alliance systems oppose each other.) In this case, Britain believed that its security depended upon helping a weaker power (the Ottoman empire) fend off the aggression of a stronger power. As a result of the British and French intervention, the Crimean War ended in Russia's defeat. Temporarily at least, the Ottoman empire remained intact, supported by other nations' balance-of-power policies.

Egypt and the Suez Canal   Although Britain opposed Russian imperialism in the Middle East, it saw nothing wrong with pursuing imperialist goals of its own. In Egypt, both Britain and France owned shares in a French company that had built the Suez Canal. This canal soon became a vital waterway for British ships trading with India. In the 1870s, Great Britain gained financial control of the canal company. In 1882, British troops were sent to Egypt to safeguard the Suez Canal and the route to India. From then until 1922, Egypt was under British protection and control.

End of the Ottoman empire   World War I (1914–1918) marked a major turning point for the Middle East. Siding with Germany in that war, the Ottoman empire's fate was linked with that of Germany's. Hoping to win independence from the Ottoman empire, various Arab armies fought against the Ottoman Turks. In the end, Germany and the Ottoman empire were defeated. The victors—Britain, France, and their allies—drew up terms of peace that left only Turkey under Ottoman control. But instead of granting the freed Arab countries their independence, the Allies devised a system for dividing up control of the Ottoman empire.

The Allies created an international organization, the *League of Nations*, for the purpose of preventing the outbreak of any more wars. Another function of the League was to oversee territories of the world that had not yet become independent nations. Included among these territories were Arab lands previously under Ottoman rule. They were referred to as *mandates* of the League of Nations. In practice, each Middle-Eastern mandate was placed under the control of a single European power. British mandates in the Middle East included Iraq, Transjordan (present-day Jordan), and Palestine. French mandates included Syria and Lebanon. For France and Britain, the chief economic benefit of their Middle Eastern mandates was the ability to exploit the rich oil resources of the region.

B. NATIONALISM IN TURKEY AND PALESTINE

Ottoman and European control of the Middle East was bitterly resented by Turks, Arabs, and other peoples living there. The Turks were impatient to gain freedom from the corrupt Ottoman government. The Arabs wanted their own nations and governments independent of foreign control.

Turkish nationalism   One of the first nations of the Middle East to achieve full independence as a modern state was the Ottoman heartland: Turkey. The Ottoman government continued to rule Turkey for only a few years after World War I. Then in 1922, it was overthrown by a remarkable Turkish military leader and nationalist, Kemal Attatürk. The next year, 1923, Attatürk was elected the first president of the new Republic of Turkey.

Attatürk wanted his country to adopt the modern practices and technologies of the West. As leader of Turkey in the 1920s and 1930s, he worked to separate the Islamic religion from the government. For example, he replaced the system of Muslim-run schools with a new system run by the government. He also replaced the Islamic legal system with a law code based on Western models. His government granted both women and men new rights, including the right to vote. Attatürk encouraged the Turkish people to wear Western-style clothing. In official documents of the republic, he replaced Arabic script with the Western alphabet. Although many Turks supported their leader's reforms, Muslims with traditional beliefs were deeply offended by them.

Conflict between Arabs and Zionists   Part of nationalism, as you know, is the idea that an ethnic group should have its own independent nation. One problem with this idea is that intense conflicts can result if different ethnic groups lay claim to the same territory. This problem was acute in the case of Palestine, one of the mandates given

Britain to govern after World War I. For centuries, both Arabs and Jews had lived on this land at the eastern end of the Mediterranean. One group wanted Palestine to become a new nation governed and controlled by Arabs. The other group wanted Palestine to become a new nation governed and controlled by Jews.

For several centuries in ancient times, the Jewish people had controlled much of Palestine. After falling to various conquerors, Palestine had been ruled by a succession of non-Jewish peoples—Assyrians, Chaldeans, Persians, Romans, Arabs, and Turks.

In the late 1800s, European Jews migrated to Palestine in increasing numbers. The immigrants and their supporters, known together as *Zionists*, hoped to establish a Jewish homeland in Palestine. (The word "Zionist" comes from "Zion," an area in Jerusalem that was the center of Jewish life in ancient times.) The Ottoman Turks refused to grant the Zionists' request for such a homeland. The British government, however, offered hope to the Zionist cause by issuing the Balfour Declaration in 1917. It declared that, in principle, Britain supported the idea of setting up a Jewish homeland in Palestine. At the same time, though, the British promised Palestine's Arab majority that their rights would be fully protected. To many, the British appeared to be making conflicting promises.

Arab nationalism   After World War I, Arab nationalism became a major force for change throughout the Middle East. Most Arabs resented the British- and French-dominated governments set up by the mandate system. While adapting to foreign rule, Arab nationalists did not give up their goal of eventually creating independent, Arab-governed states. One by one, nationalists in each territory or colony worked to persuade the Western powers to give in to the Arabs' nationalist strivings. In 1922, Britain allowed Egypt to become independent, although it remained under British military protection for many years. In 1932, Iraq was also granted independence.

The outbreak of World War II in 1939 weakened the ability of France and Britain to hold onto their mandated territories and colonies. By war's end in 1945, Syria and Lebanon had succeeded in winning their independence from France. A year later, Transjordan also became a new nation (soon named Jordan).

The last Islamic territory to break from European control was the North African country of Algeria. France had held Algeria as a colony for more than a hundred years. In the 1950s, the Algerians rose in revolt and, after a determined struggle, finally forced France to grant them independence in 1962.

The rebirth of Israel   In Palestine during the period between the two world wars, there were frequent outbursts of fighting between the Arab majority and the Jewish minority. The Jewish population in the territory grew rapidly in the 1930s. German Jews arrived by the thousands, seeking refuge from anti-Jewish persecution by the German dictator, Adolf Hitler. After World War II ended in German defeat, both the Jews and Arabs in Palestine demanded that they be given a nation of their own. The United Nations, founded in 1945 as a peace-keeping organization, arranged a compromise settlement that attempted to satisfy both Arabs and Jews. In 1947, the UN partitioned the former British mandate of Palestine into two states: one for Jews and the other for Arabs.

The nation carved out of Palestine as a homeland for Jews was called Israel. It was named after the ancient kingdom of Israel of the 10th century B.C., a time when Jews had been governed by their own kings: Saul, David, and Solomon.

Israeli War for Independence　　Israel proclaimed its existence as an independent nation in 1948. But the Arab nations of the Middle East did not accept the UN decision to create a separate Jewish state. Arab armies from Syria, Lebanon, Jordan, and Egypt attacked Israel in an attempt to destroy the new nation. Despite their superior numbers, the Arabs were defeated in the war. In 1949, they agreed to a UN-arranged armistice. They refused, however, to accept or recognize the existence of Israel as a legitimate nation.

PALESTINIAN REFUGEES: These women in a refugee camp in Jordan were among the hundreds of thousands displaced by the Arab-Israeli wars. Why has it been extremely difficult to find a peaceful solution to the Palestinian problem?

Arab refugees from Palestine   During the course of Israel's war for independence, hundreds of thousands of Arabs left their homes in Palestine. Some were forced to flee. Others left voluntarily, believing that they would soon return after a swift Arab victory. Palestinian refugees lived for years in poor conditions in camps set aside for them (chiefly in Lebanon and Jordan). They demanded the right to return to their former homeland, which they claimed should be an Arab-controlled state. Palestinian demands were supported by the Muslim states of the Middle East. Israel, however, resisted such demands, fearful of having hostile people living within its borders.

How could the nationalist demands of the Palestinians be peacefully reconciled with the national existence of Israel? Seeking a solution to this difficult question has been central to the history of the Middle East since 1949.

TWO ISRAELI LEADERS

Many Jews born outside the Middle East played a leading role in founding the nation of Israel. Among them were David Ben-Gurion and Golda Meir.

David Ben-Gurion   Israel's first prime minister was born in Poland in 1886. Enthusiastic about the Zionist cause, he emigrated to Palestine when he was 20 years old. For years, he worked in Jewish farming settlements. He became active in Palestine in the Zionist party.

| David Ben-Gurion | Golda Meir |

In the 1930s, Ben-Gurion became a leader in the Zionist movement. He challenged British control of Palestine when it appeared that the British were siding with the Arabs against the Jews. He urged Jews in Palestine to revolt against British rule. In 1948, Israel declared itself a new nation. Democratic in form, Israel's constitution provided for the election of a prime minister by the Israeli legislature, the *Knesset*. As the leader of the majority party, Ben-Gurion was elected prime minister in 1948 and served almost continuously in that office until 1963.

Ben-Gurion's domestic and foreign policies succeeded in helping Israel survive in its challenging early years. He led his new nation to victory against Arab foes in the war of 1948–1949. After that, he ordered a series of devastating strikes against Arab military targets in retaliation for repeated Arab border raids. The prime minister also encouraged the settlement of Israel's desert lands by welcoming Jewish immigrants from many parts of the world. The "Father of the Nation," as Israelis call him, died in 1973.

Golda Meir   Born in the Ukraine in 1898, Golda Meir emigrated with her family to Milwaukee, Wisconsin, in 1906. She emigrated in 1921 with her husband to Palestine, where they joined a *kibbutz* (collective farming community).

During the 1940s, she was a determined spokesperson for Israeli nationhood. She negotiated with the British regarding Israel's independence. In 1949, she was elected a member of the Knesset, where she would serve for 25 years. In 1956, she was appointed Israel's foreign minister. In the late 1960s, Ms. Meir helped bring about the merger of three political parties to form the Israeli Labour party. Soon afterward, in 1969, she was elected prime minister.

As head of Israel's government, she promoted increases in Jewish immigration and the construction of housing. Golda Meir attempted to arrange a peace settlement with Israel's Arab neighbors. But her efforts came to an unhappy end in October 1973 when neighboring Arab states launched a surprise attack on Israel (the Yom Kippur War). Weakened by the effects of cancer, she resigned as prime minister in 1974 and died four years later.

Questions for Discussion

1. Compare and contrast the lives of David Ben-Gurion and Golda Meir before Israeli independence.
2. Do you think that their experiences before 1948 affected their views and actions as Israeli leaders? Explain.

In Review

The following questions refer to Section III: The Dynamics of Change.

1. *Key terms:* Define or identify each of the following:

balance of power	League of Nations	Zionist
Suez Canal	mandate	kibbutz

2. How do the Crimean War and the building of the Suez Canal show the imperialistic interest of European powers in the Middle East?

3. Give *three* major examples of how the Middle East was changed by nationalism.

4. *Critical thinking:* "In its early stages, nationalism is often a violent and destructive force." Evaluate this statement, citing evidence from the history of the Middle East to support your view.

IV. Contemporary Nations (1950 to the Present)

In the latter half of the 20th century, several sources of conflict have kept the Middle East in a continuous state of tension and turmoil. They are the (1) ongoing conflicts between Israel and the Palestinians and between Israel and surrounding Arab nations and (2) conflict within Islam between those Muslims who accept the ways of modern and secular society and other Muslims who believe that a traditional and religious society is best. Members of the latter group are sometimes called *Muslim fundamentalists*.

A. THE ARAB-ISRAELI CONFLICT

The Israeli War for Independence (1948–1949) was only the first of four wars between Israel and its Arab neighbors.

War in the Suez   In 1956, a second war broke out over control of the Suez Canal in Egypt. Although Egypt had gained independence, the canal had for many years been owned and operated by the British as a vital link in Europe's trade with Asia. European control of the Suez Canal offended the nationalist beliefs of Egyptian President Gamal Abdel Nasser. In 1956, Nasser *nationalized* (took ownership of) the canal. Seeking to regain control, Great Britain and France attacked Egypt. Israel joined in the attack in order to halt Egyptian raids into Israel. U.S. President Dwight Eisenhower did not approve of the attacks. He feared that the Soviet Union might enter the conflict on the side of Egypt. As a result of U.S. pressure, British, French, and Israeli forces withdrew from Egypt. The Suez Canal remained under Egyptian control. UN troops, however, remained on the Israeli-Egyptian border to prevent further raids from Egypt into Israeli territory.

The Six-Day War   In 1967, a third war broke out. Jordan, Syria, and Egypt launched a joint invasion of Israel in an effort to destroy it. Because Israel took only six days to defeat the Arab armies, this war became known as the Six-Day War. Short as it was, the war had long-term consequences. Israeli forces now occupied several territories

ISRAEL AFTER THE SIX-DAY WAR

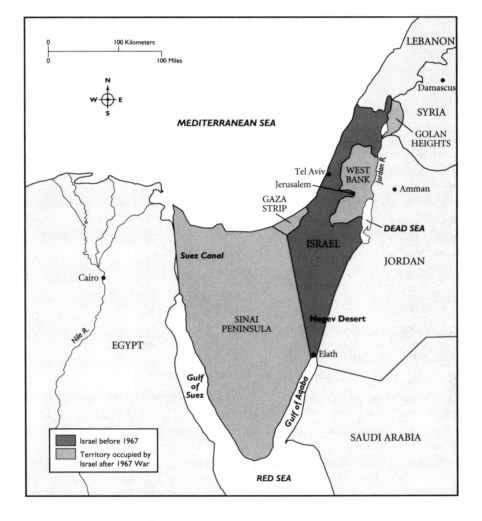

formerly held by Israel's Arab neighbors. These included the Golan Heights (taken from Syria), the Sinai Peninsula and Gaza Strip (taken from Egypt), and the West Bank of the Jordan River and East Jerusalem (taken from Jordan). Now Israel controlled the entire city of Jerusalem, not just the western half of the city that it had controlled before the war. Israeli forces continued to occupy those territories gained during the war as a means of securing Israel's borders against future attack.

The Yom Kippur War   Six years later, in October 1973, the Arabs and Israelis were at war for a fourth time. In an attempt to regain the occupied territories, the Arab nations launched a surprise invasion of Israel on the Jewish holy day of Yom Kippur. After fierce fighting and initial Arab victories, Israel drove back the Arabs in a successful counterattack. The United States used its influence to negotiate a cease-fire.

Causes of the Arab-Israeli conflict   Why have Israel and its Arab neighbors been in conflict ever since the founding of Israel? Three reasons may be given:

- The Israeli need for military security clashes with Arab demands for the return of occupied territories. On the one hand, Israel is reluctant to return these territories, fearing that the Arabs might use them as places from which to launch further attacks. On the other hand, the Arabs believe that the occupied territories belong to them, not to Israel. In fact, many Arabs believe that all of Israel should be under Arab (rather than Jewish) control.
- Religious differences are a second reason for the conflicts. The majority Islamic population of the Middle East objects to having a Jewish country in the region.
- Finally, there is a conflict of cultures. The modern, Western ways of the Israelis are viewed with suspicion by many Muslims who value the strict, traditional ways outlined in the Koran.

The Palestinian issue   After Israel's victories in the wars of 1948 and 1967, large numbers of Palestinians found temporary homes in refugee camps in Syria, Lebanon, and Jordan. The poverty of the camps and the nationalist feelings of the Palestinians gave rise to a political movement, the Palestine Liberation Organization (PLO). Headed by Yasir Arafat, the PLO's main goal was to eliminate Israel as a nation and turn the land into a Palestinian country. One of the PLO's main weapons was *terrorism* (the use of violence or the threat of violence for political purposes). For example, the PLO sent agents into Israel who killed unarmed Israeli civilians. (For a larger discussion of terrorism, see Chapter 9.)

More than a million Palestinians live in the Gaza Strip and the West Bank. Beginning in 1987, young Palestinians in these territories protested the presence of Israeli troops by throwing stones at them. Israeli forces sometimes responded to the stone throwing by firing guns at their assailants. Many of the Palestinian demonstrators were wounded, and some were killed. The *Intifada*, as the Palestinians called their uprising, attracted international attention.

Peace efforts   Many notable efforts to find peaceful solutions to the Arab-Israeli conflict have been undertaken. In 1978, U.S. President Jimmy Carter persuaded Egyptian President Anwar al-Sadat and Israeli Prime Minister Menachem Begin to travel to the United States for informal talks at Camp David, Maryland. In a dramatic reversal of former policies, Sadat and Begin agreed to a peaceful settlement of their two countries' major differences. As a result of the Camp David Accords, Israel returned the Sinai Peninsula to Egypt. For its part, Egypt became the first Arab country to give Israel formal recognition as an independent nation. Sadly, however, Sadat's peace policy cost him his life. In 1981, he was assassinated by Egyptians who opposed better relations with Israel.

The United States has sought to maintain good relations with its ally Israel as well as with Arab nations of the Middle East. Seeking to promote peace in the region, President George Bush and Secretary of State James Baker urged Israel to negotiate with the Palestinians on the future of the West Bank and the Gaza Strip. Both Israel and key Arab states appeared to take a major step toward peace when they agreed to attend a diplomatic conference in Madrid, Spain, in 1991. A series of peace talks followed in Washington, D.C.

Israeli-Palestinian agreement, 1993   An astonishing diplomatic breakthrough on the Palestinian issue took place in September 1993. Israeli Prime Minister Yitzhak Rabin agreed to recognize and directly negotiate with his country's longtime enemy, the PLO. Furthermore, he agreed to allow limited self-rule for Palestinians living in the Gaza Strip and the city of Jericho in the West Bank. For his part, PLO leader Yasir Arafat agreed to recognize the right of Israel to exist as a nation. The written agreement between the two leaders, called a Declaration of Principles, was signed in a dramatic ceremony on the White House lawn in Washington, D.C.

President Bill Clinton promised to give U.S. backing to the agreement and help negotiate the difficult issues that remained. Still unsettled were: (1) recognition of Israel by Jordan, Lebanon, and Syria; (2) the future status of Jerusalem; (3) control of the Golan Heights; (4) Israeli settlements in the West Bank; (5) the presence of Israeli troops on the Lebanese side of the Israeli-Lebanon border; and (6) the long-term future of the Gaza Strip and the West Bank.

TWO ARAB LEADERS

Two Arab nationalists did a complete turnaround in their dealings with Israel. Both the Egyptian leader Anwar al-Sadat and the Palestinian leader Yasir Arafat engaged in hostile acts against Israel early in their careers. Later, though, each came around to the idea that peace was the more realistic policy.

Anwar al-Sadat Born in Egypt into a peasant family in 1918, Sadat was just four years old when Egypt gained its independence from British control. As a youth, however, he became aware that Egypt's king often tied his country's foreign policy to that of Great Britain. After graduating from a Cairo military academy, Sadat joined a group of military officers who secretly plotted to overthrow the pro-British monarchy. For his revolutionary activities, he was twice arrested and jailed.

Released from jail the second time, Sadat once again plotted against the Egyptian king. In 1952, he and other military officers, including Gamal Abdel Nasser, succeeded in overthrowing King Farouk. In the new government headed by Nasser, Sadat held a number of high-level offices. When Nasser died in 1970, Sadat became Egypt's new president.

Anwar al-Sadat

Like most Egyptians, Sadat strongly supported Palestinians' demands for a nation of their own. He denounced Israel for occupying the Gaza Strip, the West Bank, the Golan Heights, and the Sinai Peninsula after the Six-Day War of 1967. To force Israel to surrender these lands, Egypt led the Arab nations' attack against Israel in the Yom Kippur War of 1973. But after failing to gain his objectives by military means, Sadat had a change of mind and heart. In 1977, he shocked the Arab world by traveling to Israel and speaking to the Israeli Knesset about the need for peace. This bold initiative led to the Camp David Accords of 1978 and a peace treaty with Israel the following year.

Many Arabs angrily accused Sadat of being a traitor to Arab unity and of betraying the cause of Palestinian nationhood. In 1981, he was assassinated by Egyptians who shared these views.

Yasir Arafat   This Arab leader was born to a well-to-do Palestinian family in Jerusalem in 1929. Arafat grew up during a time of frequent clashes between Arabs and Palestinian Jews over the future of the British mandate. Arafat entered the struggle by joining a group of Palestinian Arab youths engaged in *guerrilla warfare* (small bands of fighters using hit-and-run tactics against larger forces). He was one

Yasir Arafat

of the many thousands of Palestinian Arabs who abandoned their homes during the Arab-Israeli War of 1948–1949.

Arafat moved to Egypt to study, graduating with an engineering degree from Cairo University. Moving to Kuwait, he became a leader of a Palestinian Arab movement to create an independent state in Palestine. Arafat joined the PLO in the 1960s, becoming its chairman in 1969. Under his leadership, the PLO engaged in terrorist attacks against Israel. In the early 1970s, Arafat's forces in Jordan were defeated by Jordanian King Hussein I, who feared a Palestinian takeover of his government. Thus, Arafat took his forces to Lebanon. In 1974, he gained world recognition as a Palestinian leader when he was invited to address the UN General Assembly.

During the Persian Gulf War of 1991 (discussed on page 126), Arafat sided with Iraqi leader Saddam Hussein. In so doing, Arafat antagonized not only the attacked nation, Kuwait, but also most other Arab states that had formerly supported him. Aware of his weakened political position, Arafat was ready to bargain. In 1993, he agreed that the PLO would recognize Israel. In return, Israel would allow Palestinian autonomy in the Gaza Strip and the West Bank. On the White House lawn, he shook hands with the Israeli prime minister and said, "Our two peoples are awaiting today this historic hope. And they want to give peace a real chance."

Questions for Discussion

1. In what ways can both Anwar al-Sadat and Yasir Arafat be considered Arab nationalists?
2. How did Sadat's visit to Israel in 1977 and Arafat's agreement with Israel in 1993 shock the Arab world?

B. THE ISLAMIC WORLD

During the 1970s, 1980s, and early 1990s, much of the Middle East was in turmoil. The Islamic (but non-Arabic) nation of Iran underwent a revolution. The partly Islamic, partly Christian nation of Lebanon was torn apart by civil war. The Persian Gulf nations of Iran, Iraq, and Kuwait were devastated by wars. And Muslim fundamentalists asserted their growing strength.

The Shah modernizes Iran   From 1941 to 1979, Iran was ruled by *Shah* (monarch) Mohammad Reza Pahlavi. With the help of the United States, the Shah began to industrialize and modernize his country. Revenues generated by Iran's large oil industry paid for the purchase of industrial technology, consumer goods, and modern weapons. But a large number of Iranians resented the Shah's policies and methods. Critics accused the Iranian government of being highly corrupt. They hated the Shah's secret police force, which used brutal methods for crushing dissent.

The Shah's worst offense, from the point of view of devout Iranian Muslims, was his attempt to modernize society. He supported less traditional roles for women and granted women rights that were common in the West but (claimed conservative Muslims) forbidden under Islamic law. For example, women of Iran could now vote, divorce their husband, and dress as they pleased. Some discarded the traditional veil and wore Western-style clothing.

The Iranian Revolution   The Shah's policies were bitterly opposed by an Islamic religious leader, the Ayatollah Khomeini. (Ayatollah is a Muslim title for an advanced religious scholar.) He and his followers thought modern ways violated basic teachings of Islam. Furthermore, they and many other Iranians resented the lack of civil rights, the one-man rule by the Shah, and the existence of extreme poverty in the midst of economic development. In 1979, angry crowds gathered on Iranian streets and demanded an end to the Shah's regime. The Shah fled Iran and went into exile. Then the Ayatollah Khomeini became the leader of a fundamentalist government in Iran.

Khomeini did away with the Shah's modernization policies. He tried to govern strictly according to the teachings of the Koran. His government reasserted basic religious values and reestablished traditional laws and customs. Once again, for example, Iranian women were required to wear traditional Islamic dress when in public. Books, magazines, newspapers, television, and films were censored to keep out things that were considered offensive to Islam.

Iranian hostage crisis   In 1979, many Iranian revolutionaries were angered by past U.S. support for the Shah. Adding to their anger was the decision by President Jimmy Carter to allow the Shah to enter the United States for medical treatment after he had fled Iran. Some of the revolutionaries seized the U.S. Embassy in Teheran, Iran, and held some Americans hostage there. The revolutionaries demanded that the Shah be returned to Iran to be put on trial. President Carter refused this demand. Instead, the United States demanded the release of the hostages. The hostage crisis lasted for 444 days. Not until the day that

Carter left office as the U.S. president—on January 20, 1981—were the hostages released. U.S. relations with Iran have remained hostile.

The Iran-Iraq War   In 1980, a territorial dispute between Iran and Iraq led to a war that lasted eight years. Adding to the conflict was a religious rivalry between two groups of Muslims, the Shiites and the Sunnis. The Iranians were mainly Shiite Muslims, whereas Iraq's leader—Saddam Hussein—and his chief supporters were Sunni Muslims. After hundreds of thousands had died on both sides, the war finally ended in 1988 when the United Nations negotiated a cease-fire. Neither side had won the war.

Civil War in Lebanon   For much of the 20th century, Lebanon was a peaceful and prosperous nation. Its capital, Beirut, was known as the "Paris of the Middle East" because of its beauty and comfortable life-style. Lebanon's constitution had called for the two main religious groups in the country—Christians and Muslims—to share power. This arrangement worked well as long as the population of the two groups was roughly the same size. But by the early 1970s, the Muslim population had grown considerably larger than the Christian population. Lebanese Muslims wanted more power in the government. To complicate matters, Palestinian refugees living in Lebanon began to protest Lebanese policies that seemed to favor Israel's Western allies (the United States, Great Britain, and others). In 1975, a civil war erupted between Christians on one side and various Muslim groups (including Palestinians) on the other side.

As the violence continued for months and then years, neighboring nations became involved in the civil war. Syria sent troops into Lebanon to aid the Palestinians. Israel countered by sending in troops to drive the PLO out of Lebanon. (The PLO had been conducting raids from Lebanese soil into Israel.) The fighting was not only between Christians and Muslims but also between different factions within each religious group. Many civilians and soldiers were killed or wounded in the fighting. Some civilians were also held by terrorists. After 16 years of civil war, much of Beirut was destroyed.

Finally in 1991, Syria established sufficient control to negotiate and enforce a cease-fire agreement. Even so, Lebanon remains unstable and partly occupied by Syrian troops. In order to protect its northern region from attack by terrorist groups, Israel too occupies part of Lebanon—the stretch of land along the Israeli border.

Islamic fundamentalism in North Africa   In the early 1990s, groups of Muslim fundamentalists posed major challenges to the established governments of Algeria, Tunisia, and Egypt. Vital to the government of each of these three North African countries is the principle of separation of church and state. But Muslim fundamentalists oppose such a concept. They want their society to be governed strictly according to the religious laws laid down in the Koran. To protect themselves, the *secular* (nonreligious) governments of Tunisia and Egypt have made it illegal for Muslim fundamentalists to form political parties and campaign for votes. Nevertheless, opposition forces did organize and appeared to have a wide following in their societies. A few groups used terrorism in an attempt to weaken and overthrow existing governments. An opposition group in Egypt, for example, assassinated a leader of the Egyptian legislature in 1991 and killed some foreign tourists.

Algeria's government, in contrast, permitted a political party of Muslim fundamentalists to run candidates for election. This party proved far more popular than the government had expected. In national elections in 1991, the fundamentalist party won a majority of votes. But before this party could take power, a group of Algerian military leaders declared a state of emergency. Algeria's government remains under the control of the armed forces. The Muslim fundamentalists, deprived of power, are still angry and still pose a threat to the military regime.

Women in Islamic societies   One of the many issues that divides Muslims is the role of women in Islamic societies. Should women be subject to a set of restrictions that does not apply to men? For example, should women be required to cover their face when in public? To these questions, different nations of the Middle East have come up with different answers.

Algeria's constitution of 1963 guaranteed women the same rights and duties as men. In other words, it defined women's role in a modern way. In 1984, however, the Algerian government enacted a set of laws, the Family Code, that went in the opposite direction. According to this code, women cannot get married without the consent of a male guardian. Also, women cannot initiate a divorce (as men can).

Saudi Arabia is still governed by a hereditary king rather than an elected leader. The country's laws are based on traditional Islamic laws. Accordingly, it is unlawful in Saudi Arabia for a woman to leave her home unless accompanied by a man. Neither may a Saudi woman drive a car.

Other Islamic governments in the Middle East have adopted a more modern approach. In Egypt, Tunisia, and Turkey, for example, women are encouraged to attend schools and universities and seek paid employment outside the home. They have the right to vote and hold public office. In 1993, for the first time, a woman—Tansu Ciller—was elected as Turkey's prime minister. The only other female elected to such a high office in the Middle East was Golda Meir, who had led the Israeli government in the early 1970s.

IRANIAN WOMEN: Holding up a picture of the Ayatollah Khomeini, these women demonstrated their support for the Ayatollah's policy concerning traditional dress. Why do Muslim fundamentalists think it is important to maintain a strict dress code?

C. ECONOMIC DEVELOPMENT

In economic terms, the nations of the Middle East may be roughly divided into two categories: those that are oil-rich and those that are oil-poor. But not all of the countries that are oil-poor are in poor economic shape.

Wealth from oil More than half of the world's oil resources are located in a few nations of the Middle East. Most of the region's oil wealth is produced by countries on the Persian Gulf—Saudi Arabia, Kuwait, Iraq, Iran, and some smaller nations. Another major oil producer is the North African nation of Libya. The world's factories and motor vehicles depend upon oil. Thus, there is constant demand for the oil piped daily from Middle Eastern wells.

Revenues from the sale of oil have transformed the economies of Saudi Arabia, Iraq, and the other oil-rich nations. The governments of these countries have used their oil earnings to build modern highways, hospitals, housing, schools, and universities. (They have also purchased much military hardware with their oil revenues.) Although the rich in each country have benefited more than the poor, the general standard of living in the oil-rich states has gone up dramatically in recent decades.

Agriculture   Not every Middle Eastern country has become wealthy from oil. In fact, a large majority of Moroccans, Algerians, Egyptians, Turks, and others derive their income from traditional occupations. Most are either farmers or herders of sheep and goats. Today, as in the past, the chief crop of the Middle East is wheat. Other major crops include cotton, fruits, vegetables, and tobacco. Improved equipment, scientific farming methods, and increased use of irrigation have led to larger harvests throughout the region.

Overpopulation and urban poverty   In the latter half of the 20th century, the populations of major cities in the Middle East have risen spectacularly. Since 1965, Iran's capital, Teheran, has grown in population seven times; Iraq's capital, Baghdad, by almost ten times. Sadly, however, the influx of newcomers from rural areas has led to widespread urban unemployment and poverty. There are not enough jobs for all the newcomers. Nor is there sufficient housing. Millions live in crowded, sprawling shantytowns.

Israel: "Making the desert bloom"   Even though much of Israel is desert, its people have managed to convert thousands of barren acres into land for farming. They have done this by (1) increasing irrigation, (2) draining swamps, and (3) controlling soil erosion. As a result of these methods, the amount of usable cropland has increased nearly three times since independence in 1948. Although some land is farmed by individual Israelis, most of the agricultural output comes from collective or cooperative farms. People living in a rural kibbutz combine their labor and share most property in common, including the community's land, buildings, and tools.

Today, only about 6 percent of Israel's work force are employed in farming. Most Israeli workers are employed in *service industries* (trade, transportation, health, and other businesses that emphasize service) and in manufacturing. Israel's 5.3 million people enjoy a relatively high standard of living despite the fact that the country has few oil wells or other natural resources. Unfortunately, the economy has not kept up with recent waves of immigration of Jews from Russia and elsewhere. Many of these newcomers have difficulty finding jobs.

ISRAELI KIBBUTZ: The 900 residents of this kibbutz in Israel eat their meals in a communal dining hall. What is a kibbutz?

Western technology and food   Trade is vital to the survival of all Middle Eastern countries. In a desert nation like Saudi Arabia, for example, food is in short supply. Money from the sale of Saudi oil pays for the millions of tons of food that Saudi Arabia must import. At the same time, many of the world's nations could not survive without oil from the Middle East.

Modern technology imported from abroad is crucial to the Middle East's economic development. Without such technology, the oil-rich countries could not operate their oil fields. Neither would Morocco and other oil-poor nations be able to equip their farms and industries. The Middle East's trade with the rest of the world provides an excellent example of global interdependence.

In Review

The following questions refer to Section IV: Contemporary Nations.

1. *Key terms:* Identify each of the following:

Muslim fundamentalist	Intifada	secular
nationalize	Camp David Accords	service industry

2. Explain who the Palestinians are, and identify their major concerns.

3. List and briefly identify the *four* major wars that were fought between Israel and its Arab neighbors.

4. Give *one cause* and *one effect* of each of the following conflicts: (a) the Iranian Revolution and   (b) the civil war in Lebanon.

5. *Critical thinking:* "Peace cannot be achieved in the Middle East unless all nations in the region recognize Israel's right to exist." Analyze this statement and explain to what extent you either agree or disagree with it.

V. The Middle East in the Global Context

Oil from the Middle East is just one of the reasons for the Middle East's importance in international politics. The region's strategic location provides another reason that every nation in the world must be concerned about developments in the Middle East. For centuries, trade routes linking three continents have passed through the Middle East. The region's excellent ports on the Mediterranean, Red, and Arabian seas increase its value as a major highway for international trade.

A. THE POWER STRUGGLE BETWEEN THE SUPERPOWERS

During the cold war, the rival superpowers—the United States and the Soviet Union—fully recognized the region's strategic location. Both set up military bases there and competed for influence in the region by providing some Middle Eastern governments with economic and military assistance.

Turkey and NATO   The cold war began almost immediately after World War II. Fearing that Communist rebels might succeed in toppling the government of Turkey, the United States in 1947 offered Turkey millions of dollars of both economic and military aid. Helped by this aid, the Turkish government succeeded in ending the Communist threat. In 1952, it joined the United States, Canada, and many anti-Communist nations of Western Europe in a military alliance called the North Atlantic Treaty Organization (NATO). (NATO is discussed in more detail in Chapter 7.) During the cold war, Turkey was strongly committed to the Western, anti-Communist side.

Soviet troops in Afghanistan   Another Islamic country that became deeply involved in the cold war was the mountainous land of Afghanistan. In 1979, Soviet troops invaded Afghanistan, attempting to put down a rebellion against Afghanistan's Communist government. The United States supplied arms to the rebels, who managed to hold out against the Soviet invaders. The fighting continued for years. Weary of the struggle, the Soviet Union finally decided to pull its troops out of Afghanistan in 1988.

B. OPEC AND THE GLOBAL POWER OF OIL-PRODUCING NATIONS

In recent decades, the world's dependence on oil has given the oil-rich countries of the Middle East increased political and economic power. As a way of increasing their power, oil-producing nations of the Middle East (Iran, Iraq, Saudi Arabia, Kuwait, Libya, Algeria, Qatar, and United Arab Emirates) have united with other oil-producing nations outside the region (Venezuela, Nigeria, and others). In 1960, they formed the Organization of Petroleum Exporting Countries (OPEC). Its chief goal is to limit the production of oil in order to increase the price of oil in world markets. Throughout the 1970s, OPEC succeeded in keeping oil supplies down and oil prices up.

OPEC found that it could use its economic power to achieve specific political goals. In 1973, Arab nations wanted to punish the United States for supporting Israel in the Yom Kippur War. They persuaded all OPEC countries to place an embargo on shipments of oil to the United States and its allies. The embargo produced a severe shortage of oil in many countries. It also caused an alarming jump in worldwide oil prices. Suddenly, the world's major powers recognized that, at any time, their oil supplies could be reduced or cut off completely.

In the 1980s, however, oil prices declined. Thus, OPEC lost some of its former influence in world politics. But in 1990, another threat to world oil supplies arose. This time, the danger came from an ambitious Iraqi leader, Saddam Hussein (discussed on page 126).

TYPES OF GRAPHS

Graphs enable us to *see* information in a highly condensed form. You are probably familiar with the three types of graphs shown on the following pages: a line graph (A), a bar graph (B), and a circle graph (C). Each presents a different kind of information.

A *line graph* shows increases or decreases in the quantity of something over a period of time. Time is usually shown on the horizontal axis and quantities on the vertical axis.

A *bar graph* uses bars of different lengths to represent quantities. Its chief use is to compare various units (such as nations, cities, sports teams, and farmland) for specific quantities (such as size, output, and rate of growth). On some graphs, like the example on the following page, bars run vertically. On others, they may be drawn horizontally.

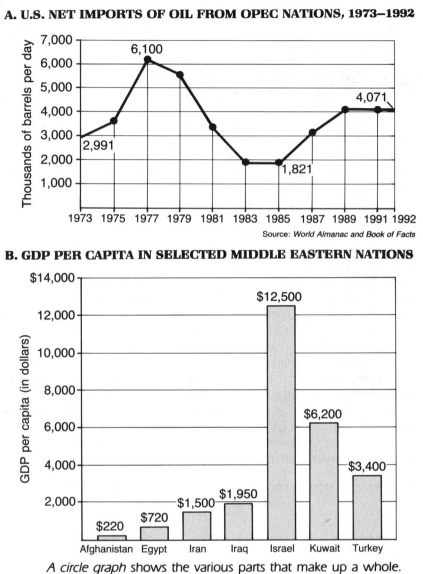

A. U.S. NET IMPORTS OF OIL FROM OPEC NATIONS, 1973–1992

Source: *World Almanac and Book of Facts*

B. GDP PER CAPITA IN SELECTED MIDDLE EASTERN NATIONS

A circle graph shows the various parts that make up a whole. The circle stands for 100 percent of something. The parts, or sections, of the circle are always labeled. The percentage for each part is usually also labeled.

Before attempting to interpret any graph, you must first look for and read its title. You will then know what the graph is about. The rest should be obvious. Test your ability to interpret information on all three types of graphs by answering the questions below about graphs A, B, and C.

C. WORLD CRUDE OIL RESERVES BY REGION, 1992

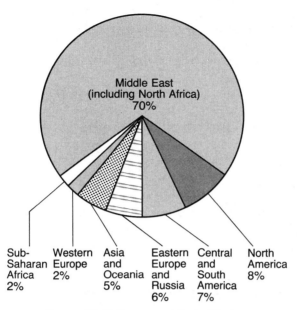

Source: *World Almanac and Book of Facts*

NOTE: GDP stands for *gross domestic product*—a measure of a nation's total wealth produced in one year. *GDP per capita* is a country's total wealth divided by its total population. It is a good measure of whether the average person in a country is relatively rich or poor.

Questions

1. In what year did the United States import the largest quantity of OPEC oil?
2. Of the countries in graph B, which *three* countries would you expect to have the highest standards of living?
3. What percentage of the world's crude oil reserves are located in the Middle East?
4. How many *million* barrels of oil per day did the United States import from OPEC nations in 1980? (Be careful.)
5. (a) Would you suspect that South Africa probably has more or less oil than Saudi Arabia? Why? (b) Which graph would best help you to prove your point?

C. IRAQ AND THE PERSIAN GULF WAR

In 1990, Iraq's military dictator, Saddam Hussein, threatened to attack a small neighboring country, Kuwait. Despite its small size, Kuwait produced even more oil than Iraq. Hussein told Kuwait to produce less so that the world price of oil would go up. (Iraq would then earn more for its own oil exports.) Furthermore, Hussein had territorial designs on Kuwait and wanted to take over its oil fields. He claimed that historically Kuwait had been a part of Iraq. On Hussein's orders, Iraqi forces invaded and occupied Kuwait in August 1990.

Persian Gulf War   Iraq's invasion of Kuwait alarmed most nations of the world, including other Middle Eastern countries. The United Nations condemned the invasion for three reasons. First, it was an act of aggression by a strong nation against a weaker one. Second, the taking of Kuwait might lead to an Iraqi conquest of neighboring Saudi Arabia, the world's largest oil-producing nation. Third, if Iraq's military action went unchallenged, Iraq might then be able to dominate other Middle Eastern countries and OPEC. A UN resolution demanded that Iraq withdraw from Kuwait by January 15, 1991. The UN authorized the use of force to liberate Kuwait if Iraq failed to withdraw by that deadline.

The United States took the lead in the international action against Hussein. It sent more than 400,000 troops to Saudi Arabia to block any Iraqi move against that country. This U.S. troop movement was known as Operation Desert Shield.

When Iraq ignored the UN deadline for withdrawal from Kuwait, the United States decided to use military force in the Persian Gulf. This action became known as Operation Desert Storm. Joined by troops from Western European, Middle Eastern, and other nations, U.S. forces attacked Iraqi positions in both Kuwait and Iraq. After only six weeks of fighting in January and February 1991, Iraqi forces were defeated and Kuwait was liberated.

War's aftermath   Despite their overwhelming military victory in the Persian Gulf War, the United States and its allies did not overthrow Saddam Hussein. Within Iraq, however, two groups rose up in rebellion against him and his government. Both the Shiite Muslims in southern Iraq and the Kurds in the north challenged Hussein's authority. To prevent Hussein's government from crushing these two foes, the United States declared a "no-fly zone" over both Shiite territory in the south and Kurdish territory in the north. Crews of U.S. planes were given orders to shoot down any Iraqi aircraft that ventured into the protected zones.

D. PERSECUTION OF THE KURDS

An issue not resolved by Iraq's military defeat is the future of the Kurds in Iraq and elsewhere. The Kurds are a distinct ethnic group and have no country of their own. They reside in an area that includes parts of Iraq, Syria, Iran, and Turkey. As a minority group, most Kurds live apart from others in these four countries. Kurds are Sunni Muslims who speak Kurdish. (Most Syrians and Iraqis speak Arabic; most Iranians speak Persian; and most Turks speak Turkish.)

Kurdish nationalists hope to set up an independent country. To achieve this goal, however, would mean taking territory from one or more of the four countries where they now live. All four countries oppose this idea. Feeling threatened by the Kurds's ambitions for nationhood, the governments of Iraq, Iran, and Turkey have persecuted the Kurds. During the Iran-Iraq War, for example, Iraq used chemical warfare to kill thousands of Kurds, including women and children. The Kurds have used violence to fight back against Iran, Iraq, and Turkey. In 1992, for example, a group of Kurdish terrorists attacked a Turkish army base.

In Review

The following questions refer to Section V: The Middle East in the Global Context.

1. *Key terms:* Define or identify each of the following:

Saddam Hussein	Persian Gulf War	Kurd
OPEC	Shiite Muslim	

2. Give *two* examples of the impact of the cold war on Middle Eastern politics.
3. Explain why OPEC was formed. How successful has it been in meeting its goals?
4. Give *one cause* and *one effect* of the Persian Gulf War.
5. *Critical thinking:* If oil is a vital resource for all nations, should its production and distribution be regulated by the United Nations? Argue either for or against this idea.

TEST YOURSELF

Multiple-Choice Questions

Level 1

On a separate sheet of paper, write the number of the word or expression that best completes each statement or answers each question.

1. The Middle East's designation as a "cultural crossroads" developed primarily as a result of the region's (1) technological achievements (2) political stability (3) geographic location (4) religious unity.

2. The Middle East has been a crossroads for trade between Asia, Africa, and Europe. Which is a major result of this fact? (1) Most of the Middle East's natural resources have been exhausted. (2) The Middle East has become a wealthy area with a high standard of living. (3) Many different cultures can be found in the Middle East. (4) The Middle East has experienced a strong sense of national unity.

3. Which statement is accurate about the geography of the Middle East? (1) Large areas of land are used for rice cultivation. (2) Most of the region has an arid climate. (3) The region experiences seasonal monsoons. (4) The region has many broad, fertile plains.

4. The early civilizations of the Nile River Valley and Mesopotamia were similar because they were (1) industrialized societies (2) monotheistic (3) dependent on fertile land (4) dependent on each other for trade.

5. In the Middle East in ancient times, the development of farming brought about (1) the establishment of permanent settlements (2) a return to a nomadic life-style (3) the rise of hunting as an important occupation (4) increased dependence on exporting oil.

6. Judaism and Christianity are similar because they (1) base their beliefs on the Koran (2) stress belief in reincarnation (3) are monotheistic (4) promote the practice of polygamy.

7. The Ten Commandments and the Five Pillars of Wisdom are similar in that they (1) established a class structure for society (2) are guidelines for living (3) consist of prayers for salvation (4) promise a happy and easy life.

8. Many Muslims live in Egypt, Nigeria, Pakistan, and Indonesia. Based on this information, which conclusion is valid? (1) Most Muslims tend to support repressive governments. (2) Islam is practiced by people of different cultures. (3) Most Muslims live in areas that are sparsely populated. (4) All Islamic nations produce surplus food for export.

9. In the Middle East during the Golden Age of Muslim culture, scholars were encouraged to (1) reject all knowledge that was Western in origin (2) ignore the achievements of Asian cultures (3) preserve and expand ancient Greek and Roman learning (4) accept religious ideas from Western Europe.

Base your answer to question 10 on the maps below and on your knowledge of social studies.

10. The changes in political boundaries shown on the maps occurred mainly because of (1) population growth (2) nationalism (3) economic development (4) communism.

MIDDLE EAST, 1910s

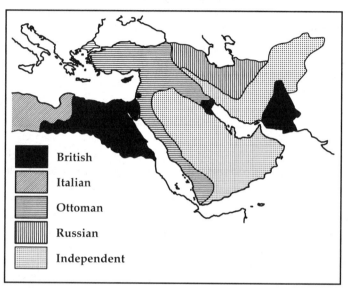

MIDDLE EAST, 1980s

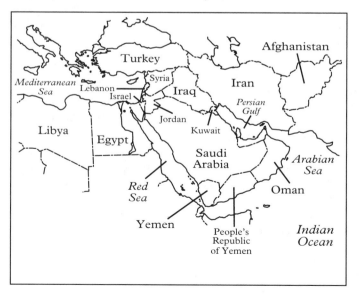

11. Which development was an important contribution of Muslim culture to civilization? (1) equal distribution of land (2) adoption of a polytheistic religion (3) advances in sciences and mathematics (4) the principle of the separation of church and state.

12. The main cause of the Arab-Israeli conflicts from 1948 to 1973 was the clash between (1) Islamic fundamentalism and Orthodox Judaism (2) Arab socialism and Israeli capitalism (3) Arab nationalism and Jewish nationalism (4) Israeli technology and Saudi Arabian economic goals.

13. Since independence in 1948, the major objective of the foreign policy of Israel has been to (1) maintain territorial security (2) mechanize its farms (3) receive military aid from the United Nations (4) sign a peace treaty with Libya.

14. Which factor served as a bond among Arab countries in the Middle East? (1) similarity of governments (2) unity under a military leader (3) reliance on the United States for aid (4) hostility toward Israel.

15. In 1979, the signing of the Camp David Accords by Egypt and Israel indicated that (1) nationalism was no longer a force in Middle Eastern politics (2) the differences between Shiite and Sunni Muslims had been settled (3) former enemies were able to negotiate (4) the Soviet Union dominated Middle Eastern affairs.

16. Which has been a major goal of both the Zionists and the Palestinians in the Middle East? (1) to unite the Middle East under their religion (2) to improve their relations with Russia (3) to become leaders in the world economy (4) to have their own independent country.

17. A major factor that contributed to terrorist activities in the Middle East was (1) a decrease in crude oil prices on the world market (2) the Palestinian effort to establish a homeland (3) the presence of United Nations forces in Syria (4) the worldwide rejection of violence as a means to end conflicts.

18. During the 20th century, a major Middle Eastern problem has been the (1) conflict between traditional culture and the push for modernization (2) refusal of industrial nations to sell weapons to Middle Eastern nations (3) decreasing birth rates in rural villages (4) denial of membership in the United Nations to Middle Eastern nations.

19. In Middle Eastern society, women have increasingly been at the center of a conflict between forces of modernization and the (1) values of traditional Islamic culture (2) pressure for a Palestinian homeland (3) shortage of capital for industrial development (4) need to reduce the birth rate.

20. During the 1980s, the economic development of Iran and Iraq was disrupted because of (1) increased emphasis on agricultural production for export (2) a war fought between these nations (3) Communist revolutionary movements in these nations (4) severe drought and famine in the area.

21. Which generalization is best supported by the reliance of many Western European nations on oil from the Middle East? (1) Most of the nations of the world are adopting command economies. (2) Nations that control vital resources are no longer able to influence world markets. (3) The goal of the world's economic planners is to decrease national self-sufficiency. (4) The nations of the world have become interdependent.

22. The Suez Canal, the Strait of Hormuz, and the Persian Gulf are important because they (1) prevent attacks on bordering nations (2) control access to vital trade routes (3) limit Russian access to ice-free ports (4) prohibit the movement of ships carrying nuclear weapons.

23. The Organization of Petroleum Exporting Countries (OPEC) was formed primarily to (1) give member nations more influence in world markets (2) force developing countries to abandon policies of nonalignment (3) help Middle Eastern nations form alliances with Western powers (4) allow the Soviet Union to develop greater influence in the Middle East.

Base your answer to question 24 on the circle graph below and on your knowledge of social studies.

WORLD'S ESTIMATED OIL RESERVES, 1990

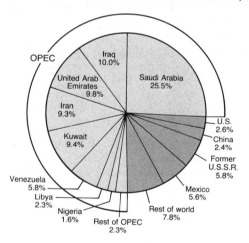

24. Which is a valid conclusion based on the information in the graph? (1) Only Middle Eastern nations are members of OPEC. (2) Events in the Middle East have little effect on world oil prices. (3) No major oil reserves exist in the Middle East. (4) Members of OPEC control approximately 75 percent of the world's oil reserves.

25. One reason that the United States and other Western powers fought in the Persian Gulf War was to (1) safeguard the flow of oil to international markets (2) end the civil war in Lebanon (3) stop the Israeli settlement of the West Bank (4) assist Iraq in its war with Iran.

Level 2

26. Which condition is a major obstacle to economic development in the Middle East? (1) use of strip mining to obtain minerals (2) reliance on capitalist economic systems (3) lack of access to world markets (4) scarcity of water resources.

27. Early civilizations in Egypt and Mesopotamia developed mainly in (1) areas with abundant mineral resources (2) valleys near rivers (3) areas with climatic diversity (4) mountainous areas.

28. The river valleys of the Tigris-Euphrates and the Nile were centers of civilization because they (1) had rich deposits of iron ore and coal (2) were isolated from other cultural influences (3) were easy to defend from invasion (4) provided a means of transportation and irrigation.

29. The religions of Judaism, Christianity, and Islam share a common belief in (1) nirvana (2) monotheism (3) reincarnation (4) animism.

30. Christianity and Islam are similar in that both (1) are polytheistic religions (2) have practiced a strict code of nonviolence (3) have the same religious holidays (4) have roots in Judaism.

31. The spread of Islam throughout the Middle East is an example of (1) national security (2) private enterprise (3) cultural diffusion (4) self-determination.

32. Which generalization is best supported by a study of the Middle East? (1) Illiteracy has become almost nonexistent. (2) Religious differences have led to serious conflicts. (3) Oil wealth has led to economic equality. (4) There are few conflicts between traditions and modernization.

33. Israel is a country that has (1) an abundance of oil (2) a democratically elected government (3) Islam as its official religion (4) friendly ties with all Islamic countries.

34. Who were David Ben-Gurion, Golda Meir, and Menachem Begin? (1) leaders of the modern state of Israel (2) scientists who developed better methods of discovering oil (3) clergy who supported Islamic fundamentalism (4) Egyptian presidents who encouraged peace with Israel.

35. The primary goal of the Palestine Liberation Organization (PLO) has been to (1) establish a home state for Palestinian Arabs (2) eliminate Communist influence in the Arab nations (3) bring about a peaceful settlement of the conflicts between Egypt and Palestinian Arabs (4) control the Organization of Petroleum Exporting Countries (OPEC).

36. Which has been a serious problem for many nations of the Middle East since World War II? (1) renewed colonial conquest by Europeans (2) the growing economic power of Japan (3) increased world demand for oil (4) conflicts between traditionalists and modernists.

37. In which of the following Middle Eastern nations is Islamic fundamentalism the major guiding force?   (1) Turkey   (2) Iran   (3) Israel   (4) Jordan.

38. The major goal of the Iranian Revolution and of the Ayatollah Khomeini was to   (1) establish closer ties with Israel   (2) prevent the expansion of communism into Iraq   (3) nationalize the oil industry   (4) create an Islamic government.

39. During the 1980s, Iran and Iraq were engaged in a war over   (1) Iran's ties with Israel   (2) territorial claims   (3) Iraq's use of terrorism   (4) the spread of communism.

Base your answer to question 40 on the cartoon below and on your knowledge of social studies.

Shanks, reprinted with permission of The Buffalo News, Inc.

40. The main idea of the cartoon is that the Middle East conflict will   (1) be confined to the Middle East   (2) be controlled by Western democracies   (3) totally destroy the Islamic religion   (4) eventually affect the entire world.

Essay Questions

Level 1

1. Certain events or occurrences in history have brought about significant changes.

Events/Occurrences
Rise of Islam
UN partition of Palestine after World War II
Westernization of Iran by the Shah
Camp David Accords by Egypt and Israel
Establishment of OPEC

Select *three* of the events or occurrences listed. For each:

- Describe the event or occurrence.
- Explain how the event or occurrence led to significant changes either in the Middle East in general or in a specific nation.

2. The Middle East faces various types of problems that affect its political development.

Problems Affecting Political Development
Warfare between Israel and Arab nations
Status of Palestinian refugees
Civil war in Lebanon
Iraq's invasion of Kuwait
Persecution of the Kurds

Select *three* of the problems listed above. For each:

- Explain how the problem affected the political development of the region.
- Discuss one specific attempt that has been made to overcome the problem.

Level 2

3. The statements below describe certain features of the geography of the Middle East.

Geographic Features
The Middle East is located in southwest Asia and North Africa.
Three-fourths of the world's oil reserves are located in the Middle East.
The Tigris-Euphrates and Nile river valleys are located in the Middle East.
Much of the Middle East has a hot, dry climate.

A. Select *two* geographic features from the list. For each feature chosen, state how it affected the history of the Middle East.

B. Base your answer to Part B on your answer to Part A. However, additional information may be included. Write an essay discussing the effects of specific geographic features on the development of the Middle East. Begin your essay with this topic sentence:

Geography has affected the development of the Middle East.

4. Throughout history, leaders have greatly influenced developments in their nation or region.

Leaders
Mohammed
Gamal Abdel Nasser
Anwar al-Sadat
Yasir Arafat
Ayatollah Khomeini
Golda Meir

A. Select *two* leaders from the list. For each leader chosen, state how she or he influenced developments in the Middle East.

B. Base your answer to Part B on your answer to Part A. However, additional information may be included. Write an essay discussing how each of the leaders influenced developments in her or his nation or region. Begin your essay with this topic sentence:

Leaders have often influenced developments in their nation or region.

CHAPTER 4

Latin America

Main Ideas

1. **GEOGRAPHIC DIVERSITY:** The varied climates and topographic features of Latin America have profoundly influenced its cultural and economic life.

2. **ETHNIC BLENDING:** In many Latin American countries, there is greater blending of racial and ethnic lines than in the United States and Canada.

3. **PRE-COLUMBIAN HERITAGE:** The Indian peoples of Latin America have preserved part of their rich heritage. They now look back to the Mayan, Aztec, and Incan periods as times of great achievement and power.

4. **CONQUEST BY EUROPEAN POWERS:** After conquering much of Latin America, Spain and Portugal exploited the region for their own economic benefit. Scarcity of Indian labor led to the importation of people from Africa as slaves.

5. **CHURCH POLICY:** The Roman Catholic Church opposed some glaring abuses of Indians' human rights. By and large, however, the Church supported the colonial governments' policies concerning treatment of Indians and other matters.

6. **REVOLUTIONS:** The examples of the American, French, and Haitian revolutions inspired Latin American colonists to revolt against Spanish rule in the early 19th century. The spread of

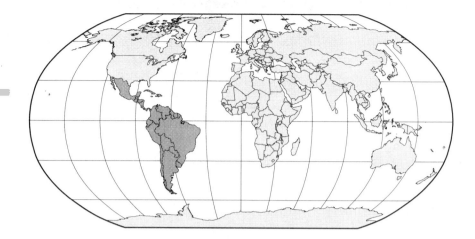

revolutionary ideas from one area to another is an example of cultural diffusion.

7. **RULE BY AN ELITE:** In the newly independent Latin American countries, most of the power was concentrated in the hands of a landowning elite. To some extent, this pattern has continued.

8. **ROLE OF THE MILITARY:** In most Latin American countries, the military has played an important and sometimes dominant role in the political system.

9. **DEMOCRATS VERSUS DICTATORS:** Some Latin American countries have succeeded in establishing a democratic tradition, while others have been ruled by dictators.

10. **U.S. INFLUENCE:** Both economically and politically, the countries of Latin America have been greatly influenced by the United States.

11. **ECONOMIC INEQUALITY:** In both the countryside and the cities, a huge gap exists between a rich minority and a poor majority. Land reform and increased industrialization would probably help reduce poverty.

12. **URBAN GROWTH:** Urbanization is occurring at a rapid pace throughout Latin America, causing the problems of poverty, pollution, crime, and overcrowding in many metropolitan areas.

Latin America: The Region at a Glance

NORTH AMERICA

CANADA

UNITED STATES

ATLANTIC OCEAN

MEXICO

Sierra Madre Mts.

Gulf of Mexico

Valley of Mexico

Havana

NETHERLANDS ANTILLES (NETH.)

ARUBA (NETH.)

DOMINICAN REPUBLIC

VIRGIN ISLANDS (U.S., U.K.)

PUERTO RICO (U.S.)

BAHAMAS

TROPIC OF CANCER

(1) Mexico City

Yucatán Peninsula

HAITI

CUBA

ST. CHRISTOPHER AND NEVIS

ANTIGUA AND BARBUDA

GUADELOUPE (FR.)

DOMINICA

MARTINIQUE (FR.)

ST. VINCENT AND THE GRENADINES

BARBADOS

TRINIDAD AND TOBAGO

BELIZE

Belmopan

GUATEMALA

Guatemala City

HONDURAS

Tegucigalpa

JAMAICA

ST. LUCIA

GRENADA

EL SALVADOR

San Salvador

CARIBBEAN SEA

(2) Panama Canal

Caracas

NICARAGUA

Managua

COSTA RICA

San José

VENEZUELA

Orinoco R.

Georgetown

Paramaribo

PANAMA

Panama City

COLOMBIA

Bogotá

GUYANA

FRENCH GUIANA (FRANCE)

SURINAME

EQUATOR

GALAPAGOS ISLANDS (ECUADOR)

ECUADOR

Quito

Amazon R.

(7)

Belém

SOUTH AMERICA

Andes Mts.

(3)

Lima

PERU

BOLIVIA

La Paz

BRAZIL

Recife

Brazilian Highlands

Brasília

PACIFIC OCEAN

Atacama Desert

(4)

Sucre

CHILE

PARAGUAY

Paraná R.

TROPIC OF CAPRICORN

Asunción

São Paulo

Rio de Janeiro

ARGENTINA

URUGUAY

Santiago

Buenos Aires

Montevideo

Río de la Plata

(6)

Pampas

★ Capital

● Other major city

0   1000 Kilometers

0   1000 Miles

N
W   E
S

FALKLAND ISLANDS (U.K.)

STRAIT OF MAGELLAN

(5)

1 MEXICO CITY: This city was the capital of the Aztec empire before Spanish invaders conquered it in 1521. Today, as home to more than 20 million people, it is the world's most populous city.

2 ISTHMUS OF PANAMA: Through this narrow strip of land, the Panama Canal was built early in the 20th century. The canal has served ever since as a major waterway for international trade. The United States is due to turn over control of the canal to Panama by the year 2000.

3 ANDES MOUNTAINS: This enormous mountain chain extends 5,500 miles along the entire west coast of South America. The mountains act as a barrier to communications between the west coast and the rest of the continent. Adapting to the mountain terrain, Indian peoples developed a civilization, which was ruled by the Incas in the 1400s and early 1500s.

4 ATACAMA DESERT: This arid part of Chile has great mineral wealth (gold, silver, copper, nitrates). A dispute over the area led Chile to fight Bolivia and Peru (1879–1883). Chile won the war and control over the area and has derived much of its wealth from the desert mines.

5 STRAIT OF MAGELLAN: This channel, 350 miles long, links the Atlantic and Pacific oceans. In 1520, Ferdinand Magellan navigated the strait on a voyage of exploration for Spain. Before the building of the Panama Canal, the strait served as an important shipping route for world trade.

6 PAMPAS: The great majority of Argentina's population lives on these fertile plains. The raising of livestock on the pampas and the export of beef are central to Argentina's economy.

7 AMAZON RIVER AND RAIN FOREST: The world's largest river flows through the world's largest rain forest. The clearing of this rain forest to promote Brazil's economic growth presents a major threat to the global environment.

8 CARIBBEAN ISLANDS (OR WEST INDIES): Because these islands were colonized by different European powers (France, Spain, Great Britain, and the Netherlands), they are divided today both culturally and politically into many small nations. The region's sunny climate makes tourism a principal industry.

I. Geography

Latin America consists of all the land in the Western Hemisphere that lies to the south of the United States. The northern part of the region includes Mexico, the eight countries of Central America (from Guatemala to Panama), and the various island nations of the Caribbean Sea. The southern part of the region consists of the 12 nations of South America. Brazil is the region's largest nation, in both area and population (over 150 million).

Why is the region called "Latin" America? It is because the two major languages spoken in the region—Spanish and Portuguese—are based on Latin (the language of the Roman empire). Another Latin language, French, is spoken in French Guiana and on a few Caribbean islands. Also helping to define Latin America is the strong influence on the region of the Roman Catholic Church.

The United States and Canada are not included in Latin America for two principal reasons. First, the great majority of people in these nations are English-speaking. English is not a Latin language. Second, before winning their independence, both the United States and Canada had been ruled by Great Britain. Most Latin American nations, in contrast, had been ruled by the Iberian countries of Spain and Portugal. (*Iberia* is the peninsula in Europe where Spain and Portugal are located.)

A. LOCATION AND SIZE

The world's two largest oceans, the Atlantic and the Pacific, separate the two continents of the Western Hemisphere (North and South America) from the other continents. For thousands of years, this fact of geographic isolation prevented the native peoples of the Americas from having contact with the cultures of Europe, Asia, and Africa.

From the Mexican-U.S. border to the southern tip of South America is a distance of about 6,000 miles. The great length of the region from north to south means that Latin America spans many climate zones. The equator crosses its central section, passing through Brazil, Colombia, and Ecuador. Here temperatures can be hot, and the climate tropical. But thousands of miles to the south, the climate is quite cold. Parts of Chile and Argentina are quite close to frigid Antarctica.

B. CLIMATES

The diverse climates of Latin America are one cause of the great diversity of Latin American cultures.

Tropical and subtropical climates of high heat and high humidity extend through much of the region, from central Mexico to southern Brazil. The high heat in this area is due to the fact that the sun's rays strike the earth almost straight down throughout the year.

RIO DE JANEIRO: This great city (population 11.1 million) is a major harbor and seaport on Brazil's Atlantic coast. How does its climate differ from that of the Amazon rain forest? (See map, page 138.)

In parts of this area, however, temperatures are moderated by one of two factors: sea breezes or high altitude. Along the coasts of these lands, ocean currents bring cool winds that provide relief from high temperatures. Areas of high altitude also have lower temperatures than surrounding lowlands. The mountainous areas of Peru and Ecuador, for example, have cool climates, even though these countries are located on or near the equator. Highland areas in parts of Brazil, Colombia, and Venezuela are also fairly cool.

No other country has more varied climates than the long, narrow, and mountainous country of Chile, in South America. Averaging only about 100 miles wide, Chile extends along the Pacific coast of the continent for over 2,600 miles. If you were to travel from the north of the country to the south, you would encounter first the extremely dry climate of Chile's Atacama Desert, then a *Mediterranean climate* (hot, dry summers; mild, moist winters), and finally a cold, wet, and windy climate near Chile's southern tip.

C. PHYSICAL FEATURES

Latin America is remarkable not only for its varied climates but also for its varied physical features.

Landforms   Second only to the Himalayas of Asia, the Andes Mountains in South America are one of the highest mountain chains in the world. Reaching heights of more than 20,000 feet, the Andes run along the entire Pacific coast of South America. From earliest times, the mountains have acted as a barrier to transportation and trade. People living on opposite sides of the Andes have largely been isolated from each other.

Another major landform, the Amazon Basin, comprises a vast area of Brazil and parts of other countries. The area is defined by the Amazon River and its hundreds of tributaries. Rains fall over the Amazon Basin on a daily basis. The hot and rainy climate supports the growth of a huge tropical rain forest. Most of the area is too hot and humid for dense human settlements. Scattered settlements of Indians, however, have long been established in the Amazon Basin. The Indians rely on the river as a source of food and a means of transportation.

Other people are also interested in the rain forest of the Amazon Basin. It is a good source of hardwood and the site of valuable mineral deposits. Non-Indians have been coming into the area in increasing numbers to exploit these resources and to set up ranches for raising cattle. Many people worry that the clearing of the rain forest for lumber and other uses could spell disaster for the earth's climate and wildlife and for the Indians who live in the rain forest. (These concerns are discussed in more detail on page 176.)

One of the driest, least habitable areas in the world is the Atacama Desert in northern Chile. Little vegetation can survive in this dry and desolate place. But the desert's rich deposits of *nitrate* (a chemical compound used in fertilizer) give the desert economic value.

The areas of South America where most people live are the (1) coastal lowlands and (2) interior plains and plateaus. One of these areas, the flat and grassy plains of Argentina, is known as the Pampas. Farmers of the Pampas grow wheat, corn, and other grains, giving the area the title of "Breadbasket of South America." To the north of the Pampas lies another important agricultural area—the Brazilian Highlands. Located just south of the Amazon Basin, its fertile soil and moderate temperatures enable farmers there to produce the world's largest crop of coffee.

Rivers   Latin America has three major river systems, all of them located in South America.

- The Amazon River begins in the Andes Mountains in Peru and runs eastward through Brazil for nearly 4,000 miles before emptying into the Atlantic Ocean. It is second only to the Nile in length. Its many tributaries make the Amazon Basin the world's largest river system.

- The Orinoco River flows through the highlands of Venezuela before emptying into the Caribbean Sea.
- The Río de la Plata forms part of the border between Argentina and Uruguay. Flowing into this wide channel are two major rivers—the Paraná and the Uruguay.

Resources   Latin America is richly endowed with mineral resources. Millions of barrels of petroleum are pumped from the wells of Mexico and Venezuela. Chile is known for its copper mines; Brazil, for its manganese mines; and Bolivia, for its tin mines.

Agricultural resources are also abundant and varied. Shipped daily from Latin American ports are large quantities of beef, wheat, and wool from Argentina, lumber from Brazil, bananas from Central America, sugarcane from the Caribbean islands, and coffee from Brazil and Colombia.

Islands of the Caribbean   A chain of islands, the West Indies, extends for a distance of almost 2,000 miles across the Caribbean Sea. The largest of these islands are Cuba, Hispaniola (Haiti and the Dominican Republic), and Puerto Rico. Most of the smaller islands were formed as the result of volcanic eruptions.

A tropical climate promotes the growth of the West Indies' principal crop and export: sugarcane. Brilliant, year-round sunshine as well as excellent beaches support a tourist industry, which is also important to the islands' economies.

As a result of differing colonial histories, the peoples of the West Indies speak a variety of languages. Dutch is spoken in Aruba; English, in Jamaica and the Bahamas; French, in Haiti and Martinique; and Spanish, in Cuba and the Dominican Republic. Some of the islands, such as Cuba and Grenada, govern themselves as independent nations. Others, such as Guadeloupe (a French possession), are still under the political control of a foreign nation. Puerto Rico has its own elected governor and legislature, but it remains a U.S. commonwealth.

In Review

The following questions refer to Section I: Geography.

1. *Key terms:* Identify each of the following:

Mediterranean climate	Amazon Basin	Andes Mountains
Pampas	West Indies	Atacama Desert

2. Compare and contrast the topography and climate of southern Chile with the topography and climate of northern Brazil.

3. Describe the Amazon Basin of Brazil. Why have many people been moving there from other parts of Brazil?

4. *Critical thinking:* The Caribbean island of Puerto Rico is part of the United States. Also, the English-speaking nation of Guyana in South America was formerly a British colony. Which of these lands should be classified as part of Latin America? (a) Puerto Rico only, (b) Guyana only, (c) both, or (d) neither. Explain your answer.

II. Early History

Scientists believe that the first humans to settle in the Western Hemisphere migrated eastward from Siberia (in Asia) to Alaska about 30,000 years ago. Over the course of thousands of years, different groups or tribes migrated widely over the land until they occupied almost every part of North and South America.

About 5,000 years ago, people in northern and central Mexico discovered a method for planting and harvesting beans, squash, and corn. As in other regions of the world, the discovery of agriculture eventually led to food surpluses. These surpluses made it possible for people to have the time and wealth to build complex societies known as civilizations.

Great civilizations developed in Latin America long before the Europeans arrived in the late 1400s and early 1500s. These invaders destroyed two of the civilizations: the Aztec empire of Mexico and the Inca empire of Peru. Much earlier, an advanced civilization created by the Mayan people of Central America had existed for hundreds of years before its mysterious decline.

A. THE MAYAN CIVILIZATION

The Mayans were an agricultural people whose civilization flourished from about A.D. 300 (a time when the Roman empire still existed) to about A.D. 900 (long after the Roman empire had fallen). The Mayans cleared areas in the dense rain forest of Central America (present-day Guatemala) using the slash-and-burn method. Their major food crops were *maize* (corn) and beans. They also grew cotton for use in making clothes.

The Mayans built a number of great cities, including Tikal, that served as administrative centers from which a ruling class of Mayan priests and nobles governed. In the cities, the Mayans constructed tall, flat-topped pyramids that housed the tombs of rulers. The pyramids also served another purpose: from the tops of the pyramids, Mayan priests observed the movement of stars and planets. The Mayans looked upon these bright objects in the night sky as gods. They believed that the gods determined everything that happened on earth: for example, whether it would rain and whether the corn would grow well.

MAYAN PYRAMID: This temple at Chichén Itzá, in southern Mexico, was one of hundreds built by the Mayans for both religious and scientific purposes. What scientific observations were made from the top of the pyramid?

Below the priests and nobles on the social scale were the merchants. They carried on an extensive trade over roads that connected the various cities. Common items of Mayan trade were jewelry, grain, salt, cloth, and animal skins.

The Mayans made a number of stunning scientific and artistic achievements. For example, they devised a calendar that was amazingly complex and accurate. Their system of mathematics included the use of zero (a concept then known to the Hindus of India but not to the Europeans). Their careful observations of the night sky enabled Mayans to predict *eclipses* (obscuring of the sun or moon by the shadow of another celestial body). Their towering pyramids were architectural wonders. Although abandoned centuries ago, some pyramids still stand. Finally, Mayans developed a written language, one based upon *glyphs* (symbolic figures or characters). Their writing is still being deciphered by scholars.

For reasons that are unclear, Mayans began abandoning most of their cities between A.D. 800 and 900. In neighboring Yucatán Peninsula (present-day Mexico), Mayan cities survived hundreds of years longer. Descendants of Mayans still live in Mexico and Guatemala.

EARLY CIVILIZATIONS OF CENTRAL AND SOUTH AMERICA

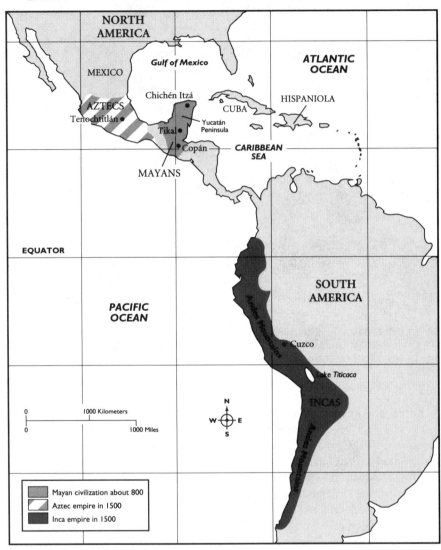

B. THE AZTEC EMPIRE

Early in the 1200s, a warlike people—the Aztecs—migrated from a barren wilderness in northern Mexico to a more fertile land on Mexico's Central Plateau. Fighting to establish themselves in their adopted land, the Aztecs acquired a reputation as fierce warriors. Eventually, they defeated in battle the more settled peoples who occupied central Mexico. They forced these people to pay *tribute* (a kind of tax that implies submission) to the Aztec ruling class.

Borrowing from earlier civilizations, the Aztecs became skilled builders. They constructed their capital city—Tenochtitlán—in the middle of a lake. They built stone bridges and causeways to connect their impressive city to the mainland. They erected huge stone pyramids and temples in the center of the city. To supply food for the city, crops were grown on floating islands in the lake. Elsewhere in the empire, of course, Aztec farmers grew their crops (maize and beans) in a more conventional manner—in the ground.

The Aztecs fashioned brilliant ornaments of gold and silver. Aztec merchants did a good business selling the handcrafted articles of Tenochtitlán to people who flocked to the city on market days.

The Aztecs worshipped many gods, especially the sun god. They believed that the sun was a god who would grow weak and die unless it was fed daily a diet of blood extracted from human hearts. To provide human victims for this god, the Aztecs constantly engaged in warfare. They would then sacrifice enemies captured in battle on the altars of the Aztec pyramids. Because of these actions (and because of the tribute they imposed), the Aztecs were feared and hated by other peoples in Mexico.

C. THE INCA EMPIRE

Completely separate from the Aztec empire in Mexico arose an even larger empire in South America. The Incas of Peru were great builders whose empire lasted approximately 100 years—from about 1440 to 1540. From their capital city Cuzco, high in the Andes, the Incas controlled a huge area that included parts of present-day Peru, Ecuador, Bolivia, Chile, and Argentina.

The Incas made use of advanced methods of agriculture. They built irrigation systems and made effective use of fertilizers. They also developed the technique of *terraced farming* (farming on level strips of land dug into the steep slopes of mountainsides).

The Incas were ruled by an absolute monarch, the "Lord Inca." They believed he was a descendant of the sun, and thus they worshipped him as a god. A highly religious people, the Incas erected temples from huge, finely chiseled blocks of stone, which weighed up to 200 tons each. Many of their temples and other stone structures still stand, having survived numerous earthquakes. For transporting goods and sending messages over vast distances across mountains, the Incas built an impressive system of stone highways and rope suspension bridges. (A *suspension bridge* is one whose roadway is suspended from two or more cables.)

The Incas put together a strong and complex government to care for the diverse needs of both cities and rural areas. The Inca monarch appointed a governor for each of the sections of the empire. Each section was subdivided into smaller districts. Those in charge of each district made sure that the resident population saved part of their food supply from good harvests for later distribution in lean years or times of famine. In this way, the government assured an adequate food supply for everyone in the empire.

The government of the Incas also managed the difficult feat of taking an accurate *census* (count) of the empire's population. It did so without the benefit of a system of writing, which the Incas lacked. Instead of written symbols like those of the Mayas and the Aztecs, the Incas kept records by tying knots in a rope device called a "quipu." A certain pattern of knots stood for a certain number.

D. NATIVE AMERICAN AGRICULTURE

For hundreds (in some cases, thousands) of years before Europeans arrived on the scene, the various peoples of Latin America had farmed the land. Their most important crops were maize, beans, and squash. In many Native American societies, the land was held and worked in common by all members of the community. This contrasts with the situation today where private ownership of land is the rule in Latin America.

LAST INCA KING OF PERU: Atahualpa (here being carried on his throne) ruled a vast empire from a capital high in the Andes. What were some of the remarkable aspects of this empire?

The Mayans and other Indian civilizations used several farming methods. These included slash-and-burn techniques, two-field farming, and irrigation. Slash-and-burn was the method used in a rain forest to quickly clear an area for farming. *Two-field farming* was a method of planting only one of two fields per season. The farmer would leave the other field to lie unplanted so that it could recover its fertility. Irrigation systems provided a regular supply of water in dry regions, thereby increasing the amount of land that could be farmed.

In Review

The following questions refer to Section II: Early History.

1. *Key terms:* Define each of the following:

   tribute   census
   terraced farming   two-field system

2. Describe *three* of the achievements of the Mayans.

3. Explain why historians consider the ancient Aztecs and Incas to have had important civilizations.

4. *Critical thinking:* Compare early American civilizations (Mayan, Aztec, and Inca) with the civilization of ancient Egypt. In your view, were Native American achievements equal to, greater than, or less than those of the Egyptians? Explain your answer.

III. The Dynamics of Change

Past generations of Americans were taught in elementary school that in 1492 Christopher Columbus "discovered" America. Today, Indian peoples and others question whether "discovery" is the right word to describe Columbus's deeds. True, his voyages across the Atlantic made Europeans aware of the existence of lands that had been previously unknown to them. But from the point of view of the Aztecs, Incas, and other native peoples, the American continents had already been discovered and settled for thousands of years. As they saw it, there was nothing *new* about the "New World." They looked upon Columbus and his crew not as discoverers, but as foreign invaders.

One fact is not in dispute. After Columbus's voyages, neither Europe nor the Americas would ever be the same again. The arrival of Spaniards and Portuguese in Latin America ended the era of great Indian civilizations. It marked the beginning of a new period of European domination. European colonization had a profound effect on the native populations. To begin with, the size of the native groups fell off drastically. Why was that? The decrease was due mainly to the diseases that Europeans brought with them. Native populations had not built up immunities to such diseases as smallpox and measles. An additional reason for the deaths of many Indians was the harsh treatment that they suffered at the hand of the conquerors.

Everywhere they went, Europeans gave names to the lands and peoples they came upon. For example, because Columbus mistakenly believed that he had found a route to the Indies of Asia, he gave the name "Indians" to the inhabitants of the lands he explored. This name has continued in use into our own times.

A. EUROPEAN EXPLORERS AND CONQUERORS, 1492–1572

Columbus and later explorers were attempting to open up a new sea route to China and India. In the 1400s, Italian city-states such as Genoa and Venice controlled the trade route to Asia that went through the eastern Mediterranean. Control of this major trade route allowed the Italians to charge high prices for Asian imports—spices, jewelry, silk, and tea. The kingdoms of Spain and Portugal were eager to find a way to break the Italian monopoly of the Asian trade.

Columbus's voyages   Christopher Columbus sailed under the Spanish flag for Queen Isabella I and King Ferdinand. Previously, Isabella and Ferdinand had each ruled separate Spanish-speaking kingdoms, Castile and Aragon. As a result of their marriage in 1469, Spain was on the way to becoming a single nation under one government. Hoping to obtain access to the fabled riches of Asia, Isabella agreed to finance Columbus's daring plan to sail across an unknown ocean. Columbus believed that by heading in a westerly direction, he would eventually reach the Far East and thereby break the Italian trade monopoly.

Columbus made a total of four voyages across the Atlantic between 1492 and 1504. He explored Cuba, other islands in the Caribbean, and the eastern coast of Central America. Until his death, Columbus clung to the belief that the lands he had explored were in Asia. He never realized that two continents, North and South America, as well as another large ocean (the Pacific), lay between Spain and China.

Portugal versus Spain   Portugal was quick to challenge Spain's claims to overseas lands, not only in the Americas but in Africa as well. In 1494, the two rival kingdoms, Spain and Portugal, accepted the pope's idea for settling their dispute. On a world map that was largely inaccurate, an imaginary north-south line was drawn through what was assumed to be the middle of the Atlantic. According to the Treaty of Tordesillas, Spain could claim lands west of this Line of Demarcation, while Portugal could claim lands east of the line. As it turned out, there was some American land to the east of the line—Brazil. A Portuguese navigator, Pedro Álvars Cabral, would confirm his country's claim to Brazil by exploring the Brazilian coast in 1500.

SPANISH AND PORTUGUESE EXPLORERS, 1492–1542

1. **Christopher Columbus.** In sailing for Spain (1492, 1493, 1498, 1502), explored the West Indies, the coast of Central America, and Venezuela.

2. **Pedro Álvars Cabral.** In sailing for Portugal, explored the coast of Brazil (1500), and secured the Portuguese claim to that country.

3. **Vasco Núñez de Balboa.** Led an expedition for Spain across the isthmus of Panama, finding a way to the Pacific Ocean (1513).

4. **Juan Ponce de León.** Explored Florida, establishing the Spanish claim to that land (1513).

5. **Hernando Cortés.** In leading an expedition for Spain (1519), conquered the Aztec empire in Mexico.

6. **Ferdinand Magellan.** In sailing for Spain (1519–1521), explored South America's east coast, navigated the Strait of Magellan, and crossed the Pacific. One of his ships became the first to circumnavigate the globe.

7. **Francisco Pizarro.** In leading an expedition for Spain (1532), conquered the Inca empire in Peru.

8. **Pedro de Mendoza.** In sailing for Spain (1536), founded the colony of Buenos Aires.

9. **Hernando de Soto.** In leading an expedition for Spain (1539–1541), explored from Florida to the mouth of the Mississippi River.

10. **Francisco de Coronado.** Led an expedition for Spain (1540) from Mexico into lands that would later become the U.S. Southwest.

11. **Juan Rodriguez Cabrillo.** In sailing from Mexico for Spain (1542), came upon San Diego harbor, California.

Spanish conquests   In less than 30 years after Columbus's first voyage, the Aztec empire was conquered by a small army of Spaniards led by Hernando Cortés. Arriving in Mexico in 1519, Cortés's band of soldiers surprised the native population with guns, horses, and armor, all of which were unknown to the Aztecs. Another factor in Cortés's success was his ability to persuade Indian enemies of the Aztecs to become the Spaniards' allies. A number of Indian groups feared the powerful Aztecs and resented paying them tribute. The previously all-powerful Aztec monarch, Montezuma II, was captured by the invaders. Eventually, he was stoned to death by his own people, who thought he had betrayed them. Cortés's victory in 1521 marked the end of Aztec rule in Mexico and the beginning of Spanish colonial rule.

Between 1531 and 1535, an ambitious and ruthless Spaniard, Francisco Pizarro, invaded the Inca empire in South America. Pizarro's forces were greatly outnumbered by the Inca army, but like Cortés's men, they had the advantage of surprise in the use of guns, horses, and armor. By a bold maneuver, they managed to capture the Inca monarch, Atahualpa. After offering to free their royal captive for a huge ransom, the Spaniards went back on their word and killed him. The Incas put up resistance to the Spaniards for years, but finally in 1572 the last part of the huge Inca empire was conquered. Meanwhile, much of the remaining lands of South America fell under the control of Spain. (Brazil remained a Portuguese colony.) Thus, in a span of less than 100 years, power in Latin America shifted from Indian civilizations to European (mostly Spanish) empires.

B. ORGANIZATION OF SPAIN'S COLONIES

During the 1500s, Spain developed a system for controlling the economic, social, and political life of its distant American territories. The Spanish landowners, soldiers, and priests who first colonized the region introduced their own culture and suppressed those of the native peoples. Devoted to the Roman Catholic Church, the Spanish colonists in the Americas did not tolerate any other religion. (The English Puritans who colonized New England in North America in the 1600s were also not tolerant of other religions.)

The Church and the Indians   Spanish conquerors of Mexico and Peru demanded that Native Americans give up their religious beliefs and adopt the Roman Catholic faith. Indeed, millions of Native Americans did begin to practice Christianity by attending worship services conducted by Spanish priests and missionaries. At the same time, however, many secretly kept their faith in traditional Indian gods and continued to observe the rituals of their pre-Christian ancestors.

The Spanish conquerors of the early 1500s treated native peoples

A MISSION IN NEW SPAIN: Founded in 1720, the Mission San Jose in San Antonio, Texas, was on the northern frontier of Spain's American empire. What was the purpose of a mission like this in colonial New Spain?

harshly and forced them to perform hard labor in mines and fields. Many thousands of Indians weakened and died under the brutal conditions imposed on them. One Spaniard who lived in the West Indies for 12 years, Bartolomé de Las Casas, was horrified by the general suffering of the native population. Las Casas, a Catholic priest, sent reports to the Spanish king and Parliament concerning the mistreatment of Indians. The king's government in Spain responded by issuing a law to protect the Indians from enslavement and other abuses of human rights.

Las Casas was one of the few figures in the Roman Catholic Church who fought for a more humane policy for Native Americans. In general, the Church had little respect for Indian cultures. It worked with the Spanish government in forcing Native Americans to submit to Spanish control.

The Church set up *missions* to care for and control Indian converts. Missions were buildings and surrounding farms that were under Church control. Native Americans living in the missions were educated in Christian doctrines and also in Spanish ways of farming and performing various skilled tasks. In the eyes of the mission *padres* (priests), education meant making the Indians adopt Spanish ways of acting and thinking. In other words, the priests tried to change the Indians' entire way of life. Mission priests also looked after the physical welfare of all residents; among other things, the priests aided the ill and the elderly.

Role of the Jesuits   The Jesuits are a society, or order, of Roman Catholic priests who stress missionary and educational work. In colonial Latin America, they were among the most active and influential missionaries. Over the course of more than two centuries, they succeeded in converting millions of Native Americans to Christianity. They founded hundreds of missions, many in remote parts of Latin America. Within their missions, Jesuits imposed strict rule, telling Indians what to do and how to do it. Resisting any outside interference in their work, the Jesuits sometimes had to close off their lands to Spanish armies.

Fearful of the Jesuits' independent power, the Spanish king in 1767 ordered them to close their missions and get out of Latin America. The expulsion of the Jesuits marked the end of an era in the history of Spanish colonial society. It did not, however, end the dominant role of the Catholic Church in the lives of America's native peoples.

Economic power of the Church   During the colonial period, which lasted into the early 1800s, the Roman Catholic Church owned most of the land in the Spanish-speaking parts of Latin America. Included among its properties were missions, ranches, buildings, and mines. The Church increased its wealth by taxing the people who worked the land. Some of the taxes paid for the Church's charitable services to the poor.

Colonial government   The royal government of Spain sent high officials to the Americas to maintain colonial rule. The most powerful of these officials, the *viceroys*, had great authority as agents of the Spanish crown. Laws created in Spain applied to all aspects of life in the American colonies.

The viceroys' colonial capitals in Mexico and Peru were separated from Spain by great distances. It took months for official communications to pass back and forth between Spain and its colonies. Because of the communication problem, in the 1500s and 1600s the viceroys had much freedom to determine which of Spain's colonial laws were to be carried out. A viceroy's rulings usually went unchallenged.

Colonial economy   The Spaniards greatly valued ownership of land because it conferred prestige as well as wealth. They looked down upon manual labor. The relatively few Spaniards who came to settle the colonies in the 1500s and 1600s were able to acquire vast holdings of land. The huge estates and the wealth that went with them soon gave rise to a small, highly privileged ruling class. This class consisted of settlers emigrating from Spain and their American-born descendants. From these beginnings, a rigid class structure developed. (In many Latin American countries, this class structure continues to the present day.)

In the 1500s, Indians were forced to do heavy manual labor for landowners and missionaries. But the Indian population declined drastically as a result of deaths from (1) the unfamiliar diseases of the Europeans and (2) harsh treatment by the conquerors. To make up

COLONIES IN THE AMERICAS, 1700

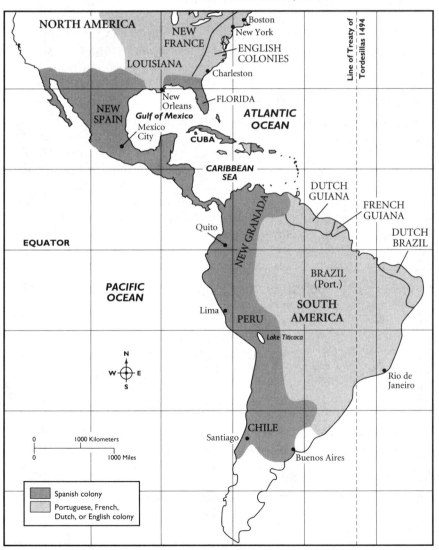

for the scarcity of Indian labor, the Spanish colonists in the 16th and 17th centuries bought enslaved Africans from slave traders. Those who survived the terrifying ocean voyage from Africa were forced to work in the gold and silver mines of Peru and on plantations throughout Latin America.

European economies were based on the idea of *mercantilism*. According to this theory, a country could enrich itself by obtaining gold and silver and other raw materials from its overseas colonies. All the European kingdoms of the 1600s and 1700s competed for wealth of this kind. From Spain's point of view, its colonies existed for basically one reason: to strengthen the treasury of the Spanish government. Thus, Spain required its colonies to send minerals and other raw materials to Spain only, and not to England or to any other nation. In addition, the colonies were allowed to purchase manufactured goods from just one source, Spain. The development of industries in the colonies was discouraged. Other European powers had similar policies toward their own colonies.

Differences between Spanish and Portuguese rule   Portuguese rule of Brazil differed in important respects from Spanish rule of Mexico and Peru. Portugal's monarchy did not attempt to closely regulate all aspects of its huge American colony. And because Portugal lacked the military power of its European rivals, the French, the Spaniards, and the Dutch were able to control parts of Brazil at various times.

The Roman Catholic Church was less influential in Brazil than in the Spanish colonies. Nevertheless, it did provide a common religion for the colonists and the various Indian peoples who occupied the Brazilian Highlands and coastal areas of Brazil.

Intermarriage and ethnic blending   In both the Spanish and Portuguese colonies, it was common for European settlers to seek marriage partners from among the women of the native population. As hundreds of thousands of Africans came to the colonies in slave ships, they likewise intermarried, with both Indians and Europeans. The offspring of European-Native American marriages were known as *mestizos*, while the offspring of European-African marriages were known as *mulattoes*. Colonists whose ancestors were entirely European were called *creoles*.

In Portuguese Brazil, the intermarriage of the races blurred racial lines even more than in Spain's colonies. In Brazil, race defined a person's social and economic status less than in other Latin American countries. For example, a person who owned a Brazilian plantation enjoyed wealth and high status regardless of his or her race. But generally, even in Brazil, those with dark skin were more economically disadvantaged than were the creoles.

Because of generations of intermarriage, the ethnic identity of Latin Americans today can be quite mixed. In Mexico, mestizos make up 60 percent of the population. In Brazil, a significant portion of the population are mulattoes. In the Dominican Republic, 73 percent of the people are racially mixed. At the same time, there are several Latin American countries where little racial mixing has occurred. Haiti, for example, is 95 percent African. Argentina is 85 percent European (chiefly Spanish and Italian).

C. WINNING POLITICAL INDEPENDENCE

Spain and Portugal managed to govern their American colonies for about 300 years—far longer than the United States has existed as a nation. But in the latter half of the 1700s, many colonists expressed growing discontent. Some wealthy landowners asked that they be allowed a voice in making laws for their society. Instead of conceding to these requests, though, Spain's monarchy continued to send officials to Latin America to rule in an authoritarian way.

Effects of the American and French revolutions   In Europe, the late 1700s was a time when educated people were debating proposed changes in government and society. This era of philosophical and scientific thinking was known as the *Enlightenment*. Among the new ideas that European thinkers discussed was the view that all people had equal rights to political liberty. (The Enlightenment is treated in more detail in Chapter 7.)

Colonists in both Latin America and North America were inspired by Enlightenment ideas to challenge the established authorities. In 1776 in the 13 North American colonies belonging to Great Britain, the enthusiasm for liberty and self-government took the form of a revolution. As a result of this American Revolution, a new, self-governing nation—the United States—came into being. A few years later, in 1789, a revolution broke out in France against the absolute rule of the French king.

The examples of the American and the French revolutions moved colonial leaders in Latin America to demand liberty for their own lands and peoples.

Napoleon's impact   In France, an ambitious soldier named Napoleon Bonaparte came to power in 1799. He disrupted Europe by successfully leading French armies as they invaded neighboring countries. One of the countries falling to Napoleon's armies was Spain, in 1808. With Spain now ruled by France, discontented Spanish colonists in Latin America had fewer ties of loyalty to the distant government across the ocean. They rose in revolt and proclaimed new republics in Mexico, Colombia, Venezuela, Chile, and Brazil (to name just a few of the nations established in the early 1800s).

Four revolutionaries   The movements for independence broke out at different times in different places. We can summarize the highlights

REVOLUTION IN HAITI: In the 1790s, while the French were experiencing their own revolution in Europe, the black majority in Haiti revolted successfully against French rule. When did other Latin American nations revolt against Spanish rule?

of the independence struggle by focusing on four of the revolutionary leaders, each of whom encouraged a spirit of nationalism.

1. Toussaint-Louverture in Haiti. Blacks on a Caribbean island were the first colonists in Latin America to achieve national independence. They lived under slavery in Haiti, which had been a Spanish colony until 1697, when France acquired it. In the 1790s, a former enslaved person named Toussaint-Louverture led a slave rebellion against the French plantation owners. Although Toussaint-Louverture was captured, his followers continued the rebellion until they finally succeeded in achieving independence for Haiti in 1804.

The Haitian revolution was the first successful black revolution against a European power. Haiti's revolutionary government promptly abolished slavery. It led the way for other American nations to do the same later in the 19th century.

2. Hidalgo in Mexico. The ringing of a church bell one September day in 1810 launched a revolution of Mexicans against Spanish rule. The revolutionary leader who rang the bell and then made a stirring appeal for liberty was Father Miguel Hidalgo. A Catholic priest, Father Hidalgo worked to force the Spaniards from Mexico and to improve living conditions of Indians. Although Hidalgo was captured and executed, other revolutionaries would obtain independence for Mexico later on, in 1821.

3. Bolívar in Colombia and Venezuela. In the northern part of South America, a youthful idealist named Simón Bolívar made this vow: "I will never allow my hands to be idle or my soul to rest until I have broken the chains laid upon us by Spain." From 1807 to 1825, Bolívar led rebel armies in lands that would eventually become the nations of Colombia, Venezuela, Ecuador, and Bolivia. At times, Bolívar faced defeat, but he eventually forced Spain to give up its South American colonies. He well earned the nickname, "The Liberator."

4. San Martín in Argentina, Peru, and Chile. Spain's colony of Peru extended down the Pacific coast of South America into what is today the nation of Chile. The man chiefly responsible for liberating this immense territory was an army officer named José de San Martín. Working from Argentina, which had gained its independence in 1810, San Martín led revolutionary armies over the Andes. Aided by a Chilean patriot, Bernardo O'Higgins, San Martín led the effort to liberate Chile, which was accomplished in 1818. He then joined forces with Bolívar in a successful effort to liberate Peru.

Formation of separate nations   Bolívar's original hope had been to create a single, unified republic in South America similar in organization to that of the United States. But disputes arose among revolutionary leaders. Bolívar's large republic of "Gran Colombia" broke apart into the separate nations of Colombia, Venezuela, and Ecuador.

In 1821 in Central America, creole leaders declared independence from Spain and created a confederation of states. By the mid-1800s, however, this Central American union had collapsed, and the separate nations of Nicaragua, El Salvador, Costa Rica, Guatemala, and Honduras had been founded.

Since the mid-19th century, no significant attempts at unifying either Central or South America have occurred. Border disputes between neighboring countries have made the prospect of Latin American unity even more unlikely. In the 1880s, for example, Chile fought a war against Bolivia, forcing the latter country to give up a coastal area rich in nitrates. In the 1930s, Bolivia lost even more land as a result of a war it fought with Paraguay.

Power of the ruling elite   In each Latin American nation, political and economic power was concentrated in the hands of an elite, primarily the landowners. They would act as masters of those employed on their *haciendas* (huge estates). In the role of protectors, the landowners would care for their peasants' basic welfare and expect total obedience in return. Most landowners were creoles; most peasants were mestizos, mulattoes, Indians, or blacks.

Military officers made up the second crucial element in the ruling elite. The army served to maintain law and order, with an army officer often heading the government. Sometimes the army caused disorder, though, when factions within the army competed for power. A general heading the government one day might be replaced the next day by an ambitious rival. Changes in government leadership would sometimes be quick and bloodless and at other times break out into civil war.

Sharing power with the landowners and military officers were high officials of the Roman Catholic Church. Like other members of the elite, most Church officials were creoles. They gave support to the existing social order and taught the masses of poor people to accept their lot without complaint. In contrast to the Church leaders, however, many village priests (especially in the 20th century) sided with the poor against the rich. Many priests have demanded radical changes in Latin American governments and societies.

Dictatorships Latin American nations called themselves *republics* (governments in which officials are elected by the voters). But most of the governments created after independence were far from democratic. From Mexico to Argentina, political power was concentrated in the hands of the elite—military officers, landowners, and high officials of the Church. From time to time, reformers would call for redistribution of land, honest elections, and greater power for the common people. But conservatives were usually able to discourage reform movements, often by jailing (or even executing) the movements' leaders.

In many Latin American countries, it was common for military officers to seize control of government by means of a *coup d'état* (a quick seizure of power by a small group). They would typically declare a state of emergency and rule the country by decree. If elections were held, the dictator or dictatorial group would manipulate the voting so that no opponent could win. Latin Americans referred to their military dictators as *caudillos*.

In the 19th century, a succession of caudillos governed Mexico. One of the most powerful and important was Porfirio Díaz, who was Mexico's president for most years between 1877 and 1911. With great political skill, Díaz won the loyal support not only of the Church and the landholding creoles but also of the mestizo majority. Encouraging foreign investors, he succeeded in building up Mexico's economy. But this success came at the expense of the laboring and peasant classes, whose standard of living remained low. Eventually, as the economy weakened, discontent with Díaz's aging dictatorship burst into open revolt. (The revolution is discussed on pages 164–166.)

Economic dependence After winning their political independence from Europe's colonial powers, the nations of Latin America had much greater difficulty winning their economic independence. In colonial times, landowners had become accustomed to regularly supplying raw materials to Spain and Portugal while importing manufactured goods from those nations. With independence, they could now sell their raw materials to other nations as well. But even with the new trading partners, the Latin American nations' economic role remained the same. They still mainly exported raw materials and imported manufactured goods.

Many Latin American countries had just one crop or one mineral to export. Honduras specialized in bananas; Colombia, in coffee; Chile, in copper; Cuba, in sugar; and Bolivia, in tin. The one-crop or one-mineral economies were extremely vulnerable to the possibility of falling prices on European and U.S. markets. In contrast, foreign suppliers of manufactured goods could usually keep their prices high.

Foreign investment   In the 19th century, the United States and the nations of Western Europe were rapidly industrializing. Businesses in these countries were looking for ways to ensure a cheap and abundant supply of raw materials. They were also looking for places to invest their money. They found Latin America ideally suited to meet their goals. Representatives of U.S. and European companies traveled to all parts of Latin America to invest in mines, oil wells, and plantations. In time, most of the industries in the region came under foreign ownership and control.

Recall that in Africa, European imperialism took the form of political control. In Latin America, Europeans did not again move in with troops and governing officials. Now they managed to have a great impact on the region by making far-ranging investments. This economic penetration was an indirect form of imperialism.

Recall also that the United States was not one of the imperial powers in Africa. In Latin America, though, it became the major force of imperialism.

Special relationship with the United States   The United States had been the first nation of the Western Hemisphere to throw off colonial rule. One of its foreign policy goals in the 19th century was to protect the newly won independence of Latin American republics. In 1823, President James Monroe issued a famous declaration, the *Monroe Doctrine*. In it, the president warned European powers not to seek new colonies in Latin America or to otherwise interfere in Latin American affairs. Implied in the warning was the idea that the United States would protect Latin American countries from outside interference. The U.S. threat was given added weight because Great Britain endorsed it. (By this time, Britain had replaced Spain as the major trading partner of many Latin American countries.)

In time, many Latin Americans came to distrust U.S. policy as expressed in the Monroe Doctrine. Instead of having Europeans interfere in Latin American affairs, it now appeared that the United States was reserving the right to interfere.

War between Texas and Mexico   In the 1820s, Texas was part of Mexico but contained only a few thousand Mexican residents (in addition to the many more Native Americans). Americans, including many slaveholding Southerners, were attracted by what they viewed as the "open land" of Texas. By the mid-1830s, there were more American settlers than Mexicans in Texas. The Americans often defied Mexico's laws, including one against slaveholding. When Mexico tried to stop further American immigration, the Americans already there revolted and declared Texas an independent nation in 1836.

Determined to put down the revolt, Mexican President Antonio López de Santa Anna led troops into Texas. His forces overwhelmed and killed the Texan defenders who were occupying the Alamo, a church mission turned into a fort. Soon afterward, however, during a battle on the San Jacinto River, the Texans captured Santa Anna, who was forced to grant their demand for independence.

Issue of Texas annexation   For nine years (1836–1845), Texas was a completely separate and independent nation: the "Lone Star Republic." Its leaders applied for admission to the Union as a state. But for years, the proposed *annexation* (formal addition) of Texas failed to receive a favorable vote in Congress. The chief obstacle was slavery. Northerners opposed annexation of Texas because slavery was well established there. Solidly supporting Texas annexation were the slave states of the South. Finally in 1845, the issue was settled in the South's favor when Congress passed a joint resolution admitting Texas to the Union as the 28th state.

Mexican-U.S. War   The territorial ambitions of the United States led to a war with Mexico. In 1846, U.S. troops were sent into Mexico over a dispute concerning the Mexican border with Texas. After two years of fighting, the Mexican government conceded defeat in 1848. As part of the peace agreement, Mexico lost California and other territories in what is now the U.S. Southwest. Another result of the war was that many Mexicans held a continuing grievance against their country's northern neighbor.

Cuba and the Spanish-American War   In 1898, the United States became involved in another war in Latin America. To support Cuban rebels in their revolution against Spanish rule, the United States declared war on Spain. U.S. victory in the war did in fact liberate Cuba from Spanish rule. In 1901, however, the U.S. Congress demanded that Cuba insert in its constitution a clause that imposed strict limits on Cuba's ability to conduct foreign policy. The United States also obtained the right to set up a military base at Guantánamo Bay on Cuba's coast. The base is still under U.S. control.

Also as a result of the Spanish-American War, Spain ceded to the United States Puerto Rico (in the Caribbean) and Guam (in the Pacific). For the bargain price of only $20 million, Spain sold the Philippines to the United States. (This sale and subsequent events in the Philippines are discussed in Chapter 5.)

U.S. military interventions   In the early 1900s, U.S. policy toward Latin America became more aggressive under the leadership of President Theodore Roosevelt. This U.S. leader extended the meaning of the Monroe Doctrine. He said that it justified sending U.S. troops into a Latin American country that failed to pay its debts to European lenders. (His reasoning was that if a Latin American country failed to pay these debts, a European power might use force to collect the money. This action would involve bringing European troops into the Western Hemisphere—a violation of the Monroe Doctrine.) Roosevelt's policy became known as the "Roosevelt Corollary to the Monroe Doctrine." Applying this policy in 1904, Roosevelt ordered troops to the Dominican Republic to collect that nation's overdue debts. Later presidents continued Roosevelt's policy of intervention by sending U.S. troops into Nicaragua, Haiti, and elsewhere.

On the one hand, U.S. intervention succeeded in helping indebted Latin American nations meet their financial obligations. Thus, no European power intervened in Latin America. On the other hand, many Latin Americans resented U.S. policy as unwanted interference in their countries' political life.

Commonwealth of Puerto Rico   Since acquiring Puerto Rico in 1898, the United States has continued to govern the island. In 1917, Congress granted the Puerto Rican people full U.S. citizenship. Then in 1952, Congress changed the status of Puerto Rico from being a U.S. territory to being a U.S. commonwealth. In part, commonwealth status means that Puerto Ricans may elect their own governor and do not have to pay U.S. income taxes. While living on the island, however, they may not vote in U.S. presidential elections. Since Puerto Ricans are U.S. citizens, they may enter or leave any part of the United States at will.

In Review

The following questions refer to Section III: The Dynamics of Change.

1. *Key terms:* Define or identify each of the following:

    mission   viceroy   caudillo
    Jesuit   mercantilism   republic

2. Explain how Spanish conquerors were able to defeat the Aztec and Inca empires relatively quickly.

3. Describe the role played by the (a) Roman Catholic Church and (b) landowning class in Spain's Latin American colonies.

4. Explain the significance of the Monroe Doctrine on U.S. relations with Latin American nations, 1823–1904.

5. *Critical thinking:* By 1900, Spain and Portugal had lost their empires in Latin America. Which groups in Latin America benefited from the change and which did not? Explain.

IV. Contemporary Nations

Early in the 20th century, two revolutions broke out that would have major effects on Latin America. First, a revolution in Mexico in 1910 forced the dictator, Porfirio Díaz, to leave office. Other changes would soon follow that challenged the social order in Mexico. Second, revolutions in Russia in 1917 resulted in the establishment of a *Marxist*, or *Communist*, government—one that is supposedly dedicated to the interests of the working class. (For an explanation of Marxist theory, see Chapter 7.)

A. LATIN AMERICAN POLITICS IN THE 20TH CENTURY

In the 20th century, politics in Latin America have, to a great extent, been dominated by revolutions and dictatorships. But there have been many examples of successful democratic societies as well.

Revolution in Mexico A successful revolt in 1910 against the dictatorial rule of Porfirio Díaz was only the beginning of a revolutionary struggle that pitted different classes of Mexicans against one another. The privileged class of landowners generally supported the military rule of one of Díaz's successors, General Victoriano Huerta. Mexico's lower and middle classes divided their loyalties among several challengers.

Two Mexican rebels—Emiliano Zapata and Francisco "Pancho" Villa—appealed to Mexico's peasants. Zapata led groups of landless peasants in raids on the properties of rich landlords. They would seize and redistribute the land by force, without compensating the former owners. Zapata wanted the Mexican government to approve his actions and to carry out more *land reform* (breaking up large estates in order to give land to landless peasants) in other parts of Mexico. Villa too supported land reform. Both rebels opposed a new government led by Venustiano Carranza.

In 1915, the United States government sided with Carranza against his opponents. It stopped the export of guns from the United States to Villa and Zapata. In 1916, Villa retaliated by leading a raid on towns in New Mexico. In the process, some 18 Americans and many more

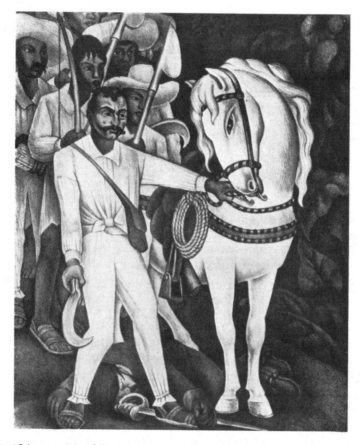

ZAPATA: This portrait of the Mexican revolutionary was created by the great Mexican artist, Diego Rivera (see page 181). Why was Emiliano Zapata regarded as a hero by millions of peasants?

Mexicans were killed. In 1916, U.S. President Woodrow Wilson sent U.S. troops into Mexico to try to capture Villa. The expedition failed to find him, so in 1917 the troops returned to the United States.

Carranza, who prevailed as Mexico's ruler, set Mexico on the road to change by supporting democratic reforms. Under a new constitition adopted in 1917, the government gained control over the Roman Catholic Church and over education in Mexico. Moreover, labor unions were recognized as lawful organizations for the first time in that country.

Carranza's successors in the 1920s and 1930s responded to the needs of workers and peasants. A strong and popular president in the 1930s, General Lázaro Cárdenas divided many large estates into smaller plots for distribution to peasants. He also gave strong support to labor unions in their struggle to win better wages and working conditions. A Mexican nationalist, Cárdenas challenged the foreign-owned oil companies in Mexico and seized control of their oil wells and other properties. Great Britain and the United States protested these actions but did not retaliate.

Dictatorship in Argentina Workers gained some influence in Argentina through the election in 1946 of a popular leader named Juan Perón. President Perón had the support of both labor unions and the military. To ensure his grip on power, he used armed squads to muzzle the press and jail political opponents.

Although he suppressed individual liberties, Perón championed the cause of Argentina's industrial workers. He made sure that workers received higher wages and better benefits. He nationalized the country's railroads and *public utilities* (companies that provide essential services, such as electricity and water, to the public). In foreign policy, Perón urged Latin Americans to follow a "third way"—a course independent of Soviet communism, on the one hand, and U.S.-led anticommunism, on the other hand. Although Perón was driven from power in 1955 by a revolt of army generals, he returned briefly in 1973 and remained president until his death the following year.

Perón's second wife, Eva (or Evita) Perón, achieved popularity of her own as a champion of the poor and of women. She collected donations of money from wealthy Argentinians and distributed the funds to the poor. She also helped Argentine women win the right to vote, in 1947. Perón's third wife (and widow), Isabel Perón, served as the country's president after Juan Perón's death, from 1974 to 1976. She was the first woman president of a nation in the Western Hemisphere.

Revolution and dictatorship in Cuba By the 1950s, two kinds of dictatorships had been established in different regions of the world. One kind of dictatorship, often labeled "rightist," got strong support from business owners and rich landowners. A second kind of dictatorship, often labeled "leftist," got support from (or ruled in the name of) the working class. The second type of dictatorship came into being in 1917 in Russia when the Communist party seized power. Dictators of Russia (called the Soviet Union beginning in 1922) claimed to be enemies of capitalism and business owners and champions of industrial workers and poor peasants. For years, revolutionaries in Latin America and other regions looked to the Soviet Union for help in overthrowing rightist military governments.

In 1959 in Cuba, revolutionary leader Fidel Castro overthrew the corrupt military regime of Cuba's longtime dictator, Fulgencio Batista. Cuba's peasants generally supported Castro because he promised land reform. Soon after coming to power, Castro welcomed the aid of the Soviet Union in transforming Cuba into a Communist state. Banning elections and suppressing freedom of speech and of the press,

Castro turned Cuba into a Communist dictatorship. He also seized many foreign-owned properties in Cuba, including those owned by U.S. businesses.

U.S. political and business leaders were angry about Castro's actions. Also, they feared that Soviet influence might spread from Cuba to other Latin American countries. In 1961, the U.S. government backed a military invasion of Cuba by Cuban exiles living in the United States. Its objective was to overthrow Castro's government. After landing on a beach on Cuba's Bay of Pigs, the invading force was quickly defeated.

In 1962, an even worse crisis arose when the United States discovered that Soviet missiles were being installed on Cuban soil. U.S. President John F. Kennedy ordered a naval blockade of Cuban waters to stop Soviet ships from bringing more missiles into Cuba. He also ordered the Soviets to remove the missiles already there. The *Cuban Missile Crisis* came dangerously close to touching off a nuclear war between the superpowers. Fortunately, however, the Soviets agreed to remove their missiles from Cuba, and the crisis passed.

Civil war in Nicaragua The Central American country of Nicaragua underwent a revolution similar to that of Cuba. In 1979, a leftist group known as the *Sandinistas* overthrew the military dictatorship of General Anastasio Somoza, whose family had ruled Nicaragua for over 40 years. Replacing Nicaragua's rightist dictatorship was a leftist dictatorship headed by Sandinista leader Daniel Ortega.

Once again, the U.S. government felt that its interests and security were being threatened by a leftist state in Latin America. It soon became apparent that the Nicaraguan government was getting aid from Cuba and the Soviet Union. In the 1980s, President Ronald Reagan persuaded Congress to give military aid to a group that was fighting to overthrow the Nicaraguan government—the *contras*. Nicaragua's long civil war ended in 1990 when the Sandinista government allowed a free and fair election to be held. The Sandinistas lost the election, and Ortega peacefully turned over the government to the election winner—Violeta Chamorro.

Trend toward more democratic government Until recently, most of the governments of Latin America were dictatorships either of the left or of the right. But recently there has been a notable trend away from dictatorships and toward greater democracy. The change in government in Nicaragua in 1990 provided just one example among many of dictators' yielding power. When Chile held democratic elections in 1990, the military regime of longtime dictator, Augusto Pinochet, came to an end. Today, almost every country of South America has a democratically elected government.

One exception to this trend toward democracy is the case of Peru under President Alberto Fujimori. In 1992, he dissolved Congress and suspended the country's constitution, claiming the need for drastic actions to fight drug lords and the terrorist group Shining Path. Despite the President's undemocratic actions, the majority of Peruvians seemed to support him. They approved a new constitution that Fujimori had wanted. Moreover, he appears to be winning the war against terrorism. In 1992, Peru's national police arrested the Shining Path leader Abimael Guzmán Reynoso. Terrorist actions have declined considerably.

Recent human rights abuses   Latin American governments have abused the human rights of political activists. In a 12-year civil war in El Salvador, for example, death squads with links to the government were blamed for the deaths of thousands of leftist opponents of the government. The civil war ended in 1992 when the government and the rebels signed a peace treaty.

For many years, a military regime in Guatemala employed death squads to terrorize that country's Indian population. Thousands of Guatemalans were massacred, and others have fled the country. In 1993, however, Guatemala got a new president, one dedicated to defending its citizens' human rights.

In the late 1980s and early 1990s in Peru, right-wing death squads were involved in killings of leftist opponents of the Peruvian government. In one incident in 1992, the squads killed nine university students and a professor. Many observers believe that Peru's military had been involved in this and other incidents, but top army officers denied the charges and refused to cooperate with nonmilitary investigations.

B. ECONOMIC DEVELOPMENT

Ever since colonial times, the farming- and mining-based economies of Latin America have had close ties to the more industrialized economies of other regions.

Dependence on foreign investments   Before World War I (1914–1918), Latin American countries were dependent mainly upon Europe for their manufactured goods. After that war, the United States became Latin America's chief trading partner and its principal source of investment capital.

Latin Americans have mixed feelings about the money that foreigners invest in their country's mines, oil wells, and large farms. On the one hand, many government leaders welcome foreign capital as absolutely necessary for economic growth and development. On the other hand, Latin Americans resent the power that foreign corporations can exercise through their control of a country's major economic resources.

DOCUMENT: AUTOBIOGRAPHY
OF A GUATEMALAN INDIAN

In 1992, the Nobel Prize for Peace was awarded to a woman from Guatemala for her efforts at championing the human rights of Guatemala's Indians. Rigoberta Menchú is herself a member of her country's largest ethnic minority, the Quiche Indians. Like most of her people, she speaks her native language, Quiche, and does not speak Spanish. At the age of 23, she told the story of her life and explained the culture of her people to a translator. The following excerpt is from her book, *I, Rigoberta Menchú.*

Two of my brothers died in the *finca* [plantation fields]. The first, he was the eldest, was called Felipe. I never knew him. He died when my mother started working. They'd sprayed the coffee with pesticide by plane while we were working, as they usually did, and my brother couldn't stand the fumes and died of intoxication. The second one, I did see die. His name was Nicolás. He died when I was eight. He was the youngest of all of us, the one my mother used to carry about. He was two then. When my little brother started crying, crying, crying, my mother didn't know what to do with him because his belly was swollen by malnutrition. . . .

Rigoberta Menchú

The little boy died early in the morning. We didn't know what to do. Our two neighbors were anxious to help my mother but they didn't know what to do either—not how to bury him or anything. Then the *caporal* [overseer] told my mother she could bury my brother in the *finca* but she had to pay a tax to keep him buried there. My mother said: "I have no money at all." He told her: "Yes, and you already owe a lot of money for medicine and other things, so take his body and leave. . . ." None of the people in our *galera* [workers' barracks] wanted my brother's body to stay there, of course, because it was upsetting. So my mother decided that, even if she had to work for a month without earning, she would pay the tax to the landowner, or the overseer, to bury my brother in the *finca*. Out of real kindness and a desire to help, one of the men brought a little box, a bit like a suitcase. We put my brother in it and took him to be buried. We lost practically a whole day's work over mourning my brother. We were all so very sad for him. That night the overseer told us: "Leave here tomorrow." "Why?" asked my mother. "Because you missed a day's work. You're to leave at once and you won't get any pay. So tomorrow I don't want to see you 'round here."

Questions

For each of the following statements, tell whether it is a fact or an opinion. *If it is an opinion,* say whether or not you agree with the opinion and explain your answer.

1. The overseer behaved badly toward the dead boy's mother.
2. Rigoberta Menchú did not witness the death of her brother Felipe.
3. The overseer ordered Rigoberta's mother to leave the plantation because she missed a day's work to arrange for her son's burial.
4. The other workers on the plantation should have done more to help the grieving family.
5. Rich landowners had too much power over the lives of their workers.

Source: *I, Rigoberta Menchú: An Indian Woman in Guatemala,* edited by Elisabeth Burgos-Debray; translated by Ann Wright. © 1984, Verso. Reprinted by permission.

Since the 1930s, when Mexico nationalized the oil properties of U.S. and British companies, several other Latin American countries have nationalized industries run by foreigners. In the 1960s, for example, Castro's Cuba nationalized all foreign-owned properties. Then in the 1970s, Venezuela's government took over complete control of that country's chief economic asset: oil.

Recently Mexico, Brazil, and other Latin American countries have been looking to Japan—the world's leading exporter of capital—to invest more money in Latin American industries. In 1990, Japanese companies invested over a billion dollars in Mexican assembly plants, many of which make goods for the U.S. market. Brazil is also attractive to Japanese investors, partly because that country has more than a million people of Japanese descent already living there.

Uneven distribution of oil   Latin America has a problem similar to that of the Middle East. Oil resources in the region are unevenly distributed. In fact, only two nations—Venezuela and Mexico—can draw upon large reserves of oil for export. Many Latin American countries have practically no oil of their own and depend on foreign sources to meet their energy needs.

Having oil resources greatly benefits the economies of Venezuela and Mexico. But it has not been an unmixed blessing. While oil brings in much needed revenue, its price moves up and down on global markets. When the price of oil dropped in the late 1980s, Mexico's government almost went bankrupt. It had gone heavily into debt to foreign bankers and had borrowed billions of dollars to finance economic development. An unexpected decline in oil prices meant that Mexico did not get the revenue it had counted on to pay its debts.

Industrialization and the debt crisis   Mexico has not been alone in its ambitious goals to industrialize. In fact, after World War II ended in 1945, every Latin American nation had plans to build factories and produce industrial goods at home instead of importing all such goods from abroad. In the latter half of the 20th century, new factories in Argentina, Mexico, and Brazil have produced everything from electric toasters to farm machinery. Industrialization was a major reason why Brazil's economy became the world's eighth largest in 1990.

Latin American economies have experienced problems as well as growth. For one thing, raising the capital for starting a sugar refinery or chemical plant usually means seeking a loan from some international banking firm. Interest payments on the borrowed money has to be paid to the bank by a certain date. Through the mid-1980s, the new and expanding industries of Latin America generally sold enough goods to meet the bank's interest charges. Then in the late 1980s, the global economy sank into a recession, and Latin American industrial firms suffered losses. In 1990, 27 countries of Latin America owed a staggering sum of $435 billion to various foreign banks.

CHILE'S MINERAL WEALTH: Copper mining is one of Chile's leading industries, and copper represents Chile's leading export. To what extent does the development of Latin America's mineral wealth depend upon foreign investments?

How can a Latin American country increase investments in its industries without relying on foreign sources of capital? Its government would have to encourage its wealthier citizens to stop investing abroad and put more of their money into domestic industries. For this to happen, the wealthy investors would have to have confidence in the political stability of the government. In the 1990s, the rapid growth rates of Latin American economies have encouraged much higher levels of investments by Europeans, Asians, and North Americans.

Problems of one-crop economies   An older economic problem has plagued Latin America for more than a century. That is the problem of a country having a *one-crop economy* (one that relies heavily on the production and sale of just one crop). For example, coffee accounts for one-third of Guatemala's exports, and sugar represents three-fourths of Cuba's exports. Such reliance on one crop practically guarantees two negative results. (1) The nation's economy is at the mercy of sharp declines in the global price of coffee, sugar, or whatever the chief crop is. (2) The soil used to grow the single crop is likely to lose its fertility over time and, thus, become less capable of yielding a good harvest.

Nevertheless, in many nations of Central America the production of a single cash crop continues to be the mainstay of their agricultural economies. So long as this pattern continues, these nations will suffer from economic dependence on shifting world markets.

Role of tourism   In almost all Latin American countries, tourism is an important and growing industry. The Mayan pyramids in Guatemala, the Inca ruins in Peru, and the beaches of various Caribbean islands attract millions of travelers from Canada, the United States, Japan, and Europe. A positive economic result of tourism is the needed revenue that flows into Latin America. But tourism is not a stable industry. If a country experiences political troubles (revolution, civil war, or acts of terrorism), its once flourishing hotels may empty.

Regional cooperation   In the 1990s, nations of Latin America have taken major strides toward increasing trade in the region and thereby improving each nation's opportunities for growth. Four South American countries—Argentina, Brazil, Paraguay, and Uruguay—signed a treaty in 1991 establishing a *free-trade zone*. In other words, each nation agreed to remove all its *tariffs* (taxes on imports) on products from the other three treaty-signing nations. Also in 1991, another free-trade pact was signed by Mexico, Venezuela, and Colombia.

A treaty that created the Western Hemisphere's largest free-trade zone went into effect in 1994. The North American Free Trade Agreement (NAFTA) provides for the elimination of tariffs and other trade barriers among the three countries of North America—the United States, Mexico, and Canada. (Several Central and South American nations have also indicated interest in joining NAFTA.) Now a business in any one of the three countries that signed NAFTA has a potential market of 380 million customers for its products. Moreover, a business has greater freedom to set up operations in any of the three countries. Many workers in Canada and the United States, however, are worried that they will lose their jobs if businesses move to Mexico to take advantage of a lower-paid work force.

Economic reforms in the 1990s   In the early 1990s, many Latin American countries were involved in a similar set of economic reforms designed to bring about prosperity. These reforms usually involved:

- bringing high rates of inflation under control
- balancing government budgets by raising tax collections and reducing government spending
- lowering tariff rates so that consumer prices of goods would be lower
- selling off government-owned industries to raise money and to attract foreign investors.

Mexico, Venezuela, Argentina, and other countries carried out these and other reforms and were generally successful. Perhaps Argentina provides the best example of an economic turnaround. Its people experienced an inflation rate of 6,000 percent in 1989; by 1993, the rate had come down to 12 percent. How did Argentina do this? The government sold most of the businesses that it had owned, including the large state oil company. It increased taxes considerably and decreased government spending, especially military spending. It lowered tariff barriers. It broke the power of labor unions. As a result of all these policies, Argentina has attracted many more foreign investors in its economy. Its people are much better off economically.

C. LATIN AMERICA IN THE GLOBAL CONTEXT

In the 20th century, the United States has exerted greater influence on Latin America than has any other nation. U.S. influence has been both economic and political. Latin Americans tended to resent U.S. policy early in the century—during the era of imperialism and military intervention discussed previously in this chapter. More recently, however, the United States has made efforts to improve its relations with Latin American nations.

Good Neighbor Policy   Early in the 1930s, U.S. President Franklin D. Roosevelt reversed the policies that had created ill will and distrust in many Latin American nations. Roosevelt pledged that his administration would follow a "Good Neighbor Policy." He said that the United States would not interfere in the political affairs of neighboring countries. During his 12 years in office (1933–1945), President Roosevelt adhered to the Good Neighbor Policy. He thereby helped improve U.S. relations with the countries of Latin America.

Organization of American States   In 1948, just three years after World War II had ended, the United States joined with other nations of the Western Hemisphere in founding a new regional organization. Member nations of the Organization of American States (OAS) agreed to (1) help settle disputes in the region through peaceful methods, (2) promote economic development, and (3) take common action to defend one another against foreign intervention in the region. Ever since its founding, the OAS has provided a means for the various nations of North and South America to resolve their differences.

Most recently, the OAS and the United States have attempted to resolve the crisis in Haiti. In 1991, Haitian military leaders ousted the country's elected president Jean-Bertrand Aristide, a Roman Catholic priest. Aristide was arrested and expelled from Haiti. People around the world protested these actions by the Haitian generals. The United States and the OAS organized an embargo of Haiti. Despite the fact that the Haitian economy was devastated by the embargo, the Haitian military refused to allow Aristide to return to power.

Cuba and the cold war   Originally, Cuba was an active member of the OAS. But after Castro came to power in 1959, Communist Cuba was accused of threatening the peace and stability of the region.

Cuba's willingness to accept arms shipments from the Soviet Union alarmed the United States and other American nations. In 1962, members of the OAS voted to ban Castro's government from participating in the organization's activities.

As a country with a Communist government, Cuba supported leftist and revolutionary movements in Nicaragua, El Salvador, and elsewhere. The United States tried to counteract Cuba's influence by giving military and economic aid to the region's conservative, anti-Communist regimes. In the 1980s, President Ronald Reagan stepped up U.S. efforts to aid anti-Communist rebels (the contras) in Nicaragua. And U.S. aid helped save El Salvador's government from being overthrown by rebel forces.

The special case of Panama   The nation of Panama has always had an unusual and special relationship with the United States. In 1903, it won its independence from Colombia through U.S. efforts. U.S. naval vessels intervened to support a small uprising in Panama against the Colombian government. Panama declared its independence, and the new Panamanian government immediately agreed to allow the United States to build and operate a canal through its lands. For many years, the United States had control over the Panama Canal and its adjacent territory, the Canal Zone. Many Panamanians, however, came to resent U.S. presence there and its control of the canal. Recognizing this fact, President Jimmy Carter in 1977 negotiated a new treaty with Panama. By its terms, the United States promised to transfer ownership of the canal and the Canal Zone to Panama by the year 2000.

U.S. intervention in Panama, however, was not yet over. In 1989, President George Bush ordered U.S. troops to invade Panama and capture its military dictator, Manuel Noriega. The U.S. government suspected Noriega of aiding international drug traffickers. Noriega was caught by the invading U.S. troops and brought back to the United States. Eventually, he stood trial here and was convicted of helping to smuggle illegal drugs into the United States. Meanwhile, the United States helped install a new government in Panama.

Global interdependence   Latin America, like other regions, is part of a world system that is increasingly interdependent. Consider the following four examples of global interdependence.

1. Multinational corporations. Whether it makes automobiles, computers, or aluminum cans, a *multinational corporation* has operations in many nations at once. It is a business organization that is truly global in scope rather than national. Large corporations originally based in Japan, the United States, or Europe have set up hundreds of manufacturing plants in the different countries of Latin America. A chief reason for doing so has been to take advantage of cheaper labor rates and more favorable taxes in the region.

2. *Patterns of migration.* Poverty is widespread in Mexico, Haiti, and some other Latin American countries. Because of this and because economic opportunities are greater in the United States, millions of Latin Americans have sought ways to come here, either temporarily or permanently. U.S. laws place restrictions on the number of people who can settle in this country each year. But economic need can be a stronger force than legal barriers. In the last decade, millions of Latin Americans have illegally entered the United States. At the same time, millions of Latin Americans have come here legally. During this period, about half of all legal immigrants to the United States have come from Latin America.

3. *Environmental problems.* Economic development can threaten the natural environment of any region of the world. But nowhere, perhaps, is the environment more threatened than in Latin America. Environmentalists are especially worried about the destruction of Brazil's rain forest. In recent years, industrial developers and miners in Brazil have opened up huge holes in the ground in order to dig for underground deposits of gold, tin, *bauxite* (an aluminum ore), and other minerals. Other developers have cut down whole forests of trees for lumber. Poverty-stricken families also have gone into the forest and burned down trees to clear the land for farming. As a result of all these activities, some of the Indians who live in the rain forest have been killed or forced to leave. Hundreds of species of tropical birds, animals, and plants have become extinct.

The burning of trees has released huge quantities of carbon dioxide into the atmosphere, possibly threatening the world's climate. Some scientists fear that the burning of rain forests contributes to a condition known as the *greenhouse effect.* They predict that, as more and more carbon dioxide enters the earth's atmosphere, the heat from the sun's rays would become trapped near the earth. (The carbon dioxide gases would act like a pane of glass in a greenhouse, thus the name "greenhouse effect.") The result would be a gradual increase in the earth's average surface temperatures. This possible change in climate, known as *global warming,* would probably melt the Arctic and Antarctic ice caps, raising ocean levels and flooding coastal areas.

4. *Traffic in illegal drugs.* Disrupting and corrupting the politics of several Latin American countries are criminal organizations that have grown rich and powerful from producing and selling illegal drugs. Drug lords in Colombia, Bolivia, and Peru are the chief importers of cocaine into the United States. Mexico is a major source of marijuana. Latin American officials who attempt to crack down on these illegal activities run the risk of being killed by members of a *drug cartel* (international organization of drug traffickers).

The United States has tried various methods for combatting the influx of drugs into the country from Latin America. It has monitored air flights and sea routes that are often used by drug traffickers. The

TRANS-AMAZONIAN HIGHWAY: Begun in the 1970s, this highway connects the formerly isolated western provinces of Brazil with the rest of the country. What might be some of the long-term effects of this road on (*a*) Brazil's economy and (*b*) the global environment?

United States has worked with Latin American armies and police forces in destroying drug crops and illegal drug laboratories in Latin American countries. It has helped train local Latin American police forces and urged them to bring drug criminals to justice. In Bolivia and Peru, the United States has sponsored programs that urge peasants to stop growing coca (which can be processed into cocaine) and instead grow some other crop. These efforts have had some success. Even so, the drug problem remains a large one for the United States and many Latin American nations.

D. SOCIAL AND CULTURAL PATTERNS

The rich cultural heritage of Latin America continues into the present. At the same time, however, forces of modern life place stress upon every society from Haiti to Argentina.

Population explosion   Latin America's population, estimated at 450 million in 1990, was more than double what it had been in 1950. At the current rate of growth, more than 100 million people will have been added to the region's population by the year 2000. Two major factors accounting for this population explosion are (*1*) improvements in public health and (*2*) inherited cultural values that stress large families and high birth rates.

Latin American economies are generally growing at a slower rate than the population. Therefore, as millions more young people come of age, they face the prospect of being unemployed much of the time.

Urban growth and poverty   Rural villages have been unable to support the growing numbers of people. As a result, millions have left rural areas in search of economic opportunities in the cities. But the cities have been unable to provide adequate housing and jobs for all the newcomers. Consequently, people have had to live in sprawling squatter settlements on the outskirts of such large cities as Lima, Peru, and São Paulo, Brazil. The squatter settlements consist of flimsy shelters with no running water or toilet facilities.

Every large metropolitan area in Latin America is trying to cope with the same set of problems. In part because of rapid urban growth, there are shortages of housing and food, congestion and overcrowding, polluted air, rampant crime, poor schools, and poor health care. The challenge for almost every Latin American government is to provide more social services for the millions of urban poor. If poverty is not significantly reduced, it is likely that revolutionary groups will continue to press for radical changes.

Families under strain   In the past, Latin Americans looked to their own families to provide stability and security. The father was an authority figure whom everyone else in the family was supposed to respect. He was both the head of household and the chief wage earner. This traditional pattern of a father-dominated household is still found throughout Latin America. The pattern, though, is beginning to break down in the cities. For decades now, women have been entering the urban work force in increasing numbers. They are no longer dependent for income upon a father or a husband. Also, among the poor residents of squatter settlements, the father may have no job or there may be no father living with the mother and children.

Unequal distribution of wealth   From colonial times to the present, Latin American society has been sharply divided between two major classes: the wealthy landowners and the poor laborers. In the 20th century, members of the middle class have become more numerous and influential in certain countries, especially in Mexico, Argentina, Costa Rica, and Chile. But in most Latin American countries, the income gap between rich and poor is more extreme than ever. According to UN estimates, about 180 million Latin Americans—40 percent of the region's population—live in poverty.

Is there a solution to the poverty problem? Since the 19th century, reformers have called for breaking up the estates of large landowners and distributing small plots to the masses of peasants. They have argued that this land reform would give millions of poor Latin American farmers a chance to rise out of poverty. Rightist dictators have

PER CAPITA GDP IN SELECTED NATIONS

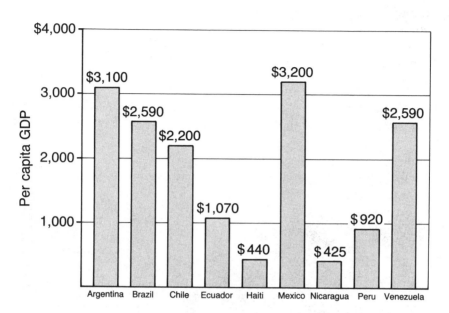

almost always resisted such demands for land reform. In a few countries—notably Mexico, Bolivia, and Chile—modest programs of land reform were carried out. For the most part, however, huge landed estates remain intact throughout Latin America. Only a small fraction of the land is controlled by those who work on it; the rest belongs to the wealthy landowning elite.

The role of education   Schools play a critical role in Latin Americans' hopes for economic progress. In the modern world, a person's *social mobility* (the degree to which one can move up from a lower class to a higher one) depends largely on how well that person is educated. The *illiterate* (those who cannot read or write) have little or no chance of rising out of poverty into the middle class. Therefore, if a government wishes to close the gap between rich and poor, it must strive to see that everyone in society is at least literate.

In recent decades, most Latin American countries have made significant progress in education. The *literacy rate* (percentage of people who can read and write) is now more than 90 percent in Cuba, Chile, and Argentina. Illiteracy is still a major problem, however, in Guatemala and Haiti, where the literacy rate is less than 60 percent. Partly because of the difficulty of transporting children to schools, the literacy rate in rural areas is usually much lower than in cities.

Cultural achievements in literature   Economic problems have not prevented Latin Americans from attaining distinction in literature. For centuries, Latin American poets, novelists, and historians have contributed to a remarkable body of literature. Foremost among the writers of the colonial era was a brilliant Roman Catholic nun from Mexico—Sor Juana Inés de la Cruz. In the 1700s, Sor Juana produced a dazzling array of literature, including plays and philosophical works.

From independence to the present day, Latin American writers have experimented with a number of literary styles and techniques. In the 1800s, Argentine poets were known for their gaucho themes. They depicted *gauchos* (South American cowboys) as romantic outlaws. In

PORTRAIT OF THE ARTIST: The Mexican artist Frida Kahlo is best known for her hundreds of sometimes realistic, sometimes fanciful self-portraits. What other Mexican artists achieved fame in the 20th century?

the late 20th century, such writers as Carlos Fuentes of Mexico and Gabriel García Marquez of Colombia have experimented with narrative techniques that blend fantasy with realism. For his novel *One Hundred Years of Solitude*, García Marquez won the 1982 Nobel Prize for Literature.

Cultural achievements in art and music   Mexican achievements in art go back to the astonishing pyramids and boldly designed stone sculptures of the Mayans and the Aztecs. Artists of the 20th century rediscovered the vivid colors and unique motifs of Aztec art and creatively incorporated them into modern paintings. In the 1930s, three Mexican artists—Diego Rivera, José Orozco, and David Siqueiros— achieved international fame with their dramatic murals depicting the history of their country. Rivera painted some of his murals in buildings in the United States. His wife, Frida Kahlo, also attained world recognition for her startling, dreamlike self-portraits.

Latin American contributions to music and dance are equally impressive. The popular dance rhythms of the rumba, tango, mambo, samba, cha-cha, and bossa nova have gained wide acceptance in the United States. From the Caribbean, both calypso and reggae have entered the mainstream of American music. Salsa, a blend of Afro-Cuban jazz and traditional Puerto Rican music, became popular in the United States in the 1980s.

In Review

The following questions refer to Section IV: Contemporary Nations.

1. *Key terms:* Define or identify each of the following:

Cuban Missile Crisis	Good Neighbor Policy	greenhouse
one-crop economy	multinational	effect
	corporation	literacy rate

2. Explain how land reform was one of the major issues of the Mexican Revolution.

3. Identify *three* economic problems faced by many Latin American nations in the 20th century.

4. Describe the impact of drug cartels on the politics of *two* Latin American nations.

5. *Critical thinking:* Evaluate U.S. actions in Latin America in the 20th century. Identify two actions that you support and two actions that you oppose. Give your reasons.

NEIGHBORS TO THE NORTH: CANADA AND THE UNITED STATES

To the north of Latin America lie two of the world's largest and most prosperous countries, Canada and the United States. Canada is the second largest country in the world; the United States is the world's strongest military power and one of the wealthiest nations. Because of their economic strength, democratic governments, and location in the Western Hemisphere, these countries have long been important to their Latin American neighbors.

Geography   Through the interior of both Canada and the United States, from the Arctic Ocean in the north to the Gulf of Mexico in the south, stretches a vast plain. Smaller plains are found along the eastern and western coasts. Most agricultural activities take place on these plains, although (due to the cold climate) farming in Canada is limited to the southern part of the country.

Mountains cover significant parts of Canada and the United States. The Rocky Mountains stretch from Alaska to the southwestern part of the United States. Smaller ranges follow the west coasts of both countries. In the east, the Appalachians consist of a range that extends from southeastern Canada to Georgia.

Both countries are fortunate to have many lakes and rivers. Much of the Mississippi River and its tributaries are navigable. So too are the five Great Lakes, four of which lie along the border between Canada and the United States. Oceangoing ships can reach the Great Lakes via the St. Lawrence River and Seaway. Because of their irregular seacoasts, both Canada and the United States have many good ports. This fact has helped both nations develop extensive trade networks.

Climate and population   Both Canada and the United States have a variety of climates. Canada, however, is generally colder than the United States because of its location farther from the equator. In fact, part of Canada (and Alaska) are within the Arctic Circle, an area so cold that trees do not grow there. The interior section of both countries have a *continental climate*—one with cold winters and hot summers. Areas along the Pacific and Atlantic oceans generally have milder winters and cooler summers than lands in the interior. Areas of western United States that are located between mountain ranges are desert-like. Southern Florida

THE CANUCKS (CANADA) AGAINST THE RANGERS (U.S.):
Competition between Canadian and U.S. hockey teams expresses
the friendly rivalry that has long existed between these neighboring
industrial powers. In what ways do the two nations share a
common culture?

has a subtropical climate; temperatures there rarely go
below freezing. The milder climates in the United States
account, in part, for its larger population—260 million—
compared to Canada's 28 million.

History   Canada and the United States have had similar
histories. Each can be divided into three eras: (1) prehistoric
settlement; (2) colonial rule; and (3) national experience
since independence.

Both Canada and the United States were settled by migrating bands of people from Asia who came to North America at different times between 30,000 and 5,000 years ago.
These Native Americans spread out across the continent,
forming many distinct societies. Although the original migrants were hunters and gatherers, some of the groups in
later times developed agricultural economies.

In the 1600s and 1700s, European powers set up colonies
in what is now Canada and the United States. The British

established 13 colonies along the Atlantic Coast (from New Hampshire to Georgia). To the north and west of these colonies, the French claimed vast lands that they called New France. To the north of New France, the British set up trading posts along Hudson Bay and claimed the surrounding area. Meanwhile, the Spanish colony of Mexico extended north into what is today the southwestern part of the United States. Florida, too, was settled by the Spaniards. As a result of a war between France and Britain, France lost its territories in North America in 1763.

Americans in the 13 British colonies declared their independence in 1776. The British fought the revolutionaries for several years, but in 1783 they signed a peace treaty that recognized the United States as a new nation. Canadian independence took place much later, and in stages. For example, in 1867 four provinces (Quebec, Ontario, New Brunswick, and Nova Scotia) formed the Dominion of Canada. The new Canadian government handled domestic affairs, but the British government still handled foreign policy. Moreover, the British monarch still served as head of state. Gradually, the Dominion added other provinces and territories. In 1931, Canada finally gained full independence (although the British monarch is still the nominal head of state).

Both before and after independence, the United States and Canada experienced waves of overseas immigration, westward expansion, and economic development. Adding to the British, French, and Native American populations of the United States came voluntary immigrants from other European countries as well as involuntary immigrants from Africa. In both Canada and the United States, non-native groups kept moving west in search of better farm lands. As they settled the land, they displaced the Native Americans. The majority of Native Americans died from European diseases, from hunger, or in battle with the settlers and their armies. In some cases, Native Americans who survived were forced to move onto reservations.

Economic patterns   At first, most settlers in Canada and the United States were engaged in farming. Not until the early 19th century did large industries develop in Massachusetts and other New England states. Often farmers and their families were hired to work in these factories. Gradually, industrialization spread to other parts of the United

States and to Canada. Both countries were blessed with rich deposits of natural resources, many rivers (which provided water power and a means of transportation), people with money to invest, and educated people to make inventions. All these factors were important in the process of industrialization. By the early 20th century, the United States had become the leading industrial nation of the world. Canada, too, became highly industrialized. Today, the populations of both countries enjoy a high standard of living.

Canada, the United States, and Mexico have long carried on a large volume of trade with one another. To increase this trade, in 1988 Canada and the United States concluded a Free Trade Agreement that would eventually eliminate duties and tariffs between the two countries. Then in 1992, leaders of Mexico, Canada, and the United States signed a similar treaty—the North American Free Trade Agreement (NAFTA). When it went into effect in 1994, it created the Western Hemisphere's largest free trade zone.

Political traditions   The governments of both Canada and the United States are democracies. But their structures are different. The Canadian government, based on the British model, has an elected, two-house legislature called the *Parliament*. The head of the executive branch, the prime minister, is elected by the majority party in Parliament. The third branch of government is an independent *judiciary* (court system). Canada still recognizes the British monarch as its *head of state* (ceremonial leader). The monarch appoints a governor general as his or her representative in Canada. Members of the upper house of Parliament, the Senate, are appointed by the governor general upon the recommendation of the prime minister. Members of the lower house, the House of Commons, are elected by the people.

The U.S. government, by contrast, lacks a parliamentary system. But like Canada, the United States has an independent judiciary and a two-house legislature. Members of both houses are elected by the people. While those in the Senate represent whole states, those in the House represent smaller electoral districts. The U.S. executive—the president—is elected in an indirect manner by the people, not by the legislature. Of course, a monarch plays no role in the U.S. political system.

TEST YOURSELF

Multiple-Choice Questions

Level 1

On a separate sheet of paper, write the number of the word or expression that, of those given, best completes each statement or answers each question.

1. The term "Latin America" most accurately refers to the (1) areas of the Western Hemisphere south of the United States (2) countries that belong to the Organization of American States (OAS) (3) continents of North and South America (4) countries that today have close economic ties with Spain.

2. A contemporary problem affecting Latin America in a major way has been (1) religious conflict (2) deforestation (3) chemical warfare (4) Islamic fundamentalism.

3. A major concern regarding the destruction of the rain forests in Brazil is that (1) cities will become seriously overcrowded (2) the temperature of the Earth's surface may increase (3) the per capita income in economically developing nations may increase (4) water supplies in these areas will increase.

4. Which generalization about the geography of Latin America is accurate? (1) Geographic features prevented foreign imperialism. (2) Harsh climatic conditions have prevented the development of large-scale agriculture. (3) The lack of geographic barriers facilitated the development of transportation and communication systems. (4) Great variations in latitude and landforms resulted in a diversity of climates.

5. Which is a valid generalization about Latin America? (1) Most Latin Americans live in isolated farm villages. (2) The majority of the governments in Latin America are Communist. (3) Most Latin Americans are descendants of immigrants from Africa. (4) Latin America is a region of racial and cultural diversity.

6. The civilizations of the Aztecs, Incas, and Mayans were similar in that all (1) spoke the same language (2) followed a monotheistic religion (3) developed cities and complex governments (4) used a complex system of writing.

7. During the colonial period, Latin American society (1) placed great value on public education (2) experienced a surplus of skilled labor (3) was organized according to a rigid class structure (4) deemphasized the role of religion.

8. Which was a characteristic of the policy of mercantilism followed by Spanish colonial rulers in Latin America? (1) The colonies were forced to develop local industries to support themselves. (2) Spain sought trade agreements between its colonies and the English colonies in North America. (3) The colonies were required to provide

raw materials to Spain and to purchase Spanish manufactured goods. (4) Spain encouraged the colonies to develop new political systems to meet colonial needs.

9. Which statement best describes a result of the scarcity of native Indian labor in Latin America during the colonial period? (1) Unskilled laborers were imported from Asia. (2) Many people from Spain and Portugal immigrated to the region. (3) Native Americans from the British colonies went south to work. (4) Large numbers of enslaved Africans were imported.

10. In Latin America, the emphasis on the role of the military and the strength of the Roman Catholic religion have their origins in (1) ancient Indian village organizations (2) cultural exchanges with the United States (3) English practices in the New World (4) Spanish colonial rule.

11. Which was a major political change in Latin America in the 19th century? (1) The political power of the Roman Catholic Church was eliminated. (2) The right to vote was extended to all people. (3) Political power was no longer held by people of European ancestry. (4) Strong nationalistic feelings led to many new nations.

12. Which statement best describes the Roman Catholic Church in most Latin American countries in the 1800s? (1) The activities of the Church were controlled by the national governments. (2) The Church confined its activities to religious matters. (3) The Church taught obedience to established authority. (4) Most people saw the Church as having little influence in daily life.

13. Which generalization is best supported by a study of the history of Latin America? (1) Protection of human rights has been a major policy of most governments. (2) Foreign powers have had little influence in the area. (3) Political power has been concentrated in the hands of the landed elite. (4) Church and state have been strictly separated.

14. During the 20th century, a major cause of political problems in Latin America has been (1) a decrease in population (2) the declining importance of international trade (3) widespread poverty (4) increasing social mobility.

15. Which is a valid statement about land distribution in many Latin American nations? (1) The Spaniards distributed land equally among the people. (2) The largest amount of land is owned by a small number of families. (3) The largest amount of land is owned by a great number of families. (4) The government owns most of the land in the name of the people.

16. Which factor best accounts for the existence of cash-crop production as the major form of agriculture in many Latin American nations today? (1) demand of world markets for such crops (2) lack of modern agricultural technology (3) inadequate supply of water and other natural resources (4) peasant ownership of most farmlands.

Base your answers to questions 17 and 18 on the graph below and on your knowledge of social studies.

**COMPARISON OF POPULATION GROWTH IN
LATIN AMERICA AND NORTH AMERICA**

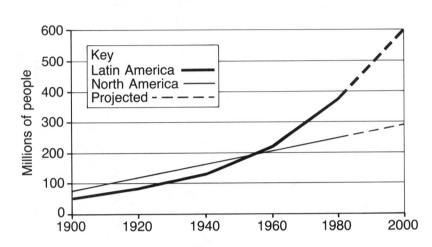

17. Based on the information in the graph, which is a valid conclusion about the populations of Latin America and North America? (1) There has always been a large difference in the population growth of Latin America and North America. (2) By the year 2000, the population of Latin America is expected to be approximately twice that of North America. (3) In 1900, the number of people in Latin America was equal to the number of people in North America. (4) In the early 1980s, the difference in population between the two regions was about 300 million.

18. Which best accounts for the situation shown in the graph? (1) decline in the standard of living in North America (2) growing trade surplus of most Latin American nations (3) improved nutrition and medical care in Latin American nations (4) increased death rate in North America due to contagious diseases.

19. The economies of most Latin American countries are characterized by (1) dependence on exporting raw materials (2) establishment of successful land redistribution programs (3) production of heavy industrial machinery (4) development of trade surpluses.

20. At the present time, which is a major economic problem for many Latin American governments? (1) increased settlement in rural areas (2) low rates of inflation (3) inability to pay foreign debts (4) lack of a chief executive.

Base your answer to question 21 on the cartoon below and on your knowledge of social studies.

21. The main idea of the cartoon is that in the early part of the 20th century   (1) South Americans asked the United States to protect them   (2) international cooperation maintained peace in South America   (3) the Monroe Doctrine was no longer enforceable (4) the United States forcefully extended its influence into South America.

22. The main purpose of the Organization of American States (OAS) is to (1) integrate the economies of Latin American nations   (2) encourage U.S. military involvement in the region   (3) destroy the power of Colombian drug cartels   (4) provide a way to resolve regional problems peacefully.

23. Since World War II, people in Latin America have moved from rural to urban areas. The major cause of this movement has been the (1) rejection of traditional customs   (2) expectation of improved economic opportunities   (3) guarantee of better housing   (4) fear of civil war.

24. Which statement concerning education in Latin America is valid?
(1) Education has often served as a vehicle for social mobility.
(2) Increased educational opportunities in rural areas have encouraged people to move from cities.   (3) Education has prevented the rise of independence movements.   (4) Latin America is the only region in which school attendance is compulsory for all children.

25. Which statement about Latin America is an opinion rather than a fact?   (1) Enslaved Africans were imported because there was a scarcity of workers.   (2) Roman Catholicism is the dominant religion of the region.   (3) Diversity exists in the physical environments of Latin America.   (4) The people of the region are less resistant to change than are people in developing countries of other regions.

Level 2

26. In Latin America, mountains have contributed to   (1) the development of good transportation systems   (2) the many climates found in the region   (3) social and political equality   (4) excellent agricultural production.

27. Most of the power in the Spanish colonies in Latin America was held by   (1) workers and peasants   (2) people who could trace their origins to Spain   (3) Indian tribal leaders   (4) people of mixed Indian and Spanish origins.

Base your answer to question 28 on the graph below and on your knowledge of social studies.

MEXICO

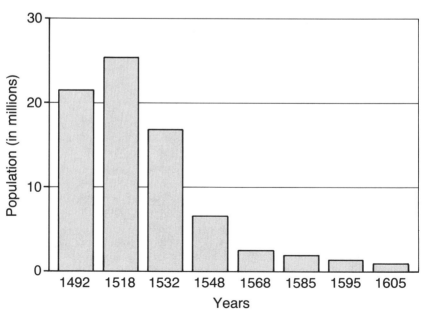

28. Which statement best explains a major reason for the trend shown on the graph? (1) The population adopted the European custom of smaller families. (2) The population was exposed to diseases from Europe. (3) Many wars decreased the population. (4) Many people moved to other areas.

29. Nationalism is most likely to develop in an area that has (1) fertile soil for agriculture (2) factories to supply consumer goods (3) a mild climate with rivers for irrigation (4) common customs, language, and history.

30. To develop nationalism, a group of people must (1) share natural resources (2) believe in the value of democracy (3) have some beliefs and values in common (4) develop a strong military force.

31. In Latin America, both Simón Bolívar and José de San Martín were leaders who (1) worked for independence (2) led Communist-inspired revolutions (3) attempted imperialistic expansion (4) wanted a return to traditional ways.

32. The Latin American leaders Simón Bolívar, Miguel Hidalgo, and José de San Martín are most closely associated with (1) independence movements (2) Communist revolutions (3) economic development (4) educational reforms.

33. "Toussaint-Louverture Defeats French Troops in Haiti"
"Bolívar Leads Revolutions in South America"
"San Martín Liberates Argentina"

These newspaper headlines refer to the growth of (1) colonialism (2) nationalism (3) Marxism (4) mercantilism.

34. Which is a reason why revolutionaries in Cuba and Nicaragua were attracted to communism? (1) Communist groups promised land reform. (2) Communist groups supported business owners. (3) Communist groups promised to support religion. (4) Communist leaders promised to end Spanish colonialism in Latin America.

35. Which situation resulted from the 1959 Cuban Revolution? (1) Cuba became a Communist nation. (2) Cuba was denied admission to the United Nations. (3) All social classes supported the new government. (4) The power of the Roman Catholic Church increased.

36. Which statement best explains the rapid population growth in Latin America? (1) Death rates for infants have decreased. (2) Family planning has been successful. (3) Many people are moving to the cities. (4) Birth control methods have been successful.

37. Which best describes the traditional family in Latin America? (1) The family unit is usually very small. (2) Teenage girls have a great deal of social freedom. (3) The family worships its ancestors. (4) The father is the head of the family.

38. The slash-and-burn method of farming has often been used in tropical regions because it (1) quickly clears a forest area (2) leads to better irrigation (3) is the main way to increase the production of crops for export to other countries (4) provides jobs for many people.

39. Which groups have most opposed social and economic changes in Latin America? (1) landowners and the military (2) students and teachers (3) middle class and union leaders (4) poor farmers and workers.

40. In Latin America, people have moved from rural villages to urban areas to (1) avoid the high cost of living in rural areas (2) escape the poor climates in rural areas (3) find job opportunities in the cities (4) live among people of different ethnic backgrounds in the cities.

Essay Questions

Level 1

1. Listed below are pairs of individuals who are associated with specific historical movements.

Pairs
Isabella I—Christopher Columbus
Hernando Cortés—Francisco Pizarro
Father Hidalgo—Toussaint-Louverture
Simón Bolívar—José de San Martín
Daniel Ortega—Fidel Castro

Select *three* of the pairs listed. For each pair selected:

- Identify the specific historic movement in which each individual was involved.
- Describe the role that each individual played in the historic movement.
- Describe the impact of the historic movement on Latin America's history

2. Various factors have had an impact on Latin America.

Factors
Population growth
Urbanization
One-crop economies
Trade relations
Foreign investments

Select *three* of the factors listed. For each one selected:

- Explain how it affected Latin America.
- Describe and evaluate an attempt made within Latin America to deal with the factor.

Level 2

3. Geographic features have influenced the development of Latin America.

Geographic Features
Andes Mountains
Amazon Basin
Pampas of Argentina
Brazilian Highlands
Atacama Desert in Chile

Select *two* of the geographic features listed. For each one chosen:

A. State one specific effect of the feature on Latin America.

B. Base your answer to Part B on your answer to Part A. However, additional information may be included. Write an essay discussing the effects of the specific geographic features on the development of Latin America. Begin your essay with this topic sentence:

> Geographic features have influenced the development of Latin America.

4. Many cultural features of Latin America were greatly influenced by Spain.

Cultural Features
Language
Religion
Social classes

A. For each of the cultural features listed above, state an important influence of Spain on the development of Latin America.

B. Base your answer to Part B on your answer to Part A. However, additional information may be included. Write an essay discussing how Spain influenced the culture of the Latin American people. Begin your essay with this topic sentence:

> Spain influenced many cultural features of Latin America.

CHAPTER 5

South and Southeast

Main Ideas

1. **IMPORTANCE OF WATER:** Irrigation is used to help increase agricultural production in those countries of South and Southeast Asia where seasonal rainfall is uneven and unpredictable.

2. **THE CASTE SYSTEM:** In South Asia, Hindu religious beliefs are closely related to a social system based on a rigid class structure.

3. **SPREAD OF BUDDHISM:** The spread of Buddhism from India into Southeast Asia is an example of cultural diffusion.

4. **CONFLICT BETWEEN HINDUISM AND ISLAM:** In India in the 1500s and 1600s, violent conflicts erupted between the followers of Islam and the followers of Hinduism.

5. **BRITISH RULE IN INDIA:** Motivated by imperialistic ideas and ambitions, Britain gradually gained control of the Indian subcontinent during the 1700s and 1800s.

6. **EXPLOITATION:** The British in India and the French, Dutch, and British in Southeast Asia exploited people's labor as well as the natural resources of the territories they controlled.

7. **IMPACT OF IMPERIALISM:** Imperialistic policies changed the economies of South and Southeast Asia and also gave rise to nationalist movements.

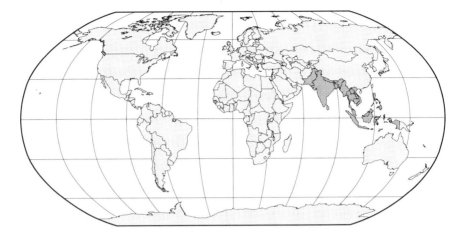

Asia

8. **INDEPENDENCE AFTER WORLD WAR II:** In the early 20th century, nationalist movements gained strength throughout South and Southeast Asia. European powers, weakened by World War II, yielded to demands for independence for many nations in the region.

9. **THE PARTITION OF BRITISH INDIA:** When India gained its independence in 1947, religious conflict caused it to divide into two nations: a Muslim one (Pakistan) and a nation with a large Hindu majority (India).

10. **POPULATION GROWTH:** In the 20th century, improvements in life expectancy, health care, and agricultural production have contributed to rapid population growth in South and Southeast Asia.

11. **POWER STRUGGLES IN VIETNAM AND CAMBODIA:** Internal struggles for power in Southeast Asia led to civil war and genocide.

12. **ECONOMIC PLANNING IN INDIA:** India's government has used economic planning to increase the nation's self-reliance and decrease its dependence on the major powers.

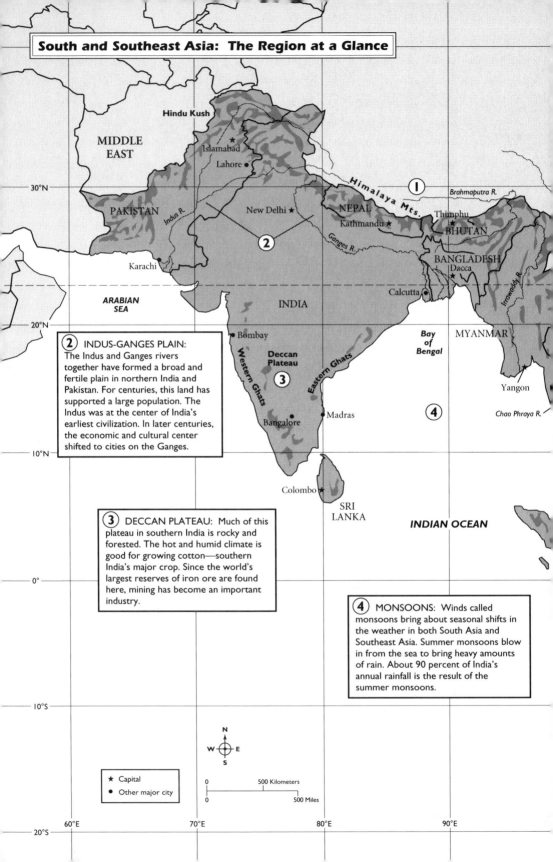

South and Southeast Asia: The Region at a Glance

Hindu Kush

MIDDLE EAST

★ Islamabad
Lahore •

PAKISTAN

Indus R.

New Delhi ★

Himalaya Mts.

NEPAL
Kathmandu ★

Thimphu ★
BHUTAN

Brahmaputra R.

Ganges R.

BANGLADESH
Dacca

Karachi •

Calcutta •

Irrawaddy R.

ARABIAN SEA

INDIA

30°N

1

20°N

• Bombay

Bay of Bengal

MYANMAR

(2) INDUS-GANGES PLAIN:
The Indus and Ganges rivers together have formed a broad and fertile plain in northern India and Pakistan. For centuries, this land has supported a large population. The Indus was at the center of India's earliest civilization. In later centuries, the economic and cultural center shifted to cities on the Ganges.

Western Ghats

Deccan Plateau

3

Eastern Ghats

Yangon

Chao Phraya R.

Bangalore •

• Madras

4

10°N

Colombo ★

SRI LANKA

INDIAN OCEAN

(3) DECCAN PLATEAU: Much of this plateau in southern India is rocky and forested. The hot and humid climate is good for growing cotton—southern India's major crop. Since the world's largest reserves of iron ore are found here, mining has become an important industry.

0°

(4) MONSOONS: Winds called monsoons bring about seasonal shifts in the weather in both South Asia and Southeast Asia. Summer monsoons blow in from the sea to bring heavy amounts of rain. About 90 percent of India's annual rainfall is the result of the summer monsoons.

10°S

N
W ✦ E
S

★ Capital
• Other major city

0   500 Kilometers
0   500 Miles

60°E   70°E   80°E   90°E

20°S

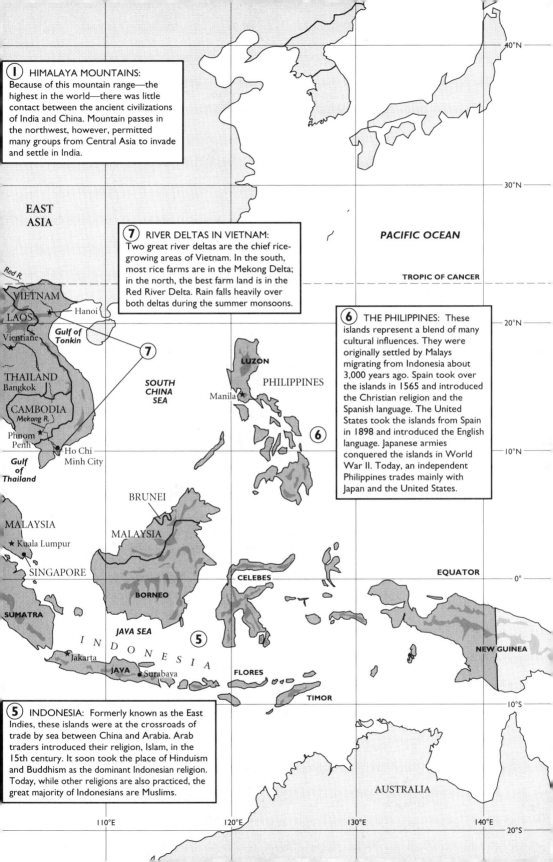

(1) HIMALAYA MOUNTAINS: Because of this mountain range—the highest in the world—there was little contact between the ancient civilizations of India and China. Mountain passes in the northwest, however, permitted many groups from Central Asia to invade and settle in India.

EAST ASIA

(7) RIVER DELTAS IN VIETNAM: Two great river deltas are the chief rice-growing areas of Vietnam. In the south, most rice farms are in the Mekong Delta; in the north, the best farm land is in the Red River Delta. Rain falls heavily over both deltas during the summer monsoons.

PACIFIC OCEAN

TROPIC OF CANCER

(6) THE PHILIPPINES: These islands represent a blend of many cultural influences. They were originally settled by Malays migrating from Indonesia about 3,000 years ago. Spain took over the islands in 1565 and introduced the Christian religion and the Spanish language. The United States took the islands from Spain in 1898 and introduced the English language. Japanese armies conquered the islands in World War II. Today, an independent Philippines trades mainly with Japan and the United States.

Red R.

VIETNAM
LAOS — Hanoi
Vientiane Gulf of Tonkin

THAILAND
Bangkok

SOUTH CHINA SEA

LUZON

PHILIPPINES

Manila

CAMBODIA
Mekong R.

Phnom Penh Ho Chi Minh City

Gulf of Thailand

MALAYSIA
★ Kuala Lumpur

SINGAPORE

BRUNEI

MALAYSIA

SUMATRA

CELEBES

EQUATOR

BORNEO

JAVA SEA

NEW GUINEA

I N D O N E S I A

Jakarta

JAVA Surabaya

FLORES

TIMOR

(5) INDONESIA: Formerly known as the East Indies, these islands were at the crossroads of trade by sea between China and Arabia. Arab traders introduced their religion, Islam, in the 15th century. It soon took the place of Hinduism and Buddhism as the dominant Indonesian religion. Today, while other religions are also practiced, the great majority of Indonesians are Muslims.

AUSTRALIA

40°N
30°N
20°N
10°N
0° EQUATOR
10°S
20°S

110°E 120°E 130°E 140°E

This chapter describes two distinct regions, South Asia and Southeast Asia. As you read, take note of the two regions' similarities and differences.

I. Geography

The major nations of *South Asia* today are India, Pakistan, Bangladesh, and Sri Lanka. It was only after World War II that these countries won their independence from British colonial rule. Before that time, the first three of these nations were referred to as "India." Thus, when we speak of Indian history before 1947, we are referring to the land that now makes up those three countries, but not Sri Lanka—an island nation off India's coast.

Southeast Asia consists of several nations located on a long peninsula as well as some island nations in the Pacific and Indian oceans. The mainland countries are Thailand, Myanmar (formerly Burma), Laos, Cambodia, Vietnam, and Malaysia. The major island nations are the Philippines, Indonesia, and Singapore.

In total area, the two regions—South Asia and Southeast Asia—are roughly the same size. Each is approximately one-third the size of the United States. Partially separating the two regions is the Bay of Bengal in the Indian Ocean. The border between Myanmar (on one side) and India and Bangladesh (on the other side) serves also as the border between Southeast Asia and South Asia.

A. THE SOUTH ASIAN SUBCONTINENT

Geographers call mainland South Asia a *subcontinent* (major subdivision of a continent) because of (1) the region's large size (larger than Western Europe) and (2) the high mountain barrier that separates South Asia from the lands to the north.

About 900 million people live in the nation of India, making it the second most populous country in the world (after China). Combined with the populations of Pakistan (about 125 million) and Bangladesh (120 million), the South Asian subcontinent has more than one billion people.

Location   As with other regions of the world, the location of South Asia has helped to shape its history and culture. The map on pages 196–197 shows that it consists mostly of a peninsula that juts into the Indian Ocean. For more than 3,000 years, South Asia has both influenced and been influenced by neighboring areas: the Middle East, Central Asia, Southeast Asia, and East Asia.

Mountains   The Himalayas stretch across the northern part of the subcontinent. The Eastern Himalayas contain the world's highest elevations, including Mt. Everest (at 29,028 feet above sea level). Because

FOODS OF SOUTH ASIA: This open marketplace in an Indian city shows some of the foods that have been cultivated in South Asia since ancient times. Which river valleys are most important to this region's agriculture?

of their height, these mountains have served as an almost impassable barrier for migrating peoples and invading armies. Thus, contact between India and China was limited until recent times. In contrast, the Western Himalayas are not as tall. They have several mountain passes—especially the Khyber Pass—over which invaders have traveled many times. As a result, many waves of migrants and invaders from Central Asia managed to cross the mountains to settle in South Asia. Among these people were followers of the Middle Eastern religion of Islam. Today, South Asia has millions of Muslims, most of whom live in Pakistan and Bangladesh.

Three other, smaller mountain ranges surround the vast Deccan Plateau in central and southern India. All three ranges present obstacles to travel. These mountains, as well as the other rough terrain of southern India help explain why India was politically divided throughout much of its history. For many hundreds of years, southern India had many small kingdoms. Its peoples spoke different languages and practiced a variety of religions. Only toward the middle of the 19th century did an outside power (Great Britain) manage to bring all of India under the control of a single government.

Rivers The region has two large and important rivers, the Indus and the Ganges. The Indus River flows southward through Pakistan into the Arabian Sea. The Ganges River flows eastward through northern India into the Bay of Bengal. Its huge delta lies in Bangladesh. Both of these two rivers are located in the northern half of South Asia.

The Indus and Ganges rivers have played a crucial role in the region. The broad, fertile valleys watered by these rivers have been excellent for farming. The rivers themselves have served as natural highways for transporting goods. By making use of these geographic benefits, people of ancient times not only cultivated crops in the Indus and Ganges valleys but also built impressive civilizations. Today, the Ganges River Valley still produces most of the rice grown in India and Bangladesh and remains one of the most densely populated areas in the world. Followers of Hinduism, the majority religion in India, consider the Ganges River to be sacred. This belief derives in part from the important role played by the river in sustaining life.

Climate Another factor that has shaped the economy and culture of South Asia is climate. The region is known for its *monsoons* (prevailing winds that change directions according to the season). In summer in India, the monsoons blow from the Indian Ocean, bringing along heavy rains. Having followed a hot, dry spring, the rainfall is vitally needed for watering farmers' crops. In the winter, the monsoons blow in the opposite direction—from the north. These winds are cold and dry. The effects of the monsoons are unpredictable. Sometimes a monsoon brings too much rain in the summer, causing floods. In other years, the summer monsoons may arrive later than normal, resulting in droughts that can be disastrous to farmers.

Rainfall is not even throughout India. Where rainfall is plentiful, rice is the major crop. Wheat requires less moisture than rice and thus can be grown in areas with less rainfall. Millet can be cultivated in the driest areas of India, such as the Deccan Plateau. The summer monsoons cannot reach the Deccan Plateau because it is surrounded by mountains.

B. SOUTHEAST ASIA

About half of Southeast Asia is a long peninsula attached to the Asian mainland. The other half consists of island nations—such as Indonesia, the Philippines, and Singapore—in the Indian and Pacific oceans. The region can be reached easily by land and sea from both China (to the north) and India (to the west). For this reason, the cultures of Southeast Asia have been subject to strong influences from China and India. From India, for example, the peoples of the Southeast Asian peninsula acquired two religions, Hinduism and Buddhism. From China, a large number of immigrants came, settling on the Malay

Peninsula (part of present-day Malaysia). There they established themselves mainly as merchants. The Chinese in Singapore and Malaysia still play a leading role in those countries' business firms.

Physical features   Several major rivers in Southeast Asia are important for transportation and agriculture. Flowing through the region from north to south are the Irrawaddy River in Myanmar, the Chao Phraya River in Thailand, and the Mekong River in Laos, Cambodia, and Vietnam. The Mekong, 2,600 miles long, provides fertile soil and water for the growth of rice and also acts as a water highway for transporting goods. The Mekong and other rivers on the Southeast Asian peninsula help make transportation possible through mountainous lands where overland travel is otherwise difficult.

Southeast Asia is rich in forests and mineral resources (especially tin and oil). Recognizing the wealth of the region's resources, Europeans competed for control of Southeast Asia during the imperialist era of the 19th and early 20th centuries (discussed later in this chapter).

Climate   Most of Southeast Asia is located in the tropical zone near the equator. The equator itself passes through most of the major islands of Indonesia. The climate of much of the region is hot and wet.

MONSOONS IN SOUTH AND SOUTHEAST ASIA

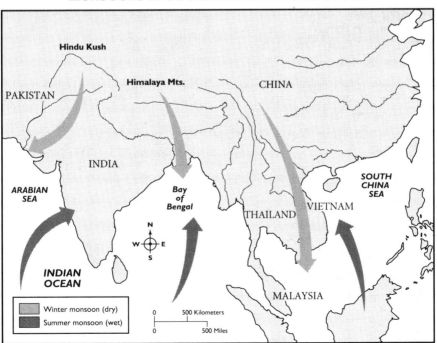

It is hot because of the region's nearness to the equator, where the sun's rays beat straight down most of the year. The climate is wet because of moisture brought by winds from surrounding bodies of water (the Indian Ocean, Pacific Ocean, and South China Sea). The region's tropical climate is suitable for growing:

- rice, the major crop of Southeast Asia
- sugarcane and coffee
- lumber and rubber, both harvested from the region's rain forests.

As in South Asia, the arrival of the wet monsoons in the summer months is crucial to the growing of crops on the mainland of Southeast Asia. Monsoons from the Bay of Bengal bring heavy rainfall to the mainland's west coast. About 100 inches of rain annually drench the Malay Peninsula and nourish growth of a dense rain forest. Some areas of the mainland are drier, mainly because mountain ranges lie between them and the coast. The wet monsoons cannot bring much rainfall over the mountains and into the interior sections.

In Review

The following questions refer to Section I: Geography.

1. *Key terms:* Define each of the following:
   subcontinent   monsoon
2. Explain the impact of monsoons on farming in both South and Southeast Asia.
3. Identify the major rivers of South and Southeast Asia and explain their importance to the regions' economies. (Refer to the map on pages 196–197 as well as to the text.)
4. *Critical thinking:* Geography can sometimes bring people together and at other times keep them separated. Explain which of these two effects has been most true of the geography of South Asia.

II. Early History

In Chapters 2 and 3, we examined the origins of the world's first civilizations in Egypt and Mesopotamia. The first civilizations in South Asia developed hundreds of years later, in the Indus River Valley. The ancient civilizations of Southeast Asia developed somewhat later than those of South Asia.

A. ANCIENT CIVILIZATIONS OF SOUTH ASIA

Between 5,000 and 4,000 years ago, farming villages along the banks of the Indus River expanded into South Asia's first cities, which were the centers of a new civilization.

Indus Valley civilization   South Asia's earliest civilization had characteristics similar to those of ancient Egypt and Mesopotamia. Its economy was based upon abundant harvests of wheat and other grains that were relatively easy to grow in the wide and fertile Indus River Valley. Food surpluses supported an urban population that lived within the walls of two major cities, Mohenjo-Daro and Harappa. Artisans in the cities knew how to work various metals—gold, silver, copper, and lead—to make tools and jewelry. To keep records, the people invented a system of writing.

The cities of the Indus Valley were carefully planned. Their streets were paved and laid out in a *grid pattern* (straight lines crossing at right angles) like that of midtown Manhattan, in New York City. Many of the buildings were made of brick. Homes often had baths that could be emptied into a drainage system that served an entire city.

Invasions   After flourishing for almost a thousand years, the Indus Valley civilization ceased to exist, for reasons that are still unclear. It is possible that the cities on the Indus River were overrun by invaders. As shown on the chart on pages 204–205, the history of South Asia often took new turns as a result of invasions.

Following the collapse of the Indus Valley civilization, fierce bands of invaders from Central Asia swept into northern India. These people, the Aryans, eventually settled in farming villages on the broad plain watered by the Ganges River. They introduced into South Asia both their language, Sanskrit, and the polytheistic religion, Hinduism. In time, powerful Aryan kings brought much of northern India under their control.

The first major dynasty to establish an empire in this region was the Maurya dynasty of the 3rd century B.C. (A *dynasty* is a succession of rulers from the same family.) The Mauryas unified much of northern India and encouraged the spread of Buddhism.

Glories of the Gupta empire   A golden age of ancient Indian culture was achieved under the Gupta monarchs. They ruled a vast northern Indian empire from about A.D. 300 to 500. (This period corresponds to the last centuries of the Roman empire, discussed in Chapter 7.) The wealth of these Gupta monarchs supported the pursuit of learning at dozens of Indian colleges and universities. Artists of the time painted stunning religious murals on the walls of Buddhist monasteries and elsewhere. Gupta doctors made major advances in surgery and the diagnosis and treatment of diseases. Indian scholars of the Gupta empire pioneered two very important concepts: zero and decimals, both of which are basic to modern mathematics. (*Decimals* comprise a numeral system based on tens.)

Eras in the History of South Asia		
Era	Time Period	Accomplishments
Indus Valley Civilization	3000–1500 B.C.	Built two major cities in the Indus River Valley—Mohenjo-Daro and Harappa.
Aryan Invasions	1500–500 B.C.	Aryans invaded India from the north; merged their beliefs with native ones to form elements of Hinduism.
Maurya Empire	300–200 B.C.	Unified much of northern India; encouraged the spread of Buddhism.
Gupta Empire	A.D. 300–500	Established a cultural "golden age" in northern India with achievements in literature, art, science, and mathematics.
Muslim Invasions (Arabs, Turks, Persians, Afghans, and Mongols)	700–1200	Introduced Islam through conquest; transmitted Indian achievements to the Middle East and Europe through trade.
Delhi Sultanate	1206–1526	Established Delhi as the capital of a large northern kingdom, which was ruled by a succession of Muslim sultans.

Mogul (or Mughal) Empire	1506–1757	Expanded Muslim control into southern India; built the Taj Mahal and other architectural marvels.
European Colonizers (Portuguese, Dutch, French, and British)	1500–1757	Gained control of ports in India and set up trading posts; introduced Christianity.
British East India Company	1600–1858	Established a trade monopoly in and political control over much of India.
Great Britain	1858–1947	Ended control by the British East India Company and added India to the British empire.

B. DEVELOPMENT OF HINDUISM

In the course of their long history, the peoples of India practiced many religions, one of the earliest being Hinduism.

Basic beliefs *Hinduism* was the traditional religion of ancient times and remains the dominant religion in modern India. Although Hindus worship hundreds of different gods, they believe that there is one spiritual force present in everything in the universe. Central to the Hindu religion are the following ideas:

- *Reincarnation* is the belief that a person's soul does not die when the body dies. Instead, it reappears after death in another living form, either in another person or in an animal.
- *Karma* is the force generated by a person's actions or deeds. According to Hindu belief, actions taken by an individual in the current life will determine that person's status in the next life. Good deeds will lead to higher status in the next life; bad deeds will lead to a lower status.
- *Dharma* refers to the set of rules or religious duties that each Hindu must exercise in her or his daily life. For example, an individual is obliged to help others and show concern for them. But each person's dharma is unique and depends largely on that person's place in society.

SHIVA THE DESTROYER: There are many Hindu gods. This statue of the Hindu god Shiva is associated with forces of destruction. Another Hindu god, Vishnu (not shown), is associated with forces of creation.

Effect on social organization   Hindu beliefs are closely related to how Hindu society is organized. Traditionally, for example, Hindus have believed in a *caste system*. A caste is a social group into which one is born. Social rules dictate how members of each caste shall live and what occupations they may enter. India today still has hundreds of castes. At the highest level of Hindu society are the *Brahmans*, members of the priestly caste, while at the lowest level are the *untouchables*.

In an earlier era, the caste into which a Hindu was born determined that person's occupation, wealth, and status throughout life. Thus, it provided one with a strong sense of social identity. A person of a certain caste could marry and have friendships with only other members of that caste. Members of the lower castes were discriminated against regularly. For example, an untouchable could not use the same village well that others used. People of lower castes were kept out of certain occupations. Even today, especially in rural areas, a person will generally associate only with others of the same caste. Discrimination based on caste still exists in India, even though the Indian constitution bans such discrimination. But the educational system and economic modernization have weakened the caste system.

C. BUDDHISM

Buddhism developed in India around 500 B.C. Its founder was a religious seeker named Siddhartha Gautama, but his followers called him Buddha, or the "Enlightened One." He believed that all forms of human suffering had a single cause: materialistic desires. He taught that by giving up all worldly desires, people could attain *nirvana* (a state of spiritual happiness and release from the otherwise endless cycle of birth and rebirth). Buddhism also incorporated the Hindu concepts of karma and dharma into its own philosophy. In India, Buddhism never grew into the dominant religion. By the process of cultural diffusion, however, Buddhism spread to other parts of Asia. It has become a major force in Southeast Asia, China, Korea, and Japan.

A BUDDHIST TEMPLE: One of the thousands of Buddhist temples in Thailand contains this golden statue of the Buddha. Who was the Buddha? What did he teach his followers?

DOCUMENTS: A SERMON BY THE BUDDHA

In the Indian city of Benares, Gautama (the Buddha) delivered a sermon to his five closest disciples, or "bhikkhus" as he called them. The following is an excerpt from that sermon.

Now, this, O bhikkhus, is the noble truth concerning suffering:

Birth is attended with pain, decay is painful, disease is painful, death is painful. Union with the unpleasant is painful, painful is separation from the pleasant; and any craving that is unsatisfied, that too is painful. In brief, bodily conditions which spring from attachment are painful.

This, then, O bhikkhus, is the noble truth concerning suffering.

Now this, O bhikkhus, is the noble truth concerning the origin of suffering:

Verily, it is that craving which causes the renewal of existence, accompanied by sensual delight, seeking satisfaction now here, now there, the craving for the gratification of the passions, the craving for a future life, and the craving for happiness in this life.

This, then, O bhikkhus, is the noble truth concerning the origin of suffering.

Now this, O bhikkhus, is the noble truth concerning the destruction of suffering:

Verily, it is the destruction, in which no passion remains, of this very thirst [desire]; it is the laying aside of, the being free from, the dwelling no longer upon this thirst.

Questions for Discussion

1. In your own words, explain what the Buddha sees as the underlying cause of suffering.
2. In your own words, explain how (according to the Buddha) one can eliminate suffering in one's life.
3. Centuries later, Thomas Jefferson wrote in the Declaration of Independence (1776) that everyone is entitled to the right of "life, liberty, and the pursuit of happiness." Do you think that the Buddha would have approved of this idea? Explain your answer.

Source: *"The Sermon at Benares," translation by Samuel Beal, copyrighted by The Open Court Publishing Company, Chicago.*

D. ISLAM

As we learned in Chapter 3, Islam originated in the Middle East in the 7th century. In the 8th century, Arab conquerors began introducing Islam into South Asia. Other Muslim invaders would come later, converting millions of people of the subcontinent. Today, Islam is the dominant religion in Pakistan and Bangladesh and the second largest religion in India.

Conflicts between Muslims and Hindus   Muslim invaders slaughtered Hindus by the hundreds of thousands and destroyed their temples. Although there were periods when the two groups got along with each other, the history of the centuries following the Muslim invasion was largely one of conflict between Muslims and Hindus. Opposition between the two groups was caused by great differences in their religious beliefs. For example:

- Muslims worship only one god; Hindus worship many.
- Muslims eat all meats other than pork. Many Hindus are vegetarians, and all Hindus refuse to eat beef; Hindus regard the cow as sacred.
- Muslims believe in the idea of social equality; Hindus developed a caste system.

TAJ MAHAL: Between 1630 and 1650, about 20,000 Indian workers labored to build this tomb for Mumta Mahal, the wife of the Mogul ruler Shah Jahan. What were some of the other achievements of the Mogul dynasty?

The Mogul empire   Muslim power was at its height in India during the years of the Mogul dynasty (1506–1757), also known as the Mughal dynasty. The Mogul monarchs succeeded in introducing Islam into southern India and in unifying much of the subcontinent. They built monuments and palaces of stunning beauty. For example, one of the most famous works of Indian architecture, the Taj Mahal, was built by a Mogul ruler as a tomb for his wife and a memorial of his love for her.

Continuing religious conflicts   Muslim-Hindu conflicts continued into the 20th century. When India achieved independence from Great Britain in 1947, it immediately divided into a Muslim nation and a Hindu one. Millions of Muslims in India had disliked being a minority in a nation dominated by Hindus. Rather than remaining within India, Muslims formed the new nation of Pakistan out of areas that were predominantly Muslim. This act led to the mass migration of Hindus and Muslims so that each would be within the borders of their respective new nation. Despite this process, millions of Muslims still live in India.

E. SIKHISM

The Sikh religion, or Sikhism, developed in India in the 15th century. It contains elements of both Islam (for example, belief in one god) and Hinduism (belief in reincarnation). Like Muslims, the Sikhs reject the caste system. Even though they borrowed from the two religions, the Sikhs have remained a separate religious group. They live primarily in northern India in the State of Punjab.

Sikhs have earned a reputation as excellent soldiers. They learned to stress military skills as they fought to free themselves from Muslim domination. Now, however, their main conflicts are with the Indian government. Many Sikhs have participated in a movement for independence from India.

F. ANCIENT CIVILIZATIONS OF SOUTHEAST ASIA

Both on the mainland and on the islands of Southeast Asia, a number of kingdoms rose to power between the 1st and 9th centuries A.D. Included among these early kingdoms were the Khmer kingdom on the Mekong River, the Pagan and Mon kingdoms on the Irrawaddy River, and several Tai kingdoms on the Chao Phraya River. Present-day nations of Southeast Asia trace their historic and cultural origins to these former kingdoms. Cambodia has its roots in the Khmer kingdom; Myanmar, in the Pagan and Mon kingdoms; and Thailand, in the ancient Tai kingdoms.

Cultural diffusion in Southeast Asia   Traveling monks and merchants introduced the three major religions of South Asia—Hinduism,
Buddhism, and Islam—to the various lands of Southeast Asia. Many
thousands of Chinese who migrated to Thailand, the Malay Penisula,
and other parts of Southeast Asia brought along a philosophy called
Confucianism (discussed in Chapter 6). When European explorers and
missionaries arrived in this region in the 1500s and 1600s, Southeast
Asians were introduced to another major religion, Christianity.

The temples and artistic treasures of Southeast Asia reflect that
region's religious diversity. The golden spires of beautiful Buddhist
temples are found throughout Myanmar, Thailand, and elsewhere. In
Cambodia, tourists seek out Angkor Wat, a huge stone temple erected
in the 12th century by the Khmer people. It honors the Hindu god
Vishnu. Its massive walls and inner shrines (now in ruins) display
thousands of wonderfully sculpted stone figures depicting Hindu
myths.

In Malaysia and Indonesia today, Islam is the dominant religion. In
fact, there are more Muslims in Indonesia than in any single country
of the Middle East.

Ethnic diversity in Southeast Asia   The ethnic character of Southeast Asia is even more mixed than its religions. In the prehistoric past,
dozens of ethnic and racial groups settled in the area: the Khmers in
Cambodia, the Malays on the Malay Peninsula, the Burmese in Myanmar—to name just a few. Later migrations from China and South Asia
added to the ethnic mix.

Increasing the cultural diversity even further, Europeans introduced their languages to the areas they colonized. Native peoples
learned to speak French in Indochina (present-day Laos, Cambodia,
and Vietnam), English in Burma (Myanmar) and the Malay Peninsula,
Dutch in the Netherlands East Indies (Indonesia), and Spanish in the
Philippines.

In Review

The following questions refer to Section II: Early History.

1. *Key terms:* Define or identify each of the following:

reincarnation	dharma	untouchable
karma	caste system	nirvana

2. Compare the Gupta and Mogul empires of India in terms of
   (*a*) cultural achievements and (*b*) religious life.

3. State *two* major beliefs of each of the following religions: (*a*) Hinduism and (*b*) Buddhism.

4. *Critical thinking:* "Basic differences in religious belief make it extremely difficult for Hindus and Muslims to understand each
   other." Present arguments either for or against this statement.

Comparing Religions of South and Southeast Asia			
Religion	Nations Where Religion Is Widely Practiced	Historic Origins	Central Beliefs
Hinduism	India, Nepal	Developed out of the religious practices of the Aryans, who invaded India around 1000 B.C.	While worshipping many gods, Hindus believe in one supreme force. Good ethical behavior means carrying out duties (dharma).
Buddhism	Myanmar, Thailand, Malaysia, Sri Lanka, Bhutan, Vietnam	Founded in Northern India in the 5th century B.C. by the followers of Siddartha Gautama (the Buddha).	By meditating deeply and giving up worldly desires, Buddhists seek to attain enlightenment—complete understanding of the divine.
Islam	Pakistan, Indonesia, Bangladesh, Malaysia, India	Founded in the Middle East in A.D. 622 by Mohammed.	Muslims believe in one god, Allah. They practice their faith daily by observing the moral laws contained in the Muslims' holy book, the Koran.
Confucianism	Vietnam	Founded in China in the 5th century B.C. by the followers of Confucius, a Chinese philosopher.	Confucianists study the teachings of Confucius for ideas on how to live a good, moral life—one that contributes to social harmony.

| Christianity | Philippines | Founded in the Middle East in the 1st century A. D. by followers of Jesus. | Christians believe in the ethical teachings of Jesus as contained in the Christian Bible. They worship Jesus as "Christ"—a savior. |

III. The Dynamics of Change

As you know, Spanish ships under Christopher Columbus sailed west across the Atlantic in 1492. Soon afterward, in 1498, Portuguese ships under Vasco da Gama sailed south and east around Africa. The major goal of both explorers was to reach the East Indies (a term used then to describe India and Southeast Asia) and gain access to the area's spices and jewels. Following the voyages of Columbus, da Gama, and later explorers, European kingdoms began a worldwide quest for trade and colonies. Between 1500 and 1900, Spain, Portugal, Britain, France, and other European nations gained economic and political control over large parts of the world, including South and Southeast Asia.

A. THE BRITISH IN INDIA

A business firm called the British East India Company got the British involved in India. In the 1600s, this company made agreements with the Mogul rulers of India for trading rights. The British fought the French in the Seven Years' War (1756–1763) in part to secure the British East India Company's monopoly of these rights. The eventual British victory in this war cleared the way for British domination of the Indian subcontinent.

Sepoy Mutiny   In 1857, Indian soldiers under British command rebelled against foreign rule and influence. Their revolt is known in the West as the "Sepoy Mutiny," but Indians call it the "Anglo-Indian War of 1857." The *sepoys* were Indians who served as soldiers for a European power. The immediate cause of their revolt was the British requirement that they use a new rifle with cartridges that the sepoys believed were greased with animal fat. In firing the rifles, the sepoys had to bite the cartridge for speedy reloading. Such a practice angered Hindu soldiers, who viewed the cow as sacred, and also Muslim soldiers, whose religion forbade them to eat pork. The British East India Company put down the rebellion with help from the British government. It was apparent, though, that the trading company was unable to control the subcontinent of India. As a result, in 1858 power was transferred to the British government, which remained in control until India achieved independence in 1947.

SEPOY MUTINY: The uprising of Indian soldiers in 1857 against their British commanders shocked Great Britain into changing its policy toward India. What new policy was adopted?

Reasons for British success   Several factors allowed the British to conquer and rule India.

- India had long been divided into many states, each with its own ruling prince. In order to prevent the princes from uniting against them, the British adopted a strategy known as "divide and conquer." This meant that the British would ally themselves with some Indian princes against others.
- Religious conflicts between Hindus and Muslims prevented the development of national unity.
- The British used their advanced military technology to suppress Indian resistance.

Imperialist motives   Pursuing an imperialist policy in the late 1800s, the British introduced major changes in India. Their chief purpose in doing so was to benefit Britain's industrial economy while also strengthening British control over India. The changes included:

- building railroads in order to help the British to transport natural resources, workers, and troops
- building irrigation systems in order to increase the production of Indian cotton destined for British textile mills

- operating schools to educate an Indian elite as loyal subjects of the British government
- providing modern medicines and methods of sanitation to prevent epidemics among Indians (and also to protect the health of British families living in India)
- using Indians as soldiers in the army and as civil service workers in the government to assist the British in ruling Indian society. (Such a policy was known as "divide and rule.")

B. GROWING NATIONALISM AND EVENTUAL BRITISH WITHDRAWAL

Without intending to do so, the British introduced the Indian people to the idea that people of an area who share common values and traditions should control their own government. What accounted for this growth of nationalism in India in the early 20th century?

- Indians came to resent their British rulers, who sometimes showed a superior attitude and treated Indian traditions with contempt. For example, Indians encountered "Europeans Only" signs on trains and at the doors of private clubs.
- The thousands of Indians who attended British schools read about and learned to value Western ideas, such as democracy, nationalism, and self-determination. (Notice that in this case, cultural diffusion moved from a Western culture to an Eastern one.)
- Indian leaders of unusual ability gave strength to two political parties that were dedicated to winning national independence. The Indian National Congress (later known as the Congress party) attracted mainly Hindus to its ranks. Its chief leader in the early 20th century was a nationalist named Mohandas Gandhi. A second party, the Muslim League, consisted of Indian Muslims who wanted an end to British rule. Its leader was Mohammed Ali Jinnah.

Gandhi's leadership Gandhi was so revered by his millions of followers that they called him Mahatma, meaning the "Great One." Gandhi and his Indian National Congress party helped free India from British control by using nonviolent means of protest. Believing that violence against the British would only lead to more violence, Gandhi in the 1920s urged Indian people to oppose British rule through *civil disobedience* (refusal to obey laws that one considered unjust). Those participating in Gandhi's campaign refused to pay taxes, boycotted British-made goods, and joined in peaceful protests and marches.

One of Gandhi's most dramatic protests was the "March to the Sea" in 1930. After the thousands who participated in this march reached the sea, they made salt from the water. Their purpose was to get around a British law that required Indians to buy salt only from the British.

Gandhi and his followers were often jailed for their actions. But Gandhi insisted that his nonviolent deeds were morally justified as a means of winning independence. To demonstrate his deep personal commitment to a cause, Gandhi would sometimes undertake a long period of *fasting* (refusing to eat).

Gandhi devised unique ways of strengthening the spirit of Indian nationalism. He urged Indians to wear traditional Indian garments rather than Western-style clothing. To make traditional cloth in traditional ways, he encouraged people to use hand-operated spinning wheels rather than to depend on machine-made goods from British factories. He hoped to overcome the hostility between Hindus and Muslims by urging both groups to join in the common struggle for independence. He reached out to the untouchables and urged others to treat them fairly.

Gandhi's nonviolent methods of protest had an effect beyond his own country. In the United States during the 1960s, Martin Luther King, Jr., would use similar methods of nonviolence and civil disobedience to protest the denial of civil rights to African Americans. For example, King went to jail (as Gandhi had done) for leading peaceful demonstrations against laws that he opposed.

MOHANDAS GANDHI: Gandhi (right) was one of the great nationalists of the 20th century. What was his approach for achieving political change?

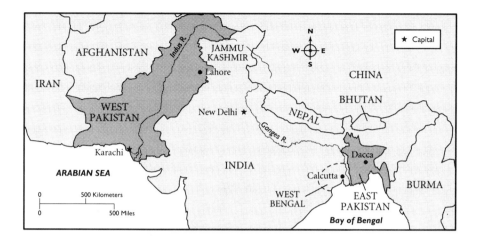

Independence   The final stage in the Indians' struggle for independence began during World War II (1939–1945). Indian political leaders agreed to halt protest activities during the war in exchange for Britain's promise to grant India independence after the war. In fact, in 1947 Great Britain kept its word by granting India independence. But violence immediately broke out between Indian's major religious groups: Hindus and Muslims. While trying to put a stop to the violence, Gandhi was assassinated by a Hindu fanatic. The Indian subcontinent was then divided into three pieces. The central piece, where Hindus were in the majority, became the Republic of India. The two Muslim-dominated areas (one on either side of India) became known as West Pakistan and East Pakistan. From 1948 to 1971, these two territories made up the new Muslim nation of Pakistan.

C. THE COLONIAL EXPERIENCE IN SOUTHEAST ASIA

The history of European influence in Southeast Asia is similar to the history of British influence in the Indian subcontinent. Beginning in the 1500s when Spain took over the Philippines, most of Southeast Asia fell under the colonial control of various Western nations. As in India, nationalist movements for independence arose in the early 20th century and gained success as a result of World War II.

Rival trading companies   The East Indies (islands that now make up Indonesia) were once a prime target for the ambitions of various European trading companies. In the 1500s, the Portuguese dominated trade in the spices grown on those islands. But in the 1600s, armed ships of the Dutch East India Company managed to gain trade supremacy. By 1750, the Dutch had won a monopoly on the trade from the islands and had established firm control over major East Indian seaports.

Colonial rule   By 1800, the government of the Dutch nation (the Netherlands) had taken control of the islands of the East Indies and ruled them as an overseas colony. (A similar transfer of power would take place in India, where in 1858 the British East India Company would surrender control to the British government.) Dutch colonists in the 1800s adopted a policy of "forced cultivation." They forced people on the islands to plant coffee and other cash crops. While this imperialist policy contributed to the Dutch economy, it disrupted the traditional way of life of the local population.

Also in the 1800s, other European powers gained control of every part of the Southeast Asian mainland except the Kingdom of Siam (present-day Thailand). Great Britain ruled Burma (present-day Myanmar) as an eastern province of its Indian empire and developed the island of Singapore into a major seaport for British trade throughout Asia. France brought under its control a number of separate kingdoms and ruled them as the French colony of Indochina.

To the north of the Netherlands East Indies lay the Philippines, an island chain that had fallen under Spanish control as early as the 1500s. In 1898, the United States defeated Spain in the Spanish-American War. The Filipinos had been fighting for their independence from Spain when the U.S. Navy arrived. The Filipinos celebrated the U.S.

COLONIAL RULE IN SOUTHEAST ASIA, 1900

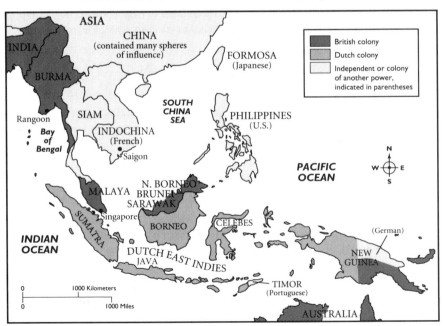

naval victory at Manila Bay, fully expecting independence to be the result. Instead, they were bitterly disappointed by the U.S.-Spanish treaty of peace, which called for the transfer of the Philippines to the United States.

The Philippine people could not accept the idea of being traded from one colonial power to another. In 1899, rebel troops that had fought against Spain turned their weapons against U.S. forces. To put down the uprising, U.S. President William McKinley sent 70,000 additional troops to the Philippines. After nearly three years of intense fighting in Philippine jungles, U.S. forces finally prevailed. The last rebel band surrendered in 1902.

By acquiring the Philippines, the United States became involved in the politics of Southeast Asia. U.S. naval bases in the Philippines and elsewhere in the Pacific would present important targets for Japanese attacks in 1941 and in later years of World War II.

Nationalist independence after World War II Early in the 20th century in Southeast Asia, various nationalist groups led movements for independence similar to Gandhi's movement in India. As with India, the independence efforts were helped by World War II. Japanese armies swept through all of Southeast Asia in 1941 and 1942, defeating and driving from power the Dutch, French, British, and U.S. defenders. Although Japan was eventually defeated in the war, the colonial powers were unable to fully restore their former control in Southeast Asia.

Fulfilling an earlier promise, the United States granted the Philippines its independence in 1946. The Netherlands, in contrast, hoped to regain control of its colony in the region, the Netherlands East Indies. But a strong independence movement led by a nationalist named Sukarno forced the Dutch to grant the people of the islands their independence in 1949 as the new nation of Indonesia.

France was at first determined to prevent Indochina from gaining independence. But a Vietnamese leader, Ho Chi Minh, was even more determined to free his country from foreign control. In 1946, forces led by Ho began a guerrilla war against the French. After losing a major battle at Dien Bien Phu in 1954, the French decided to withdraw from Indochina. Thus, Laos and Cambodia won their independence as new nations. A divided Vietnam also came into being. While a Communist government led by Ho Chi Minh controlled North Vietnam, an anti-Communist government controlled South Vietnam.

In Review

The following questions refer to Section III: The Dynamics of Change.

1. *Key terms:* Define or identify each of the following:

Sepoy	"divide and rule"	fasting
"divide and conquer"	civil disobedience	

2. In separate columns, list (a) the positive effects and (b) the negative effects of British colonial rule of India.

3. Explain how each of the following led to India's independence: (a) nationalism, (b) Gandhi's leadership, and (c) World War II.

4. *Critical thinking:* "In their rule of South and Southeast Asia, the Western colonizers planted the seeds of their own overthrow." (a) Explain what you think this statement means. (b) Present evidence to support or refute the statement.

IV. Contemporary Nations

Eventually after World War II, every former colony in both South Asia and Southeast Asia became an independent nation. Various kinds of governments came to power in the region. India, for example, became a parliamentary democracy. Pakistan was for many years ruled by military officers. North Vietnam (and later all of Vietnam) was under the control of a Communist dictatorship. Let us look first at India, the most populous country in the two regions, to see how that government dealt with a range of challenges.

A. PROBLEMS OF INDEPENDENCE IN INDIA

India adopted the system of government that the British had introduced, parliamentary democracy. (Britain's government is discussed in Chapter 7.) The members of India's popularly elected legislature (called the Parliament) chose the country's chief executive (the prime minister). When India became independent in 1947, Jawaharlal Nehru became its first prime minister and dominant political leader, serving for the next 17 years. Nehru was strongly influenced by Gandhi's philosophy of nonviolence. He too was a nationalist who stressed the unity of India by trying to overcome religious differences between Muslims and Hindus. In world affairs, he was best known for his policy of nonalignment. He refused to take sides in the cold war rivalry between the United States and the Soviet Union.

Religious and cultural disputes Despite Nehru's efforts toward national unity, religious and cultural differences continued to cause trouble for India. The partition of India into separate Hindu and Muslim nations caused enormous suffering. In the late 1940s, millions of people in the two countries were forcibly resettled. Many Muslims in India migrated to Pakistan, while many Hindus in Pakistan migrated to India. In the process, thousands were killed. The forced migrations increased the existing regional problems of poverty, famine, disease, and homelessness. In addition, the territory of Kashmir, in northern India, became a longlasting source of tension between Pakistan and India. Both nations claimed Kashmir. Both nations are still dissatisfied with the pieces of Kashmir that each received under a UN agreement in 1949.

Civil strife continues in India   Many Indians still feel stronger ties to their religious and cultural group than to the nation as a whole. The Sikh minority, for example, has demanded *autonomy* (self-government) for Punjab, a state in northern India where most Sikhs live. The dispute between the Sikhs and the Indian government has led to major episodes of violence. In 1984, the Indian Army seized the Sikhs' Golden Temple at Amritsar. Over 600 people were killed in the incident. In retaliation, Sikh extremists assassinated Prime Minister Indira Gandhi, the daughter of Nehru. Seven years later, in 1991, Rajiv Gandhi, Indira's son and successor as prime minister, was also assassinated, but by another rebel group.

Also disturbing Indian unity in the 1990s have been new outbreaks of religious strife between Hindus and Muslims. Even though the overwhelming majority of its population is Hindu, India has a sizable Muslim minority (11 percent of all Indians). In the northern states of Jammu and Kashmir, Muslims are demanding either independence or union with Pakistan. Violent clashes between Muslims and Hindus have resulted in many deaths.

B. PAKISTAN AND BANGLADESH

When Pakistan was established as a nation in 1947, its lands consisted of two separate areas. The central government, located in West Pakistan, sent administrators to East Pakistan to enforce national laws. But economic and cultural differences between the two sectors posed a serious problem. West Pakistan was more industrialized and prosperous than East Pakistan. Most people in West Pakistan spoke Urdu; most people in East Pakistan spoke Bengali. Bengali traditions of East Pakistan differed from the traditions of West Pakistan. In many ways, the Bengalis felt that they had closer ties to the people of West Bengal, a state of India.

In 1971, East Pakistanis rioted against the Pakistan government, accusing it of being dominated by West Pakistanis. With the help of the Indian Army, the East Pakistanis succeeded in establishing their independence as a new nation: Bangladesh. Now there were three major nations on the South Asian subcontinent. In the northwest was Pakistan (formerly West Pakistan). In the northeast was Bangladesh (formerly East Pakistan). And in the center was India. (See the map on page 217.)

TRADITIONAL WAYS: These women of Bangladesh still use centuries-old methods for threshing wheat. Why might some of these people or their neighbors feel the need to move to a large city? What problems would they encounter there in adapting to urban life?

C. SOCIETY IN INDEPENDENT INDIA

India's population (some 900 million) is the world's second largest. Its growth rate is also among the world's highest, largely because of improvements in health care. In the next century, India is expected to overtake China as the world's most populous country.

The rapidly growing population has placed a great strain on India's limited resources. Moreover, economic growth has not kept pace with population growth, resulting in a continuing low standard of living. India's government has tried to control population growth by supporting the use of birth control devices and voluntary sterilization. These efforts, however, have had only limited success since many Indians resent them. Traditionally, Indians have viewed large families as an economic asset. At least in rural areas, more children mean more hands that can work to help bring in more money.

Effects of urbanization on traditional values Today, as in the past, a large majority of Indians live in rural villages. There the caste system and other traditions are strongest. In recent decades, however, economic change has caused millions of villagers to move to India's crowded cities. Over time, these migrants and their children may begin to lose touch with their traditions. For example, urban women may decide to marry whom they please rather than follow the traditional custom of *arranged marriages* (ones in which the choice of a partner is dictated by the parents). Women in India's cities have greater independence than do village women because the former are generally better educated and many work outside the home.

Urbanization has weakened the caste system. Indians who live and work in cities cannot avoid mixing with people from different backgrounds and castes. (Remember that in traditional India, members of one caste were not even supposed to eat with members of another.)

The Indian government has declared the caste system illegal and has banned discrimination against the untouchables. In rural areas, however, the caste system still influences the lives of millions of people. Here we see an example of the gap that sometimes develops between a nation's laws, on the one hand, and traditional customs, on the other.

D. INDIA'S ECONOMY

India's economy is partly socialistic. It consists of a number of state-run enterprises as well as many private businesses.

Industrial growth   As India's first prime minister, Nehru advocated *democratic socialism*. Under this economic and political system, the democratically elected central government takes a leading role in promoting economic growth. India set up a series of five-year plans that spelled out the nation's economic goals and priorities. One major goal was to speed up the rate of industrialization. Nehru and his successors recognized that India's industries were far behind those of the West. Many of India's manufactured products were the work of *cottage industries* (ones based in the home) where workers used simple tools. By stressing the building of factories, India's economic planners hoped to decrease dependency on foreign imports and make their country more self-reliant.

To encourage industrialization, India set up a reserve bank. It controls the supply of money in the economy. It also provides funds for expanding state-owned, large-scale industries (railroads, steel, chemicals, and others).

Economic planning and large, government-owned industries have negatively affected India's ability to compete in world markets. India's economy has not kept pace with the rapidly growing economies of nations, such as South Korea and Taiwan, where free enterprise plays a greater role. The Indian government is beginning to give up some of its control over the economy, allowing more private ownership of industries. It also is encouraging more investments by foreigners.

The Green Revolution in agriculture   One of India's critical needs is growing enough crops to feed its huge and growing population.

Through the 1950s and 1960s, India's harvests fell far short of its people's needs. It had to import much of its food from other nations, including the United States and Canada.

In recent decades, however, India has greatly increased its production of rice, wheat, and other crops. Because of improved farm machinery, fertilizers, new varieties of seeds, and pesticides, crop yields on a given piece of land are much higher than in the past. The dramatic gains in agriculture in India and elsewhere in South and Southeast Asia are part of the worldwide Green Revolution. Despite these improvements, though, India must still import a portion of its food supply.

Continued dependence on foreign capital Since independence, India has not attracted enough foreign investment capital. This fact has hindered economic development. Nevertheless, in the 1980s India obtained an increase in both foreign loans and foreign aid. To encourage investments in India's industries, the government offered tax advantages to foreign companies and individual investors. In addition, much foreign aid came from the United States, the Soviet Union, Western European countries, and international banking organizations. The flow of loans, investments, and aid has spurred India's economic growth. However, the continuing violence between religious groups has discouraged some foreign investors. Indian business leaders have demanded strong government action to control disorders.

Problems of rural and urban poverty In India, poverty remains a major problem in both rural and urban areas. In the countryside, farmers still depend upon the monsoon cycle, which at times can bring too much rain and at other times can bring extended periods of drought. Farming villages are often unable to support their growing populations. As a result, people from rural areas tend to migrate to urban areas, which are already severely overcrowded. Unemployment in the cities is widespread. Even college graduates have difficulty finding employment. Many graduates choose to emigrate to other countries in search of work, causing what has been termed a *brain drain* (emigration of many professional workers to other countries).

E. COMPETING ECONOMIC SYSTEMS IN SOUTHEAST ASIA

In Southeast Asia, some nations practice capitalism, while others practice communism.

Capitalist countries Leading examples of capitalist, or free enterprise, countries in Southeast Asia are Malaysia, Singapore, and Thailand. In the 1970s and 1980s, these countries experienced rapid economic growth, partly as a result of investments by major Japanese and U.S. corporations. Indonesia and the Philippines are other important capitalist countries of Southeast Asia. Leading the surge of economic growth in Southeast Asia have been the oil, electronics, textile, and tourist industries. In the 1990s, large Southeast Asian companies have been investing in other Asian markets. China especially has attracted Southeast Asian investors.

Communist countries By 1975, all three nations of Indochina—Vietnam, Cambodia, and Laos—had adopted the economic and political system known as communism. As we learned in Chapter 1, Communist countries have command economies. In these countries, both agriculture and industry are under the complete control of the Communist party, which also runs the government. Today, the Communist countries of Southeast Asia rank among the poorest in Asia. In part, this situation came about because these countries lost much of the economic support they had been getting from the Soviet Union. The Soviet Union dissolved into a number of independent republics in 1991. The main republic, Russia, has neither the resources nor the will to continue economic aid to Communist nations.

A series of wars was also partly responsible for the economic plight of the Communist countries of Southeast Asia. These wars—the Vietnam conflict and the Cambodian civil war—will be discussed later in this chapter. Before these conflicts of the 1960s and 1970s, Cambodia, Laos, and Vietnam made up an area known as the "rice bowl" of Asia. Now these three countries must import rice to feed their populations. To stimulate economic growth, the government of Vietnam has encouraged more private business activity and foreign investment.

PLANTING RICE FIELDS: This scene in modern Vietnam shows how rice has been cultivated in Southeast Asia for centuries. Seedlings are transplanted in the fields.

F. THE GLOBAL CONTEXT

After World War II, the cold war rivalry between the United States and the Soviet Union affected international politics everywhere, including South and Southeast Asia.

Rivalry between India and Pakistan   *Third world* was a term that came into common use early in the cold war. It referred to those nations that refused to enter into alliances with either the anti-Communist bloc of nations (the "first world") or the Communist bloc (the "second world"). Third world nations tried to follow a policy of neutrality, or nonalignment. Under Nehru's leadership in the 1950s and early 1960s, India followed such a policy. It acted as the leader of other third world countries in the United Nations. India received aid from both the United States and the Soviet Union. It distrusted the United States, however, because of the U.S. policy of giving military aid to Pakistan, a hostile neighbor.

In the cold war, Pakistan allied itself with the United States against China and the USSR. Pakistan also wanted protection from its neighbor India. In 1954, Pakistan became part of the Southeast Asian Treaty Organization (SEATO), whose members pledged themselves to protect one another from any attack by another country. SEATO members included the United States, France, Great Britain, Australia, New Zealand, the Philippines, and Thailand. As a military ally, Pakistan received much military and economic aid from the United States. This aid continued even after Pakistan withdrew from SEATO in 1972. (SEATO dissolved in 1977.) India protested against U.S. aid to Pakistan and turned more to the Soviet Union for aid to counter the growth of Pakistan's military power.

Since the end of the cold war in 1991, India and Pakistan have been changing their foreign relations. Recognizing that its longtime policy of nonalignment no longer has any meaning in the post-cold war era, India has been improving its relations with the United States. Its aid from Russia has been cut off due to that power's financial difficulties. At the same time, U.S. military aid to Pakistan has been cut off, in part because of suspicions that Pakistan has been assembling nuclear weapons.

Civil war and genocide in Southeast Asia   After World War II, several nations in Southeast Asia engaged in fierce struggles for power between Communist forces and their opponents. Much of the fighting through the 1950s, 1960s, and 1970s was done by the Vietnamese, Laotians, and Cambodians themselves. Arms, however, were supplied by outside powers. The Soviet Union and China supported the Communist forces, while the United States supported the anti-Communist ones. By 1965, U.S. troops were drawn into the Vietnam War. As members of SEATO, Thailand, New Zealand, and Australia also participated in the conflict on the side of the anti-Communists.

1. War in Vietnam. The origins of the Vietnam War date back to the early 1940s when a nationalist movement led by Ho Chi Minh fought for Vietnam's independence, first from the Japanese and then (after 1945) from the French. France finally withdrew from Vietnam in 1954. At a peace conference that year, Vietnam was divided into northern and southern sections, each with its own government. Elections were supposed to be held to unify the nation. After elections failed to take place, Ho's Communist government of North Vietnam began fighting the U.S.-backed, anti-Communist government of South Vietnam. From 1965 to 1973, U.S. troops fought alongside the South Vietnamese in a costly and unsuccessful effort to defeat Communist forces, which included the Vietcong (South Vietnamese Communists). At one point in the 1960s, more than 500,000 American soldiers were involved in the conflict. Then the number was gradually reduced. In 1973, the United States withdrew from Vietnam after having negotiated a peace agreement with North Vietnam. But two years afterward, in 1975, South Vietnam's government fell under the control of North Vietnam. Both parts of Vietnam were then politically reunited in a single nation under Communist control. The capital of the former South Vietnam, Saigon, was renamed Ho Chi Minh City.

A problem remaining from the Vietnam War is U.S. concern about more than 2,000 U.S. soldiers who are listed as "missing in action" (MIA). The United States insists that Vietnam account for each and every MIA and, if any are still alive, let them return to the United States. Until Vietnam cooperates on this matter, the United States is refusing to exchange ambassadors with that country. The U.S. government did, however, lift a long-standing trade embargo on Vietnam in 1994.

2. Cambodian genocide. In 1975, a group of Communists called the Khmer Rouge came to power in Cambodia. They used terror to further revolutionary goals. Once in power, the Khmer Rouge began a policy of forced migration and extermination of potential rivals. All citizens were forced to leave Cambodia's capital, Phnom Penh. Huge numbers of these people were sent on forced marches to remote sections of the country. Many died from starvation or disease, while others were killed by Khmer Rouge troops. The Communists tolerated no opposition. Probably as many as one million people lost their lives in Cambodia due to the Khmer Rouge's acts of *genocide*. (Genocide is the deliberate killing of members of an ethnic, religious, or political group.)

In 1979, Vietnamese troops invaded Cambodia and drove the Khmer Rouge from power. The Vietnamese installed a different Communist government in Cambodia, but one loyal to Vietnam. For years, forces of the new government and the Khmer Rouge fought a civil war. Then in 1991, the United Nations helped arrange an agreement that ended the civil war. According to this peace agreement, Communist and non-Communist political parties in Cambodia were to participate in free

CORAZON AQUINO: As president of the Philippines, Corazon Aquino acted as commander in chief of the armed forces. In what way was her presidency more democratic than that of predecessor, Ferdinand Marcos?

elections and share power. In 1993, a UN-sponsored national election brought to power a new *coalition government* (a government in which two or more political parties rule in an alliance). The Khmer Rouge, however, refused to give up their arms and were excluded from the government.

Governmental changes in the Philippines

The United States retook the Philippines from Japanese forces during World War II. But after the war, in 1946, the United States granted the Philippines its independence. U.S.-Filipino ties have remained strong. For example, until 1992 the United States continued to operate two major military bases in the Philippines.

One of the best-known Filipino leaders after the war was President Ferdinand Marcos (1966–1986). He ordered the military to fight Filipino Communist guerrillas and Filipino Muslims who wanted a separate nation. He also acted in dictatorial ways, violating the human rights of members of other political parties. In 1986, a presidential election was held in which Marcos was declared the winner. Most neutral observers, however, claimed that the elections involved cheating and that another candidate had really won. That person was Corazon Aquino, the widow of an opponent of Marcos's who had been slain several years earlier under suspicious circumstances. Key military leaders withdrew their support for Marcos and gave it to Aquino.

As the new president, Aquino led the Philippines toward greater democracy. A free press, free elections, and rival political parties developed under her leadership. A new president was elected to office in 1992, but Aquino's democratic reforms remain intact.

In Review

The following questions refer to Section IV: Contemporary Nations.

1. *Key terms:* Define or identify each of the following:

    autonomy   brain drain   Green Revolution
    democratic socialism   third world   genocide

2. Identify *one* major economic or political problem faced by each nation after it won independence: (*a*) India,   (*b*) Pakistan,   (*c*) Vietnam, and   (*d*) the Philippines.

3. Give *one* cause for each of the following conflicts: (*a*) Sikh rioting in India and   (*b*) the Vietnam War.

4. *Critical thinking:* Do you think the United States involvement in the Vietnam War was justified? Explain your answer.

NEIGHBORS TO THE SOUTH: AUSTRALIA AND NEW ZEALAND

South of the equator, to the south and east of Indonesia, are located two important island nations, Australia and New Zealand. They are separated from each other by about 1,200 miles of ocean water. Because Australia and New Zealand were colonized by the British, they both have strong cultural and economic ties to Great Britain and other Western nations.

Geography   The two islands that make up New Zealand (called simply North Island and South Island) have a climate that is both mild and wet. Most days of the year, rain falls over the islands' hilly and mountainous terrain. In such a climate, the forests that cover one-fourth of the land grow lush and green. Pasture grasses also thrive, as do the millions of sheep that graze on New Zealand's rolling acres. The sheep and cattle in the country outnumber the human population (3.5 million) by a ratio of 25 to 1.

Unlike mountainous New Zealand, Australia is comprised largely of a flat plateau and a semidesert. Only along the continent's eastern coast does one find a long chain of

AUSTRALIA AND NEW ZEALAND

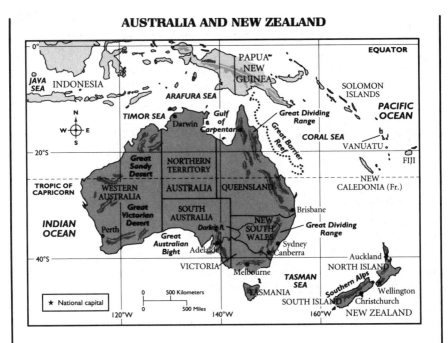

mountains. Known as the Great Dividing Range, these mountains intercept moist ocean breezes and cause life-giving rain to fall on the coastal plain to the east. The great majority of Australia's 18 million people live on or near this well-watered strip of coastal land. The vast interior of central Australia, known as the *outback*, receives very little rain. There are widely scattered sheep ranches and mining towns in this region, but the outback is too dry and barren to support large human populations.

History The history of Australia and New Zealand may be divided into three major eras: (1) prehistoric settlement, (2) British colonial rule, and (3) nationhood in the 20th century.

Australia was originally settled by a hunting people who probably migrated there from Indonesia about 40,000 years ago. The *Aborigines* (as the British were to call them) adapted their culture not only to the well-watered coastal plains but also to the harsh environment of the outback.

Many thousands of years passed before the first groups of human settlers arrived on the remote islands of New Zealand. They probably came from other islands in the Pacific, perhaps paddling long canoes over hundreds of miles of open water. The *Maoris*, as these people are called, arrived in New Zealand sometime in the 1300s. An agricultural people, they were extremely skillful in the arts of boat-making, weaving, and sculpting ceremonial masks.

The British period of New Zealand's and Australia's histories began in the late 1700s. A British geographer and naval officer, Captain James Cook, explored both islands of New Zealand in 1769. The next year, he sailed along Australia's eastern coast and gave it the name New South Wales. What practical use could be made of these remote lands on the other side of the world from Britain? The British government decided to turn New South Wales into a prison colony and thereby solve the problem of London's badly overcrowded jails. For 80 years (1788–1868), British courts would commonly order convicted criminals and debtors to be "transported" to the prison camps of New South Wales, Australia. After their sentences ended, many prisoners remained in Australia to become farmers and ranchers.

British pioneers started settling New Zealand in the early 1800s. They brought in sheep from Australia. Soon large herds of the wool-producing animals were thriving on New Zealand's grassy hills.

Both the Aborigines and the Maoris suffered from the arrival of newcomers. The foreigners' diseases as well as their guns severely reduced the native populations. In New Zealand, prolonged warfare with British settlers ended in 1872 in the Maoris' defeat. Today, the Maoris make up nine percent of New Zealand's population, while the Aborigines account for less than two percent of all Australians. New Zealand's constitution guarantees the Maoris representation in that country's legislature.

The period of national independence for both Australia and New Zealand began early in the 20th century. Great Britain granted self-rule to Australia in 1901 and to New Zealand in 1907. Both countries, however, remained within the British Commonwealth. In major wars of this century (World War I, World War II, the Korean War, and the Vietnam War), troops from Australia and New Zealand took heavy casualties fighting beside allied forces from the United States and other Western nations.

Political traditions   Following in the British tradition, the governments of both Australia and New Zealand are multiparty democracies. Each has the following: (1) a written constitution, (2) an elected, two-house legislature similar to the

British Parliament (discussed in Chapter 7), and (3) a prime minister elected by the majority party in the legislature.

In 1893, New Zealand became the first nation in the world to grant women voting rights equal to those of men. (U.S. women had to wait until 1920 to be guaranteed such rights.) In addition, the *secret ballot* originated in Australia, a measure that makes elections more democratic.

Economic patterns   By every measure, living standards in both Australia and New Zealand rank among the world's highest. In both nations, more than four-fifths of the population live in cities and towns. Almost every household has a television, a telephone, and an automobile. The literacy rate is close to 100 percent. The governments of both countries provide "free" (tax supported) health services.

Australia's high standard of living is based largely upon its agricultural and mineral wealth. For more than a century, Australia has been one of the world's top exporters of wool, beef, and wheat. In addition, Australian mining companies have profited from the land's rich deposits of gold, silver, bauxite, coal, iron, nickel, and uranium.

Much of New Zealand's wealth comes from the huge quantities of wool that it sells on world markets. Among its other major industries are processed foods and forest products.

TEST YOURSELF

Multiple-Choice Questions

Level 1

On a separate sheet of paper, write the number of the word or expression that, of those given, best completes each statement or answers each question.

1. Population density is greatest in the northern part of India because (1) people tend to settle along the seacoast (2) the population centers in China are easy to reach from this area (3) the major river systems are located in this area (4) families in this area traditionally are larger than families in southern India.

2. Which is a major effect of geography on South and Southeast Asia? (1) Monsoons help determine the types of agricultural products grown. (2) The wealth of natural resources led to early industrialization. (3) Climatic conditions have led to chronic food shortages. (4) Geography has created a sense of unity among all the peoples.

3. In South and Southeast Asia, the continued importance of the monsoon cycle indicates that these regions are (1) becoming major exporters of oil (2) developing heavy industry (3) dependent on farming to sustain their economies (4) opposed to the use of nuclear power.

4. Which is a valid statement about the role of religion in modern India? (1) Buddhism has replaced Hinduism as the major religion. (2) Religion has lost most of its influence and importance. (3) Religion and politics are rigidly separated. (4) Religious beliefs and social structure are closely related.

5. Which statement was true of the caste system in traditional India? (1) Members of different castes often intermarried. (2) Caste membership determined a person's occupation. (3) The highest caste was composed of untouchables. (4) The caste system had little effect on daily village life.

6. When I go to the office, I put on my shirt and I take off my caste; when I come home, I take off my shirt and I put on my caste.

   What idea can be inferred from this quotation? (1) The caste system continues to influence Indian society. (2) The caste system has been rejected by most Indians. (3) Successful urban workers in India belong to the same caste. (4) The Indian government officially supports the caste system.

7. Religious differences between Muslims and Hindus in South Asia after World War II led to (1) increased control by the British colonial

government   (2) an arbitrated settlement by the United Nations
(3) the creation of the nations of India and Pakistan   (4) increased
Communist influence in the region.

8. Which generalization best explains the creation of the nations of
India and Pakistan in 1947?   (1) Armed conflict is necessary for independence movements to succeed.   (2) Religious conflicts may
have a strong influence on political events.   (3) Industrialization
needs to reach a high level before a nation can become independent.
(4) Similar geographical and historical conditions may promote unity
between nations.

9. The Sepoy Mutiny in India   (1) restored power to the hereditary
monarchies   (2) attempted to reject the traditional culture in the
country   (3) resisted foreign influence in the country   (4) reestablished the power of religious leaders.

10. Which factor contributed most to Great Britain's control over India
until after World War II?   (1) the diversity and the lack of unity of
the Indian population   (2) the location of the Indian subcontinent
(3) British empathy for social conditions in India   (4) British support
of the Indian Congress party.

11. Europeans were able to dominate much of South Asia in the 19th
and 20th centuries primarily because   (1) Christianity appealed to
the people of the region   (2) Europeans had more advanced technology   (3) Hindus did not believe in the use of military force
(4) few natural resources were found in the region.

12. The government of Great Britain built railroads, schools, and irrigation systems in colonial India primarily to   (1) prepare India for
independence   (2) strengthen its political and economic control in
India   (3) secure favorable trading arrangements with different Indian leaders   (4) help India maintain its traditional cultural systems.

13. The primary goal of the Indian National Congress (1885–1947) was to
(1) reform the Hindu religion   (2) partition India between Muslims
and Hindus   (3) create a socialist economy   (4) gain independence
from Great Britain.

14. Which method did Mohandas Gandhi use in his campaign to win
independence for India?   (1) refusing to cooperate with the British
government   (2) leading armed uprisings against the authority of the
British   (3) enlisting foreign help in driving the British from India
(4) requesting that the United Nations order the British to leave India.

15. Which action best expresses Mohandas Gandhi's concept of civil disobedience?   (1) A British army outpost was bombed to protest the
British presence in Northern Ireland.   (2) Citizens in the United
States went to jail for peacefully demonstrating against segregation
laws.   (3) French citizens wrote letters to their government to oppose
arms sales to Iraq.   (4) Supporters of Ferdinand Marcos attempted
a coup d'état against the Philippine government.

Base your answer to question 16 on the passage below and on your knowledge of social studies.

> "...But there come some occasions ... when he considers certain laws to be so unjust as to render obedience to them a dishonor. He then openly and civilly breaks them and quietly suffers the penalty for their breach...."

16. This passage supports the use of   (1) military force   (2) civil disobedience   (3) appeasement   (4) retaliation.

17. During the 1980s, national unity in India was hindered by   (1) a foreign policy of nonalignment   (2) continued fear of attack from the Soviet Union   (3) political interference from China   (4) conflicts among Sikhs, Hindus, and Muslims.

18. In India, migration of people from rural areas to urban areas has resulted in   (1) an increase in the number of people involved in agriculture   (2) the strengthening of the caste system   (3) more limitations on the freedom of women   (4) a weakening of traditional values and the caste system.

19. A major problem faced by South and Southeast Asian nations today is that   (1) increased immigration has created high levels of employment   (2) industrial development has hindered democratic reform   (3) rapid modernization has led to a shortage of agricultural products   (4) economic growth has not kept pace with population growth.

20. Which was a result of the other three?   (1) Pakistani government officials from West Pakistan sent to administer East Pakistan   (2) the creation of the nation of Bangladesh   (3) the existence of cultural and economic differences between East and West Pakistan   (4) rioting in East Pakistan in 1971.

21. Which condition has most stimulated economic growth in India in the 1980s and 1990s?   (1) a small urban population   (2) an increasing infant mortality rate   (3) increased investment of capital   (4) a diversity of languages.

22. India has developed a mixed economy that   (1) guarantees government control over the economy   (2) provides open competition without government interference   (3) blends free enterprise with socialism   (4) relies on the traditional barter system.

23. Which was a result of India's policy of nonalignment?   (1) India kept its defense spending at a low level.   (2) The Indian government was successful in limiting population growth.   (3) The Indian government worked to reduce religious conflicts.   (4) India accepted aid from both the United States and the Soviet Union.

24. Which has been characteristic of several Southeast Asian countries since World War II?   (1) internal struggles for power that have led to political instability   (2) isolation from the influence of the superpowers   (3) democratic governments based on the principles of the

French Revolution   (4) fundamentalist Islamic governments supported by Iran.

25. Which was a major result of the end of the Vietnam War?   (1) North and South Vietnam were politically reunited.   (2) India improved its relations with the United States.   (3) The United States increased its political influence in Southeast Asia.   (4) Most Southeast Asian nations adopted a democratic form of government.

Level 2

26. Early civilizations in India developed mainly in   (1) areas with abundant mineral resources   (2) valleys near rivers   (3) areas with climatic diversity   (4) mountainous areas.

27. India is considered a land of many cultures and languages mainly because of its   (1) open immigration policies   (2) colonial past   (3) historical ties to China and Japan   (4) geographic diversity.

28. Monsoons are most important to   (1) urban dwellers   (2) farmers   (3) industrial workers   (4) government officials.

29. Which of the following is the best example of cultural diffusion?   (1) Hinduism is the major religion in India.   (2) Buddhism spread from India to China.   (3) Hindi is the main language in India.   (4) India is a land of many villages.

30. Which has been one effect of the traditional caste system in India?   (1) It has provided many opportunities for advancement.   (2) It has provided equal wealth among the people.   (3) It has provided people with a sense of identity.   (4) It has provided political rights to all people.

Base your answers to questions 31 and 32 on the advertisement below and on your knowledge of social studies.

"Wanted: Brahman woman for Brahman man, aged 30 years. Engineer, having own factory. Father is a doctor, and brothers are lawyers."

31. The newspaper in which this advertisement appeared is most likely located in   (1) Vietnam   (2) Cambodia   (3) Philippines   (4) India.

32. Which is a conclusion that can be made about the society described in this advertisement?   (1) Rural areas have many unmarried people.   (2) Most of the people are Muslims.   (3) Education is not valued.   (4) Traditional values continue to be important.

33. Which action was most opposed by Mohandas Gandhi?   (1) using violence to obtain independence   (2) boycotting foreign businesses   (3) engaging in protest marches   (4) supporting Indian businesses.

34. The idea of nonviolent resistance is best illustrated by   (1) U.S. involvement in Vietnam   (2) conflict between Hindus and Muslims in India   (3) genocide in Cambodia   (4) India's struggle for independence from Great Britain.

Base your answer to question 35 on the cartoon below and on your knowledge of social studies.

Now, remove that and fix this one.

IBH Publishing Co., Bombay, India

35. The cartoon illustrates India's problems with (1) a poor transportation system (2) government aid (3) conflict between religious groups (4) the monsoon cycle.

Base your answer to question 36 on the headlines below and on your knowledge of social studies.

> "Sri Lanka rice production increases by 32% in two years"
> "Philippines end more than 50 years of rice imports"
> "India's wheat and rice production increases greatly"

36. The developments referred to in the headlines were most directly the result of the (1) Commercial Revolution (2) Green Revolution (3) Cultural Revolution (4) Industrial Revolution.

37. When India became independent, it was partitioned (divided) into India and Pakistan because of   (1) religious differences between Hindus and Muslims   (2) economic concerns   (3) health and medical problems   (4) conflicts between people in rural and urban areas.

38. In India, the caste system has been weakened most by   (1) aid from the United States   (2) movement of people to the cities   (3) use of the military to enforce laws   (4) increased farm production.

39. During the 1980s and 1990s, a major problem in India has been (1) interference by China   (2) the decline of the Hindu religion (3) the threat of invasion from Russia   (4) violence resulting from cultural differences.

40. In India, the traditional role of women has changed during the 20th century mainly because of the   (1) movement of people from rural to urban areas   (2) use of nonviolent protest methods   (3) growth of political unrest   (4) influence of Hinduism.

Essay Questions

Level 1

1. Below are listed major headlines associated with South and Southeast Asia.

Headlines
"Sepoy Mutiny Breaks Out"
"Indira Gandhi Assassinated"
"Green Revolution Aids Indian Economy"
"Ho Chi Minh Leads Revolution Against the French"
"Mass Executions Occur in Cambodia"

Select *three* of the headlines listed above. For each headline selected:

● Discuss one major cause of the event.

● Discuss one political, economic, or social effect of the event.

2. The story of history indicates that the attempt to solve one problem sometimes leads to other problems.

Attempted Solutions
Farmers rely on monsoon cycle for agricultural production
British gain control of India (1858)
India gains independence (1947)
Pakistan formed as a separate nation (1947)
Migration of people from rural to urban areas

Select *three* of the attempted solutions. For each solution selected:

● Describe how the solution attempted to solve a specific problem.

● Describe how this attempted solution created another problem.

Level 2

3. The statements below describe certain features of the geography and climate of South and Southeast Asia.

Features
The Himalayan Mountains stretch across northern India.
River valleys are located in northern India.
The Deccan Plateau is located in central and southern India.
Monsoons blow across South and Southeast Asia.

A. Select *three* of the features described above. For each feature selected, state one specific effect.

B. Base your answer to Part B on your answer to Part A. However, additional information may be included. Write an essay discussing the effects of specific geographic features on the development of South and Southeast Asia. Begin your essay with this topic sentence:

> Geography has affected the development of South and Southeast Asia.

4. Throughout history, leaders have greatly influenced developments in their nation or region.

Leaders
Siddhartha Gautama (Buddha)
Mohandas Gandhi
Jawaharlal Nehru
Ho Chi Minh
Corazon Aquino

A. Select *three* of the leaders listed above. For each leader selected, state one way in which the leader has influenced developments in his or her nation or region.

B. Base your answer to Part B on your answer to Part A. However, additional information may be included. Write an essay discussing how each of the leaders influenced developments in his or her nation or region. Begin your essay with this topic sentence:

> Leaders have often influenced developments in their nation or region.

CHAPTER 6

East Asia

Main Ideas

1. **GEOGRAPHIC ISOLATION:** Ancient China was geographically separated from other early civilizations, a fact that explains why the Chinese believed they were superior to all others.

2. **CONFUCIAN IDEAS:** Confucius's teachings about family relationships, society, and politics became the basis of Chinese civilization for many centuries.

3. **RISE AND FALL OF DYNASTIES:** For centuries in China, periods of strong dynastic rule alternated with periods of weakness and disorder.

4. **WEAKNESSES OF THE OLD ORDER:** In the 19th century, corrupt government as well as a lack of advanced military technology made China an easy target for Western imperialists.

5. **COMMUNIST TRIUMPH:** After a long struggle, the Chinese Communist party led by Mao Zedong came to power in 1949.

6. **RECENT ECONOMIC CHANGES:** Since Mao's death in 1976, some farms and industries have been privatized. This had led to an impressive growth in the economy.

7. **CULTURAL BORROWING:** Living on islands off the East Asian mainland, the Japanese have been able to borrow selectively from foreign cultures without being overwhelmed by them.

8. **SCARCITY OF RESOURCES:** Scarcity of arable land and mineral resources has forced the Japanese to use intensive farming methods and to trade for vital raw materials.

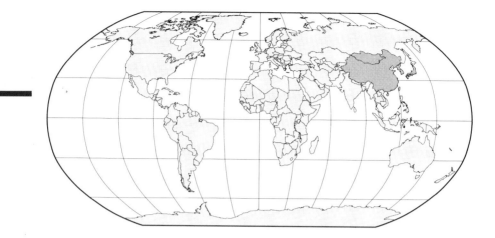

9. **SHINTOISM:** Japan's native religion emphasizes the worship of nature.

10. **FEUDALISM:** During Japan's feudal period, power was divided among large landowners, who commanded armies of samurai (warriors or soldiers).

11. **MODERNIZATION:** In the late 19th century, Japan's government and elite class concentrated on adopting the industrial technologies of the West.

12. **IMPERIALIST AGGRESSION:** In the 1930s and 1940s, Japan colonized weaker neighbors in Asia and became involved in a war with the United States and its allies.

13. **ECONOMIC COMPETITION:** Increasingly, Japan has turned to advanced technology and foreign trade and investment to improve its economic position in world markets.

14. **CULTURAL IDENTITY:** While borrowing some aspects of their culture from China, the Korean people have always maintained a separate identity.

15. **JAPANESE OCCUPATION:** For 50 years (1895–1945), Japan exercised imperialist control over Korea.

16. **WAR BETWEEN THE TWO KOREAS:** After World War II, Korea was divided into two parts—Communist North Korea and non-Communist South Korea. War between the two Koreas and their allies (1950–1953) ended with a truce.

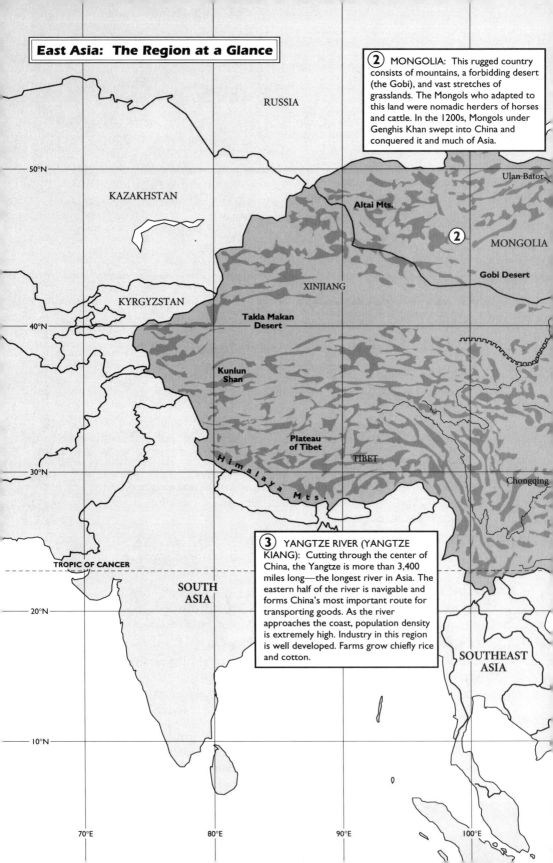

East Asia: The Region at a Glance

② MONGOLIA: This rugged country consists of mountains, a forbidding desert (the Gobi), and vast stretches of grasslands. The Mongols who adapted to this land were nomadic herders of horses and cattle. In the 1200s, Mongols under Genghis Khan swept into China and conquered it and much of Asia.

RUSSIA

KAZAKHSTAN

Ulan Bator

Altai Mts.

② MONGOLIA

Gobi Desert

KYRGYZSTAN

XINJIANG

Takla Makan
Desert

Kunlun
Shan

Plateau
of Tibet

TIBET

Chongqing

Himalaya Mts.

TROPIC OF CANCER

SOUTH
ASIA

③ YANGTZE RIVER (YANGTZE KIANG): Cutting through the center of China, the Yangtze is more than 3,400 miles long—the longest river in Asia. The eastern half of the river is navigable and forms China's most important route for transporting goods. As the river approaches the coast, population density is extremely high. Industry in this region is well developed. Farms grow chiefly rice and cotton.

SOUTHEAST
ASIA

50°N

40°N

30°N

20°N

10°N

70°E   80°E   90°E   100°E

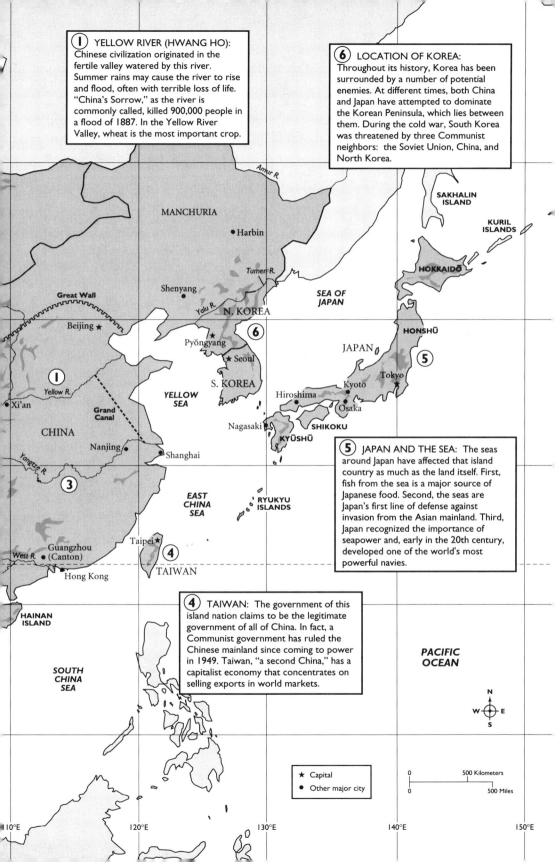

① YELLOW RIVER (HWANG HO): Chinese civilization originated in the fertile valley watered by this river. Summer rains may cause the river to rise and flood, often with terrible loss of life. "China's Sorrow," as the river is commonly called, killed 900,000 people in a flood of 1887. In the Yellow River Valley, wheat is the most important crop.

⑥ LOCATION OF KOREA: Throughout its history, Korea has been surrounded by a number of potential enemies. At different times, both China and Japan have attempted to dominate the Korean Peninsula, which lies between them. During the cold war, South Korea was threatened by three Communist neighbors: the Soviet Union, China, and North Korea.

⑤ JAPAN AND THE SEA: The seas around Japan have affected that island country as much as the land itself. First, fish from the sea is a major source of Japanese food. Second, the seas are Japan's first line of defense against invasion from the Asian mainland. Third, Japan recognized the importance of seapower and, early in the 20th century, developed one of the world's most powerful navies.

④ TAIWAN: The government of this island nation claims to be the legitimate government of all of China. In fact, a Communist government has ruled the Chinese mainland since coming to power in 1949. Taiwan, "a second China," has a capitalist economy that concentrates on selling exports in world markets.

Amur R.

MANCHURIA

• Harbin

SAKHALIN ISLAND

KURIL ISLANDS

Tumen R.

Shenyang •

HOKKAIDŌ

SEA OF JAPAN

Great Wall

Yalu R.

N. KOREA

Beijing ★

HONSHŪ

Pyŏngyang ★

⑥

JAPAN

⑤

Seoul ★

Tokyo ★

① Yellow R.

Kyoto

Xi'an •

YELLOW SEA

S. KOREA

Hiroshima •

Grand Canal

CHINA

Osaka •

Nanjing •

Nagasaki •

SHIKOKU

KYŪSHŪ

③

Shanghai •

Yangtze R.

EAST CHINA SEA

RYUKYU ISLANDS

Taipei ★

④

Guangzhou • (Canton)

West R.

TAIWAN

Hong Kong

HAINAN ISLAND

PACIFIC OCEAN

SOUTH CHINA SEA

N
W ✛ E
S

★ Capital
• Other major city

0   500 Kilometers
0   500 Miles

110°E   120°E   130°E   140°E   150°E

Even though it is only part of a continent, East Asia is one of the world's largest regions, both in area and in population. It contains one of the world's oldest civilizations—China—and also one of the world's most modernized nations—Japan. Other nations of East Asia are North and South Korea, Mongolia, and the island of Taiwan.

I. China: Geography

The more than one billion people who live in China today make that country the most populous nation on earth. In area, it is third in size after Russia and Canada. China's capital is Beijing.

A. PHYSICAL FEATURES

Three great rivers flow through the broad and fertile valleys of eastern China. The Yellow River (Hwang Ho) flows through northeastern China, the Yangtze River (Yangtze Kiang) through central and eastern China, and the West River (Hsi Chiang) through southeastern China. Since early times, the land watered by these rivers has been cultivated by Chinese farmers. Today, as in the past, most people live in the eastern part of China. This is where nearly all of China's fertile farmland is located.

Surprisingly, only about 13 percent of China's total land area can be successfully farmed. Stretching for vast distances to the north and west of the river valleys are barren lands that are sparsely settled. Such land comprises about two-thirds of China. The Gobi Desert in the north is dry and barren. A mountainous region and high plateau extending westward into Tibet is extremely rugged.

Responding to this geographic challenge, the Chinese have developed expert methods for working the soil, fertilizing it, irrigating as needed, and rotating crops. These methods help boost production from each precious acre. They are all examples of *intensive farming methods* (ones used to cultivate the land to its maximum extent).

China's densely populated river valleys are cut off from other heavily populated regions of the world by the mountains and deserts to the north and west and by the Pacific Ocean to the east. As a result, Chinese civilization developed in relative isolation. For many centuries, the Chinese regarded their own civilization as the only one that existed and looked upon all foreign peoples as barbarians. In other words, geographic isolation led to ethnocentrism—the idea that one's own culture is superior to all others.

B. CLIMATE

China's climate is as varied as its terrain. The desert lands in the northwest have cold winters and hot, dry summers. The northeast, though cool and fairly dry, has enough moisture for the Chinese to

RICE PADDIES IN EASTERN CHINA: This land near the Yangtze River is part of the great rice-producing region in China. How do agricultural conditions here differ from those in (a) the Yellow River Valley and (b) western China?

grow wheat. In contrast, southern China has a climate similar to that of neighboring parts of Southeast Asia: humid and hot. The warm, wet climate helps Chinese farmers grow huge quantities of rice. In the summer months, wet monsoons blow northward across China's coastal areas and river valleys and bring heavy rainfall. In the winter, the monsoons blow over China from the north, bringing cold, dry winds.

In the spring, the amount of rain that falls over different parts of China can be either heavy or light. If it is unusually heavy, rivers like the Yellow and the Yangtze are apt to flood their valley and bring terrible loss of life. If little rain falls, there is danger of drought and massive starvation. From time to time throughout their history, the Chinese have suffered from these two calamities: floods and drought.

C. ETHNIC GROUPS

As much as 94 percent of China's population belong to the dominant ethnic group—the Han Chinese. But because China's population is so huge, there are also more than 60 million people in China who belong to various ethnic minorities. Chief among them are the Mongols, Koreans, Manchus, and Tibetans.

The nearly two million Tibetans who live in the western part of China have suffered from harsh rule ever since the 1950s, when

Chinese Communists came to power there. A highly religious people, the Tibetans developed their own distinct branch of Buddhism many centuries ago. Although China has long claimed Tibet as part of its nation, Tibetans do not accept Chinese rule and are seeking independence. Tibet's Buddhists recognize their religious leader, the Dalai Lama, as the true leader of Tibet.

II. China: Early History

Chinese civilization originated about 4,000 years ago in villages and cities along the Yellow River in the north. Gradually the kingdoms on this river extended their power southward. Eventually they gained control of the rice fields of the Yangtze River Valley. It took several hundred years before the rice-growing region in the south was joined politically with the wheat-growing region in the north.

A. CHINESE CIVILIZATION DEVELOPS

Until the 20th century, the history of Chinese civilization was largely a history of ruling dynasties.

Shang dynasty A dynasty of kings with the family name of Shang ruled for hundreds of years until the family lost power in 1122 B.C. Even during this early period, Chinese civilization was remarkably advanced. The Shang dynasty was noted for:

- a system of writing that used thousands of picture symbols to represent objects and ideas
- the weaving of silk cloth from the threads of silkworms
- a method for casting large and artistically designed objects of bronze
- the use of wheeled, horse-drawn chariots in warfare.

Chou dynasty Another family, the Chou, seized power from the Shang and founded a new dynasty in 1122 B.C. Over time, Chou rulers lost strength. They permitted powerful landlords within their kingdom to rule over local territories as independent states. For hundreds of years, these states warred among themselves. It was during this period of turmoil that a teacher and scholar named Confucius sought moral solutions for China's troubled society (see the next page).

Ch'in dynasty The founder of a new dynasty in 221 B.C. had the family name of Ch'in. His armies succeeded in ruthlessly crushing opposition and bringing all the rival states under central control. The first Ch'in ruler established an empire and protected it from foreign attack by ordering millions of peasants to build a huge wall—the Great Wall of China—all along the empire's northern frontier.

EXPANSION OF THE CHINESE EMPIRE

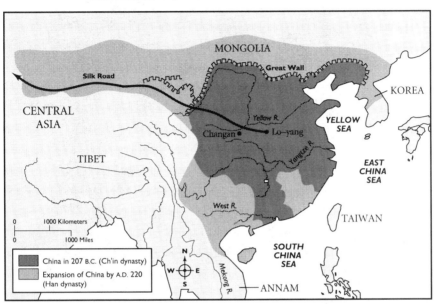

Han dynasty   The Ch'in dynasty lasted less than 20 years. The leader of a popular revolt against the Ch'in tyrant established the Han dynasty, which expanded the empire into Central Asia. During the four centuries of Han rule, the Chinese ruling class adopted a philosophy that has influenced Chinese culture and politics ever since. It was the philosophy that had been taught by the revered Chinese scholar, Confucius.

B. THE PHILOSOPHY OF CONFUCIUS

Confucius (551–479 B.C.) believed that there was a natural harmony and order to the universe. He thought that social relationships among people would also be harmonious if everyone understood his or her proper role in a family. A key element in family relationships was a respect for age. Sons were required to obey their fathers, and younger brothers had to recognize the higher status of older brothers. Women of all ages were considered inferior. However, children were expected to respect both mother and father. The family was viewed as a miniature society. If the members of each family attained harmony, then it followed (according to Confucius) that the entire kingdom or empire would also attain the ideal of perfect harmony and order.

In effect, *Confucianism* was a moral code for regulating all family relationships. It placed greater emphasis on the harmony of the group

CONFUCIUS: For more than 2,000 years, this teacher and *sage* (wise philosopher) influenced Chinese civilization. What did he teach? Who studied his teachings?

than on the welfare of the individual. Thus, family members were expected to fulfill their roles and sacrifice their personal goals to the larger good of the family.

Importance of education   A key element in Confucian philosophy was education. Confucius believed that the knowledge of music, poetry, history, and philosophy would lead people to act ethically and wisely. Education would lead to right conduct; in turn, right conduct would lead to a good society. Because of the Confucian stress on education, scholars were highly respected and were made officials in the emperor's government.

Mandate of heaven   Confucius was also concerned about the proper relationship between the ruler and the common people. In ancient China, it was commonly believed that the emperor could keep his *mandate of heaven* (right to rule) only as long as he ruled wisely and in the best interests of the people. Later philosophers argued that rebellions against weak or unwise rulers were justified because these rulers had forfeited their "mandate of heaven."

C. OTHER PHILOSOPHIES AND RELIGIONS

Although Confucianism had the greatest influence on Chinese society, it was by no means China's only philosophy or religion. Taoism and Buddhism also became popular during the Han dynasty.

Taoism   According to the religion of Taoism, people should learn from nature how to behave and think. For example, by observing the ways of a spring breeze or a running brook, people could put themselves in touch with a divine force. They would learn to behave in a simple and natural way rather than strive to follow formal rules and obligations of society. Living apart from society, Taoists hoped to achieve inner peace and harmony by acting in accordance with the ways of nature.

Buddhism   As we discussed in the last chapter, the religion of Buddhism originated in India around 500 B.C. Buddhist monks taught people the importance of trying to shed all their worldly desires. The religion spread to China during the first century A.D. Converts to Buddhism learned techniques for *meditation*—the practice of sitting and focusing one's thoughts for many minutes (or for hours) at a time. After the fall of the Han dynasty in A.D. 220, Buddhism enjoyed widespread popularity and spread to all parts of China. Chinese Buddhists modified the religion in many ways. They mixed in elements from their own culture, such as the Chinese emphasis on harmonious living.

D. GOLDEN AGE OF CHINESE CIVILIZATION

During the Middle Ages, a time when Western Europe was relatively weak and divided, China's civilization entered into a period of unrivaled cultural achievement. Its golden age spanned two dynasties, the T'ang and the Sung.

Achievements of the T'ang dynasty   The imperial family of the T'ang dynasty ruled China for almost 300 years (618–907). The emperor and his advisors lived in splendor in the Chinese capital of Changan. Within the walls of this huge city—the largest city in the world at the time—lived about a million people. (By contrast, London, England, would not achieve a population that large until about 1800.)

The early years of the T'ang were noted for good government and general prosperity. One of the first T'ang emperors, T'ai Tsung

(626 –649), dedicated himself to governing the empire and conducting his own life strictly according to the teachings of Confucius. He surrounded himself with scholar-officials who were also devoted to the Confucian ideal. The emperor used a system of competitive examinations to ensure that every official in the empire was well educated in Confucius's teachings. Anyone wishing to enter government service—or *civil service*—had to take a series of exams on the Confucian classics. Only the most able scholars, as determined by the tests, were accepted into the ranks of China's governing class. This system of competitive examinations continued in China from T'ang times to the modern era.

During the T'ang dynasty, the arts flourished in China. Every Confucian scholar was expected to demonstrate skill with a brush in painting landscapes and writing poems. In the early 700s, a number of poets attained fame for their brilliant observations on life and nature. T'ang poets Li Po and Tu Fu have a reputation in China similar to that of Shakespeare's in Europe and elsewhere.

One of the technological achievements of the T'ang dynasty was the invention of a system for printing books using carved, wooden blocks, each of which could print a page. (Western Europe did not begin to use block printing until 500 years later.)

Achievements of the Sung dynasty   About half a century of disorder followed the collapse of the T'ang dynasty. But a new dynasty, the Sung (960–1279), once again gave China a long period of economic prosperity, political stability, and cultural achievement. During this era, the economic center of China shifted from the wheat farms of the north to the rice farms of the south. Revolutionary in its effect was the discovery of a method for growing two crops of rice every year instead of one crop. The increased food supply enabled China's population to reach 100 million in Sung times. This figure surpassed the population of any other kingdom or empire at the time.

In science and technology, Sung China was also well ahead of the West. The following inventions (some originated even before the Sung) were in use in China long before their appearance in Europe:

- windmill (used to draw water out of a well)
- the magnetic compass and ship's rudder (for navigation)
- gunpowder (used in making fireworks)
- mechanical clock
- movable type (used in printing books)
- water-powered machinery (used in making clothing and other textiles)
- blast furnace (for making iron tools)
- paper money (to replace copper coins, which were in short supply).

From the point of view of Chinese women, the Sung dynasty imposed additional burdens and hardships. It was during this time that the practice of footbinding became common. Young girls' feet would be tightly bound to prevent them from growing. Women had difficulty walking on their deformed feet, but such feet were considered beautiful.

E. MONGOLS AND MANCHUS

Chinese dynasties would usually come to an end as a result of both internal and external pressures. Internally, the Chinese would often suffer from corruption among high officials and from the practice of overtaxing the common people. Externally, the empire's armies would be unable to defend the northern frontier against fierce attacks by nomadic "barbarians." In the 1200s, a weakened Sung dynasty became victim to external dangers. From the north (present-day Mongolia), Mongols rode into China on their war horses and set up their own dynasty under Kublai Khan. One of those who served the Mongol emperor was a foreigner from Italy, Marco Polo. Upon his return to Italy, Marco Polo wrote about his experiences in China. His writings stimulated interest in China among Europeans.

Mongol rule lasted less than a hundred years. The Chinese managed to overthrow the Mongols and establish a new dynasty, the Ming, in 1368. During its height, art and literature flourished. Eventually, however, the Ming dynasty also weakened, and another northern invader, the Manchus, swept into China. The Ch'ing dynasty established by the Manchus in 1644, like its predecessors, was strong in the beginning. But the Manchus entered a corrupt stage in the 1800s. This time, the foreign "barbarians" who took advantage of a dynasty's declining power came from Europe.

In Review

The following questions refer to Sections I (China: Geography) and II (China: Early History).

1. *Key terms:* Define or identify each of the following:

intensive farming	mandate of heaven	civil service
Tibet	dynasty	meditation

2. Give *two* examples of how China's geography has influenced its history and culture.

3. Explain the differences between Confucianism and Taoism.

4. *Critical thinking:* Compare China's golden age—the T'ang and Sung dynasties—with the golden age of Islam (review pages 100–101). (a) What, if anything, was similar about these two civilizations? (b) What was different?

Eras in the Early History of China (to 1912)

Dynasty	Time Period	Achievements
Shang	about 1766–1122 B.C.	Developed (1) a system of writing, (2) horse-drawn chariots, (3) silk weaving, and (4) bronze objects.
Chou	about 1122–256 B.C.	Powerful nobles established semi-independent states. Confucius taught a philosophy of moral values and family relationships.
Ch'in	221–206 B.C.	Established China's first empire. Built large section of the Great Wall.
Han	206 B.C.–A.D. 220	Established Confucianism as the accepted philosophy of the empire. Expanded the empire into Central Asia. Buddhism introduced into China.
Sui	A.D. 581–618	Reunified China after a long period of disorder. Built the Grand Canal linking northern and southern China.
T'ang	618–907	Attained high level of prosperity and stability. Scholars and poets flourished.
Sung	960–1279	Increased rice production. Invented gunpowder,

Sung (continued)		magnetic compass, and movable type. Created magnificent landscape paintings and *porcelains* (type of pottery).
Mongol rule	1279–1368	China added to vast Mongol empire. Marco Polo was employed by Mongol Emperor Kublai Khan.
Ming	1368–1644	Drove out the Mongols and restored Chinese rule. Art and literature flourished.
Manchu rule (Ch'ing dynasty)	1644–1912	Early period of strength (to 1800) followed by period of weakness and corruption (to 1912). Failed to defend China from Western imperialism.

III. China: Dynamics of Change

Like the Mongols before them, the Manchus quickly adopted many aspects of Chinese civilization, including both respect for Confucian scholarship and contempt for foreigners. Manchu emperors took the Chinese view that peoples outside China were uncivilized.

A. CHINA'S RELATIONSHIP WITH THE WEST

Through the 1700s, merchants from Great Britain, France, and other European nations wanted to trade Western manufactured goods for fine Chinese porcelains and other beautifully crafted objects. But the Manchu emperors placed severe limits on the foreigners' activities in China. The emperors and their Chinese advisers took the traditional view that the "barbarians" from the West could offer nothing valuable to a civilization as advanced and self-sufficient as China's.

What the Manchu government failed to understand was that Western Europeans had taken one of China's own inventions, gunpowder, and used it to build their military power. The Chinese used explosives not to propel cannonballs and bullets, but simply to send up fireworks on ceremonial occasions. Unwilling to learn from the West, Manchu rulers failed to equip their armies with modern weapons. They were thus unprepared to defend the empire against European aggression. In addition, Western Europe had begun the process of industrialization. China, on the other hand, had not yet begun to industrialize (even though its discoveries in science were far ahead of Europe's).

The Opium War   In the early 1800s, British merchants in China finally found an item of trade that many Chinese wanted to buy. The item was opium, a mind-altering drug made from a poppy plant grown in British India. Many people in the upper ranks of Chinese society became addicted to opium. The Manchu emperor banned the drug from China because of its destructive effects on people's health.

The British, however, would not accept the Manchu ruler's anti-opium decree. When Chinese authorities tried to stop traffic in the drug, British gunboats opened fire. Thus began a three-year conflict (1839–1842) known as the "Opium War." During this war, British firepower, especially that of the British Navy, prevailed over the poorly equipped Manchu forces. China was forced to make several humiliating concessions to its Western foe. It ceded the island of Hong Kong to Great Britain. It opened up five other seaports to British merchants. (Earlier, the British could conduct trade only in the city of Canton.) In addition, British citizens who committed crimes on Chinese soil were granted the right to be tried in British courts (instead of in Chinese ones). The Chinese considered such a *right of extraterritoriality*, as it was called, an insult.

Spheres of influence   After the British victory in the Opium War, other European powers wanted to gain similar privileges and trading opportunities for themselves. In the late 1800s (the Age of Imperialism), European nations competed for spheres of influence in China. A *sphere of influence* was an area in which China granted special and exclusive rights to a foreign nation. Each favored nation enjoyed the exclusive privilege of trading and conducting business in its own sphere. By 1900, much of China had been carved into spheres of influence by Europe's major powers: Britain, France, Germany, and Russia. In addition, Japan also claimed a sphere of influence in Korea after having defeated China in the Sino-Japanese War of 1894–1895. (Before this, Korea had been closely allied with China.)

Many reformers in China recognized that their country needed to industrialize, fight corruption, and learn techniques of modern warfare. But despite past failures and humiliating treaties with foreign powers, the Manchu government in Peking was slow to act.

SPHERES OF INFLUENCE IN CHINA

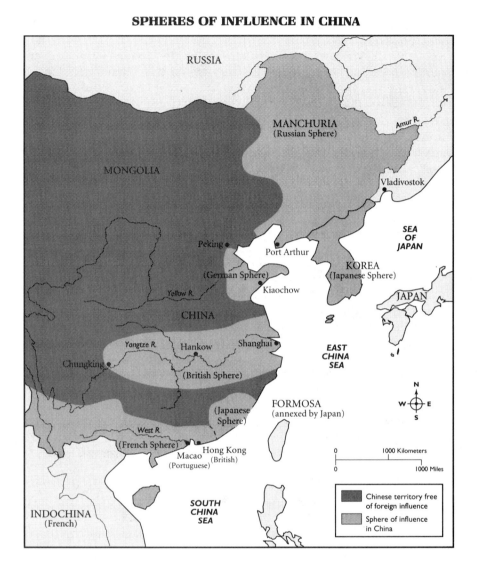

Secret societies and rebellions Many Chinese bitterly resented the decline of their once great empire and its treatment by foreigners from the West. After China's defeat in the Opium War, some Chinese joined a number of secret societies that plotted revolt against the Manchu government, which they blamed for China's decline.

The first massive popular uprising against Manchu rule broke out in 1849. It continued for 15 violent years. Participants in the Taiping Rebellion, as the uprising was called, won control over much of northern China. But some European nations, fearing that their economic interests were threatened, helped the Manchus crush the rebellion.

An incredible 20 million people perished in the civil war before it finally ended in 1864.

In 1899–1900, a secret society known as the Boxers launched an assault against all foreigners. This was called the "Boxer Rebellion." Unlike rebels in the Taiping Rebellion, the Boxers supported Manchu rule and were encouraged by the empress of China. The Boxers hoped to restore China's traditional ways and independence from foreign dominance. During the rebellion, hundreds of Christian missionaries were slaughtered. Eventually, a combined military force of Europeans, Americans, and Japanese ended the rebellion. The victors forced China to pay the foreigners a large *indemnity* (sum of money in payment for damages suffered).

B. FROM EMPIRE TO REPUBLIC

A number of Chinese nationalists and reformers hoped to bring China into the modern world by adopting some political and economic ideas from the West. One such nationalist and reformer was a Chinese revolutionary named Sun Yat-sen. He led several rebellions against Manchu rule, all of them unsuccessful. Then in 1911, a small revolt in one part of China spread quickly to Beijing, the Chinese capital. The last emperor of China, a six-year-old boy, was overthrown. After thousands of years, the Chinese monarchy dissolved. The rebels under Sun Yat-sen proclaimed a republic and proceeded to draw up a constitution.

Sun Yat-sen hoped that the new China would be founded on three principles: (1) nationalism (ridding China of foreign dominance), (2) democracy (establishing a popularly elected government), and (3) industrialization.

Soon after the revolution, China broke up into separate districts, each under the control of a different warlord. (A *warlord* is a military leader who uses his command of his army to rule over part of a country.) For several years, the republic was even weaker than the monarchy had been.

Chiang Kai-shek and the Kuomintang   In the 1920s, one of Sun Yat-sen's followers managed to defeat the warlords and bring most of China under the control of a central government. This leader, Chiang Kai-shek, used his control of a political party—the Kuomintang, or Nationalist party—to govern China in a dictatorial fashion. Peasants, who had suffered poverty and oppression under the Manchus, were no better off under Chiang's government. They paid heavy taxes to landlords as they had done for centuries. In addition, Chiang's government was generally corrupt. High officials would use public funds to enrich themselves instead of providing needed public services.

MAO ZEDONG AND CHIANG KAI-SHEK: During World War II, Mao (left)
and Chiang (right) cooperated. But after this 1946 banquet and toast, they
became enemies again. What was the final outcome of their rivalry?

C. FROM CAPITALISM TO COMMUNISM

Challenging the Nationalist party's grip on power was a party that
claimed to speak for China's peasants and factory workers—the
Chinese Communist party. It was modeled after the Soviet Communist
party, which had seized power in Russia in 1917 (discussed in Chapter
8). Its leader, Mao Zedong, condemned the corrupt practices of
Chiang's government. The Communists gained popularity throughout
the 1920s and 1930s for several reasons. First, the Communists promised to carry out the program of the Chinese people's hero, Sun Yat-
sen. Second, many Communists lived among the common people in
the villages and shared their hardships. Third, Communists promised
to reform the system of land ownership by giving peasants ownership
of the land they worked. Finally, communism emphasized the needs
of the group over those of the individual. This idea was similar to the
Confucianist emphasis on the needs of Chinese society over those of
the individual.

The Nationalists under Chiang almost succeeded in destroying their
Communist enemies. In 1934, a defeated Communist army barely escaped from Chiang's forces by retreating over rugged terrain into a

remote part of China. Those who survived this 6,000-mile Long March—including Mao Zedong—gained a reputation as heroes of the Communist movement.

In 1937, the Nationalists and the Communists agreed to end their civil war temporarily and turn both of their forces against the invading Japanese. After World War II ended, however, the Chinese civil war resumed. The Chinese Communists received military aid from the Soviet Union. Meanwhile, the Chinese government received massive amounts of aid from the United States. But the government failed to win the loyalty of the people, and the Communists steadily gained popular support. In 1949, the Communists triumphantly marched into Beijing and proclaimed the People's Republic of China. Mao Zedong quickly established himself as the Communist dictator of mainland China. Chiang fled with his Nationalist forces to the island of Taiwan. Still backed by the United States, Chiang's government claimed to make laws for all of China. In fact, it controlled only Taiwan.

In Review

The following questions refer to Section III (China: The Dynamics of Change).

1. *Key terms:* Define or identify each of the following:

   right of extraterritoriality   Boxer Rebellion   capitalism
   sphere of influence   indemnity   communism

2. Give *two* examples of Western imperialism in China in the 19th century.

3. Summarize the political troubles of the Chinese republic under Sun Yat-sen and Chiang Kai-shek.

4. *Critical thinking:* How do you explain the Communists' rise to power by 1949? Give *two* reasons that you think are the most important.

IV. China: Contemporary Society

Ever since the Communist takeover in 1949, mainland China has undergone revolutionary changes in its economic, political, and social life. The "second China," Taiwan, has also changed greatly as it has adjusted its capitalist economy to the demands of a new era.

A. THE GOALS OF MAO ZEDONG

From 1949 until his death in 1976, Mao Zedong dominated the government of China. As a leader with Marxist, or Communist, ideas (discussed in Chapter 7), he hoped to replace capitalism with a system operated by and for the working class (peasants and factory workers). He had specific goals for transforming Chinese society:

- Politically, he wanted to establish a one-party dictatorship.
- Socially, he aimed to eliminate the rich merchants and landowning classes and wipe out the extreme differences between rich and poor.
- Economically, he wanted to place China's factories, farms, and all other means of production under the direct control of the Communist government.
- Internationally, he aimed to build China's power and prestige and make China a leader in world affairs.
- Culturally, Mao aspired to get rid of Confucianism and replace the Confucian literary classics with Communist works. Toward this end, every Chinese citizen was required to memorize passages from the "Little Red Book," a book containing Mao's words of advice on communism.

B. METHODS OF CHANGE

In the 1950s, Mao adopted revolutionary methods for achieving his goals. He proclaimed the Communist party to be China's only legal party. Moreover, all candidates for elected office had to be Communists. As head of the party, Mao had dictatorial power to set overall policy for China's central government. In effect, his power was as absolute as that of the Chinese emperors had been.

Mao moved quickly to revolutionize both the Chinese economy and Chinese society. The government seized farmland from landlords and redistributed it to millions of landless peasants. In the process, many thousands and perhaps millions of resisting landlords were killed as "counterrevolutionaries." The government also took over all of China's factories, stores, and railroads and placed them under the control of Communist managers. The Communists made an effort to equalize the economic status of men and women by having authorities assign jobs without regard to one's gender.

All social institutions were placed under the control of the state. It ran the schools, which were required to promote Communist values. Newspapers, books, and other publications were also run by the government. The media's main function was to win popular support for Mao's policies. The arts, such as theater, dance, and painting, also had one main purpose: to instruct the people in Communist ideology. Propaganda in all forms—posters, movies, speeches, newspaper articles—portrayed Mao as a kind of god who could do no wrong. Dissent was not tolerated. Anyone who expressed ideas different from the "party line" was subject to punishment.

C. FAILURE OF THE GREAT LEAP FORWARD

Mao thought that the Chinese nation was capable of modernizing and industrializing almost overnight. In 1958, he announced a five-year plan for economic growth in both industrial and agricultural production. He called this plan the "Great Leap Forward."

To help achieve this plan, factory workers were asked to work long hours to meet production goals. They operated machinery around the clock. Managers allowed no time for keeping the equipment in good condition, so that the machinery soon broke down. Peasants throughout China were ordered to produce iron from small, quickly constructed iron mills near their homes. But their methods were so inefficient that little iron was produced. Meanwhile, the vital task of growing food was neglected.

Mao hoped to increase farm production by introducing the commune system. A *commune* combined hundreds of smaller farms into a single working unit. Wages and work assignments were set by the managers of the commune. Family members were often forced to live apart since men, women, and children had separate quarters. Demoralized by the radical changes in their way of life, commune workers fell far short of the production quotas assigned to them.

To please Mao, Communist officials reported huge increases in food production at a time when, in fact, millions were starving. The Great Leap Forward proved a failure. It was abandoned only because of continued food shortages and a decline in industrial output.

D. THE CULTURAL REVOLUTION

In the mid-1960s, Mao attempted to create radical social change. He called upon young Chinese to shout revolutionary slogans and to round up anyone suspected of being "old-fashioned" or anti-Communist. Young people were urged to leave school and to "learn revolution by making revolution." Wearing red badges on their arms, they were known as the Red Guard. Their mission, said Mao, was to bring about a Cultural Revolution in China by arousing people's enthusiasm for Mao's teachings.

Many of the Red Guards were former students from large cities who had left school to live and work with the peasants in the countryside. Wherever they went, the Red Guards acted as the eyes and ears of the government. They would accuse many of their elders of lacking revolutionary spirit. Their victims would be arrested, denounced, and humiliated in public.

The upheavals of the Cultural Revolution caused immense human suffering as well as major damage to China's economy. Mao finally called a halt to the movement in the early 1970s.

CULTURAL REVOLUTION: Marching through Beijing in 1966, these Red Guards carried a portrait of their hero, Mao Zedong. What was Mao's purpose in launching the Cultural Revolution?

E. CHINA AFTER MAO

After Mao's death in 1976, groups of high-ranking Communist officials competed for control of the party and the government. One of these groups, later called the "Gang of Four," was led by Mao's widow, Jiang Qing. The four leaders plotted to seize control of the government. Before they could do so, however, they were arrested. At their trial, they were convicted of committing political crimes. Jiang Qing received a suspended death sentence.

Economic development under Deng Xiaoping   The most influential leader to emerge after Mao's death was Deng Xiaoping. Though a Communist revolutionary like Mao, Deng wanted to see China concentrate on taking practical steps toward achieving economic growth. He called his program of economic reform the "Four Modernizations" because it called for progress in four areas: agriculture, industry, science, and defense.

In agriculture, Deng hoped to increase food production by applying some of the principles of a free market system. Communes have been broken up into smaller units. In the unit assigned to them, an individual family agrees to produce a certain quantity of rice or other product for government purchase. Any surplus over this amount can be sold by the family for its own profit. Under this system, farmers can reap the rewards for successfully managing and working the land.

A CHANGE IN POLICY: In 1979, Mao's successor, Deng Xiao Ping (waving), traveled to the United States to meet with President Jimmy Carter. How did Deng change China's economic policies?

In industry, too, Deng has applied principles of the free market. The government now encourages foreign trade and investment in China. Factory managers are given greater responsibility in making decisions. Individuals are even allowed to open small businesses and run them for profit. As a result of the new policies, China has significantly increased its industrial output. Workers have been able to purchase many more consumer goods than before. Despite its gains in industry, however, China still has an economy that is overwhelmingly agricultural.

China's universities have expanded their science programs. Research has led to advances in fertilizers, pesticides, and irrigation methods and has played an important role in increasing China's agricultural production.

In defense, China has made efforts to modernize its armed forces. It has developed nuclear weapons (including nuclear bombs and missiles) and has equipped its air force with high performance jet fighters.

Population control One obstacle to China's economic growth has been its huge population. Providing food and housing for a billion people can absorb so much land and labor that little is left for anything else. To overcome this problem, China's Communist government has tried to discourage people from having many children. Married couples in China's cities are permitted to have just one child without penalty, while those in rural areas are permitted to have two children. If they have more, they pay a penalty in the form of reduced income, a less desirable job, or poorer housing. There is also the threat of forced abortions. So far, the policy has worked to slow China's population growth.

F. CHINA IN THE GLOBAL CONTEXT

As soon as the People's Republic of China was established in 1949, it became involved in the cold war in international affairs.

Relations with Russia China's relations with its northern neighbor, the Soviet Union, underwent a complete reversal during the cold war. Shortly after coming to power, Mao signed a treaty of friendship with the Soviets. For years, China received a large amount of Soviet economic and military aid. Moreover, the Chinese adopted many Soviet methods of organizing a state-run economy. Through the 1950s, the two largest Communist nations—the Soviet Union and China—seemed to be natural allies.

In the 1960s, however, signs of strain and even hostility developed between them. Mao began to denounce the approach to communism taken by Soviet leaders. He actively supported the spread of communism through war and revolution, while the Soviet Union emphasized *peaceful coexistence* (getting along with one's enemies). He rejected the idea that the Soviet Union should be the only leader of the Communist world. As a Chinese nationalist, Mao became suspicious of the Soviets' military buildup in Central Asia. On their part, the Soviets were alarmed by China's testing of nuclear weapons. The split between the Chinese and the Soviets finally led to open conflict in the form of border wars on China's northern boundary. A major war was avoided, but friction between the Communist powers continued.

Relations with the United States In 1949, U.S. leaders were not happy after learning that Mao's Communist army had won control over mainland China. The United States refused to recognize the Communist government as legitimate and maintained diplomatic relations only with Chiang Kai-shek's government on Taiwan. This policy of U.S. hostility toward Communist China continued for more than 20 years.

During the 1950s, there was a serious danger of war breaking out directly between China and the United States. As part of a UN effort in the Korean War (1950–1953), U.S. troops fought against both North Korean and Chinese forces (discussed on pages 295–296). At one point during the conflict, U.S. General Douglas MacArthur proposed bombing targets in China, but President Harry Truman refused to be drawn into a wider war against China and possibly the Soviet Union. Thus, the Korean War continued with heavy casualties on both sides until a cease-fire was arranged in 1953. In another Asian war (in Vietnam in the 1960s and early 1970s), China gave aid to the North Vietnamese. At the same time, the United States sent troops to fight on the side of the South Vietnamese government.

A dramatic change in U.S.-Chinese relations occurred in 1972 when President Richard Nixon traveled to Beijing to meet with Mao and other Communist leaders. The American and Chinese leaders agreed to open up cultural and trade relations between their countries. Finally in 1979, the United States established full diplomatic relations with the government of the People's Republic of China.

Mao's successor, Deng Xiaoping, was particularly interested in improving relations with the United States. He hoped that U.S.-Chinese trade would contribute to his goal of strengthening China's economy. As part of his strategy, Deng encouraged thousands of Chinese students to attend colleges and universities in the United States. He hoped that, upon their return to China, these students would apply their knowledge to help China modernize.

Student protests in Tiananmen Square   Having learned about Western democracies, students in China began to demand greater individual freedom and democracy in their own country. But Deng's government, while encouraging a certain amount of free enterprise in the marketplace, would not allow free expression of political ideas. The Communist leadership was determined to maintain its power and perceived the student movement as a threat. It also feared that an open political system would lead to civil war.

The conflict between the government and the students came to a tragic conclusion in 1989. Thousands of students gathered in Tiananmen Square in Beijing. For several days, they made speeches proposing democratic changes in the political system. Many workers joined the demonstrations. The government responded by sending in tanks and soldiers to fire upon the unarmed demonstrators. As a result, large numbers of protesters were killed and wounded. Many others were arrested, placed on trial, and imprisoned.

Viewed on television by millions of people around the world, the "Tiananmen Square Massacre" had a negative effect on China's relations with the United States. Protesting the killings, the United States temporarily suspended trade with China. Eventually, however, economic relations between the two countries were restored. Leading intellectuals and other Chinese continue the demands for democracy.

China's role in the United Nations   A major international dispute of the cold war era involved China's membership in the United Nations. Since its founding in 1945, the United Nations had granted China a permanent seat on the powerful UN Security Council. However, when China became Communist in 1949 and the Nationalists fled to Taiwan, a question arose as to which of the two competing governments would be allowed UN membership. Would it be Chiang Kai-shek's Nationalist government in Taiwan or Mao Zedong's Communist government in Beijing? For years, the United States used its influence in the United Nations to keep Taiwan's anti-Communist government as the UN member.

In 1971, however, a majority of UN members voted to admit representatives from the People's Republic of China rather than from Taiwan. Ever since, China's Communist regime has been a permanent member of the UN Security Council.

The status of Taiwan and Hong Kong The islands of Taiwan and Hong Kong, located off the Chinese coast, are currently outside the control of the People's Republic of China. The larger island, Taiwan, is still claimed by the Communist government as a part of China. In practical terms, however, China recognizes that a major war would have to be fought to take possession of Taiwan. Currently, there appears to be little danger that Taiwan will lose its independence as a separate nation.

In contrast, Hong Kong, one of the last imperialist holdings of Great Britain, will soon change its status. It had been governed as a British colony ever since British victory in the Opium War in 1842. According to a British-Chinese treaty signed in the mid-1980s, Hong Kong will be turned over to the People's Republic of China in 1997. However, it will be allowed to keep its booming capitalist economy for the following 50 years. Many residents of Hong Kong are nervous about the prospect of their wealthy city falling under Communist rule. They fear that Hong Kong will lose the democratic institutions developed under British rule.

G. TAIWAN: AN ECONOMIC SUCCESS STORY

In 1949, two million Chinese fled mainland China and sought safety from the Communist army on the island of Taiwan. The island is mountainous, and only one-quarter of its land can be cultivated. Even so, the newcomers to the island were able to adapt successfully and build an economy that today is one of the strongest and fastest growing in the world.

Taiwan is one of several Asian nations that have recently made impressive gains in their standard of living. It is considered one of the four East Asian "tigers"—the others being Hong Kong, Singapore, and South Korea. Taiwan's success, like that of the other economic "tigers," is based upon its ability to manufacture low-priced but high-quality goods for export and sale on the world market. These include such consumer goods as clothing, electronics, and processed foods. As a result of their country's booming economy, the Taiwanese people have improved their own economic well-being. For example, they have 200 times as many televisions and cars as they had 20 years ago.

In Review

The following questions refer to Section IV (China: Contemporary Society).

1. *Key terms:* Define or identify each of the following:

   Great Leap   Cultural Revolution   peaceful coexistence
     Forward   Four Modernizations   Tiananmen Square
   commune

2. Give evidence in support of this statement: "Mao's government was an example of a totalitarian state."

3. Explain how Deng Xiaoping's policies differed from those of Mao.

4. *Critical thinking:* Do you think that the Chinese people now believe that communism is an undesirable system? Explain your answer and give specific evidence to support your view.

TEST YOURSELF

Multiple-Choice Questions on China

Level 1

On a separate sheet of paper, write the number of the word or expression that, of those given, best completes each statement or answers each question.

1. Which feature of Chinese agriculture led to the development of the other three?   (1) growing rice and grains for their high food value   (2) constructing irrigation systems   (3) scarcity of fertile land   (4) intensive farming methods.

2. Which is the main reason for the heavy population concentration in the eastern regions of the People's Republic of China?   (1) The Chinese capital is located in the east.   (2) Most of China's fertile farmland is located in the east.   (3) Most of China's oil resources are located in the Yangtze River Valley.   (4) Overland trade with China's neighbors declined.

3. In traditional Chinese culture, which philosophy or religion had the greatest influence on the development of social order and political organization?   (1) Taoism   (2) Buddhism   (3) Confucianism   (4) Marxism.

4. Confucianism emphasizes the idea that   (1) government should own the means of production   (2) economic success is more desirable

than knowledge and learning   (3) each person has an important responsibility to family and society   (4) an individual's personal goals are more important than the goals of the group.

5. In ancient China, one effect on government of the teachings of Confucius was the high status of   (1) soldiers   (2) merchants   (3) farmers   (4) scholars.

6. "By nature men are pretty much alike; it is learning and practice that set them apart."—Confucius.

This statement suggests that significant human differences in the world are mostly due to differences in   (1) physical appearance   (2) inherited characteristics   (3) emotions   (4) culture.

7. A goal common of Confucianism, Taoism, and Buddhism is to   (1) establish peace and harmony   (2) provide the basis for democratic government   (3) limit the power of the emperors   (4) promote individual artistic creativity.

8. During the centuries of dynastic rule, the Chinese rejected other cultures as inferior to their own. This situation illustrates the concept of   (1) ethnocentrism   (2) imperialism   (3) social mobility   (4) cultural diffusion.

9. During the 19th century, Western nations were able to gain control over parts of China mainly because   (1) the Chinese had a strong tradition of nonviolence   (2) China lacked the military technology needed to stop these ventures   (3) China was promised aid to its industries   (4) the Chinese lacked a strong cultural identity.

Base your answers to questions 10 and 11 on the cartoon below and on your knowledge of social studies.

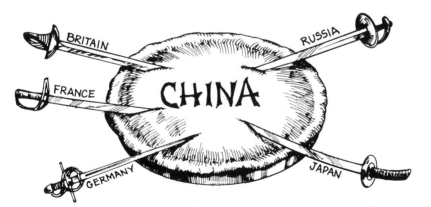

10. The cartoon depicts the   (1) ethnocentrism of the Chinese during the Manchu Ch'ing dynasty of the 17th century   (2) separation of China into spheres of influence by 19th-century imperialist nations   (3) military aid given to Chinese revolutionaries by the Soviet Union during the 1940s   (4) favored trading-partner status awarded to China by many Western European countries in the 1980s.

11. The situation depicted in the cartoon was brought about by (1) economic agreements with Western nations (2) the low level of cultural and economic development in China throughout its history (3) the military weakness of China and the European desire for expansion (4) the alliance of the Soviet Union with the Chinese Communists and the aid given to the Nationalists by Western Europe.

12. Both the Taiping Rebellion and the Boxer Rebellion attempted to rid China of (1) Mongol control (2) illegal drug traffic (3) Communist influence (4) foreign domination.

13. Which segment of Chinese society gave the most support to the Communists during the 1930s and 1940s? (1) peasants (2) religious leaders (3) landowners (4) bureaucrats.

14. The Chinese Communists won popular support during the 1930s and 1940s partly because they (1) gave merchants leadership positions in the Communist party (2) accepted advanced military technology from Western nations (3) emphasized the needs of the rural peasant population (4) cooperated with the Japanese.

15. In China, the terms "Long March," "Little Red Book," and "Great Leap Forward" are most closely associated with the (1) economic policies of the Kuomintang (2) expulsion of foreigners during the Boxer Rebellion (3) foreign policy under Deng Xiaoping (4) leadership of Mao Zedong.

16. In 1958, China's Great Leap Forward called for programs designed to (1) break up the communal farm system (2) slow down industrial expansion and devote more resources to agricultural growth (3) restore a capitalist economic system (4) increase both industrial and agricultural production.

Base your answers to questions 17 through 19 on the passage below and on your knowledge of social studies.

> When I was young, the Chairman promised us all food. He promised that we would never go hungry again or be without work. My family was led to a village where we became members of a production team. We worked hard, long hours but we were fed every day. The commune prospered at first, but soon people did not meet their quotas and we did not increase our production. We all received the same amount of rice; it didn't matter how much work we did.
>
> With the new Chairman, things are different in our village. The government has given us plots of land to work as our own, though I still put in time as a commune worker. We can now keep the amount we produce above the quota set by the government. This has made most of us work harder and the government quotas are being met for the first time in years.

17. The Chairman mentioned in the first paragraph was most likely (1) Sun Yat-sen (2) Deng Xiaoping (3) Chiang Kai-shek (4) Mao Zedong.

18. According to the first paragraph, which is the most likely reason that agricultural production quotas were not met? (1) The workers felt threatened by the government. (2) The workers had little to gain by working hard. (3) The workers were hungry and could not work. (4) The workers were young and inexperienced.

19. Under the new Chairman, mentioned in the second paragraph, which economic idea was introduced to increase production? (1) scarcity (2) tax reform (3) free enterprise (4) collectivism.

20. During the 1980s, a major goal of China was to (1) accelerate economic growth (2) encourage the growth of traditional religions (3) establish a federal system of government (4) protect individual liberties.

21. Which statement about the economy of China in the 1980s and 1990s is most accurate? (1) China surpassed the United States in steel production. (2) China's economy slowed down because of a lack of natural resources. (3) China increased its industrial capacity and foreign trade. (4) China's economy suffered from overproduction of consumer goods.

22. A major reason for China's growing economic success is that (1) the Chinese government is permitting a certain amount of free enterprise (2) there was a return to the policies of Mao Zedong (3) the Communist government was overthrown and replaced by a democratic government (4) the Chinese government is discouraging the growth of small businesses.

23. In China, a major result of Deng Xiaoping's policies has been (1) an improved standard of living for many people (2) an increase in totalitarian control (3) a strengthening of the landlord system (4) a greater respect for Confucian scholars.

24. Which statement best describes the status of women in traditional China? (1) Women were encouraged to obtain an education. (2) Women were expected to run for political office. (3) Women were considered inferior. (4) Women were encouraged to work outside the home.

25. Which fact about China has been a cause of the other three? (1) The present economy of China has trouble providing for all the needs of the people. (2) The Chinese government has set limits on the number of children married couples may have. (3) Chinese cities have a severe shortage of housing. (4) For most of the 20th century, China's population grew rapidly.

Level 2

26. Most of China's population settled (1) in deserts (2) in the mountains (3) in river valleys (4) within rain forests.

27. In China, people in different regions wear different types of clothing and eat different types of food. This is most likely the result of (1) orders from the government (2) European imperialism (3) Chinese nationalism (4) geography and climate.

28. Which statement best explains why most of the population of China lives in the eastern part of the nation? (1) The best agricultural land is in the east. (2) The largest forests are in the east. (3) The best protection against military attack is in the east. (4) The largest oil deposits are in the east.

29. The philosophy of Confucius emphasizes (1) respect for elders (2) class warfare (3) a military life (4) owning land.

30. Before the 20th century, China was ruled by (1) dynasties (2) democratic governments (3) Communists (4) religious leaders.

31. In the 1800s, China became a victim of foreign imperialism because it was (1) more industrialized than the European countries (2) known for its great literature and art (3) located close to Europe (4) a militarily weak nation.

32. The Boxer Rebellion was an attempt to (1) end poverty in China (2) make China democratic (3) increase trade between China and Europe (4) drive foreigners out of China.

33. From 1912 to 1950, China's political history was characterized by (1) rule by emperors (2) democratic rule (3) violent conflicts (4) imperialist control by foreign powers.

34. In the 1930s and 1940s, many Chinese peasants supported the Communists because the Communists promised (1) land reform (2) peace with Japan (3) the restoration of the Manchu dynasty (4) aid from industrialized countries.

35. The ideas of Confucius and Mao Zedong both emphasized (1) industry rather than agriculture (2) competition rather than cooperation (3) the group rather than the individual (4) religious values rather than economic profits.

36. In China, the goal of the Cultural Revolution was to (1) establish China's military superiority in Asia (2) increase industrial and agricultural production (3) end Manchu rule (4) increase the emphasis on the teachings of Mao Zedong.

37. A major problem for China has been (1) the size of its population (2) a lack of mineral resources (3) a lack of workers (4) too much rainfall.

38. In the second half of the 20th century, China's political leaders have been especially concerned with (1) increasing the population density in the cities (2) controlling population growth (3) returning to traditional values (4) establishing colonies throughout Asia.

39. During the 1980s, China was successful in (1) increasing its industrial production (2) gaining colonies throughout Asia (3) remaining isolated from the rest of the world (4) ending Communist rule.

40. During the 1980s and 1990s, China has attempted to (1) increase trade with the West (2) return to isolationism (3) develop democratic institutions (4) end all birth control practices.

Essay Questions on China

Level 1

1. Every significant event has causes and results. Some significant events in China's history are listed below.

Events
The Opium War (1839–1842)
The Boxer Rebellion (1899–1900)
Manchu dynasty overthrown (1911)
Communists defeat Nationalists (1949)
The Great Leap Forward (1950s)
The Cultural Revolution (1960s)
Tiananmen Square demonstrations (1989)

Select *three* of the events listed above. For each event chosen:

- Discuss one major cause of the event.
- Discuss one major result of the event.

2. Ideas, policies, and actions adopted by leaders affect their people in many ways. Some important individuals in China's history are listed below.

Leaders
Confucius
Sun Yat-sen
Chiang Kai-shek
Mao Zedong
Deng Xiaoping

Select *three* of the leaders listed above. For each of the leaders chosen:

- Explain one basic idea, policy, or action.
- Describe one major change brought about by the individual's idea, policy, or action.

Level 2

3. The statements below describe certain features of the geography and climate of China.

Features
The major rivers of China form fertile valleys in the eastern part of the country.
Western and northern China consist of mountainous terrain and deserts.
Monsoons bring heavy rainfall to southeastern China.

A. State one specific effect for each of the features described in the statements above.

B. Base your answer to Part B on your answer to Part A. However, additional information may be included. Write an essay discussing the effects of specific geographic features on the development of China. Begin your essay with this topic sentence:

Geography has affected the development of China.

4. The people of China have faced a number of problems throughout their history. Some of these problems are listed below.

Problems
Overpopulation
Foreign domination
Internal conflicts
Dictatorship

A. Select *three* of the problems listed. For each problem selected, state one cause and one result.

B. Base your answer to Part B on your answer to Part A. However, additional information may be included. Write an essay discussing the causes and results of China's problems. Begin your essay with this topic sentence:

China has faced many problems throughout its history.

V. Japan: Geography

Japan is an *archipelago*—a group of many islands. It consists of four main islands and many other smaller ones. Located on the largest island, Honshu, is Japan's capital, Tokyo (the fourth largest city in the world).

A. THE EFFECTS OF JAPAN'S LOCATION

Japan is surrounded by water—the Pacific Ocean to the east and the Sea of Japan to the west. Notice on the map on page 243 that southern Japan lies just 100 miles from the southern part of the Korean peninsula. About 700 miles of sea separate southern Japan from the east coast of China. Northern Japan is just a few hundred miles from a section of the Russian coast.

Because Japan is separated by water from the East Asian mainland, it has been able to maintain its political and cultural independence. In addition, because Japan is fairly near both Korea and China, it has always been in a position to borrow ideas and technologies from civilizations on the mainland.

In past centuries, Japan's government sometimes chose to limit its contacts with the outside world. Its separateness as an island country allowed it to adopt such a policy. In more recent times, however, Japan has recognized that it cannot afford to be isolated. Its economic existence depends heavily on world trade and world finance.

FOOD FROM THE SEA: Japan leads the world in the size of its fishing industry. How is the importance of fishing for Japan explained by aspects of Japan's geography?

B. THE EFFECTS OF JAPAN'S TOPOGRAPHY

Over three-quarters of the land area of Japan is mountainous. This fact creates three problems for the Japanese. (1) Their buildings and transportation networks are sometimes threatened by volcanic eruptions and earthquakes. (2) Only a small percentage of land is *arable* (suitable for farming). (3) The lack of available living space causes people to crowd together in densely populated urban areas.

The Japanese have attempted to overcome the scarcity of farmland in four ways. First, throughout their history they have harvested the fish of the surrounding seas. Today, Japan is one of the major fishing nations of the world. Second, the Japanese have successfully cultivated mountainous areas, using the technique of terraced farming. Along the sides of the mountains, farmers cut level patches of land, or terraces, for growing crops. Third, using intensive farming methods, the Japanese have made effective use of every available acre of level land. Fourth, they currently make up for any shortages by importing food from other countries.

Adjusting to the high density of their population, the Japanese typically build small homes on narrow plots of land or occupy small apartments in high-rise buildings in the cities. Also, the scarcity of good land forces them to be extremely efficient producers of both agricultural and industrial goods.

The rivers of Japan, unlike the major rivers of China, are too short and contain too many rapids to be useful for transportation. Their main use is to help irrigate the rice paddies.

C. THE EFFECTS OF CLIMATE AND NATURAL DISASTERS

The surrounding seas help to give much of Japan a temperate climate. On the central island of Honshu, mildly warm summers are followed by mildly cool winters. More extreme temperatures and seasons occur at either end of the country: hot summers on the southernmost island, cold winters on the northernmost island. It often rains in Japan, a fact that encourages the cultivation of rice, Japan's major crop.

Destructive forces of nature are a major danger in Japan. Each year, more than a thousand earthquake tremors shake the islands. Any one of Japan's 30 active volcanoes could erupt at any time. Furthermore, the islands are subject to vicious winds known as *typhoons*. (A typhoon is a large system of winds that rotates around a center.) Finally, Japan's shores are sometimes pounded by huge *tidal waves* caused by earthquake activity.

Forces of nature have played an important role in the Japanese religion of *Shintoism*. People of ancient Japan were struck with awe in witnessing the violent fury of nature—a volcano erupting, an earthquake shaking, a typhoon blowing, or a tidal wave slamming into the shore. The Shinto religion was a response to the violence of nature— and also to its beauty. Shintoism's central belief is that spirits inhabit and control natural objects such as mountains, rivers, and winds. Shinto believers pray to these spirits. Shintoism emphasizes respect for ancestors and loyalty to family and nation. It serves as a unifying force in Japanese life.

D. THE EFFECTS OF RESOURCE SHORTAGES

The Japanese people have always had to devise creative solutions to overcome their most serious problem—a scarcity of resources. Scarcity of land for farming has caused the Japanese to become efficient producers of food crops, such as rice, and to eat fish instead of beef for protein. (Not many cattle are raised in Japan, since cattle grazing demands much land.)

Although it lacks such raw materials as oil and iron, Japan has managed to become one of the major industrial nations of the modern world. It has done so by devising ways to make finished goods efficiently. Japan has sold these goods as exports and has imported oil, iron, and other needed raw materials. In short, modern Japan has achieved a high standard of living because its advanced technology and efficiently produced goods have been exchanged for the resources it has needed.

VI. Japan: Early History

Unlike the early civilizations of China, India, Egypt, and Mesopotamia, the civilization of Japan did *not* originate in a broad and fertile river valley. As late as 200 B.C., while the Chinese were building the Great Wall, the Japanese were still a hunting people who were only beginning to learn to farm. They acquired their civilization largely by learning all that they could from the much older civilization of nearby China.

A. BORROWING CULTURAL WAYS FROM ABROAD

More than once in Japan's history, government leaders have consciously chosen to adopt the advanced ways of a foreign culture.

Learning from China In the 7th century A.D. (the 600s), a Japanese prince decided that the time had come to learn the civilized ways of the empire of China. The prince ordered trusted members of his court to go to China for the purpose of mastering all aspects of Chinese civilization. They studied its arts, religions, philosophies, government, and written language. Returning to Japan, the travelers taught members of Japan's leading families how to write and paint in the Chinese manner. Eventually, the Japanese developed their own written characters, which were similar in style to those of China.

Learning about Buddhism A major religion also came to Japan from abroad. You have read how Buddhism had originated in India and then spread to China. This religion also entered Korea and from there was introduced into Japan. Just as the Chinese had modified Buddhism to suit their own culture, the Japanese did the same. Elements of Japan's native religion, Shintoism, affected the imported religion of Buddhism. Buddhist temples and Shinto shrines coexisted and were located throughout the Japanese archipelago.

B. THE FEUDAL PERIOD (1185–1600)

A curious fact of history is that at one time Japanese society and the kingdoms of medieval Europe were organized in much the same way. In the 1200s and 1300s, the social and economic system in both areas was feudalism. (Cultural diffusion cannot account for this coincidence, since during this era there was no contact between Japan and Europe.)

SAMURAI'S SUIT OF ARMOR: The samurai was covered from head to foot in armor that gave protection while also allowing maximum freedom of movement. What was the samurai's role in medieval Japanese society?

In Japan, as in Europe, *feudalism* was a system by which lords (large landowners) obtained military services from those who had pledged loyalty to them. In other words, a feudal lord could raise an army by calling together warriors who owed allegiance to him. In Europe, such warriors were called knights; in Japan, they were called *samurai*. Acting as military commanders, the feudal lords would lead their samurai armies into battle. A characteristic of Japanese feudalism was that all the people knew their place in a rigid class system. The peasants (who owned no land) were at the bottom of society, the samurai in the middle, and the feudal lords at the top. (Feudalism in Western Europe is discussed in Chapter 7.)

The samurai made up a paid military caste. They followed a strict code of ideal warrior behavior. According to their code of *Bushido*, "the way of the warrior," the samurai were expected to defend their lords and each other to the death. Every samurai's chief possession was his sword, which hung at his side. The samurai code helped foster a militaristic tradition in Japanese society.

Japan's most powerful feudal lords were in charge of large regions. The lord who was appointed to govern the country as a whole was known as the *shogun*. During the feudal period (1185–1600), the emperor had less real power than the shogun, who was always the leader of the strongest family or clan in Japan. After he had appointed the shogun to run the government, the emperor did little more than serve as a religious leader and a symbol of Japanese unity. In short, during the feudal period, power was (1) based on class relationships and (2) centered in a military ruler, the shogun.

C. JAPANESE APPROACH TO NATURE AND THE ARTS

In feudal Japan, a distinctive culture developed. The various arts that flourished in the feudal period expressed the Shintoist belief that nature was divine and should be revered. The same arts are still an important part of Japanese culture.

The Japanese tea ceremony, for example, an elaborate ritual involving the preparing and serving of tea, is meant to put people in touch with the inner spirit. Painted screens and ink drawings are other traditional arts, both of which use nature as subjects. The art of *origami* involves the folding of paper into the shape of flowers, animal figures, and other natural objects. Poets who write *haiku*, a traditional form of Japanese unrhymed poetry, look to nature for their inspiration. A Japanese garden is a work of art that is meant to inspire viewers of its rocks, streams, and plants to meditate deeply.

In Review

The following questions refer to Sections V (Japan: Geography) and VI (Japan: Early History).

1. *Key terms:* Define or identify each of the following:

typhoon	Shintoism	samurai
tidal wave	feudalism	shogun

2. Give *two* examples of how Japan's geography has affected its history and culture.

3. Explain the role played by cultural diffusion in Japan's early history.

4. *Critical thinking:* "The Japanese people turned a handicap into an advantage." (a) What is Japan's chief geographic handicap? (b) How have the Japanese successfully adapted to this handicap?

VII. Japan: The Dynamics of Change

Beginning in the 1600s, powerful shoguns brought peace and unity to Japan by putting an end to a series of wars between rival clans. During this time, every shogun had the power of a military dictator. Although the position of emperor was kept, he remained in the background. His status and prestige were used, however, to support the policies of the shogun.

Shoguns looked with suspicion upon foreigners from Europe, who in the early 1600s arrived in Japan in increasing numbers. Fearing aggression from these "foreign devils," one shogun ordered the massacre of Christian missionaries and their Japanese converts and forbade Europeans from trading with Japan. Although there were no more massacres, other shoguns also adopted antiforeign and isolationist policies. For more than 200 years, Japan was closed to world trade.

A. COMMODORE PERRY AND THE OPENING OF JAPAN

In 1853, Commodore Matthew Perry of the U.S. Navy led an expedition to Japan. His purpose was to convince Japanese leaders to open their ports to U.S. trade. Perry's ships shot off their cannons, and members of the expedition displayed goods made by U.S. industrial technology. Japanese leaders, including the shogun, soon became convinced that their country could not long defend itself in the modern world unless it began to change its traditional ways. As a result of Perry's visit, Japan in 1854 opened its ports to trade with the United States and later with other Western nations.

B. MEIJI RESTORATION (1868–1912)

Instead of strengthening the shogun's power, the new trade with the West caused his downfall. Powerful lords accused the shogun of giving in to the demands of foreigners. In 1868, the lords managed to overthrow the shogun and declare Emperor Meiji the true head of government. In fact, the leaders of this bloodless revolt now shared power with the emperor. They called their new regime the Meiji Restoration.

Industrial progress The new regime adopted the goal of quickly catching up with the industrial progress of the Europeans and the Americans. Remember that more than a thousand years earlier, a Japanese prince of the 7th century had decided to catch up to the advanced civilization of China. Now the ruling group of the Meiji Restoration was determined to master the advanced technologies of the West. Japanese students were sent abroad to learn about Western factories, railroads, and communications systems. What they learned

COMMODORE PERRY: This is a Japanese artist's depiction of the chief U.S. naval officer who visited Japan in 1853. How did Commodore Perry change Japan's relationship with the West?

was rapidly put into practice in Japan. Railroads were built and telegraph systems installed. Modern Japanese factories were soon turning out great quantities of textiles and other manufactured goods for sale to foreign markets.

Leading the effort to industrialize Japan were the wealthy families that controlled Japan's largest banks and industries. Powerful combinations of banks or industries were known as the *zaibatsu*. Many of them had close ties to the political leaders who had brought about the Meiji Restoration. Together the Japanese industrialists and the high officials close to the emperor were the nation's new ruling class.

Revolutionary changes The industrialization of Japan was only one of the ways in which the Meiji leaders imitated the West. Other changes in society and politics were just as revolutionary.

1. Politically, the government became highly centralized. It took power away from local lords and governments. Tokyo replaced Kyoto as Japan's capital. A written constitution was adopted in 1889. It provided for an elected *Diet* (parliament) similar to the lawmaking bodies in Western Europe. The government was not truly democratic, however, since the hereditary emperor had far greater power than the elected legislature. For example, the constitution gave to the emperor the power to command the army and navy, make war and peace, and dissolve the lower house of the legislature at will.

2. *Militarily, a new Japanese army and navy were created.* They were based on the German model, which was considered the best in Europe at the time. All young Japanese men would now be subject to a military draft. Since there would no longer be a separate role for the samurai, many of them rioted against the new order.

3. *Socially, remnants of feudalism were abolished.* The great lords yielded control of their lands to the government. In return, they and their families were promised permanent seats in the upper house of Japan's new Diet. The government allowed peasants to own their own land and become independent farmers. To make economic opportunities more widely available to the middle and lower classes, the government established a public education system for all. From then on in Japan, a person's future would depend much more on ability and skill than on class or caste.

C. JAPANESE EXPANSION AND WORLD WAR II

Japanese leaders feared that a lack of natural resources might prevent Japan from building a strong industrial economy. As they well knew, Japan had relatively small amounts of oil, coal, and iron ore. To obtain these needed raw materials as well as an expanded food supply, Japan's government launched a plan to invade weaker neighbors and take over their mineral-rich lands. In doing so, Japan was following the example of European imperialists.

Japan's expansion in Asia began in 1894 with an attack on China. After a brief but decisive war, Japan gained control of the Chinese island of Taiwan, which was renamed "Formosa." Next, Japan went to war with Russia and won another impressive victory. As a result of the Russo-Japanese War of 1904–1905, Japan gained control of Korea and in 1910 officially declared Korea to be Japanese territory. Japan also received from Russia the southern half of Sakhalin Island and Russia's sphere of influence in southern Manchuria (in China).

Japan entered World War I in 1914 as an ally of Great Britain. It took advantage of China's military weakness to occupy the German-held Shantung Peninsula, on China's east coast. It also obtained German-held islands in the Pacific.

Rise of the militarists   In Japan in the 1920s, a bitter conflict developed between two groups concerning Japan's foreign policy goals. One group was made up of politicians in the legislature who wanted Japan to remain at peace with the West and who opposed a policy of military expansion. Another group was made up of young army officers who were extreme nationalists. They were frustrated by the government's failure to act more aggressively in Asia.

Two disasters played into the hands of the militarists. In 1923, a terrible earthquake destroyed much of Tokyo and Yokohama, killing about 143,000 people. Then in the 1930s, the entire industrial world was in a severe economic crisis, the Great Depression. Both disasters, especially the economic collapse, caused extreme hardship in Japan. In troubled times, many people tend to seek quick and dramatic solutions to their society's problems. The Japanese militarists' criticism of government policy and demands for aggressive action had much wider appeal in the troubled and depressed decade of the 1930s.

Invasion of China   Anxious to demonstrate Japan's military power, Japanese army officers began to act on their own. In 1931, they used a small incident in Manchuria as an excuse to start a war with China over that territory. The government in Tokyo felt obliged to back the army, which quickly succeeded in occupying Manchuria. Other nations of the world viewed this act as aggression and as a threat to world peace. The League of Nations condemned Japan for its invasion of Manchuria. Despite this condemnation, Japan remained in control there, renamed the area "Manchukuo," and established a puppet government.

By 1937, Japan's military had gained considerable power within the government. Thus, when the Japanese army attacked eastern China, it quickly won the government's backing. From then until the end of World War II, the militarists would dominate the government.

World War II   Japan made plans to extend its control to the Philippines, Dutch East Indies (now Indonesia), and the mainland of Southeast Asia. It began to establish an empire in the Pacific known as the "Greater East Asia Co-Prosperity Sphere." In 1940, a year after war had broken out in Europe, Japan joined with Germany and Italy in a military alliance known as the Rome-Berlin-Tokyo Axis.

The United States now put pressure on Japan to stop its aggression. Declaring a trade embargo, President Franklin Roosevelt cut off shipments to Japan of U.S. gasoline, scrap iron, and steel. Anticipating that its conflict with the United States might eventually lead to war, Japan decided to strike the first blow. On December 7, 1941, hundreds of Japanese planes bombed a U.S. fleet anchored at Pearl Harbor in Hawaii. The surprise attack led the United States to declare war on Japan. Soon after, Japan's allies—Germany and Italy—declared war on the United States.

By 1942, Japan's powerful navy had gained control of many of the islands in the southern Pacific. Its armies occupied territories extending in a huge arc from Manchuria in the north to the Dutch East Indies in the south. French Indochina, Malaya, the Philippines, Burma, and Hong Kong, were all occupied by the Japanese. Then in a series of bloody battles (1942–1945), the United States and its allies forced the Japanese to retreat. The cost in lives in these battles was very high for both sides.

Toward the end of World War II, U.S. planes dropped two atomic bombs on Japan. One fell on the city of Hiroshima and the other, on the city of Nagasaki. These bombs were unlike anything the world had ever seen. The devastating destruction of these bombs and the loss of life caused Japan to surrender unconditionally in the summer of 1945.

D. THE OCCUPATION AND RECONSTRUCTION OF JAPAN (1945–1952)

After World War II, U.S. military forces occupied Japan and required the defeated nation to adopt a more democratic form of government. A new constitution adopted in 1947 replaced the earlier one of the Meiji period. According to the 1947 constitution:

- The Japanese people were to be the source of power for the government. (Formerly, all power had originated with the emperor.)
- The emperor was to serve only in a ceremonial role as a symbol of the nation.
- All Japanese adult citizens had the right to vote.
- Rival political parties would be free to compete in elections for seats in the Diet, the Japanese legislature.
- An independent court system was established.
- Japan would abolish its armed forces (except for small self-defense forces) and would pledge never to go to war again.

The postwar economy of Japan also underwent major reforms. The zaibatsu were broken up. This reform, however, did not last long, and the zaibatsu again became powerful. Large agricultural estates were broken up into smaller farms. Many landless farm workers received their own land. Aided by U.S. financial and technical assistance, Japan was able to rebuild and modernize its factories in a remarkably short time.

VIII. Japan: Contemporary Society

Today, Japan is one of the most prosperous and technologically advanced nations in the world. At the same time, it faces serious problems that are quite similar to the problems of past generations. One problem is economic: How can large numbers of people continue to support themselves in a country that has few of the natural resources needed for industrial growth? A second problem is cultural. Ever since

CROWDED SUBWAYS: At the rush hour in Tokyo, commuters are jammed into subway cars by white-gloved "pushers." What are some of the problems of urban living in Japan?

World War II, the Japanese have been influenced by Western fashions in dress, entertainment, and consumer goods. Some Japanese worry that a Western life-style may eventually erode their culture's traditional values.

A. CROWDED CITIES AND POPULATION CONTROL

Japan is no larger than California, yet its population of 125 million is half that of the United States. Also, because much of Japan is mountainous, the Japanese people are crowded together in the remainder of the country. In the cities, where three-fourths of the people live, housing shortages and overcrowding are facts of life. Japan's government encourages family planning, a policy which has had some success in slowing down the rate of population growth.

B. CHANGING STATUS OF WOMEN

Before World War II, the women of Japan were in an inferior position relative to that of men. Women had few rights. They could not vote. They could not work in industries or in the professions. They were limited to wearing a traditional style of dress. Most marriages were arranged. With few exceptions, admission to universities was reserved for men only.

As Japan became a more democratic nation after World War II, the second-class status of Japanese women began to change. Women received the right to vote. They began to work outside the home as both industrial workers and professionals. Adopting the Western approach to love and marriage, they began to marry according to their own choice of partner, rather than following their parents' choice. Western fashions became commonplace in the cities of Japan. Women as well as men were now admitted to universities. Such changes have not only given women more freedom but have also enabled them to make greater contributions to Japan's economy. Japanese women have rarely occupied leading roles in business or government. But this situation may be changing. In 1993, for the first time, a woman was selected to preside over the Japanese Diet.

C. CHANGES IN FAMILY LIFE

In past centuries, the Japanese family followed the Confucian model. Relations in the family were based upon the teachings of the Chinese philosopher Confucius. (Here we see another example of cultural diffusion.) Women of the family were expected to obey the men. The father was the head of the household. His authority extended down to each son, beginning with the eldest. The eldest son and his wife were expected to live with the son's parents. The role of younger women was limited to performing household chores. But older women (the grandmother and mother-in-law) had considerable authority managing the household. Strict loyalty to the family was expected of all family members.

After World War II, family patterns underwent significant change. Most families now live in large cities. The small size of city apartments makes it difficult for large, extended families to live together. In addition, as children become young adults, they commonly choose to live near their jobs and not with their parents. Moreover, as women enter the workplace, they tend to acquire some independence and freedom of choice at home.

Changes in the traditional family have had both positive and negative consequences. As parental authority weakens, children have a greater opportunity to make their own decisions. They can now pursue careers of their own choice instead of following their father's choice. Nevertheless, the modern family may no longer be able to provide all its members with the same degree of emotional and economic support as families had previously provided.

Despite the many changes in postwar Japan, family ties and bonds of loyalty are still strong.

D. ECONOMIC DEVELOPMENT

In losing World War II, Japan had to abandon its plan of relying upon military force to obtain needed raw materials. But the problem of scarce resources remained as serious as ever. How could Japan rebuild its industrial economy and pay for all the oil and iron it needed to sustain such an economy? Its main wartime foe, the United States, proved to be a generous and helpful occupying power. Wanting Japan to succeed under its new democratic constitution, the U.S. government gave millions of dollars in aid to help rebuild Japan's war-torn cities.

An "economic miracle"   Japan's new strategy for economic success was to manufacture industrial products and sell them abroad. Business leaders in Japan saw an opportunity to produce automobiles and electronic products more efficiently and at less cost than Western businesses could. They also hoped to build upon Japan's prewar success as a major producer of steel, machinery, and ships. In the 1950s and 1960s, it became clear to all observers that the Japanese strategy was working. An increasing number of products made in Japan were sold all over the world. New glass-and-steel office buildings, banks, and hotels replaced the bombed-out buildings of wartime. Japan's rapid rise to prosperity was referred to as an "economic miracle."

Factors in Japan's success   The success of Japan's businesses rests partly on their organizational and management techniques. In Japan, the factory or other workplace functions like an extended family. Once they join a company, Japanese workers can expect to be employed there for their entire working lives. In return for job security, workers develop a feeling of loyalty to the company. They actively seek ways to perform their jobs better and more efficiently. Suggestions for improvement may come from any employee, not just from managers. As a result, employees at all levels tend to maintain their self-esteem and sense of pride in their jobs.

A second factor in Japan's success has been its ability to adopt new and advanced technologies—"high tech," as it is sometimes called. Success in the production of electronics, computers, and automobiles depends partly upon research (making new discoveries in science and technology). It also depends upon devising techniques for applying those discoveries to the production of goods. Japan's ability to stay ahead in the high-tech race is based partly upon its successful educational system. Students are motivated to study hard to achieve top grades. In addition, Japanese businesses are willing to invest in long-range projects that will not bring immediate profits. Japan has also demonstrated an ability to borrow and build upon research carried out in other countries.

A third factor promoting success has been the close cooperation between Japan's government and major Japanese corporations. First, the government identifies areas of economic opportunity. Then it gives strong support to Japanese firms that attempt to expand their sales in these areas. Also, the government has shielded Japanese industries and agriculture from foreign competition by placing restrictions on goods imported into Japan. For example, for many years few American automobiles and little American rice could be found in Japan due to import barriers.

A fourth factor promoting economic prosperity has been the small amount of money that the Japanese government spends on national defense. The Japanese constitution prohibits Japan from having regular armed forces. Instead, ever since 1945, the United States has assumed responsibility for defending Japan from any aggressors.

ECONOMIC GROWTH OF JAPAN
(COMPARED TO GERMANY AND THE UNITED KINGDOM)

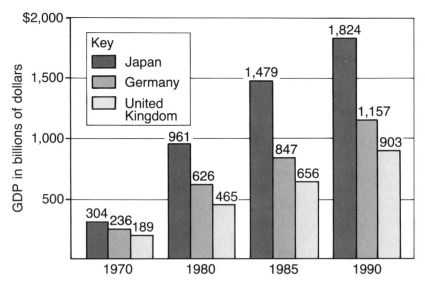

Trade and Investment To maintain its economic position, Japan must sell more of its own goods abroad than what it buys from other nations. In other words, it must have a *favorable balance of trade* (value of a country's exports exceeds the value of its imports). Year after year, Japan has achieved this goal. Its success in international trade caused the value of its currency, the Japanese yen, to rise in relation to other

DRAWING CONCLUSIONS FROM TABLES

Which nation of East Asia has the highest standard of living? Do the two Communist nations in this region have a generally higher or lower standard of living than their non-Communist neighbors? The table below helps us to make such comparisons.

Standard of Living in Five East Asian Countries

	Column 1 GDP per capita (dollars)	Column 2 TV sets per 1,000 people	Column 3 Passenger cars per 1,000 people	Column 4 Physicians per 10,000 people
China	360	125	1	15
Japan	19,100	555	30	17
S. Korea	6,300	111	45	10
N. Korea	960	11	NA*	27
Taiwan	8,790	313	125	11

*Not available

Studying the column heads The key to interpreting this table—or any table of numbers—is to pay close attention to the column heads. In this case, column 1 is labeled "GDP per capita (dollars)." (See the glossary for a definition of gross domestic product [GDP] per capita.) The word in parentheses, "dollars," tells you that the numbers in this column are to be read like this: GDP per capita in China: 360 *dollars*. As you look down the column, just say to yourself "dollars" for each number that you read.

Also notice that the other column heads read ". . . per 1,000 people" or ". . . per 10,000 people." Why do you suppose the statistics are given in these terms instead of as total quantities (so many million TV sets in Japan, for example)?

Questions

1. Which East Asian nation has (a) the highest GDP per capita; (b) the most passenger cars per 1,000 people and (c) the fewest physicians per 10,000 people?
2. Why would it be incorrect to conclude from the table that Taiwan has more passenger cars than Japan?
3. Does any one nation in the table exceed the others in all four categories?
4. Using information from the table, demonstrate that the standard of living of East Asia's Communist nations is generally above or below that of the region's non-Communist nations. Support your position with specific data.

currencies. In the 1980s, Japanese companies greatly increased their investments overseas. For example, they established automobile plants in the United States and purchased American real estate. Also, Japan granted large sums of financial aid to less industrialized nations to help them purchase Japanese goods. Japan's trade position and financial strength make Japan one of the world's economic superpowers.

Effects on Japanese society   The booming economy has had a profound effect on Japanese society. It has produced a large middle class with a high standard of living. As members of the middle class increase their incomes, they spend more on consumer goods, take vacations abroad, and develop a strong demand for Western products. Despite increased exposure to the West, the Japanese still maintain aspects of their traditional culture, such as Shintoism, the Japanese garden, Japanese style of homes, and reverence for the emperor. Their urban culture is modern but also distinctly Japanese.

E. JAPAN IN THE GLOBAL CONTEXT

The Japanese are well aware that their prosperity is based on world trade and the interdependence of nations. They depend on other countries for natural resources. Meanwhile, other countries depend on Japan for industrial products. To make up for its scarcity of iron ore and oil, Japan must import huge quantities of these resources. Japan must import much of its food, too. It is the world's largest importer of agricultural products (including wheat, corn, citrus fruits, and beef).

Relations with the United States   Japan's success in selling its goods on world markets has cut deeply into U.S. sales both at home and abroad. As a result, the United States has an unfavorable balance of trade with Japan. This has led to tensions between the two countries. Frustrated by unsuccessful attempts to sell certain U.S. goods to Japan, some American manufacturers have complained that the Japanese discriminate against foreigners trying to do business in their country. Ever since the 1970s, the U.S. government has put pressure on Japan to open up its markets to American goods. Some U.S. business and government leaders have called for increased tariffs on imports from Japan—a step that would have damaged Japan's economy. To avoid high U.S. tariffs, Japan has made some concessions in its trade practices.

Today, U.S. exports to Japan are increasing. American-made machinery, equipment, and other manufactured goods are now found more frequently in Japan. Even U.S. rice is now being sold in Japanese stores.

Relations with other nations The United States is by no means the only nation whose trade and defense policies are important to Japan. Its relations with various nations of Asia and Europe are also critical to Japanese hopes for continued economic growth in the 1990s.

1. *China and Korea*. Japan views China as a huge market for Japanese technology. Hoping to expand sales to the world's most populous nation, Japanese business firms have undertaken a number of joint economic ventures in China. China recognizes that its developing economy could benefit from Japan's advanced technology. At the same time, however, China also sees risks in opening up its economy to Japanese penetration. The Chinese have not forgotten the harsh treatment they received from Japanese occupying forces during the 1930s and 1940s.

The people of North and South Korea also remember the Japanese occupation of Korea (1910–1945) with bitterness. Nevertheless, Japan carries on an extensive trade with South Korea. In the post-cold war era, Japan aims to normalize relations with North Korea and expand its trade with that country.

2. *Southeast Asia*. Japan invests heavily in industrial enterprises in Thailand, Malaysia, and other nations of Southeast Asia. Here too, however, Japan's activities are viewed with distrust by people who remember Japanese military invasions during World War II.

3. *Russia*. Ever since the Russo-Japanese War of 1904–1905, Japan and Russia have regarded each other as potentially hostile powers. In recent years, these countries have been disputing control of the Kurile Islands, which stretch from northern Japan to Russian Siberia. The Soviets occupied these islands during World War II. Today, the Japanese would like to see them returned. This disagreement has held back significant Japanese financial aid to Russia.

Defense policy in the post-cold war era Japan was demilitarized after its defeat in World War II. Still in force is an article in the Japanese constitution of 1947 that forbids Japan from organizing an army and navy. During the cold war, Japan looked to the United States to provide military protection against possible attack from its Communist neighbors (China, North Korea, and the Soviet Union). But now that the cold war is over, Japan is under pressure to redefine its role in the international community. Its foreign policy in the 1990s involves seeking answers to the following questions:

- Should Japan be permitted to rearm in light of its aggressive foreign policies in the 1930s and early 1940s?
- Should Japan bear some of the costs of its own defense, costs that the United States has been largely bearing?

China and Japan in the 20th Century

	China	Japan
1900–1914	Boxer Rebellion challenges Western imperialism. Manchu dynasty falls; revolution led by Sun Yat-sen establishes a republican government.	Japan defeats Russia in Russo-Japanese War (1904–1905). Industrialization continues under Meiji leaders.
World War I (1914–1918)	Rival warlords divide China. One of the rival governments declares war against Germany, 1917.	Japan declares war against Germany, 1914; Japan seizes China's Shantung Peninsula.
1919–1936	Chiang Kai-shek and Kuomintang (Nationalist party) establish strong central government (1928). Civil war with Communists begins.	Military officers challenge Japan's civilian government. Great Depression weakens government's efforts to hold back militarists' influence. Japanese invade and occupy Manchuria (1931).
War in Asia and World War II (1937–1945)	Civil war suspended as Nationalists and Communists join forces to fight Japanese invaders. Japanese troops occupy eastern China. With help of U.S. military aid, Chiang's government survives the war.	Japanese forces invade eastern China (in 1937). They also conquer a vast area in Southeast Asia and the Pacific. Their attack on Pearl Harbor (1941) brings the United States into the war. Japan surrenders after

- Should Japanese forces take part in UN-sponsored military actions, such as the Persian Gulf War of 1991? (Japan had an interest in this war since most of its oil supplies come from the Middle East. Japan gave financial support to the allied war effort but sent no troops. Members of the Japanese Self-Defense Forces did participate in a large UN peacekeeping operation in Cambodia in 1993. The UN effort successfully organized free elections in that country.)

World War II (continued)		suffering a series of defeats and mass destruction from two atomic bombs.
Cold war, first phase (1945–1970)	Civil war resumes. Communists win. Nationalists under Chiang are forced to flee to Taiwan (1949). Mao Zedong's Communist government revolutionizes life in China by setting goals for economic development (Great Leap Forward) and encouraging violent political action (Cultural Revolution).	Japan, under U.S. occupation, adopts new, democratic constitution and demilitarizes the country. United States signs defense pact with Japan, promises aid in case of Soviet or Chinese attack. Japan rapidly rebuilds and by 1970 has achieved an "economic miracle."
Cold war, second phase (1971–1990)	U.S. President Richard Nixon meets with Mao in China, opening a new chapter in U.S.-Chinese relations. Following Mao's death (1976), Deng Xiaoping leads economic reform of China, allows some free enterprise, and invites foreign investments.	Japan enters period of booming economic growth; becomes a world leader in the manufacture of computers, automobiles, and other products. Government and industry cooperate to secure new markets for Japanese exports. United States accuses Japan of unfair trade practices, seeks solution to huge U.S.-Japanese trade deficit.

In Review

The following questions refer to Sections VII (Japan: The Dynamics of Change) and VIII (Japan: Contemporary Society).

1. *Key terms:* Identify each of the following:

Meiji Restoration Diet	zaibatsu "economic miracle"	Greater East Asia Co-Prosperity Sphere favorable balance of trade

2. State *four* ways in which the Meiji Restoration changed Japan.

3. Explain the significance of each of the following: (a) Commodore Matthew Perry's expedition in 1853, (b) the Japanese invasion of Manchuria in 1931, (c) the Japanese attack on Pearl Harbor in 1941, and (d) the Japanese constitution of 1947.

4. Provide *four* reasons for Japan's economic successes in the decades after World War II.

5. *Critical thinking:* "In the long run, Commodore Perry's success in 1854 led to the rise of Japan as an economic and military power." (a) How would you interpret this statement? (b) Do you agree with it? Explain your answer.

IX. Korea

Shaped like a large thumb, the peninsula of Korea is connected to the northeastern corner of China and points toward the southernmost island of Japan. Korea was one nation until the end of World War II. Then it became divided between a Communist North Korea and a non-Communist South Korea.

A. GEOGRAPHY

Korea's geography sets it apart from its powerful neighbors—China, Russia, and Japan. The peninsula is bordered by seas on three sides. Korea's northern border consists of two rivers—the Yalu and the Tumen—and a rugged mountain range. For many hundreds of years, the seas and mountains have helped Korea maintain its independence.

Landforms Running down the center of the Korean peninsula from north to south is a region of heavily forested mountains. On the western side of these mountains, Korean farmers grow crops of wheat (in the north) and rice (in the south). As in Japan, there is a scarcity of good farmland. In fact, only about one fifth of Korea is capable of being cultivated. These fertile lands are mainly in the coastal lowlands, where most Koreans live.

Korea's rivers are generally longer, deeper, and more useful than Japan's rivers. Several are deep enough to be navigated. Three of Korea's major cities—P'yŏngyang in North Korea and Seoul and Pusan in South Korea—are located on major rivers.

SEOUL, SOUTH KOREA: This busy city of about 11 million people is the capital of one of the "Four Tigers" of East Asia. What are the others? What do all four have in common?

Climate   North Korea's climate is considerably colder than that of South Korea. In the south, summers are warm and rainy. This climate enables rice to be grown as the main crop. In the north, crops of wheat, barley, and soybeans are better suited to a shorter growing season.

Up and down the peninsula, Korean agriculture depends on the seasonal monsoons that blow across East Asia. A summer monsoon brings the heaviest rainfall. The rice fields in the south receive more than twice as much rain as the wheat fields in the north.

Resources   While South Korea has the better climate for agriculture, North Korea is richer in mineral resources for industry. In the northern mountains, there are large deposits of coal, tungsten, iron ore, and magnesium. North Korea makes use of these resources in its factories. South Korea, on the other hand, must import most of its mineral ores. Even so, the south's industrial output is greater than that of North Korea, largely because South Korea's capitalist economy is more efficient and more modern than North Korea's Communist economy.

B. EARLY HISTORY

Korean civilization began later than China's but earlier than that of Japan. Koreans made the crucial transition from using stone tools to using bronze tools around 900 B.C.

Unification of the three kingdoms   For hundreds of years, the Korean peninsula was divided into three powerful kingdoms, which were often at war with one another. One of these kingdoms, Silla, finally attained supremacy over the others and brought all of Korea under its control in A.D. 676. Then in 935, after another power struggle among rival kingdoms, the peninsula was unified under a new ruling family—the Koryo dynasty.

In 1392, the Koryo dynasty was replaced by the Yi dynasty. For the next five centuries (until 1910), the Yi dynasty ruled Korea.

Culture   Like most civilizations, the early civilization of Korea was partly original and partly borrowed. The landowning aristocrats who formed the ruling class followed two religions that came from China. (These are examples of cultural diffusion.) They relied upon Confucianism for its ethical teachings. At the same time, they worshipped at Buddhist temples in hopes of attaining spiritual fulfillment. Even today, many Korean families mix their religions. One family member may be chiefly Buddhist while another living in the same household may be chiefly Confucianist.

Originally, Korea's system of writing was borrowed from China and consisted of thousands of characters. In the 1400s, however, Koreans devised an alphabet of just 24 characters—an alphabet that is still in use today. Koreans valued education and scholarship as much as the Chinese did. They too required their government officials to pass a competitive civil service examination based upon knowledge of the Confucian classics.

The Koreans were the first people in East Asia to invent a system of movable type for printing books. By this system, each letter of the alphabet was on a separate block and could be moved to make up different words. The Koreans were printing books by this method as early as 1234—more than 200 years before the process was first used in Europe.

Relations with China and Japan   Throughout much of its history, Korea feared three potential enemies: the empire of China, the Mongols to the north of China, and the empire of Japan. During Korea's Middle Ages (about 600 to 1500), the chief threat came from the Mongols. Since China also feared the Mongols, Korea usually regarded China as an ally. Korea maintained good relations with China by paying tribute to the Chinese emperor.

In the 1200s, the Mongols overwhelmed the Chinese defenders of the Great Wall, swept through China, and overthrew the Sung Dynasty. They then invaded Korea. The Koreans battled the Mongols off and on for 30 years. Eventually, they signed a peace treaty that gave the Mongols some privileges and power but kept Korea independent.

Some 350 years later, in the 1590s, the Koreans were twice challenged by invasion forces from Japan. Even Buddhist priests joined in the struggle to defeat the invaders. A great naval battle won by the

Koreans helped to drive off the attackers. Thus, Japan's first attempts to dominate Korea ended in defeat.

C. THE DYNAMICS OF CHANGE

The commercial ambitions of Europe presented the next major challenge to Korea's independence. To counter this threat, Korea's government adopted an isolationist policy similar to that of Japan. Beginning in the 1600s, it refused to permit merchants from any European nation to trade at a Korean port.

Korea under Japanese rule   In the late 1800s, Korea came under pressure from Japan, the United States, and the European powers to change its isolationist policy. Reluctantly, Korea's government signed a treaty of trade and friendship with Japan. Soon afterward, it also opened its ports to manufactured goods from the West.

Slow to adopt modern ways, Korea's government was poorly prepared to defend Korea from the imperialist ambitions of Japan. In 1894, Japan fought a brief but decisive war against China. As a major outcome of this war, China agreed to let Japan dominate Korea. (Traditionally, China had viewed Korea as belonging within its sphere of influence.) Japanese troops in Korea made sure that the Korean government followed Japan's overall policy. In 1910, Japan completed its takeover by deposing the Korean emperor and declaring Korea to be a part of Japan.

From 1910 to the end of World War II in 1945, Korea was under Japanese rule. The Japanese forced the Koreans to industrialize. Japan's rule was harsh and bitterly resented by the Korean people. But the factories built during this period helped Korea develop a modern economy.

Division of Korea   Japan lost control of Korea during the last few months of World War II. When the war ended, Soviet troops occupied the northern part of Korea while U.S. troops occupied the southern part. As a temporary measure, the Soviets and Americans agreed to recognize the 38th parallel (line of north latitude) as the dividing line between their areas of control. Then the Soviets helped a Communist government to take power in the north. A non-Communist government was formed in the south after UN-sponsored elections were held. Thus, two Koreas came into being: North Korea with its capital at P'yŏngyang and South Korea with its capital at Seoul. The dividing line between them remained the 38th parallel.

Korean War   In June 1950, North Korean troops began a massive invasion of South Korea. The United Nations denounced the invasion and authorized UN members to give military aid to South Korea. Many nations took part in the military expedition to rescue South Korea. The largest number of troops came from the United States.

UN armies under the command of U.S. General Douglas MacArthur at first succeeded in pushing back the North Korean offensive. After UN forces advanced deep into North Korean territory, Communist China's leader, Mao Zedong, intervened in the conflict by sending Chinese armies to the aid of the North Koreans. After intense fighting and heavy losses, the conflict became stalemated near the 38th parallel. By 1953, North and South Korea agreed to a cease-fire, which ended the fighting. However, no peace treaty was signed. U.S. troops still patrol the border between the two Koreas.

D. CONTEMPORARY SOCIETY

Since the war, the two Koreas have followed very different paths. North Korea remains a Communist country whose economy—like that of China—is controlled by the state. South Korea's economy—like that of Japan—is based upon free enterprise.

North Korea today A Communist dictator, Kim Il Sung, controlled North Korea's government from 1948 to 1994. Kim maintained a tight grip on every aspect of North Korea's political, economic, and social life. Children in North Korea's schools learned to speak of Kim as their "Great Leader" and one who could do no wrong.

Like other Communist leaders (Stalin in the Soviet Union and Mao in China), Kim set ambitious goals for industrializing his country. Drawing upon its rich mineral resources, North Korea's state-controlled industries did make considerable progress—though less so than did the booming industries of South Korea.

In the early 1990s, the United States and other nations were troubled by reports that North Korea was secretly manufacturing nuclear weapons. Kim's government refused to allow UN inspectors to determine whether or not the report was true. (North Korea was one of many nations that had signed a Nuclear Nonproliferation Treaty; signers of this treaty pledged to prevent the spread of nuclear weapons to nations that did not already possess them.) The U.S. government in 1993 urged an economic boycott of North Korea until such time that the North Koreans would cooperate with the UN inspectors.

South Korea today Until recently, there was little democracy in South Korea. While the government allowed elections, there was only one party and it had strong ties to the military. Thus, Syngman Rhee, South Korea's first president, controlled elections and suppressed opposition groups. The first election in South Korea in which two parties competed freely for votes took place in 1987. Since then, the government has become more democratic and respectful of human rights.

In recent decades, South Korea's economy has grown at a rapid rate. Along with Hong Kong, Singapore, and Taiwan, it is one of the "four tigers" of Asia—countries that have become major competitors in the world marketplace. South Korea's success, like that of Japan, is based upon (1) a highly educated and skilled labor force and (2) government policies that encourage the manufacturing of goods for export. South Korea has been able to produce steel more cheaply than either Japan or the United States. In the United States, many consumers have purchased South Korean automobiles and electronic goods. As a result of their country's economic growth, South Koreans have increased their average income sixfold in a 30-year period.

In Review

The following questions refer to Section IX: Korea.

1. *Key terms:* Define or identify each of the following:

   Koryo dynasty   P'yŏngyang   "four tigers"
   38th parallel   Seoul

2. Compare North and South Korea in terms of their (a) natural resources and (b) economic and political systems.

3. Describe Korea's relations before World War II with (a) China and (b) Japan.

4. *Critical thinking:* "The current division between North and South Korea is artificial, and therefore it is unlikely to last long." Evaluate this statement, explaining why you either agree or disagree with it.

TEST YOURSELF

Multiple-Choice Questions on Japan and Korea

Level 1

On a separate sheet of paper, write the number of the word or expression that, of those given, best completes each statement or answers each question.

1. Japan is made up of a chain of islands called (1) an archipelago (2) a peninsula (3) a delta (4) an atoll.

2. In Japan, which condition was the cause of the other three? (1) Most of the nation is mountainous with little arable land. (2) Farmland is cultivated intensively. (3) Japanese housing consists of high-rise apartments or small houses on small lots. (4) The sea is used as a major source of food.

3. Which statement best describes an effect that geography has had on Japan? (1) Japan's smooth coastline has prevented the development of a fishing industry. (2) Japan's large plains have made wheat growing a primary industry. (3) The lack of important natural resources has led Japan to depend on trade with other nations. (4) The location of Japan has encouraged great ethnic diversity within the nation.

4. Even though Japan has few natural resources, it has a high standard of living mainly because it has (1) developed technology that can be exchanged for the resources it needs (2) printed more money whenever living standards have started to decline (3) imported most manufactured goods (4) produced goods and services without obtaining natural resources.

5. Before Commodore Matthew Perry's expedition in 1853, Japan's major foreign influence was (1) Russia's need for warm-water ports (2) the introduction of advanced technology from the United States (3) France's quest for new colonies (4) China's religion, art, and writing.

6. One factor that accounted for Chinese influence on traditional Korean and Japanese cultures was the (1) continuous warfare among the countries (2) geographic locations of the countries (3) refusal of Western nations to trade with Japan and Korea (4) annexation of Japan and Korea into the Chinese empire.

7. Which characteristic is found in traditional Japanese society? (1) Each person is considered equal. (2) The rights of the individual are more important than those of the family. (3) Women are expected to be obedient to men. (4) Young people are free to choose their occupation.

8. Which was a characteristic of feudalism in Japan? (1) The middle class acquired more power than any other class did. (2) A unified nation was ruled by an absolute monarch. (3) The army encouraged strong nationalistic feelings among the people. (4) All the people knew their roles in a rigid class system.

9. In medieval Japan, the feudal system was dominated by (1) middle-class merchants (2) peasant farmers (3) radical revolutionaries (4) warrior aristocrats.

10. In Japanese history, what was the impact of the Meiji Restoration (1868–1912)? (1) Japan adopted an isolationist policy. (2) Contact with Western nations encouraged Japan to industrialize. (3) Chinese influence on Japanese literature and the arts was limited. (4) Japan adopted a feudal society.

11. Japan during the Meiji Restoration was similar to Japan after World War II in that during both of these periods Japan (1) limited political freedoms and pursued a foreign policy of isolationism (2) increased the powers of the samurai (3) underwent political reform and economic expansion (4) was ruled by dictators and the military.

12. Which was a major justification used by Japan for empire building in the 1930s and 1940s? (1) revenging attacks by aggressive neighbors (2) promoting immigration of foreigners (3) spreading the Buddhist religion (4) obtaining food and raw materials.

13. A comparison of Japan's policies before 1945 with its policies in effect after 1945 indicates that (1) reduction in spending on military goods leads to economic depression (2) dependence on foreign trade usually leads to a weakened national economy (3) territorial aggression is not necessary to secure national economic goals (4) democratic institutions hinder economic growth.

14. Democracy in modern Japan resulted primarily from (1) Shinto and Buddhist beliefs about equality and justice (2) reforms imposed by the United States after World War II (3) a history of imperial justice under the constitution of the emperor (4) the diffusion of ideas and practices from China and Korea.

15. Since World War II, which development has occurred in the Japanese economy? (1) Japan has become self-sufficient since it now possesses adequate natural resources. (2) Japan has achieved a favorable balance of trade. (3) Japan has returned to a strong emphasis on agriculture. (4) Japan has a shortage of skilled workers.

16. One reason for the emergence of Japan as a world economic power is Japan's (1) development of nuclear power (2) abundance of fossil fuels (3) strong tradition of military rule (4) business enterprises and organizations.

17. South Korea's present-day industrial success is largely the result of (1) dependence on loans from Western European nations (2) abundant natural resources of iron and petroleum (3) an educated, highly skilled work force (4) strong military forces and imperialism.

18. Which statement best describes conditions in Japan today? (1) Japan is a modern society that is completely self-sufficient. (2) Japan has continued to rely on China and Korea for its cultural values and technological development. (3) Japan has remained a primarily agrarian society with an emphasis on maintaining traditional values. (4) Japan has adopted modern technological advances while maintaining aspects of the traditional culture.

19. Which statement best describes Korea since the end of World War II? (1) A united Korean nation has become a major force in world politics. (2) South Korea has adopted a policy of imperialism toward other nations. (3) Korea has been divided by the politics of the cold war. (4) North and South Korea have entered into an alliance with Japan.

20. Since the early 1970s, Japan has become more independent of U.S. policies because (1) Japan opposes the U.S. policy of détente with Communist countries (2) Japan has emerged as an economic superpower (3) the United States has failed to honor its commitments to defend Japan (4) Japan is so militarily strong that it no longer needs U.S. help to protect itself.

21. In recent years, which factor has been a major reason for the economic tensions between the United States and Japan? (1) Japan has imported more from the United States than it exported to that country. (2) The United States has refused to place quotas on Japanese goods. (3) The United States has imported more from Japan than it has exported to Japan. (4) Japan has lowered tariffs on goods imported from the United States.

Base your answers to questions 22 and 23 on the cartoon below and on your knowledge of social studies.

Henry Payne, reprinted by permission of UFS, Inc.

22. The main idea of the cartoon is that the current relationship between the United States and Japan (1) may lead to the destruction of Japan's traditional culture (2) has prevented U.S. trade with other countries (3) has been more beneficial to Japan than to the United States (4) has had a negative impact on the economies of both countries.

23. Which person would be most likely to agree with the point of view expressed in the cartoon? (1) an American importer of Japanese cars (2) an unemployed American factory worker (3) a prosperous Japanese farmer (4) the Japanese Minister for Economic Affairs.

Base your answers to questions 24 and 25 on the cartoon on page 301 and on your knowledge of social studies.

24. What is the main idea of the cartoon? (1) The Japanese should trade only with the United States. (2) The United States has threatened to use tariffs to protect its industries from Japanese competition.

"Don't worry, I'll only use it if I fall behind."

Stephen Austin/Rothco Cartoons

(3) Sports competition between the United States and Japan can have an effect on reducing tariffs.   (4) United States tariffs have hurt post-war Japanese economic development.

25. Which situation led to the idea presented in the cartoon?   (1) the unfavorable United States balance of trade with Japan   (2) the superior quality of goods made in the United States   (3) the takeover of Japanese businesses by Americans   (4) the Japanese defeat in World War II.

Level 2

26. Korea is a peninsula that is located closest to   (1) India   (2) Africa   (3) the Middle East   (4) China.

27. In Japan, a major economic problem has been the lack of   (1) natural resources   (2) investment capital   (3) skilled labor   (4) experienced management.

28. Japan became a major fishing nation because most of its land is made up of   (1) deserts   (2) mountains   (3) rain forests   (4) plateaus.

29. Before the 1800s, Japan   (1) adopted aspects of Chinese culture   (2) sold raw materials to other nations   (3) spread its religion to other societies   (4) conquered nearby Asian nations.

30. A major belief of Shintoism is that (1) animals are sacred (2) there is only one God (3) people should follow their desires (4) ancestors should be respected.

31. Feudal society in Japan was dominated by (1) a powerful shogun (2) the emperor (3) the legislature (4) religious leaders.

32. Before Commodore Matthew Perry's naval visit in 1853, Japan was (1) involved in international trade (2) a colony of China (3) isolated from world affairs (4) an imperialistic nation.

33. Japanese ports were opened to world trade as a result of (1) Commodore Perry's expedition (2) the Meiji Restoration (3) the Russo-Japanese War (4) World War II.

34. The samurai of Japan were influential during a period of (1) weak central government (2) increasing nationalism (3) religious and political reform (4) invasions by foreigners.

35. Early in the 20th century, Korea was under the political control of (1) China (2) the Soviet Union (3) Japan (4) the United States.

36. In the period before World War II, Japan followed a policy of (1) isolationism (2) imperialism (3) international cooperation (4) disarmament.

37. Which reform took place in Japan after World War II? (1) Japan's industry was destroyed. (2) The emperor's position was abolished. (3) Japan became a democracy. (4) Labor unions were declared illegal.

38. The economic success of Japan will most likely lead to (1) its loss of influence in Asia (2) the end of individual freedoms in Japan (3) its conquest of other countries (4) its increased influence in world affairs.

39. A study of Japanese society today will lead to the conclusion that Japan has (1) become completely Westernized (2) rejected modern ideas (3) been able to blend traditional and modern ways of thinking (4) become dependent on other Asian nations for new ideas.

40. Which statement concerning modern Japan is most accurate? (1) Japan is a major trading nation. (2) Japan's army is one of the largest in the world. (3) Japan shows little concern for its environment. (4) Japan has given up all its traditions.

Essay Questions on Japan and Korea

Level 1

1. Throughout history, major developments have had effects on the geographic area in which they occurred. Some significant developments in the history of Japan and Korea are listed below.

Developments
Shintoism
The Meiji Restoration (1868–1912)
Japanese rule of Korea (1910–1945)

Establishment of a democratic government in Japan (1945–1952)
Japanese industrial development (1950 to the present)
The Korean War (1950–1953)

Select *three* of the developments listed above. For each development chosen:

- Describe the development.
- Discuss one factor that led to the development.
- Explain how Japan was affected by the development.

2. Nations and regions often adopt ideas and practices from other parts of the world. For example, both Japan and Korea have experienced cultural diffusion from   (a) China and   (b) the West.

Select *either* Japan *or* Korea. For the nation chosen:

- Describe one Chinese idea or practice and one Western idea or practice that influenced the nation.
- Discuss the effects of the Chinese and Western ideas or practices on the nation.

Level 2

3. The statements below describe certain features of the geography and climate of Japan.

Features
Japan is a group of islands separated from the rest of Asia.
Most of Japan is made up of mountains.
Japan's rivers are short and contain rapids.
Japan has abundant rainfall.

A. Select *three* of the features described in the statements above. For each feature chosen, state one specific effect on Japan.

B. Base your answer to Part B on your answer to Part A. However, additional information may be included. Write an essay discussing the effects of specific geographic features on the development of Japan. Begin your essay with this topic sentence:

Geography and climate have affected the development of Japan.

4. The people of Japan have faced a number of problems throughout their history. Some of these are listed below.

Problems
High population density
Scarcity of raw materials and natural resources
Attempts to increase Japanese imports of U.S. goods
Tradition versus modernization

A. Select *three* of the problems listed above. For each problem chosen, state one cause and one result.

B. Base your answer to Part B on your answer to Part A. However, additional information may be included. Write an essay discussing the causes and results of Japan's problems. Begin your essay with this topic sentence:

Japan has faced many problems throughout its history.

CHAPTER 7

Western Europe

Main Ideas

1. **WARM-WATER PORTS:** Easy access to warm-water ports and navigable rivers have encouraged cultural diffusion and trade both within Western Europe and outside the region.

2. **GREEK AND ROMAN CULTURE:** Both ancient Greece and ancient Rome strongly influenced European history in later eras.

3. **MEDIEVAL SOCIETY:** During the Middle Ages, Europeans developed an economic system known as manorialism and a social system called feudalism. Moreover, the Roman Catholic Church provided stability, order, and unity.

4. **RENAISSANCE:** The Renaissance was a time of renewed interest in Greek and Roman cultures. It also represented a shift from an emphasis on spiritual matters to a concern with earthly pursuits.

5. **REFORMATION:** In the 1500s, several groups of Christians revolted against the pope's authority and practices of the Roman Catholic Church. This Protestant Reformation led to political and religious conflicts throughout much of Western Europe.

6. **EXPLORATION:** The Age of Exploration (1450–1750) marked the beginning of Western European domination in the Western Hemisphere and parts of Africa and Asia.

7. **ORIGINS OF A MARKET ECONOMY:** A market economy and modern capitalism developed in the 1500s and 1600s.

8. **INDUSTRIAL REVOLUTION:** By emphasizing machine production and the factory system, the Industrial Revolution in

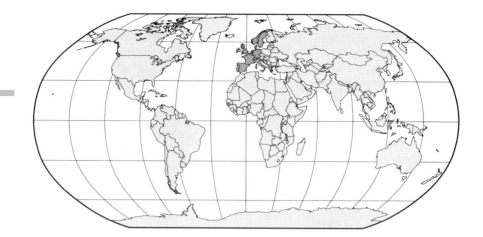

the 1700s and 1800s brought great changes to Western European society, and eventually to the entire world.

9. **IMPERIALISM:** Western European nations sought raw materials and new markets in other regions through a policy of conquest and colonization.

10. **WORLD WAR I (1914–1918):** Nationalism, imperialistic rivalries, militarism, and opposing alliance systems caused a regional conflict to escalate into a major world war.

11. **TOTALITARIANISM:** In Germany, Italy, and the Soviet Union in the 1930s, military action was glorified, opposition was not tolerated, and human rights were suppressed.

12. **WORLD WAR II (1939–1945):** Aggression by Nazi Germany, Italy, and Japan caused the outbreak of the most destructive war in history. One result of this war was the Holocaust—the killing of millions of Jews by Nazi Germany.

13. **COLD WAR:** After World War II, the United States and the Soviet Union emerged as the world's superpowers. Competition between them shaped the policies of nations around the world for 45 years.

14. **EUROPEAN UNION:** Most nations of Western Europe are removing trade barriers in an attempt to unify the region economically and draw member nations closer together politically.

Western Europe: The Region at a Glance

ARCTIC OCEAN

30°W 20°W 10°W 0° 10°E 20°E 30°E 40°E 50°E

★ Reykjavik
ICELAND

NORWEGIAN SEA

ARCTIC CIRCLE

65°N

⑧ NORWAY SWEDEN
Oslo
Stockholm ★

NORTHERN IRELAND SCOTLAND
NORTH SEA
DENMARK
BALTIC SEA

55°N

IRELAND
Dublin ★ UNITED KINGDOM (Great Britain)
★ London
WALES
ENGLISH CHANNEL
Thames R.

①
BELGIUM
NETHERLANDS
★ Amsterdam
Copenhagen

② ⑦
Elbe R.
Berlin ★
Great European Plain
GERMANY
Oder R.

EASTERN EUROPE

ATLANTIC OCEAN

Brussels ★
Seine R.
Rhine R.
Paris ★ LUXEMBOURG
Loire R.
Rhone R. Bern ★ ⑥ AUSTRIA
Vienna ★

FRANCE
SWITZERLAND
Alps
Danube R.

45°N

Ebro R. Pyrenees
Po R. Apennines
BLACK SEA

PORTUGAL
Madrid ★
Lisbon ★
SPAIN
③
BALEARIC IS. (Sp.)
CORSICA (Fr.)
SARDINIA (It.)
Tiber R.
Rome ★
ITALY
④
ADRIATIC SEA
GREECE
AEGEAN SEA

SICILY (It.)
IONIAN SEA
MALTA
Athens ★
⑤
CRETE (Gr.)

35°N

MEDITERRANEAN SEA

★ Capital

N
W E
S

NORTH AFRICA

25°N

0 ____ 300 Kilometers
0 ____ 300 Miles

1 GREAT BRITAIN: A narrow body of water, the English Channel, separates this island nation from most of the rest of Europe. This fact has enabled the British to defend their land from invasion. Good harbors and closeness to the sea help explain why the British developed both a strong merchant class and a strong navy.

5 GREECE: Western civilization originated with the culture of the ancient Greeks. A mountainous land, Greece was not easily united. Instead of one state or empire, the Greeks formed many city-states that competed with one another for trade and power. The spirited competition helped produce a culture that valued individual effort, achievement, democracy, and free inquiry.

2 THE LOW COUNTRIES: Three nations—the Netherlands, Belgium, and Luxembourg—occupy a flat coastal plain near the North Sea. Much of the Netherlands is below sea level. To keep the land from being flooded, the Dutch maintain an elaborate system of dikes. Excellent harbors (Amsterdam, Rotterdam) have enabled the Dutch to become rich through overseas trade.

6 ALPS MOUNTAINS: This mountain range—the highest in Europe—provided a natural border for several nations: Italy, France, Austria, Germany, and Switzerland. The Alps served as a natural barrier between central and southern Europe until the Romans were able to build roads through some of its passes.

3 IBERIAN PENINSULA: Two nations, Spain and Portugal, make up this subregion. A mountain range, the Pyrenees, separates the peninsula from neighboring France. Harbors on the Atlantic Ocean enabled Spain and Portugal to take the lead in the Age of Exploration in the 15th and 16th centuries.

7 GREAT EUROPEAN PLAIN: Stretching from northern France through the Low Countries eastward into Germany and Poland, this broad and fertile plain is the best agricultural land in Europe. Since the area is both valuable and difficult to defend, its history has been one of frequent warfare among neighboring states.

4 ITALIAN PENINSULA: This long peninsula occupies a commanding position in the Mediterranean Sea. In ancient times, the city of Rome gained control of the peninsula. Using its central location to advantage, Rome eventually conquered all lands on the Mediterranean, including North Africa and much of Western Europe and the Middle East.

8 SCANDINAVIA: Two peninsulas—Denmark and Norway/Sweden—make up the most northerly subregion in Western Europe. In the Early Middle Ages, the people of these peninsulas were known as Vikings. Sailing boldly across the North Sea in their long boats, they raided and plundered widely along Europe's coasts and up its rivers.

I. Geography

The continent of Europe consists of two main regions—Eastern Europe (described in Chapter 8) and Western Europe. One special characteristic of Western Europe is that it is bordered on three sides by water. Thus, the economic, political, and social life of the region have been strongly influenced by the nearby oceans and seas. On the map on page 306, notice the location of the Atlantic Ocean and the Mediterranean, North, and Baltic seas.

A. RELATIONSHIP TO THE SEAS AND OCEANS

Because Western Europe is small and much of it consists of peninsulas and islands, a high percentage of the region's 370 million people live on or near a coastline. The uneven coastline provides a large number of ports and harbors for fishing boats, merchant ships, and naval fleets. Many Western Europeans make a living from the seas—whether by fishing, trading manufactured goods and food products, or serving tourists in seaside resorts.

Western Europe is fortunate to have many navigable rivers. These include the Seine River in France, the Rhine in Germany, the Danube in Austria, the Po in Italy, and the Thames in Great Britain. The major rivers of Western Europe have been connected by canals, producing great stretches of navigable waterways. The inland waterways, along with the seas and oceans, have encouraged cultural diffusion and economic interdependence within the region. They have also helped sustain contacts and trade with nations in other regions of the world.

B. TOPOGRAPHY

Western Europe's diverse topography includes mountains, lowlands, and plateaus.

Mountains   Western Europe has a number of mountain ranges, the highest and most rugged of which are the Alps. Centered in Switzerland, the Alps form a land barrier between Italy and countries to the north. Another mountain range, the Pyrenees, separates Spain from France. These mountain chains have discouraged movement by land, but people have been able to get around them easily by sea. In Switzerland, Greece, Italy, and elsewhere, many people have lived in villages isolated from others by mountains.

Lowlands   Found along coastlines and in river valleys, lowland areas or plains cover about one-fourth of Western Europe. The largest stretch of lowlands is the Great European Plain. It begins in the west in France, extends north into Belgium, the Netherlands, Germany, and Denmark, and continues east all the way to the Ural Mountains in

RIVER BARGES ON THE RHINE: The Rhine River flows through the center of Europe from southern Germany to the North Sea. What other Western European rivers are important highways of trade?

Russia. The rich soil of the lowlands has attracted large numbers of settlers. Throughout European history, easy travel over lowland areas has encouraged migration, trade, and foreign invasions.

Plateaus   Flat highland areas, or plateaus, cover the central regions of Spain, France, Germany, and Austria. While some crops are grown on the plateaus, the grazing of livestock is more common in these areas.

C. CLIMATE

Much of Western Europe has a mild climate. Winters are not too cold, and summers are not too hot. This moderate climate is due in part to the location of the region in a temperate zone. Another moderating force is the *North Atlantic Drift* (warm ocean currents in the Atlantic Ocean). Winds from the ocean provide moderate temperatures and plentiful rainfall to agricultural areas along the Atlantic Coast. The North Atlantic Drift also helps keep Western European ports ice-free all winter. Ports that are always or almost always ice-free are called *warm-water ports*.

More severe is the climate of Iceland, Norway, Sweden, and Finland. Because parts of these countries are located near or above the Arctic Circle, temperatures can be very cold.

In southern Europe, lands bordering the Mediterranean Sea have a Mediterranean climate: hot, dry summers and cool, rainy winters. This climate, found in Italy, Greece, and parts of Spain and France, supports the growing of grapes, olives, and citrus fruits, all of which are exported in large quantities.

D. RESOURCES FOR HEAVY INDUSTRY

Western Europe has large deposits of coal and iron ore, both of which are important in making steel. In addition, the region contains a number of fast-moving rivers that have been dammed to provide hydroelectric power. These factors have helped make Great Britain, Germany, and France industrial giants. The other countries of Western Europe also are industrialized. Great Britain and Norway have discovered large reserves of oil in the North Sea. These reserves, however, are not sufficient to supply all of Europe's needs. Thus, Western European countries must import much of the oil that they need from the Middle East and elsewhere.

In Review

The following questions refer to Section I: Geography.

1. *Key terms:* Define or identify each of the following:

   Great European Plain   warm-water port
   North Atlantic Drift

2. State how each of the following geographic features has affected the culture and history of Western Europe: (a) mountain ranges, (b) rivers, and   (c) access to the sea. (Refer to the map on page 306 as well as to the text.)

3. *Critical thinking:* Western Europe is divided into many relatively small nations. How does the region's physical geography help to explain this fact?

II. Early History

The first major civilizations in Western Europe—ancient Greece and Rome—developed in lands bordering the Mediterranean Sea.

A. ANCIENT GREECE

Because the land was mountainous, the original settlers of the Greek peninsula lived in isolated villages. Gradually these villages developed into *city-states*—independently governed cities that controlled surrounding areas of farmland. The culture of the ancient Greeks reached its greatest height between 500 and 400 B.C., a time that has been called the "Golden Age of Greece." During this period, the city-state of Sparta (in southern Greece) concentrated on training its citizens for military service. The city-state of Athens (in eastern Greece) was more famous for its democratic political system and achievements in the arts and sciences. At times, Sparta and Athens went to war with each other. At other times, they were military allies. The Spartans, with the better army, were strongest on land. The Athenians were the better naval power (in part because they had many ships engaged in trade around the Mediterranean).

Birth of democracy   Ancient Athens was the first society to adopt democratic practices. In ancient times, most societies around the world were governed either by monarchs or by small groups of nobles. In the city-state of Athens, however, the right to discuss public issues and make decisions was given to all *citizens* (people who owe allegiance to and are entitled to protection from a state). All citizens were considered equal before the law. Any citizen accused of crime had the right to a trial by a jury of fellow citizens. But citizens of Athens had responsibilities as well as rights. For example, they had to take up arms and defend the city in times of war.

Athens was considered a direct democracy rather than an indirect one. In an *indirect democracy* (such as we have in the United States), citizens elect representatives to pass laws. In a *direct democracy*, citizens meet together in an assembly and decide by majority vote what laws shall be adopted for the community.

Political life in ancient Athens was democratic, but only in a limited way. Most people were not citizens. These non-citizens included all women, slaves, and foreigners living in Athens. Only free, male Athenians could vote, hold public office, or even own property. Although democracy in Athens was far from perfect, it prepared the way for later democracies, such as our own.

The questioning spirit   Perhaps the first people to search for truth through experimentation and logical analysis were the people of ancient Athens. For using this approach in studying and treating diseases, Hippocrates is considered the father of medicine. (Previously, people had believed that diseases were caused by evil spirits.) The philosopher Socrates won fame in ancient Greece for his method of inquiry. He believed that truth can be discovered by asking a series of questions and challenging accepted beliefs. This technique has become known as the "Socratic method."

Plato, a follower of Socrates, emphasized such qualities as wisdom, truth, courage, justice, and reason as ideal virtues. Because he thought such virtues were rare, Plato rejected the idea of democracy. Instead, he proposed an ideal republic governed by a philosopher-king who would know how to act in the best interests of society. Plato's most famous student was Aristotle. Among Aristotle's many contributions was *logic*, a set of rules for reasoning. Aristotle also believed in a philosophy of moderation, or avoiding extremes in living one's life.

DOCUMENT: LAST DIALOGUE OF SOCRATES

The Athenian assembly wrongly convicted the Greek philosopher Socrates of trying to corrupt the city's youth with his teachings. For this, he was sent to prison and condemned to die. After being condemned, Socrates discussed with friends whether it was right or wrong for him to escape from prison, as they urged him to do. His friend Plato recorded what Socrates said in a conversation with a friend named Crito. The following is an excerpt from that dialogue.

SOCRATES: Then we must do no wrong?

CRITO: Certainly not.

SOCRATES: Nor, when injured, injure in return, as the many imagine; for we must injure no one at all?

CRITO: Clearly not.

SOCRATES: Again, Crito, may we do evil?

CRITO: Surely not, Socrates.

SOCRATES: And what of doing evil in return for evil, which is the morality of the many—is that just or not?

CRITO: Not just.

SOCRATES: For doing evil to another is the same as injuring him?

CRITO: Very true.

SOCRATES: Then we ought not to retaliate or render evil for evil to anyone, whatever evil we may have suffered from him. But I would have you consider, Crito, whether you really mean what you are saying. For this opinion has never been held, and never will be held, by any considerable number of persons. . . . Tell me, then, whether you agree with and assent to my first principle, that neither injury nor retaliation nor warding off evil by evil is ever right. . . .

Questions for Discussion

1. How does this dialogue illustrate the Socratic method?
2. What evil or wrong has been done to Socrates?
3. Do you think Socrates is arguing for or against the idea of avoiding death by escaping from prison? Why?
4. Do you agree or disagree with Socrates "that neither injury nor retaliation nor warding off evil by evil is ever right"? Explain your answer.

Source: Plato, "Crito." Translated by B. Jowett. Reprinted in *Plato*. New York: Walter J. Black, 1942.

Greek culture   The Greeks believed in the pursuit of excellence. This ideal was reflected in their art, architecture, sports, and literature. In art, Greek sculpture aimed to portray the ideal human body in a natural and graceful style. A famous work that reflects this ideal is *The Discus Thrower*, a statue that shows a Greek athlete at his best.

In architecture, the most famous example of the Greek classical style is the Parthenon, a temple in Athens. Large and graceful columns form the outside of this magnificent marble structure.

In sports, the Greeks set standards of excellence for athletes through regular competitions. In fact, the Greeks began the tradition of the Olympic Games, which they held every four years in Olympia.

In literature, Greek poets were the first to write plays for the stage. Their earliest dramas were *tragedies*, plays that portray human conflicts from which there can be no escape. For example, in *Antigone*, a tragedy by Sophocles, the king's niece must decide whether or not to bury the body of her deceased brother. To bury her brother would mean defying the king's command. To fail to bury her brother, however, would anger the gods. For choosing to bury her brother, Antigone is condemned to death. Later plays, such as those of Aristophanes, were *comedies*—humorous plays that poke fun at certain people or social customs.

Probably the most famous works of Greek literature were written by a blind poet, Homer. His two great epic poems, the *Iliad* and the *Odyssey*, told of a war against the people of Troy and the adventures of one of the war's survivors, Odysseus.

THE PARTHENON: This great temple of Athens, now in ruins, was built during the Greek golden age (5th century B.C.) in honor of the Greek goddess Athena. What aspects of Greek civilization are still part of our own civilization?

B. WARFARE IN ANCIENT GREECE

As stated earlier, Sparta and Athens sometimes joined together in war and sometimes fought against each other.

The Persian Wars (490 B.C.–479 B.C.)   While the Greek city-states were starting to develop their civilization, Persia was extending its power over most of neighboring Asia Minor (present-day Turkey). Because Greek colonies in Asia Minor rebelled against Persian rule, a war broke out between Greek city-states and Persia. Although greatly outnumbered, the Greek soldiers defeated the Persians on the Plains of Marathon in 490 B.C.

A second Greek victory took place ten years later, in 480 B.C., after the Spartans had fought to the death at Thermopylae to defend a strategic mountain pass against the invading Persian army. Although the outnumbered Spartans were finally defeated, they provided Athens with enough time to prepare for a Persian attack. In a major naval battle, the Athenians defeated the Persian navy. In the next year, 479 B.C., the Persians were again defeated, this time by a Spartan army. Having been defeated on both land and sea, the Persians left Greece. In the end, Greece had saved itself from Persian control against great odds.

GREECE IN THE PERSIAN WARS

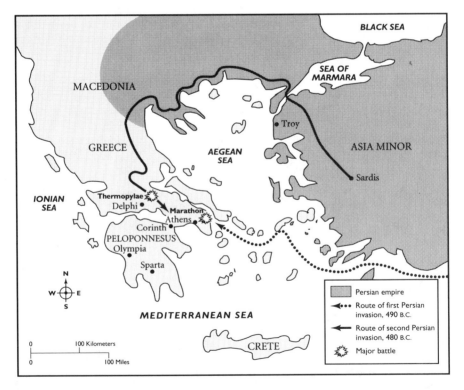

The Peloponnesian Wars (431 B.C.–404 B.C.)   The Greek victories in the Persian Wars did not bring a lasting alliance between Sparta and Athens. From 431 to 404 B.C., Athens and its allies fought Sparta and its allies for control of the Peloponnesian Peninsula in southern Greece. Although Sparta would eventually win the wars, all the participating city-states were weakened by the conflict.

C. THE HELLENISTIC EMPIRE

The warfare just described would lead to the rise of a new empire in Greece. Macedonia, a kingdom to the north of Greece, took advantage of the weaknesses of the Greeks. By 338 B.C., its leader, Philip II, was able to unify most of Greece under Macedonian rule. Philip II admired Greek culture. He even hired Aristotle to teach his son, Alexander, about it. The king hoped to further expand his empire and to spread Greek ideas and culture. But Philip II was assassinated in 336 B.C. and was succeeded by Alexander.

Through invasions and conquests, Alexander the Great created a vast empire in only 13 years. This Hellenistic empire stretched as far south as Egypt and as far east as the Indus River Valley (in modern-day India). Alexander's conquests were important in that they led to the diffusion of Greek culture throughout the empire, and beyond.

The Greeks were also influenced by the people whom they conquered. They adopted many customs and beliefs from the Persians, Egyptians, and Phoenicians. This era of cultural diffusion and exchange is known as the "Hellenistic Period."

Alexander died at age 33. His rule of the empire was divided among three of his generals. Hellenistic culture, however, flourished for

EMPIRE OF ALEXANDER THE GREAT

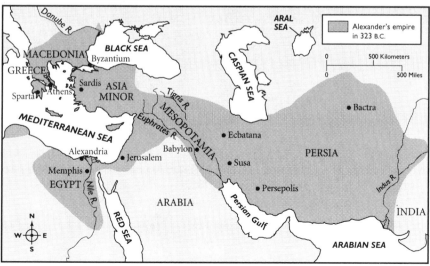

several hundred years more. In art, the Greeks of the Hellenistic Period portrayed the human body even more realistically than before. In science, several important advances were made. Aristarchus developed the theories that the sun is the center of the universe and that the earth revolves around the sun. Eratosthenes was able to accurately estimate the circumference of the earth. Another major achievement of the Hellenistic Period was the founding of hundreds of schools and libraries in major cities in Europe, North Africa, and the Middle East. The largest and most famous library of its time was established in Alexandria, Egypt.

D. THE ROMAN REPUBLIC

In 509 B.C., at a time when the Greeks were building their civilization, neighboring people in and around Rome (on the Italian peninsula) set up a republic. They had a republican form of government in which citizens elected officials to govern them.

Social classes   Roman laws in the early years of the republic favored the wealthy landowners, known as *patricians*. Farmers, merchants, and all other citizens were *plebeians*. At first, plebeians were not protected by the law, nor could they vote or hold office. In addition to these two social classes of citizens were the slaves—foreigners who had been captured in wars. Slaves in the Roman republic had no rights.

Women could be citizens, but no women were permitted to vote or hold political office. A woman was always legally subordinate to a man—first to her father, and after she married, to her husband.

Government organization   The Roman republic had separate branches of government in order to prevent any one person or group from becoming too powerful. An executive branch was headed by two consuls, each elected to a one-year term. A legislative branch consisted of a Senate that represented the patrician class and an Assembly that represented the plebeian class. The Assembly elected ten tribunes, who had the power to veto Senate-passed laws that might harm the plebeians.

In a later era, both the British Parliament and the U.S. Congress would follow the model of the two-house Roman legislature.

Law and justice   Originally, Roman laws were not written down. Plebeians were sometimes punished for breaking laws that they did not know existed. Then in 451 B.C., some basic Roman laws were written down and assembled in a collection called the *Roman Law of the Twelve Tables*. The following important concepts formed the basis of Roman law:

- All citizens are equal under the law.
- An accused person is innocent unless proven guilty.
- An accused person has the right to know his or her accuser.
- People should not be punished for what they think.
- An accused person has the right to a trial by jury (first practiced by the Greeks).
- Records of judges' decisions are kept for use in subsequent cases.

Initially, Roman law offered only limited human rights. For example, it did not allow a plebeian to marry into a patrician family. Eventually, however, people's rights were expanded. Enslaved people gained the right to purchase their freedom and become citizens. Slavery for debt was banned. Moreover, women gained the right to make their own wills and business arrangements and to control their own money and property.

E. MILITARY CONQUESTS

The lands that the Romans controlled expanded through the centuries. In the early republic, only a small area along the Tiber River in Italy was Roman. By 290 B.C., the republic had grown to include almost

SLAVERY IN THE ROMAN EMPIRE: Following the Roman conquest of Iberia (present-day Spain and Portugal), captives such as these were sold into slavery. What were other effects of Roman rule over conquered lands?

ROMAN EMPIRE AT ITS HEIGHT

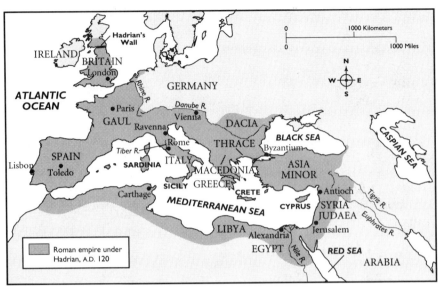

all of the Italian Peninsula. By the next century, Rome would extend
its rule to include North Africa, Spain, Sicily, Sardinia, and Corsica.
How did Rome become so powerful?

In part, the Roman expansion was due to its strong army. It was
divided into units called *legions*, which in turn were divided into
small, effective units of 80 to 100 men. The Roman republic put much
emphasis on military service. All male, adult citizens had to serve
either in the army or the navy. In a series of wars, the Punic Wars
(264–146 B.C.), the Romans established their power by defeating Car-
thage, a strong city-state on the North African coast. But this victory
did not come easily. Before then, the Carthaginian general Hannibal
had invaded Italy and badly damaged the Roman army. Rome
achieved victory only when it succeeded in attacking the city of Car-
thage itself.

From republic to empire   In the 1st century B.C., a series of crises
and civil wars caused the Roman republic to be replaced by a more
dictatorial form of government—the Roman empire, which was ruled
by an emperor. The career of Julius Caesar marked the beginning of
the end for the republic. As a military leader, Caesar gained fame from
his successes leading Roman legions in the conquest of Gaul (France).
He returned to Rome with his army to become dictator for life. Under
his strong leadership, Caesar reformed both the tax system and the
calendar. He also extended citizenship to non-Romans. But some sen-
ators, jealous of Caesar's powers, assassinated him in 44 B.C.

A civil war followed Caesar's death. The ultimate winner of the war
was a young politician named Octavian. He persuaded the Senate to

give him the title Augustus and to grant him the combined powers of consul, tribune, commander of the army, and chief religious leader. From that point on, the Roman world was governed by a series of authoritarian emperors.

F. ACHIEVEMENTS OF THE ROMAN EMPIRE

The Roman conquest of Greece, Macedonia, Syria, and Egypt brought the Romans into close contact with Greek culture. In their art, architecture, literature, and religion, the Romans often relied upon the cultural patterns of the Greeks. But in many cases, they made important contributions of their own. Roman architecture was noted for its use of the arch, column, and dome. Both arches and columns were adapted from Greek examples, while large domes were a Roman invention. A fine example of a large, domed building built by the Romans is the Pantheon, which still stands in Rome. It was erected to honor the Roman gods, many of whom were the same as Greek gods and goddesses but with different names. For example, Athena became the Roman goddess Minerva; Zeus became the Roman god Jupiter.

Roman art was greatly influenced by the realism of Hellenistic art. A favorite form of Roman sculpture, for example, was the portrait bust.

Roman literature often reflected Greek influences. For example, in his *Aeneid*, the Roman poet Virgil imitated the structure of the *Iliad* and the *Odyssey*, by Homer. Romans helped to transmit Greek culture to much of Western Europe by translating works of Greek literature into Latin. Since Latin was the language of the Romans, it became the official language of the Roman empire and spread over much of Western Europe. Italian, Spanish, French, and Portuguese are all based on Latin.

In the field of engineering, the Romans invented cement (a mixture that enables stones to adhere to each other). The cement, together with paving stones, enabled Romans to build thousands of miles of wide roads. Previously, most roads in Western Europe had been dirt roads. Now the Romans could create a system of roads and bridges to move goods and troops between Rome and the various provinces. The Romans also built an elaborate system of *aqueducts* to transport water from the countryside to the cities. The aqueducts, together with major sewer systems and public baths, enabled the Romans to build large cities without fear of major outbreaks of diseases. The impact of Rome on other societies and the pattern in which Roman roads were laid out led to the often-quoted saying, "All roads lead to Rome."

The Romans built an extensive trading network that linked all parts of their empire. Trade also extended beyond the empire as far as Central Africa, India, and China. The Romans spent huge sums of gold and silver for imported Chinese silks and spices. Excessive purchases of Asian luxuries weakened the Roman empire's economy and may have been a factor in the empire's decline.

THE ROMAN FORUM: The forum of ancient Rome consisted of temples to various gods and government buildings where public business was conducted. What aspects of Roman civilization were borrowed from the Greeks?

Spread of Christianity A new religion, Christianity, arose in the Middle East during the time this region was part of the Roman empire. For 300 years, the religion spread slowly but steadily into areas under Roman control. At first, Roman emperors viewed the religion as a threat and persecuted those who practiced it. The Christian belief in one god challenged the official Roman religion, which recognized many gods.

In A.D. 313, the Roman emperor Constantine I ended the persecution of Christians and gave government protection to Christianity. Then in 392, Christianity became the Roman empire's official religion. As a result of this change in official policy, Christianity became the dominant religion in both Western and Eastern Europe. This religious change brought with it a number of other changes that were to shape Western culture for centuries. To Christianity, for example, we derive our system for counting years. The initials A.D. stand for *anno Domini*, a Latin phrase meaning "the year of the Lord"; B.C. stands for "before Christ."

A new capital In addition to changing the empire's religious policy, Emperor Constantine also changed its capital. In A.D. 330, he moved the capital from Rome to the eastern part of the empire (in present-day Turkey). Named Constantinople in honor of the emperor, the city was later renamed Istanbul by the Turks. Constantinople had an excellent location on the passage between the Mediterranean and Black seas. Emperor Constantine thought the new location of the capital would be safer from foreign invasions than Rome had been. He was right. Even after the fall of the Roman empire in 476, its eastern counterpart—the Byzantine empire—remained a strong power.

Greek (not Latin) was the official language in the eastern empire. Nevertheless, Byzantium enabled many Roman political and cultural contributions to survive. In addition, because Christianity was its official religion, the empire helped this religion to spread. One Byzantine emperor, Justinian (527–565), was able to expand the empire to include much of the old Roman empire, including all of Italy and parts of Spain, North Africa, and Syria. (For more on the Byzantine empire, see Chapter 8.)

G. DECLINE OF THE ROMAN EMPIRE

The size, power, and influence of the Roman empire gradually declined, for various reasons.

Internal factors   To some extent, the Roman empire was a victim of its own successes. For example, as the empire grew larger, more and more captured people were made slaves. Enslaved people made up an increasingly larger percentage of the population. Their influence was particularly felt during slave uprisings, which weakened the empire. The most famous uprising was led by a slave named Spartacus in 73 B.C. For two years, Spartacus and some 90,000 other slaves carried out acts of destruction in central and southern Italy.

Many *peasants* (farmers with little or no land of their own) also became dissatisfied with their situation. As the empire grew, large quantities of grain were imported from outside Italy. As a result, the price of grain that the peasants sold kept going down. Thus, peasants' incomes went down, and many peasants were forced to sell their land to owners of large estates. Instead of growing grain, these large landowners made greater profits by grazing cattle and sheep or growing grapes and olives, often with slave labor.

As the empire grew, the government found that it needed larger armies to protect the empire. To pay for these armies, the government imposed higher taxes on Roman citizens. With higher taxes, many citizens found that their standard of living was declining.

Because of outbreaks of diseases and a low birth rate, Roman citizens experienced a declining population. Yet the Roman government and army kept growing in size. As a result, more and more foreigners had to be brought into the government and the army. The patriotism of foreigners, however, was weaker than that of Roman citizens. Also, a succession of incompetent Roman emperors weakened the loyalty of Roman citizens to their state.

External factors The major external threat facing Rome was that of invasions by less civilized Germanic peoples from the north. These invaders included the Visigoths, Ostrogoths, Franks, and Vandals, all of whom had been forced out of their own lands by the Huns, a fierce group of people from Central Asia. The Germanic groups sought refuge within the Roman empire. They ended up, however, destroying it. The Roman army was too weak to control these peoples or even to protect the city of Rome. In A.D. 410, a Germanic leader, Alaric, invaded Rome and looted it. Then in 476, a Germanic general, Odoacer, came to Rome and made himself the Roman ruler. This last date is generally considered the end of the western half of the Roman empire. The eastern half continued as the Byzantine empire.

In Review

The following questions refer to the history of Greek and Roman civilizations, as discussed on pages 310–322.

1. *Key terms:* Define or identify each of the following:

   city-state   plebeian   Hellenistic empire
   direct democracy   patrician   Roman Law of
                                     the Twelve Tables

2. In separate columns, list *three* cultural achievements of each of the following: (a) Greeks and (b) Romans.

3. Compare and contrast the political systems of Athens and the Roman republic.

4. Provide *three* causes of the decline of the Roman empire.

5. *Critical thinking:* What aspects of our own civilization originated with the ancient Greeks and Romans?

H. THE EARLY MIDDLE AGES (A.D. 500–1000)

Historians of European history call the years 500–1500 the Middle Ages or the Medieval Period. The first 500 years of this era are known as either the Early Middle Ages or the Dark Ages. Times were "dark" in the sense that levels of learning and culture were not as great as they had been earlier, during Greek and Roman times. Moreover, there was more instability. Nevertheless, it was during this period that the foundations were laid for Europe's future development.

Economic activity With the decline of the Roman empire came a decline in commerce and cities in Western Europe. Bridges, roads, and sewage systems were not maintained. There was less trading and selling of goods. People left the cities and towns for the countryside. As before, most people made their living in agriculture, but now mostly in *subsistence farming*. People grew only enough food to feed their families. Surplus crops (those that can be sold) were rare.

Political activity The kingdoms that developed in the Early Middle Ages were relatively small and weak. One exception was the Frankish kingdom, which included most of present-day France and the western half of present-day Germany. The Franks were a Germanic people who had settled in this area and then adopted the Christian religion. An important Frankish leader, Charles Martel, organized an army to fight the Moors, a Muslim people who were invading from Spain. In 732, Martel's forces defeated the Moors at the Battle of Tours. This victory stopped the Moors from advancing any farther into Europe, but the Moors continued to rule in Spain for hundreds of years. (For more on the Moors, see page 330.)

Charlemagne The strongest Frankish ruler (and one of the greatest leaders in European history) was Martel's grandson Charlemagne. Ruling from 768 to 814, Charlemagne carved out an empire that included present-day France, Germany, Austria, northern Italy, and a portion of Spain. Because he helped spread Christianity to new areas, the *pope* (head of the Christian Church in Rome) gave the Frankish king the title "emperor of the Romans." (Later Germanic rulers so honored would be called "Holy Roman emperors.")

Charlemagne instituted a number of reforms. Learning and scholarship in Western Europe had declined since the fall of the Roman empire. Few people (even among the clergy) knew how to read and

CHARLEMAGNE'S EMPIRE, 814

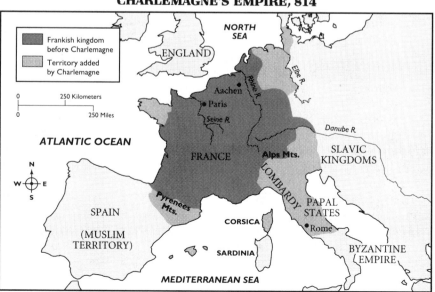

write. Many of the accomplishments of the Greeks and Romans had been forgotten. Charlemagne worked to reverse this. He set up a school in which the clergy were taught reading and writing. He urged scholars to copy ancient Greek and Roman manuscripts.

Another of Charlemagne's reforms had important social consequences. He gave large estates to those nobles who had served him in the army or in government. This practice was one factor in the rise of feudalism, described below.

The Vikings   In the 9th century, after the decline of Charlemagne's empire, bands of Viking fighters attacked Western Europe. The Vikings were a Germanic farming people who lived in Scandinavia. Many were also sailors who built sturdy "long ships" capable of sailing on the often stormy Atlantic. Viking sailors gained a reputation as fierce fighters and raiders. The first Vikings who attacked settlements on the coasts of England, Ireland, Scotland, and the Frankish kingdom were mainly interested in plunder. Later, some Vikings settled down in these areas to live and rule. Danish Vikings, for example, conquered and ruled England several times. Norwegian Vikings sailed west and set up colonies in Iceland, Greenland, and North America. Swedish Vikings set up trade routes through lands that later became Russia. (The "Rus," as the Swedish Vikings in Russia were called, are discussed in Chapter 8.)

Most Vikings were not raiders or traders but remained in Scandinavia as farmers. There they became more a part of the mainstream of Western European society after Christian missionaries converted them. Eventually they would set up the independent kingdoms of Denmark, Sweden, and Norway.

Feudalism   Following the breakup of Charlemagne's empire, there was no strong central authority in Western Europe. Economic disorder and constant warfare threatened people's security. Feudalism, which flourished in Western Europe from approximately 800 to 1300, met people's needs for economic security and protection.

Feudalism in medieval Europe was an economic, political, and social system based on the concept of protection. Under this system, strong local rulers often had more power than kings. How did the feudal system work? A king would grant a large piece of land, or *fief,* to an individual noble (lord) in return for political and military support. Those who received these large estates would, in turn, grant smaller pieces of land to lesser lords in return for loyalty and protection. Nobles who received grants of land in this manner were known as *vassals.* Most vassals were *knights,* trained soldiers who swore allegiance to a greater lord and were obligated to defend him. Knights were expected to follow a code of *chivalry.* This code described appropriate and acceptable behavior, such as assisting women and children, exhibiting bravery in battle, and demonstrating respect and courtesy.

Below the landholding noble class were the common people—the artisans and peasants. They performed economic functions in return for their lord's protection. *Artisans* were skilled workers who provided many needed goods and services. Peasants worked their lord's land and supplied the lord's household with food.

Manorialism   During the medieval period, an economic system known as *manorialism* developed. It was closely associated with feudalism. Basic to this system was the *manor*, a large piece of land on which were located the lord's house or castle, a church, and cottages for the peasants and artisans. The manor was *self-sufficient*, meaning that all economic and social needs of its residents could be met within the boundaries of the manor. The peasants lived on the manor and tended the fields. They grew the manor's food, while artisans produced all the manor's furniture, clothes, weapons, and tools. The manor church, presided over by a priest, served as the center of religious and social activities. Most peasants were *serfs*. They were not free to leave the lord's manor to work elsewhere. Even if the manor changed hands, the serfs remained tied to the land.

The medieval church as a unifying force   During the disorder of the Early Middle Ages in Western Europe, the Christian Church provided a sense of stability and unity. Religion was a way of life that influenced people's thinking and actions from birth to death.

A MEDIEVAL MANOR

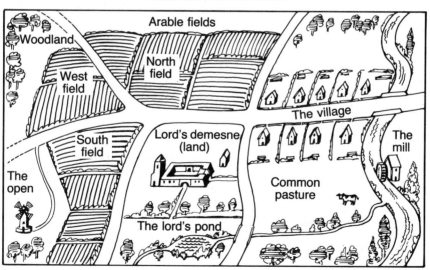

Since there was no other central authority in Western Europe, the pope in Rome occupied that position in most people's eyes. Christians from Ireland to Italy looked to the pope to provide religious, moral, and sometimes even political leadership. The pope's authority was dramatically demonstrated when Pope Leo II crowned Charlemagne in the year 800. Even emperors kneeled before the pope.

The Church allowed no disagreements with its beliefs. It demanded that every Christian accept its rulings on religious matters. Those who dared challenge Church doctrines were denounced as *heretics*. They could be *excommunicated* (expelled from the Church) and, thus, denied hope of *salvation* (going to heaven).

The Church performed the important tasks of preserving European literacy and learning. Monks busied themselves copying classic Greek and Latin texts. Ordinary people sought the help of priests in reading and writing letters. Even the lord of the manor needed a local priest's help in keeping records.

I. THE LATER MIDDLE AGES (1000–1500)

After the year 1000, Western Europeans saw many changes in their social, economic, and political lives. The many small kingdoms of Western Europe began to develop political strength and size. There were more frequent wars between armies of knights. At the same time, medieval towns developed in size, wealth, and importance.

Agricultural revolution During the Later Middle Ages, agricultural production was greater than it had been earlier. Not only could manors easily supply their own needs (as before), they could now produce a surplus that could be sold to others. The increased agricultural production was due, in part, to methods introduced in the Early Middle Ages. They were the:

- *Three-field system.* Under this system, a manor's fields would be divided into three parts. In any given year, various crops would be planted on two of the fields, while the third field would lie *fallow* (unplanted). Then by rotating the crops, nutrients in the soil would be replenished. This system cut losses caused by crop failures.
- *Horse collar.* Previously, oxen had been used to plow most fields. The invention of the horse collar allowed the speedier horse to plow more efficiently than the ox.
- *Iron-tipped plow.* Adding an iron tip to the previously all-wood plow improved the medieval peasants' ability to turn over the soil.

Growth of trade and towns Trade, which had declined during the Early Middle Ages, began to increase again as Western Europe became safer for merchants. Moreover, manors began to produce food surpluses that were sold for cash. More people now had money with which to buy goods. For example, landlords were now more likely to buy needed tools, clothing, and furniture from merchants than to have these goods made on the manor. At first, trade fairs became popular places to buy and sell goods. Merchants with goods to sell would travel from fair to fair. Later, they preferred to set up permanent shops in a town or a city.

As more merchants and artisans settled in towns, the towns began to increase in size. Because they were located on both sea and land routes of trade, certain towns in Flanders, northern Germany, and northern Italy became busy industrial and commercial cities.

Guilds With the growth of towns came the rise of a new social class in Western Europe—the middle class. It consisted of neither peasants nor lords, but of those in between—the merchants and artisans. Each of these two groups formed guilds to govern their own economic life.

Working in small shops, artisans specialized in making goods of all kinds—shoes, hats, jewelry, barrels, wine, baked goods, and so on. Each group of artisans (shoemakers, hatters, jewelers, etc.) organized its own *craft guild*. The guild would train young workers, known as *apprentices*, in the skills of the craft. It would also set prices, wages, working conditions, and quality standards for the making of goods. Most members of the craft guilds were male artisans. In the textile industry, however, women made up a majority of some of the weaving guilds.

Medieval merchants bought and sold goods made by others. Their *merchant guilds* set prices and quality standards for goods sold in town. They also set restrictions on outsiders who wanted to trade in a town. In buying a shipment of goods, guild members might pool their resources in order to spread the risk of loss. Merchant guilds became quite powerful and often served as a form of town government.

The Crusades In a series of wars (1096–1291) known as the *Crusades*, armies of Christians marched or sailed from Europe to the Middle East in an effort to recover the Holy Land from the Seljuk Turks, a Muslim people. The Holy Land included the city of Jerusalem and surrounding areas called Palestine.

The First Crusade began in 1096 at the urging of Pope Urban II. The armies from Europe captured Jerusalem in 1099 and then set up four Christian states in the area. Eventually, however, Muslim forces won back these territories one by one. As a result, other Crusades set out from Europe in the 12th and 13th centuries, but these expeditions were not successful.

Results of the Crusades Although they failed militarily, the Crusades had several lasting results:

1. *Cultural diffusion.* Europeans came into contact with the more advanced Muslim culture of the Middle East. Stimulated by this contact, European scholars began to explore new ideas in science, philosophy, and literature.

2. *Increased world trade.* Crusaders returned to Western Europe with a desire for goods previously unavailable to Europeans: perfumes, sugar, pepper, silks, and certain dyes. Arab merchants purchased these goods from the Middle East, India, and China. The Venetians, who had built large ships to transport Crusaders, now used the ships to trade with the Arab merchants and bring the goods to Europe. Growing interest in this trade and in lands to the east would lead Marco Polo to visit China in the 1270s.

3. *Persecution of Jews and Muslims.* The religious zeal connected with the Crusades may have been one of the causes of the increased religious intolerance and persecution of the Later Middle Ages. Crusaders in Jerusalem slaughtered Jewish and Muslim residents. Other Crusaders on their way to the Middle East attacked non-Christian communities in Eastern Europe. In some areas of Western Europe, Jews were forbidden to own land and were denied citizenship. Some guilds banned Jews from membership, which meant that they could not practice certain professions. In many towns, Jews were forced to live in neighborhoods separate from Christians. These areas became known as *ghettos.*

Later, certain countries expelled all Jews except those who converted to Christianity. For example, Jews were expelled from England in 1290, from France in 1306, and from Spain in 1492. Spain forcibly converted or expelled Muslims as well.

FOUR CRUSADES

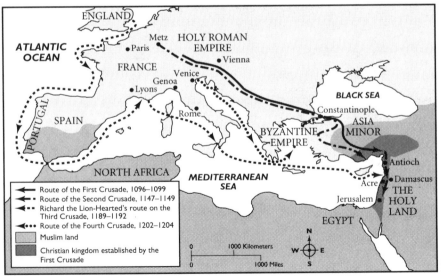

NOTRE DAME CATHEDRAL, PARIS: The pointed arches at the base of this building, the "rose" (circular) stained-glass window above, and the tall towers are hallmarks of the Gothic style of architecture. How does this style differ from the classical style as shown on page 313?

The Church's influence on culture Cultural achievements of Western Europeans during the Later Middle Ages usually were associated with the Roman Catholic Church. In architecture, for example, people spent much money and devoted years of labor to building large stone *cathedrals* (churches that are the official seat of a bishop). In an architectural style known as Gothic, churches were decorated with stained-glass windows, sculptures, and paintings—all on religious themes. Inside the churches and monasteries were kept *illuminated manuscripts* (hand-copied Bibles that were elaborately illustrated). Much of the music created during this period was church music. *Notation*, the recording of musical notes on paper, was a medieval invention.

Education Most schools of this period were associated with the Roman Catholic Church and were set up to train its clergy. Universities were founded, however, that trained people for other careers as well, such as in medicine and law. Important universities of the Middle Ages were established in Paris, the Italian cities of Salerno and Bologna, and the English towns of Cambridge and Oxford.

Emerging nation-states During the Later Middle Ages, *nation-states* began to emerge in Western Europe. These were large areas in which people shared a common culture and language and were governed by a central government. By the year 1500, nation-states had been formed in England, France, Spain, Portugal, Denmark, and Sweden, but not in Germany or Italy. In each case, the formation of a nation-state was marked by an increase in the powers of the monarchy at the expense of the powers of the nobility.

- *France*. In 987, the French king Hugh Capet ruled only a small area around Paris. Later French kings gradually gained more territory. But beginning in the 12th century, the English gained large parts of what are now French lands. Not until 1453 were the English driven out of all but a small area of France.

- *England*. In 1066, William the Conqueror and his army crossed the English Channel from Normandy (part of present-day France) and gained control over most of England. He appointed his Norman warriors as feudal lords there. But to keep royal control, he forced everyone in England to swear primary loyalty to him, the king, not to the feudal lords. William's grandson Henry II ruled an even greater area—England, Scotland, Wales, and a large part of France. Henry II's son John was less successful. Some of the English lords objected to the heavy taxes he imposed on them. They were also angry that lands had been lost in northern France. As a result, in 1215 the lords forced King John to sign the Magna Carta, a document that listed the feudal rights of the nobility in England. The document set a *precedent* (legal example) in England that a monarch's powers could be limited by the law.

- *Spain*. After the Moors had invaded what is now Spain and Portugal in the 8th century, the Iberian Peninsula was ruled by various Muslim states and Christian kingdoms. Gradually, Christian kingdoms such as Castile and Aragon expanded by defeating the Moors. In 1469, the royal heir of Castile, Isabella, married the royal heir of Aragon, Ferdinand, thereby uniting most of Spain. During their reign, their armies conquered Granada, the last Muslim state in Spain.

In Review

The following questions refer to the history of Western Europe from about 500 to about 1500, as discussed on pages 322–330.

1. *Key terms:* Define each of the following:

subsistence farming	artisan	guild
vassal	serf	nation-state

2. State who the Vikings were and what lands they conquered and settled.

3. Explain the difference between the feudal system and the manorial system.

4. Explain the long-term effects of medieval improvements in farm technology.

5. *Critical thinking:* Create a dialogue between two English brothers, Edward and John. Imagine that both are vassals to the recently crowned king, Richard I (1189–1199). Edward urges the king to participate in a crusade, while John advises against such a move. Use your dialogue to explore both the risks and the rewards of participating in the Crusades.

III. The Dynamics of Change

Medieval Europe slowly made the transition into the modern era during the period of cultural awakening and renewal that historians call the Renaissance.

A. THE RENAISSANCE

The Renaissance was the period from approximately 1300 to 1600 when the artists and writers of Western Europe expressed renewed interest in the cultures of ancient Greece and Rome. Renaissance means "rebirth"—in this case, the rebirth of classical learning.

Origins in Italy   The Renaissance began in the Italian city-states in the 14th century and later spread to Spain, France, England, the Netherlands (Holland), and other countries of Western Europe. Italy was in the forefront in the general increase of trade and the growth of towns (discussed on pages 326–327). The merchants and bankers who had grown wealthy from trade helped support the achievements of the Renaissance. For example, a family of bankers in Florence, the Medici, financed much of the art and architecture that made Florence a leading Renaissance city.

In both art and literature, the leaders of the Italian Renaissance showed enthusiasm for every aspect of ancient Greek and Roman culture. They were also more interested in secular, or worldly, affairs than medieval thinkers had been. Renaissance thinkers emphasized *humanism*, the idea that each individual was unique and had great worth in this world. As in Greece's "Golden Age," Renaissance thinkers emphasized questioning. This challenging of authority and increase in secular concerns eventually led to a decrease in the power of the Roman Catholic Church.

A RENAISSANCE PORTRAIT: The *Mona Lisa* by Leonardo da Vinci is probably the most famous portrait ever painted. How does it show a change in subject and theme from the art of the Middle Ages?

Art   The most famous artists of the Italian Renaissance were probably Leonardo da Vinci (1452–1519) and Michelangelo (1475–1564). Leonardo da Vinci achieved fame for his paintings *Mona Lisa* and *The Last Supper*. He was an architect and inventor as well as a painter. His drawings of a parachute and a flying machine show that he was far ahead of his time. Michelangelo is best known for his mural paintings on the ceiling and walls of the Sistine Chapel in Rome. These paintings and his powerful sculptures (such as his statue of David) are noted for their realistic depiction of the human body. Michelangelo was also partly responsible for designing the dome of St. Peter's Church in Rome.

In addition to producing beautiful works, artists of the Renaissance were among the first to use *perspective* in paintings and drawings. This technique gave a feeling of depth to a two-dimensional scene.

Literature   The Renaissance in Italy also produced great writers, including Francesco Petrarch (1304–1374) and Niccolò Machiavelli

(1469–1527). Petrarch created the *sonnet*, a 14-line poem. His work became a model for European poets of later times. Machiavelli's *The Prince* served as a handbook for rulers of the day. It advised rulers on ways to achieve and maintain power.

Renaissance Spain produced a great writer in Miguel de Cervantes (1547–1616). His novel *Don Quixote* makes fun of the ways and thoughts of medieval knights. In Renaissance England, William Shakespeare (1564–1616) wrote many great plays, including comedies such as *The Taming of the Shrew*, tragedies such as *Hamlet*, and histories such as *Julius Caesar*. Shakespeare's masterful use of language, his understanding of human follies, and his skill at interweaving plots and subplots account for his reputation as one of the world's greatest playwrights.

The printing press   Literature of the Renaissance was given a boost by the introduction of the printing press. This invention had long been in use in China and Korea. But it was unknown in Europe until a German inventor Johannes Gutenberg began printing books using metal, movable type around 1450. With Gutenberg's printing press, the Bible and other books could be produced in multiple copies at lower prices. Literature could be made available to thousands of people, not just to a few monks and scholars. As more books became available to more people, ideas spread more quickly.

B. THE REFORMATION AND COUNTER-REFORMATION

The questioning spirit of the Renaissance influenced those individuals who would become key figures in the Reformation. Early in the 1500s, Christians in a number of Northern and Central European nations protested against some of the practices and policies of the Roman Catholic Church. Because their movement involved both reform of the Church and protests against the pope's power, it was known as the *Protestant Reformation*.

The Protestant Reformation   In 1517, the Protestant Reformation began when a German monk, Martin Luther, published his "Ninety-Five Theses." This document criticized the Roman Catholic Church and called for reform of certain Church practices of the time, including the sale of *indulgences* (pardons for sins granted by officials of the Roman Catholic Church). In northern Germany, indulgences were sold as pardons from God for sins that one had committed. Luther argued that forgiveness is achieved only through faith in God, not with indulgences. Luther also believed that individuals should read and interpret the Bible for themselves rather than rely upon the pope and priests to do this for them. He said that the Bible is the final religious authority, not the pope or a Church council.

Luther and his supporters also opposed two other Church practices: *nepotism* (the awarding of high Church positions on the basis of family relationships) and *simony* (the buying and selling of Church positions).

Luther's ideas and his questioning of traditional authority were attacked by Pope Leo X, who excommunicated him in 1521. Luther's ideas, however, won the support of many followers, including powerful princes who ruled various states in northern Germany. In addition to liking Luther's ideas, some German rulers became Lutherans in order to seize properties of the Roman Catholic Church. They also saw it as a way to weaken the power of the Holy Roman emperor, Charles V. Lutheranism replaced Catholicism as the established religion throughout northern Germany and in Sweden, Norway, and Denmark.

Other Protestant religions developed in other parts of Western Europe. In Geneva, Switzerland, a French religious thinker, John Calvin (1509–1564), agreed with Luther's idea that the Bible is the only religious authority for Christians. In addition, Calvin introduced the doctrine of *predestination*, the idea that a person's salvation was determined at birth. One could not gain admittance to heaven by trying to lead a moral life since one's admittance had already been determined.

CATHOLIC AND PROTESTANT EUROPE, 1600

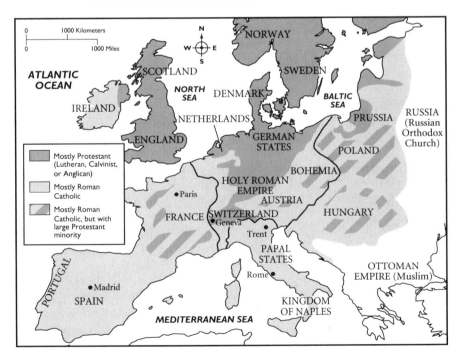

But leading a moral life might be a sign that one was among those chosen to go to heaven. To Calvin, a moral life did not permit music, dancing, and card playing. Christians from several other European countries traveled to Switzerland to hear Calvin preach. They returned home and organized Protestant religions based on Calvin's ideas. Among the new Calvinist groups were the Puritans in England, the Presbyterians in Scotland, and the Huguenots in France.

Another Protestant revolt occurred in England, where King Henry VIII set up the Anglican Church in 1534. He broke with the Roman Catholic Church because of the pope's refusal to grant the king a divorce from Catherine of Aragon, a Spanish princess. Another factor behind the king's action was his desire to gain control over the Catholic Church's extensive properties in England. After he broke with Rome, Henry VIII created the Anglican Church, also known as the Church of England. Thus, England became a Protestant nation with the monarch acting as the leader of the newly formed church. To this day, the Anglican Church is the dominant religion in England.

The Counter-Reformation   As Protestantism spread, Christians who remained faithful to the Roman Catholic Church took various measures to both combat Protestantism and reform their own Church. Their movement is known as both the *Counter-Reformation* and the Catholic Reformation. In the Council of Trent (1545–1563), Catholic Church leaders banned nepotism and simony. The Council also called for tight controls on the sale of indulgences. (After the Council disbanded, the Church banned the sale of indulgences altogether.)

Also in the 1500s, the Catholic Church put greater emphasis on educating Catholics and converting Protestants and other non-Catholics. Much of the responsibility for these efforts was placed upon the Jesuits (Society of Jesus), organized by Ignatius of Loyola in 1534. Jesuit missionaries succeeded in converting many Native Americans in North and South America to Catholicism. Their work explains in part why Latin America today is largely Roman Catholic. The Jesuits also helped prevent Poland, Hungary, and southern Germany from becoming Protestant. Another Catholic group established at this time, the Ursuline Order of nuns, concentrated on educating young women.

Other attempts by the Roman Catholic Church to combat Protestantism included the *Index* and the Inquisition. The *Index* was a list of books that Catholics were prohibited from reading because the works contained ideas that differed from Church teachings. The *Inquisition*, a special Church court that had been set up several centuries earlier, aimed to suppress *heresies* (beliefs that were counter to official Church doctrines). This committee of high Church officials had the power to arrest, imprison, and even execute those who preached "false" doctrines. The Inquisition was strongest in Spain and Italy.

Persecution of non-Christians During the Reformation and Counter-Reformation, there was increased persecution of non-Christians in Western Europe, especially Jews. For example, Jews were expelled from many parts of Italy. In cities from which they were not expelled, such as Rome, they were forced to live in ghettos. As a result of these actions, many Jews resettled in the Ottoman empire, whose Muslim government was more tolerant.

Religious wars The Protestant Reformation and the Catholic Church's responses to it led to social and political conflicts.

1. French Civil War. In the late 1500s in France, Huguenots (a Protestant sect) and Catholics fought a bloody civil war over such issues as religious freedom and which group would control the French crown. In one especially bloody incident, the St. Bartholomew's Day Massacre of 1572, thousands of Huguenots were killed by supporters of the Catholic king. The French Civil War was finally resolved in 1598 in favor of the Catholics. Nevertheless, the French king, Henry IV, granted the Huguenots freedom of worship and the right to serve in government.

2. Thirty Years' War. From 1618 to 1648, the many Protestant and many Catholic states in Germany fought each other in a religious war that caused much devastation. Various foreign powers took sides in the war, including Denmark, Sweden, and France. In the Treaty of Westphalia that ended the war, Lutheran, Calvinist, and Catholic rulers in Germany all received the right to determine the religion of their respective states.

3. English Civil War. This long war (1640–1660) is discussed on page 343.

C. THE AGE OF EXPLORATION

During the 1400s and 1500s, change was occurring in all areas of European life. The Renaissance resulted in sweeping changes in art and literature. The Reformation introduced revolutionary changes in the Christian religion. Also beginning in the 1400s (and continuing into the 1700s), there took place a dramatic and world-changing expansion of geographic knowledge. During this Age of Exploration, Western Europe set up global empires and trading networks. For the first time, the various regions of the world became interconnected through trade.

The Age of Exploration began about 1450. Before that date, Western Europe had existed in relative isolation from the Americas, most of Africa, and much of Asia. During the next 300 years, European nations established regular contacts with these regions. By 1750, European armies, navies, and merchant ships had achieved both political and economic dominance in many parts of the world. How did this transformation come about?

Causes   The roots of European expansion can be traced back to the Crusades (1096–1291). Remember that the Crusades awakened Europeans' desire for luxuries from Asia: silks, spices, and perfumes. Then the published stories of Marco Polo, an Italian who had traveled to China in the late 1200s, aroused further interest in the riches of Asia. Other factors also came into play:

- *Fall of Constantinople.* In 1453, the capital of the Byzantine empire, Constantinople, fell to the Ottoman Turks. Previously, the city had served as an important trading center in which Italian merchants traded for Asian spices and other goods. The loss of this city to an unfriendly power gave Europeans a reason to seek other trade routes to Asia.

- *Italian trade monopoly.* The Italian cities with ports on the Mediterranean Sea had long enjoyed a monopoly in European trade with the Middle East and Asia. With this monopoly, the Italians were able to control the prices of imports throughout Europe. As a result, Spain and Portugal were seeking new routes to Asia— ones that would break the Italian monopoly. Soon England, France, and the Netherlands would also seek new trade routes.

- *New technology.* Inventions made it possible for Western Europeans to improve their ability to navigate ships on ocean waters. The magnetic compass, originally invented in China, made it easier to steer a ship in the right direction. The *astrolabe*, improved by Muslim navigators in the 12th century, allowed sailors to determine how far north or south they were from the equator. Finally, a small, three-masted sailing ship known as a *caravel* was developed by the Portuguese in the 1400s. Caravels were able to survive storms at sea better than earlier-designed ships.

- *Religious and economic motivations.* Both religious and economic motives led Europeans to take on the dangerous and costly voyages of exploration. Many Europeans believed that it was their Christian duty to convert people of other lands to their religion. At the same time, explorers hoped to find new sources of gold and silver in lands across the oceans.

Portuguese and Spanish exploration   European voyages of exploration began with a Portuguese ruler, Prince Henry the Navigator. In the early 1400s, Prince Henry set up a school of navigation in Portugal. Students of this school—Portuguese sea captains and navigators— soon were sailing south along the coast of Africa. There they set up a series of trading posts to obtain gold, ivory, and slaves. Later Portuguese rulers also encouraged and financed voyages, including one by Bartholomeu Dias. In 1488, Dias sailed around the Cape of Good Hope, the southern tip of Africa. Realizing that Dias had found a passage to India, the Portuguese monarchy sent Vasco da Gama on another voyage farther around Africa and on to India, which he reached in 1498.

EARLY VOYAGES OF EXPLORATION

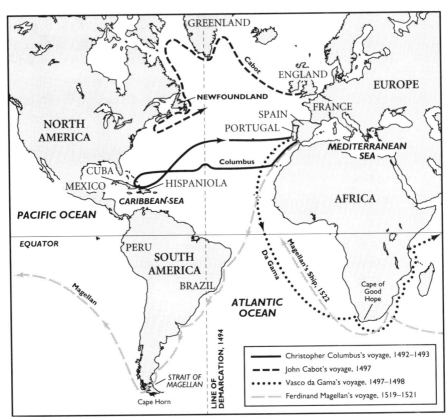

Competing with the Portuguese, Spanish rulers also began financing voyages of exploration. In 1492, Christopher Columbus convinced Queen Isabella I and King Ferdinand of Spain to support his voyage west across the Atlantic. Columbus expected to reach Asia by sailing westward. In this way, he hoped to find a faster route than the one around the tip of Africa. Instead, Columbus and his crew became the first people from Europe since the Vikings to encounter the lands that were soon to be named "America."

Another famous explorer who sailed for Spain was Ferdinand Magellan, who led the first expedition to sail around the world. His fleet sailed west and south around the tip of South America and then west across the Pacific Ocean. Magellan did not live to see the success of his expedition. He was killed by native people in the Philippines in 1521. But one of his ships made it back to Europe in 1522. (Other Spanish and Portuguese explorers and conquerors are discussed on pages 150–152.)

Explorations by other European powers England, France, and the Netherlands were also interested in overseas exploration. In 1497, English King Henry VII sent John Cabot west to find a sea route to Asia. Instead, Cabot reached the coasts of Newfoundland, Nova Scotia, and New England. More than a century later, in 1607, the first permanent English settlement in North America was established at Jamestown, Virginia.

Sailing for France in 1524, Giovanni da Verrazano searched in vain for a Northwest Passage through North America to Asia. In 1534, Jacques Cartier went on a similar quest and explored the St. Lawrence River. The first French settlement in North America was Quebec, founded by Samuel de Champlain in 1608.

The Dutch, too, went in search of a Northwest Passage and ended up settling in North America. In the 1620s, they established the colony of New Netherland along the banks of the Hudson River.

Effects of European expansion What were the consequences of European exploration from the point of view of Africans and Native Americans? For the most part, the effects were tragic and devastating.

From Africa in the 1500s, Portugal and Spain began the practice of shipping enslaved people across the Atlantic to colonies in Central and South America. Many Africans died during the passage to America, largely because of the inhumane treatment they suffered on the slave ships. The slave trade either removed or killed hundreds of thousands of young Africans. As a result, much of Africa's social and political structure was weakened. (For more on the Atlantic slave trade, see Chapter 2.)

Also destructive were the effects of European colonization on Native Americans. The Europeans in both North and South America introduced diseases against which Native Americans had no immunity. These European diseases proved to be far more deadly than European guns. Death rates among Native Americans from smallpox, measles, and other foreign diseases were so high that much of the native population died.

Many of the Native Americans in the French and English colonies of North America who survived diseases and warfare lost their lands to European settlers. In the United States in the 1800s, many were forced to live on reservations (often just barren tracts of land). Nevertheless, Native Americans in both North and South America tried to preserve their own cultures. They rejected European notions that their cultures were "primitive" or "inferior."

European rivalries The nations of Western Europe were affected in many ways by their overseas colonies. For one thing, political rivalries among European nations were now carried out on a global scale. England, for example, wanted some of the gold that Spain was now bringing back from its mines in Peru. Thus, Queen Elizabeth I encouraged English pirate ships to attack the gold-filled Spanish ships that were returning to Spain from colonies in Latin America. Angered by these pirate attacks and fearful of the growing naval power of England, Spain went to war against England. It sent a huge fleet of warships—the Spanish Armada—to attack the English coast in 1588. The expedition ended, however, in a crushing Spanish defeat. From this point on, English naval power was dominant in the Atlantic Ocean.

In the 1600s and 1700s, several wars were fought between England and France over the possession of colonial territories. In one of these wars (known in Europe as the "Seven Years War," 1756–1763), Great Britain finally emerged victorious over France. The same war was also fought in North America, where it was known as the "French and Indian War." British victory in this global conflict gave Britain possession of French Canada as well as control of scattered territories in India.

The Commercial Revolution Sweeping economic changes in Europe accompanied the building of overseas empires. Among these changes were: (1) a change from a feudal system and manorial economy to a capitalist economy based on trade; (2) a shift in economic power from the Italian city-states to nations on the Atlantic coast (chiefly England, France, Spain, and the Netherlands); and (3) a new economic policy called mercantilism. Collectively, these economic changes of the 1500s and 1600s are referred to as the *Commercial Revolution.*

Slowly replacing the feudal and manorial system of the Middle Ages was the economic system known as capitalism. It depended on merchants and bankers to use their money (or capital) to invest in business ventures in hopes of making a profit. During the Commercial Revolution, merchants and bankers in the growing cities of Western Europe successfully applied the capitalist system by investing in colonies and various overseas trading ventures.

Governments also played a role in the Commercial Revolution by adopting the policy known as mercantilism. According to mercantilist theory, a nation was economically strong if it managed to accumulate more gold and silver than any rival kingdom. One way to obtain such precious metals was to dig them from colonial mines. Another way was to sell goods abroad while protecting domestic industries from foreign competition. According to mercantilist theory, colonies could be useful to a kingdom's goal of building a favorable balance of trade. Their chief economic role was to provide raw materials for industries in the ruling country. The laws of France, England, and the other European powers prohibited their colonies from manufacturing goods and also prohibited them from importing anything from any other country. Colonies could import manufactured goods only from the ruling country, thereby adding to that country's economic wealth.

In Review

The following questions refer to historic changes in Western Europe from about 1300 to about 1600, as discussed on pages 331–340.

1. *Key terms:* Define or identify each of the following terms:

humanism   *Index*   Age of Exploration
indulgence   Inquisition   Commercial Revolution

2. Explain what the Renaissance was and why it began in Italy.

3. Compare the causes of the Protestant Reformation with those of the Counter-Reformation (or Catholic Reformation).

4. State *one* major achievement of each of the following: (*a*) Michelangelo, (*b*) Johannes Gutenberg, (*c*) John Calvin, (*d*) Prince Henry the Navigator, and (*e*) Ferdinand Magellan.

5. *Critical thinking:* Which do you think had a greater impact on European society: Luther's writings or Columbus's explorations? Explain your answer.

D. ABSOLUTE MONARCHS IN FRANCE, LIMITED MONARCHS IN ENGLAND

In the 1500s and 1600s, several monarchs in Western Europe attempted to rule their kingdoms as if all power belonged to them alone. They were known as absolute monarchs. These monarchs believed that (*1*) all power to govern rested in their hands and (*2*) their authority came directly from God. As such, they claimed to rule by *divine right*.

Louis XIV of France   Probably the best example of an absolute monarch was Louis XIV of France. From the 1660s until his death in 1715, Louis had enormous influence on the cultural and political life of Europe. He set the standard for other absolute monarchs to follow. To strengthen the French economy, Louis gave support to new industries, encouraged overseas trade, and set up French colonies in North America. But he also engaged in a number of costly wars that severely taxed the French people and built up huge debts. Louis XIV spent additional large sums of money to build a magnificent palace at Versailles. The thousands of French nobles who came to live a luxurious court life at Versailles competed with one another to be counted among the king's favorites. Perhaps Louis XIV's main legacy was that he left France with a bankrupt treasury.

England's tradition of limited monarchy   The English monarchs were not as absolute as those in France. As early as 1215, King John of England had agreed to the terms of the Magna Carta (discussed on page 330). Later, it became customary in England for the king to seek the consent of an advisory body, Parliament, for major policies such as raising a new tax.

QUEEN ELIZABETH I: Here England's most popular queen is honoring
Sir Francis Drake for capturing treasure from Spanish ships. Why were
the monarchs who followed her—James I and Charles I—less popular?

The strongest English monarch of the 1500s was Queen Elizabeth
I. During her long reign (1558–1603), England began its rise as a strong
commercial and naval power. Because of the queen's wise decisions
and popularity, the English Parliament generally went along with the
laws and taxes that she requested.

Elizabeth's successors, in contrast, were much less popular. Both
James I and Charles I offended members of Parliament by claiming
the right to rule without consulting Parliament. Parliament voted to
challenge Charles I by issuing the Petition of Right in 1628. This document said that Parliament must approve all requests by a monarch
for taxes and loans. It further stated that no person could be imprisoned without a specific charge first being issued by authorities.

The triumph of Parliament Charles I decided to defy Parliament and act without its approval. In 1640, a civil war broke out between the king's supporters and those who sided with Parliament. The latter group consisted mainly of Puritans—English Protestants who wanted to reform the Anglican Church. (The king's supporters, with their long-flowing hair, were known as Cavaliers. The opponents of the king were known as Roundheads because of their short hair.) By 1646, the king's forces had been defeated. Charles I was put on trial by Parliament, found guilty of treason, and beheaded in 1649.

Control of the English government was now in the hands of Oliver Cromwell, the Puritan leader of Parliament's army. Until his death in 1658, Cromwell ruled as a dictator (called "Lord Protector"). The Puritans' strict dress rules and social customs were imposed on all English people. Many of the English found Cromwell to be as tyrannical as past kings had been.

After Cromwell's death, a new Parliament restored the monarchy. The new king, Charles II, again made the Anglican Church the official one. But this king also came into conflict with Parliament. As one result of the conflict, Parliament passed the Habeas Corpus Act in 1679. It provided that no individual could be held in prison without being informed of the charges for the arrest. Following Charles II as British king was James II, a Roman Catholic. Fearing that this king intended to make England a Catholic country, Parliament removed him from office.

To take the place of James II, Parliament invited William and Mary, Protestant rulers of the Netherlands, to assume the English throne. Lacking support in England, James II fled to France. This peaceful transfer of power became known as the "Glorious Revolution of 1688." As a condition to gaining the throne, William and Mary were required to sign the English Bill of Rights, in 1689. This document provided that Parliament had the right to meet regularly to pass laws, to approve all taxes, and to control the army. Members of Parliament were guaranteed freedom of speech. The document also included the right to bail and a speedy trial. With this document, much of the English monarchy's power passed to Parliament.

E. THE SCIENTIFIC REVOLUTION

During the Middle Ages, most Europeans had relied on religious authority to explain natural events, such as the movement of the stars, sun, and moon across the night's sky. Scholars also knew what the ancient Greeks and Romans had written about these matters. In the 1500s and 1600s, a *Scientific Revolution* took place in which emphasis was put on observation and experimentation. Scholars began to reject the explanations of natural phenomena given by both the Roman

THE GOVERNMENT OF GREAT BRITAIN

For hundreds of years, England and its northern neighbor, Scotland, existed as separate kingdoms. This fact changed in 1707 when the English and Scottish parliaments agreed to a union to be called Great Britain. Since our own U.S. government is partly based on the British example, we should understand how Great Britain's government was organized.

In Great Britain today, two political parties—the Conservative party and the Labour party—compete to control a majority of votes in Parliament. The British two-party system goes back to the early 1700s when a group of politicians called Tories competed with another group called Whigs. (In general, the Tories tended to favor conservative policies, compared to the somewhat more liberal Whigs.)

During the same period—the reign of George I (1714–1727)—the British cabinet system of government originated. The king began the practice of choosing his chief advisers and ministers from the majority party in Parliament. At the time, the Whigs were in control, so George I chose all Whig leaders to form his *Cabinet*, a council of ministers. The chief leader of the Whig party, Sir Robert Walpole, acted as the leader of the king's Cabinet. He became known as the *prime minister*. In effect, the prime minister and the Cabinet ran the government. The king simply endorsed the policies recommended by his ministers. That is the way the British system has worked ever since.

Unlike the United States, Great Britain does not have a written constitution. Instead, its government is based on a series of laws, traditions, and customs that have been accepted over a long period of time. For example, although parliamentary elections in Britain are scheduled every five years, they may be held sooner if the House of Commons (the lower and more powerful house of Parliament) votes "no confidence" in the prime minister. Under these circumstances, the prime minister will call for new elections.

Although it has no written constitution, the British government has a long tradition of respecting citizens' rights to freedom of speech, press, and religion. British citizens are also guaranteed legal rights such as those enjoyed by U.S. citizens. Underlying these rights are the principles of equality before the law and justice for all.

British parliamentary democracy is a *unitary system of government* rather than a federal one. Power resides in a central government rather than being divided between a central government and state governments, as in the United States.

WESTMINSTER HALL, LONDON: Here the two houses of the British Parliament meet. What are the differences between the House of Commons and the House of Lords?

Catholic Church and the ancient Greeks and Romans. Major contributors to the Scientific Revolution were Nicolaus Copernicus, Galileo Galilei, and Sir Isaac Newton.

Copernicus (1473–1543) A Polish astronomer, Copernicus challenged the belief that a stationary earth was the center of the universe. This view had long been supported by the Church. Through reasoning and observation, Copernicus concluded that the earth and other planets revolved around a stationary sun. Fearful of prosecution, Copernicus refused to allow his writings to be published until he was near death. As he feared, Church authorities condemned his book.

Galileo (1564–1642) An Italian astronomer, mathematician, and physicist, Galileo built a telescope that enabled him to make detailed observations of stars, planets, and the moon. His observations confirmed those of Copernicus. In 1633, the Inquisition summoned Galileo to Rome and ordered him to renounce his views publicly. The Catholic Church put him under house arrest. Although Galileo was silenced, his views would form the basis for future scientific theories and discoveries.

Newton (1642–1727) An English physicist and mathematician, Newton discovered important laws of motion, including the law of gravity. According to Newton, the sun, the earth, and other bodies have gravitational pulls. These pulls explain why planets remain in orbit around the sun, why the moon remains in orbit around the earth, and why objects on planets fall in only one direction—downward.

Scientists like Newton and Galileo also were among the first to use the *scientific method*. In other words, they would conduct experiments and make careful observations before drawing conclusions. Many advances were made in medicine, biology, mathematics, and physics. Moreover, people who specialized in social sciences (such as political science and history) thought that they could use similar methods in their own fields of study.

F. THE ENLIGHTENMENT

In the 1700s, leading thinkers of Western Europe looked to the future with optimism. They thought that the future could be shaped and directed by reason. They believed that society was based on natural laws. As a result, they challenged the power of absolute monarchs and the idea that a monarch ruled by divine right. Historians have labeled this period "The Age of Enlightenment" or "The Age of Reason."

In Great Britain, John Locke (1632–1704) was a leading Enlightenment figure. This English philosopher is best known for his work *Two Treatises of Government*. Locke wrote that life, liberty, and property were *natural rights*, rights with which all persons are born. He stated that people gave up total freedom in return for protection from a ruler. Thus, it was the ruler's responsibility to protect the natural rights of the people. If a ruler failed to carry out this responsibility, the people had the right to overthrow their government.

France was represented in the Enlightenment by several influential thinkers, including:

- **Baron de Montesquieu (1689–1755)**, a French author. He is best remembered for his monumental work *The Spirit of the Law*. In it, he wrote that the ideal government should be separated into three branches. The legislative branch would pass laws; the executive branch would carry out the laws; and the judicial branch would interpret the laws. The purpose of this separation was to prevent any one individual or group from becoming too powerful and thereby gaining total control of the government. Montesquieu's ideas became the basis for the separation of powers clauses in the U.S. Constitution.

- **Voltaire (1694–1778)**, a French author and probably the most influential Enlightenment figure. Like Montesquieu, he was a great admirer of the English system of government. He wrote essays, plays, and letters that attacked various injustices in France by both the monarchy and the Catholic Church. He condemned abuse of power by the monarchy, class privileges, torture, slavery, censorship, and religious intolerance. Voltaire argued that the best form of government was a monarchy that had a constitution, a strong parliament, and civil rights for all. Voltaire was both imprisoned and exiled for expressing his views.

- Jean-Jacques Rousseau (1712–1778), a Swiss writer who lived most of his life in France. There he wrote novels, philosophical works, and an autobiography, *Confessions.* In his most famous book, *The Social Contract,* he rejected the way that society was then organized. Rousseau proposed a different way of governing—one in which the will of the people would guide the decisions of government. He wrote that people are born good but are corrupted by the environment: "Man is born free, and everywhere he is in chains."

WOMEN OF THE ENLIGHTENMENT: A number of women, including Madame de Staël of France (above), organized gatherings of leading thinkers of the Enlightenment and wrote important essays of their own. How did ideas of the Enlightenment challenge the absolute monarchs of the 18th century?

Impact on political revolutions The writers of the Enlightenment had a major impact on both European and American societies. Their ideas formed the intellectual basis for the American and French revolutions (and for later independence movements in Latin America). For example, Locke's ideas on natural rights and the right to overthrow one's government influenced American revolutionary leader Thomas Jefferson. Locke had written, "Man has the right to defend his life, liberty, and property against those who would take it away." Later, in the Declaration of Independence, Jefferson would write that all people had an equal right to "life, liberty, and the pursuit of happiness."

In Review

The following questions refer to historical changes in Western Europe from about 1500 to 1789, as discussed on pages 341–348.

1. *Key terms:* Define or identify each of the following:

Oliver Cromwell	Cabinet	unitary system of government
English Bill of Rights	prime minister	Age of Enlightenment

2. Compare England's monarchy under William and Mary with France's monarchy under Louis XIV.

3. State at least one effect that writers of the Enlightenment had on the history of Western Europe or some other region.

4. *Critical thinking:* State whether each of the following can be proved or disproved scientifically: (*a*) James I's claim to rule by divine right, (*b*) Jefferson's claim that all people have rights to "life, liberty, and the pursuit of happiness." and (*c*) Galileo's claim that all objects fall at a fixed rate. Explain each answer.

G. THE FRENCH REVOLUTION (1789–1799)

A revolution against the French monarchy broke out in 1789. This upheaval proved to be a dynamic agent of change not only for France but also for other nations of Europe. Eventually, the ideas of the French Revolution would influence nations in other regions as well.

Long-range causes Political, economic, and social factors all played a part in causing the revolution.

1. *Political causes.* An underlying cause of the revolution was the regular abuse of power by the French monarchy. Holding absolute power, a French king could order the arrest of anyone on any charge and could hold secret trials without juries.

2. *Economic causes.* A chief economic factor was the unfair system of taxation in France. For more than a century, heavy taxes had been levied to pay for the costly wars of three kings named Louis (Louis XIV, XV, and XVI). The burden of paying these taxes fell on the middle and lower classes, with the peasants paying the highest taxes. Members of the upper class (nobles and clergy) were exempt from paying any taxes at all. Of course, taxpayers resented this.

3. *Social causes.* A major social cause was the unequal structure of French society. At the top of society, the higher clergy and the nobles formed a small but privileged class. The Roman Catholic Church owned half of the land in France but paid no property taxes. Nobles enjoyed a life of luxury and were supported by government pensions. The *bourgeoisie* (members of the middle class, including shopkeepers) were angry about the restrictions placed upon them. There were limits as to how far they could advance in government and Church employment. They (as well as the peasants) had no say on how much taxes they had to pay.

Meeting of the National Assembly   The immediate cause of the French Revolution was the financial situation of the monarchy. As a result of past wars and extravagant living at Versailles, King Louis XVI's government was nearly bankrupt. To raise taxes, Louis decided in 1789 to call a meeting of the Estates General. This legislative body, which had not met in 175 years, was divided into three estates, or social classes. The First Estate represented the clergy, the Second Estate represented the nobility, and the Third Estate represented the middle and lower classes. Voting took place by estate. Consequently, although the Third Estate had the most members and represented 95 percent of the population, it could be outvoted two to one by the First and Second Estates. Angered by this situation, the Third Estate refused to take part in deliberations. Joined by a few priests from the First Estate, they formed a National Assembly in which representatives would vote as individuals rather than by estate. Moving to a nearby tennis court, they took an oath (the Tennis Court Oath) not to disband until they had written a new constitution for France. Unsure of what to do, the king took no action. Then desperate for new taxes, he finally recognized the National Assembly as legitimate.

Despite the king's agreement with the National Assembly, many people in Paris did not trust him. They believed that Louis XVI would call in troops to stop the National Assembly from functioning. Thus, they took matters into their own hands. On July 14, 1789, crowds stormed the Bastille, a Paris prison, hoping to find weapons with which to fight the king's army. Although there were few weapons in the Bastille, its takeover was considered a victory for the masses. (Today, this event is celebrated in France every July 14 as Bastille Day.)

THE TENNIS COURT OATH: This painting shows members of the Third Estate meeting on a tennis court in the king's palace at Versailles in 1789. What was decided at this meeting? Why did this event have revolutionary consequences?

While crowds were gathering in Paris, peasants throughout France were staging their own protests. They invaded the houses of nobles, destroyed nobles' property, and seized records of peasants' feudal obligations to nobles.

Phases of the revolution The French Revolution went through three phases.

1. Years 1789–1792. This first phase was moderate and was led by members of the middle class. During this period, the National Assembly adopted the Declaration of the Rights of Man. This document introduced the slogan "Liberty, Equality, Fraternity" and declared that "men are born free and remain free and equal in rights." Included in these rights were liberty, property, and resistance to oppression. The National Assembly also abolished feudal dues, limited the powers of the king, and gave the government the power to make appointments in the Roman Catholic Church. It also seized Church lands, selling them at low prices to peasants.

Fearful that the king would use troops to end the revolution and abolish reforms, a group of women marched on Versailles (located outside of Paris). This "women's march" forced King Louis XVI and

Queen Marie Antoinette to return to Paris. Shortly thereafter, the king and queen attempted to flee from France. But they were captured by forces loyal to the revolutionaries and returned to Paris.

2. Years 1792–1794. The second phase of the revolution was the most *radical* (extreme) of the three. During this period, a new group of revolutionaries came to power and executed the French king and queen. The new leaders organized a Committee of Public Safety for the purpose of arresting and executing anyone thought to be "an enemy" of the revolution. Georges-Jacques Danton and Maximilien Robespierre became the most powerful and feared members of this committee. In the "Reign of Terror" that followed, the committee condemned to death thousands of innocent people. Many were executed by a new instrument for beheading known as the *guillotine*. In 1794, Robespierre sent Danton to his death; later that year, Robespierre himself was guillotined. With that event, the Reign of Terror ended.

3. Years 1795–1799. In the third phase of the revolution, a conservative, five-man Directory governed France. This government proved to be weak and ineffectual. In 1799, a popular general, Napoleon Bonaparte, staged a coup d'état. He overthrew the Directory and brought the French Revolution to an end.

Foreign reaction The revolutionary events in France greatly worried the monarchs of Europe. They feared that the French Revolution and its ideals of liberty, equality, and fraternity would spread to their own kingdoms and challenge their rule. Thus, several monarchs joined forces in an attempt to suppress the revolution by invading France. They were unsuccessful, however, largely because nationalist feelings caused many French people to support their government. In addition, talented generals in the French armed forces (such as Napoleon Bonaparte) provided military leadership.

Results of the revolution The French Revolution had several important results. First, political power in France shifted to the bourgeoisie. French nobles, who had been dominant under the monarchy, saw a sharp decline in their powers. Second, there was increased nationalist feelings, both in France and elsewhere. Finally, the ideals of the French Revolution (liberty, equality, and fraternity) spread to other parts of Europe, and eventually throughout the rest of the world.

H. NAPOLEON'S EMPIRE (1799–1815)

For 15 years, one man—Napoleon Bonaparte—dominated France and much of Europe.

Foreign wars France was at war during most of Napoleon's reign. In fact, Napoleon often led the French and allied forces, which at one point occupied much of the European continent. At different times,

French forces defeated the Austrian, Prussian, and Russian armies. Of the European powers, only Great Britain stayed undefeated. Its superior navy commanded the sea lanes in northern Europe. In 1805, a British fleet under Admiral Horatio Nelson won a decisive battle against the French off the coast of Spain at Cape Trafalgar. By failing to defeat the British Navy, Napoleon had no chance of invading Great Britain.

Napoleon's many victories on land allowed him to place his relatives on thrones in Italy, Spain, and the Netherlands. He also formed new states that were dependent for their existence upon France: the Confederation of the Rhine (part of present-day Germany) and the Duchy of Warsaw (part of present-day Poland).

In 1812, Napoleon made a major strategic error by invading Russia and then staying there too long. The French army was able to move deep into Russia and defeat a Russian force near Moscow. Then, however, winter set in. Lacking supplies for the bitter cold weather, Napoleon ordered a retreat. During the retreat, the French suffered overwhelming losses from attacking Russian forces. As a result, Napoleon was never again able to organize a large enough army to defeat France's many enemies. In 1815 at Waterloo, Napoleon's troops were defeated by combined British and Prussian armies. The victors at Waterloo took Napoleon prisoner and forced him to spend the rest of his life in exile. The new French ruler was a monarch with limited powers—Louis XVIII.

Domestic achievements   Napoleon is remembered for his accomplishments inside France almost as well as he is remembered for his military victories abroad. He restored social order among the French people, most of whom were tired of years of violence and disorder. Napoleon did this by setting up a dictatorship, serving initially as first consul and later as emperor.

Although there was a dictatorship, Napoleon allowed religious freedom. He ended the government's persecution of the Roman Catholic clergy, a practice that it had begun during the French Revolution. He also abolished discrimination against Jews, which had been taking place for centuries.

Under Napoleon's leadership, the French government created the Code Napoleon. This set of laws applied to all of France, replacing the many confusing local and regional laws. The Code emphasized important rights, such as trial by jury, the right to choose one's occupation, and equality before the law for all men. It eliminated all restrictions that still existed in regard to serfdom and feudalism. Concerning women, however, the Code said that they could not buy or sell property and had only limited legal rights. In effect, women now had fewer rights than they had had during the French Revolution.

NAPOLEON'S EMPIRE, 1812

Napoleon centralized education, which had earlier been the responsibility of the Catholic Church. For the first time, the French government paid teachers' salaries and set national educational standards. Other domestic reforms included the establishment of a Legion of Honor to reward those who served France and a Bank of France to control French currency.

Napoleon's legacy abroad Napoleon introduced reforms wherever the French army went. Restrictions against Jews, such as forcing them to live in ghettos, were abolished. In parts of Europe, religious tolerance became more widespread. The French introduced the Code Napoleon in conquered countries, thereby replacing laws that had retained aspects of feudalism and serfdom. Nobles lost much of their power in these countries. Appointments and promotions in government offices came to be based more on merit than on social class.

On the negative side, Napoleon was a dictator. He did not allow freedom of speech, the press, or assembly. The French secret police arrested critics of Napoleon. Moreover, his ambitious foreign policies led to the death of millions of Europeans—both civilians and soldiers. Today, the question of whether Napoleon was more of a hero or a villain is still being debated.

I. THE RISE OF NATIONALISM

Napoleon made another important contribution to European history. He contributed to the rise of nationalism throughout the continent. Nationalism is the feeling of loyalty to a region whose inhabitants share a common history, language, and tradition. It often leads to a desire among those who share these characteristics to form their own nation-state. It sometimes leads people who already have their own state to want to make it larger or stronger. In France, Napoleon encouraged the teaching of patriotism in the schools. His military victories inspired nationalism among the French people.

At the same time, the spirit of nationalism was aroused in reaction against French rule and influence in the countries that France had conquered. The Spaniards and Portuguese, for example, rose up against their French rulers and declared the independence of their nations. Many Germans began to hope for the time when all German-speaking states in Central Europe would be united under one government. Italians were also inspired to think of their long-divided land as a single nation with a common culture.

Concert of Europe   In the decades after Napoleon's final defeat in 1815 at the battle of Waterloo, the leaders of Europe's major powers (Austria, Prussia, Russia, and France) met from time to time. Known as the "Concert of Europe," this group was fearful of the growth of nationalism and sought to control its impact. Troops from these powers intervened against nationalist uprisings that threatened the powers of European monarchs. Since Prince Metternich, the Austrian foreign minister, was the leader of the Concert of Europe, the period from 1815 to 1848 has been called the "Age of Metternich."

Italian unification   For centuries after the fall of the Roman empire, Italy had consisted of a number of city-states and small kingdoms. The Papal States, for example, were separate from the Kingdom of Sardinia. Italians began to wonder why they did not have a single state for all Italian-speaking people. Three Italian leaders were chiefly responsible for gaining Italian unification in the 1850s and 1860s. They were: Giuseppe Mazzini (sometimes called the "soul" of the movement), Camillo di Cavour (the "brain" of the movement), and Giuseppe Garibaldi (the "sword" of the movement).

Mazzini was a writer who dreamed of a unified, democratic Italy. To achieve this goal, he founded an organization known as "Young Italy." He also wrote inspiring books and essays about his dream.

Cavour served as prime minister of Sardinia, one of the larger Italian states. Through a series of brilliant diplomatic maneuvers and wars, he managed to unite most of the Italian city-states and kingdoms by 1860.

UNIFICATION OF ITALY

Garibaldi provided the revolutionary force (the "Red Shirts") that overthrew the government of Sicily in southern Italy. Then Cavour and Garibaldi helped to join this area with the Kingdom of Sardinia in 1861. Thus, the king of Sardinia, Victor Emmanuel II, became king of Italy. The process of Italian unification was completed with the addition of Rome in 1870.

German unification   At about the same time, German nationalism helped bring about the creation of a united Germany. Before the 1860s, the German-speaking part of Europe had consisted of many independent states. King Wilhelm I came to the throne of Prussia in 1861 with the goal of uniting Germany under the leadership of Prussia by force of arms. His strong-willed and able prime minister, Otto von Bismarck, helped the Prussian king achieve his goal through a policy he called "blood and iron." This meant that Prussia would be willing to fight for a unified Germany.

German unity was achieved in several steps. In 1866, Prussia engaged Austria, the other major German state, in warfare and then defeated it. As a result, Prussia annexed several states in northern

Germany. In 1867, Bismarck pressured other German states to join with Prussia in a North German Confederation. Bismarck then maneuvered France into declaring war against Prussia. Prussian troops quickly defeated the French in 1871. In the peace treaty ending the Franco-Prussian War, Prussia gained the French territories of Alsace and Lorraine. After the war, a group of German states in the south voluntarily joined the German confederation under Prussian leadership. Germany was now united as a nation. Its emperor, or kaiser, was Wilhelm I.

Self-determination   Both Italy and Germany provided examples of countries in which the force of nationalism brought several independent states together to form a new nation. Nationalism also worked the opposite way—separating a large state into several smaller ones. In the 19th century, people in different regions began to demand self-determination, the right of national groups under the rule of others to declare independence. In Latin America, most of the European colonies fought for and achieved independence in the early 1800s (discussed in Chapter 4). In Europe, Greece won its independence from the Ottoman empire in 1830. In the same year, Belgium separated from the Netherlands.

UNIFICATION OF GERMANY

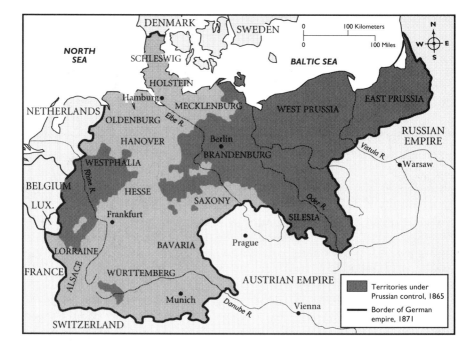

In Review

The following questions refer to the French Revolution, Napoleon, and nationalism, as discussed on pages 348–356.

1. *Key terms:* Define or identify each of the following:

   bourgeoisie　　　　National Assembly　　　　Code Napoleon
   Third Estate　　　　Reign of Terror　　　　self-determination

2. Identify *one* political, *one* social, and *one* economic cause of the French Revolution.

3. Explain why Napoleon's invasion of Russia was considered to be a major mistake for him and for France.

4. Identify those individuals who were most responsible for　(a) the unification of Italy and　(b) the unification of Germany.

5. *Critical thinking:* On balance, would you say that Napoleon accomplished more good than harm—or more harm than good? Try to prove your conclusion by listing positives in one column and negatives in another.

J. THE INDUSTRIAL REVOLUTION

Nationalism was a powerful political force that would ultimately change the world. Another powerful agent for change was the economic revolution in the way goods were made. Beginning in England in about 1750, people began to manufacture goods in factories instead of at home. Moreover, they began to make things by machine rather than by hand. These changes greatly increased the quantity of manufactured goods while also reducing their cost. As a result of this Industrial Revolution, cheaper goods would become available to more people all over the world.

Preconditions　The Industrial Revolution began in England for several reasons. First, England had a large supply of coal and iron. Second, labor was widely available there as a result of the country's growing population and the movement of unemployed farm workers to the cities. Third, England's many navigable rivers and canals made it relatively easy to transport raw materials to and finished goods from the factories. Fourth, demand for England's goods was strong because the English population was growing rapidly and the English colonists in America were required by mercantilist laws to purchase manufactured goods only from the home country. Finally, England had a well established and growing middle class that specialized in trade. As capitalists, members of this class were looking for new opportunities to invest their money, such as in the building of factories.

The factory system   The English textile industry was the first to develop the *factory system*, the production of goods in a factory instead of in the homes of workers. Under the factory system, large numbers of people worked together in large buildings. The machinery used in these factories made production more efficient than was possible working in cottages with hand tools.

The factory system was first used to produce cotton textiles. The invention of new machines for spinning and weaving cotton increased production in this industry. For example, the *spinning jenny* increased the output of cotton thread by spinning eight threads at one time from cotton fibers. The *power loom* enabled workers to weave cloth from threads more quickly by using water power. The ability of British factories to increase the output of cotton thread led to an increased demand for cotton fiber. In the late 18th century, an American inventor, Eli Whitney, created the *cotton gin*, a machine that could separate seeds from raw cotton much faster than human labor could.

Another invention that greatly increased textile production was the *steam engine*, developed by a Scot named James Watt in the 1760s. Before this invention, factories had to be located along the banks of a fast-moving stream or river in order to harness water power. With the steam engine, power was produced by the burning of coal. This was a great advantage for the British, who had large deposits of coal. Now factories could be located away from rivers and streams.

Steam power was also used in other industries beside textiles. In iron mills, flour mills, breweries, and other types of factories, steam power greatly increased production.

Railroads and steamboats   The use of steam also led to major improvements in transportation—changes that contributed to the Industrial Revolution. Steam power enabled the growth of railroads, which in many places replaced transportation on rivers and canals. By 1850, railroad lines connected most of the major cities in England and some cities on the European continent. Finally, the steamboat was invented in 1807 by Robert Fulton, an American. Used on rivers, lakes, and oceans, the steamboat would increase the speed with which people and goods could be transported across water.

The Industrial Revolution elsewhere   Soon after the Industrial Revolution began in England, it spread to France, Belgium, northern Germany, and elsewhere. By 1850, much of Western Europe was industrializing. The Industrial Revolution also took place in the United States because of its many natural resources, large labor supply, railroad and canal networks, and technological advances. By the end of the 19th century, the United States replaced Great Britain as the leading industrial nation in the world. In the 20th century, the Industrial Revolution would spread to almost every part of the globe.

INVENTIONS OF THE 19TH CENTURY

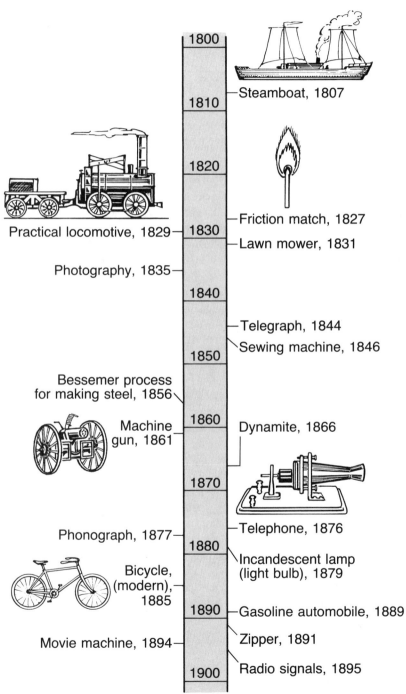

1800

Steamboat, 1807

1810

1820

Practical locomotive, 1829 — 1830 — Friction match, 1827
— Lawn mower, 1831

Photography, 1835 —

1840

— Telegraph, 1844
Sewing machine, 1846

1850

Bessemer process
for making steel, 1856

Machine 1860 Dynamite, 1866
gun, 1861

1870

Telephone, 1876

Phonograph, 1877 — 1880
Incandescent lamp
Bicycle, (light bulb), 1879
(modern),
1885
1890 — Gasoline automobile, 1889

Movie machine, 1894 — Zipper, 1891

1900 — Radio signals, 1895

K. EFFECTS OF THE INDUSTRIAL REVOLUTION

The Industrial Revolution transformed life in Europe. In addition to its many economic effects, it gave rise to several political and social movements of great importance.

Increased interdependency   As we just learned, the Industrial Revolution, which began in England, soon spread to other parts of the world. Because of industrialization, nations produced more goods, which resulted in a need to trade more with one another. In this way, the Industrial Revolution made the nations of the world more interdependent.

Labor reforms   In the early 1800s, working conditions in British factories and mines were terrible. Workers toiled 12 to 16 hours a day for little pay. It was common for whole families to work together—mother, father, and even little children. They often worked in poorly ventilated areas with no safety devices on machines. These conditions led to many work-related injuries and deaths.

In response to poor working conditions, the British Parliament passed several factory reform laws in the 1800s. The Factory Act of 1833 limited children to working an eight-hour day. Later laws provided additional reforms. For example, one law prohibited boys under 13 and all women from working underground in the mines. Another law set the maximum workday for all workers at ten hours. Other laws set minimum safety standards in factories.

Urbanization   Another result of the Industrial Revolution was the growth of cities in Western Europe. In part, this urbanization was due to a general population explosion in Europe. People were living longer, and women were having babies at an earlier age.

Other factors behind urbanization involved changes in agriculture. New machines were invented that made agriculture more productive and profitable. As farming became more productive, farms needed fewer workers. At the same time, some English farmers began to acquire lands by fencing off, or enclosing, common lands that had previously been used by villagers as pastures. This *enclosure movement*, as it was called, resulted in larger and more efficient farms. But many of the farmers who could no longer use the lands that had been held in common abandoned farming and migrated to the cities in search of work. There many of them were employed in the newly opened factories and other businesses.

Urban dwellers often lived in crowded, unsanitary conditions. Not enough housing was built for all the urban newcomers. Millions of workers were forced to live in homes that lacked proper sewage systems and ventilation.

EFFECTS OF THE INDUSTRIAL REVOLUTION: This engraving shows a street scene in London in the mid-1800s. Why did the Industrial Revolution increase urban crowding and poverty?

Political reforms   The Industrial Revolution resulted in the growth of the middle class in Great Britain. In the early 1800s, however, the British upper class still controlled political power. This control was made possible by property qualifications for voting. Thus, only about 6 percent of males in Britain could vote for representation in the House of Commons (the lower house of Parliament). Because membership in the House of Lords (the upper house) was hereditary, it too was still controlled by the upper class.

A growing number of people in the middle class (such as industrialists, doctors, lawyers, bankers, and merchants) demanded to participate in government. The Reform Bill of 1832 satisfied much of the middle class by reducing property and financial qualifications for voting. Now about 20 percent of all males could vote. The act also changed representation in Parliament by increasing the number of members from the growing urban areas and decreasing the number from rural ones. Thus, the act eliminated what were called "rotten boroughs," underpopulated regions that were overrepresented in Parliament. The Reform Bill of 1867 further increased the number of voters. It eliminated property qualifications for male factory workers. Later bills gave the vote to male farm workers as well. Women in Great Britain did not gain the right to vote until 1918 (for those over age 30) and 1928 (for those over age 21).

In France, the vote was extended in 1830, but only slightly. In 1848, however, all adult men got the suffrage. French women did not get the vote until 1945.

Laissez-faire capitalism   During the Industrial Revolution, Scottish economist Adam Smith developed an important theory about capitalism. In his book, *The Wealth of Nations* (1776), Smith called for an end to tariffs, mercantilism, and other government regulations affecting the economy. Instead, he proposed free trade and free competition, which he claimed would benefit everyone. His idea of no government interference in business affairs is called laissez-faire (a French phrase meaning "leave it alone"). Smith's economic philosophy influenced not only political leaders in Great Britain, but leaders in other industrialized nations as well, including the United States.

Labor unions   To protect themselves from poor working conditions and low wages, workers organized labor unions in Great Britain and other industrialized countries. In the 1800s, these unions were organized mainly by crafts. There were unions of carpenters, printers, and so on. Members sometimes went on strike to obtain better working conditions and higher pay. Most Western European governments banned labor unions in the early 1800s. In time, however, as the size and power of the working class grew, laws were changed to permit labor unions to operate.

Socialism   During the 19th century, many critics blamed the capitalist system for the terrible working and living conditions of the new industrial workers. Among the critics of capitalism, the *socialists* were the most vocal. They believed that government should play a major role in improving working and living conditions. Most socialists believed that government should own the means of production—land, machinery, and factories. Socialists also called for the government to provide people in need with a range of social services, such as health care. Another group of socialists called for people to join together to form their own ideal communities. In such communities, homes, land, and businesses would be owned by all, collectively. Advocates of these communities were known as *utopian socialists*.

Karl Marx was one of the leading socialists of the 1800s. He developed the theory of communism. Born in Germany, Marx eventually settled in England. In 1848, he and fellow socialist Friedrich Engels wrote their most famous work, *The Communist Manifesto*. In it, they expressed the idea that history was an ongoing class struggle between the rich and the poor. Marx also discussed the future, claiming that, like the past, it too will be determined by economic forces. He stated that competition among businesses would force prices to come down. As prices declined, profits for business owners would also be reduced. One way for businesses to increase profits would be to force workers to accept lower wages or to work longer hours at no additional pay. Marx called this idea the "theory of surplus value" because the profits came from this extra, or "surplus," labor of workers.

Marx also believed that competition among businesses would force business owners to increase production by replacing workers with machines. As a result of this *automation*, unemployment would increase significantly. Marx predicted that Europe's industrial economy would undergo frequent periods of unemployment and depression. He further predicted that conditions of labor and wages would worsen until workers, unable to survive, would be driven to revolution. This revolution, claimed Marx, would be successful, with the victorious *proletariat* (workers) replacing the bourgeoisie as rulers, and socialism replacing capitalism as the economic system.

Marx believed that after the revolution a temporary dictatorship would be necessary to protect the interests of workers. Eventually, Marx claimed, all class differences would disappear; there would then be no conflicts or wars and no need for a state. He labeled this stateless, all-workers society "communism" since he believed that workers in it would work for the benefit of the community rather than for their own, individual gains.

In the late 1800s in most Western European countries, political parties were formed that were based on the theories of Karl Marx. (In other chapters—4, 6, and 8—we describe how Marxists in the 20th century came to power in Cuba, China, Russia, and elsewhere.)

L. AGE OF IMPERIALISM

In the late 19th and early 20th centuries, the industrialized nations of Western Europe competed to take control of new colonies in Africa and Asia. Their efforts to build colonial empires gave a name to their

GREEDY JOHNNIE: This 1896 cartoon commented on the imperialist scramble for overseas colonies. Who are the competitors? Why is Britain called "Greedy Johnnie"?

era: the "Age of Imperialism." Imperialism refers to the practice of strong nations taking control of weaker areas. The Western European nations were able to dominate others because of their technological and military superiority.

Motives for imperialism   Behind the race for colonies were economic, political, and social motives. Economically, the Industrial Revolution brought about an increasing supply of manufactured goods. Needing new markets for these goods, the Europeans looked for colonies to serve that need. The industrial nations also required new sources of raw materials. Many of these could be obtained cheaply in Asia and Africa. Another economic motive was the belief that colonies offered excellent opportunities to invest money.

Politically, some Europeans wanted colonies to strengthen national pride. People thought that they would feel more important if their government had an empire. Moreover, colonies were thought to give nations some military advantages. Some naval officers, for example, wanted island colonies as naval bases and coaling stations for their warships.

Socially, many Europeans believed that it was their duty to spread the benefits of their culture to other peoples. These supposed benefits included Christianity, medical and scientific advances, and Western educational systems. This idea was expressed at the time in the poem "The White Man's Burden" by Rudyard Kipling.

Competition for colonies   When the scramble for colonies began in 1878, certain European nations already had centuries of experience governing overseas empires. Great Britain, for example, controlled the South Asian subcontinent, the Malay Peninsula, Burma, Singapore, and Hong Kong. In the South Pacific, lands under British control included New Zealand and Australia. Furthermore, Britain already ruled many African colonies. The British liked to boast: "The sun never sets on the British empire." France, the Netherlands, and Portugal also had important overseas empires.

The scramble for colonies in Africa was begun by King Leopold II of Belgium. He had become interested in Africa following the explorations of Henry Stanley and David Livingstone. In 1878, Leopold II's agents seized the Congo (present-day Zaire) and set up a colony to be ruled directly by the Belgian monarch. Then France and Britain added more colonies to their empires in Africa. Germany and Italy, two nations lacking empires, also succeeded in acquiring a few African colonies. The orderly division of Africa into European colonies was agreed upon at the Berlin Conference (1884–1885). At the same time, France expanded its control over Indochina. In addition, China was divided up into various spheres of influence (discussed in Chapter 6).

Opposition to imperialism   Not everyone in Western Europe was convinced that imperialism was a good policy. In fact, it had many critics, who argued as follows:

- Imperialism was morally wrong. European governments denied basic political rights to people in their colonies.
- The high expense of governing an overseas colony was often well above the revenues and profits derived from exploiting that colony.

- The competition for colonies increased political and military tensions among European powers. In fact, imperialism was partly responsible for several wars. For example, in the Fashoda Incident (1898), Britain and France nearly went to war in the Sudan before resolving their dispute. In the Boer War (1899–1902), Great Britain fought descendants of Dutch settlers for control of portions of South Africa. And as we will discuss in the following section, imperialism was also an underlying cause of World War I.

In Review

The following questions refer to the Industrial Revolution and imperialism, as discussed on pages 357–366.

1. *Key terms:* Define or identify each of the following:

    factory system   laissez-faire   automation
    enclosure movement   utopian socialism   proletariat

2. Provide at least *two* reasons why the Industrial Revolution began in England.

3. Identify *three* effects of the Industrial Revolution on European society.

4. Compare and contrast Adam Smith's economic theories with those of Karl Marx.

5. *Critical thinking:* Was imperialism a positive or negative force for change? Explain your answer.

M. WORLD WAR I (1914–1918)

World War I was originally known as the "Great War." It involved all of the European powers and many of their colonies. Eventually, the United States, Japan, and China were also drawn into the conflict.

Long-range causes The long-range causes of World War I originated in the 19th century. They were:

- *Nationalism.* As discussed previously, feelings of nationalism ran high in the 19th and early 20th centuries. For example, French nationalists hoped to regain Alsace and Lorraine, which had been lost to Germany in the Franco-Prussian War, 1870–1871. Meanwhile in Eastern Europe, Poles, Serbs, Croats, Czechs, and other ethnic groups desired to break away from the Austro-Hungarian empire and set up independent nations of their own.

- *Militarism.* A nation's policy of building up its armed forces with the goal of having more military power than its rivals is called *militarism.* For example, in the years before World War I, Germany attempted to build a powerful navy capable of challenging Great

Britain, which had the world's strongest navy at that time. Another example of militarism was the competition among the major powers of Europe to enlarge their armies and equip them with superior weapons. In particular, France and Germany, fearing each other, built up their respective armies.

- *Imperialism.* Germany's attempts to acquire African colonies were viewed by Great Britain and France as challenges to their own empires in Africa. For example, in 1905 and again in 1911, France and Germany narrowly avoided war when Germany refused to accept French claims to Morocco. Both incidents were resolved through compromise, with France retaining the greater amount of territory in Africa each time.

- *Alliances.* The major European nations attempted to maintain a balance of power by means of opposing alliance systems. Member nations of each alliance pledged to fight together against a common enemy if any member were to be attacked. Germany, Austria-Hungary, and Italy, for example, formed the Triple Alliance. (In 1914, Italy dropped out of the Triple Alliance and was replaced by Turkey.) These nations became known as the "Central Powers" because of their location in Central Europe. Great Britain, France, and Russia formed an alliance known as the Triple Entente. Together these nations were known as the "Allies." Each of the major nations also had alliances with less powerful nations. Thus, on the eve of World War I, Europe was divided into two alliance systems.

In the 20 years before 1914, tensions between rival powers had been steadily building in Europe. The British were concerned about

EUROPE IN WORLD WAR I

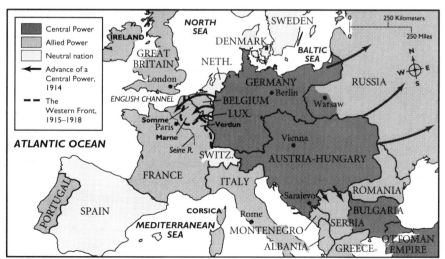

Germany's ambitions for colonies and a strong navy. They also feared competition from Germany's growing industrial economy. Leaders of Austria-Hungary were increasingly worried about the rebellious feelings of the Slavic peoples within the empire. They were also concerned about Russia's support for Serbia. Russians, in turn, worried about Germany's support of Austria-Hungary.

Short-range causes The spark that ignited World War I was an assassination on the streets of Sarajevo on June 28, 1914. This city is in Bosnia-Herzegovina, then part of the Austro-Hungarian empire. The victims of the shooting were the heir to the throne of Austria-Hungary, Archduke Francis Ferdinand, and his wife. The assassin was a Bosnian Serb and a member of a secret band of Serbian nationalists opposed to Austro-Hungarian rule. He hoped to unite the Serbian-populated part of the Austro-Hungarian empire with independent Serbia.

Austria-Hungary blamed Serbia for the assassination. It presented Serbia with an *ultimatum* (list of final demands). Even though Serbia agreed to most of the demands, Austria-Hungary declared war on Serbia on July 28, 1914. The next day, its heavy guns began bombarding Belgrade, the Serbian capital.

Austria-Hungary's allies and Serbia's allies readied their respective armies for war. A huge Russian army prepared to defend Serbia. Recognizing that Germany would defend Austria-Hungary against Russia, France and Great Britain prepared for war to defend themselves and their Russian ally. On August 3, German armies marched into Belgium, considered the best invasion route for attacking France. This German invasion violated Belgian neutrality and caused Great Britain to declare war against Germany and Austria-Hungary. By the end of the first week of August, the major powers of Europe were at war.

War strategies and use of new technologies In the early months of the war, German armies swept through Belgium and into northern France. A desperate French counterattack on the Marne River near Paris finally stopped the German advance. After that, the opposing armies dug themselves into defensive positions. Over hundreds of miles of French countryside, they dug a series of interconnecting trenches to establish what became known as the Western Front. Between the opposing armies' trenches lay a narrow strip of battlefield known as "no-man's-land." Soldiers ordered to climb out of their trenches to attack the enemy were raked by enemy machine-gun fire and killed by the thousands. After three years of attacks and counterattacks, the Western Front moved no more than a few miles in either direction. This *trench warfare* resulted in stalemates and terrible losses of life on both sides.

Two weapons were introduced in the war that greatly increased the death toll. (1) The machine gun was widely used to defend a trench against enemy attackers. (2) Poison gas, which could be carried by wind currents into enemy trenches, was first used by the Germans, in 1915. One type—mustard gas—attacked the skin, causing large blisters, terrible pain, and sometimes death.

Other weapons introduced during the war included tanks and long-range artillery. At sea, Germany nearly crippled the British merchant fleet with another new weapon, the submarine. In the air, both sides used airplanes for the first time. Combatants in airplanes spied on enemy positions and fought each other in aerial "dogfights."

Wartime changes   In 1915, Italy joined the Allies after the Allies had secretly promised Italy additional territory at the expense of Austria-Hungary. In 1917, the United States entered the war on the side of the Allies after repeated German submarine attacks had resulted in the loss of U.S. merchant ships and lives in the Atlantic Ocean. Also in 1917, Russia dropped out of the war after a Communist revolution overthrew Russia's government.

The war ends   By 1918, German troops had become exhausted and demoralized. Germany had suffered heavy losses as its new advances in France were pushed back. Thus, workers and soldiers in Germany were ready to rebel. The emperor fled the country, and socialists in Berlin seized power. The new German government agreed to sign an *armistice* (agreement to stop fighting) and conceded defeat. The armistice that brought the war to an end on November 11, 1918, took place on the 11th hour of the 11th day of the 11th month.

N. RESULTS OF WORLD WAR I

The war had significant effects on the people and nations of Europe as well as on nations outside Europe.

Social changes   The war was terribly destructive. It caused the deaths of some ten million soldiers and roughly the same number of civilians. Many other Europeans were wounded or had their homes, farms, or workplaces destroyed.

During the war, the great number of men serving in the armed forces led to labor shortages in the warring nations. As a result, women were asked to take factory and office jobs that had previously been held only by men. After the war, many of these women kept their jobs. The war experiences led more women to demand the right to vote. Women in Germany, Austria, and Great Britain gained that right after the war ended.

Labor unions in each country enthusiastically supported the war effort. This support enabled labor leaders (along with business leaders) to be represented when each government planned its war economy.

The participation by labor unions in the war effort earned them new social respectability.

Also resulting from the war were two Russian revolutions of 1917. These revolutions were caused in part by the hardships and heavy casualties suffered by the Russian people in the war.

Fourteen Points   Other long-term consequences of the war were spelled out in the terms of peace. Early in 1918, months before the war had ended, U.S. President Woodrow Wilson had issued his ideas for a peace settlement that would be fair to all nations—victors and vanquished alike. Because it listed 14 terms of peace, his proposal was known as the "Fourteen Points."

At the heart of Wilson's plan was the idea of self-determination. He wanted Poles, Czechs, and other national groups to have the opportunity to form independent nation-states. The last of Wilson's Fourteen Points was the idea of creating a League of Nations. The main purpose of this peacekeeping organization would be to reduce the chances of future wars.

Treaty of Versailles   In early 1919, representatives of the Allies met in France to impose peace terms on Germany. (Germany was not invited to the conference.) Ignoring many of the Fourteen Points, British and French representatives wanted to treat Germany harshly. They wanted to blame Germany for the war, receive payments for war damages, and take measures so that Germany would never again rise as a major military power. In general, their views prevailed over those of Wilson.

The treaty that finally emerged, the Treaty of Versailles (1919), provided the following:

- Alsace-Lorraine (German territory since 1871) would again be part of France.

- Poland, which had been under Russian rule for more than 100 years, would again be independent. It would receive land from Germany that would connect Poland to the Baltic Sea. This former German territory became known as the Polish Corridor.

- Germany would lose all of its overseas colonies, including those in Africa.

- France would receive all of the coal mined in Germany's coal-rich Saar Basin for 15 years.

- Germany would be required to pay a huge amount of money as *reparations* (payment for war damages).

- Germany would be made to disband its armed forces. It would further agree not to have an army of more than 100,000 people.

- Germany would be required to *demilitarize* (remove troops and armaments from) the Rhineland, a territory in western Germany.

EUROPE AFTER THE TREATY OF VERSAILLES, 1919

- Germany would accept full responsibility for causing the war. This provision was known as the "war guilt clause."
- A peacekeeping organization, the League of Nations, would be created to reduce the chances of future wars.

A separate treaty with Austria dissolved the old Austro-Hungarian empire. In its place, the treaty created four new republics: Yugoslavia, Czechoslovakia, Austria, and Hungary. Austria and Hungary were each reduced to a fraction of their former size.

President Wilson viewed the Treaty of Versailles as severe, but supported it because it included the creation of the League of Nations. Also, his idea of self-determination became a reality—for at least one national group—with the creation of Poland. The U.S. Senate, however, failed to ratify the treaty because of fears that membership in the League of Nations would draw the United States into wars.

The terms of the treaty caused bitterness and resentment among Germans since Germany was forced to accept the blame for the war and pay huge sums in war damages. German bitterness would become one of the factors leading to a second world war only 20 years after the treaty was signed.

O. THE RISE OF MILITARY DICTATORSHIPS

In the 1920s, many observers recognized that the peace created at Versailles was a fragile one. In the 1930s, that peace was threatened from three sources: a Nazi regime in Germany, a Fascist dictatorship in Italy, and a military dictatorship in Japan. Most dangerous to the peace of Western Europe was the rise to power of the German leader, Adolf Hitler. How did Hitler come to power?

Germany's economic troubles After Germany's surrender in World War I, a new government known as the Weimar Republic was established. Leaders of this government were democratically elected, and basic freedoms were guaranteed in a constitution. The new republic, however, was too weak to deal with Germany's problems. In 1919, the first year of peace, Germany faced an economic crisis—lack of money. The Versailles Treaty required Germany to pay huge reparations to Great Britain and France. To do this, the Weimar government printed large amounts of paper money. As a result, German money lost most of its value and became almost worthless. Prices for goods soared—a condition known as *inflation*.

Economic conditions worsened in the early 1930s as inflation was followed by a worldwide depression. The "Great Depression," as it was called, was characterized by massive unemployment, low wages, and little international trade. In Germany, many people lost faith in their government. They hoped extremist political groups, such as the Nazi party, could provide answers to their problems.

The Nazi rise to power "Nazi" was the shortened name for the National Socialist German Workers' party. During the 1920s, an angry war veteran, Adolf Hitler, used rallies, racist slogans, and emotional speeches to win popular support for this extremist party, which began with only a handful of members. He organized a private army known as the "Brown Shirts." For the country's problems, Hitler blamed Jews, Communists, the Versailles Treaty, and the Weimar government. Demonstrations, physical attacks upon Jews, and street fights with Communists became commonplace. As the 1930s began, the Nazis were the second largest party in Germany.

In 1933, the president of the Weimar Republic invited Hitler to act as the government's new chancellor. Hitler used this position and the Nazi party to gain total control over the German government. He eliminated all opposition, leaving only the Nazi party in power. The government became a dictatorship. *Nazism*, with its racist language and nationalistic ideas, appealed to many Germans who were angry and confused over their economic troubles and still bitter about their nation's military defeat in World War I.

Totalitarian society Hitler's Germany was totalitarian—marked by total government control over all aspects of society and a lack of freedom of speech, press, and assembly. In Nazi Germany, all forms of communication—including newspapers, magazines, radio, and film—came under government control. The Nazis set up special military units (the SS) and secret police units (the Gestapo) to eliminate all those viewed by the Nazis as enemies. Fair and public trials were ended. Other totalitarian features included the abolition of labor unions, the banning or burning of books considered to be anti-German (such as those written by Jewish authors), the creation of a Hitler Youth Movement, control over the arts and education, and the use of children to spy on their parents. Many of Hitler's ideas were contained in his book, *Mein Kampf* (*My Struggle*).

Racism and anti-Semitism   *Racism* is the belief in the superiority of one racial group over others. *Anti-Semitism* is a specific form of racism directed against Jewish people.

Anti-Semitism in Europe has had a long history. During the Middle Ages and the Renaissance, Jews were expelled from Spain, Portugal, several Italian cities, and parts of Germany. Many European Jews had been forced to live in separate, walled-off sections of their cities known as ghettos. In Russia, Jews had been the victims of frequent *pogroms*—organized attacks that took the lives of thousands of Jews and destroyed their homes. In a technique known as *scapegoating*, the Russian government unfairly blamed Jews for the problems confronting Russia. (For more on the situation in Russia, see Chapter 8.)

In Germany, Adolf Hitler's rise to power depended to a large extent on his ability to make use of anti-Semitism and scapegoating. Once in office, Hitler also used the *big lie technique*: the idea that a lie repeated often enough is soon believed. One of Hitler's major lies was the idea of the Aryan race. Hitler claimed that the Germans descended from a special race of people known as Aryans. These people were distinguished from others, he said, by their fair skin, blond hair, and blue eyes. He considered Jews, Slavic peoples, Gypsies, and many others as inferior beings.

In the 1930s, Germany passed laws that denied German Jews the right to practice their professions, the right to citizenship, and other civil rights. In schools, Jewish children were segregated from others. All Jews were required to wear the Star of David as a means of identification. Beatings of Jews on the streets and destruction of Jewish homes, synagogues, and businesses became common. The worst of these outbreaks occurred on "Kristallnacht" (the night of broken glass) in 1938. By the late 1930s, many Jews had either fled Germany or been sent to concentration camps. The worst, however, was yet to come. (For a discussion of the Holocaust, see pages 381–382.)

Other dictatorships   Hitler's Nazi regime was just one example of the fascist governments that were prominent during the 1930s.

Fascism is a system of government that demands total obedience to a powerful dictator, uses force and censorship to eliminate opposition, preaches an extreme form of nationalism, and glorifies militarism.

The first nation in Europe in which fascism won power was Italy. Shortly after World War I, Italy suffered from weak political leadership and high unemployment. In 1922, under the leadership of Benito Mussolini, a fascist party seized power after a march on Rome. Using force to establish his dictatorship, the fascist leader ended freedom of the press, arrested and killed political opponents, disbanded labor unions, and abolished opposition parties. By seeking military conquests, Mussolini hoped to regain the glory that was once Rome's. Thus, Italian armies attacked the African kingdom of Ethiopia in 1935. The Ethiopians put up a stubborn resistance but eventually surrendered to the invader.

Then in 1936, Italy formed a military alliance with Nazi Germany. The two powers began aiding fascists in Spain who were fighting to overthrow the Spanish Republic. The Spanish Civil War ended in 1939 with a victory by the fascist leader Francisco Franco. Italian aggression continued in 1939 when Italy invaded and seized Albania, a small country in the Balkans.

Asia also felt the effects of the increasing power of fascism. In Japan in the 1920s and 1930s, military leaders began to dominate the government. Their fascist beliefs and dictatorial methods resembled those of the fascists of Germany and Italy. Wanting Japan to be the supreme power in East Asia, the military leaders greatly expanded Japan's army and navy. In 1931, Japanese troops invaded China's northern province of Manchuria. (This and other Japanese acts of aggression are discussed in Chapter 6.)

In Review

The following questions refer to World War I and the rise of dictatorships in the 1920s and 1930s, as discussed on pages 366–374.

1. *Key terms:* Define or identify each of the following:

militarism	Fourteen Points	inflation
ultimatum	demilitarize	anti-Semitism

2. Explain how a murder in Sarajevo led to the outbreak of World War I. (In your answer, discuss the alliance systems and other causes of international tension.)

3. Identify *three* ways in which World War I was different from earlier wars.

4. Give reasons for the rise of Nazism in Germany.

5. *Critical thinking:* Propose *two* changes in the Treaty of Versailles that *might* have prevented the rise of Hitler to power. Give reasons for each proposed change.

P. CAUSES OF WORLD WAR II

The direct causes of World War II were acts of military aggression by three powers: Germany, Italy, and Japan. A contributing cause was the failure of the League of Nations and democratic governments to take strong actions against the aggressors.

Military aggression   Japan's invasion of Manchuria in 1931 and Italy's invasion of Ethiopia in 1935 were among the earliest acts of aggression to threaten world peace. But the most serious challenge came from Hitler's intention to create a new German empire. This he called the "Third Reich." In violation of the Treaty of Versailles, Germany built up its military forces. In 1936, Germany moved its army into the demilitarized Rhineland. In 1938, Germany sent its troops into Austria and annexed this German-speaking country. Later that year, Germany demanded control of the German-speaking part of Czechoslovakia known as the Sudetenland.

Appeasement at Munich   Remembering the terrible destruction of World War I, both British and French leaders were reluctant to become involved in another war. They hoped that a policy of appeasement might satisfy Hitler and preserve the peace of Europe. *Appeasement is the policy of yielding to the demands of a rival power in order to avoid armed conflict.* At a conference in Munich, Germany, in 1938, British and French leaders gave in to Hitler's demands to annex the Sudetenland. Hitler promised that Germany would not demand any more territory. However, only a few months after the conference, in 1939, Germany occupied the remainder of Czechoslovakia. Then Germany threatened Poland.

Inaction by the international community   Why did the League of Nations fail to act to stop aggression in the 1930s? After all, this organization had been created after World War I to maintain international peace. The League was handicapped by two main weaknesses. (1) The United States and the Soviet Union—two of the world's major powers—failed to join. (2) The League could not force member nations to contribute military forces or to support its decisions.

U.S. and Soviet policies   The United States and the Soviet Union might have acted on their own to stop Hitler's acts of aggression. Why did they fail to do so?

Many Americans in the 1930s were disillusioned with the results of World War I. They thought that the war had accomplished nothing

NAZI AND ITALIAN AGGRESSION BEFORE WORLD WAR II

worthwhile and that millions had died in vain. They were determined to keep their country out of any future war that might break out in Europe. In addition, Americans were preoccupied with the problems of the Great Depression. Following public opinion, lawmakers in the U.S. Congress passed a series of Neutrality Acts. These acts forbade the sale or shipment of arms to nations involved in war.

What kept the Soviet Union from acting? Soviet dictator Joseph Stalin believed that his country's military forces were not strong enough to fight Germany without the support of allies. After Great Britain and France failed to stand up to Hitler, Stalin stunned the world in 1939 by signing a nonaggression pact with Germany. In this pact, the USSR and Germany agreed that neither nation would attack the other if a war broke out in Europe. Germany also secretly agreed to permit Russia to seize the Baltic nations of Estonia, Latvia, and Lithuania.

German Invasion of Poland   The nonaggression pact assured Hitler that his planned invasion of Poland would not cause the Soviet Union to take up arms against him. In September 1939, German tanks and planes began a devastating attack on Poland. This time, instead of continuing to appease Hitler, Great Britain and France both declared war against Germany. They also declared war against Italy and Japan, two nations that had previously entered into an alliance with Germany. Thus, war in Europe automatically resulted in war in Asia as well.

Q. WORLD WAR II

The first year of World War II was a triumph for the Axis powers (Germany, Italy, and Japan) and a disaster for the Allies (Great Britain and France).

German advances Advancing swiftly across the Polish border in 1939, wave after wave of German tanks, infantry, and planes forced Poland to surrender within only 30 days. The German method of attack was so rapid and overwhelming that it was named *blitzkrieg*, German for "lightning war."

In 1940, using the same method of attack, German armies swept into Denmark, Norway, the Netherlands, Belgium, and Luxembourg. France managed only a brief resistance before it too fell to the Nazis, in June 1940. With France beaten and the Soviet Union pledged not to take up arms against Germany, Great Britain was the only European nation with a chance of stopping Germany. Hitler planned to invade England in September 1940. To weaken his enemy, he ordered thousands of German planes to bomb London and other British cities. In this "Battle of Britain," British air raid sirens warned civilians each night of German attacks. British cities were heavily bombed and suffered major damage.

The Royal Air Force was able to save Britain from defeat by shooting down enough German planes to cause Hitler to call off the invasion. British Prime Minister Winston Churchill paid tribute to the Royal Air Force by declaring that "never in the field of human conflict was so much owed by so many to so few." Great Britain struggled alone for months as the last major foe of Nazism to resist conquest. Recognizing the burden placed on Great Britain, Churchill noted that "if the British Empire and its Commonwealth last for a thousand years, men will still say: 'This was their finest hour.' "

End of Soviet-German cooperation The most important turning point in the war was Hitler's decision to invade the Soviet Union, in June 1941. This decision proved to be a fatal mistake for Hitler. The Soviet Union now became an ally of Great Britain. More important, Germany had to move many of its troops to the Eastern Front (Russia), thus preventing an adequate defense of its Western Front. At first, Germany gained much territory in the East, moving to the outskirts of

CHURCHILL AND THE BATTLE OF BRITAIN: To rally the fighting spirit of the British people, Prime Minister Winston Churchill would walk through bombed out areas of London shortly after the German bombs hit. Why was the Battle of Britain crucial to the chances of victory for the Allies?

Moscow and Leningrad. After these initial successes, however, the Germans encountered fierce Soviet opposition at the Battle of Stalingrad (1942–1943). After losing this battle, the Germans began a two-year retreat back to Germany.

End of U.S. neutrality Another important turning point in the war was the U.S. decision to enter the war on the side of the Allies. In December 1941, the U.S. Congress declared war on Japan after Japan had launched a surprise attack on the U.S. naval base at Pearl Harbor in Hawaii. The U.S. declaration, in turn, caused Germany and Italy to declare war on the United States. As a result, the United States committed itself to defeat Germany and Italy as well.

Allied victories in North Africa and Europe It took the Allies more than three years (1942–1945) to win back the territories Germany had conquered. In 1942, a British force defeated a German force in a tank battle at El Alamein, in Egypt. The battle was significant because it stopped the German offensive in North Africa led by General Erwin Rommel. The Germans in North Africa then retreated west to Tunisia. There in 1943, combined assaults by British and U.S. armies forced the surrender of the German army in North Africa. From their African bases, the Allies invaded the Italian island of Sicily. They then began a long and bloody campaign to liberate the rest of Italy. In the same year, Mussolini was forced from power, and German troops occupied the northern part of Italy.

On June 6, 1944 (known as "D-Day"), Allied forces left England in a massive effort to liberate France from German control. Crossing the English Channel, the Allies achieved their objective of securing beach-heads on the coast of Normandy. It was the largest sea-to-land assault in history. Allied forces, under the command of U.S. General Dwight Eisenhower, fought for control of Normandy, and later for all of France. They liberated Paris in August 1944 and then pushed eastward toward Germany.

From the east, Soviet troops also moved rapidly toward Germany. In April 1945, U.S. and Soviet troops met for the first time on German

ALLIED DRIVE TO VICTORY IN EUROPE, 1943–1945

territory. Sensing that the end was near, Hitler committed suicide. Germany surrendered unconditionally on May 7, 1945, ending the war in Europe.

Allied victory in the Pacific   After Japan had attacked Pearl Harbor in 1941, it achieved a number of military victories and extended its power across much of East and Southeast Asia and over many Pacific islands. Japanese forces took Indochina from the French and the Netherlands East Indies from the Dutch. They also took the British colonies of Burma, Malaya, Singapore, and Hong Kong and the U.S. territory of the Philippines. To win back these lands, the United States and its allies fought a long and difficult campaign. In this campaign, the United States developed a strategy (called "island-hopping") of attacking key islands on the way to Japan. Fighting on these islands was fierce and cost many lives on both sides. After the United States dropped two atomic bombs on the Japanese cities of Hiroshima and Nagasaki, Japan finally surrendered, on August 14, 1945.

Wartime conferences, 1943–1945   During the last years of the war, U.S., British, and Soviet leaders met three times—at Teheran (in Iran), at Yalta (in the Soviet Union), and at Potsdam (in Germany). At these meetings, they discussed military strategy as well as plans for dealing with the postwar world. The three major powers agreed to the following:

- Germany would be disarmed after the war.
- Germany would be divided into four zones of occupation (British, U.S., French, and Soviet).
- War criminals in both Germany and Japan would be put on trial.
- Japan would be occupied chiefly by U.S. troops.
- Some Polish territory would be granted to the Soviet Union; some German territory would be granted to Poland.
- A United Nations would be set up.

R. RESULTS OF WORLD WAR II

World War II was the most destructive war in history. In past wars, the greatest loss of life had been suffered by armies in the field. World War II, however, was a *total war* (one in which civilian populations were often targets as were military units, supply lines, and factories).

Wartime destruction   Some 35 million Europeans died in the war, as many as 20 million of them Soviet citizens. Millions of Asians and more than 400,000 Americans also died in the conflict.

Destruction from the air played a major role in the war. On each mission, huge bombers dropped thousands of tons of bombs on enemy targets. German bombers destroyed large sections of London. In retaliation, British and U.S. bombers destroyed the German cities of Dresden, Hamburg, and Stuttgart as well as much of Berlin. The dropping of two atomic bombs on Japanese cities (Hiroshima and Nagasaki) killed more than 100,000 people instantly. Thousands of other Japanese died later from the effects of nuclear radiation. Even to this day, the dropping of the atomic bombs on civilians continues to be debated. Supporters argue that it shortened the war and saved American lives. Opponents argue that the number of civilian deaths and the extent of property destruction could never be justified.

The Holocaust   Beginning in 1941, Hitler extended his persecution of Jews to the ultimate extreme. In a policy he called "the final solution," Hitler tried to rid Europe of all Jews through genocide. The systematic killing of six million European Jews by the Nazis later became known as the *Holocaust*. During the years of the Holocaust (1941–1945), Jews from Germany and German-occupied countries were taken from their homes and transported to concentration camps. There Jewish men, women, and children were sent to gas chambers (disguised as shower rooms) where they were murdered with a poison gas. Other Jews were worked to death, starved, or shot. For example,

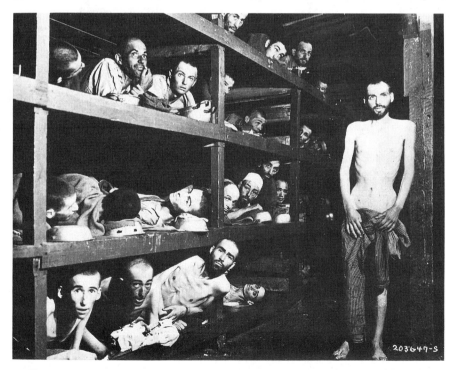

BUCHENWALD CONCENTRATION CAMP: These Jews were among the survivors of the Holocaust. Millions of other victims of Nazi genocide did not survive. What led to cruelty and injustice on such a massive scale?

in a concentration camp in Auschwitz, Poland, thousands of people were killed each day. Various other groups that Hitler considered inferior (such as Communists, Gypsies, Poles and other Slavic peoples, and homosexuals) also died in the concentration camps.

By the end of the war, the Jewish population of Europe had almost been wiped out. For example, Poland's Jewish population of 3 million in 1939 had been reduced to approximately 120,000 by 1945. Within Poland, one dramatic example of Jewish resistance occurred in the Warsaw Ghetto where, in 1943, the remaining Jewish residents resisted Nazi forces for almost a month.

Nuremberg trials   Many people in the Allied countries wanted to punish Nazi leaders for their part in the Holocaust and other acts that they labeled "war crimes." From November 1945 to October 1946, the Allies held a series of trials in Nuremberg, Germany. The defendants were former military and political leaders of Nazi Germany. Of 24 defendants, 19 were convicted and, of these, 10 were executed. Other military trials held in Germany for some 500,000 former Nazis led to lesser punishments. Similar war-crime trials were held in Japan after the war. The war-crime trials in Nuremberg and Japan established the principle that national leaders could be held responsible for "crimes against humanity." Individual leaders could no longer use the excuse that they were following the official policy of a government.

Divided Europe   World War II ended with Soviet troops occupying part of Germany and most of Eastern Europe. The Soviet Union now was the strongest military power in Europe. Western European countries had to deal with the new threat of Communist expansion at a time when they were struggling to rebuild their economies.

Global impact   During the war, the U.S. economy had grown stronger, while European economies had become weaker. Moreover, the United States had become a military superpower. As a result, after the war the United States took a larger role in world affairs.

In Africa and Asia, the European imperialist nations no longer had the economic or military strength to keep control of their colonies. As a result, independence movements in the colonies gained strength during and after the war.

United Nations   The failure of the League of Nations to prevent World War II led Allied leaders to replace it with a stronger peacekeeping organization. Founded in April 1945, the United Nations included in its membership both the United States and the Soviet Union—two major powers that had not joined the League. The inclusion of all the major world powers in the United Nations has allowed it to be more successful than the League of Nations had been.

HOW THE UNITED NATIONS IS ORGANIZED

The largest body in the United Nations is the General Assembly, which consists of representatives from all member nations. Its main purpose is to provide a forum for the discussion of international issues in the hope of resolving conflicts peacefully. On resolutions that come before the General Assembly, each nation is entitled to one vote.

A smaller UN body, the Security Council, consists of five permanent members and ten nonpermanent ones. The permanent members are China, France, Great Britain, Russia, and the United States. The ten nonpermanent members are elected for two-year terms by the General Assembly. The Security Council is responsible for maintaining international peace and security. It can call upon member nations to take action in a crisis. Such action may take the form of economic sanctions or military intervention. A resolution to act must be approved by nine members, including all five permanent members of the Security Council. A negative vote by any of these permanent members is a *veto* of the proposed action, resulting in its defeat.

The Security Council sometimes votes for prompt action against aggressor countries. Since the United Nations does not have its own army, it relies upon troops supplied by member nations to carry out its decisions.

Special UN agencies carry out various functions. An Economic and Social Council works to reduce hunger and improve health care in poorer countries. A Secretariat serves as the administrative agency of the United Nations. It is headed by the secretary general, who is the chief officer of the United Nations. An International Court of Justice decides legal questions referred to it by disputing nations.

The United Nations in action On occasion, the United Nations has resorted to force to stop an act of aggression. For example, in the early 1950s UN troops were called upon to help South Korea when it was attacked by North Korea. In the early 1960s, UN troops were sent into Africa when civil war erupted in the Congo. More recently, the United Nations took military action after Iraq had invaded Kuwait. In 1991, a United Nations coalition led by the United States launched a massive air and ground attack on Iraqi positions in both Kuwait and southern Iraq. Thus, Iraq was quickly defeated.

In addition to taking military action, the United Nations also provides humanitarian aid. For example, in Somalia in

A MEETING OF THE UN SECURITY COUNCIL: Who are the permanent members of this body? What are its responsibilities?

East Africa, the United Nations helped end a famine caused by warfare among different clans. Humanitarian aid to people in Bosnia (in the former Yugoslavia) kept many of them from starving from the effects of a civil war.

The United Nations, however, has had less success in its efforts to settle major conflicts. In the Middle East, for example, there have been four major wars between Arab nations and Israel in a conflict that has continued for more than 40 years. The United Nations was unable to prevent any of these wars from breaking out. In the 1990s, the UN has been no more successful using peacekeeping forces to stop a civil war in the former Yugoslavia.

The United Nations can only be as effective as its member states wish it to be. The special interests of the major powers have often prevented the UN Security Council from acting in a crisis. During the cold war, the Security Council could not take a stand on such matters as the Vietnam War and the Soviet invasion of Afghanistan because the Soviets would routinely veto proposals by the United States, France, and Great Britain. Even after the cold war, a major power can still block UN action. For example, Great Britain has been opposed to having the United Nations address a major conflict between Catholics and Protestants in Northern Ireland (a British territory). (For a description of this conflict, see Chapter 9.)

In Review

The following questions refer to World War II, its causes, and its consequences, as discussed on pages 375–384.

1. *Key terms:* Define or identify each of the following:

   appeasement   D-Day   Holocaust
   blitzkrieg   total war   "war crime"

2. Explain how Hitler's invasion of the Soviet Union can be regarded as a turning point in World War II.

3. Compare the United Nations with the League of Nations in terms of (a) membership and   (b) power to keep the peace.

4. *Critical thinking:* Could Great Britain, France, the Soviet Union, and the United States have done anything before September 1939 to prevent the outbreak of World War II? Explain your answer.

IV. Contemporary Nations (1945 to the Present)

After World War II, Western European countries were confronted with a number of challenges. These included (1) how to respond to the Soviet Union's continued occupation of Eastern Europe; (2) how to deal with demands for independence from the colonies of European powers; and (3) how to rebuild their economies.

A. CONFLICTS OF THE COLD WAR

Soviet troops continued to occupy Eastern Europe after World War II. In that region, the presence of Soviet troops and rigged elections in Poland, Hungary, and other countries brought Communists to power. In a speech in 1946, former British Prime Minister Winston Churchill said that an "iron curtain" had descended across the continent of Europe. He claimed that Soviet control in Eastern Europe was so complete that there would be little contact between people of that area and people in the democracies of Western Europe. These Eastern European nations became known as *satellites* of the Soviet Union because their policies were dictated by Soviet leaders.

With Western Europe devastated as a result of World War II, the responsibility for resisting future Soviet expansion fell to the United States. The United States adopted a policy of *containment*, which meant that the United States would consistently try to stop Soviet expansion.

Truman Doctrine   A civil war in Greece presented the U.S. containment policy with its first major test. In 1947, the Greek government was in serious danger of being overthrown by Greek Communists. If Greece became Communist, it was thought that Greece would then come under Soviet influence—and later so would Turkey. U.S. President Harry Truman decided to oppose the Communist pressure by providing Greece and Turkey with $400 million in military aid. The program of giving U.S. aid for this purpose was called the Truman Doctrine. As hoped, U.S. aid did help Greece and Turkey deal successfully with the Communist threat, and both Greece and Turkey remained free from Soviet influence.

Marshall Plan   Western Europe's economies were devastated by World War II. The war had caused tremendous physical damage, and there was little money for rebuilding. In postwar France and Italy, Communist parties made the most of people's discontent by winning large numbers of supporters in elections. Responding to the economic and political turmoil in Europe, U.S. Secretary of State George Marshall in 1947 proposed a plan to give generous amounts of U.S. aid. The U.S. Congress adopted the Marshall Plan, which authorized more than $12 billion in economic assistance to Western European countries. The purpose of the plan was to provide the financial means for nations to help themselves. The plan worked. By 1951, Communist control of France and Italy was no longer a serious possibility, although the Communist parties in both countries remained strong.

Division of Germany   After the war, Germany was occupied by four wartime allies—Great Britain, France, the United States, and the Soviet Union. Each of these powers occupied a different section of Germany, and also a different section of the German capital, Berlin. It soon became clear that the Soviet approach to occupying and administering its territory in eastern Germany was very different from the American, British, and French approach in western Germany. There, the three nations managed to work out a common policy for disarming, rebuilding, and bringing democracy to their areas. The Soviets, in contrast, forced the East Germans to accept a Communist system that was harsh and undemocratic. As a result of these differences, Germany was divided into two parts in 1949. West Germany became an independent state with free elections. East Germany became a Communist-controlled Soviet satellite.

Berlin Blockade and Airlift   The U.S. containment policy took a slightly different form in Berlin. This city is situated within that part of Germany that was under Soviet control. In 1948, the Soviet Union announced that the British, French, and Americans could no longer use existing land routes to Berlin from western Germany. Thus, food and other vital supplies would no longer be able to reach the people in West Berlin by trains or trucks. (West Berlin was the part of the city that the Soviets did not control.) President Truman ordered the U.S.

DIVIDED GERMANY AND BERLIN, 1948

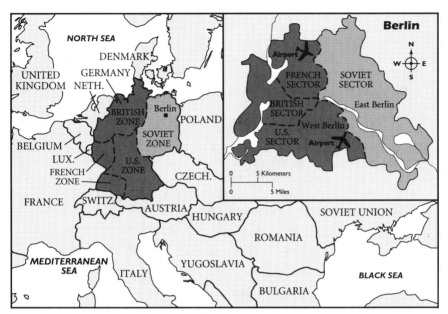

Air Force to fly in supplies to West Berlin. This operation, known as the Berlin Airlift, continued day after day for almost a year. Finally in 1949, the Soviet Union yielded to Western determination. It ended its blockade of land routes to West Berlin.

The conflict over Berlin was an example of the cold war, the conflict between the United States and the Soviet Union that involved threats and competition but not actual warfare.

NATO The Soviet Union and its *bloc* (group) of satellites in Eastern Europe threatened the security of Western Europe. Recognizing a common danger, nations on both sides of the Atlantic formed an alliance called the North Atlantic Treaty Organization, or NATO. The treaty establishing NATO in 1949 was signed by 12 countries: Great Britain, France, Italy, Belgium, the Netherlands, Denmark, Norway, Portugal, Luxembourg, Iceland, Canada, and the United States. (Greece and Turkey joined NATO in 1952; West Germany, in 1955; and Spain, in 1982.) In the treaty, members agreed "that an armed attack against one or more of them in Europe or North America shall be considered an attack against all." The common defense of NATO members rested on a shield-and-sword concept. European and U.S. ground troops would act as a "shield" against any Soviet attack. U.S. atomic weapons would act as the "sword."

The purpose of the NATO alliance was to deter the Soviet Union from aggression and thus avoid war. It is an example of cooperation between the United States and Western Europe and has led to a high degree of security. As will be discussed in Chapter 8, the USSR set up the Warsaw Pact in 1955 as an alliance to counter NATO. NATO still exists today, even though the Soviet Union and the Warsaw Pact were dissolved in 1991. In 1994, some of the nations of Eastern Europe and Russia established a friendly relationship with NATO known as the "Partnership for Peace."

Berlin Wall   During the 1950s, many East Germans escaped their country by crossing into East Berlin, and from there into West Berlin. This exodus hurt the East German economy and embarrassed the Communist regime. As a result, in 1961 East Germany built the Berlin Wall, a barrier of concrete and barbed wire designed to separate East and West Berlin. The flow of refugees dwindled. The Berlin Wall became a symbol of the failure and repression of the Communist East German dictatorship as well as of Soviet Communism.

German reunification   In 1989, the Berlin Wall was torn down by Berlin residents as part of an anti-Communist revolution against the East German government. The East German rulers fell from power. In 1990, East Germany joined with West Germany to form a reunified Germany. (For more about these events, see pages 463–464.)

B. COLLAPSE OF THE COLONIAL EMPIRES

After World War II, the colonial empires of Western European powers collapsed. In Asia, Africa, and the Middle East, one colony after another demanded national independence. Weakened by the war, the colonial powers were eventually forced to yield to the pressures for self-determination.

The story of the breakup of colonial empires is told elsewhere. For accounts of the various struggles for national independence, see the relevant sections in Chapters 2, 3, 4, 5, and 6.

British and French experiences   The experiences of the British and French in losing their empires were very different. British colonial policy changed in 1946 when the Labour party, which had long opposed colonialism, came to power. Moreover, the British government had earlier promised Mohandas Gandhi that India would receive its freedom when World War II ended. In addition, the cost of maintaining colonies had become very expensive. Thus, as we learned in Chapter 5, India and Pakistan became independent in 1947. The next year, Burma and Ceylon received their freedom and, in 1957, so did Malaya. In West Africa, Ghana received its independence from Great Britain in 1957. The last British colony in Africa to receive independence was Southern Rhodesia (now Zimbabwe) in 1980.

The French government was more resistant to the idea of losing its empire. It fought several wars to suppress independence movements. For example, in Indochina France fought nationalist forces led by Ho Chi Minh from 1946 to 1954. After the loss of a major battle at Dien Bien Phu in 1954, France withdrew from Indochina. In Algeria in North Africa, the French fought an independence movement during the 1950s. The conflict was settled when Algeria received its independence in 1962. Before and after independence, about one million French settlers left Algeria and moved to France.

European relations with former colonies   Many nations that were once under colonial rule still maintain special ties to Western Europe. For example, India, Nigeria, Kenya, and other former colonies of Great Britain are members of the Commonwealth of Nations. The 50 nations that belong to this voluntary association enjoy special trade advantages, such as reduced tariffs.

France and Belgium also maintain important trade relations with their former colonies. For example, the former French colony of Morocco exports one-fourth of its goods to France. The former Belgian colony of Congo (now Zaire) exports more than one-third of its goods to Belgium. Also, a special military relationship exists between France and some of its former colonies. For example, in 1994 French troops entered Rwanda to provide humanitarian aid and protection to its civilian population in Rwanda's civil war.

C. EUROPE'S ECONOMIC REVIVAL

The major goal of Western European countries after World War II was to rebuild their shattered economies. Eventually, they succeeded in restoring prosperity. The most important factors in Western Europe's recovery were: (1) economic aid from the United States in the form of the Marshall Plan; (2) Western Europe's skilled work force; (3) a strong regional demand for consumer goods, such as new cars and appliances; and (4) the reduction of trade barriers within the region.

From Common Market to European Union   Many Western Europeans believed that prosperity would come sooner if their governments reduced regional trade barriers. As a result, in 1952 France, West Germany, the Netherlands, Belgium, Luxembourg, and Italy formed the European Coal and Steel Community. It removed tariffs between member countries on coal, iron ore, and steel. It also regulated production of these goods in the community.

In 1957, the same six countries expanded the concept by creating the European Economic Community (EEC or Common Market). It was designed to eliminate all tariff barriers among member states. Eventually, the organization grew as Great Britain, Greece, Portugal, Spain, Ireland, and Denmark joined.

The initial success of the Common Market led member nations to set up a more ambitious plan known as the European Community (EC). Its goals include the free flow of goods, services, people, and capital among member nations. Plans have also been discussed for a single European currency, a single European bank, and eventual political union. If such a union is achieved, it would, among other things, set a common foreign policy for all member nations. These goals face major opposition among Western Europeans who are reluctant to give up their national sovereignty. In 1994, the European Community became known as the European Union (EU).

International trade   In addition to trading with one another, members of the European Union are also part of a world trade network. Member states have joined the General Agreement on Tariffs and Trade (GATT), first negotiated in 1947. As a worldwide agreement by over 100 nations, GATT has reduced tariffs and attempted to eliminate other barriers to trade. GATT members continue to meet regularly in order to further reduce tariffs and trade barriers.

Individual Western European countries have long been major trading partners with the United States. Moving in both directions across the Atlantic Ocean are vast quantities of automobiles, electronic goods, machinery, agricultural products, beverages, and other items. But despite the overall cooperation between Western Europe and the United States, disagreements have arisen. The EU, for example, provides subsidies to protect some products that compete with U.S.-made ones. A *subsidy* refers to money provided to a private business by a government. This government aid allows private businesses and farmers to sell their products at reduced prices and still make a profit. Many critics of subsidies claim that they allow one nation's businesses to have an unfair advantage in the sale of their products. For example, in 1992 the United States objected to French subsidies for soybeans that kept U.S. soybeans out of European markets.

The welfare state   Another issue of the post-World War II era has been the role of the government in caring for people's economic and social needs. A number of Western European countries decided that government's role in the economy should be greatly expanded. Great Britain and Sweden took the lead in establishing a form of socialism known as the *welfare state*. A welfare state is a nation whose government assumes responsibility in providing for most of the essential needs of its citizens. For example, in the 1950s, the British government adopted a number of welfare measures. These included a package of unemployment and retirement benefits for all workers and a program of free medical coverage for all citizens. To pay for these services, the government increased income taxes greatly, especially on the incomes of the wealthy and upper middle class. The British government also took over some of the nation's major industries. These included the railroads, coal mines, and iron and steel mills. In other industries and in farming, private ownership remained the rule.

Trend toward privatization   Many Western Europeans did not approve of the welfare state and government ownership of industries. During the 1980s, their opposition became stronger. Conservative parties came to power in Great Britain, Sweden, and elsewhere. They cut back or eliminated certain social programs. They also *privatized* (sold to private owners) some of the government-owned industries. The force behind privatization was British Prime Minister Margaret Thatcher, who dominated British politics during the 1980s. She was the first woman elected to lead a major European nation.

In a related trend, Western European governments are giving more direct support to private industry. They are taking an active role in establishing industrial guidelines and in financing large industrial projects. For example, the governments of Britain, France, and several other nations provided billions of dollars of aid to design and build Airbus, an airplane that soon became a leader in the world aircraft market. Airbus competed directly with non-subsidized airplanes made in the United States.

THATCHER AND MITTERRAND: In 1986, British Prime Minister Margaret Thatcher and French President François Mitterrand signed a treaty for constructing a tunnel under the English Channel. How does this "Chunnel" illustrate a recent trend toward greater European unity?

D. LIVING IN A CHANGING WORLD

Throughout the 20th century, Western Europe has undergone rapid social and cultural changes in response to even more rapid technological changes.

Changing work force   Both the Commercial Revolution in the 1500s and the Industrial Revolution in the 1800s greatly accelerated the movement of people from farms and rural villages to major urban centers. In the 20th century, the trend has grown even stronger. In France today, only 9 percent of the labor force are agricultural. In Britain, less than 2 percent of the labor force are farm workers.

Major changes are taking place in the types of occupations held by most people. Western Europe is moving from an *industrial age* to a *post-industrial age*. In the industrial age, most Western European workers were employed in manufacturing industries. Today in the post-industrial age, many Western Europeans work in major service industries, such as finance, government, education, retail sales, health care, and transportation.

Changes in literature and art   As Western Europe became more urbanized, writers and artists began depicting the human costs of adapting to a rapidly changing world. The French novelist Jean-Paul Sartre expressed the idea that life has no ultimate meaning. He believed that individuals must create their own standards of right and wrong, of good and bad. Such a philosophy, known as *existentialism*, had wide influence among intellectuals in the mid-20th century. An Irish playwright, Samuel Beckett, experimented with new theatrical techniques for portraying the loneliness and alienation of modern life. His *Waiting for Godot* (1952) shows people unsuccessfully searching for spiritual guidance. Another existentialist, Simone de Beauvoir, studied the position of women in society in her book *The Second Sex* (1953).

European artists were inventive in breaking away from the romantic and realistic styles of painting and sculpture of earlier periods. Instead of painting scenes and objects in great detail, French *impressionists* such as Claude Monet and Georges Seurat invented the technique of applying paint on a canvas in short strokes and tiny points of color to suggest the vivid interaction of form, color, and light. The Spanish artist Pablo Picasso experimented even more boldly with various ways of depicting the human body as a jumbled assembly of cubes and triangles. Many artists of the 20th century were *abstractionists* who created drawings, paintings, and sculptures that had no identifiable subject.

Social justice and human rights   One value that has long been important in Western Europe is the belief in the dignity and worth of the individual. It may have been first expressed by the ancient Greeks. It was carried forward by the thinkers of the Enlightenment and the French Revolution. This belief in human rights is now an ideal of the United Nations and of democratic reformers in all nations.

Although human rights were severely abused by fascist regimes of the 1930s and 1940s, progress has been made since then in guaranteeing basic rights to various peoples of Western Europe. For example, women have won recognition as the equals of men in terms of their legal and political rights. In theory, women's right to equal economic opportunities has also been granted. In practice, however, there is still a wide gap between the average incomes of male and female workers.

Not everybody in Western Europe respects the human rights of others. For example, in Germany groups of *neo-Nazis* (people who support the policies of Hitler's Nazis) have attacked a number of refugees and foreign workers living in the country. Turks, Arabs, Africans, Gypsies, and refugees from various Eastern European countries have been subjected to beatings, firebombings, and other acts of violence. Similar attacks have taken place elsewhere in Western Europe, including France, Spain, Italy, and Greece.

In Review

The following questions refer to Section IV: Contemporary Nations (1945 to the Present).

1. *Key terms:* Define or identify each of the following:

"iron curtain"	subsidy	post-industrial age
satellite	welfare state	existentialism

2. List and briefly identify *three* U.S. actions or policies that helped Western European nations defend against communism and the Soviet Union.

3. State *three* ways in which the economies of Western Europe have changed since World War II.

4. *Critical thinking:* Some people question whether NATO has a useful function to perform in the post-cold war era. If you lived in Western Europe today, would you want NATO to continue? Why or why not?

TEST YOURSELF

Multiple-Choice Questions

Level 1

On a separate sheet of paper, write the number of the word or expression that, of those given, best completes each statement or answers each question.

1. The ancient Greek city-state of Sparta (1) was primarily concerned with the health of its people (2) was a powerful military state (3) granted universal suffrage to its people (4) placed great emphasis on literature and the arts.

2. Which was a major characteristic of democracy in ancient Athens? (1) All adult male citizens were eligible to vote. (2) All residents were given voting rights. (3) Women were allowed to vote in major elections. (4) Slaves were permitted to vote in major elections.

3. A major contribution of the Roman republic to Western European culture was the (1) concept of government by laws (2) belief that political power should be controlled by the military (3) establishment of agricultural communes (4) rejection of the concept of slavery.

4. One result of the fall of the Roman empire was (1) a renewed interest in education and the arts (2) a period of disorder and weak central government (3) an increase in trade and manufacturing (4) the growth of cities and dominance by the middle class.

5. Which was a characteristic of feudalism? (1) Land was given in exchange for military service and other obligations. (2) Government was made up of a bureaucracy of civil servants. (3) Power rested in the hands of a strong central government. (4) Unified national court systems were developed.

6. "All things were under its domain ... its power was such that no one could hope to escape its scrutiny." Which Western European institution during the Middle Ages is best described by this statement? (1) the guild   (2) knighthood   (3) the Roman Catholic Church (4) the nation-state.

7. In Europe, a long-term effect of the Crusades was (1) the strengthening of the feudal system (2) the adoption of Islamic religious practices (3) an increased demand for goods from the East (4) increased European isolation.

8. How did the humanists of the Renaissance differ from the traditional medieval philosophers? The humanists (1) had a greater interest in the spiritual life of people (2) lacked interest in ancient Greek and Roman culture (3) rejected Christian principles (4) emphasized the importance of the individual.

9. Which was an immediate result of the European Age of Exploration? (1) Islamic culture spread across Africa and Asia. (2) European influence spread to the Western Hemisphere. (3) Independence movements developed in Asia and Africa. (4) Military dictatorships were established throughout Europe.

10. Which long-term effect did the Magna Carta and the establishment of Parliament have on England? (1) The system of mercantilism was strengthened. (2) The power of the monarchy was limited. (3) The new American form of government was adopted. (4) The influence of the middle class was reduced.

11. Which was a result of the Protestant Reformation in Europe? (1) The Catholic Church accepted the dominance of the new Protestant religions in Italy, France, and Germany. (2) Spain became a predominantly Protestant nation. (3) Catholic Church leaders refused to make any changes in Church practices. (4) The power of the Catholic Church in Europe was weakened.

Base your answers to questions 12 and 13 on the speakers' statements below and on your knowledge of social studies.

> Speaker A: By nature, men are free, equal, and independent. No one can be put out of this estate and subjected to the political power of another without his own consent.
>
> Speaker B: The question arises about whether it is better to be loved more than feared or feared more than loved. The reply is that one ought to be both feared and loved, but it is much safer to be feared than loved.
>
> Speaker C: Society's interests are best served by open and free competition. The laws of nature dictate that the struggle of the marketplace produces the best results.
>
> Speaker D: Does anyone believe that the progress of this world springs from the mind of majorities and not from the brain of individuals?

12. Which speaker supports the ideals of democracy? (1) A (2) B (3) C (4) D.

13. The ideas of the capitalist system are best supported by Speaker (1) A (2) B (3) C (4) D.

14. Which was a result of the Commercial Revolution? (1) decline in population growth in Europe (2) shift of power from Western Europe to Eastern Europe (3) spread of feudalism throughout Western Europe (4) expansion of European influence overseas.

Base your answer to question 15 on the map below and on your knowledge of social studies.

15. The map illustrates the concept of (1) mercantilism (2) isolationism (3) socialism (4) feudalism.

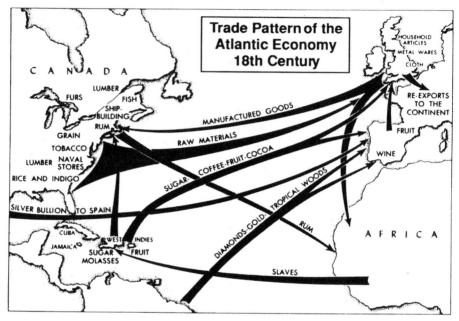

Trade Pattern of the Atlantic Economy 18th Century

16. Which statement reflects an argument of Enlightenment philosophers against the belief in the divine right of kings? (1) God has chosen all government rulers. (2) Independence is built by military might. (3) A capitalist economic system is necessary for democracy. (4) The power of the government is derived from the governed.

17. In a number of European countries in the 1800s, which situation was a result of the influence of Napoleonic invasions? (1) increase in religious conflict (2) rise of nationalist movements (3) decentralization of governmental power (4) economic depression.

18. A major result of the Industrial Revolution in Europe was (1) an increase in the size and influence of the middle class (2) an increase in the percentage of people engaged in farming (3) a decreased life expectancy and an increased infant mortality (4) a reliance on subsistence economies.

Base your answer to question 19 on the drawing on the next page and on your knowledge of social studies.

19. The drawing illustrates workers' reactions to which development of the Industrial Revolution? (1) machines replacing workers (2) slum housing conditions (3) rise of unions (4) equal sharing of profits with workers.

**ANGRY WORKERS SMASH A SPINNING JENNY IN
19th-CENTURY ENGLAND**

*Base your answer to question 20 on the table below and on your knowledge
of social studies.*

**Social Origins of Members of the British Cabinet
(19th and 20th centuries)**

Class	1868–1886	1886–1916	1916–1935	1935–1955	1955–1970
Aristocracy	55%	49%	23%	21%	13%
Middle class	45	49	57	58	72
Working class	—	3	19	21	14

20. Which generalization is supported by the information in the table?
(1) The influence of political parties has steadily increased.   (2) The
middle class has played an increasingly significant role in British
government.   (3) Labor unions have little influence on Cabinet decisions.   (4) The aristocracy plays the most important role in British
government today.

21. In his writings, Karl Marx maintained that history is primarily   (1) a
compromise between rulers and the ruled   (2) an ongoing class conflict between the rich and the poor   (3) a long struggle by groups to

achieve representative democracy   (4) a religious conflict between Eastern and Western groups.

22. The major factor that enabled some Western European nations to dominate large parts of Asia and Africa in the 19th and early 20th centuries was the   (1) technological and military superiority of these European nations   (2) acceptance of Christianity by many Asians and Africans   (3) desire of Asians and Africans for European raw materials   (4) refusal of Asians and Africans to fight against European imperialism.

Base your answer to question 23 on the cartoon below and on your knowledge of social studies.

23. What is the main idea of the cartoon?   (1) Many people assisted Western nations in acquiring overseas colonies.   (2) Western imperialism involved the exploitation of people and resources in the colonies.   (3) Many job opportunities were created by Western colonization.   (4) Western imperialism improved the quality of life for people in the colonies.

"Learning civilized ways is hard work!"

Base your answer to question 24 on the graph on the next page and on your knowledge of social studies.

24. Which is an accurate statement based on the information in the graph?   (1) In 1914, Austria-Hungary attempted to end the arms race in Europe.   (2) In 1914, the five major European powers spent more on military programs than on any other program.   (3) In 1914, Russia was the most militaristic of all the European nations.   (4) In 1914, Germany spent more money on its military than did any other European nation shown.

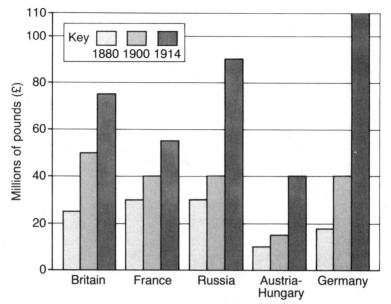

MILITARY SPENDING

Key: 1880 1900 1914

Millions of pounds (£): 110, 100, 80, 60, 40, 20, 0

Britain, France, Russia, Austria-Hungary, Germany

25. During the 1930s, a joint act of appeasement by the British and French was   (1) signing a treaty with Germany to outlaw nuclear weapons   (2) allowing Czechoslovakia's Sudetenland to be taken over by Germany   (3) entering into a defensive alliance with the United States   (4) supporting independence for German colonies in Africa.

26. Which belief is common to both 17th-century absolutism and 20th-century totalitarianism?   (1) A two-party political system is essential for a stable society.   (2) Separation of church and state should be encouraged.   (3) Dissenters are dangerous and should be punished.   (4) The state should establish a strong public school system.

Base your answers to questions 27 and 28 on the passage below and on your knowledge of social studies.

The important lesson wasn't so much the Nazis' extraordinary evil but that it could happen with the participation of so many, the indifference of many more, that humanity has no guarantees against its vicious streaks except its own conscience, for which each individual is responsible.... The effort for decency and justice must go on every day, everywhere.

27. In the passage, the term "extraordinary evil" refers to the   (1) Berlin Blockade   (2) Marshall Plan   (3) cold war era   (4) Holocaust.

28. What is the main idea of the passage?   (1) A nation's wartime policies should not be subjected to moral standards.   (2) Individuals who follow the orders of their superiors should not be prosecuted for their actions.   (3) In time of war, the end justifies the means.   (4) Individuals have an obligation to oppose immoral policies.

29. Which situation contributed to Adolf Hitler's rise to power in Germany after World War I? (1) support of Hitler's radical policies by the Social Democrats in the Reichstag (2) strong feelings of resentment and nationalism built up by economic and political crises (3) refusal by the League of Nations to admit Germany as a member (4) violence and terrorism promoted by Germany's former enemies.

30. A major reason that the United Nations has been more successful than the League of Nations is that the United Nations has (1) had greater participation on the part of the major powers (2) avoided programs to aid economic development in developing nations (3) eliminated war among its members (4) removed all trade barriers between members.

Level 2

31. The ancient Athenians are credited with (1) inventing and using the wheel (2) eliminating slavery (3) establishing governments that had democratic elements (4) inventing the printing press.

32. Important long-term contributions of ancient Greek and Roman civilizations are mainly found in the area of (1) military technology (2) religious doctrine (3) economic policy and planning (4) government and law.

33. In medieval Europe, the feudal system was dominated by (1) middle-class merchants (2) serfs (3) revolutionaries (4) strong local rulers.

34. Which statement best describes society under the influence of medieval Christianity? (1) Religion was a way of life that governed people from birth to death. (2) Religion permitted the freedom to choose how people would worship. (3) Religion played a major role only in the lives of the clergy. (4) Religion influenced society by stressing the equality of all religions.

35. The Magna Carta was important to the development of democracy because it (1) limited the power of the monarch (2) created a two-house legislature (3) took land away from the nobles (4) extended the right to vote to peasants.

36. Which feature was typical of Greece during the Golden Age and Italy during the Renaissance? (1) voting by both men and women (2) racial diversity (3) social equality (4) a questioning spirit.

37. The religious diversity in Western Europe is mainly the result of (1) the Congress of Vienna (2) World War II (3) the French Revolution (4) the Protestant Reformation.

38. Two main features of a capitalistic economic system are (1) powerful labor unions and fixed prices (2) tariffs and state ownership of basic industries (3) free trade and free competition (4) central planning by government and full employment.

39. The writers and philosophers of the Enlightenment believed that government decisions should be based on   (1) religious beliefs   (2) the divine right of kings   (3) natural laws and reason   (4) traditional values.

40. Nationalism is most likely to develop in an area that has   (1) land suited to agriculture   (2) industry to supply consumer demands   (3) a moderate climate with rivers for irrigation   (4) common customs, language, and history.

41. The beginning of the Industrial Revolution depended on   (1) the support of the Catholic Church   (2) an increased number of farmers   (3) technological advances   (4) political reforms.

42. Karl Marx believed that a revolution by workers was more likely to occur as a society became more   (1) religious   (2) militarized   (3) industrialized   (4) democratic.

43. Before World War II, Great Britain adopted a policy of appeasement in order to   (1) form an alliance with Italy   (2) encourage democracy in Eastern Europe   (3) avoid war with Germany   (4) change the frontiers of France and the Soviet Union.

44. The Holocaust in Europe is an example of   (1) interdependence   (2) segregation   (3) genocide   (4) empathy.

45. The North Atlantic Treaty Organization is an example of   (1) an attempt to prevent the spread of Soviet power   (2) United States efforts to gain foreign territory   (3) the failure of capitalism   (4) United Nations interference in the affairs of member nations.

Essay Questions

Level 1

1. Changes in society have been brought about by individuals in various ways.

Individuals
Queen Isabella I
Martin Luther
Napoleon Bonaparte
Giuseppe Garibaldi
Otto von Bismarck
Karl Marx
Adolf Hitler

For each of *four* individuals listed above:

- Describe a specific policy or idea of that individual that brought about change.
- Explain how that individual's policy or idea had either a positive or negative effect.

2. Certain events or occurrences in history have brought about significant changes.

Events/Occurrences
Pope Urban II calls for Crusades (1095)
The Glorious Revolution in England (1688)
The French Revolution (1789–1799)
Archduke Francis Ferdinand is assassinated (1914)
The Holocaust (1941–1945)
The United Nations is established (1945)

For each of *four* events or occurrences listed above:

● Describe the event or occurrence.
● Discuss one cause of the event or occurrence.
● Explain how the event or occurrence led to significant changes in
  a specific nation or region.

Level 2

3. Western Europe has a great diversity of geographic features.

Geographic Features
Mountains
Lowlands
North Atlantic Drift
Mediterranean climate
Irregular coastline
Rivers and canals

A. Select *four* of the geographic features listed. For each feature chosen, state one specific effect on the political, economic, or social
development of Western Europe.

B. Base your answer to Part B on your answer to Part A. However,
additional information may be included. Write an essay discussing the effects of specific geographic features on the development
of Western Europe. Begin your essay with this topic sentence:

Many geographic features have influenced the
development of Western Europe.

4. Below are listed several periods in the history of Western Europe.

Historical Periods
Ancient Greece
Renaissance
Age of Enlightenment
Industrial Revolution
Age of Imperialism

A. Select *three* of the historical periods listed. For each period chosen, state an effect of Western Europe on another region of the world.

B. Base your answer to Part B on your answer to Part A. However, additional information may be included. Write an essay discussing the effects of each period on other regions of the world. Begin your essay with this topic sentence:

> Various historical periods in Western Europe have had important worldwide effects.

CHAPTER 8

Russia and Eastern

Main Ideas

1. **ABSENCE OF WARM-WATER PORTS:** For centuries, a chief goal of Russian foreign policy was to obtain access to warm-water ports.

2. **CULTURAL HERITAGE:** The Christian Orthodox religion and the arts of the Byzantine empire were adopted by Russia during the Early Middle Ages.

3. **DIVERSE ETHNIC GROUPS:** Slavs, Bulgars, and Magyars were among the many different groups that settled the region.

4. **ABSOLUTISM UNDER THE CZARS:** Russian czars were monarchs who ruled with absolute power.

5. **WESTERNIZATION:** Czar Peter the Great (1682–1725) introduced Russians to technologies and customs from Western Europe.

6. **CONDITION OF THE SERFS:** Millions of Russians toiled as peasants with few rights and no property until Czar Alexander II liberated them in 1861.

7. **NATIONALISM IN THE BALKANS:** Eager to break away from the Ottoman and Austro-Hungarian empires, many ethnic groups in the Balkans fought for national independence.

8. **WORLD WAR I AND REVOLUTION:** Russian participation in World War I was a major cause of the March 1917 Revolution (in which Czar Nicholas II was overthrown) and the November 1917

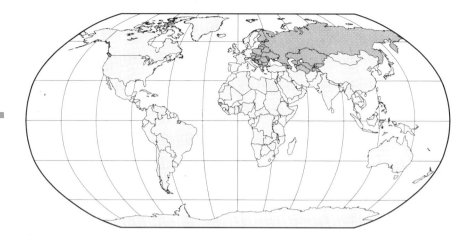

Europe

Revolution (in which the Bolsheviks established a Communist government based on the ideas of Karl Marx).

9. **TOTALITARIANISM UNDER STALIN:** The Bolsheviks, led by V. I. Lenin, immediately set up a dictatorship. Under Lenin's successor, Joseph Stalin, the Soviet Union became a totalitarian state with a planned economy.

10. **SATELLITE NATIONS OF EASTERN EUROPE:** Shortly after World War II, the governments of Eastern Europe fell under Communist control and became satellites of the Soviet Union.

11. **GORBACHEV'S REFORMS:** The last Soviet leader, Mikhail Gorbachev, allowed greater political freedom and attempted economic reforms by introducing elements of capitalism.

12. **REVOLTS IN EASTERN EUROPE:** Nationalism and the failure of Communist economies in Eastern Europe resulted in rebellions against Communist governments and against Soviet control.

13. **BREAKUP OF THE SOVIET UNION:** Nationalist independence movements in the various republics of the Soviet Union helped cause that nation to dissolve in 1991.

14. **UNSTABLE GOVERNMENTS AND CIVIL WARS:** Ethnic conflicts and distrust led to civil wars in Yugoslavia and in some of the former republics of the Soviet Union.

Russia and Eastern Europe: The Region at a Glance

② BALTIC SEA: In the early 1700s, the Russian czar Peter the Great built a new capital at St. Petersburg in order to command an outlet to this sea. Russian trade with the West depends greatly on Baltic Sea routes. In the 20th century, the Soviet Union took over the Baltic nations of Latvia, Estonia, and Lithuania in order to strengthen its control of the sea.

① POLAND: Since 1025 when the first Polish king was crowned, the boundaries of this state have changed many times. In the 18th century, the state disappeared altogether when it was partitioned, or divided, among three powers (Russia, Prussia, Poland). Because Poland lies across a wide plain, its eastern and western frontiers are difficult to defend.

③ URAL MOUNTAINS: This low mountain range forms part of the boundary between Europe and Asia. Since the Middle Ages, the mountains have been mined for their rich mineral resources, including salt, silver, gold, and asbestos.

ARCTIC OCEAN

NOVAYA ZEMLYA

BARENTS SEA

• Murmansk

Kola Peninsula

• Arkhangelsk

Ural Mts.

Siberian Plain

Ob R.

Yenisei R.

FINLAND

WESTERN EUROPE

Helsinki •

Lake Ladoga

St. Petersburg •

② BALTIC SEA

ESTONIA

LATVIA

LITHUANIA

Volga R.

★ Moscow

⑦

RUSSIA

• Yekaterinburg

Novosibirsk •

RUSSIA

POLAND

★ Minsk

BELARUS

Great European Plain

CZECH. REP.

Warsaw ★

Oder R.

Vistula R.

HUNG.

Kiev ★

Don R.

Prague

Danube R.

★ Budapest

Dnieper R.

Dniester R.

Volgograd

CASPIAN SEA

KAZAKHSTAN

Altai Mts.

Lake Balkhash

SLOVAKIA

MOLDOVA

UKRAINE

Donets Basin

ARAL SEA

SLOVENIA

CROATIA

ROMANIA

Crimea

BLACK SEA

GEORGIA

Tbilisi

UZBEKISTAN

Bishkek ★ Alma-Ata

BOSNIA & HERZEGOVINA

BULGARIA

⑥

Tashkent •

KYRGYZSTAN

Sarajevo

⑧

Caucasus Mts.

Tien Shan

YUG.

ARMENIA

Dushanbe •

Ashkhabad •

TAJIKISTAN

Belgrade

Yerevan

ALBANIA

MACEDONIA

MEDITERRANEAN SEA

AZERBAIJAN

Baku

TURKMENISTAN

⑧ THE BALKANS: This mountainous region in southeastern Europe is made up of many countries, including Albania, Yugoslavia, Macedonia, Bulgaria, Bosnia, and the European part of Turkey. Ethnic conflicts in this region (they still exist) were one of the causes of World War I.

⑦ VOLGA RIVER: This river, the longest in Europe, is a major transportation route through the most heavily populated part of Russia. Canals link the Volga with the Baltic Sea, the Barents Sea, and the Black Sea.

| 10°E | 20°E | 30°E | 40°E | 50°E | 60°E | 70°E | 80°E | 90°E |

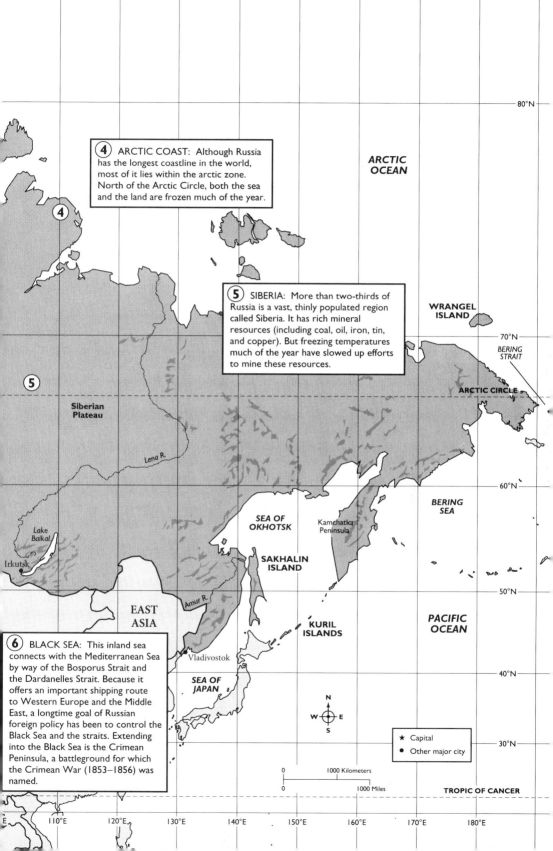

4 ARCTIC COAST: Although Russia has the longest coastline in the world, most of it lies within the arctic zone. North of the Arctic Circle, both the sea and the land are frozen much of the year.

5 SIBERIA: More than two-thirds of Russia is a vast, thinly populated region called Siberia. It has rich mineral resources (including coal, oil, iron, tin, and copper). But freezing temperatures much of the year have slowed up efforts to mine these resources.

6 BLACK SEA: This inland sea connects with the Mediterranean Sea by way of the Bosporus Strait and the Dardanelles Strait. Because it offers an important shipping route to Western Europe and the Middle East, a longtime goal of Russian foreign policy has been to control the Black Sea and the straits. Extending into the Black Sea is the Crimean Peninsula, a battleground for which the Crimean War (1853–1856) was named.

ARCTIC OCEAN

WRANGEL ISLAND

BERING STRAIT

ARCTIC CIRCLE

Siberian Plateau

Lena R.

SEA OF OKHOTSK

Kamchatka Peninsula

BERING SEA

Lake Baikal

Irkutsk

SAKHALIN ISLAND

EAST ASIA

Amur R.

KURIL ISLANDS

PACIFIC OCEAN

Vladivostok

SEA OF JAPAN

N
W ✦ E
S

★ Capital
● Other major city

0   1000 Kilometers
0   1000 Miles

TROPIC OF CANCER

80°N
70°N
60°N
50°N
40°N
30°N

110°E   120°E   130°E   140°E   150°E   160°E   170°E   180°E

I. Geography

The region described in this chapter is the largest in the world in area. It consists of the (1) nation of Russia, (2) nations of Eastern Europe, and (3) nations of Asia that once were part of the Russian and Soviet empires. Since the breakup of the Soviet Union in 1991, the region has undergone profound political and economic changes.

A. LOCATION

Locate the Ural Mountains and the Caucasus Mountains on the map on pages 406–407. Geographers use these mountain ranges to mark the division between Europe and Asia. Notice that the world's largest nation, Russia, lies on both sides of the Urals. Thus, there is both a European Russia and an Asian Russia. Most Russians live on the European side of the Urals. On the Asian side is a vast and thinly populated land that stretches for thousands of miles all the way to the Pacific.

European Russia is included in what is known as Eastern Europe. This region stretches from the Urals in the east to the western borders of Finland, Poland, the Czech Republic, Slovakia, Hungary, and Slovenia. During the cold war, most of the nations of Eastern Europe had Communist governments. The end of the cold war and the breakup of the Soviet Union gave rise to many new or newly independent nations with non-Communist governments. These new nations of Eastern Europe are: the Czech Republic, Slovakia, Croatia, Slovenia, Macedonia, Bosnia-Herzegovina, Ukraine, Belarus, Moldova, Lithuania, Latvia, and Estonia. Because three of these countries (Lithuania, Latvia, and Estonia) are located on the Baltic Sea, they are sometimes referred to as the "Baltic countries."

Three former Soviet republics in the Caucasus—Armenia, Azerbaijan, and Georgia—form a distinct subregion. Azerbaijan is predominantly Muslim, while most people in Armenia and Georgia are Christians. Azerbaijan is blessed with oil reserves, which have been exploited since the 19th century. In contrast, Georgia and Armenia have relatively few valuable natural resources.

Forming another distinct subregion are five new republics of Central Asia that were once part of the Soviet Union. Located to the south of Russia, each of these nations has a Muslim majority. They are: Kazakhstan, Uzbekistan, Tajikistan, Kyrgyzstan, and Turkmenistan.

B. TOPOGRAPHY

The topography of this vast region (Russia, Eastern Europe, and Central Asia) consists of plains, plateaus, and mountains.

Plains The previous chapter described the Great European Plain, which extends across much of the European continent. From Western

SHEEP FARMING IN GEORGIA: Since Georgia was once part of the Soviet Union, this mountainous land belongs to the same region as Russia does. It is located in the Caucasus Mountains.

Europe, this lowland area continues into northern Poland and then becomes quite wide through European Russia. Continuing east, it stops at the Ural Mountains, then resumes on the other side of the Urals as the West Siberian Plain. Smaller plains are found in Hungary, Romania, and elsewhere.

Plateaus A plateau stretches across Siberia, a vast subregion that forms much of the Asian part of Russia. Siberia's climate is too cold for agriculture. Its huge forests, however, are a good source of lumber, and its mineral wealth includes both gold and diamonds.

Mountains In addition to the Urals, Russia has other mountain ranges, including several along its Pacific coast. Some of the mountains there are active volcanoes. The Caucasus Mountains form Russia's southern border with Georgia and Azerbaijan.

A much higher mountain range is found in Central Asia. Two nations in that region, Tajikistan and Kyrgyzstan, are completely mountainous, with elevations reaching up to 24,590 feet.

In the southern part of Eastern Europe are found relatively low-lying mountains. One mountain range, the Carpathians, provided somewhat of a barrier protecting Romania and Slovakia from invaders from the north. Another mountain range, the Transylvanian Alps, cuts through Romania. The Balkan countries of Yugoslavia, Croatia, Bosnia-Herzegovina, Bulgaria, Macedonia, and Albania are extremely mountainous.

C. RELATIONSHIP TO THE SEAS AND OCEANS

Russia has fewer warm-water ports than any other major country. Most of Russia's long coastline along the Arctic Ocean is blocked with ice for much of the year. Russia has another long coastline along the Pacific. But few people live along this coast, and the Pacific ports are frozen during the winter.

Russia's main trading routes to the seas and oceans pass through the Barents and Baltic seas (in the northwest) and the Black Sea (in the southwest). Sailing from Murmansk, a ship can make it through the Barents Sea to the Atlantic Ocean. Sailing from a Baltic port, a ship can cross into the North Sea near Denmark and reach the Atlantic Ocean. Sailing from a Black Sea port, a ship can reach the Mediterranean Sea by passing through two straits, the Bosporus and the Dardanelles. For centuries, securing access to warm-water ports on the Baltic and Black seas was a major goal of Russian foreign policy.

D. RIVERS

In Eastern Europe, major rivers include the Danube, which flows into the Black Sea, and the Oder, which flows into the Baltic. In European Russia, major rivers include the Volga, which flows into the Caspian Sea, and the Don, which flows into the Black Sea. Boats from the Volga can reach the Don via a canal. Most of Siberia's rivers flow north to the Arctic Ocean, a fact that limits their usefulness for trade. In fact, because all of Russia's major rivers flow either in a northerly or a southerly direction, the Russians have had difficulty transporting goods from east to west and back.

E. CLIMATE

The climate of this huge region varies greatly, especially as one travels from north to south (or from south to north). The Arctic Circle passes through northern Russia and Finland. Here it is very cold most of the year. In this Arctic zone, the usually frozen and treeless land is known as *tundra*. The ground thaws on top during a brief summer. But underneath is *permafrost* (permanently frozen soil). Few people live in this zone.

South of the tundra lies a wide band of forested land called the *taiga*. Covering most of Siberia and the northern part of European Russia, the taiga consists mainly of conifers (cone-bearing trees).

Most of Eastern Europe, including European Russia, consists of a mixed-forest zone. Where trees have been cleared, the land produces rich crops, since summers are warm and rainfall is plentiful. The winters here are cold, however, as Arctic winds sweep down from the north.

South of the mixed-forest zone, in Ukraine and Russia, lies a broad belt of rich agricultural land. These are the *steppes*, areas of flat, semidry grasslands. The rich soil of the steppes supports the growing of wheat and corn, often with the aid of irrigation.

Farther south and to the east, the climate becomes hot and dry. Much of Central Asia, for example, is a desert. Its high mountains block winds carrying moisture from reaching the lowland areas. Enough rain falls, however, to permit sheep grazing and cotton growing.

F. NATURAL RESOURCES

Russia is rich in mineral resources, including oil, natural gas, iron, coal, manganese, gold, and copper. It also has the world's largest forest reserves, which provide Russians with a plentiful supply of lumber. Large amounts of mineral resources have gone untapped because of their location beneath the frozen tundra and dense forests. Russia's resource-rich environment helped it to become an economic power. However, the inefficient use of these resources by the Soviet government was one reason for the breakup of the Soviet Union.

Other nations of Eastern Europe are not as rich in mineral resources and sources of energy. Nevertheless, Poland, Slovakia, and the Czech Republic have large coal deposits. Hungary has large deposits of bauxite (an ore used in making aluminum). Romania has valuable reserves of petroleum and natural gas.

Agriculture is important in all Eastern European countries. Ukraine was long known as "the breadbasket of the Soviet Union" because of its rich farmlands. About 40 percent of Eastern Europe's land is arable. A mild climate combined with broad stretches of good farmland have enabled Poland, Hungary, the Czech Republic, and other nations to produce large quantities of grains, potatoes, and other vegetables.

G. GEOGRAPHIC INFLUENCES ON HISTORY

Because much of their territory is a broad plain, Russia and other Eastern European countries lie open to attack and invasion. They have few defensible borders. Poland lies on a major invasion route and has been attacked and *partitioned* (divided up) several times. For long periods, it has ceased to exist as an independent country. Napoleon's armies (in the early 1800s) as well as Hitler's armies (in the 20th century) were able to overrun Poland and part of Russia.

While lacking defensible frontiers, Russia has sometimes been aided by its large land area and severe winters. The invading armies of both Napoleon and Hitler found themselves trapped in Russia during the winter months. The sheer size of the country meant that supply lines of the invaders had to be long and thinly stretched. Forced to retreat, both the French and the German invading forces suffered heavy losses.

In Review

The following questions refer to Section I: Geography.

1. *Key terms:* Define or identify each of the following:

   the Caucasus (subregion)   permafrost   steppe
   tundra   taiga

2. Explain the significance to Russia of (a) warm-water ports, (b) access to the Bosporus and the Dardanelles, and (c) the Volga and other major rivers.

3. Explain the connection between Russia's climates and its vegetation zones.

4. *Critical thinking:* Would you expect the cultures of people living in present-day Russia to be more diverse or less diverse than those of Western Europe? Explain.

II. Early History

Much of the early history of Eastern Europe and Russia involves the history of the Slavs.

A. SLAV MIGRATION

During the time of the Roman empire, most Slavic people lived north of the Carpathian Mountains (in present-day Poland). Beginning in the 400s, waves of invaders sweeping through Eastern Europe forced many of the Slavs to move. The Slavs split into three groups. The southern Slavs moved to the Balkans. They are the ancestors of the various ethnic groups who now populate that region: Slovenes, Serbs, Croats, and Macedonians. The western Slavs settled in what is now the Czech Republic, Slovakia, and Poland. The eastern Slavs moved into the territory that is now Ukraine, Belarus, and Russia.

B. THE BYZANTINE EMPIRE

Both the Slavic and non-Slavic peoples of Eastern Europe were strongly influenced by the most powerful state in that region, the Byzantine empire. Recall that this empire started as the eastern half of the Roman empire. At its height, the Byzantine empire dominated an area almost as large as the entire Roman empire had been. Its capital, Constantinople, was located near the strategic waterways—the Bosporus and the Dardanelles—that controlled trade between the Black and Mediterranean seas. The empire based its wealth and power upon control of trade through southeastern Europe.

The Byzantine empire lasted for nearly a thousand years, from 476 until the Turks captured Constantinople in 1453. Its most famous emperor, Justinian I (527–565), is known for enlarging the empire and for giving its people a new law code based upon older Roman laws. For many centuries, Byzantium was far stronger than the feudal kingdoms of Western Europe. It carried on an extensive trade with Asia and preserved much of Greek and Roman culture.

Byzantine culture was more Greek than Roman. The people of the empire used the Greek alphabet rather than the Latin one. They also established a form of Christianity known as the Greek Orthodox Church. Their religion differed from the Roman Catholicism of Western Europe in several ways. The head of the Greek Orthodox Church was the patriarch of Constantinople, not the pope in Rome. Greek Orthodox priests could marry, while Roman Catholic priests could not. In addition, the prayers and rituals of the two churches differed.

The Balkans   The borders of the Byzantine empire often came under fierce attack from neighboring peoples of Eastern Europe. In about 670, the Bulgars, a nomadic people from Central Asia, swept into Byzantine territory in the Balkans and turned that mountainous land into a Bulgar empire. Although not originally Slavic, the Bulgars became so through intermarriage with southern Slavs.

Another threat to Byzantine power came in the early 900s when a warlike people, the Magyars, invaded a country that, centuries later, would become Hungary. Eventually the Magyars settled down in the Danube River basin and adopted the life-style of their Slavic neighbors.

In the late 800s, people living in the Balkans were converted to Greek Orthodox Christianity by missionaries from Byzantium. Two of the missionaries, Cyril and Methodius, invented the first Slavic alphabet (known as *Cyrillic*), which is still in use.

C. EARLY RUSSIA (RUS)

The Slavs that settled in present-day Ukraine, Belarus, and Russia were mostly farmers and hunters. Some engaged in trading goods with Byzantium, the capital of the Byzantine empire. They traveled by boat down the Dnieper River and across the Black Sea. In about 860, Vikings from Sweden began invading the area and taking over the trade routes, including the trading centers of Novgorod and Kiev. Some of the major "goods" that they sent to Byzantium were slaves—Slavic people whom they had obtained as tribute from the various Slavic communities.

Kievan Rus   In 882, a Viking named Oleg organized Rus—the first kingdom of the various eastern Slav settlements. Oleg became its grand prince, and other Vikings became princes and *boyars* (nobles) of this kingdom. As the Vikings intermarried with the Slavs, the two cultures fused. Kiev, the capital of present-day Ukraine, was then the capital of Rus. (The name "Rus" later became "Russia.")

Cultural influences on early Russia Byzantine culture influenced Russian culture in many ways. In 988, the Russian grand prince, Vladimir I of Kiev, converted to Orthodox Christianity. His conversion led to the adoption of the Orthodox Church as the official religion of Russia. Also during this period, Russians of Kiev adopted the Cyrillic alphabet, which is the basis for the Russian and Ukrainian written languages.

Russian art and architecture were also influenced by contact with Byzantine civilization. The icons, mosaics, and domes found in Russian churches are all based upon Byzantine influences. An *icon* is a representation of a sacred Christian figure. It may be a painting or a carved object. A *mosaic* is a pattern made from small tiles of glass, gold leaf, or marble.

KIEVAN RUS AND THE BYZANTINE EMPIRE

EASTERN ORTHODOX CHURCH: The onion domes on this church in
Moscow are typical features of religious architecture in Russia. When
and how did Christianity come to Russia?

D. RELIGIOUS DIFFERENCES AMONG
   EASTERN EUROPEANS

Not all the peoples of Eastern Europe adopted the religion and
culture of Byzantium. The northern Slavs who settled in Poland and
the Magyars of Hungary became Roman Catholics. Religious differences between the Orthodox Christians of Russia and the Roman

Catholics of Poland were to have long-term political effects. As we shall see, the Poles and the Russians fought many wars with each other. Their hostility was based partly on cultural differences and partly on competition for power and land.

E. RUSSIA UNDER THE MONGOLS

In the 13th century, medieval kingdoms of Asia and much of Europe were conquered by the Mongols from East Asia. Led by Genghis Khan ("Great Ruler"), Mongol armies swept through Kiev and surrounding areas, having already conquered China and part of India. The Mongols burned the city of Kiev and went on to dominate Russia for 240 years (from the 13th to the 15th centuries). The Mongols also made raids as far west as Poland, Hungary, and Bulgaria, but they did not remain in these places.

Mongol rule in Russia was extremely harsh. The conquerors relied on force and fear to maintain their power. Severe punishments, including death, were common for minor offenses. The Mongols kept the Slavic princes in power as long as the princes collected taxes for the Mongol *khan* (ruler). Any Slavic community that refused Mongol demands was attacked and burned to the ground.

Effects of Mongol rule   Historians actively debate the effects of the long rule of the Mongols over Russia. Some say that the autocratic system of government adopted later by the czars (and even later by modern dictators) had their roots in Mongol rule. Indeed, it is easy to see how later rulers might admire the strict control that the khan had

MONGOL EMPIRE, 1300

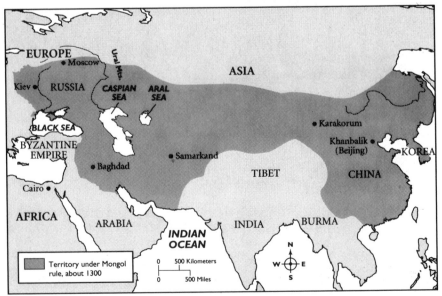

over his large empire. Russia, however, lacked democratic institutions long before the Mongols arrived. The czars' use of secret police, torture of political prisoners, and centralized government may have had other origins.

Some historians say that Mongol rule cut off the Russians from contact with Western Europe and with the Byzantine empire. They point out that Russians did not experience the Renaissance and Reformation as did Western Europeans. Other historians claim the opposite—that Russians' ties with other areas became even greater during the time the Mongols were in control. In fact, they claim, the Mongols encouraged Russian foreign trade so that the Mongols could collect more taxes from the Russians.

Most historians agree on at least one effect of Mongol rule on Russian history. It contributed, they say, to the rise of Moscow as the new center of power in Russia, replacing Kiev. Previously, Moscow had been an unimportant town lying far to the north of Kiev. To avoid the Mongols, many Russians moved away from Kiev and settled in and around Moscow. Moreover, a prince of Moscow persuaded the Mongols to appoint him grand prince of Russia. This position was especially important because the grand prince was in charge of collecting taxes for the Mongols. To further add to Moscow's prestige, the grand prince of Moscow persuaded the metropolitan of Kiev, the main church leader of the eastern Slavs, to live in Moscow.

In Review

The following questions refer to Section II: Early History.

1. *Key terms:* Define or identify each of the following:

Slav	Bulgar empire	boyar
Cyrillic	Kievan Rus	icon

2. Explain how each of the following played a role in shaping Russian culture: (*a*) eastern Slavs,   (*b*) Vikings, and   (*c*) Eastern Orthodox Church.

3. Explain how the Mongol conquest of Russia helped in the rise of Moscow to power over its Russian neighbors.

4. *Critical thinking:* To what extent, if at all, did the Mongol conquest significantly influence Russian culture and politics? Explain your answer.

III. The Dynamics of Change

From the end of the period of Mongol rule in 1480 to modern times, Russians saw the rise of a centralized, autocratic state, the expansion of the country into an empire, and the subjugation of minorities.

A. THE RISE OF MUSCOVY

In addition to being aided by Mongol policies, Muscovy (Moscow and the area it controlled) grew in size and power because of the abilities of its rulers.

Ivan III "the Great" (1462–1505)   Czar Ivan III doubled the area that Moscow ruled to include the rival cities of Tver and Novgorod. Realizing that the Mongols' power had weakened, he stopped paying tribute to them. In effect, this meant that Muscovy was now free of Mongol control. Ivan III gained the title "the Great" by building beautiful churches and palaces in Moscow and surrounding the city with a wall. The section enclosed by this wall became known as the Kremlin. Ivan gained prestige by marrying Sophia, the niece of the last Byzantine emperor. After the Byzantine empire had fallen in 1453 to the Turks, Moscow saw itself as the successor to the Byzantine empire and as the main defender of the Orthodox Christian religion. The rulers of Moscow began calling themselves *czar* (Russian for caesar or emperor) in imitation of the Byzantine emperors.

Ivan IV "the Terrible" (1533–1584)   This czar expanded the Russian state to the east by defeating Mongol armies at Kazan and Astrakhan and by subduing native peoples in Siberia. He was less successful in expanding to the west. Ivan IV became known as "the Terrible" for the ruthless ways in which he treated his subjects. New social institutions of Ivan IV's time included:

- *Feudalism.* Previously the boyars had been free to serve the princes and grand prince at will. Their lands were private property and were passed on from generation to generation. Ivan III and Ivan IV changed the relationship between the czar and the boyars. Lands could now be taken away from nobles at will. As new Russian lands were conquered or as lands were seized from boyars, the czar gave these lands to new nobles who would agree to serve him. This relationship was similar to the feudal relationships that had developed between kings and vassals in Western Europe during the Early Middle Ages (discussed in Chapter 7).

- *Serfdom.* As the nobles of Russia were becoming less free, so too were the peasants. Peasants had traditionally been able to move about freely. Under Ivan IV, many ran away to escape serving in the army and to avoid paying rising taxes. Some settled to the south and east on lands recently conquered. Groups of these runaways became known as Cossacks. To prevent this flight of peasants from continuing, the Russian government made many peasants *serfs*, people obligated to serve a landlord for life. As in Russia, serfdom was also introduced in Poland, Bohemia, and

EXPANSION OF RUSSIA

other parts of Eastern Europe at this time. This change in social status ran counter to the trend in Western Europe, where most serfs had already been freed.

B. RUSSIA UNDER PETER THE GREAT

In 1613, people in Moscow witnessed the crowning of a new czar, Michael Romanov. While this ruler was not outstanding, he did establish a dynasty—the Romanov dynasty—that would rule Russia until 1917. Of all the Romanovs, the czar who had the greatest impact on Russian society was Peter Romanov—Peter I "the Great." During his long reign (1682–1725), Peter I successfully pursued two major policies: (1) Westernization and (2) expansionism.

THE BUILDING OF ST. PETERSBURG: Czar Peter the Great (standing to the left of the map) supervised the building of his new capital. Why did he choose to move the capital from Moscow to a location on the Baltic Sea?

Westernization As a young man, Peter was eager to learn all that he could about the technologies and culture of Western Europe. He was convinced that the only way for Russia to become a major military power was through *Westernization* (adoption of Western ideas). He traveled to Holland and England to observe Western ways. After his return, he introduced Russia to a host of sweeping reforms.

Peter the Great reorganized the Russian army according to Western models and created a Russian navy. To encourage business activity, he invited European skilled workers and businesspeople to come to Russia. The government organized mining companies and factories and forced serfs to work in them. Nobles were required to serve either in the military or in the government.

Wanting Russians to adopt Western fashions, Peter the Great required Russian men to cut off their beards and women to stop wearing veils. More important was Peter's decision to move Russia's capital from Moscow to an entirely new city, St. Petersburg. The czar himself supervised the building of the new capital, which provided Russia with its first port on the Baltic Sea. Peter called it a "window on the West."

Expansionism   Ever since the rule of Ivan the Great in the 1400s, Russia had aggressively pursued a policy of *expansionism* (adding territories to a nation). In 1682, Peter the Great's first year as czar, Russia was already three times larger than the rest of Europe. The country continued to expand under Peter. In the early 1700s, Russia fought and won several wars with Sweden and Poland, thereby gaining land along the Baltic Sea (present-day Estonia and Latvia).

C. RUSSIA UNDER CATHERINE THE GREAT

Later in the same century, another strong ruler, Catherine II (1762–1796), continued Russia's expansionism. She too was known as "the Great" because of Russia's military victories during her rule. Defeating

CATHERINE AND THE SERFS: Touring parts of her empire, Catherine the Great (in the carriage window) was shown only villages and serfs' cottages that looked prosperous. What was the true condition of the serfs under the czars?

both the Ottoman empire and the Tatars (a Central Asian people), Russia gained the Crimean Peninsula and other lands along the Black Sea. The conquered territories included Odessa, a valuable warm-water port that today is in Ukraine. Just as important were Catherine II's gains in Poland. Russia joined with Prussia and Austria in partitioning Poland among them. After three such partitions (in 1772, 1793, and 1795), Poland no longer existed. (Poland would not regain its independence until 1918.) The areas in Poland that Russia acquired would become the present-day nations of Belarus, Lithuania, and parts of Ukraine.

Catherine II also continued Peter the Great's policy of Westernization. She made French the language of the Russian court and encouraged the nobility to read the works of French Enlightenment authors (discussed in Chapter 7). She invited many Western European authors, artists, and musicians to move to Russia. Catherine II saw herself as enlightened, but she remained an absolute ruler. Western ideas reached only the nobility and a small middle class. The serfs continued to suffer. For example, a rebellion of peasants in 1773–1774 was ruthlessly suppressed by the Russian government.

D. NAPOLEON'S INVASION

Russia was one of Europe's great powers in the early 1800s. It played a major role in bringing about the military defeat and final downfall of Napoleon Bonaparte. In Chapter 7, we discussed the mistake that Napoleon made in invading Russia in 1812. The French forces burned Moscow but then winter set in. Far from home and without adequate supplies, the French army retreated. But as it withdrew, Russian forces attacked and inflicted terrible losses. These losses contributed to Napoleon's defeat two years later.

DOCUMENTS: TOLSTOY'S *WAR AND PEACE*

A Russian count, Leo Tolstoy, achieved fame as a novelist in the late 19th century. In one of his masterpieces, *War and Peace* (1869), he weaves into a fictitious story many passages that describe and comment on Napoleon's fateful invasion of Russia in 1812. The following passage is Tolstoy's account of the French army in full retreat.

One army fled, the other pursued. From Smolensk the French had the choice of several different roads, and one would have thought that during their stay of four days there they might have determined the enemy's position, might have devised some advantageous plan and undertaken something new. But after the four-day halt, without maneuvers or plans, the mob ran along the beaten track, neither to the right nor to the left, but on the old—and worst—road, through Krasnoe and Orsha.

Expecting the enemy in the rear and not in front, the French hastened on, spreading out and becoming separated from one another by as much as twenty-four-hours' march. In advance of them all, fled the Emperor [Napoleon], then the kings, then the dukes. The Russian army, expecting Napoleon to take the road to the right beyond the Dnieper—the only reasonable thing for him to do— themselves turned to the right and came out onto the highway at Krasnoe. And here, as in a game of blindman's buff, the French ran into our vanguard. Seeing the enemy unexpectedly, the French were thrown into confusion, stopped dead in panic, then resumed their flight, abandoning their comrades in the rear. . . .

From Orsha they fled along the road to Vilna. . . . At the Berezina they were again thrown into confusion, many were drowned, many surrendered, but those who managed to cross the river pressed on. Their Supreme Commander donned a fur coat, got into a sledge, and sped on alone, deserting his comrades. Those who could get away did so, and those who could not—surrendered or died.

Questions for Discussion

For each multiple-choice question, select what you think is the best answer. Give a *reason* for your choice.

1. From clues in the reading, you can assume that the Dnieper and the Berezina were (a) roads (b) mountains (c) rivers (d) armies.
2. What appears to be the author's view of Napoleon? Tolstoy (a) admires Napoleon for his courage (b) admires Napoleon for his brilliance as a general (c) dislikes Napoleon because of his reckless tactics (d) regards Napoleon as a coward who thinks only of his own safety.
3. Which of the following phrases best characterizes the movement of armies that Tolstoy describes? (a) orderly progress (b) general confusion (c) skillful maneuvering (d) determined resistance.

Source: Leo Tolstoy, *War and Peace.* Translated by Ann Dunnigan. New York: New American Library, 1968.

E. DISCONTENT AND REFORM

Like the czars before them, both Peter the Great and Catherine the Great were autocrats. An *autocrat* is a ruler who holds absolute power over a society. The power of the czar went unquestioned until early in the 19th century. Then, stirred by the liberal ideas of the French Revolution, a few Russian thinkers began to challenge the laws and customs that oppressed the lower class.

Decembrists' revolt   In December 1825, after the death of Czar Alexander I, a group of Russian army officers with liberal ideas attempted to take power. The new czar was to be Nicholas I. But the "Decembrists," as the officers became known, declared their support for Nicholas's brother Constantine. (Constantine had already renounced his claim to the throne.) By so doing, the officers hoped to gain power, establish a constitutional monarchy, and abolish serfdom.

After the Decembrists' revolt failed, Nicholas I (1825–1855) suppressed liberal and revolutionary ideas in Russia. He also sent troops into Poland in 1830 and Hungary in 1848 to put down rebellions.

Complaints against serfdom   Although Peter the Great and Catherine the Great had introduced Russia to Western ideas, they did so mainly for the benefit of the small upper class—the nobles. The basic

RUSSIFICATION

By the late 19th century, the territory ruled by Russia was very large. As a result of the expansionist policies of the czars, the Russian empire now included the huge Asian land of Siberia, the Central Asian lands of Kazakhstan and Turkistan, the Caucasus nations of Armenia and Georgia, and the Eastern European lands of Ukraine, Finland, Estonia, Latvia, Lithuania, and part of Poland. The diverse peoples within this large empire spoke different languages, belonged to various religions, and practiced different customs.

In the 1880s and 1890s, the Russian government feared that some of the non-Russian peoples in the empire might rebel. To prevent this, the government attempted to make the non-Russian nationalities give up their own languages and adopt Russian. The official policy was called *Russification*. Thus, for example, in Poland and the Baltic states, instruction in schools had to be given in the Russian language.

Many Russians at this time thought that faith in the Orthodox Church was a sign of loyalty to the czar. Thus, for political as well as religious reasons, Orthodox Christian missionaries were sent to the Volga River Valley to convert Muslim Tartars. Jews in the Russian empire became the victims of campaigns by Russian nationalists.

POGROM IN KIEV: In the 1800s, Russian Jews were frequently set upon and beaten by mobs. The police offered no protection. How did such pogroms affect immigration to the United States?

Jews were forced to live in the western part of the empire (chiefly Poland and Ukraine). In this "Pale of Settlement," as it was called, they were sometimes forced to move from town to town by official decree. The worst abuses against Jews were government-sponsored attacks, or *pogroms*. Stirred up by government propaganda, mobs of Russian peasants would assault Jews and burn down their homes without fear of punishment. As a result, thousands of Jews were killed. The pogroms and other forms of persecution caused many Jews to emigrate from Russia to the United States in the late 19th and early 20th centuries.

economic needs of the peasants were ignored. Moreover, peasants were heavily taxed to pay for the country's many wars of expansion.

Peasants formed an overwhelming majority of the population. While many had been freed, more than half of them were still serfs by 1850. Serfs were not permitted to leave the land of their own free will. However, their landlords could sell them to other landowners with or without the land. Serfs could not marry without the consent of the landowners. In criminal cases and legal disputes, peasants were subject to decisions of landowners, from which there was no appeal.

Defeat in the Crimean War Those who disapproved of Russia's social system were further upset by Russia's defeat in the Crimean War, fought against the Ottoman empire. Major battles of this war (1853–1856) took place in the Crimea, a peninsula extending into the Black Sea. Russia hoped to win from the Ottoman Turks an outlet from the

Black Sea to the Mediterranean Sea. However, since both Britain and France feared a Russian presence in the Mediterranean, they entered the war on the side of the Ottoman empire. As a result, the Russians suffered a crushing and humiliating defeat.

The war revealed the weaknesses of the Russian army, which lacked modern arms. It also demonstrated that Russia had neither the industries nor the railroads needed to supply a modern army.

Reforms of Alexander II   In 1855, while the Crimean War was still being fought, Czar Nicholas I died and was replaced by his son, Alexander II (1855–1881). Unlike his father, Alexander II sympathized with those who wished to reform Russia's social system. Acting on his liberal beliefs, he issued a decree that abolished serfdom in Russia in 1861. Thus, people could no longer be bought or sold. They could marry whom they choose, own property, and go into occupations and businesses.

Alexander II introduced other reforms as well. He wished to reduce the powers of the Russian nobility. As a result, local assemblies called *zemstvos* were set up in each region. These assemblies included representatives not only of the nobility but of the peasants and townspeople as well. In addition, the reform-minded czar introduced a new judicial system based on the ideas of equality before the law and trial by jury. He required local governments to establish elementary schools for all children. He urged Russian universities to grant teachers greater freedom to speak out on political issues.

Alexander II's reforms, though well intended, did not solve Russia's social problems. Although millions of serfs were freed by Alexander's decree, they were far from satisfied. The freed serfs were given some land to farm. But for years they were required to pay fees for this land. Most peasants found that they could not earn enough from their small plots to pay these fees as well as taxes and their own living expenses. As a result, many peasants rioted to protest their poor conditions.

In Review

The following questions refer to the rise of Muscovy and the Russian empire, as discussed on pages 417–426.

1. *Key terms:* Define or identify each of the following:

   serfdom   autocrat   Russification
   Westernization   zemstvo   pogrom

2. Identify one major reform of each of the following rulers: (a) Peter the Great and   (b) Alexander II.

3. Describe the extent of Russian territorial expansion from 1460 to 1900.

4. *Critical thinking:* Do you think that Peter I and Catherine II deserved their honorary titles of "the Great"? Explain your answer.

F. STRUGGLES FOR INDEPENDENCE IN EASTERN EUROPE

Nationalism was an especially explosive force for change in the 19th century. Most of the peoples of Eastern Europe were under the control of one of three empires. (1) In central Europe, the Austrian empire controlled Czechs, Slovaks, Hungarians, and others. (2) In southeastern Europe, the Ottoman empire controlled Serbs, Bulgarians, Romanians, and others. (3) Finally, as we have read, the Russian empire controlled Poles, Ukrainians, Byelorussians, Lithuanians, Latvians, and others.

Creation of Austria-Hungary In all three empires, several nationalities tried to gain their independence. In 1848, Hungarians revolted against the Austrian empire, but the revolt was crushed. In 1866, after Austria had lost a war with Prussia, the Hungarians again demanded independence. Instead, the Hungarians settled for a compromise—a new empire known as Austria-Hungary. It had a *dual monarchy*, with the Austrian emperor also serving as the Hungarian king. Although the Hungarian part of the empire had its own capital city and parliament, Austria dominated the union.

Polish nationalism Recall that Poland had lost its independence after Russia, Prussia, and Austria had partitioned it three times (in 1772, 1793, and 1795). During the 1800s, the Poles who lived under Russian rule made two attempts to regain their independence. Both attempts were crushed by Russian armies.

New nations in the Balkans Far more successful were struggles for independence against the rule of the weakening Ottoman empire. Russia defeated that empire in the Russo-Turkish War of 1877–1878. As a result of this war and the Conference of Berlin that followed, three nations in the Balkans—Serbia, Montenegro, and Romania— gained their independence from the Ottoman Turks. Another nation, Bulgaria, broke away from Ottoman rule in 1908.

G. CONFLICT IN THE BALKANS

Although the Ottoman empire was weakened, it still controlled some territory in the Balkans in the early years of the 20th century.

First Balkan War (1912–1913) Leaders of several Balkan nations thought the Ottoman empire was too weak to retain all of its territory. As a result, Bulgaria, Serbia, Montenegro, and Greece went to war together against the Ottoman empire. They easily defeated the Turks and gained Ottoman territory. Austria-Hungary, however, prevented Serbia from gaining what it wanted most: an outlet to the Adriatic Sea.

Instead, Austria-Hungary brought about the creation of a new, Muslim country on the Adriatic—Albania.

Second Balkan War (1913)   Dissatisfied with the borders created earlier in the year, the Balkan countries involved in the First Balkan War (as well as Romania) fought Bulgaria. As a result of this Second Balkan War, Bulgaria became smaller, while the Ottoman empire and Serbia grew larger.

Even after two wars, most of the people in the Balkans were dissatisfied because various nationalities were still under the control of Austria-Hungary or the Ottoman empire. Nationalist ambitions in the Balkans would soon contribute to the outbreak of World War I (discussed in Chapter 7).

H. THE INDUSTRIAL REVOLUTION COMES TO RUSSIA

Russia did not begin to industrialize in a meaningful way until the 1890s—more than a century after the Industrial Revolution had started in Great Britain. Industrialization in Russia was directed mainly by the government. A major step was the construction of the 5,000-mile-long Trans-Siberian Railroad, which linked the Ural Mountains with Vladivostok, on the Pacific coast. The government encouraged foreign investments, which provided much of the capital needed to begin new industries. By 1900, Russia was the world's second largest producer of petroleum and the fourth largest producer of steel. Other important industries included textiles, coal, and chemicals.

With industrialization came the growth of an urban working class. Recruited from the peasantry, the new industrial workers often lived in crowded, unsanitary barracks. Many of them were women, since employers found that they could pay women less than men. Workers in 19th-century Russia made up only a small portion of the population. They were concentrated, however, in Moscow, St. Petersburg, and other industrial centers where they would have great influence on the revolutions of the early 20th century. It is important to remember, though, that most of the Russian population were peasants.

I. THE PATH TOWARD REVOLUTION

In the late 19th and early 20th centuries, many Russians wanted to make great changes in their government and society. Some favored turning the Russian state into a constitutional democracy similar to the British and French governments. Others had more extreme ideas for change.

Radical groups   Several groups advocated violence and terror to bring about change. They attempted to assassinate Czar Alexander II several times, and in 1881 they succeeded. The assassination, however, did not change Russia. The next czar, Alexander III, imposed a harsher rule.

Another radical group, the Social Democrats, were Marxists who wanted industrial workers to rise up against the capitalist class and seize economic and political power. In 1903, the Social Democrats split into two groups—Bolsheviks and Mensheviks—each of which became a separate party. The Bolsheviks, led by V. I. Lenin, wanted radical changes and a small, tightly controlled party. The Mensheviks were less extreme and believed in a party open to all.

The Bolsheviks would eventually take control of the Russian government. But first, the Russian monarchy was weakened by three events: (1) Russia's defeat in a war with Japan, (2) an uprising in the Russian capital, and (3) Russia's participation in World War I.

Russo-Japanese War   In 1904, war broke out between Russia and Japan over the control of Manchuria, a province in northern China. The Russians were defeated by the Japanese in both land and sea battles. When the war ended in 1905, Russia had to leave Manchuria and turned over to Japan the southern half of Sakhalin Island (which Russia had received from Japan in 1875).

Russians were angry that their government had fought the war so poorly. Japan's victory was the first by an Asian power against a European one in modern times.

Revolution of 1905   Angered by the Russian government's loss in the war and by its continued denial of basic human rights, many Russian people called for changes. On a Sunday in January 1905, a group of workers and their families marched peacefully on the czar's Winter Palace in St. Petersburg to deliver a petition. The unarmed protestors were fired upon by Russian troops. This event, known as "Bloody Sunday," triggered a wave of protests among workers, peasants, and soldiers. Workers in several cities formed *soviets* (councils or assemblies) that organized *general strikes* (agreements among various groups of workers not to go to work).

Fearful of losing power, Czar Nicholas II (1894–1917) agreed to demands for an elected legislature. In March 1906, the first elections were held for this newly established legislature, known as the Duma. The czar, however, retained a veto power over legislation and the right to appoint all ministers. The Duma proved to have much less real power than reformers had wished.

Losses in World War I   The final blow to the Russian monarchy came about as a result of the terrible suffering caused by World War I. Russia entered that war in 1914 as an ally of Great Britain and France. In the course of the war, the Russian army suffered millions of casualties, major defeats in battle, and the loss of Polish and Ukrainian territories.

Within Russia, people suffered from inflationary prices, low wages, and shortages of food in the cities. Sometimes workers went on strike to obtain higher wages and more food.

J. THE RUSSIAN REVOLUTION OF 1917

The 1917 revolution in Russia occurred in two stages. First, there was a revolution in March against the czar. This was followed by a second, more radical revolution in November.

The March Revolution of 1917   Contributing to the monarchy's downfall were: (1) the general suffering caused by World War I, (2) the failure of the modest reforms introduced in 1905, and (3) the failure of Russia's monarchy to respond to workers' demands for change. The March Revolution began when food shortages led to riots and strikes. Demanding food and protesting government policies, thousands of workers and students marched through the streets of Petrograd (as St. Petersburg was then called). When the czar ordered his troops to end the riots by firing on the protestors, the soldiers refused and joined the demonstrators. Feeling isolated, the last Russian czar, Nicholas II, *abdicated* (gave up the throne).

Declaring an end to the monarchy, a group of revolutionaries formed the *Provisional* (temporary) *Government*. It introduced democratic ideals, such as equality before the law. It promised freedom of religion, speech, and assembly. It allowed labor unions and permitted strikes.

The Bolshevik Revolution (November 1917)   The same problems that had brought down the czar now confronted the Provisional Government. World War I continued, and so did Russia's involvement and heavy losses in the war. Under the new government, food shortages and inflation continued. In addition, the Provisional Government was faced with a threat by those who favored the czar's return. The continuing crisis presented an opportunity for a radical group such as the Bolsheviks to seize power.

Lenin and the Bolsheviks urged soldiers to desert their units and encouraged peasants to seize land. They promised to take Russia out of the war if the Bolsheviks came to power. Lenin's slogan "Peace, Land, and Bread!" appealed to thousands of desperate Russians. Another of Lenin's slogans was "All Power to the Soviets!" Soviets of workers had been formed in the major Russian cities. There were also peasant soviets in the countryside and military soviets in the armed forces.

In November, the Bolsheviks overthrew the Provisional Government in Petrograd. They arrested government officials and the czar. Soviets in Moscow, Petrograd, and other major cities pledged their support to the new government.

K. EASTERN EUROPE AFTER WORLD WAR I

Besides contributing to the collapse of the Russian monarchy, World War I also sealed the fate of the Austro-Hungarian empire. Having been defeated, Austria-Hungary ceased to exist after the war. Taking its place were four nations: Austria and Hungary, which became separate states each greatly reduced in size, and the new nations of Czechoslovakia and Yugoslavia. Poland and several other Eastern European states also gained their independence as a result of the peace treaty signed at Versailles in 1919—the Treaty of Versailles. (See the map on page 371.)

Czechoslovakia   This newly formed nation consisted of two major population groups: the Czechs in the western part of the country and the Slovaks in the eastern part. There were also several ethnic minorities, including a sizable German population in an area known as the Sudetenland. Recall that in the 1930s, Nazi Germany's ambitions concerning the Sudetenland would help disrupt the peace of Europe.

Yugoslavia   In 1918, various Slavic peoples of the defeated Austro-Hungarian empire had ambitions for nationhood. The nation that finally took shape consisted of three main sections: (1) the former nation of Serbia, (2) the former nation of Montenegro, and (3) lands occupied by various other Slavic ethnic groups including the Slovenes, Croats, and Bosnians. This new nation, given the name Yugoslavia in 1929, was dominated from the beginning by the Serbs.

Poland   After more than a hundred years of foreign domination, Poland was reborn as an independent nation. The peacemakers at Versailles put together a large Polish state consisting of lands once held by Germany, Austria-Hungary, and Russia.

Other nations   For having sided with the victorious Allies during the war, Romania was rewarded with territories taken from Austria-Hungary and Russia. In contrast, both Hungary and Bulgaria lost territory after having been defeated in the war.

In 1917 and 1918, four nations on the Baltic Sea—Finland, Estonia, Latvia, and Lithuania—declared their independence from Russia. Following World War I, the victorious Allies recognized them.

L. THE SOVIET UNION UNDER LENIN

In Russia, the Bolshevik seizure of power in Petrograd in 1917 was only the beginning of a long and violent struggle. The struggle was waged in two ways. First, the Bolsheviks had to maintain their power against foreign enemies as well as against opponents within Russia. Second, Bolshevik leaders fought among themselves over the type of

LENIN: Addressing Russian troops in Moscow in 1919, V. I. Lenin urged support for the Bolshevik government. What groups and nations were then opposed to the Bolsheviks?

society Russia was to have and which Bolshevik would run the country.

Peace with Germany One of Lenin's first acts after coming to power was to take Russia out of the war against Germany. For Russia, the price of peace turned out to be quite high. By the Treaty of Brest-Litovsk (signed in March 1918), Russia gave to Germany and Austria-Hungary a number of lands: Poland, Byelorussia, Estonia, Latvia, and Lithuania. It also recognized the independence of Ukraine, Finland, and Georgia. In all, Russia lost about a third of its population, a third of its agriculture, and half of its industry. (Russia would win back some of these lands in the civil war that was just beginning.)

Civil war There were people both outside of and within Russia who opposed the Bolshevik Revolution and viewed it with fear.

Leaders of other nations were afraid that the Bolsheviks might stir up class warfare in their own countries and encourage workers to revolt against their governments. It was well known that the Bolsheviks were followers of German socialist Karl Marx and that Marx had called upon factory workers all over the world to rise up against the capitalist system. Hoping to overthrow Bolshevism (or communism) in Russia, the Allies sent a small number of troops to that country in 1918, the final year of World War I. Taking part in this military expedition were troops from France, Italy, Great Britain, Japan, and the United States.

The Bolsheviks' chief foes, however, were not the foreign troops but Russians and other ethnic groups within Russia who bitterly resisted Bolshevik rule. For three years, 1918–1921, opposing armies fought each other in a civil war. The "Reds" (Communists) battled the "Whites" (opponents of communism), who were aided by the Allies. The civil war ended in 1921 in total victory for the Red Army and Lenin's government—but only after millions of deaths and widespread misery from famine and disease.

Establishing the Soviet Union   In 1922, five years after their revolution, the Bolsheviks gave the Russian empire a new name. Four republics under Bolshevik control (Russia, Ukraine, Byelorussia, and Transcaucasia) signed a treaty of union creating a nation known as the Union of Soviet Socialist Republics (USSR). In time, it became better known as the Soviet Union. Later, other republics entered (or were forced into) the union. By the 1940s, the Soviet Union consisted of 15 republics. Although each of the republics had its own government, they were all strictly controlled from Moscow, the Soviet capital.

Lenin's policies   How were Karl Marx's theories about the working class to be turned into practice? Did communism require that *every* industry and *every* farm be taken over by the government and managed as public property? As the leader of Russia's newly formed Communist government, Lenin was called upon to answer these questions.

At first, Lenin ordered the Red Army to seize control of all privately owned factories and turn them over to the Communist government. This resulted in a sharp decline in industrial production. Lenin also encouraged peasants to take land away from wealthy landowners and the Russian Orthodox Church. Because of these actions and because of the general disorders of the civil war, not enough food reached the cities. Famine became widespread.

Therefore in 1921, Lenin changed his approach. He announced the New Economic Policy (NEP). Instead of having all economic resources fall under state control, Lenin's NEP permitted a limited amount of private ownership of these resources and the selling of goods for private gain. Individual Russians could once again own small businesses. And peasant farmers could again sell surplus crops for profit. The government, however, kept control of heavy manufacturing and the transportation and banking industries. While the NEP was in force (1921–1928), the Soviet economy improved, showing increased production and reduced shortages.

In Review

The following questions refer to changes in Russia and Eastern Europe from the 1880s to the early 1920s, as discussed on pages 427–433.

1. *Key terms:* Define or identify each of the following:

dual	"Bloody Sunday"	Treaty of
monarchy	Provisional	Brest-Litovsk
soviet	Government	New Economic Policy

2. Explain the role played by each of the following in causing the downfall of the czarist government in March 1917: (a) the Russo-Japanese War and (b) World War I.

3. State *three* ways in which the map of Eastern Europe changed as a result of World War I.

4. *Critical thinking:* (a) Explain why Russia was ripe for revolution in 1917. (b) Do you think the Bolshevik victory in November was inevitable? Why or why not?

M. THE SOVIET UNION UNDER STALIN

Lenin's death in 1924 led to a power struggle among the top leaders of the Communist party. For a few years, it was not clear who would take Lenin's place as the new Communist dictator. Would it be the organizer of the Red Army—Leon Trotsky? Or would it be the general secretary of the Communist party—Joseph Stalin?

Stalin's rise to power Trotsky and Stalin had conflicting views about the future of communism. Trotsky favored a policy of promoting workers' revolutions throughout the world. Stalin, in contrast, wanted to concentrate on building up the power of the Soviet Union. He opposed Trotsky's ideas for using Soviet resources to help foreign revolutionaries.

Stalin used his position as Communist party boss to defeat Trotsky and exile him from Russia. Stalin then attacked those party leaders who had just recently supported him against Trotsky. Thus, by 1929 Stalin had defeated all other rivals and was in complete control of the Soviet government.

One of Stalin's first acts as dictator was to abandon Lenin's New Economic Policy. Under Stalin, all economic resources in the Soviet Union would be controlled by the government. Such an economic system (in which the government makes all major economic decisions) is known as a command economy.

Five-year plans For centuries, Russia's economy had been chiefly agricultural, not industrial. Stalin hoped to change the Soviet economy by developing its industries in a very short time. To accomplish this goal, the Soviet government set production targets for every industry. All managers and workers in the steel industry, for example, would be told how much steel to produce within a five-year period. The quantity demanded in the fifth year of the plan was always far higher than the quantity demanded in the first year. Each *five-year plan*, as it was called, was followed by a new five-year plan with even higher goals for production.

At first, the five-year plans for industries appeared to work. By the end of the first such plan (1928–1932), Soviet industrial output had doubled. Five years later, it had doubled again. But these gains had terrible human costs. Millions of workers were forced to relocate and work at low wages in coal mines, steel mills, weapons plants, and other expanding industries. They often had to work long hours. As consumers, Russians had fewer goods to purchase than before the revolution, since the five-year plans stressed heavy industry rather than consumer goods.

Collectivization   The five-year plans also called for a new system for organizing farm production. The government ordered small farms to be joined together to form larger, "collective farms." Farmers who had previously worked their own small plots now had to turn over their land, livestock, and equipment to those collectives. The farmers would then work the land together. Some of the collective farms were owned and operated by the government. The process for changing from private farms to collective farms was called *collectivization*.

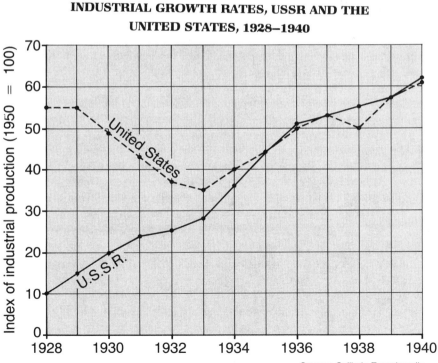

INDUSTRIAL GROWTH RATES, USSR AND THE UNITED STATES, 1928–1940

Source: *Collier's Encyclopedia*

In the state-run farms, the Soviet government determined what crops were to be grown by each collective and what prices the government would pay for them. These payments were shared by members of the collective. Workers on the collectives received wages.

Reign of terror   The wealthier Russian farmers, called *kulaks*, and millions of poorer peasants resisted collectivization. Stalin responded by ordering all resisting farmers to be treated as enemies of the Communist revolution. In the government's anti-kulak campaign (1932–1937), about three million people—both poor and wealthy farmers—were either executed, deported, or sent to labor camps, where they often starved to death. Millions more starved from the famine caused by the failure of Stalin's agricultural policies.

Stalin's reign of terror was not limited to farmers. He conducted massive *purges* (removals) of those he accused of being disloyal to the regime. Leading Soviet citizens, including top-ranking Communist officials and army officers, were removed from office, arrested, and placed on trial. At the trials, the accused were forced to confess to crimes that they had not committed. They were then either executed or sent to labor camps, where many died. Between 1934 and 1938, millions of people were arrested, tortured, imprisoned in labor camps, or executed. In 1940, the exiled Leon Trotsky was assassinated in Mexico, most likely by Stalin's agents.

Totalitarian control   The killing of peasants and the purging of government officials were just two of the techniques that Stalin employed to create a totalitarian police state. The Soviet secret police force, begun under Lenin, expanded operations under Stalin. Russians became afraid to speak openly about any subject, aware that they might be arrested for their words. Information in Soviet newspapers and magazines and on radio programs and newsreels was little more than propaganda praising Stalin and attacking those whom he chose to purge.

To keep ethnic minorities under control, Stalin renewed the czarist policy of Russification. He made the Russian language the official language of all Soviet republics. Whether schools were in Russia or in the non-Russian republics, all instruction had to be in the Russian language. The top government official in a republic was often an ethnic Russian.

Stalin's power as the dictator of a totalitarian state was greater than the absolute power that the Russian czars had had. Loyalty was measured according to whether or not a person agreed with Stalin's policies. Under both Lenin and Stalin, people were taught that the needs of the state were more important than the rights of individuals.

THE COMMUNIST PARTY AND
THE SOVIET GOVERNMENT

In theory, the Soviet Union's government was limited by a written constitution. In practice, however, the government was a dictatorship of the Communist party. Although the Soviet constitution listed the rights of citizens, it placed greater emphasis on social control and law and order. Most important, the constitution provided for the existence of only one political party, the Communist party. Thus, whoever controlled this party also ruled the Soviet Union.

Communist party organization The most powerful leaders of the Communist party were (*1*) the general secretary and (*2*) the Politburo—a small group that assisted the general secretary in running the party. In theory, these leaders were elected by a larger group, the Central Committee. In turn, members of this committee were theoretically elected by an even larger body, the Party Congress. Finally,

ORGANIZATION OF THE COMMUNIST PARTY

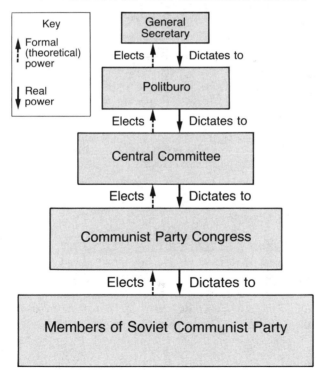

delegates to the Party Congress were elected by those Soviet citizens who belonged to the Communist party. Membership in this party was not open to everyone. In fact only about 5 percent of the Soviet Union's population were admitted into the Communist party. These privileged citizens were the only ones who could hold political office.

On the surface, the system appeared to be democratic. In reality, however, the party leaders at the top—the general secretary and the Politburo—dictated all nominations for party and government offices. Thus, for example, party officials were selected by party leaders at the top rather than by party members or by ordinary citizens. Party leaders told lower-ranking Communists how to vote on every issue.

Soviet government organization   All Soviet citizens, not just the Communists, could vote in elections for government officials. But since the candidates were selected by the leaders of the Communist party (the only party), voters had no choice but to approve or not approve the party candidates.

Voters elected the members of the legislative branch, known as the Supreme Soviet. This body in turn elected the leaders of the executive branch, known collectively as the Council of Ministers. The ministers in turn elected a premier as head of the Soviet government. Once again, the system seemed democratic and subject to voter control. In fact, the general secretary of the Communist party dictated what laws were to be passed by the lower-ranking Communists who sat in the Supreme Soviet. Furthermore, the general secretary could choose also to be premier, as Stalin did in 1941. Nobody else in the Politburo dared to object.

N. WORLD WAR II

The Soviet Union was not the only totalitarian state in Europe in the 1930s. Recall that the 1930s was the decade in which Adolf Hitler and the Nazi party rose to power in Germany. The Communist dictator of the Soviet Union and the Nazi dictator of Germany regarded each other as enemies. Stalin suspected that Hitler intended to use Germany's military might to gain territory in both Western and Eastern Europe. He also knew that Soviet forces would be too weak to stop Hitler unless they were backed up by the British and the French. But, as discussed in Chapter 7, Britain and France decided to appease Hitler in 1938. They gave in to the German dictator's demands to occupy the Sudetenland in Czechoslovakia. Realizing that he could not count on other powers to help resist German aggression, Stalin made a sudden shift in policy that shocked the world.

Nonaggression pact of 1939   In 1939, Stalin signed a pact with Hitler. In this nonaggression pact, as it was called, the Soviet Union and Germany pledged not to attack each other if a war broke out in Europe. Hitler agreed to this pact (even though the German dictator was a bitter enemy of communism) because the pact removed the Soviet Union as a potential enemy in a war that he planned to begin soon. Stalin agreed to the pact because his country was unprepared to fight Germany at that time. Also, the German and Soviet dictators secretly agreed to divide up territories in Eastern Europe once war broke out. (Thus, Estonia, Latvia, and Lithuania would be incorporated into the Soviet Union. Poland would be divided between the two powers.)

Beginning of the war   Only one week after signing the nonaggression pact, Hitler started World War II in Europe by ordering a German army to invade Poland. This event caused Great Britain and France to declare war against Germany. It also caused Stalin to send Soviet troops into that part of Poland that had once been under Russian rule. Germany occupied western Poland, while the Soviet Union occupied eastern Poland. Thus, from 1939 until the last months of the war, Poland was once again an occupied country.

Soviet forces also invaded other territories in Eastern Europe. On Stalin's orders, they attacked Finland, Romania, and the Baltic states of Estonia, Latvia, and Lithuania. The Soviets managed to subdue and occupy the Baltic states and take one section of Romania. The Finns put up a fierce resistance but finally agreed in 1940 to surrender about 10 percent of their territory to the Soviet Union.

At the same time, other parts of Eastern Europe fell under Hitler's control. The fascist governments of Hungary, Romania, and Bulgaria were pressured into joining an alliance with the Axis powers (Germany and Italy). The nations of Greece and Albania fell to Axis invaders. Although Axis forces attacked and occupied Yugoslavia, resistance fighters in that country gave the occupying armies trouble throughout the war.

In one part of Yugoslavia, the Germans set up the puppet state of Croatia. The Croatian government, headed by a fascist, built concentration camps for Jews, Gypsies, and Serbs. In these camps, thousands were put to death.

German invasion of the Soviet Union   The nonaggression pact did not long protect the Soviet Union from Hitler's ambitions for conquest. In June 1941, German forces struck deep into Soviet territory. They rapidly took control of the rest of Poland, the Baltic states, Byelorussia, and much of Ukraine and western Russia. German troops reached the outskirts of Moscow and Leningrad (formerly St. Petersburg). Overwhelmed by German firepower, the Soviets adopted a *scorched earth policy*. As they retreated, they destroyed crops, homes, factories, and other resources to keep them from falling into German hands. The strategy succeeded in cutting off supplies that the Germans needed to maintain their invasion. Eventually, winter set in and German troops froze in the bitter cold.

While Germany was fighting the Soviet Union in 1941 on its Eastern Front, it was doing well on its Western Front (discussed in Chapter 7). France and the low countries had easily fallen to Nazi forces. Great Britain was being bombed.

In 1942, the war in Russia reached a climax as the Germans attacked and surrounded the cities of Leningrad (in the north) and Stalingrad (in the south). Despite relentless bombardments and widespread hunger and starvation, the Russians held their ground. In Stalingrad, they fought off German assaults for six months. Finally in 1943, the Russians launched a counteroffensive there that forced the Germans to retreat. The Russian victory at Stalingrad, where the Germans lost 200,000 troops, was a turning point in the war. From then on, the Soviets were on the offensive against a retreating German army.

By 1944, the Soviets had regained all the territories originally lost to the invaders. They also had won control of much of Eastern Europe (Bulgaria, Hungary, Czechoslovakia, Romania, and Poland). Early in 1945, Soviet forces were near Berlin, Germany. There they were met by their Western allies—British, Canadian, and U.S. forces that had previously liberated France and swept through Western Germany. In May, Germany surrendered and the war in Europe ended.

Wartime losses and destruction   World War II took a heavy toll on Soviet life and property. More than 20 million Soviet citizens—both soldiers and civilians—lost their lives in the war, and millions more were wounded. The loss of property was enormous. Entire villages (as well as railroads, factories, and mines) were destroyed. Stalingrad and much of Leningrad lay in ruins.

The Eastern European countries also suffered heavy losses. In Yugoslavia, one and a half million people died; in Poland, the death toll came to some six million. Many of these deaths were the result of Hitler's policy of genocide against the Jews of Europe (discussed in Chapter 7).

U.S. military aid   During World War II, relations between the Western democracies and the Soviet government improved. Both sides had a common interest in defeating Nazi Germany. One sign of improved U.S.-Soviet wartime relations was the shipment of U.S. military supplies to the Soviets.

YALTA: In February 1945, Sir Winston Churchill (left), Franklin D. Roosevelt, and Joseph Stalin met at Yalta, in the Soviet Union. There the leaders of Great Britain, the United States, and the Soviet Union agreed, among other matters, to transfer some Polish territory to the USSR.

Even before the United States entered the war against Germany in December 1941, it had begun a program of aid to Great Britain. Known as "Lend-Lease," it supplied Great Britain with war materials on credit. By 1945, the program had delivered about $49 billion worth of war materials to a total of 35 nations. About one-fifth of this aid, including shipments of U.S.-made trucks and jeeps, was sent to the Soviet Union. The Lend-Lease aid helped the Soviets avoid defeat during the difficult years of 1941 and 1942.

Wartime conferences Anticipating victory, the Soviet, British, and U.S. leaders met three times during World War II to discuss both military strategy and the terms of peace. At the first two wartime conferences at Teheran (Iran) in 1943 and Yalta (Soviet Union) in 1945, the "big three" consisted of Soviet Premier Joseph Stalin, British Prime Minister Winston Churchill, and U.S. President Franklin Roosevelt. At the third conference, at Potsdam (Germany) in 1945, President Harry Truman represented the United States in place of Roosevelt, who had died a few months earlier.

At the "big three" conferences, important decisions were made concerning the politics of postwar Europe. The leaders of the three powers agreed to the following:

- Germany would be disarmed after the war.
- Germany and its capital, Berlin, would be divided into four zones of occupation (British, French, U.S., and Soviet).
- The Soviet Union would receive a part of eastern Poland.
- Poland would receive some German territory.
- Liberated from German control, the various nations of Eastern Europe would elect new governments. (Since Soviet troops had occupied these nations in the process of defeating German forces, the Soviets were in a position to dominate and control the elections.)

Some critics of these wartime agreements accused the U.S. and British leaders of "giving away" Eastern Europe to the Soviets. Defenders of the agreements argued that since Soviet troops already occupied this region, the Americans and the British would have had to risk war with the Soviet Union in order to remove Soviet troops.

O. EASTERN EUROPE AFTER WORLD WAR II

After World War II, the Soviet Union carried out—at least in part—the terms of the agreement at Yalta. As agreed, the Soviets permitted elections to be held in Poland, Hungary, and the other Eastern European countries that they were occupying. They made sure, however, that the elections were won by Communist party candidates. If the postwar elections had been free and fair, the Communists may not have come to power in these countries.

Methods of Communist takeover Between 1945 and 1948, Soviet agents in Poland, Hungary, Bulgaria, and Romania resorted to various tactics for controlling election results. They threatened opposition candidates, destroyed anti-Communist newspaper offices, and stuffed ballot boxes with Communist votes. National leaders who opposed the Soviet Union were either arrested and executed or forced to flee the country. The last of the Eastern European nations to lose its independence was Czechoslovakia. In 1948, Czech Communists and their Soviet backers carried out a coup in which they forced democratically elected leaders to leave office. The Communists then rigged the next election so that they could not lose.

The Communist governments of Eastern Europe imitated the Soviet system. They nationalized (took ownership of) heavy industries, turned privately owned farms into collective farms, and enacted five-year plans. They used secret police forces to eliminate political opposition. They tried to discourage religious activities, fearing that religious beliefs might compete with loyalty to the state. But many people in Eastern Europe refused to give up their religion. Throughout the years of Soviet control, the Roman Catholic Church and certain other religions remained important institutions.

Soviet satellites   Since the Soviets had put them into power, the Communist dictators of Eastern Europe generally took orders from Moscow. Their nations were like satellites revolving in the orbit of Soviet power and control. Thus, the countries were called "Soviet satellites."

After the war, Soviet troops continued to occupy Germany's eastern zone. Thus, East Germany also became a Soviet satellite. Here the Soviets took apart German factories and shipped them to the Soviet Union. Defending these acts, Soviet leaders argued that the factories were a form of reparation for the many Soviet factories that had been destroyed during the Nazi invasion.

In Review

The following questions refer to the Soviet Union under Stalin until the end of World War II, as discussed on pages 434–443.

1. *Key terms:* Define or identify each of the following:

    five-year plan   kulak   scorched earth policy
    collectivization   purge trial   the "big three"

2. Describe *two* methods used by Stalin to maintain and expand his power as the Soviet dictator.

3. Explain how most of the countries of Eastern Europe became Communist states after World War II.

4. *Critical thinking:* Do you think that Stalin made a wise decision in agreeing to the nonaggression pact with Hitler? (Evaluate the decision from the point of view of Soviet national interests.) Give reasons for your answer.

IV. Forty Years of the Cold War (1945–1985)

Soon after World War II ended in 1945, an intense rivalry developed between the Soviet Union and its wartime ally, the United States. This rivalry—the cold war—was a conflict between two opposing economic systems (communism and capitalism) and two opposing political systems (dictatorship and democracy).

A. CAUSES OF THE COLD WAR

Chapter 7 described how the cold war affected Western Europe. This chapter looks again at the conflict between the Soviet Union and the United States. Both sides in the conflict had reasons for hostility and distrust.

Soviet distrust of the United States   The Soviets feared the United States for a number of reasons.

- For a few years after the war (1945–1949), the United States was the only nation in the world that possessed atomic weapons.
- The U.S. economic system was capitalist in that most of its businesses were privately owned and operated for profit. The *ideology* (belief system) of Soviet communism taught that there was bound to be violent conflicts between a capitalist nation and a Communist one.
- The Soviet Union regarded the anti-Communist policies of the United States as hostile. Chief among such policies were the Truman Doctrine, the Marshall Plan, and NATO (all discussed in Chapter 7).
- The Soviets opposed the unification of the three western zones in Germany. They feared a strong and united Germany, since the Soviet Union had already suffered terribly from German invasions during the two world wars.

U.S. distrust of the Soviet Union   The United States also had strong reasons for its distrust.

- Soviet troops remained in Eastern Europe after the war. U.S. leaders objected, claiming that this occupation violated wartime agreements and extended Soviet power over a large area.
- Soviet troops in Eastern Europe threatened the security of Western European nations.
- In the 1940s, Communist parties were gaining strength in several countries of Western Europe, including Greece, Italy, and France.
- The Soviet Union attempted to spread communism around the world by aiding nationalist uprisings and revolutions. In fact, by 1949 Communist forces had come to power in China and North Korea and were threatening to take over French Indochina.
- Also significant were the differences in political systems. The United States was democratic while the Soviet Union was totalitarian.

B. AREAS OF CONFLICT

The cold war lasted for more than four decades. During that time, competition between the world's two most powerful nations took many forms.

An arms race   In 1945, the United States had dropped two atomic bombs on Japan to end World War II. In 1949, the Soviet Union exploded its first atomic bomb. In 1952, the United States developed a more powerful nuclear weapon, the hydrogen bomb. But only one year later, the Soviet Union announced that it too had developed a hydrogen bomb. Year after year, the superpowers spent huge sums of money building up their nuclear arsenals. They kept inventing new weapons systems, including land- and sea-based missiles and long-range bombers (all capable of being equipped with nuclear weapons). The world lived in fear that someday these weapons might be used in a war capable of destroying all life on the planet.

A space race In 1957, the Soviet Union took the lead in the space race by launching *Sputnik I*, the first space satellite. The Soviets followed this feat in 1961 with another first—the launching into orbit of a satellite with a human inside. The United States matched that feat the next year. Then in 1969, two U.S. astronauts walked on the moon's surface, an event that astonished the world and gave the United States the lead in the space race. Later, both countries launched space stations, communication and weather satellites, and spacecraft directed at other planets.

Espionage Both superpowers maintained huge spy and intelligence-gathering organizations. The Soviet Union's spy agency and secret police force, the KGB, placed spies in the United States and in almost every other country in the world. The U.S. Central Intelligence Agency (CIA) established a worldwide spy network for the United States.

Propaganda Making great efforts to influence world public opinion, both the Soviets and the Americans conducted campaigns of propaganda. For example, the United States created Radio Free Europe, which broadcast information that had been unavailable to the people of Eastern Europe.

Alliances Both superpowers signed treaties of alliance in which they pledged to defend their allies against attack. The Soviet Union allied itself with other Communist nations. Soviet allies included Communist China (through the 1950s) and Cuba (after Castro came to power in 1959). The most important and enduring alliances of the Soviet Union were those with the satellite countries of Eastern Europe. The Warsaw Pact of 1955 provided that Soviet troops be stationed in Eastern European countries to defend them against the NATO alliance.

Military and economic aid During the cold war, most nations of the world were *not* allied with either the Soviet-dominated Communist bloc or the U.S.-dominated Western bloc. Nevertheless, as we discussed in previous chapters, the cold war rivals attempted to influence the politics of third world nations in Latin America, Africa, Asia, and

ALLIANCES IN THE COLD WAR

the Middle East. In the 1960s, for example, President John F. Kennedy began a program called the "Alliance for Progress." Under this program, the United States offered billions of dollars in economic aid to the countries of Latin America. A major purpose of this aid was to defeat Soviet and Cuban efforts to spread communism in that region. (It was hoped that U.S. aid would reduce Latin Americans' economic discontent, which Communists used to promote revolution.)

In addition to economic and technical aid, the two superpowers also extended military aid to various governments. In the Middle East, for example, large quantities of Soviet military aid went to Egypt and Syria. The United States also gave military aid to countries in the Middle East: Jordan, Saudi Arabia, and Israel.

Proxy wars Although the United States and the Soviet Union never fought each other, they did engage in *proxy wars*. That is, they gave military support to opposing sides in wars fought outside their own borders. Two such wars were fought in Asia: the Korean War in the early 1950s and the Vietnam War in the 1960s and early 1970s. A great number of U.S. troops were involved in both of these conflicts. Even though Soviet troops were not used in either war, Soviet military aid provided important support for the forces of both North Korea and North Vietnam. (For more about these two wars, see Chapters 5 and 6.)

C. REVOLTS IN EASTERN EUROPE

Why did the hostilities of the cold war fail to lead to a military conflict between the United States and the Soviet Union? One reason was that each of the two superpowers recognized that certain territories or regions belonged within their rival's sphere of influence. Soviet leaders understood that attempts to take over Latin American countries would be viewed as threats to the United States. At the same time, U.S. leaders understood that the nations of Eastern Europe lay within the orbit of the Soviet Union. Both superpowers fully recognized the danger of nuclear war if either interfered in the other's zone of special interest.

In the 1950s and 1960s, for example, major revolts broke out in Eastern Europe against Communist rule. In Hungary in 1956 and again in Czechoslovakia in 1968, Soviet tanks moved in to put down the uprisings. Although the United States protested the Soviet actions, it did not intervene to give support to the "freedom fighters."

Uprising in Poland, 1956   One of the first anti-Soviet and anti-Communist revolts occurred in Poland. In 1956, Polish workers and consumers rioted against price increases and shortages of consumer goods. Poland's Communist government used military force to crush the protests.

Uprising in Hungary, 1956   Inspired by the Polish example, Hungarians also revolted. For a few days, rebels succeeded in setting up an independent government. They demanded the withdrawal of Soviet troops. Instead of backing down, the Soviet Union sent massive numbers of troops and tanks into Hungary and regained control.

Uprising in Czechoslovakia, 1968   A reform-minded Communist leader, Alexander Dubček, came to power in Czechoslovakia in 1968. Dubček hoped to create a more democratic nation by allowing freedom of speech and the press. In the spring of 1968 (called the "Prague spring"), many Czechoslovakians in their capital of Prague began to express themselves openly and to criticize Communist policies. The Soviet Union, fearful of losing control, ordered troops into Czechoslovakia to occupy the country. Dubček was replaced, and tight government censorship was reestablished.

D. CRISES IN BERLIN AND CUBA

In the early 1960s, two crises brought the superpowers to the brink of war. At this time, the Soviet leader was Nikita Khrushchev and the U.S. president was John Kennedy.

Berlin, 1961 Recall that after World War II, the Soviets occupied East Germany while the Western allies (the United States, Britain, and France) occupied West Germany. Berlin was also divided into four zones of occupation. Since Berlin was located within East Germany, the Western allies had to pass through the Soviet zone of occupation in order to reach the city. This situation gave the Soviets an advantage in controlling Berlin. In 1948, they tried to take over all of Berlin by announcing that the Western allies could no longer use the roads and railroads leading into the city. The United States responded with the Berlin Airlift, which forced the Soviet Union to end its blockade. The cold war conflict over Berlin continued through the 1950s.

In 1961, the conflict developed into another major crisis. The Soviet leader, Khrushchev, demanded that the Western powers pull out of West Berlin. Speaking for the United States and its NATO allies, President Kennedy refused to yield. In fact, to show U.S. determination, Kennedy visited Berlin just as the East Germans were erecting the Berlin Wall to divide the city. The president pledged that his country would never abandon the people of West Berlin. (For more about the Berlin Wall, see Chapter 7.)

Cuba, 1962 More dangerous than the Berlin crises was the Cuban Missile Crisis of 1962. In Chapter 4, we discussed how Soviet missiles were secretly shipped into Cuba and how U.S. President Kennedy ordered a naval blockade of that country to keep Soviet ships away. If any Soviet ship had tried to break through the blockade, the United States might have responded by launching a nuclear attack against Soviet targets. Fortunately, Khrushchev recognized that the United States viewed Soviet missiles in Cuba as a threat to U.S. security. He ordered Soviet ships sailing to Cuba to turn around. The crisis finally passed when Khrushchev agreed to remove all missiles from Cuba.

E. REDUCING COLD WAR TENSIONS

So frightening was the Cuban Missile Crisis that it marked a turning point in the cold war. After that crisis, the Soviet Union and the United States looked for ways to reduce the danger of nuclear war.

Nuclear test ban and the hot line In 1963, the two superpowers (together with Great Britain) signed a Nuclear Test-Ban Treaty. In this treaty, they agreed to end the testing of nuclear weapons in the atmosphere, in outer space, and under water. In the same year, a *hot line* (electronic link by telegraph and teleprinter) was set up to prevent accidental nuclear war. Connecting the offices of the U.S. president and the Soviet leader, the hot line gave the two leaders a means of communicating directly with each other in times of crisis.

"Let's Get A Lock For This Thing"

"Let's get a lock for this thing"—from *Herblock: A Cartoonist's Life* (Lisa Drew Books/Macmillan Publishers, 1993)

THE NUCLEAR THREAT: The leaders depicted in this 1962 cartoon are John F. Kennedy and Nikita Khrushchev. After the Cuban Missile Crisis, how did they attempt to "get a lock for this thing"?

Détente   In the early 1970s, President Richard Nixon and Soviet leader Leonid Brezhnev attempted to reduce cold war tensions and minimize the chance of a nuclear war. Their policy was known as *détente*, a French word meaning "to relax." In this case, the goal was to relax tensions and improve relations between the two superpowers.

SEEKING DÉTENTE: Soviet leader Leonid Brezhnev (left) met with U.S. President Richard Nixon at a Soviet Black Sea resort in 1974.

In 1972, Nixon traveled to Moscow to meet with Brezhnev. The U.S. president agreed to end a U.S. trade ban of 1949, which had prohibited the shipping of U.S. goods to the Soviet Union. To help the Russian people through a bad food shortage, Nixon declared that the Soviets could purchase as much as $750 million worth of U.S. wheat. This agreement came to be known as the U.S.-Soviet "grain deal." It was a good example of détente, since it showed that the rival superpowers could reach agreement on certain issues.

SALT I Treaty   On his trip to Moscow in 1972, Nixon made another important agreement with Brezhnev. The two leaders signed an arms control treaty that set a limit on the number of offensive and defensive missiles that each power could have. Their agreement, later ratified by the U.S. Senate, was called the Strategic Arms Limitation Talks (SALT) I Treaty.

Helsinki Accords   Another example of improved U.S.-Soviet relations in the 1970s was a diplomatic conference in Helsinki, Finland. In the Helsinki Accords of 1975, the United States and its NATO allies agreed to respect the Soviet sphere of influence in Eastern Europe. For their part, the Soviet Union and its Eastern European allies agreed to respect the human rights of their citizens, including the freedom to travel. In later years, however, the United States accused the Soviet Union of violating the Helsinki Accords by preventing thousands of Soviet Jews from leaving the country.

Scientific cooperation and cultural exchanges   Science and the arts also played a role in improving U.S.-Soviet relations in the 1970s. For example, in a cooperative scientific venture in 1975, U.S. and Soviet spaceships linked up in space. Astronauts from both countries conducted joint scientific experiments while orbiting the earth.

Cultural exchanges also promoted goodwill between the superpowers. Soviet dance troupes such as the Bolshoi Ballet and the Kirov Ballet often toured the United States. In exchange, U.S. performers, including Louis Armstrong and Billy Joel, toured the Soviet Union.

SALT II Treaty   Extending the SALT I agreement on arms control, Soviet and U.S. negotiators agreed to further limit the number of long-range offensive missiles that each superpower could have. Completed in 1979, the SALT II Treaty also would have limited each power's long-range bombers. This treaty, however, was not ratified by the U.S. Senate because of the Soviet invasion of Afghanistan in 1979.

F. RENEWAL OF COLD WAR TENSIONS (1979–1985)

The Soviet invasion of Afghanistan began a brief period of increased tensions between the superpowers.

Invasion of Afghanistan   In the 1970s, the Soviet Union supported a Communist government in Afghanistan. Then in 1978, with Soviet backing, a group of radical Afghan Communists seized power.

Soviet troops moved into Afghanistan in 1979 to support the new Communist government. But Afghan rebels, fighting in the rugged Hindu Kush Mountains, put up a fierce resistance. The war for control of Afghanistan dragged on for years at great cost and loss of life on both sides.

The United States opposed Soviet involvement in Afghanistan, fearing that the Soviets might use it as a base for seizing the oil fields in the Persian Gulf. To retaliate for Soviet aggression, President Jimmy Carter cut back U.S. grain shipments to the Soviet Union. He also announced that U.S. athletes would not go to Moscow in 1980 to participate in the Summer Olympic Games. Most important, the United States supplied military aid to the rebel forces fighting the Soviet-backed government in Afghanistan.

U.S. arms buildup   After Ronald Reagan was elected president in 1980, he persuaded Congress to finance a huge increase in spending on weapons systems and the armed forces. This U.S. military buildup came as a direct challenge to the Soviet Union. Returning to the hostile language of the cold war, Reagan referred to the Soviet Union as an "evil empire."

In Review

The following questions refer to Soviet-U.S. relations during the cold war, as discussed on pages 443–452.

1. *Key terms:* Define or identify each of the following:

    arms race   Warsaw Pact   hot line
    space race   Cuban Missile Crisis   détente

2. Give one example of a U.S. action and one example of a Soviet action for each of the following: (a) cold war alliances,   (b) military and economic aid, and   (c) proxy wars.

3. Explain how *one* of the following was an arena for conflict between the superpowers: (a) Berlin,   (b) Cuba, and   (c) Afghanistan.

4. Explain what happened in each of the following years to either increase or decrease cold war tensions: (a) 1956,   (b) 1962, (c) 1972, and   (d) 1979.

5. *Critical thinking:* In your view, which *two* conflicts during the cold war involved the greatest danger of triggering a nuclear showdown between the superpowers? Explain your answer.

G. SOVIET DOMESTIC POLITICS

Leading the Soviet Union through nearly four decades of the cold war were three Communist dictators: Joseph Stalin, Nikita Khrushchev, and Leonid Brezhnev. How did each leader approach the Soviet Union's political and economic problems at home?

Stalin's last years   After World War II ended in 1945, Stalin resumed the government's five-year plans. Once again, he concentrated on building up heavy industries and military production. By 1950, Soviet industrial production was second only to that of the United States. In contrast, consumers continued to suffer from shortages of clothing, electronic appliances, and other basic consumer goods. Workers' wages remained low.

In the postwar years, agricultural production in the Soviet Union failed to increase. In 1947, people in Ukraine and southwestern Russia suffered a terrible famine. Harsh government policies as well as a drought were responsible. The Soviet government had forced Ukrainian and Russian peasants to deliver grain to the cities, even though these farmers did not have enough grain to feed themselves.

Adding to the sufferings of the postwar period was Stalin's continued use of labor camps. Many Soviet soldiers who returned home from German prison camps were either shot or sent to labor camps in Siberia. Why? They were considered disloyal for having been taken alive as prisoners. Millions of others in labor camps were the victims of Stalin's many new purges. The victims included not only political and military leaders but also leaders of Soviet culture—musicians, artists, writers, and scientists.

The Khrushchev era　After more than 25 years of dictatorial rule, Stalin died in 1953. His death touched off a power struggle among top Communist officials. After a brief period of time, Khrushchev emerged as the most powerful of these officials. In 1956, he surprised those attending a Party Congress by criticizing some of Stalin's methods. He attacked the former dictator's campaign of terror in the 1930s and his leadership during World War II.

Khrushchev followed up his speech of criticism with a de-Stalinization campaign—efforts to allow greater freedom. Some victims of Stalin's purges were released from labor camps. Censorship in the arts and literature was lifted slightly. Writers could now openly criticize Stalin's policies and actions. If they expressed disapproval of Khrushchev, however, they could still be penalized.

The Soviet economy made some progress in the Khrushchev era. Khrushchev's five-year plans put new emphasis on producing consumer goods—a policy that made Khrushchev popular with the Soviet people. Khrushchev also made reforms in agriculture, but food production remained inadequate. Unlike Stalin (who had let people starve during years of poor harvests), Khrushchev in 1963 ordered massive purchases of grain from the United States and other countries.

The Brezhnev era　In 1964, a group of high-ranking officials in the Communist party forced Khrushchev to resign. For a few years, Leonid Brezhnev (the new party secretary) and Alexei Kosygin (the new premier) shared power. In the early 1970s, Brezhnev emerged as the stronger of the two.

During the Brezhnev era (1964–1982), it became clear that the Soviet economy was growing too slowly to keep pace with industrial production in the West. Construction of missiles and other weapons consumed a large part of the Soviet budget. Agricultural production was still low. In some years, the Soviet Union again had to import large quantities of wheat and other crops.

Another problem during the Brezhnev years was that many Russians had become unhappy with the Communist system. In theory, all workers under communism were to receive equal incomes and benefits. In practice, Communist leaders and high officials enjoyed special privileges and received expensive consumer goods (such as Western cars and clothing), while the average worker lived poorly. People noticed corruption among important officials, but most kept silent for fear of being arrested. As did earlier leaders, Brezhnev used the KGB to eliminate political opposition. Writers of *underground literature* (illegal writings that criticized government policies and were published or passed on secretly) were subject to being arrested and either imprisoned or sent to mental institutions. (During Stalin's time, those arrested for the same "crimes" would have been executed.) Despite this strict control by the government, a number of citizens persisted in writing and distributing underground literature.

Brezhnev's death in 1982 led to another power struggle among high-ranking Communists. Two elderly leaders followed each other in quick succession as general secretary of the party. When the second of them died in 1985, a younger man, Mikhail Gorbachev, came to power as the new general secretary. Gorbachev was determined to completely reform the Soviet economic and political system. He had no intention of ending Communist rule in Russia or of breaking up the Soviet Union. As we now know, however, that is eventually what happened.

Before describing the collapse of the Soviet empire, let us look at Soviet society as it existed when Gorbachev came to power.

H. SOVIET SOCIETY

The Soviet Union consisted of 15 republics. Each republic—including the largest, Russia—had a mixed population of ethnic and religious minorities.

Ethnic mix   The largest ethnic group, the Russians, made up about half of the Soviet Union's 280 million people in 1985. The second largest group, the Ukrainians, made up 16 percent of the population. The remainder of the Soviet people included Byelorussians, Uzbeks, Armenians, Georgians, and dozens of other distinct groups, each with its own language and traditions.

Religions   When the Communist party came to power in 1917, it opposed religious practices and developed a propaganda campaign against religion. Thus, by 1985 the majority of the Soviet people belonged to no organized religion. Defying the government, about 20 percent of the people still practiced the Russian Orthodox religion in 1985. Another 10 percent of the population were Muslims, most of them living in Central Asia (north of Iran and Afghanistan). A few million Roman Catholics, Jews, and Protestants also lived in the Soviet Union.

UNDERSTANDING CHRONOLOGY

Russia was ruled by a Communist government for almost 75 years. To understand what happened to the Soviet empire between 1917 and 1991, you need to know when and in what order major changes occurred in Soviet leadership and policy. The time line below presents a partial summary of major eras in Soviet history.

As drawn, the time line is incomplete. It shows only three major eras in Soviet history. Complete the time line yourself by doing the following:

1. Copy the time line on this page onto a sheet of paper. To give yourself ample room, draw the time line across the full *length* of the paper.
2. Use a different color or shading pattern (stripes, dots, and so on) to represent each of the following eras:
   A. FIRST FIVE-YEAR PLAN
   B. STALIN'S PURGES
   C. COMMUNIST TAKEOVER OF EASTERN EUROPE
   D. KHRUSHCHEV IN POWER
   E. YEARS OF DÉTENTE
3. Use the letters A–E to label each shaded section of the time line.
4. Referring to the chronology of events on page 460, select *six* specific events to place on the time line: (a) three events from the years before the cold war and (b) three events during the cold war. To see how events may be placed on a time line, refer to the model time line on page 23.

ERAS IN SOVIET HISTORY

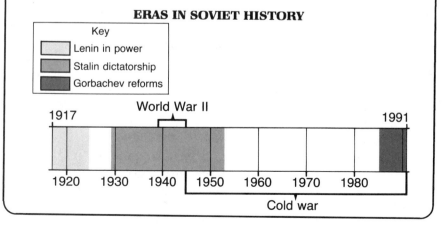

Key
Lenin in power
Stalin dictatorship
Gorbachev reforms

World War II
1917   1991
1920   1930   1940 | 1950   1960   1970   1980
Cold war

The Communist government discriminated against people of any faith who practiced their religion. Jews, however, generally suffered worse treatment than other groups. Recall that pogroms in czarist Russia had killed many thousands of Jews and destroyed their property. Russification policies under Stalin resulted in the purges and deaths of additional thousands of Jews. During the cold war, the Soviet government placed severe restrictions on its people's freedom to travel and emigrate. In the 1970s, however, détente with the West and heavy U.S. pressure caused the Brezhnev government to allow Jews to leave the country. Since then, large numbers of Jews have emigrated, chiefly to Israel and the United States.

Women in the work force   The Soviet Constitution of 1936 guaranteed equal rights to women and men. According to Communist beliefs, Soviet women were to have equal opportunities for employment outside the home. As a result, the vast majority of Soviet women had jobs throughout most of their adult lives. They worked in every occupation and profession. For example, in the 1980s, about 70 percent of Soviet doctors were women. In fact, the percentage of women employed as doctors, lawyers, and engineers was higher in the Soviet Union than in the United States.

Nevertheless, Soviet women did not have the same opportunities as men to rise to top positions. In Soviet schools, for example, most teachers were women, while most administrators were men. The male-dominated Communist party admitted few women into its upper ranks.

Arts and sciences   The Soviet government viewed the arts as a form of state propaganda. During the 1920s and 1930s, it demanded that Soviet art, film, drama, and literature portray workers as heroes struggling against their "oppressors," the capitalist class. This approach to art was called *socialist realism*.

Government censors prohibited works of art and literature that did not meet official guidelines. For example, Russian poet and novelist Boris Pasternak won the Nobel Prize for Literature in 1958 for his novel *Doctor Zhivago*. It was banned in the Soviet Union, however, because it gave a negative view of the Bolshevik Revolution. Another writer, Alexander Solzhenitsyn, was deported in 1974 for allowing his three-volume study, *The Gulag Archipelago*, to be published in the West. The book was a long and revealing description of Soviet labor camps. It too was banned in the Soviet Union.

Soviet scientists also were made to serve the interests of the state. A brilliant Soviet physicist, Andrei Sakharov, was largely responsible for developing the first Soviet hydrogen bomb. In time, however, Sakharov spoke out against nuclear testing. He wrote a book attacking the Soviet government's practice of suppressing the free exchange of ideas.

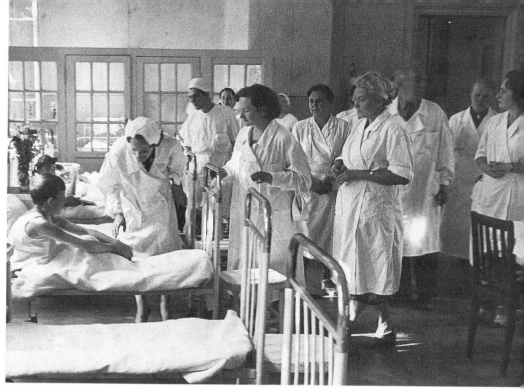

SOVIET WOMEN: A large majority of Soviet doctors were women. Does this fact prove that Soviet men and women had equal career opportunities? Explain.

In 1975, the government cut off Sakharov's contacts with universities outside the Soviet Union. He could no longer work as a scientist, and he was forced to live in isolation away from Moscow. Sakharov's ideas about democracy would once again be heard after Mikhail Gorbachev came to power in 1985.

In Review

The following questions refer to Soviet domestic policies during the cold war, as discussed on pages 452–457.

1. *Key terms:* Define each of the following:

   underground literature   socialist realism

2. State *three* ways in which Khrushchev's policies differed from those of Stalin.

3. Describe the effects of the Soviet system on: (a) writers and artists,   (b) scientists, and   (c) women.

4. *Critical thinking:* "A government that suppresses criticism and dissent is bound to be corrupt." Do you think that this statement accurately describes what happened to the Soviet government? Why or why not?

V. Contemporary Nations

For seven years (1985–1991), Gorbachev struggled to increase the output of the Soviet economy by reforming the Soviet state. His reforms did not work, and, consequently, the Soviet Union broke up.

A. WEAKNESSES OF THE SOVIET ECONOMY

Gorbachev was well aware that the Soviet economy was weak. In fact, in 1985 it was approaching a state of near collapse. At fault was the Communist system itself, which failed to produce enough goods and services to supply the basic needs of the Soviet people. The system did not work well for several reasons.

Lack of flexibility   In the Soviet Union's command economy, economic decisions were under the command, or direction, of the central government. The Soviet government determined what products to produce, what services to provide, and what prices to charge for these goods and services. Prices usually had no relationship to the costs of production. Nor did the price of a product, such as a television set, reflect consumer demand for it. Government agencies that controlled factory production often ordered too many of some products and too few of others. As a result, there were both waste and shortages.

Lack of incentives   A second weakness of the Soviet economy was that workers had little incentive to improve their performance on the job. The government employed them and guaranteed them a certain wage whether or not they worked hard. How much a worker earned was not related to how much he or she produced. Thus, there was low worker productivity.

Overemphasis on military goods   A nation has only a certain amount of natural resources. If it uses these resources to produce guns, for example, then it cannot use these same resources to produce other items. For more than 40 years during the cold war, Soviet leaders devoted a large percentage of their country's resources to producing military equipment (in order to compete in the arms race). Little remained to provide for people's basic needs, such as food, clothing, and housing. Even less was available for luxury items, such as automobiles. Soviet stores often had shortages of many products. Consumers were forced either to do without or to wait in long lines at poorly stocked government stores.

Corruption   In the Soviet Union, people bribed government officials to get around established rules and regulations. They made payments to government officials to speed up the process of acquiring permits and approval forms. A *black market* (system for selling goods illegally) was created by private businesspeople to supply products that could not easily be found in state-run stores. Black marketeers sold both domestic and foreign-made items for profit, usually at prices higher than those allowed by the government.

Agricultural problems   For years, agricultural output in the Soviet Union fell far below the government's goals. One reason for this failure was the lack of incentives for farmers to produce a surplus. Farmers were poorly paid, and crop prices were determined by the government. If a collective farm failed to meet the goals set for it, individual farmers were not held responsible. A second reason for low food production was the system of centralized planning, which often failed to take into account the needs of local collective farms. For example, a collective might have had good farm equipment but no means of fixing the equipment when it broke down.

To remedy these problems, Soviet leaders introduced minor incentives to improve production. For example, increased production by a worker was sometimes rewarded with a special vacation. Honors and awards were given to those who produced more than others. On the collective farms, farmers were allowed to sell produce from their own small plots of land and keep the profits. In fact, these small plots were usually more productive than the lands of the collective farm. Even these incentives, however, failed to significantly increase farm production overall.

A SOVIET COLLECTIVE FARM: In 1963, residents of this collective farm in the Soviet Union walked by posters advertising goals for future food production. What were the actual results of collective farming?

RISE AND FALL OF THE SOVIET UNION, 1917–1991

November 1917: Bolshevik party seizes power in Petrograd.

1918–1921: Red Army fights civil war against anti-Communists.

1921: Lenin announces his New Economic Policy.

1922: Communist government establishes USSR, or Soviet Union.

1924: Lenin dies.

1928–1932: First Five-Year Plan is carried out.

1929: Stalin assumes dictatorial powers.

1934–1938: Stalin orders a number of "purge trials."

1939: Stalin and Hitler sign a nonaggression pact.

1941–1943: German troops invade the Soviet Union.

1945: Agreement at Yalta permits Soviets to supervise elections in Eastern Europe.

1949: Soviets explode a nuclear weapon.

1953: Stalin dies.

1955: Warsaw Pact is formed.

1957: Soviets launch *Sputnik I.*

1962: Cuban Missile Crisis almost leads to a nuclear showdown.

1964: Brezhnev replaces Khrushchev as the Communist party leader.

1972–1979: Détente governs Soviet and U.S. foreign policy. Soviet economy declines.

1979: Soviet forces invade Afghanistan.

1985: Gorbachev comes to power as the Communist party leader.

1986: Gorbachev announces policies of glasnost and perestroika.

1989: Soviets permit free elections that would eventually topple Communist governments in Poland, Czechoslovakia, and elsewhere in Eastern Europe. Berlin Wall comes down.

1990: Leaders of Baltic republics call for independence. East and West Germany are reunited.

June 1991: Boris Yeltsin wins Russia's first direct election for president.

August 1991: Attempted coup by Soviet hard-liners fails.

December 1991: Russia and Ukraine vote for independence. Gorbachev resigns as head of the Soviet government. The Soviet Union is dissolved.

B. ATTEMPTS AT REFORM

Gorbachev hoped to revive the Soviet economy and to make the Communist system more democratic. To achieve these goals, he introduced a number of sweeping reforms.

Glasnost   Gorbachev told the Soviet people that he wanted them to be able to speak and write openly on public issues. Unlike in the past, there would be no penalties for doing so. Gorbachev's policy of inviting public discussion and free speech was called *glasnost* (openness). Soviet newspapers and television news programs were now free to criticize government policies and to report on world and national events without censorship. Under glasnost, Soviet citizens could practice any religion without state interference. After years of living in exile, the famed Soviet scientist Andrei Sakharov was welcomed back to Moscow.

Perestroika   Reforms aimed at reviving the Soviet economy were called *perestroika* (restructuring). Gorbachev encouraged local government officials, factory managers, and collective farm directors to make their own decisions rather than take orders from the central government. He wanted workers' wages and government payments to factories and collective farms to rise or fall depending on each producer's success in increasing output. In short, perestroika involved

CAPITALISM IN THE NEW RUSSIA: On a Moscow street, books are sold for a profit by an enterprising merchant. How does Russia's current economic system differ from the former Soviet system?

moving away from a command economy toward a system in which local factories and farms made decisions more freely.

Besides changing the rules for factories and farms, Gorbachev also encouraged people to form privately owned businesses. The business owners would decide for themselves what goods or services to offer for sale and what prices to charge for them.

Opening the political process Gorbachev also changed the political system to allow Soviet citizens real choices when they voted in elections. In the past, the Communist party had provided voters with only one list of candidates. In effect, voters had no choice except whether or not to approve the party's list. Gorbachev opened up the election process by allowing several candidates to compete for the same office. At first, all candidates had to be members of the Communist party. Soon, however, non-Communists were also allowed to run for election to the Congress of People's Deputies and other government posts.

In the separate republics that made up the Soviet Union, greater political openness led to nationalist movements for autonomy (self-government). Nationalist candidates in Lithuania, Latvia, Estonia, and other republics won election to their republics' legislatures. In 1990, all the republics passed laws stating that if a conflict existed between a republic's law and a Soviet (national) law, the republic's law was supreme.

C. CHANGES IN FOREIGN POLICY

Gorbachev recognized that too much of his country's economic resources had been devoted to the arms race. The Soviet Union could no longer afford to stretch its resources in an effort to match U.S. armaments. The Soviet leader therefore decided to seek new agreements with the United States on arms control.

The INF Treaty On three occasions, Gorbachev met with U.S. President Ronald Reagan to discuss arms control and other issues. Their third meeting took place in 1987 in Washington, D.C. Here the two leaders made a major breakthrough by signing a treaty that provided for all U.S. and Soviet intermediate-range missiles in Europe to be removed and dismantled. (Intermediate-range missiles could travel hundreds of miles, compared with long-range ICBMs, which could cross oceans.) The treaty was called the Intermediate-Range Nuclear Forces Treaty, or INF Treaty.

Other agreements Later U.S.-Soviet agreements went beyond the INF Treaty. In 1990, Warsaw Pact and NATO countries, including the Soviet Union and the United States, agreed to make large reductions in their nonnuclear forces in Europe. After the signing of this

Conventional Forces in Europe (CFE) Treaty, the Soviet Union with-drew many of its troops and arms from Eastern Europe.

Another treaty, signed in 1991, was the first U.S.-Soviet agreement to sharply reduce (not just limit) each country's long-range nuclear weapons. The Strategic Arms Reduction Talks (START) Treaty did not go into effect before the breakup of the Soviet Union later in 1991.

Soviet withdrawal from Afghanistan   The last major dispute in the cold war involved the Soviet effort to put down a rebellion against Communist rule in Afghanistan. Despite years of fighting, the Soviet army had failed to defeat rebel forces there. Throughout the long struggle, the rebels had received U.S. military aid. The Soviets had used up a vast amount of its resources in the war. Finally, Gorbachev de-cided to withdraw all Soviet forces from Afghanistan, a process that was completed in 1989.

D. REVOLUTIONS IN EASTERN EUROPE

Communism in the various nations of Eastern Europe worked no better than it did in the Soviet Union. Economic production was low. Basic freedoms were denied. Corruption among top Communist of-ficials was widespread. In addition, the Poles, Hungarians, Czechs, and other peoples of Eastern Europe were dissatisfied about being dominated by a foreign power, the Soviet Union. Earlier revolts against Communist rule and Soviet domination (in Poland, Hungary, and Czechoslovakia) had been crushed. In the late 1980s, however, Gor-bachev's reforms gave Eastern Europeans hope for democratic change in their own nations. In fact, Gorbachev himself put pressure on Com-munist parties in Eastern Europe to allow voters more choices. Throughout Eastern Europe, free choice led to the overthrow of communism.

Poland   Poland led the way in winning independence from Soviet control. Strikes by Polish workers forced Poland's Communist govern-ment to hold free elections in 1989. A labor union, Solidarity, ran can-didates and won a large number of seats in the Polish legislature. In 1990, the head of Solidarity, Lech Walesa, was elected Poland's pres-ident. The freely elected Polish government moved quickly to change the old command economy into a free market system.

East Germany   In the late 1980s, East Germany's Communist gov-ernment also lost power. Hoping to gain popular support, the govern-ment permitted East Germans to travel freely to West Germany. As a result, the Berlin Wall, a symbol of the cold war, became unnecessary, since there were no longer any East German restrictions on travel. In November 1989, ordinary Germans from both sides of the wall began tearing it down. The East German government now felt pressured to

END OF THE BERLIN WALL: In 1989, the Soviet and East German
governments permitted crowds of Berliners to break down the wall that
had divided their city for decades. How did this event mark a major
change in the politics of Eastern Europe?

schedule elections in which non-Communists could participate. In
May 1990, the non-Communists won the election, and Communist
rule in East Germany came to an end.

One of the first goals of the new East German government (as well
as of the West German government) was to reunify East and West
Germany into one nation. World War II allies Great Britain, France, the
United States, and the Soviet Union agreed to permit reunification. In
October 1990, West Germany and East Germany came together to form
one country.

European nations were concerned about the possible military
power of a united Germany. The new German government, however, pledged never again to take military action against Germany's
neighbors.

Hungary In Hungary also, Communist power was swiftly and
peacefully swept aside. In 1989, the country's Communist party renamed itself the "Socialist party" and promised free elections. In the
elections of 1990, the former Communists lost to a coalition of
non-Communists.

Czechoslovakia Responding to demonstrations by anti-Communists in 1989, Czechoslovakian leaders allowed the formation of a
coalition government in which non-Communists were in a majority.
Because the change was so peaceful, it was called the "Velvet Revolution." The nation's parliament elected as president Václav Havel, a
playwright who had been imprisoned by the Communists for participating in a Czech human rights movement during the 1970s.

Bulgaria   Pressure from reformist Bulgarian leaders forced longtime Communist dictator Todor Zhivkov to resign in November 1989. The Bulgarian government held free elections in 1990, but the Communists (now named "Socialists") did not lose their control of the government until the fall of 1991.

Albania   The transition from Communist dictatorship to democracy was relatively peaceful in Albania. Beginning in 1991, the Communist regime allowed multiparty elections. In 1992, Albanians elected their first non-Communist government since 1944.

Romania   In 1989, Romanians experienced widespread anti-Communist demonstrations. In response, longtime ruler Nicolae Ceauşescu launched bloody attacks against the demonstrators. He vowed to remain in power. Within days of these attacks, however, he was overthrown and executed. Former Communists remained in control of Romania until 1991, when non-Communists won parliamentary elections.

Yugoslavia   As in other Eastern European countries, people in Yugoslavia demonstrated in 1990 for multiparty elections, and the Communists gave up their monopoly of political control. In the republics of Slovenia and Croatia, where the demonstrations had been the most widespread, non-Communists won elections in 1990. (For more on Yugoslavia, see pages 467–468.)

E. END OF THE SOVIET UNION

As one Eastern European country after another ended Communist rule, the various nationalities in the Soviet Union increased their demands for either autonomy or full independence. By the end of 1990, the three Baltic republics—Lithuania, Latvia, and Estonia—had all voted to break away from the Soviet Union and become independent nations. Soviet leaders, however, refused to allow this.

Within the Republic of Russia, people were divided in their political loyalties. Despite Gorbachev's reforms, the Soviet Union faced economic collapse. Consumer goods were in short supply, and inflation could not be controlled. Some Russians believed that Gorbachev's reforms did not go far enough. They proposed ending communism immediately and turning over most state industries to private owners. The newly elected president of the Russian republic, Boris Yeltsin, was among those who advocated more private ownership of property. At the other extreme were Russian Communists who were alarmed by Gorbachev's policies. They were upset that the Soviet empire had lost control of Eastern Europe and the Baltic republics. They also wanted the government to keep many of its state-owned factories and farms. Several of these opponents of reform plotted to seize power in a coup d'état.

The August coup In August 1991, while Gorbachev was on vacation, a small group of Communist leaders announced that they were taking control of the Soviet government. This group, however, managed to hold power for only three days. Defying their decrees, thousands of Russians (including Russian President Boris Yeltsin) stood on top of barricades in front of the Russian Parliament Building in Moscow. The crowd refused to allow Soviet troops to enter the building. When coup leaders ordered the troops to fire on the demonstrators, the troops refused. The coup had failed, and its leaders were jailed.

Gorbachev returned to power but now faced the challenge of a popular and powerful Yeltsin. Throughout the Soviet Union, the Communist party was widely blamed for the coup. Hoping to remain in power as a non-Communist leader, Gorbachev resigned as the Communist party's general secretary and dissolved the party's Central Committee. By the end of August 1991, all activities of the Communist party had been suspended and the Soviet Union had ceased to be a Communist state.

Independent republics After the failed coup and the end of Soviet communism, the Soviet Union quickly broke up. One by one, the various remaining republics that had made up the empire declared their independence. On December 8, 1991, Yeltsin (as Russia's president) was joined by the presidents of Ukraine and Belarus in signing an agreement creating a loose union of their three Slavic republics. They called it the "Commonwealth of Independent States (CIS)." Later, other republics of the former Soviet Union joined with them. Several did not join, including Latvia, Lithuania, and Estonia. Since the Soviet Union no longer existed, Gorbachev resigned and retired to private life.

In Review

The following questions refer to the decline and fall of the Soviet Union, as discussed on pages 458–466.

1. *Key terms:* Define or identify each of the following:

black market	perestroika	Commonwealth of
glasnost	August coup	Independent States

2. Identify and explain *four* weaknesses of the Soviet economic system in the 1980s.

3. Identify *two* changes in the Soviet domestic policy and *two* changes in Soviet foreign policy under Mikhail Gorbachev.

4. List *five* key events in the decline of Soviet power in Eastern Europe, 1989–1991.

5. *Critical thinking:* (*a*) How would you evaluate Gorbachev's attempts to revive the Soviet Union? (*b*) To what extent, if at all, do you think that Gorbachev's policies were responsible for the breakup of the Soviet Union? Explain your answer.

F. CHANGES IN EASTERN EUROPE

After breaking away from Soviet control, the nations of Eastern Europe struggled through the difficult years of making the transition from communism to a free market system.

Privatizing Industry The new multiparty democracy in Poland took major strides toward privatizing the Polish economy. The reforms led to high rates of unemployment and inflation. Other countries in the region, including Hungary, Czechoslovakia, and Bulgaria, made similar efforts to privatize their industries and farms. Hungary's new government had great success in developing trade with Germany and other Western countries. Major multinational corporations have opened production facilities throughout Eastern Europe and are now selling their products in these new markets.

Integrating the German economy The joining of the two econmies of East and West Germany presented an unusual challenge. As a number of poorly run industries were closed down after German reunification in 1990, the East Germans suffered high rates of unemployment. To lift the economy of the former East Germany out of its depressed state, Germany's government has invested billions of dollars in its eastern section. The area's economy, however, is still in trouble. Furthermore, the costly government attempts to aid the East Germans have caused huge budget deficits, inflation, and rising unemployment in all of Germany.

The breakup of Czechoslovakia In some countries of Eastern Europe, independence from Soviet control has led to increased nationalism among ethnic groups. In Czechoslovakia, Slovaks resented the fact that the central government was largely controlled by Czechs. Slovak nationalism soon became a strong force. In 1992, the Slovak Parliament voted to separate the Slovak state from the Czech state and become an independent nation. Václav Havel, who had been elected Czechoslovak president in 1989, was opposed to this division and resigned. The Czechs and Slovaks decided to create separate nations. On January 1, 1993, Czechoslovakia divided into two smaller nations: the Czech Republic and Slovakia.

The breakup of Yugoslavia Unlike the peaceful breakup of Czechoslovakia, ethnic conflicts in Yugoslavia led to civil war. Founded after World War I, Yugoslavia consisted of six republics. One of these republics, Serbia, exercised the most control. In June 1991, two of the

Yugoslav republics—Croatia and Slovenia—declared their independence as new nations. Later on, two other republics—Macedonia and Bosnia-Herzegovina (often called Bosnia)—also declared their independence.

Because the Serbs dominated Yugoslavia, they opposed the breakup of the country. Serb leader Slobodan Milosevic said that Serbia would agree to the breakup only if Serbia were given the right to annex the portions of Croatia, Bosnia, and Macedonia that had large Serbian populations.

In 1991, a bloody civil war broke out in Croatia between Croats and Serbs. Troops from Yugoslavia's army (which was dominated by Serbs) were sent into Croatia to support the Serbs living there. By early 1992, that war was halted by a UN-sponsored cease-fire. Shortly thereafter, a civil war broke out in Bosnia. Bosnia was populated by three major groups—Muslims, Serbs, and Croats. Many Bosnian Serbs were opposed to Bosnia's declaration of independence and initiated fierce fighting against the Bosnian army. Serbian and Croatian forces were sent to Bosnia to support their respective ethnic group. The civil war resulted in thousands of deaths. The Muslims were the major losers in this conflict. Victims of "ethnic cleansing," some two million Muslims were forced out of areas that they had shared with either Serbs or Croats. They became refugees within Bosnia or else were driven out of the country altogether. Many Muslims (as well as some Croats and Serbs) were held prisoner, tortured, raped, or massacred.

In 1992, the United Nations imposed a trade and oil embargo (ban) on Yugoslavia, which now consisted of the republics of Serbia and Montenegro. The United Nations also organized shipments of food and medicine to starving communities in Bosnia and prohibited Serbian airplanes from flying over Bosnia. In addition, the United States organized airlifts of food and clothing to Muslim communities that could not be reached by truck. These efforts, however, failed to end the bloodshed or the terrible, inhuman conditions.

G. CONFLICTS IN THE CAUCASUS AND CENTRAL ASIA

The collapse of the Soviet Union in 1991 led to independence for its republics. With independence, however, has come increased conflict among various ethnic groups and nationalities.

Civil wars in the Caucasus South of Russia, three small republics lie in an area that extends across and south of the Caucasus Mountains. All three—Georgia, Armenia, and Azerbaijan—were torn by civil wars in the early 1990s. In Georgia, two provinces with ethnic minorities attempted to win their independence. One of these provinces,

Abkhazia, contained a large number of Muslim people who wished to throw off Georgian rule. In the other province, South Ossetia, most of the people favored union with Russia. In both of these provinces, heavy fighting has taken place.

In Azerbaijan, civil war has broken out between ethnic Armenians (who are mostly Christians) and ethnic Azeris (who are mostly Muslims). Fighting is concentrated in the province of Nagorno-Karabakh. Here 75 percent of the people are ethnic Armenians. The Armenians have been fighting to win control of this province and join it to Armenia. The civil war within Azerbaijan has led to armed conflict between that country and neighboring Armenia. Armenian forces have gained control of much of western Azerbaijan.

Civil war in Moldova Another civil war broke out between two of Moldova's ethnic groups. The majority of Moldovans are Romanian in language and culture. A Russian minority there, fearing that Moldova might unite with neighboring Romania, established their own small republic in eastern Moldova, which they call the "Trans-Dniesterian Republic." This breakaway republic, however, is not recognized by any other nation.

Republics of Central Asia As the Soviet Union broke up in 1991, five independent nations were formed in Central Asia: Kazakhstan,

A MUSLIM FAMILY IN UZBEKISTAN: Uzbekistan was once the chief cotton-growing area in the Soviet Union. What troubles might it have in adjusting to independence?

Kyrgyzstan, Tajikistan, Turkmenistan, and Uzbekistan. Each nation has a Muslim majority and also a sizable minority of ethnic Russians. In Tajikistan, conflict between Muslims and Russians over sharing power within the government has led to the outbreak of a civil war. Russia has sent 20,000 troops to Tajikistan to support the Russian minority.

Of the Central Asian nations, Kazakhstan is the largest in both population and area. Its economy is also better off than those of other Central Asian nations, largely because Kazakhstan has sizable deposits of oil. Since approximately 37 percent of the population are ethnic Russians, Kazakhstan has had close relations with Russia and has actively supported the Commonwealth of Independent States. It has agreed to get rid of its nuclear weapons.

H. UKRAINE AND BELARUS

Russia's western neighbors Ukraine and Belarus are also struggling to adjust to being newly independent countries in the post-cold war era of the 1990s.

Ukraine   Since its independence in December 1991, Ukraine has been a nuclear power. This is because the former Soviet government had stored nuclear weapons in Ukraine (and in three other republics—Russia, Kazakhstan, and Belarus). At first, Ukraine's political leaders promised to transfer the country's nuclear weapons to Russia to be destroyed. Later, they became concerned that Russia might not destroy the weapons. Therefore, they announced that Ukraine would keep some of the weapons. Still later, Ukrainian leaders agreed to give them up.

Another problem involves Russia's desire to get back the Crimea from Ukraine. This peninsula along the Black Sea had been transferred from Russia to Ukraine in a 1954 agreement. Today, the majority of Crimea's population consists of ethnic Russians. Many of them want Crimea to join the Russian Republic. The Ukrainian government opposes such a transfer of territory.

Ukraine's government has been slow to privatize state-run industries and move toward a free market system. The country had been a major producer of coal and steel and a major exporter of wheat and other crops. Since independence, however, industrial and agricultural production have declined and the economy has suffered from high rates of inflation and unemployment.

Belarus   Before becoming independent, Belarus was known as the republic of Byelorussia. This new nation also inherited nuclear weapons from the former Soviet Union. It has since transferred some of these weapons to Russia to be destroyed and promises to transfer the remainder by the late 1990s. Belarus's capital, Minsk, serves as the capital of the Commonwealth of Independent States. Belarus's ties with Russia remain strong.

I. THE NEW RUSSIA

In leaving the Soviet Union, Russia faced the huge challenge of trying to build a stable, democratic political system and a productive economy. Since the time of the Bolshevik Revolution in 1917, the Russians had spent 74 years under a Communist system that was controlled by the state. Now they had to make the difficult move to a free society.

Economic changes   Under Boris Yeltsin's leadership as president, Russia is dismantling its command economy. It is changing its economic system from state control of all industries and farms to a system based on competition among privately owned businesses operated for profit. One method of making such a change is known as *privatization*. State-owned companies are being sold to private individuals, both Russians and foreigners. In some cases, state industries are being turned over to *joint-stock companies* (business organizations that raise capital by the sale of shares of ownership). Russians with money to invest can become part owners in the new companies. To spur privatization, the Russian government gave all Russian citizens a document that they can convert into shares of ownership in companies that had previously been state-owned. The Russians have the choice of holding onto these shares as an investment or selling them to other Russians for ready cash.

Another way of changing the economic system is allowing the formation of new businesses. On the streets of Moscow and other cities, Russians have set up privately owned booths that sell a wide range of goods, from television sets to boots, from coffeemakers to tea. Other Russians have set up their own restaurants and stores, which compete with state-run ones. Goods that are not available in state-owned stores are often available in the new privately owned stores and in the outdoor booths.

The change to private ownership has been a slow process. In fact, Russian politicians and economists debate among themselves as to how quickly the change should be made. Each reform has severe economic consequences. Unemployment results from the decreased production that comes about when inefficient factories close or when factories that once produced armaments are converted to peacetime uses. Some businesses have let go workers who had previously been kept on the payroll by the government even though they were not needed. Many Russians would like to see the Russian government

New Nations of Eastern Europe and Central Asia

Nation (year of independence)	Earlier Status	Population	Ethnic Groups (not all groups listed)
Armenia (1991)	part of Soviet Union	3,415,000	Armenians 93%
Azerbaijan (1991)	part of Soviet Union	7,450,000	Azeris 82% Russians 6% Armenians 6%
Belarus (1991)	part of Soviet Union	10,373,000	Byelorussians 80% Russians 13%
Bosnia and Herzegovina (1992)	part of Yugoslavia	4,365,000	Muslim Slavs 43% Serbs 31% Croats 17%
Croatia (1991)	part of Yugoslavia	4,784,000	Croats 78% Serbs 12%
Czech Republic (1993)	part of Czechoslovakia	10,400,000	Czechs 94% Slovaks 4%
Estonia (1991)	part of Soviet Union	1,607,000	Estonians 62% Russians 30%
Georgia (1991)	part of Soviet Union	5,570,000	Georgians 70% Armenians 7% Russians 6% Azeris 5% Ossetians 3%
Kazakhstan (1991)	part of Soviet Union	17,101,000	Kazakhs 40% Russians 37% Germans 6% Ukrainians 5%
Kyrgyzstan (1991)	part of Soviet Union	4,567,000	Kyrghizis 52% Russians 21% Uzbeks 13%
Latvia (1991)	part of Soviet Union	2,728,000	Latvians 54% Russians 33%
Lithuania (1991)	part of Soviet Union	3,788,000	Lithuanians 80% Russians 9% Poles 7%
Macedonia (1991)	part of Yugoslavia	2,050,000	Macedonians 68% Albanians 20%

Moldova (1991)	part of Soviet Union	4,458,000	Moldovans 65% Ukrainians 14% Russians 13%
Russia (1991)	part of Soviet Union	149,527,000	Russians 82% Tatars 3% Ukrainians 3%
Slovakia (1993)	part of Czechoslovakia	5,300,000	Slovaks 87% Hungarians 10%
Slovenia (1991)	part of Yugoslavia	1,974,000	Slovenes 91%
Tajikistan (1991)	part of Soviet Union	5,680,000	Tajiks 62% Uzbeks 23% Russians 8%
Turkmenistan (1991)	part of Soviet Union	3,838,000	Turkmens 72% Russians 9% Uzbeks 9%
Ukraine (1991)	part of Soviet Union	51,994,000	Ukrainians 73% Russians 22%
Uzbekistan (1991)	part of Soviet Union	21,626,000	Uzbeks 70% Russians 11%

Analyzing the data

1. Which nations outside Russia have sizable Russian minorities (10 percent or more of the population)?
2. Which of the nations listed have ethnic majorities that represent more than 90 percent of the population?
3. From each of the following groups, identify the nation that has the largest population: (a) former republics of Yugoslavia, (b) former Soviet republics in the Caucasus, and (c) former Soviet republics on the Baltic.

retain ownership of large industrial plants and state farms in order to keep people employed.

Another consequence of the economic changes has been inflation. Previously, the Soviet and Russian governments controlled prices of certain basic products, such as milk, bread, and medicines. Prices remained low because the government subsidized industries that produced these and many other products. Economic reformers, however, have been pushing the government to drop these subsidies and price controls and allow prices to rise. In that way, the reformers maintain, people will be encouraged to start new businesses to produce these goods. Inflation has already had an unfortunate impact on the elderly and on others who have fixed incomes. Their incomes provide them with enough money to buy only a fraction of the goods they could previously afford.

There are also problems of corruption and increased criminal activity. Russian society is no longer under tight government control. Criminal gangs are taking advantage of the situation. They force owners of new businesses to pay "protection" money or face being murdered. And as under the Soviet regime, many government officials are corrupt. To get official approval to operate new businesses, for example, people often have to pay bribes.

Political changes Russia's economic problems have made it more difficult for Yeltsin to deal with his many political opponents. Blaming Yeltsin for the continuing shortages and high prices of goods, many members of the Russian Parliament in 1992 and 1993 worked to block his policies. Some tried to oust Yeltsin from the presidency. (The Parliament had been elected when the Soviet Union still existed. Because of the election rules in effect then, most of the members of Parliament were Communists or former Communists.)

In September 1993, Yeltsin announced that he was dissolving Parliament and scheduling new elections in December. The Parliament reacted by declaring Yeltsin's actions unconstitutional and ordering

TURMOIL IN THE NEW RUSSIA: What events in 1993 led to the drawing of this cartoon? Why is Boris Yeltsin shown in a white hat while Parliament wears a black hat?

him to resign. Yeltsin refused. In October 1993, the conflict erupted into street fighting and bloodshed in Moscow. Supporters of the anti-Yeltsin group attacked police lines and stormed a few government buildings. Yeltsin responded by ordering tanks to open fire on the Parliament Building, which the anti-Yeltsin forces had occupied. After a few hours, government troops loyal to Yeltsin managed to defeat Yeltsin's opponents and arrest their leaders (including leaders of Parliament).

In December 1993, Russians voted on a new Constitution and on representatives to a new Parliament. Yeltsin was pleased that the new Constitution was approved because it gave the office of the president greater powers and took away some powers from Parliament. Yeltsin was less pleased with the makeup of the new Parliament. There were even more of Yeltsin's opponents in this Parliament than in the previous one. The opponents—both Communists and ultranationalists—were united on at least one matter: restoring Russia's prestige, its empire, and its military power. Their speeches attempted to stir up Russians' discontent with the economy.

Yeltsin's conflicts with his opponents continue. Wishing Yeltsin's reform efforts to succeed, U.S. President Bill Clinton visited Russia in 1994 and offered continued U.S. support to the Russian government. The United States has pledged billions of dollars to aid Russia's struggling economy.

Loose ties to the CIS   After the breakup of the Soviet Union in late 1991, it was unclear what role would be played by the new Commonwealth of Independent States. Originally, it was supposed to help member nations coordinate their economies and military defense systems. Thus far, however, the CIS has been a weak organization. Instead of retaining a common currency (the ruble), some member nations have developed their own. Instead of having a single military policy, Ukraine and Russia have disputes concerning the control of nuclear weapons located in Ukraine. Also, there is debate about the role of Russian troops in other Commonwealth nations.

As the dominant member of the CIS, Russia has taken over the seat in the UN Security Council once held by the Soviet Union.

End of the arms race   The end of communism in the former Soviet Union brought an end to both the cold war and the arms race. In February 1992, President Boris Yeltsin met with U.S. President George Bush. They pledged to remove any remaining traces of the cold war and declared that Russia and the United States do not view each other as enemies. The United States also received assurances that the nuclear missiles of the Soviet Union (which were then located in Russia, Ukraine, Belarus, and Kazakhstan) would remain under central control. Since then, Ukraine, Belarus, and Kazakhstan have agreed to dismantle and turn over the nuclear weapons in their lands to Russia.

In December 1992, Bush and Yeltsin met again, signing START II, a treaty that called for deep cuts in the nuclear arsenals of their two countries. The United States pledged to reduce its total number of nuclear warheads from about 10,000 to no more than 3,500 by the year 2003. In response, Yeltsin declared that Russia would cut its warheads to 3,000 by that date.

In Review

The following questions refer to the post-cold war era, as discussed on pages 467–476.

1. *Key terms:* Define each of the following:

   "ethnic cleansing"   joint-stock company

2. (a) Identify *three* civil wars that erupted in new nations of Eastern Europe and the former Soviet Union in the early 1990s.
   (b) State who were the opposing sides in each of these wars.

3. State what have been Yeltsin's major problems in the following areas: (a) the Russian economy, (b) political control, and (c) control over nuclear weapons.

4. *Critical thinking:* (a) Choose one of Yeltsin's major problems and propose two alternatives for dealing with it. (b) Assuming that you were advising Yeltsin, explain which alternative you think he should adopt. Justify your choice.

TEST YOURSELF

Multiple-Choice Questions

Level 1

On a separate sheet of paper, write the number of the word or expression that, of those given, best completes each statement or answers each question.

1. Peter the Great and Catherine the Great changed Russia by (1) abolishing all social class distinctions (2) becoming constitutional monarchs (3) preventing wars with neighboring nations (4) introducing Western ideas and customs.

2. Which statement best explains why many Jews left Russia during the late 1800s? (1) There was tremendous overcrowding in the regions of Russia where most of the Jews lived. (2) The Jews experienced many forms of discrimination and persecution. (3) The climate of Western Europe was better suited to the Jews' tradition of farming. (4) The Jews were forced to work in Russian factories.

3. Throughout the 1800s, Russia was interested in acquiring Turkish territory mainly because Russia wanted to (1) maintain peace in the Middle East (2) obtain access to the Mediterranean Sea (3) reestablish the Byzantine empire (4) obtain the rich farmland of the Anatolian Plateau.

4. Which generalization is best supported by a study of the politics of the Balkan Peninsula before World War I? (1) Conflicting national interests threatened world peace. (2) The Soviet Union maintained a policy of isolation in spite of tensions in this region. (3) Rapid industrialization increased economic stability in this region. (4) The desire to control oil supplies was the main cause of global conflict.

Base your answer to question 5 on the cartoon below and on your knowledge of social studies.

5. What is the main idea of the cartoon? (1) Russia spent too much for defense during World War I. (2) The czar expected widespread unemployment after World War I. (3) Russian military leaders were confident of victory over the Germans. (4) There was widespread discontent in the Russian army during World War I.

Adapted from K.R. Chamberlain's drawing
that originally appeared in *Masses*, Jan. 1915

At Petrograd
Russian Officer: "Why these fortifications, Your Majesty?
Surely the Germans will not get this far!"
The Czar: "But when our own army returns—?"

6. Which situation resulted from the Russo-Japanese War of 1904–1905? (1) Japan lost its status as a world power. (2) The Japanese emperor encouraged reforms in Russia. (3) Dissident groups challenged the power of the Russian czar. (4) Russia gained control of China and Japan.

7. The Russian peasants supported the Bolsheviks in the 1917 revolution mainly because the Bolsheviks promised to (1) establish collective farms (2) maintain an agricultural price-support system (3) bring modern technology to Russian farms (4) redistribute the land owned by the nobility.

8. Which statement best describes the political situation in the Soviet Union immediately after Lenin's death in 1924? (1) The nation adopted a constitutional monarchy. (2) Trotsky and his followers assumed full control of the Communist party. (3) Popular elections were held to choose a new general secretary of the Soviet Communist party. (4) A power struggle developed among Communist party leaders.

9. The main purpose of the many purges and public trials that took place in the Soviet Union in the 1930s was to (1) force Jewish people to leave the Soviet Union (2) eliminate opposition to Joseph Stalin and his government (3) establish a free and independent court system in the Soviet Union (4) reform the outdated and inadequate agricultural system.

10. In Eastern Europe after World War I, the greatest obstacle to national unity in many nation-states was the (1) great ethnic diversity found in the region (2) economic dependence of Eastern Europe on Japan (3) acceptance of democratic traditions by most Eastern Europeans (4) expansion of United States influence in the region.

Base your answer to question 11 on the passage below and on your knowledge of social studies.

> **ARTICLE 50** In accordance with the interests of the people and in order to strengthen and develop the socialist system, citizens of the USSR are guaranteed freedom of speech, of the press, and of assembly, meetings, street processions and demonstrations.
>
> Exercise of these political freedoms is ensured by putting public buildings, streets and squares at the disposal of the working people and their organizations, by broad dissemination of information, and by the opportunity to use the press, television, and radio.—*Excerpt from the Constitution of the Soviet Union.*

11. Which conclusion can be reached by a comparison of events in the Soviet Union and this passage from the Constitution of the Soviet Union? (1) Constitutional rights guarantee a free society. (2) A national constitution always guarantees human rights. (3) A constitutional guarantee must be very specific in order to be effective. (4) A government can sometimes ignore constitutional guarantees.

12. Which is an accurate statement about the Soviet economy under the leadership of Joseph Stalin? (1) A large selection of consumer goods became available. (2) The Soviet Union increased its industrial output by developing heavy industry. (3) Private farmers were encouraged to sell their surplus produce in an open market. (4) The government reduced its role in planning industrial production.

Base your answer to question 13 on the cartoon below and on your knowledge of social studies.

BY JEFF MACNELLY FOR THE CHICAGO TRIBUNE

Reprinted by permission: Tribune Media Services.

13. What is the main idea of the cartoon? (1) The Soviet Union's military exercises destroyed large areas of farmland. (2) The central planners of the Soviet Union did not promote industrial development. (3) The economy of the Soviet Union was dominated by the agricultural production of small landowners. (4) In the Soviet Union, modernization efforts focused too much on the military.

14. Which is generally a characteristic of a Communist economy? (1) Investment is encouraged by the promise of large profits. (2) The role of government in the economy is restricted by law. (3) Government agencies are involved in production planning. (4) Entrepreneurs sell shares in their companies to the government.

Base your answer to question 15 on the quotation below and on your knowledge of social studies.

> From Stettin in the Baltic to Trieste in the Adriatic, an iron curtain has descended across the Continent. Behind that line lie all the capitals of the ancient states of central and eastern Europe. Warsaw, Berlin, Prague, Vienna, Budapest, Belgrade, Bucharest and Sofia, all these famous cities and the populations around them lie in what I might call the Soviet sphere, and all are subject, in one form or another, not only to Soviet influence, but to very high, and in some cases increasing measure of control from Moscow.—*Winston Churchill.*

15. What is the main idea of this quotation? (1) The Soviet Union has expanded its influence throughout Eastern Europe. (2) The Soviet Union has helped the nations of Eastern Europe improve their standard of living. (3) The democratic nations of Western Europe have stopped the expansion of Soviet influence in the world. (4) The Soviet Union will support Communist revolutions in Southeast Asia.

Base your answer to question 16 on the map below and on your knowledge of social studies.

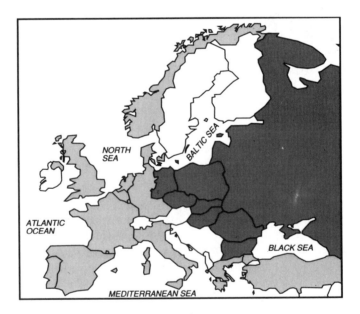

16. The map illustrates a division of Europe that led to the creation of the (1) Axis and the Allied powers (2) North Atlantic Treaty Organization (NATO) and the Warsaw Pact (3) Triple Alliance and the Triple Entente (4) United Nations and the League of Nations.

Base your answer to question 17 on the cartoon below and on your knowledge of social studies.

17. What is the main idea of the cartoon?   (1) The economies of Eastern Europe satellite nations were stronger than the Soviet economy. (2) The Soviet Union produced more industrial goods than China. (3) The standard of living in Communist nations needed improvement.   (4) Most Communist nations were wealthier than capitalist nations.

EVERY MAY DAY, I KEEP HOPING **SOMEONE** WILL BE ABLE TO MARCH IN THIS PART OF THE PARADE...

CAVALCADE OF COMMUNIST COUNTRIES WITH A VIABLE ECONOMY

Wiley Miller © 1988 San Francisco Examiner

18. The Soviet Union's involvement in Afghanistan was motivated mainly by a desire to   (1) exploit the mineral resources of the region (2) support a Communist government   (3) stop the expansion of Japan into the Middle East   (4) establish an independent nation-state in the region.

19. The experiences of the Soviet Union in Afghanistan in the 1980s suggested that   (1) communism was a growing force in the world (2) guerrilla forces could win wars without aid from other nations (3) large-scale industry was necessary to win wars   (4) powerful nations could not always force their will on others.

20. Which is a valid statement about the Soviet Union from the time of the Bolshevik Revolution through December 1991?   (1) Education was limited to the Communist party elite.   (2) Demand for consumer goods exceeded production.   (3) Military expenditures were low. (4) Industrialization did not occur.

21. In the Soviet Union, Lenin's New Economic Policy (NEP) and Gorbachev's policy of perestroika were similar in that each   (1) included some practices of capitalism   (2) rejected central government involvement in the economy   (3) established a series of five-year plans for economic growth   (4) linked economic growth to military strength.

22. "The Soviet people want a clear perspective ... unconditional democracy ... glasnost in all things, big and small ... respect for hard work ... and faithful service for the cause and the good of society." The main idea of this quotation was that (1) the political system of a Communist nation could not be changed   (2) foreign aid was needed to achieve economic stability   (3) the nation had been damaged by civil unrest   (4) both increased freedom and greater dedication to the public good were needed.

23. Which is a valid statement about the reunification of East and West Germany in 1990?   (1) East German prosperity made reunification desirable for West Germany.   (2) Reunification was linked to the withdrawal of United States forces from Western Europe.   (3) Reunification occurred despite concerns of other European nations over the power of a united Germany.   (4) A reunified Germany promised to withdraw from the North Atlantic Treaty Organization (NATO).

24. Events in both Eastern Europe in the early 1900s and in the Soviet Union in the late 1980s were mainly the result of   (1) movements toward the repression of individual rights   (2) declines in the use of advanced technology   (3) the influence of religion on government   (4) challenges by ethnic groups desiring independence.

25. A major development in relations between the Soviet Union and the United States occurred in the late 1980s when the two nations agreed to   (1) purchase all their oil from Mexico   (2) withdraw from the United Nations   (3) eliminate a group of nuclear missiles from Europe   (4) ban arms sales to developing nations.

Level 2

26. The early history of Russia was most influenced by its lack of (1) warm-water ports   (2) mineral deposits   (3) different climates (4) navigable river systems.

27. An influence that spread from the Byzantine empire to early Russia was the   (1) Orthodox Christian religion   (2) use of the Latin alphabet   (3) beginning of democracy   (4) factory system.

28. Which term best describes the political system in Russia before the 20th century?   (1) democratic republic   (2) absolute monarchy (3) parliamentary democracy   (4) military dictatorship.

29. Which term best describes the position of Jews in czarist Russia? (1) political leaders   (2) persecuted minority   (3) wealthy landlords (4) military leaders.

30. Changes in Russia after the Communist revolution of 1917 resulted in   (1) a two-party political system   (2) increased power for ethnic minorities   (3) a limited monarchy   (4) a union of socialist republics.

31. Lenin is best remembered as   (1) the last Russian czar   (2) the leader of the Communist revolution in 1917   (3) the leader who Westernized Russia   (4) the leader who replaced Joseph Stalin.

32. Joseph Stalin's leadership of the Soviet Union led to   (1) democratic reform   (2) private industry   (3) religious freedom   (4) terror and abuse of human rights.

33. The expansion of communism into Eastern Europe was a direct result of   (1) the Crimean War   (2) the Napoleonic Wars   (3) World War I   (4) World War II.

34. In the 30 years after World War II, which area was most influenced by the Soviet Union?   (1) Southeast Asia   (2) North Africa   (3) Eastern Europe   (4) Central America.

35. The "cold war" was the term used to describe   (1) ethnic conflicts among Eastern Europeans   (2) conflicts between Eastern Europe and the Soviet Union   (3) fighting in the former Yugoslavia   (4) political conflicts between the Soviet Union and the United States.

36. The events that took place in Hungary in the 1950s and in Czechoslovakia in the 1960s demonstrated the Soviet Union's   (1) support of nationalism among satellite nations   (2) influence on the economies of developing nations   (3) determination to maintain political control over Eastern Europe at the time   (4) attempts to promote its artistic and literary achievements in Western Europe.

37. Economically, the Soviet Union most emphasized the production of   (1) automobiles for export   (2) building materials for luxury housing   (3) consumer goods   (4) heavy industrial goods.

38. Which provided the best example of a command economy in the Soviet Union?   (1) large private corporations   (2) private farms   (3) subsistence agriculture   (4) five-year plans.

39. Mikhail Gorbachev is best remembered for his attempts to   (1) conquer Eastern Europe   (2) increase the size of the military   (3) reduce travel and trade   (4) increase political and economic freedoms.

40. After the collapse of the Soviet Union, the first leader of an independent Russia was   (1) Leon Trotsky   (2) Nikita Khrushchev   (3) Leonid Brezhnev   (4) Boris Yeltsin.

Essay Questions

Level 1

1. Throughout history, basic political, social, and economic rights of some groups were violated in Russia and Eastern Europe.

Groups of People
Jews in Russia and the Soviet Union
Serfs on Russian estates
Purged officials in the Soviet Union under Stalin
Peasants in the Soviet Union under Stalin
Eastern Europeans in satellite nations
Muslims in Bosnia-Herzegovina

For each of *three* of the groups listed, use specific historical information to explain how that group's basic political, social, or economic rights were violated.

2. Every significant event has causes and results. Some significant events are listed below.

Events
Serfdom in Russia ends (1861)
Russian Revolution of 1905 attempts to overthrow czarist rule
Romanov dynasty overthrown (1917)
Bolsheviks overthrow Provisional Government (1917)
Soviet Union enters World War II (1941)
Soviet Union collapses (1991)

Select *three* of the events listed above. For each event selected:

- Discuss a major cause.
- Discuss an important result.

Level 2

3. Listed below are certain geographic features of Russia.

Geographic Features
A frozen tundra covers northern Russia.
Arctic winds sweep across much of Russia in the winter.
A plain stretches across Eastern Europe into Russia.
Russia contains valuable natural resources.
Many rivers in Russia flow in a north-south direction.

A. Select *three* of the geographic features listed above. For each feature chosen, state how it affected the history of Russia.

B. Base your answer to Part B on your answer to Part A. However, additional information may be included. Write an essay discussing the effects of specific geographic features on the development of Russia. Begin your essay with this topic sentence:

Geography has affected the development of Russia.

4. National leaders have had a great impact on Russia, the Soviet Union, and Eastern Europe.

National Leaders
Peter the Great
Catherine the Great
V. I. Lenin
Joseph Stalin
Lech Walesa
Mikhail Gorbachev
Boris Yeltsin

A. Select *three* of the national leaders listed. For each one chosen, state an action or policy with which that leader is associated.

B. Base your answer to Part B on your answer to Part A. However, additional information may be included. Write an essay explaining how the actions or policies of the leaders influenced their nation. Begin your essay with this topic sentence:

Leaders have often influenced the development of their nation.

CHAPTER 9

The World Today

Main Ideas

1. **WORLDWIDE HUNGER:** Hunger, which exists in all countries, can be caused by economic, environmental, political, social, and technological factors.

2. **ECONOMIC INTERDEPENDENCE:** Because national economies have become interdependent, economic decisions made in one nation affect other nations.

3. **DEBTS OF DEVELOPING COUNTRIES:** The large debts owed by many developing countries have become increasingly difficult to repay.

4. **CHANGING FAMILY PATTERNS:** Traditional family patterns are changing throughout the world as cultures become more industrialized and urbanized.

5. **OVERPOPULATION:** An area is said to be overpopulated when the resources of the region are insufficient to meet the basic needs of the people. Many global problems, such as hunger, poverty, and unemployment, are closely tied to overpopulation.

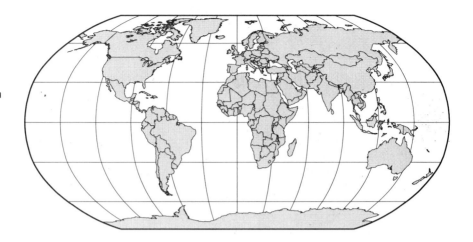

6. **ACID RAIN:** All nations have a common interest in controlling acid rain, which damages the global environment.

7. **HUMAN RIGHTS:** In its Universal Declaration of Human Rights, the United Nations has declared that all people possess basic political, social, and economic rights.

8. **TERRORISM:** Extremist groups often use terrorism to achieve their goals.

9. **COMPUTER REVOLUTION:** Like the Commercial and Industrial revolutions of the past, today's Computer Revolution has changed the way people live and work.

10. **MEDICAL ISSUES:** Advances in medical technologies have created moral or ethical issues concerning the fair and proper use of these technologies.

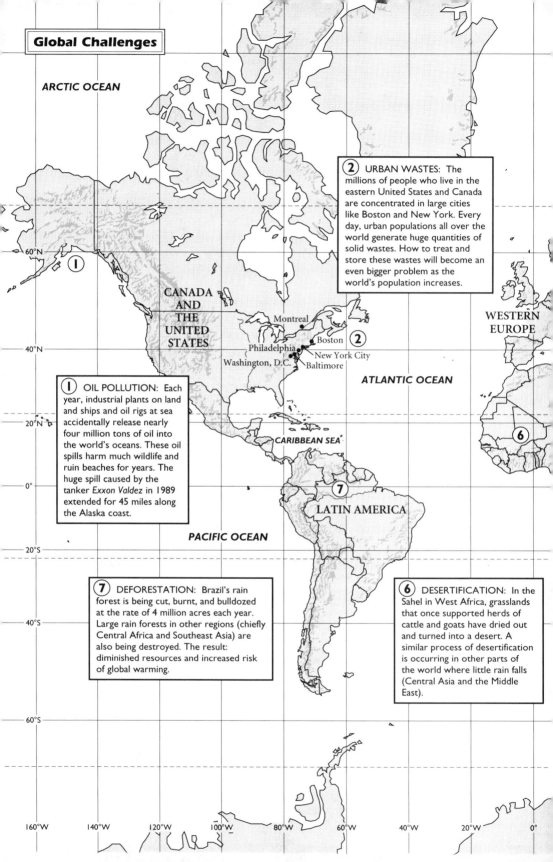

Global Challenges

ARCTIC OCEAN

2 URBAN WASTES: The millions of people who live in the eastern United States and Canada are concentrated in large cities like Boston and New York. Every day, urban populations all over the world generate huge quantities of solid wastes. How to treat and store these wastes will become an even bigger problem as the world's population increases.

60°N

①

CANADA AND THE UNITED STATES

Montreal

WESTERN EUROPE

40°N

Boston **2**

Philadelphia
New York City

Washington, D.C.
Baltimore

ATLANTIC OCEAN

1 OIL POLLUTION: Each year, industrial plants on land and ships and oil rigs at sea accidentally release nearly four million tons of oil into the world's oceans. These oil spills harm much wildlife and ruin beaches for years. The huge spill caused by the tanker *Exxon Valdez* in 1989 extended for 45 miles along the Alaska coast.

20°N

CARIBBEAN SEA

6

0°

7

LATIN AMERICA

PACIFIC OCEAN

20°S

7 DEFORESTATION: Brazil's rain forest is being cut, burnt, and bulldozed at the rate of 4 million acres each year. Large rain forests in other regions (chiefly Central Africa and Southeast Asia) are also being destroyed. The result: diminished resources and increased risk of global warming.

6 DESERTIFICATION: In the Sahel in West Africa, grasslands that once supported herds of cattle and goats have dried out and turned into a desert. A similar process of desertification is occurring in other parts of the world where little rain falls (Central Asia and the Middle East).

40°S

60°S

160°W 140°W 120°W 100°W 80°W 60°W 40°W 20°W 0°

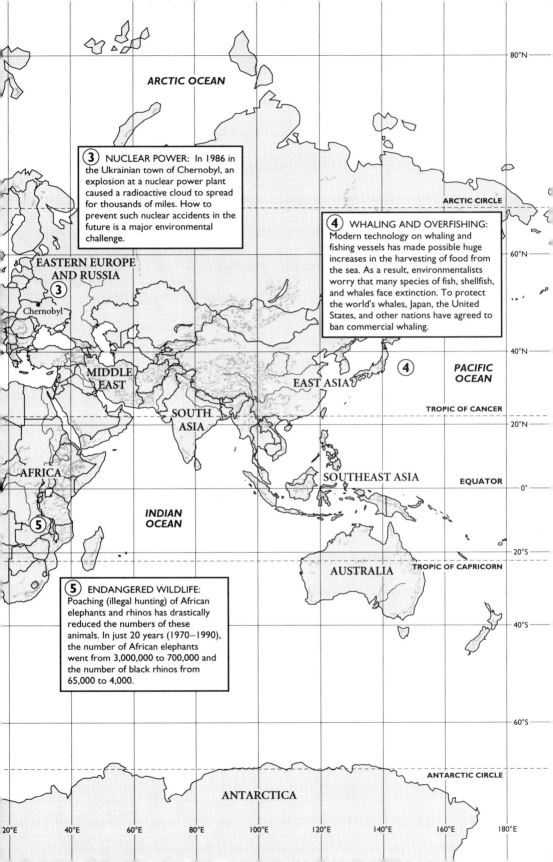

ARCTIC OCEAN

80°N

3 NUCLEAR POWER: In 1986 in the Ukrainian town of Chernobyl, an explosion at a nuclear power plant caused a radioactive cloud to spread for thousands of miles. How to prevent such nuclear accidents in the future is a major environmental challenge.

ARCTIC CIRCLE

4 WHALING AND OVERFISHING: Modern technology on whaling and fishing vessels has made possible huge increases in the harvesting of food from the sea. As a result, environmentalists worry that many species of fish, shellfish, and whales face extinction. To protect the world's whales, Japan, the United States, and other nations have agreed to ban commercial whaling.

60°N

EASTERN EUROPE AND RUSSIA

3

Chernobyl

MIDDLE EAST

40°N

EAST ASIA

4 PACIFIC OCEAN

SOUTH ASIA

TROPIC OF CANCER

20°N

AFRICA

SOUTHEAST ASIA

EQUATOR 0°

INDIAN OCEAN

5

20°S

AUSTRALIA TROPIC OF CAPRICORN

5 ENDANGERED WILDLIFE: Poaching (illegal hunting) of African elephants and rhinos has drastically reduced the numbers of these animals. In just 20 years (1970–1990), the number of African elephants went from 3,000,000 to 700,000 and the number of black rhinos from 65,000 to 4,000.

40°S

60°S

ANTARCTIC CIRCLE

ANTARCTICA

20°E   40°E   60°E   80°E   100°E   120°E   140°E   160°E   180°E

In an interdependent world, all regions are affected by the same forces and all face similar problems. In previous chapters, we observed how population growth has created problems in Africa and East Asia. We studied the effects of industrialization and environmental pollution in Latin America and Western Europe. We saw the impact of terrorism on the politics of the Middle East and South and Southeast Asia. Now in this chapter, we will look at these and other forces of change as they affect *every* continent and region of the globe.

Although made up of distinct regions and areas, the world today may also be viewed as a single global environment, almost as if it were encased in a huge bubble. In such a world, the specific problems of one nation may soon become the common concerns of every nation. With that in mind, let us now take a global view of the following areas of concern:

- problems of developing nations
- environmental problems
- changes in global politics after the cold war
- the impact of new technologies
- social and cultural changes.

I. Problems of Developing Nations

One way of classifying the nations of the modern world is in terms of their economic development. A nation could be classified as relatively wealthy or poor, as either highly industrialized or slightly industrialized, and as either "developed" or "developing."

A. DEFINING "DEVELOPED" AND "DEVELOPING"

Those nations of the world that are highly industrialized and have a high standard of living are called *developed nations*. Leading examples of such nations are the United States, Canada, the nations of Western Europe, and a few nations of East Asia (such as Japan, Taiwan, and South Korea).

Having passed through the Industrial Revolution, many developed nations are now in a stage of development called the *post-industrial revolution*. In a post-industrial nation like the United States, large numbers of workers are employed in service occupations such as banking, education, health care, and entertainment. A smaller percentage of workers are employed in factories than before.

Many nations of the world are still changing from a labor force that is largely agricultural to one that is largely industrial. In the Southeast Asian nation of Vietnam, for example, about 65 percent of the labor force is engaged in farming and only about 8 percent in manufacturing. In the African nation of Liberia, more than 80 percent of the workers are engaged in agriculture. Both Vietnam and Liberia are examples of *developing nations*—nations whose economies are more agricultural than industrial and whose standard of living is relatively low.

Some nations cannot easily be classified as either developed or developing. The economy of Mexico, for example, presents a mixed picture: 24 percent of the labor force is engaged in agriculture, 64 percent in industry and services. Thus, Mexico is neither as industrialized as Japan (75 percent in industry and services) nor as agricultural—or "developing"—as either Vietnam or Liberia.

B. COMPARING "HAVE" AND "HAVE-NOT" NATIONS

In terms of material possessions, the developed nations of the world are much wealthier than the developing nations. Other factors distinguish these two types of countries. Look at some of the differences between the United States (a developed nation) and Zaire (a developing nation) in the following table.

A Comparison of Two Nations

Categories	United States	Zaire
Population	260 million	39 million
GDP per capita	$22,470	$180
Passenger cars per 100,000	56,000	61
Television sets per 100,000	77,000	59
Literacy	97 percent	72 percent

The differences in living standards between some countries and others can be huge. Because of the size of these differences, developed nations such as the United States are often said to be the "have" nations of the world. By contrast, developing nations such as Zaire are considered the "have-not" nations.

C. HUNGER

Hunger exists in wealthy countries as well as in poor ones. In the poorer developing nations, however, the problem is often more severe and widespread.

Famine in East Africa   In large areas of East Africa, millions faced starvation and death in the 1980s and early 1990s as a result of a terrible drought and military conflict. For example, in Ethiopia, lack of rainfall caused crops to fail and herds of animals to perish. Villagers and nomadic herders wandered hundreds of miles in search of food and water. An estimated one million people died of hunger within a period of just two years, 1984–1985.

Many tons of food were donated and shipped to Ethiopia by various countries, religious groups, and international organizations. The relief supplies saved many lives. Unfortunately, military conflicts and corruption prevented much of the aid from reaching the people who most needed it. Some of the food was seized by armed gangs and sold for profit.

In Somalia, a civil war among rival armies forced farmers off their land and cut off food supplies to the cities. Food would be seized by each of the rival armies to prevent the other from getting it. In the Sudan, fighting between the Muslim population in the north and the Christian population in the south has led to many deaths, widespread hunger, and much destruction of land and property.

Causes Hunger in East Africa has been caused by environmental factors (the drought) and by political factors (civil wars and corruption). There are also economic causes of hunger. For example, workers who are either unemployed or have low-paying jobs may find it impossible to buy enough food for their families. When food prices go up during a period of food scarcity, the poor have an even harder time. In addition, the ranks of the urban unemployed are often swelled by refugees from other countries and migrants from rural areas. The newcomers to the cities may be seeking jobs, fleeing armed conflict, or leaving farmland that has become unproductive. Whatever brings them, their numbers add to the overall problem of urban unemployment, food shortages, and hunger.

Search for solutions Hunger persists despite advances in agricultural technology. Scientists had originally hoped that the Green Revolution (discussed in Chapter 2) would solve the problem of world food shortages. Beginning in the 1960s, they had developed new varieties of rice, corn, and wheat that were far more productive than older varieties. At first, high-yielding wheat in India and high-yielding rice in Southeast Asia succeeded, as hoped, in expanding the world's food supply.

Unfortunately, methods for growing the improved grains also damaged the environment. The insects that attacked the new crops were controlled by the use of *pesticides* (chemicals used to kill pests such as insects). These toxic chemicals, however, also killed birds and other animals and caused harm to humans.

The Green Revolution did not work well in many parts of Africa where soil conditions were poor. In fact, attempts to increase crop yields weakened the soil further and helped to turn millions of acres into desert lands. As we discussed in Chapter 2, the process of desertification has had a terrible effect on the economies of many African nations.

D. ECONOMIC TIES TO THE DEVELOPED NATIONS

Ever since World War II, the developing nations of Africa, Asia, and Latin America have received various forms of aid from the United States and other developed nations. This aid for economic development may come in the form of (1) loans, (2) grants of money, and (3) *technical assistance* (help in learning new technologies).

Impact of multinational corporations   Another major influence on developing nations is multinational corporations. While the headquarters of these huge businesses are usually located in a developed country, their factories, mines, and sales outlets are found throughout the globe. In both developed and developing nations, multinational corporations offer employment to millions. Their business activities stimulate economic growth and industrial development.

Companies choose to set up plants in developing nations for two main reasons. (1) Workers in developing countries are accustomed to receiving wages far below average wages in the United States, Japan,

VOLKSWAGEN PLANT IN BRAZIL: A German manufacturer operating in a South American country is one example of a multinational corporation. What are other examples?

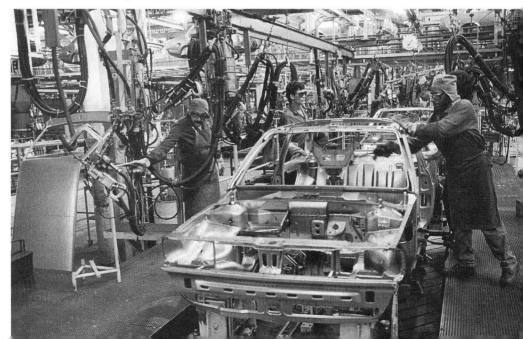

and other developed countries. (2) Raw materials can be obtained cheaply in developing countries. A company can save the expense of shipping copper ore, for example, from Zaire if it operates a copper refinery close to the copper mines of Zaire. Thus, cheaper labor rates and savings on transportation and raw materials cause manufacturing companies to open up plants in developing countries.

By reducing costs, a multinational corporation can sell its products at lower prices throughout the world. This trend is partly responsible for the high standard of living enjoyed in the United States and other developed countries.

The burden of debt   For decades, developing nations have depended upon loans to finance industrial projects. The loans come from various sources: the governments of developed nations, foreign banks, and international organizations such as the International Monetary Fund and the World Bank. Often, however, developing nations are unable to pay back the loans. They then become heavily indebted to the governments, banks, or institutions that had made the loans.

The poorer nations resent the economic dominance of the wealthier nations. They argue that, in the long run, the entire world benefits from the development of their economies. Therefore, they urge increased international cooperation and financial aid. At UN meetings and other international conferences, developing countries often call upon industrialized countries to either increase their investments or to provide relief from the crushing burden of debt that they face. In response, the United States has lowered the interest rates on loans made to several countries, including Mexico and Brazil.

E. URBANIZATION

Another problem that all developing nations face is the movement of people from rural to urban areas. There are two main reasons why this shift in population—known as urbanization—takes place. First, large families in rural villages may find that there is not enough work or food to support all family members. Forced to leave home, young people hope to find some way of earning money in the cities. Second, some people move to cities to escape a famine or a violent conflict. For example, in Peru, the terrorist activities of the Shining Path revolutionaries caused thousands of peasants to flee to the cities.

The problems of the growing cities are great. There is rarely adequate housing for all the newcomers. Most of them are forced to live in shacks or primitive shelters made of old materials. Such temporary structures lack proper sanitation facilities. Under such conditions, diseases can spread rapidly. The newcomers may be jobless for long periods. In desperation, some may resort to begging, stealing, or drug use.

F. EDUCATION

Compared with industrialized countries where almost everyone can read and write, many developing countries have low rates of literacy. In the Latin American nation of Guatemala, for example, only about half the population is literate. In the African nation of Mozambique, less than 20 percent of the people can read and write. One reason for these low rates of literacy is that both Guatemala and Mozambique have suffered from civil war for many years.

In recent years, literacy rates have been rising in many developing nations. In the age of computers, however, people must achieve more than basic literacy. As countries develop, their economies have a growing need for highly educated workers, managers, and technicians. But since developing nations have limited funds to build and staff schools, they cannot afford to get large numbers of students through high school. Therefore, a high percentage of children attend school for only a few years before entering the work force.

A few students may go abroad to attend a university in a developed country. Often they choose to remain in that country instead of returning home. The unfortunate result is a "brain drain." The developing nations lose the expert knowledge and services of their best educated young people.

G. OVERPOPULATION

In most nations of the world, the population is growing. But the population of poorer, developing nations is growing at a much faster rate than that of wealthier, developed nations. Why is this so? Population growth occurs whenever the *birth rate* (number of births per thousand people) is greater than the *death rate* (number of deaths per thousand people). In both developed and developing nations, the death rate has declined in recent decades because of advances in medical care. At the same time, the birth rate in the United States and other developed nations has also declined as more couples adopt birth control methods to limit family size and young people delay families until they are older. In such countries, population growth from year to year is small. In many developing countries, however, the birth rate remains as high as ever. Thus, there is a greater difference in these countries between birth rates and death rates. (See the graphs on page 526.)

For example, Africa's population growth rate of 3.2 percent a year is the highest in the world. If it continues at this rate, nearly 30 African nations will double their present population in less than 25 years.

Developing countries have generally had high birth rates, especially in rural areas. This is because parents view having many children as an economic advantage. The more children who are born, the greater the chance that some of them will grow up to contribute their labor to the family. Furthermore, methods of birth control are not always taught or encouraged in traditional cultures.

Population gains from year to year have increased the problems of developing countries. Some say that there is overpopulation. It is difficult to raise a country's standard of living when the country's population is at such a level that natural resources are not available to meet the population's needs. Two problems mentioned earlier, hunger and illiteracy, are directly linked to this problem of overpopulation. In addition, the poverty of the urban and rural poor adds to the political problems of a nation. As population growth drives up the total number of jobless in the cities and landless in the countryside, the problem becomes worse. The jobless and the landless may become so angry that they take violent action against the government.

In Review

The following questions refer to Section I: Problems of Developing Nations.

1. *Key terms:* Define or identify each of the following:

   developed nation   technical assistance
   developing nation

2. Identify *three* major problems of developing nations. For each problem, provide an example of a country that has this problem.

3. Explain why the original successes of the Green Revolution have been limited.

4. *Critical thinking:* "It is in the interest of the United States to promote economic development of third world nations." Would you agree or disagree with this statement? Provide reasons to support your position.

II. Environmental Problems

As the 20th century comes to an end, people of all nations have become more aware of chemicals polluting the air and water, of garbage piling up in landfills, and of plants and animals becoming extinct. Both developed and developing nations contribute to these environmental problems. Both have an interest in seeking solutions.

A. LONG-TERM CAUSES OF ENVIRONMENTAL DAMAGE

In modern times, there are two major developments that are chiefly responsible for polluting the globe. One development, the Industrial Revolution, led to the invention of coal-burning and oil-burning machines, which pollute the air with chemicals. A second development has been the rapid growth of the world's population in the 20th century. As the population has increased, more industrial products have been produced and sold. This has led to increased output of industrial wastes.

The rapid increase in the world's population has occurred during the same time in which the world has become industrialized. In 1850, the world had a population of about one billion. Within the next hundred years, the population had more than doubled to 2.5 billion. The figure reached 4.5 billion in 1980 and 5.5 billion in 1990. It will likely reach 6 billion by the end of the century. As these numbers keep increasing, environmental problems get worse.

B. WATER POLLUTION

Two major causes for the pollution of lakes, rivers, and oceans are industrial wastes and raw sewage. Lacking the necessary funds, many developing nations do not have the sewage treatment plants that are needed to control water pollution.

Oil spills at sea further pollute the earth's water. One of the largest oil spills occurred in 1989 when the tanker *Exxon Valdez* struck a reef off the coast of Alaska. The accident caused the deaths of large numbers of fish, birds, and other wildlife.

Fertilizers are another common pollutant. Farmers use fertilizers to grow their crops. When excess rain causes fertilizer to flow off a field, it usually ends up in a river or a lake, where it causes excess plant life to grow. The process deprives the water of the oxygen that fish need to survive.

C. LAND POLLUTION

One form of land pollution results from the disposal of *wastes* (garbage). There has been an increase in solid wastes as populations have expanded. Local governments have deposited the garbage in dumps. But as the demand for land has increased, there are fewer good sites for depositing solid wastes. One alternative is the burning of trash. This process creates energy that can be turned into electrical power. Since incinerator plants are expensive, few developing nations have such waste treatment plants.

Another form of land pollution results from efforts to dispose of chemical and nuclear wastes in the ground. When these *toxic* (poisonous) wastes are stored in metal containers and buried, they pose dangers to the environment. The containers might eventually leak and pollute surrounding land and waters.

D. AIR POLLUTION

As societies become more industrialized and urbanized, the air becomes more polluted. Emissions from factories, homes, businesses, and power plants cause air pollution. So too do emissions from cars, trucks, buses, and airplanes. As a result, developed countries now have laws regulating air pollution. Developing countries often lack such laws. This is because they are more concerned with modernizing than with preserving the environment.

Acid rain   One form of air pollution is *acid rain* (rain or snow with a high concentration of acids). The chief sources of the problem are the chemicals discharged from factories, power plants, and vehicles, which combine in the air and fall to the earth as acid rain. This rain causes lakes and streams to become more and more acidic, killing fish and plants.

Like other environmental hazards, acid rain recognizes no national boundaries. Wind currents carry the source of pollution for hundreds and even thousands of miles. Thus, acid rain that originates in one country may fall in another. For example, half of the acid rain that falls in Canada originates in the United States.

Depletion of the ozone shield   Environmentalists also worry about holes in the *ozone shield*, a layer of ozone gas high above the earth's surface. This ozone layer absorbs much of the sun's ultraviolet rays. These rays are harmful to living things and can cause skin cancer. The ozone shield is damaged by *chlorofluorocarbons*, or CFCs, chemical gases resulting from the manufacture of refrigerator coolants and foam containers. Scientists believe that CFCs have opened up holes in the ozone shield, including a huge one above Antarctica.

Destruction of the rain forests   The daily destruction of Brazil's rain forests is another major threat to the global environment. Similar destruction is also taking place in the rain forests of sub-Saharan Africa, Southeast Asia, and elsewhere.

The world's tropical rain forests are mostly located in developing countries. On the one hand, the people of these countries need the income from mining, ranching, or logging in the rain forests. On the other hand, clearing the rain forests destroys many species of plants and animals. Also, the burning of millions of trees causes carbon dioxide to build up in the atmosphere. This condition leads to the greenhouse effect.

AIR POLLUTION: People living in Mexico City are frequently affected by a heavy layer of smog that hangs over their city. How might such air pollution be brought under control?

Greenhouse effect   In the 1980s, scientists warned that the burning of trees and emissions from power plants, factories, and vehicles cause a buildup of carbon dioxide in the atmosphere. The gases act like a greenhouse, trapping the sun's rays in the atmosphere and causing a slight increase in average temperatures. Because of this greenhouse effect, scientists are predicting a gradual change in climate (known as *global warming*) that would some day melt the Arctic and Antarctic ice caps, causing flooding of coastal cities around the world. It would also harm many forms of plant and animal life, possibly even human life.

E. MANAGING SCARCE RESOURCES

Related to the problem of a polluted environment is the problem of decreasing energy supplies. In an industrial economy, the burning of two fossil fuels, oil and coal, is the principal cause of pollution and global warming. As world population increases, it is almost certain that the use of both oil and coal will increase and lead to problems. The worldwide supply of oil will steadily diminish. Some scientists predict that the world could run out of oil as early as the year 2030. If this happens, factories and power plants could switch to coal, which pollutes the air more than oil does. Coal's increased use would add to environmental pollution.

What can be done? Nations of the world have several ways of dealing with future shortages of fossil fuels. First, developed nations like the United States and Canada could take steps to slow down their use of energy. They could follow the example of Japan, a highly industrialized nation that manages to consume energy at less than half the rate of the United States. For example, people could make greater use of *public transportation* (buses, subways, trains) and drive more fuel-efficient cars.

A second solution to the problem of scarce energy resources is to rely more on renewable sources of energy. For example, scientists and engineers have devised systems for heating and air conditioning homes with *solar energy* (heat from the sun's rays). Other forms of renewable energy include river currents, winds, ocean tides, and *geothermal energy* (heat from within the earth). Engineers are currently at work experimenting with new technologies that may some-day make greater use of these powerful forces of energy.

Nuclear energy   Another alternative to the burning of fossil fuels is *nuclear energy* (energy produced by the splitting of an atom). Some countries, such as France and Japan, rely heavily on nuclear power plants to provide the country's electrical needs. Those favoring the use of nuclear energy say that it is a clean, efficient, and relatively inexpensive alternative to coal and oil.

Nevertheless, there is growing concern about the risks posed by using nuclear energy. Opponents point out that nuclear power plants contain radioactive materials. If released into the air, even in small doses, such materials can cause cancer. Large amounts of released radiation would cause widespread deaths and birth defects in future generations. Accidents have occurred in some nuclear power plants, including a dangerous breakdown in 1979 at the Three Mile Island reactor in Pennsylvania. In 1986, an even worse accident took place at the Chernobyl nuclear power plant in the Soviet Union. It resulted in the spread of radiation over much of Europe and the loss of lives in Ukraine, where the plant is located.

Another concern regarding nuclear power plants involves nuclear wastes, which are radioactive. There are not enough safe places to store these wastes for the hundreds of thousands of years they take to decay. Few Americans want nuclear wastes stored near them.

F. NEED FOR GLOBAL COOPERATION

Today, it is generally understood that a nation's environmental problems cannot be solved by that nation acting alone. Instead, nations must seek ways to cooperate and take common action against a common problem—the polluting of the planet Earth. In recent years, a number of international conferences on the global environment have made notable progress.

Protecting the ozone layer Meeting in Montreal, Canada, in 1988, representatives from 27 nations including the United States agreed to limit the production of CFCs—the chemicals that were damaging the ozone layer. Another international conference in London in 1990 went even further. The 31 participating nations agreed to eliminate all CFC production by the year 2000.

Earth Summit of 1992 A major step toward global cooperation was taken in 1992 when 178 countries sent representatives to the largest environmental conference ever held. At this "Earth Summit" in Rio de Janeiro, Brazil, several agreements were reached on various environmental problems:

- an agreement on limiting the economic development of the rain forests
- an agreement on reducing gases that contribute to the greenhouse effect (carbon dioxide emitted by factories, power plants, and motor vehicles)
- an agreement on protecting plant and animal species from the threat of extinction
- an agreement (called the Rio Declaration) on the responsibilities of nations to protect the environment while also developing their industries.

DRAWING CONCLUSIONS FROM GRAPHS

At the current rate of consumption, how quickly will the world run out of oil? To what extent are the major industrialized nations polluting the atmosphere? Which of the world's regions consume the greatest amount of energy?

The answers to these and other questions about the global environment are found in the accompanying six graphs. Notice that three types of graphs (line, bar, and circle) are presented in pairs. Compare the two graphs that make up each pair. Then determine whether each statement at the bottom of page 504 draws a correct or incorrect conclusion from the data given.

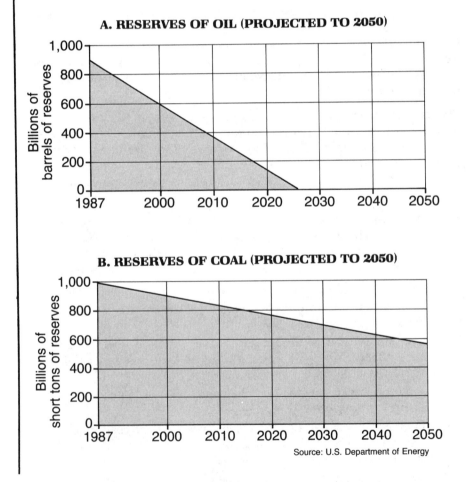

A. RESERVES OF OIL (PROJECTED TO 2050)

B. RESERVES OF COAL (PROJECTED TO 2050)

Source: U.S. Department of Energy

C. COUNTRIES WITH THE HIGHEST
YEARLY EMISSIONS OF CFCs, 1991

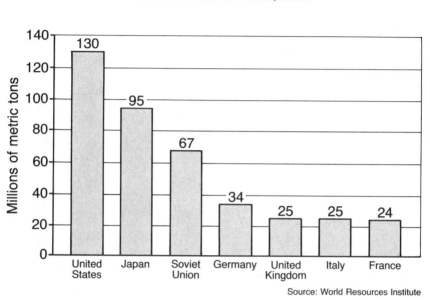

Source: World Resources Institute

D. COUNTRIES WITH THE HIGHEST YEARLY EMISSIONS OF
CARBON DIOXIDE FROM AUTOS AND INDUSTRY, 1991

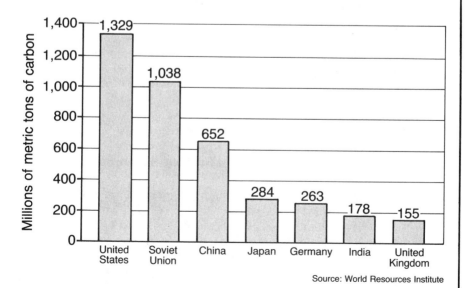

Source: World Resources Institute

E. WORLD POPULATION, 1992   **F. ENERGY USE, 1992**

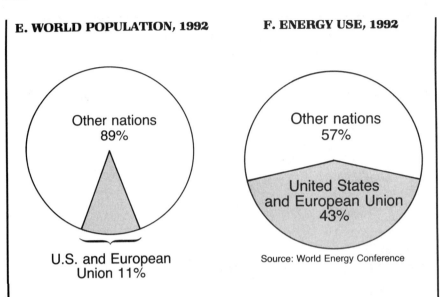

Questions

By referring to the graphs, determine whether each statement is *true* or *false*. Or you may find that there is not enough information in the graphs to prove or disprove a statement. In that case, answer: *not enough information*.

1. At the current rate of consumption, both oil and gas reserves will disappear altogether by the year 2050.
2. The United States and Japan produce the highest levels of CFCs, but the auto and industrial emissions in these countries are below the world average.
3. Although they have less than 20 percent of the world's population, the United States and Western Europe account for more than 40 percent of the world's energy use.
4. The world's reserves of oil are declining at a faster rate than its reserves of coal.
5. In 1992, energy use in the Soviet Union was below that of the United States.
6. No nation of Latin America equaled Germany's high levels of carbon dioxide emissions in 1991.

In Review

The following questions refer to Section II: Environmental Problems.

1. *Key terms:* Define or identify each of the following:

toxic waste	ozone shield	solar energy
acid rain	global warming	geothermal energy

2. Explain how increases in the world population put increasing pressures on the global environment.

3. Select *two* environmental problems. For each (a) state the nature of the problem and   (b) identify a proposed solution to the problem.

4. *Critical thinking:* "Global problems are the result of billions of individual actions." (a) Suggest *three* ways in which your actions affect the global environment. (b) Suggest one way in which a change in your actions could take pressure off the environment.

III. Changes in Global Politics

Today, the entire world is still adjusting to the collapse of the Soviet Union in 1991 and the end of the cold war. What have been some of the consequences of this dramatic change in global politics?

A. NEW CHALLENGES IN THE POST-COLD WAR ERA

During his presidency (1989–1993), George Bush spoke hopefully of the beginning of a "new world order." But so far, there appears to be no clear pattern of order emerging. Instead, there is division, conflict, and disorder in various regions of the world. The new facts of political life in the post-cold war era are as follows:

1. U.S. supremacy Throughout the cold war, two superpowers—the United States and the Soviet Union—had maintained a global balance of power. Now that the Soviet Union no longer exists, only one superpower remains. In the 1990s, the military power of the United States is clearly superior to all others. But the U.S. role in the new era has yet to be defined. A possible role for the world's strongest power is to continue to take the lead in resolving international conflicts. In the Persian Gulf War of 1991, for example, the United States successfully organized the coalition of nations that defeated Iraq. In 1993,

President Clinton acted as host for the signing of a historic agreement between leaders of Israel and the PLO (discussed in Chapter 3).

2. Increased nationalism   Following the breakup of the Soviet Union in 1991, many newly independent nations have come into being. Czechoslovakia divided into two new nations, the Czech Republic and Slovakia. Four republics of Yugoslavia (Croatia, Slovenia, Bosnia, and Macedonia) also declared their independence. The Soviet Union divided into 15 independent nations. Civil wars in some of these nations may lead to further divisions. Nationalism also led to the joining together of East and West Germany.

3. Ethnic strife   Soviet power during the cold war had helped to keep ethnic disputes in Eastern Europe, the Caucasus, and Central Asia from erupting into armed conflict. After Soviet power ended, however, old hostilities surfaced, and brutal civil wars broke out in Bosnia, Croatia, Azerbaijan, and elsewhere.

4. Struggling democracies   It is hardly surprising that Russia, Poland, and other Eastern European countries are having trouble adjusting to conditions of freedom. Each nation has had to overhaul its entire economic and political system and do so almost overnight. The changes required are no less revolutionary than those associated with the French Revolution 200 years earlier. Like the French in 1789, many Eastern Europeans had high hopes for sudden improvement in their economic lives. So far, these hopes have not been met. In Poland, privatization caused the closing of dozens of old, state-run factories, whose inferior products could not be sold on world markets. In Russia, political quarrels intensified between pro-democracy leaders like Boris Yeltsin and his nationalist opponents. In time, democracy in Eastern Europe can settle into a stable pattern, but first, there must be encouraging signs of economic progress.

5. Reduced aid to the "third world"   During the cold war, the world was viewed as being divided among three groups of nations. The non-Communist nations of the West were in the "first world." Communist nations allied with the Soviet Union were in the "second world." The developing nations of Africa, Asia, and Latin America were referred to as the "third world."

To influence third world nations, the Soviet Union and the United States provided them with large amounts of economic and military aid. With the end of the cold war, however, the need to influence developing countries by giving such aid is less urgent. Nevertheless, the United States continues to give aid to some developing countries for the purpose of boosting their economies, supporting democracies, and helping populations avoid starvation.

6. Role of the United Nations   During the cold war, the rivalry between the superpowers had often prevented the United Nations from taking effective action in a crisis. A proposal for action would usually be vetoed in the UN Security Council by either the Soviet Union or the United States. Now that the cold war has ended, there are fewer disagreements among members of the Security Council. Russia and the United States have jointly approved various peacekeeping missions by UN forces in civil wars in Bosnia, Somalia, and elsewhere.

B. PROTECTING HUMAN RIGHTS

Several major issues from the cold war era have carried over into the present. One such issue is how to protect people who live in countries whose governments violate basic human rights.

Defining human rights   In 1948, the United Nations General Assembly approved a document called the Universal Declaration of Human Rights. The list of basic rights included in this document was based largely on earlier documents that were important to the development of Western democracies (for example, the British Magna Carta of 1215 and the U.S. Declaration of Independence of 1776). The UN document, however, went beyond the earlier documents by including not only civil and political rights but also economic and social rights.

The Declaration of Human Rights included such civil and political rights as freedom of speech and religion, the right to fair trial, and the right to participate in government. Economic rights included the right to work, join labor unions, and maintain a decent standard of living. Social rights included the freedom to marry and raise a family, receive a basic education, and maintain one's culture.

Since 1948, the United Nations has remained committed to the protection of human rights throughout the world. Its Commission on Human Rights investigates reports of human rights abuses and tries to stop governments from violating these rights.

Major violations of human rights   Despite its Declaration of Human Rights, the United Nations lacks the power to force governments to respect basic political rights, such as freedom of speech and freedom of religion. Thus, in every region of the world, certain governments regularly violate the rights of citizens in an effort to eliminate opposition to their rule.

Some of the worst human rights violations of the cold war period occurred in South Africa, the Soviet Union, Cambodia, and Uganda. Let us review them briefly:

- In South Africa, the government's policy of apartheid violated the rights of millions of South African blacks. Politically, black South Africans could not vote or hold office. Economically, they could work only in the lowest-paying occupations. The identification passes that they were required to carry violated their right to travel freely. (For more about apartheid, see Chapter 2.)

DOCUMENT: THE UNITED NATIONS UNIVERSAL DECLARATION OF HUMAN RIGHTS

Adopted in 1948, the UN Declaration of Human Rights consists of 30 main articles. Quoted below are Articles 1–5, which list political rights, and Articles 23–24, which list economic rights.

Source: *The Human Rights Reader*, Revised Edition. Edited by Walter Laqueur and Barry Rubin. New York: New American Library, 1990.

ARTICLE 1

All human beings are born free and equal in dignity and rights. They are endowed with reason and conscience and should act toward one another in a spirit of brotherhood.

ARTICLE 2

Everyone is entitled to all the rights and freedoms set forth in this Declaration, without distinction of any kind, such as race, color, sex, language, religion, political or other opinion, national or social origin, property, birth or other status.

Furthermore, no distinction shall be made on the basis of the political, jurisdictional or international status of the country or territory to which a person belongs, whether it be independent, trust, non-self-governing or under any other limitation of sovereignty.

ARTICLE 3

Everyone has the right to life, liberty and the security of person.

ARTICLE 4

No one shall be held in slavery or servitude; slavery and the slave trade shall be prohibited in all their forms.

ARTICLE 5

No one shall be subjected to torture or to cruel, inhuman or degrading treatment or punishment.

.   .   .   .

ARTICLE 23

1. Everyone has the right to work, to free choice of employment, to just and favorable conditions of work and to protection against unemployment.

2. Everyone, without any discrimination, has the right to equal pay for equal work.

3. Everyone who works has the right to just and favorable remuneration insuring for himself and his family an existence worthy of human dignity, and supplemented, if necessary, by other means of social protection.

4. Everyone has the right to form and to join trade unions [labor unions] for the protection of his interests.

ARTICLE 24

Everyone has the right to rest and leisure, including reasonable limitation of working hours and periodic holidays with pay.

Questions for Discussion

1. Do you think the economic rights listed in this document are as important as those political rights that are listed? Why or why not?
2. Which rights, if any, were violated by (a) Soviet policies during the cold war and (b) the apartheid policies of South Africa's government?
3. Which of the human rights listed above are guaranteed to U.S. citizens by the U.S. Constitution? (Referring to an encyclopedia, an almanac, or a textbook in U.S. history, look up the first ten amendments to the U.S. Constitution. These ten amendments are called collectively "the Bill of Rights.")

- In the Soviet Union, thousands of *dissidents* (those who disagree with official policies) were sent to forced labor camps in Siberia. By punishing people for speaking out, the Soviet government violated their right to freedom of speech. Jews and others who wished to emigrate to other countries were denied their basic right to leave a country (discussed in Chapter 8).

- When a Communist group (the Khmer Rouge) seized power in Cambodia in 1975, they adopted a policy of genocide against their political opponents. They executed hundreds of thousands of people, including Buddhist monks, former government officials, and anyone suspected of supporting the former government. The basic rights of these people, including the right to a fair trial, were violated (discussed in Chapter 5).

- In Uganda in the 1970s, military dictator Idi Amin also adopted a policy of genocide against political opponents as well as against ethnic groups other than his own. In effect, his rule violated almost every one of the human rights identified by the United Nations (discussed in Chapter 2).

GENOCIDE IN UGANDA: This pile of skulls gives horrifying proof of the massacres ordered by Uganda's political leaders in the 1970s and 1980s. When such acts occur, should the United Nations send in troops to protect the innocent?

In the early 1990s, the collapse of communism in the Soviet Union and the end of apartheid in South Africa eliminated some of the worst human rights violations. However, serious violations still continue throughout the world. For example, military governments in many African nations routinely mistreat political opponents and wage war on rival ethnic groups. In the Latin American nation of Guatemala, the government has employed death squads that have killed thousands of Indians and people suspected of being revolutionaries. In the Middle East, Saddam Hussein's government in Iraq has waged war against that country's Kurdish population in the north and Shiite Muslims in the south. In Eastern Europe, Serbian armies have carried out a policy of "ethnic cleansing" against the Muslim population of Bosnia. In East Asia, China's Communist government continues its long-standing policy of prohibiting opposition in Tibet. Following the killing of students and other protestors in Tiananmen Square in 1989, China's leaders have continued to violate the human rights of dissident groups despite strong protests by the United States.

C. COPING WITH TERRORISM

Another major challenge of the post-cold war era is how to deal with terrorist attacks and threats. Terrorism refers to the use or threat of violence for political purposes. Victims of terrorism could be anyone: the leader of a country, other government officials, business leaders, ordinary citizens, or tourists. Terrorists aim to spread fear and to disrupt the normal operations of a government and society. They usually belong to small, well-organized groups that sometimes have the secret financial support of governments that do not respect international law.

In recent years, terrorist acts in several nations have killed thousands of people and disrupted the lives of thousands of others. For example:

In Northern Ireland About two-thirds of the population of Northern Ireland are Protestants. Most of these people want their section of Ireland to remain under British rule. In contrast, many Roman Catholics in Northern Ireland want their region to unite with the Irish Republic, an overwhelmingly Catholic nation. They argue that British rule is a form of colonialism. For decades, a group called the Irish Republican Army (IRA) has conducted a campaign of terrorist bombings and shootings in an effort to end British control of Northern Ireland. IRA terrorists have set off a number of bombs in Northern Ireland and other parts of Great Britain. Protestant extremists have also used terrorism against Catholics in Northern Ireland. Since the mid-1970s, over 2,000 deaths have resulted from acts of terrorism by Protestant or Catholic extremists.

In the Middle East   For many years, the Palestine Liberation Organization (PLO) used terrorism against Israel in its attempt to turn that country into a homeland for Palestinians. PLO terrorists regularly attacked Israeli settlements, buses, beaches, and airplanes. They even carried out attacks outside of Israel. In 1972, they murdered 11 Israeli athletes who had gone to Munich, West Germany, to participate in the Olympic Games. In 1985, PLO terrorists hijacked an Italian cruise ship, the *Achille Lauro*, and killed one of its American passengers, an elderly Jewish tourist.

The PLO was not the only group in the Middle East to resort to terrorism. A group of Iranian revolutionaries (supported by the Iranian government) held more than 50 Americans as hostages in Teheran in 1979 and 1980. During the civil war in Lebanon in the 1980s, a terrorist attack killed 241 U.S. Marines. (Some of these events are discussed in Chapter 3.)

In Germany   In the 1990s, neo-Nazi extremist groups in Germany have used terrorism against immigrants in an attempt to force the

WORLD TRADE CENTER BOMBING, 1993: A bomb planted by terrorists in one of the world's tallest office buildings caused major property destruction and six deaths. What motivates such acts of terrorism?

German government to change its immigration policies. Most attacks were directed against Gypsies, Turks, and refugees from Eastern Europe. These attacks have resulted in several deaths, some property damage, and widespread fear.

In the United States　In 1993, a number of terrorists bombed the World Trade Center in New York City, one of the world's largest office buildings. Six people were killed, many were injured, and thousands of workers had to be evacuated. The incident spread fear among Americans that terrorists might strike anywhere. Those convicted of planting the bomb were from Sudan and Egypt. Possible reasons for the attack included anger at the U.S. government for supporting the Egyptian government and Israel.

In Colombia　In the South American country of Colombia, members of drug cartels have used bombings and assassinations to try to force the Colombian government to stop its antidrug campaign.

In Review

The following questions refer to Section III: Changes in Global Politics.

1. *Key terms:* Define or identify each of the following:
   "new world order"　　　　　　　　　　dissident
   UN Declaration of Human Rights　　　　IRA
2. Identify *three* characteristics of world politics in the post-cold war era and give an example of each.
3. For each of the following regions, give an example of a human rights violation:　(a) Africa,　(b) East Asia, and　(c) Southeast Asia.
4. *Critical thinking:* If you were the UN secretary general, which of these problems would you consider the most important for the United Nations to attend to:　(a) human rights violations,　(b) terrorism, or　(c) ethnic strife? Explain your answer.

IV. Changes in Technology

In the world today, a technological revolution is taking place that has brought great changes in our society and in other developed nations. Since the computer is a leading factor in that revolution, some observers have called it the *Computer Revolution*. But as we will see, more is involved in the post-industrial age than the computer.

A. THE COMPUTER REVOLUTION AND INFORMATION AGE

The impact of the Computer Revolution on our times is similar to the impact of the Industrial Revolution a century ago. The computer has already changed the way people live and work and will continue to do so for decades to come.

Origins   The computer is a machine that uses electronic circuits to store and sort vast quantities of information, or data. Its origins date back to the early mechanical calculators developed in the 1600s by a French mathematician, Blaise Pascal. The age of electronic computers, however, did not begin until a machine known as ENIAC was assembled at the University of Pennsylvania in the 1940s. Consisting of thousands of vacuum tubes, this huge machine was only slightly more powerful than one of today's small, hand-held calculators.

By the early 1950s, computers were being mass produced and sold to government agencies and large corporations. By the 1960s, a new generation of computers, using small transistors, could process data ten times faster than earlier models.

The silicon chip   A major breakthrough in 1969 would soon make computers widely available to a great number of individuals and small businesses. This was the invention of the *silicon chip*, a tiny square of *silicon* (a chemical element) with electronic circuits printed on it. Powerful, compact computers made from these chips could process much more information at higher speeds than ever before. Equally important, they could be mass-produced at relatively low costs.

Uses of the personal computer   By the early 1980s, millions of people were able to afford computers for their personal use at home. Every year, U.S. and Japanese manufacturers introduced new models that were both more powerful and less expensive than the preceding year's models. During the first four decades of the Computer Revolution (1950–1990), businesses, schools, hospitals, science labs—in fact, every institution in society—found hundreds of uses for their new "thinking machines." For example:

- Bankers, stockbrokers, and employees of insurance companies used them to keep track of millions of financial transactions.
- Airports used them to control the traffic of arriving and departing planes.
- Schools used them for everything from teaching math to setting up exchanges of electronic information with classrooms in foreign countries.
- Teenagers used them to play video games.

- Writers and students drafted and edited papers by using computerized word processors instead of typewriters.
- Manufacturers used computer-operated robots to assemble everything from kitchen appliances to jet engines.
- Scientists and engineers used computers to try out theories about how some mechanical or natural system (such as a jet engine or the body's circulatory system) would respond under a variety of conditions. For example, an engineer could test the design of a new aircraft or missile by actually seeing on the computer monitor how the craft would function at a velocity of X and an altitude of Y. By entering different data for X and Y, the engineer could, in effect, determine whether the craft would fly or crash.

Entering the Information Age   Computers are a major part—but by no means the only part—of an electronic system of communication that reaches around the world. Through a device known as a *modem*, a computer in one city can instantly gain access to vast quantities of information from around the country. The computer does this by sending and receiving information over telephone lines.

"Excuse me, I'm lost. Can you direct me to the information superhighway?"

Drawing by W. Miller; © 1994 The New Yorker Magazine, Inc.

INFORMATION SUPERHIGHWAY: What problems do some people have adjusting to fast-changing computer technologies?

In the telecommunications industry, a new technology has been invented that is vastly superior to ordinary copper wire as a medium for transmitting information over phone lines. This new synthesized material, called *fiber-optic cable*, is replacing the old network of copper wires. The nation's communications system will soon be able to handle an almost limitless information flow. In the early 1990s, President Bill Clinton and Vice President Albert Gore talked about the need to build an *information superhighway* made of fiber-optic cable.

Though the future is always hard to predict, these are some of the changes that we may begin to see soon:

- Instead of separate telephones, televisions, and personal computers, these devices would be combined into a single interacting system. The TV monitor would display every kind of information: computer data and video games as well as TV entertainment over hundreds of cable channels.

- Instead of relying on textbooks as the main medium of instruction in schools, students would obtain much of their education from interacting with a computer terminal. Studying any topic, they could instantly display on a classroom's electronic screen whatever they wished to see and use: text, photographs, statistics, graphs, relevant video scenes, and so on.

- Instead of daily commuting to an office, more and more workers would work at home. They would interact by phone and computer (now all one system) to solve problems, buy and sell goods, and transmit writing or artwork over the information superhighway.

Related developments   Other changes in technology in the last half of this century have quickened the pace of modern life. For example, the Concorde jet, first developed in Western Europe, flies at 1,500 miles per hour and makes it possible for a traveler to cross the Atlantic Ocean in little more than two hours. High-speed trains have also been developed. Japan's bullet trains speed commuters to and from Tokyo and other cities at the rate of 120 miles per hour.

In the field of communications, photocopying machines make it possible for people to copy information instantly and cheaply. In addition, since the late 1980s *fax* (facsimile) machines have made it possible to transmit printed information over telephone wires. The *facsimilies* (exact copies) of printed material may be transmitted anywhere in the world. Photocopying and fax machines represent the greatest advances in reproducing the printed word since the development of the printing press in the Middle Ages.

Space technology   During the cold war, the Soviet Union and the United States competed with each other in launching satellites and space capsules into space (discussed in Chapter 8). The end of the cold war brought an end to this space race. Competition has given way to cooperation. Today, scientists from around the world help to launch space probes and analyze the data transmitted from them.

One of the major benefits of space exploration has been the development of communications satellites. Hundreds of these devices now orbit the earth. Acting as electronic relay stations, the satellites pick up signals from the earth and transmit them to earth-based stations around the world. Thus, data entered into a computer in Tokyo or Paris or New York can be relayed via satellite to any place on earth. Traveling at the speed of light, the communication is picked up instantly by the receiving computers. Distances between places no longer matter in the satellite-linked communications system that has turned the world into a "global village."

Adjusting to the new technology   Any revolutionary change in technology is bound to produce some negative effects. For example, as a labor-saving device in the workplace, the computer has been responsible for the loss of thousands of factory and office jobs. Nevertheless, the computer has also created new jobs and careers for specialists and managers trained in computer science.

Some people fear that the computer poses a potential danger to a person's fundamental right to privacy. For example, for a small user's fee, a computer operator can receive a listing of names of people who had once been arrested or failed to pay a debt. Some computer experts have accessed the files of schools, businesses, and government agencies. What could stop these computer experts from gaining access to embarrassing or harmful information? What could prevent abuse by government officials who do not respect individual rights? Should there be laws regulating the use of computerized records?

Another issue concerns the effects of the computer on social classes in both developed and developing countries. Some social scientists predict that the computer will widen the gap between the rich and the poor. They argue that only the best educated will have the skills and training needed to compete for high-paying technical and professional jobs of the future. In their view, the majority of people will find employment only in lower-paying service jobs. At the same time, the economic gap between developed and developing countries may also become greater in the Computer (or Information) Age. Social scientists point out that education and high literacy rates are the key to a nation's future. If that is the case, then developed nations with high rates of literacy have a great advantage over developing nations in their ability to make changes. For example, in China, only 3 percent of high school graduates go on to college, while in the United States more than 30 percent of high school graduates do so.

B. MEDICAL BREAKTHROUGHS

There have been many remarkable advances in medicine in the 20th century. Perhaps the most important result of these medical advances was a dramatic increase in life expectancy in every part of the world. For example, in the United States, a person born in 1920 could expect to live to the age of 54, while a person born in 1994 could expect to live to age 76.

New cures for diseases In 1900, there were no known cures for such common diseases as typhoid, measles, and polio. Over the next 60 years, advances in medical science eliminated these three diseases as major threats. For example, in the 1950s Dr. Jonas Salk of the United States developed a polio vaccine. Vaccines for the prevention of other diseases have also been extremely effective. Today in many parts of the world, children receive one vaccine for diphtheria, tetanus, and whooping cough and another vaccine for measles, mumps, and rubella. Such vaccinations have greatly improved children's chances for survival into adulthood.

Early and accurate diagnosis of diseases is often extremely important for their successful treatment. This aspect of medicine has been improved through the development of various scanning devices. Through the use of X-ray, ultrasound, and magnetic resonance imaging (MRI) machines, physicians can get clear and accurate images

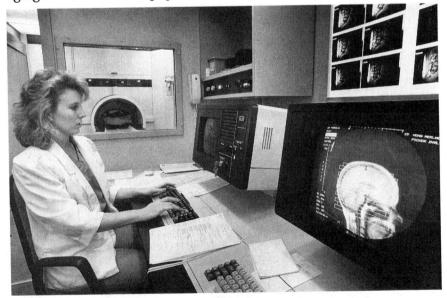

MEDICAL TECHNOLOGY: Computerized methods such as magnetic resonance imaging (MRI) allow doctors to "see" inside a patient's body. How do such methods also add to the increased costs of health care?

within a patient's body. Scanning techniques enable doctors to detect cancerous tumors at an early stage. For example, the X-ray examination known as *mammography* has led to the earlier detection and treatment of breast cancer in women.

Other recent medical advances include organ transplants, bypass surgery (for victims of heart disease), and laser technology. Newly discovered drugs are able to stabilize blood pressure, heartbeats, and emotional disorders. Breakthroughs in the treatment of cancer include *chemotherapy* (chemical treatment) and *radiation therapy* (X-ray treatment).

In developing nations, organizations such as the World Health Organization (WHO) and the United Nations International Children's Emergency Fund (UNICEF) have helped to carry out many medical advances. Much remains to be done, however. In many poorer nations, the infant mortality rate is still high. In Ghana, for example, 86 out of 1,000 infants die at birth (compared to just 7 infant deaths out of 1,000 in Germany).

C. PROBLEMS OF MODERN MEDICINE

The impressive successes of modern medicine have had some unforeseen consequences. These include ethical questions and the problem of financing health care.

Ethical questions   An ethical question is one that involves distinguishing between "right" (proper or moral) conduct and "wrong" (improper or immoral) conduct. For example, if a person has no hope of recovery from an injury or illness and is in constant pain, should that person be kept alive indefinitely through the use of life-sustaining equipment? In deciding this question, a person may consider both (a) the expense of using the equipment and (b) the quality of life of the person being kept alive. If that person is in a permanent coma or is "brain-dead," should that person be helped to live on?

Another ethical problem in medicine is the question of who shall receive scarce replacement organs (such as the heart or liver) or use expensive equipment (such as a kidney dialysis machine) that can help save lives. Shall the decision be based on factors such as a patient's wealth, age, or possible value to society? A related ethical question involves providing expensive equipment and drugs to people in developing nations who cannot afford them. Should wealthier nations supply such equipment and drugs to poorer nations or should the wealthier nations concentrate on saving lives within their own borders?

Financing health care   A major problem in the medical field has been the increasing cost of health care. In the United States, for example, average health care costs for an individual rose from $591 in 1975 to more than $2,600 in 1991. It is estimated that by year 2000, average health care costs for an American will increase to more than $5,000. Americans are not alone in having this problem. Rising health care costs are causing financial crises for people throughout the world. Many people are not able to pay for even inexpensive drugs and procedures, let alone the expensive ones.

Most developed countries have some form of national health plan where the central government pays either all or most of the costs of doctors' services and hospital care. Everyone, poor and rich alike, has an equal right to use the plan. It must be remembered, however, that no government services are free. Ultimately, whether the service is road repair, school instruction, or health care, taxpayers pay for what the government provides. Thus, nations that have government-spon-sored health plans also must collect more in taxes, mainly from people of upper and middle incomes.

The AIDS epidemic All the techniques known to medical science have not been enough to stop the spread of the deadly disease known as acquired immuno-deficiency syndrome (AIDS). The cause of the disease, a virus known as HIV, is passed from one infected person to another through sexual contact, direct contact with bodily fluids such as blood, or by sharing needles used to inject drugs. Since the first cases of AIDS appeared in 1981, more than 160,000 people in the United States have died of the disease. In many African nations, the AIDS epidemic has been much more devastating. In 1994, of the more than 14 million people worldwide who had been affected with the HIV virus, some 9 million were in Africa. Unless a remedy is found, by the year 2000 the number of infected persons is expected to climb to 40 million. Scientists around the world are actively attempting to find a cure for the disease.

In Review

The following questions refer to Section IV: Changes in Technology.

1. *Key terms:* Define or identify each of the following:

Information Age	fiber-optic cable	communications
silicon chip	information superhighway	satellite
		chemotherapy

2. Provide an example of how the computer has revolutionized life in recent times.

3. Identify *two* ethical problems that have arisen because of advances in technology.

4. *Critical thinking:* Changes in technology have greatly affected the way people live. (a) Prepare a chart in which you contrast life

today in the Information Age with life around 1900.   (*b*) Which two changes since 1900 do you consider the most positive and which two do you consider the most negative? Explain your answers.

V. Changes in Culture and Society

The saying, "It's a small world," has become a common expression. Largely because of electronic technologies (computers, television, communications satellites), the various cultures and nations of the world are in close communication on a daily basis. We have read that throughout history, cultural diffusion has been a powerful force for change. With a greater number of cultural contacts taking place than ever before, we can expect cultural diffusion to change the world even more rapidly in the future.

The conflicts created by rapid cultural change are evident in all the world's regions. This has been noted in previous chapters. Now let us look at these conflicts from a global viewpoint.

A. CONFLICTS BETWEEN TRADITION AND MODERNIZATION

Can a society adopt modern technologies without either changing or giving up its cultural traditions? In many societies, especially in the developing world, there are sharp disagreements between those who wish to maintain traditions without change and those who are more willing to change their customs and beliefs. As we have read, many Islamic nations of the Middle East are torn between Muslim traditionalists (such as the fundamentalists) and Muslims who wish to modernize.

Saudi Arabia is an example of a nation that has balanced the forces of tradition and modernization. The Saudis' great oil wealth has enabled them to build modern facilities such as airports, office buildings, and universities. At the same time, the people of Saudi Arabia have maintained their traditional values and religious beliefs. Islamic law, for example, still exerts a powerful influence on all aspects of Saudi society.

Japan is another nation that has managed to strike a balance between a traditional culture and a modern economy. The Japanese are in the forefront of modern science and technology. At the same time, traditional values such as respect for elders and strong family ties still play an important role in their lives.

Impact of Western culture on the non-Western world Popular forms of entertainment (movies, television shows, pop music) have

U.S. MOVIES IN JAPAN: This movie theater in Japan is showing the American-made film *Back to the Future*. How does the motion picture industry reflect global interdependence?

become an important aspect of culture in all nations of the world. As the leading creator of all forms of mass entertainment, the United States has probably spread the knowledge of its own culture and values more widely than any other nation. Since 1993, for example, movie audiences from Rio de Janeiro, Brazil, to Jakarta, Indonesia, have enjoyed the dazzling special effects in Steven Spielberg's science fiction thriller, *Jurassic Park*. In fact, judging by box office attendance, this U.S.-made film was the most popular movie of the year in Brazil, Indonesia, Malaysia, Japan, Thailand, Lebanon, and Egypt. Television shows like "The Simpsons" and "Seinfeld" also have been watched by millions in every region of the world.

Could U.S. exports of movies, television shows, videos, rock music, T-shirts, soft drinks, and fast-food hamburgers be viewed as a form of cultural imperialism? Those who are suspicious of U.S. power argue that they are. In contrast, millions of others argue that the popularity of U.S. products simply means that people the world over enjoy outstanding entertainment or products, no matter where they come from.

Impact of non-Western cultures on the West In an interdependent world, cultural influences extend in all directions. In Chapter 2, we learned that African music, dance, and art have influenced American jazz, contemporary dance, and modern art.

Just as U.S. fashions in dress and entertainment have been adopted in Asia, certain aspects of Asian cultures are now popular in the United

States and other Western nations. For example, beginning in the 1960s, a number of religious cults based on Hinduism and Buddhism gained a wide following in the United States. Millions of Americans learned Yoga exercises in meditation (techniques borrowed from India) and mastered Japanese methods of self-defense (the martial arts of jujitsu, karate, and judo). Popular alternative forms of medicine include the ancient Chinese art of *acupuncture*—placing needles at precise points in the body to affect healing and to relieve pain.

African Americans have consciously looked to the varied cultures of Africa to strengthen their identity and pride. Many have adopted hairstyles and fashions in dress similar to those commonly worn in Nigeria or Senegal. In addition, many thousands of African Americans (including champion boxer Muhammad Ali and political activist Malcolm X) have adopted Islam as their religion. Colleges and universities have helped spread knowledge of African culture by offering courses in African studies.

B. CONFLICTS BETWEEN ECONOMIC COMPETITION AND COOPERATION

Formerly, the competition that dominated world politics was the cold war rivalry between the United States and the Soviet Union. In the world today, the competition is mainly economic in nature. Thus, developed and developing nations are seeking to build stronger economies by increasing their exports and gaining a larger share of world trade. As in any competition, there are both winners and losers. Some nations like Japan, South Korea, and Germany have greatly increased their exports. Other nations like the former Communist states of Russia and Romania are having great difficulty in gaining a share of the world markets for their products.

In their approach to trade, every nation must choose between two policies. One policy, known as *protectionism*, attempts to place barriers in the way of foreign imports coming into the country. The most common trade barrier is a tariff, or tax on imports. The chief argument for protectionism is that a nation's industries are protected against competition from low-priced foreign imports. The opposite policy, known as "free trade," removes barriers to trade and encourages nations to buy and sell each other's goods openly and without restriction. The chief argument for free trade is that it rewards the most efficient producers, just as free competition in sports rewards the best athletes. Thus, each nation will export the products it produces most efficiently.

Trade disputes between Japan and the United States   For years, the world's leading industrial nations have competed to sell similar products to the same international markets. Japanese cars, for example, compete with cars made in Germany, Britain, France, Italy, and the United States. Gold necklaces made in Hong Kong compete on world markets with gold necklaces made in India and South Africa.

As discussed in Chapter 6, the United States has strongly objected to Japan's trade policies. It has complained that its huge trade deficit with Japan (over $50 billion in 1993) was largely the result of "unfair" Japanese trade barriers. For example, U.S. manufacturers of computer chips and other products have found it difficult to sell to Japanese companies. U.S. farmers ran into trade barriers that blocked the sale of American rice and apples, even though their costs for producing these goods were lower than Japanese costs.

Regional trading blocs   On the one hand, economic competition between nations seems greater than ever in the post-cold war era. On the other hand, there is a strong trend toward greater economic cooperation. The most visible signs of such cooperation are the many agreements that established free trade zones. Chief among them are:

  1. *The European Union.* The members of this Western European economic union have agreed to eliminate tariffs in their region and to seek adoption of a common currency (discussed in Chapter 7). The most prosperous nations of Eastern Europe—Poland, Hungary, and the Czech Republic—are considering joining the organization.

  2. *General Agreement on Tariffs and Trade (GATT).* Ever since the 1940s, the nations signing this agreement (now numbering over 100) have participated in a series of talks concerning trade issues. From time to time, they have made agreements to remove trade barriers. In 1993, the seventh round of talks (held in Uruguay) resulted in major reductions in tariff rates among participating nations.

  3. *The North American Free Trade Agreement (NAFTA).* U.S. approval of this agreement in 1993 established the largest free trade zone in the world. Canada, the United States, and Mexico agreed to gradually end tariffs on goods traded among the three countries. Tariffs on some goods were to be eliminated immediately, while other tariffs were to be removed over a 15-year period.

  4. *The Commonwealth of Independent States (CIS).* Although the Soviet Union broke up, most of the former members of that union are attempting to coordinate their economic and trade policies (discussed in Chapter 8).

  5. *Other Regions.* The Organization of African Unity (discussed in Chapter 2) continues its efforts at strengthening the economies of African nations. And many of the nations of Latin America have entered into trade pacts that have either lowered or eliminated trade barriers in that region.

C. CONFLICTS IN MULTICULTURAL SOCIETIES

As we have seen, migration has been a major cause of change throughout the history of every region. We have studied the effects of Aryans migrating into India, Goths migrating into Western Europe, Turks migrating into Eastern Europe, Aztecs migrating into central Mexico, Dutch and British migrating into South Africa, Mongols migrating into Russia, and Russians migrating into Siberia.

In our own times, migration continues as Haitians seek asylum in the United States to escape from poverty and dictatorship. Mexicans seek employment in the United States. Romanians and Bulgarians seek a better life in Germany. And Russian Jews seek freedom and economic opportunity in Israel and the United States. (Of course, these are just a few examples of the many major migrations of the past and present.)

Many nations today are populated by a mixture of ethnic groups. The United States provides a leading example of such a multicultural society. Its racial and ethnic mixture is the result of people from all parts of the world joining the Native Americans, who were already here. Although the United States has had racial and ethnic conflicts, citizens today think of themselves both as Americans and as members of ethnic groups. The challenge for each American today is to find the common values that help one to live alongside and participate with other Americans of different backgrounds. The motto on the Great Seal of the United States is "E Pluribus Unum," meaning "Out of Many, One." It could well be the motto for the whole world.

In Review

The following questions refer to Section V: Changes in Culture and Society.

1. *Key terms:* Identify each of the following:

    acupuncture   protectionism   multicultural society

2. Give *two* examples of the impact of non-Western cultures on Europe and the United States.

3. Explain why many nations have entered into regional trade pacts. (In your answer, provide one example of such a pact.)

4. *Critical thinking:* "The whole world would benefit if all nations eliminated all their tariffs." Present one argument either for or against this idea.

TEST YOURSELF

Multiple-Choice Questions

On a separate sheet of paper, write the number of the word or expression that, of those given, best completes each statement or answers each question. NOTE: Some of the questions that follow are based upon your knowledge and understanding of concepts that apply to several regions. To answer these questions, you may need to review material covered in previous chapters. You may also wish to consult the Glossary for terms such as social mobility *and* tradition.

Level 1

1. The major cause of the high birth rates in most developing nations has been   (1) the need for a large urban work force   (2) a desire to counteract an increasing death rate   (3) a need to replace people killed during civil wars   (4) traditional beliefs and the economic need to have large families.

Base your answer to question 2 on the graphs below and on your knowledge of social studies.

BIRTH AND DEATH RATES, 1850–1977

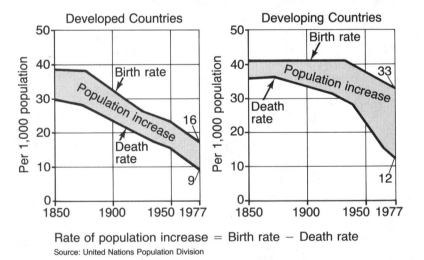

Rate of population increase = Birth rate − Death rate
Source: United Nations Population Division

2. Which statement is best supported by the information in the graphs? (1) Population growth in both developed and developing countries will reach the same rate.   (2) By the year 2000, the developing countries will reach the point of zero population growth.   (3) Population growth since 1900 has largely been due to a drop in the death rate. (4) Population growth since 1900 has largely been due to an increase in the birth rate.

Base your answer to question 3 on the graph below and on your knowledge of social studies.

WORLD POPULATION, 1500–2000

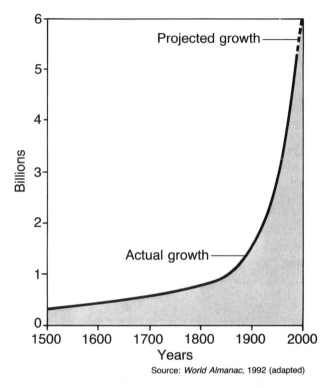

Source: *World Almanac*, 1992 (adapted)

3. Which is the most valid conclusion based on the graph? (1) The most rapid rate of growth occurred before 1800. (2) The world's population will remain the same after 2000. (3) The number of children per family has been steadily increasing. (4) The growth rate of the world's population has been increasing.

4. A comparison of a world map that shows physical features with a world map that shows population density would most likely lead to the conclusion that (1) physical features are not related to where people live (2) physical features determine a nation's system of government (3) the most industrialized countries are in the Southern Hemisphere (4) the areas with the best water resources are often the most heavily populated.

5. During the 1970s and 1980s, India and China attempted to improve the quality of life for their people and to increase economic growth by (1) changing the political structure (2) adopting policies to limit population growth (3) encouraging farmers to move to the cities (4) seeking overseas colonies.

6. In developing nations, people have moved from rural villages to urban areas to (1) avoid the high cost of living in rural areas (2) escape the poor climates in rural areas (3) find job opportunities in the cities (4) live among people of different ethnic backgrounds in the cities.

7. Which is a feature of most traditional societies? (1) political equality of men and women (2) extended family system (3) ease of upward social mobility (4) involvement of all adults in decision making.

8. Which situation generally occurs in a society as a result of urbanization? (1) Opportunities for social mobility increase. (2) Ties to extended families are strengthened. (3) Poverty in rural areas is eliminated. (4) Population in rural areas increases.

Base your answer to question 9 on the cartoon below and on your knowledge of social studies.

Dana Summers © 1994, The Washington Post Writers Group. Reprinted with permission.

9. What is the main idea of the cartoon? (1) Industrialized nations have provided little in the way of famine relief. (2) Ethiopians had no real need for foreign relief aid. (3) Sometimes foreign aid does not go to the groups who need it the most. (4) Countries frequently fight wars because of a lack of food.

10. The Green Revolution has partly succeeded because it has (1) promoted democratic reform (2) increased agricultural productivity in some regions (3) introduced Western culture and values (4) established economic equality among the people.

11. Which factors are usually found in developing nations? (1) high level of productivity and high standard of living (2) dependence on agricultural production and low standard of living (3) high level of productivity and low population growth rate (4) decline of industrial production and high population growth rate.

12. The basic characteristic of subsistence agriculture is that farmers (1) produce mostly staple crops to sell (2) sell large portions of their crops at the market price (3) produce crops mainly for their own immediate use (4) produce crops according to government orders.

13. Which generally occurs as a nation moves from an agricultural economy to an industrialized economy? (1) There is a greater need for education and training. (2) Larger families are needed to meet economic and social goals. (3) The number of people at the poverty level increases sharply. (4) There is a renewed emphasis on traditional values.

14. Which is a major problem facing many of the poorer developing nations in the 1990s? (1) Food production is inadequate. (2) There are too many technically skilled workers. (3) European armies dominate these nations. (4) Too many consumer goods are produced.

15. Which statement describes most nations that depend on one crop or product for export? (1) They are frequently affected by world market conditions. (2) They experience periods of rapid industrialization. (3) They have Communist governments. (4) They encourage subsistence-level agriculture.

16. Which condition is most necessary to the process of industrialization in a society? (1) dependence on subsistence agriculture (2) creation of a one-crop economy (3) availability of investment capital (4) capture of foreign lands.

17. During the 1980s, a major problem in many economically developing countries was the (1) fear of competition with industrialized countries (2) decreasing numbers of potential employees in these countries (3) increasing foreign debt in these countries (4) shortage of markets in industrialized nations.

18. During the 1970s and 1980s, the Palestine Liberation Organization (1) adopted passive resistance as a way to deal with enemies (2) used terrorism as a means of achieving goals (3) became allied with the United States and Western Europe to defeat communism (4) refused support from religious groups and organizations.

19. A major cause of the continued conflict in Northern Ireland has been (1) opposing dynastic claims (2) religious differences (3) interference from the superpowers (4) industrial rivalry.

20. The main concern regarding the destruction of the rain forests is that (1) cities will become seriously overcrowded (2) the temperature of the earth's surface may increase (3) per capita income in economically developing nations may increase (4) water supplies in economically developing nations will increase.

21. Acid rain damage, contamination from nuclear accidents, and deterioration of the earth's ozone layer indicate a need for (1) the elimination of fossil fuels (2) international cooperation and communication (3) high tariffs and a favorable balance of trade (4) nationalization of major industries.

22. Which is a valid statement about infectious diseases and epidemics? (1) Modern medicine has discovered effective treatments for several infectious diseases and epidemics. (2) The AIDS epidemic is limited to countries of the Western Hemisphere. (3) In the 20th century, oceans and seas prevent diseases from spreading from one continent to another. (4) Most diseases are limited to industrialized nations.

Base your answer to question 23 on the graph below and on your knowledge of social studies.

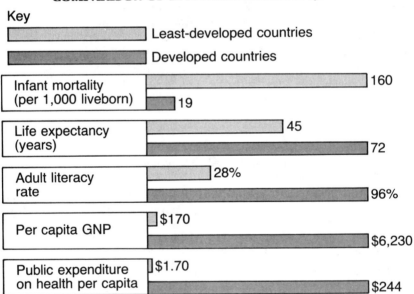

COMPARISON OF INTERNATIONAL INEQUALITIES

Key
- Least-developed countries
- Developed countries

Infant mortality (per 1,000 liveborn)	160 / 19
Life expectancy (years)	45 / 72
Adult literacy rate	28% / 96%
Per capita GNP	$170 / $6,230
Public expenditure on health per capita	$1.70 / $244

Source: United Nations Children's Fund (UNICEF)

23. A valid conclusion that can be made is that nations with a low per capita GNP have (1) greater life expectancy (2) greater public expenditure on health per capita (3) a high infant mortality rate (4) a high adult literacy rate.

24. Since World War II, economic conditions in developing nations have undergone great changes mainly because of (1) a greater tolerance of minorities (2) the introduction of modern technology (3) the establishment of democratic governments (4) a decrease in nationalistic feelings.

25. Industrialization in developing countries has most often resulted in (1) mass migrations from rural to urban areas   (2) fewer educational and employment opportunities   (3) strengthening of traditional values and family patterns   (4) decreased use of natural resources.

Level 2

26. The extended family and subsistence farming are most associated with   (1) developed nations   (2) urban areas   (3) industrial societies   (4) rural areas.

27. Which of the following is a major trend in developing nations today? (1) return to village life   (2) population shifts from rural to urban areas   (3) increasing barriers to international trade   (4) increasing medical benefits to workers and farmers.

28. Which of the following is the most likely cause of famine?   (1) International agencies refuse to provide food aid.   (2) There is little knowledge of farming methods.   (3) Long dry spells may ruin the soil. (4) Farmland has been destroyed in order to build factories.

29. Which of the following is most associated with a traditional society? (1) subsistence agriculture   (2) large-scale factories   (3) high-speed railroads   (4) large urban centers.

30. In developing nations of the world, modernization requires (1) strong military governments   (2) many different cultures   (3) religious unity   (4) investment capital.

31. The United States sells oil to Japan while Japan sells automobiles in the United States. Which is a valid conclusion based on this statement?   (1) There are many barriers to international trade.   (2) Japan and the United States are self-sufficient.   (3) Japan and the United States trade only with each other.   (4) We live in an interdependent world.

32. The Earth Summit of 1992 and the North American Free Trade Agreement are examples of   (1) military alliances   (2) human rights agreements   (3) imperialism   (4) international cooperation.

33. Which of the following is a result of the collapse of the Soviet Union? (1) There is full cooperation among the former republics.   (2) There is decreased involvement by the United Nations in world affairs. (3) A number of armed conflicts have developed in Eastern Europe and Central Asia.   (4) Russia has regained control over the former republics.

34. A possible effect of the destruction of the rain forests is that   (1) cities will become overcrowded   (2) all nations will become more interdependent   (3) terrorism will increase   (4) the temperature of the earth's surface may increase.

35. In some regions, the Green Revolution has   (1) promoted democratic reforms   (2) increased agricultural output   (3) introduced Western culture and values   (4) established economic equality.

36. Which was a method used by the Irish Republican Army (IRA) and the Palestine Liberation Organization (PLO) to achieve their goals? (1) terrorism   (2) nuclear weapons   (3) pollution of the environment (4) withholding financial aid.

37. Chernobyl and Three Mile Island are most associated with the problem of   (1) desertification   (2) deforestation   (3) acid rain   (4) nuclear accidents.

38. The end of apartheid in South Africa has been a major gain for (1) communism   (2) human rights   (3) the PLO   (4) religious fundamentalism.

39. In which two societies did acts of genocide occur?   (1) Cambodia and Uganda   (2) India and Great Britain   (3) Germany and Switzerland   (4) Egypt and Saudi Arabia.

40. Some nations of Asia are developing nuclear weapons. This is a good example of   (1) interdependence   (2) technological diffusion (3) resource management   (4) genocide.

Essay Questions

Level 1

1. Many problems face the nations of the world today. Some of these problems are listed below.

Problems
Air pollution
Deforestation
Disposal of nuclear wastes
Overpopulation
World hunger

Select *three* of the problems listed above. For each problem selected:

● Explain one cause and one effect.
● Describe one way that governments or groups have attempted to solve the problem.

2. When controversial topics are examined, there are always opposing viewpoints. Each statement below expresses a viewpoint about a controversial topic.

Statements
The computer has benefited people in the 20th century.
Terrorism is an appropriate means to bring about change.
The Chinese government has a right to limit family size.
Urbanization has been beneficial to developing nations.
European influences have benefited other parts of the world.

Select *three* of the statements listed above. For each statement selected, discuss one argument for and one argument against the statement.

Level 2

3. There are many environmental problems in the world today.

Environmental Problems
Acid rain
Depletion of the ozone layer
Greenhouse effect
Water pollution
Desertification

A. Select *three* of the environmental problems listed above. For each problem selected, state one cause.

B. Base your answer to Part B on your answer to Part A. However, additional information may be included. Write an essay in which you discuss causes for the environmental problems listed above. Begin your essay with this topic sentence:

> There are important causes for the world's environmental problems today.

4. Human rights violations have occurred in many nations in recent years.

Nations
South Africa
Soviet Union
Cambodia
El Salvador
Bosnia-Herzegovina

A. Select *three* of the nations listed above. For each nation selected, state one example of a human rights violation.

B. Base your answer to Part B on your answer to Part A. However, additional information may be included. Write an essay in which you explain how human rights were violated in at least three of the societies listed above. Begin your essay with this topic sentence:

> Human rights violations have occurred in many nations in recent years.

APPENDIX

PREPARING FOR AN EXAM IN GLOBAL STUDIES

You are approaching the end of a challenging course in Global Studies. You have been introduced to hundreds of names, events, and terms concerning the history and geography of eight major regions of the world. It is a vast subject. How can you prepare yourself for a final exam that covers so much information?

The test-taking tips that follow will help you to review the main ideas and most significant facts associated with Global Studies. They will also provide you with strategies for answering multiple-choice and essay questions. By reviewing the highlights of the course and practicing test-taking strategies, you can go into a standardized or final exam confident of a successful outcome.

I. Developing a Test-Taking Strategy

In preparing for any test, it is important to determine (1) how much time remains between now and the test date and (2) the kind and amount of material that should be reviewed. Here is a formula for test-taking success:

> Long period of review (three weeks or more) + Organized plan of study = Knowledge of the material = High test score.

An opposite approach (a short period of cramming and no organized plan of study) will probably produce a negative result.

A. HOW TO STUDY FOR THE FINAL EXAM

Instead of cramming your test preparation into a short time, you will have much greater success if you follow these guidelines:

- Separate the course of study into distinct units, devoting at least two days (preferably four days) of study to each unit.
- Create a daily schedule for studying. Make sure that this schedule allows you sufficient time to cover the full course before the exam date.
- Before going to new material, allow about 15 minutes for reviewing what you had studied the day before.
- Study at times when you are alert rather than late at night when you may be tired and unable to concentrate.
- Study in a quiet place with few distractions. Avoid such diversions as talking on the telephone or keeping one eye on a television show and the other eye on your study notes.

B. WHAT TO STUDY

When reviewing each chapter, always try to focus on the most important terms, people, and ideas. To help you, these are listed in the following section, one list for each chapter of the text.

II. A Plan for Reviewing Global Studies

What follows is a method for linking your study of each chapter to its key terms, people, events, and ideas. Allow two study sessions for studying Chapter 1, "How the World Changes," and two to four sessions for each subsequent chapter.

A. HOW THE WORLD CHANGES

Begin your review by making sure you understand the meaning of key geographic and historical terms. There is a high likelihood that you will encounter most of these terms in the multiple-choice section of a Global Studies exam.

Exercise 1: Identifying terms   On a piece of paper, write a phrase or sentence defining each term listed below. Then check the accuracy of your definition by looking at the Glossary (pages 565-576). Revise your original definition if you find that it is inaccurate or incomplete. Do *not* simply copy the Glossary definition. By using your own words, you will better remember the meaning of each term.

Key Terms in Geography and History

absolute monarchy	ethnic cleansing	population density
anthropology	ethnocentrism	prehistoric culture
archeology	extended family	region
capitalism	free enterprise	revolution
climate	historic culture	socialism
command economy	Industrial Revolution	social revolution
communism	interdependence	subregion
cultural diffusion	irrigation	technological innovation
democracy	market economy	totalitarianism
dictatorship	nationalism	traditional economy

Exercise 2: Questions on key terms   On a standardized or final exam, you can expect to find several questions that test your understanding of key terms. Four questions of that type are presented here. To deal with this kind of question, do the following: (*a*) identify each key term being tested; (*b*) think to yourself what the term means; and (*c*) look for an answer that either defines or expresses the meaning of the term. Practice this test-taking strategy for each of the following questions.

1. Nationalism is most likely to develop in an area that has   (1) land suited to agriculture   (2) adequate industry to supply consumer demands   (3) a moderate climate with rivers for irrigation   (4) common customs, language, and history.

2. Cultural diffusion occurs most rapidly in societies that   (1) adhere to traditional social values   (2) have extended families   (3) come into frequent contact with other groups   (4) have a strong oral history.

3. Which statement is most characteristic of totalitarian governments?   (1) Local media report a variety of opinions concerning government policy.   (2) The judiciary is independent of the executive branch of government.   (3) Human rights are constitutionally guaranteed for all people.   (4) Loyalty is measured by the extent to which a person agrees with government policy.

4. The best example of nationalism is   (1) the people of India demanding independence from Great Britain   (2) a medieval lord raising an army to protect his manor   (3) the peacekeeping forces of the United Nations patrolling in Lebanon.   (4) Spain declining to join the North Atlantic Treaty Organization (NATO).

Note: Question 4 differs from the others by giving specific historical events. Do you have to remember and understand all of these events (e.g., UN actions in Lebanon, Spain's policy toward NATO) in order to answer the question? No, you do not. In fact, you will more likely choose the correct answer if you think only about the definition of the key term, nationalism. You know that nationalism often means a people's desire to win independence from foreign rule. Knowing this, you can locate the answer readily and eliminate the other choices.

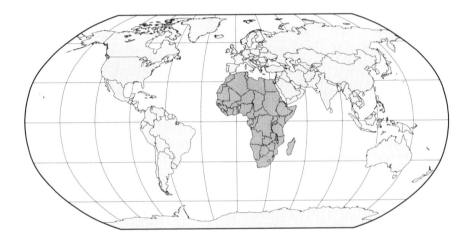

B. AFRICA

On a final or standardized Global Studies exam, you can expect that most of the multiple-choice questions will deal with a specific region. To be fully prepared for the set of questions on Africa, do the following:

- Review the Main Ideas listed on pages 38–39. Simply by reading these pages, you will be reminded quickly of the central themes in African geography and history.
- Study the map of Africa on page 40. Referring to the numbered boxes connected to this map, make a list of at least five ways in which Africa's geography has influenced its history. (Your list will help you prepare for both the multiple-choice and essay portions of the exam.)
- Carry out the following two suggested exercises:

Exercise 1: Identifying terms   On a piece of paper, write a phrase that identifies each item listed in the following table. Refer to the

Glossary for general terms (such as *rain forest*) and to information in Chapter 2 for the names of people, places, and events. An effective way to master every item on the list is to work with another student as a "quiz partner." One partner reads from his or her list of identifying phrases. The other partner gives a person, event, or term associated with each phrase. After completing a set of ten terms, reverse roles.

African Geography	African History	Contemporary Affairs (since 1945)
desertification	Axum	African National Congress
Great Rift Valley	animism	Idi Amin
Nile River	Ghana	apartheid
rain forest	imperialism	F. W. de Klerk
Sahara	Koran	homelands
Sahel	Kush	human rights
savanna	David Livingstone	Jomo Kenyatta
sub-Sahara	Mali	Nelson Mandela
	pharaoh	Kwame Nkrumah
	polytheism	Organization of African Unity
	pyramid	Pan-Africanism
	slave trade	self-determination
	Songhai	Bishop Desmond Tutu
	Henry Stanley	
	Zimbabwe	

Exercise 2: Eliminating incorrect answers The following set of five questions represent the kind of multiple-choice questions on Africa that are likely to appear on a standardized or final exam. As you answer each question, practice the strategy of eliminating those choices that you think are clearly incorrect. One way to do this is to turn each choice into a question. Consider, for example, this example:

Example: A major result of the development of civilization in Egypt was the (1) conquest and settlement of Western Europe (2) establishment of a democratic system of government in Egypt (3) establishment of trade routes between Egypt and other kingdoms (4) decline of agriculture as an important occupation in Egypt.

Think to yourself: Did the ancient Egyptians conquer and settle Western Europe? (No, choice 1 is out.) Did ancient Egypt have a democratic system of government? (No, the pharaoh, a monarch, had absolute power; choice 2 is out.) Did ancient Egypt trade with other kingdoms? (Probably; keep choice 3 as a possible answer.) Did agriculture decline as an occupation in ancient Egypt? (Probably not, since Egyptian civilization was based on farming in the Nile Valley; choice 4 is out.) The answer is now clear (choice 3) because three other choices have been eliminated.

1. Which statement best describes the effects of the geography of Africa? (1) Geography has encouraged physical mobility throughout Africa. (2) The geography of Africa has hindered economic development. (3) The geography of Africa has stimulated political and cultural unity. (4) The geography of Africa has resulted in most African countries having similar economic and social systems.

2. During the 19th century, the African continent was affected most by (1) the Commercial Revolution (2) the introduction of socialism (3) the Crusades (4) European imperialism.

3. During the 1950s and 1960s, the history of most African countries was characterized by (1) colonization by imperialist nations (2) the achievement of political independence (3) a sharp decrease in the birth rate (4) a decline in population.

4. The term "Pan-Africanism" can best be defined as a movement whose purpose is to (1) promote African unity (2) support cultural diversity (3) encourage European investment in Africa (4) advocate a return to colonial conditions.

5. In the Republic of South Africa, the government's apartheid policy was based primarily on the concept of (1) justice under the law (2) nativism (3) racial segregation (4) economic specialization.

Exercise 3: Answering an essay question Some essay questions on standardized and final exams require students to explain how certain governments have violated the rights of its people. Consider the following essay question:

Throughout history, governments have violated the political and human rights of various groups. These violations have led to nationalist movements.

Victims of human rights abuses in Africa
Africans under European colonial rule
Blacks in the Republic of South Africa under apartheid
Ugandans during the reign of Idi Amin

For *two* of the groups listed above,

- Explain how the rights of the group were violated.
- Describe what was done to eliminate the abuse or abuses of rights.

After answering the above question, select *one* region other than Africa where human rights have been violated. List at least *three* violations of human rights in the selected region.

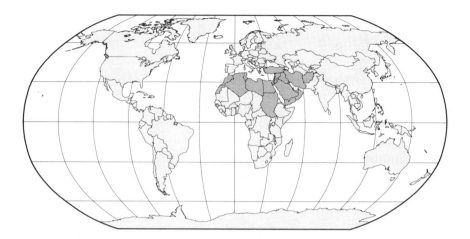

C. THE MIDDLE EAST

To be fully prepared for an exam's multiple-choice questions on the Middle East, do the following:

- Review the Main Ideas about the Middle East, listed on pages 86–87.
- Study the map of the Middle East on pages 88–89. Referring to the numbered boxes on this map, make a list of at least *five* ways in which the Middle East's geography has influenced its history.
- Complete the following exercises:

Exercise 1: Identifying terms   On a piece of paper, write a phrase that identifies each item listed below. Refer to the Glossary for general terms (such as monotheism) and to information in Chapter 3 for names of people, places, and events. Study with a "quiz partner" (see the instructions on page 539. Africa, Exercise 1).

Middle East Geography	Middle East History	Contemporary Affairs (since 1945)
Arabian Peninsula	Balfour Declaration	Yasir Arafat
Bosporus and Dardanelles	Christianity	Menachem Begin
Fertile Crescent	Code of Hammurabi	David Ben-Gurion
Gaza Strip	Islam	Intifada
Jerusalem	Judaism	Saddam Hussein
Mecca	Kemal Atatürk	Ayatollah Khomeini
Mesopotamia	Mohammed	Kurd
Persian Gulf	Ottoman empire	Golda Meir
Sinai Peninsula	Shiite Muslim	Muslim fundamentalist
Strait of Hormuz	Sumer	Gamal Abdel Nasser
Suez Canal	Sunni Muslim	Persian Gulf War
West Bank	Zionism	Anwar al-Sadat

Exercise 2: Multiple-choice questions   One type of question in final or standardized exams in Global Studies ask you to find what several people, places, or events have in common. Consider this example:

Example: The river valleys of the Tigris-Euphrates, the Nile, and the Indus were centers of civilization because they each   (1) had rich deposits of iron ore and coal   (2) were isolated from other cultural influences   (3) were easy to defend from invasion   (4) provided a means of transportation and irrigation.

At first, such a question may appear more challenging than others. In fact, however, it could be *easier* than others if you know how to approach it. In the above example, you may have forgotten about the Indus River civilization. Suppose, though, that you are familiar with the other two civilizations mentioned. Focus on the civilization about which you know the most. When you answer the question for that civilization, you probably have answered it correctly for the other two as well.

Practice this strategy on the following questions.

1. Gamal Abdel Nasser, Mao Zedong, and Simón Bolívar were similar because they each   (1) promoted nationalism among their peoples   (2) believed in Marxist principles   (3) modeled their political actions on religious doctrine   (4) taught respect for established authority.

2. Notre Dame Cathedral in Paris, the Dome of the Rock in Jerusalem, and the Great Pyramid in Egypt are examples of   (1) architectural accomplishments that reflect religious beliefs   (2) the influence of Buddhist architecture on conquered nations   (3) buildings of the post-industrial era   (4) the influence of cultural diffusion on contemporary architecture.

3. The Strait of Hormuz, the Suez Canal, and the Strait of Gibraltar are important because they   (1) prevent attacks on bordering nations   (2) control access to vital trade routes   (3) limit Russian access to warm-water ports   (4) prohibit the movement of ships carrying nuclear weapons.

4. A problem that faced the Austro-Hungarian empire, the Ottoman empire, and the Soviet Union was the (1) effect of urbanization on a rural population (2) monopoly of the traditional church (3) inability to produce modern weapons (4) tension among many different ethnic groups.

5. A major cause of conflict in both Northern Ireland and Lebanon has been (1) opposing dynastic claims (2) religious differences (3) interference from the superpowers (4) industrial rivalry.

Exercise 3: Answering essay questions Some essay questions on final or standardized exams require you to explain how developments that take place in one region affect other regions of the world. For example:

Throughout history, major developments have had effects beyond the regions in which the changes occurred. The following are associated with the Middle East.

Developments in the Middle East
Birthplace of major civilizations
Birthplace of major religions
Formation of the Organization of Petroleum Exporting Countries (OPEC)
Establishment of Israel
Creation of the Palestine Liberation Organization (PLO)
Rise of Islamic fundamentalism
Iraqi invasion of Kuwait.

Select *three* of the developments from the list. For each one selected:

- Describe the development.
- Use specific examples to show how the development affected a region other than the Middle East.

After answering the above question, select a different region. List *five* developments in the chosen region that affected other regions. Then write an essay on *three* of them.

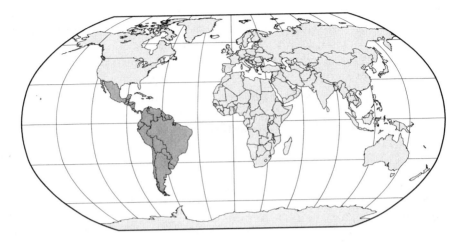

D. LATIN AMERICA

To prepare for multiple-choice questions focusing on Latin America, do the following:

- Review the Main Ideas listed on pages 136–137.
- Study the map of Latin America on page 138. Referring to the numbered boxes connected to this map, make a list of at least *five* ways in which Latin America's geography has influenced its history.
- Complete the following exercises:

Exercise 1: Identifying terms   On a piece of paper, write a phrase that identifies each item listed below. Refer to the Glossary for general terms (such as mercantilism) and to information in Chapter 4 for the names of people, places, and events. You might benefit by studying with a "quiz partner."

Latin American Geography	Latin American History	Contemporary Affairs (since 1945)
Amazon River	Aztec	Alliance for Progress
Andes Mountains	Simón Bolívar	Fidel Castro
Atacama Desert	caudillo	contra
Brazilian rain forest	Hernando Cortés	Cuban Missile Crisis
Caribbean Sea	hacienda	Manuel Noriega
Central America	Inca	North American Free
creole	Mayan	Trade Agreement
mestizo	mercantilism	Organization of American
mulatto	Montezuma	States
Pampas	Toussaint-Louverture	Sandinista
Panama Canal	Juan Perón	

Exercise 2: Stress on diversity In a course in Global Studies, *diversity* is an important word. Partly because every region has diverse geographic features, it also has diverse cultures. Knowing this fact will help you with certain exam questions that have "diversity" or "variety" as one of the choices. If the choice suggests that a certain region lacks diversity, you can be certain that choice is the wrong one. In contrast, you have a good chance of being right if you select an answer that describes a region as diverse or varied. Some of the questions below enable you to practice this strategy.

1. Which generalization about the geography of Latin America is accurate? (1) Geographic features prevented foreign imperialism. (2) Harsh climatic conditions have prevented the development of large-scale agriculture. (3) The lack of geographic barriers has helped transportation and communication to develop. (4) Great variations in latitude and landforms have resulted in a diversity of climates.

2. In Latin America, the mountainous terrain has contributed to (1) the development of a good infrastructure (2) the varied climates found in the region (3) social equality and political unity (4) extensive agricultural production.

3. Which group has most frequently opposed social and economic changes in Latin America? (1) landowners (2) students (3) Roman Catholic priests (4) peasants

4. In many Latin American nations, reliance on the production of a single cash crop has led to (1) economic dependence on other nations (2) rapid repayment of foreign loans (3) a high per capita gross national product (4) development of a strong industrial economy.

5. Which is a valid generalization about Latin America? (1) Most Latin Americans live in isolated farm villages. (2) The majority of the governments in Latin America are Communist. (3) Most Latin Americans are descendants of immigrants from Africa. (4) Latin America is a region of racial and cultural diversity.

Exercise 3: Answering an essay question Some essay questions on Global Studies exams require students to explain how geographic features affect the way of life in a region. For example:

Geographic features can influence the development of a region.
Geographic Features in Latin America
Andes Mountains
Amazon River
Atacama Desert
Brazilian rain forest
Pampas

Select *three* geographic features from the list. For each feature selected, discuss how it has had either a positive or negative effect on
the development of Latin America.

   After answering the above question, select a region other than Latin
America. List *five* geographic features that have affected the region.
Then write an essay in which you discuss how *three* of the geographic
features have affected the development of the region.

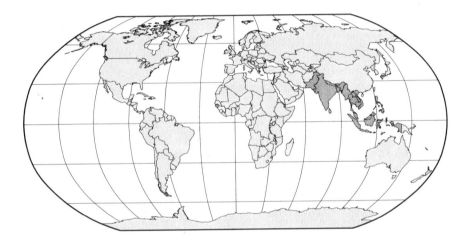

E. SOUTH AND SOUTHEAST ASIA

   To prepare for the multiple-choice questions on this region, do the
following:

● Review the Main Ideas listed on pages 194–195.

● Study the map of South and Southeast Asia on pages 196–197. Referring to the numbered boxes on this map, make a list of at least
   five ways in which the geography of South and Southeast Asia has
   influenced its history.

● Complete the following exercises:

Exercise 1: Identifying terms   On a piece of paper, write a phrase
that identifies each item listed in the following table. Refer to the
Glossary for general terms and to information in Chapter 5 for the
names of people, places, and events. You might want to study with a
"study partner."

Geography	History	Contemporary Affairs (since 1945)
Bangladesh	Aryan	Indira Gandhi
Ganges River	Buddhism	genocide
Himalaya Mountains	caste system	Khmer Rouge
Indonesia	civil disobedience	Jawaharlal Nehru
Indus River	Congress party	partition of India
Malay Peninsula	Mohandas Gandhi	third world
Malaysia	Gupta empire	Vietnam War
monsoon	Hinduism	
Pakistan	Ho Chi Minh	
Philippines	Indochina	
Singapore	Indus Valley	
Vietnam	civilization	
	Mughal empire	
	Muslim League	
	reincarnation	
	Sepoy Mutiny	

Exercise 2: Multiple-choice questions To answer each of the following multiple-choice questions, use one or more of the test-taking strategies learned earlier. You will find questions that (a) involve defining a key term, (b) contain topics and events common to several different regions, or (c) mention cultural or geographic diversity. First, identify the type of question. Then use the appropriate strategy for answering it.

1. A study of untouchables and Brahmins in India and a study of Native Americans and people of European descent in some Central American nations indicate that   (1) class systems exist in many parts of the world   (2) low levels of technology create divisions between people   (3) there is a new unity among the poor of the world   (4) people live as equals throughout the world.

2. Which is a result of India's policy of nonalignment?   (1) India has kept its spending on welfare at a low level.   (2) The Indian government has been successful in limiting population growth.   (3) The Indian government has worked to reduce religious conflicts.   (4) India accepted aid from both the United States and the Soviet Union.

3. In recent years, India and China have attempted to improve the quality of life for their people and to increase economic growth by   (1) changing the political structure of the countries   (2) adopting policies to limit population growth   (3) encouraging farmers to move to the cities   (4) seeking overseas colonies.

4. Which is a valid generalization that can be made about Southeast Asia?   (1) A common religion gives cultural unity to the region. (2) Diverse geographic conditions have led to cultural diversity. (3) Most people live in the cities.   (4) Every nation in the region has a democratic government and capitalist economy.

5. The best example of nationalism is   (1) UN intervention in the Korean War   (2) British colonial policies in India in the 19th century   (3) the Vietnamese struggle to win independence from the French   (4) the peace treaty ending World War I.

6. The process of cultural diffusion is best illustrated by   (1) the spread of Buddhism from India to other parts of Asia   (2) Gandhi's methods for opposing British colonialism   (3) the partition of India in 1947   (4) the granting of independence to the Philippines.

Exercise 3: Answering essay questions   Some essay questions on final or standardized exams require students to explain how religions have influenced the culture or cultures of a region. For example, look at the following:

Religions have had a major impact on the lives of people in specific regions.

Religions—Regions
Hinduism—South Asia
Buddhism—Southeast Asia
Islam—South Asia

For each of the religions listed above:

- Describe one major belief or practice of the religion.
- Discuss how this belief or practice has affected the social, economic, or political life of the peoples of the region with which the religion is paired.

After answering the above question, select a region that has been affected by either Christianity or Judaism, or by both. Then discuss how a belief in or practice of Christianity or Judaism has affected the people of the region.

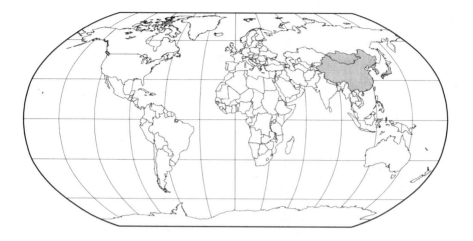

F. EAST ASIA

To prepare for questions on China, Japan, and other nations of East Asia, do the following:

- Review the list of Main Ideas on pages 240–241.
- Study the map of East Asia on pages 242–243. Referring to the numbered boxes on this map, make a list of at least *five* ways in which East Asia's geography has influenced its history.
- Complete the following exercises:

Exercise 1: Choosing facts to support a statement   Your total score on the essay part of the final or standardized exam can count almost as much as your total score on the multiple-choice section. The essay questions are similar in form to those given at the end of every chapter in this text. Each of these questions begins with a generalization. For example:

1. Throughout history, people have taken actions to oppose those in power.
2. Nationalism and imperialism have often been the cause of military conflicts.
3. Geographic factors affect the development of nations throughout the world.
4. Religion has often strongly influenced many aspects of culture in society.
5. Revolutions can be political, social, and/or economic. They produce long-term effects on regions and countries.

Copy the previous statements into your notebook. Make each statement the heading for a different page. Under each statement, list names, events, and terms (from the following lists) that you could use to support the statement in an essay. Finally, choose *three* of the statements and write a one- or two-paragraph essay on each.

Chinese Geography	Chinese History	Contemporary Affairs (since 1945)
Beijing	Boxer Rebellion	Cultural Revolution
Gobi Desert	Chiang Kai-shek	Deng Xiaoping
Hong Kong	Confucius	Great Leap Forward
Taiwan	Great Wall	Mao Zedong
Tibet	Long March	Red Guard
Yangtze River	Manchu	Taiwan
Yellow River	Mongol	Tiananmen Square
	Opium War	
	sphere of influence	
	Sun Yat-sen	
	Taiping Rebellion	
	Taoism	

Japanese Geography	Japanese History	Contemporary Affairs (since 1945)
archipelago	Bushido	Constitution of 1947
tidal wave	Greater East Asia Co-Prosperity Sphere	Diet
Tokyo	Hiroshima/Nagasaki	Economic Miracle
typhoon	Meiji Restoration	favorable balance of trade
	Pearl Harbor	
	Perry's expedition	
	samurai	
	Shintoism	
	shogun	

Exercise 2: Interpreting political cartoons   You can expect that a few of the multiple-choice questions on a final or standardized exam in Global Studies will be based on political cartoons. You can improve your chances for correctly answering these questions by doing the following:

1. *Before* reading the question, study the cartoon carefully. Try to determine whether the cartoon refers to an event that happened in the distant past or to a fairly recent event. Visual clues will help. Images of technology of the past —a sword or cannon—may suggest that the cartoon is based on events that happened long ago. If the cartoon characters are in modern dress, you know that the cartoon has a modern theme.

2. Recognize whether or not the cartoon is commenting about some political event. Make an educated guess about what that event might be. For clues, look at everything in the cartoon: its title, labels on the cartoon figures, statements in the cartoon bubbles (if any), and expressions on the faces of figures.

Often the joke in a political cartoon comes from its use of irony. Irony means saying the opposite of what is actually meant. Consider, for example, the punch line in the cartoon on page 552. The armed figures representing China's government are quoted as saying: "Well, we sort of gave in to their demands." Did they really give in to the students' demands by killing them? Of course not. The killers' excuse for their actions is nonsense. The cartoonist is mocking the Chinese officials by putting words in their mouths that are obviously false or absurd.

3. Now turn to the question and consider your choices. Eliminate any statements that seem to contradict what you know to be true. (For example: "Totalitarian governments allow free expression of political ideas.") Since most cartoons take a negative or critical view of government policy, look for a statement that expresses such a viewpoint. If you have no idea what the cartoon is about, choose the answer that seems to you most negative or critical.

Practice this cartoon-reading strategy by answering the following questions.

Base your answer to questions 1 and 2 on the cartoon below and on your knowledge of social studies.

1. The cartoon depicts the   (1) favored trading-partner status awarded to China by many Western European countries in the late 20th century   (2) Russo-Japanese War in the early 1900s   (3) separation of China into spheres of influence in the late 1800s (4) ethnocentrism during the Ming dynasty in the 1500s.

2. The situation depicted in the cartoon was brought about by the (1) economic agreements with Western nations signed by Deng Xiaoping   (2) low level of cultural and economic development in China throughout its history   (3) military weakness of China and the European desire for expansion   (4) alliance of the Soviet Union with the Communists and the aid given to the Nationalists by Western European countries.

Base your answer to question 3 on the cartoon below and your knowledge of social studies.

Steve Kelley/Copley News Service

3. The cartoon supports the idea that   (1) maintaining peace and order are the most important responsibilities of governments (2) many young people cannot understand the value of democratic principles   (3) peaceful protests may not succeed against a totalitarian government   (4) totalitarian governments allow free expression of political ideas.

Exercise 3: Answering essay questions   Some essay questions on
final exams require students to explain how nations have been influenced by economic developments. For example, consider the
following:

Economic developments have had major political, economic, and
social effects on specific nations and on the global community.

Economic developments
The Industrial Revolution in the 19th century
Economic modernization in the 20th century

For each of the economic developments listed above:

● Discuss a major effect of the economic development on *either* China
  or Japan.
● Discuss a major effect of the economic development on any *one*
  nation of Western Europe, Africa, Latin America, or the Middle East.

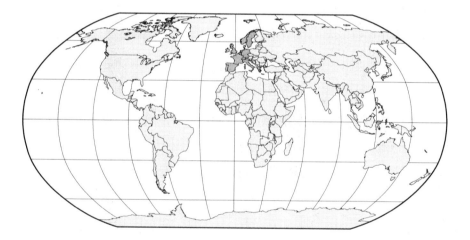

G. WESTERN EUROPE

Be aware that a standardized or final exam in the course will give
equal weight to all regions. There will be no more questions on Western Europe than there are on East Asia or Latin America. Therefore in
reviewing for the exam, you should spend the same amount of time
on this region as on the others.

Review the Main Ideas on pages 304–305 and the map on page 306.
Then complete the following exercises:

Exercise 1: Mastering graph questions   In the multiple-choice section of the exam, at least one question will be based on information presented in the form of a graph. As an example, bar graphs like the one below use parallel bars to compare quantities and to answer questions such as whether one nation has more or less of something than another nation. Thus, the key words to look for (as you read your four choices) are: *most, more, less,* and *least*. Any choice that lacks one of these words is probably the incorrect answer. But be careful. In the question below, even though choice 2 has "more" in it, it is an incorrect answer. Why? Even though choice 3 has "most" in it, it too is an incorrect answer. Why?

Analyze both the following graph and the choices to the question. For *each* choice, explain why it is either the correct answer or one of the incorrect answers.

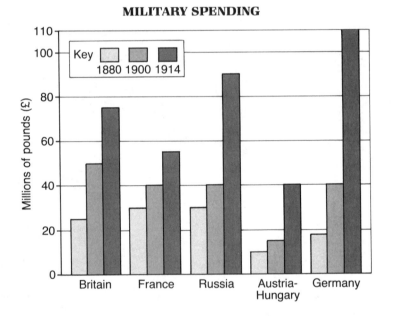

1. Which is an accurate statement based on information in the graph?
(1) In 1914, Austria-Hungary attempted to end the arms race in Europe.   (2) In 1914, the five major European powers spent more on military programs than on any other program.   (3) In 1914, Russia was the most militaristic of all the European nations.   (4) In 1914, Germany spent more money on its military than did any other European nation.

Exercise 2: Three time lines   On three separate pieces of paper, create three time lines showing major events in the history of Western Europe. The first time line should extend from 500 B.C. to A.D. 1500. On it, place the *italicized events* listed in Column A below. On a second time line (from 1500 to 1900), place the *italicized events* listed in Column B. On a third time line (from 1900 to the present), place the *italicized events* listed in Column C. (For a model, refer to the time line on page 359.)

A. History to 1500	B. History, 1500–1900	C. 20th Century
Alexander the Great conquers Egypt	Age of Absolutism	appeasement
Athens	*Otto von Bismarck unifies Germany*	*Atlantic Charter*
Julius Caesar murdered	*Napoleon Bonaparte's coup d'etat*	*Axis Powers*
Charlemagne crowned	John Calvin	*Berlin Airlift*
Christopher Columbus's first voyage	*Oliver Cromwell governs England*	Winston Churchill
Crusades begin	*Declaration of the Rights of Man*	containment
direct democracy	divine right	European Community
Magna Carta	Enlightenment	fascism
manorialism	*French Revolution begins*	Fourteen Points
Middle Ages	*Galileo's discoveries*	*Great Depression begins*
Michelangelo	*Industrial Revolution begins*	*Adolf Hitler comes to power*
Plato	John Locke	*Holocaust begins*
pope	Martin Luther	Iron Curtain
Renaissance begins	*Ferdinand Magellan's voyage*	League of Nations
Roman Catholic Church	Karl Marx	Marshall Plan
Roman empire	Baron de Montesquieu	Nazism
Socrates on trial	Isaac Newton	Nuremburg Trials
	Ninety-Five Theses	Sudetenland
	Protestant Reformation	*Margaret Thatcher becomes prime minister*
	Scientific Revolution	*Treaty of Versailles*
		Truman Doctrine
		United Nations

Exercise 3: Identifying terms   On a piece of paper, write a phrase that identifies each non-italicized item from the previous list. For the meaning of general terms (such as direct democracy), refer to the Glossary. For the names of specific people and historic eras, refer to the Index and to Chapter 7.

Exercise 4: Answering essay questions   Some essay questions on final exams require students to support generalizations with specific facts. For example, consider the following statements:

Statements

1. Throughout history, the lives of people have been shaped by the forms of government under which they live.
2. Religion has often strongly influenced many aspects of a region's culture.
3. Nationalism has been a major force in shaping world events.
4. In the 20th century, international organizations have been formed to meet both national and global needs and interests.

Copy each statement into your notebook. Under each statement, give *three* facts from the history of Western Europe that you could use to support the generalization.

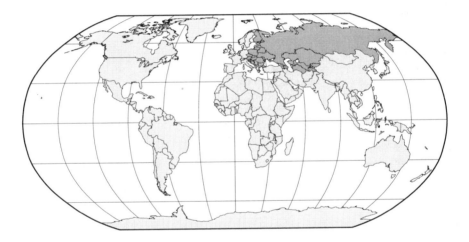

H. RUSSIA AND EASTERN EUROPE

To prepare for exam questions on this region, review the Main Ideas on pages 404–405 and the map on pages 406–407. Then complete the following exercises:

Exercise 1: Organizing names, events, and terms   Unlike earlier lists, the names, events, and terms that follow are listed at random. They will have far greater meaning if you sort them into five categories: "Geography," "History to 1500," "History, 1500–1917," "Era of the Soviet Union," and "Post-Cold War Era." Enter these categories in your notebook. Allow enough space under each category for listing up to 15 names, events, and terms.

Names and Terms

Joseph Stalin	collectivization	Alexander
Ural Mountains	tundra	Solzhenitsyn
Warsaw Pact	Byzantine empire	Peter the Great
Russo-Japanese War	Eastern Orthodox Church	Battle of
Ivan the Great	Crimean War	Stalingrad
Mikhail Gorbachev	Duma	Boris Yeltsin
steppe	Nikita Khrushchev	Marshal Tito
"Peace, Land, and Bread!"	V. I. Lenin	New Economic
pogrom	Serbia	Policy
Nicholas II	perestroika	kulak
Cyrillic	nonaggression pact	Siberia
Mongol empire	Leonid Brezhnev	Black Sea
Russification	Catherine the Great	Lech Walesa
privatization	Decembrists	five-year plan
Leon Trotsky	serfdom	glasnost
zemstvo	détente	Solidarity
purge	Baltic Sea	Volga River
permafrost	Berlin Wall	black market
underground literature	Yalta Conference	

Exercise 2: Analyzing essay questions   You may have gained much information in preparing for an exam. However, you can spoil your chances of doing well on it if you neglect to follow the instructions for answering essay questions. The instructions can be complicated. Consider this question from an actual standardized exam:

Thoughout history, both men and women have had an impact on their times. They have played various roles.

Roles
Scientist
Political reformer
Social reformer
Writer
Revolutionary

A. Select *two* roles from the list. For *each role* selected, identify *one* man or woman who played the role in a specific African, Asian, Latin American, Middle Eastern, or European nation.

B. Describe an action, discovery, or work of *each* individual identified in Part A, and discuss the individual's impact on the political, economic, or social development of his or her nation or society.

In answering Part A of this question, suppose that you had decided to write about Lenin (a Russian revolutionary) and Mao Zedong (a

Chinese revolutionary). For this answer, you would be given only half credit because you selected just one role (revolutionary) instead of the two roles that were called for in the question.

To make sure that you are following instructions, make a chart like this:

Roles	*Examples*
1. Political reformer	Mikhail Gorbachev
2. Revolutionary	V. I. Lenin

Notice that the instructions do *not* indicate that you must choose people from different countries. Therefore the above answer (with two people from Russia) should receive full credit.

Turning to Part B of the question, notice the two key words: "describe" and "discuss." These words suggest that you should write two short paragraphs for each of your chosen leaders:

● one paragraph describing an action by Gorbachev

● one paragraph discussing the impact of Gorbachev's action on the Soviet Union

● one paragraph describing an action by Lenin

● one paragraph discussing the impact of Lenin's action on Russia or the Soviet Union.

Now answer the above essay question, using as examples people other than Gorbachev and Lenin.

I. THE WORLD TODAY

In the essay section of the exam, at least one question will focus on current world problems. Here is an example of such a question:

Since World War II, many areas of the world have been affected by problems.

Problems
Deforestation
Desertification
Terrorism
Air and water pollution
Depletion of the ozone layer
Human rights violations

Choose *three* problems from the list. For *each* problem chosen,

● Select a world region (such as Latin America, Africa, East Asia, or Western Europe) and explain how the problem has been a concern in the region since World War II.

- Explain *one* specific way the problem has had global effects.

You must cite a different region for each problem chosen.

Exercise 1: Charting your answer   An excellent method for preparing to answer such a question is to create a chart for yourself. Select three problems from the list—the three about which you know the most. On the left side of a piece of paper, list your choices. Along the top of the paper, write the regions mentioned in the question. Then for each of the selected problems, think of an example of that problem occurring in one of the regions.

The resulting chart might look like this:

	Latin America	Africa	East Asia	Western Europe
Deforestation	Destruction of the Brazilian rain forest			
Terrorism				IRA bombings in Northern Ireland
Human rights violations			Tiananmen Square, 1989	

This technique helps you in two ways. First, it clarifies your choices. Second, it ensures that your answer will satisfy the requirements of the question.

Create your own chart, using examples different from those in the sample chart.

Exercise 2: Writing the essay   The following question is almost identical in form to the question in Exercise 1. However, different problems have been listed. Practice your skill at essay writing by answering all parts of the question as instructed. Use the chart technique as just described.

Since 1980, many regions of the world have been affected by problems.

Problems
acid rain
depleted ozone layer
greenhouse effect
drug cartels
overpopulation
AIDS
ethnic and religious conflicts
debts of developing nations

Choose *three* of the problems listed. For each problem chosen:

- Select one of the following regions: Latin America, Africa, Eastern Europe, South Asia, or Southeast Asia. Explain how the problem has been a concern in that region since 1980.
- Describe one specific plan for solving the problem. You must use a different region for each problem chosen.

III. More Tips on Answering Test Questions

If you carry out the study plan just described and complete the exercises, you will have practiced a number of strategies for successful test taking. Here are some additional tips that will improve your chances of success in answering both multiple-choice and essay questions.

A. MULTIPLE-CHOICE QUESTIONS

In most standardized Global Studies exams, each multiple-choice question consists of four possible answers, only one of which is correct. How do you increase your chances of selecting the correct answer? Most important, of course, is how much you know about the subject. Even if you are well prepared, however, you can still make unnecessary mistakes by answering questions too hastily. Before answering each question, *take enough time to consider all choices.* If you are not sure about your answer, put a mark next to the question. If you have time near the end of the exam, return to the marked questions and consider your choices a second time.

Marking the standardized exam booklet When given to you at the beginning of the test, an exam booklet on a standardized test is your property. Unless you are specifically instructed not to do so, you may mark and make notes in the booklet. Cross out unlikely answers. Underline key words. Write notes to yourself in the margins. (For other types of exams, check first with the proctor or your teacher before you mark the booklet.)

B. ESSAY QUESTIONS

In most final or standardized exams, one key to success in answering essay questions is to consider the various choices of topics *before* you begin to write.

The five-minute scan Before writing an essay answer, give yourself plenty of time—at least five minutes—to read all the essay questions. Recognize that you may have two kinds of choices to make:

(1) You may have to choose from among a number of questions. For example, the instruction at the beginning of the essay section could read: "*Answer three questions from this part.*" Then if seven questions are given, you can eliminate four of them and write essays on the remaining three.

(2) Within a question, you may have a choice of topics. Every chapter in this text offers practice in handling essay questions of this type.

As you read each question, decide whether you think you know a lot, a fair amount, or a little about the general subject. You might even rate each question according to how well you can handle it. Give a question a *4* rating if it seems easy, a *1* if it seems too difficult. (A rating of *3* or *2* falls somewhere in between.)

Practice this strategy now by reading and rating the following seven questions. You would, of course, choose to write about the three questions that receive your highest ratings. (The questions were those used in a recent New York State Regents exam.)

Part II

ANSWER THREE QUESTIONS FROM THIS PART.

1. Throughout history, groups of people have taken actions to oppose those in power.

   Groups
   Arab Palestinians in the Israeli-occupied territories
   Philosophers of the Enlightenment in France
   Solidarity in Communist Poland
   Sikhs in India
   Boxers in China
   Contras in Nicaragua
   African National Congress (ANC) in the Republic of South Africa

   Select *three* of the groups listed. For each one selected:

   ● State a major goal of the group.
   ● Discuss how the group tried to achieve this goal.

2. Nationalism and imperialism have often been the cause of military conflicts.

   Conflicts
   Hundred Years' War
   19th-century revolutions
      in Latin America
   Napoleonic wars
   Sepoy Mutiny
   World War I
   Vietnam War
   Persian Gulf War

Choose *three* of the conflicts listed. For each conflict chosen, discuss how nationalism *or* imperialism led to the conflict. In your discussion of each conflict chosen:

- Include the historical background of the conflict.
- Explain the specific role of nationalism *or* imperialism as a cause of the conflict. [You must state whether you are discussing nationalism *or* imperialism.]

3. Throughout history, the ideas of leaders have affected their nations. The statements below express the ideas of the leader with whom they are paired.

I am the State. — Louis XIV, France
Promote the upright and banish the crooked, then the people will be submissive. — Confucius, China
Here I stand. I cannot do otherwise. — Martin Luther, a German state
Peace, Bread, Land! — V. I. Lenin, Russia
The Three Principles: the people's livelihood, the people's democracy, the people's nationalism. — Sun Yat-sen, China
The best way of gaining our freedom is not through violence. — Mohandas Gandhi, India

Select *three* of the statements listed. For each one selected:

- Explain the idea of the leader as expressed in the statement.
- Describe how the leader's ideas were carried out in his nation.

4. The nations and regions of the world face various types of problems that affect economic development.

Problems Affecting Economic Development
Shortage of investment capital — Eastern Europe
Desertification — African Sahel
Overpopulation — China
Shortage of natural resources — Japan
Pollution — Western Europe
Dependence on a one-product economy — Latin America

Choose *three* of the problems from the list. For each one chosen:

- Explain how the problem has affected the economic development of the nation or region with which it is paired.
- Discuss *one* specific attempt that has been made by that nation or region to overcome the problem.

5. Geographic factors affect the development of nations throughout the world.

Geographic Factors — Nations
Mineral resources — Great Britain *or* Zaire
River systems — Egypt *or* China
Mountains — Chile *or* Greece
Location — Italy *or* Korea
Climate — Russia *or* India
Strategic waterways — Panama *or* Turkey

Select *three* of the geographic factors listed. For each one selected, discuss how the geographic factor affected the political *or* economic development of *one* of the nations with which it is paired.

6. Throughout history, the basic political, social, and economic rights of some groups have been violated.

Groups of People
Serfs on European medieval manors
Untouchables in India
Jews in Europe during World War II
Peasant farmers in Latin America
Women and children during the early Industrial Revolution
Kurds during the 20th century
Dissidents in the Soviet Union under Stalin

Select *three* groups from the list. For each one selected, use specific historical information to explain how the group's basic political, social, *or* economic rights were violated.

7. Certain events or occurrences in history have brought about significant changes.

Events/Occurrences
Voyages of Columbus
Glorious Revolution in England
Failure of the Weimar Republic in Germany
Defeat of Japan in World War II
Westernization of Iran by Shah Pahlevi
Signing of the Camp David Accords by Egypt and Israel
Adoption of glasnost in the Soviet Union

Select *three* of the events or occurrences listed. For each one selected:

● Describe the event or occurrence.
● Explain how the event or occurrence led to significant changes in a specific nation or region.

Following the command words   Be sure to observe the word of command that tells you how to handle a question. One question may direct you to *identify* topic X. Only a sentence or two is required to carry out this direction. Another question may direct you to *describe* topic Y. You can satisfy this direction by writing a paragraph that simply tells about the topic without offering any analysis or evaluation. A third question may direct you to *discuss* topic Z. Here you must write a paragraph that combines descriptive statements with statements of analysis or evaluation—for example, whether you think Z had a positive or a negative effect. A fourth question might ask you to *show* how X had an effect on Y. In this case, you should write a paragraph in which you cite a specific example that illustrates the given idea.

C. CHECKING YOUR WORK

If time remains after you have written your last essay, take every available minute to review your work—both your multiple-choice answers and your essays. Have you answered every question? Have you completely carried out every direction? Have you numbered your essays? Can you recall something that you were unable to remember on your first attempt? In other words, take the time to fully review and improve your answers—and your final score.

GLOSSARY

abdicate to give up the throne

Aborigine a native person of Australia

absolute monarchy a system of hereditary rulers who try to keep all political power in their hands

abstractionist an artist who creates objects or images that are not similar to forms in the real world

acid rain rain or snow with higher than normal acidity

alms charity

animism a belief that spirits inhabit both living and nonliving things

annexation the act of making an area that belongs to one country part of another country

anthropology the scientific study of human cultures—both past and present

anti-Semitism a form of racism directed against Jewish people

apartheid the policy of South Africa's former white-controlled government to keep the races from mixing

appeasement a policy of yielding to demands of a rival power in order to avoid war

aqueduct a structure used to carry large volumes of flowing water over distances

arable suitable for farming

archeology the study of material remains of past human societies

archipelago a group of many islands

arid dry

armistice an agreement to stop fighting

arranged marriage one in which the choice of partners is decided by both sets of parents

artifact an object created by a culture in the past

artisan a skilled worker who provides services or makes a product

astrolabe a navigational device that tells how far north or south one is from the equator

autocrat a ruler who holds absolute power

automation the replacement of workers by machines

autonomy the quality of being self-governing

balance of power a world situation whereby two equally strong powers or alliances oppose each other

bar graph a graph that compares various quantities using bars of different lengths

bauxite an aluminum ore

big lie technique the deliberate gross distortion of the truth

birth rate number of births per thousand people

black market an illegal trade in goods

blitzkrieg a rapid military attack over a large area, first used by the Germans in 1939

bloc a group

boyar a Russian noble

Brahman a member of the highest caste in Hindu society

brain drain the continued emigration of many of a country's educated people

broken projection a way of representing the major continents fairly accurately in terms of shapes and relative sizes

Bronze Age a period of human culture marked by the use of bronze tools and weapons, 4000–3000 B.C.

Buddhism the religion founded by Siddhartha Gautama in India around 500 B.C.

Bushido the code of behavior of the samurai, Japanese warriors of feudal times

cabinet a council of ministers who advise the head of a government

capital money needed to start or expand a business; also tools, machines, and buildings used to manufacture products

capitalism an economic system based on private ownership of capital goods and a free market

caravel a small, sturdy, three-masted sailing ship

cardinal a high official of the Roman Catholic Church

caste system hereditary social system that involves rules and roles for members of each caste

cathedral a large church that is the official seat of a bishop

caudillo the Spanish word for military dictator

census a count of an area's population

chemotherapy a cancer treatment using chemicals

chivalry a code of behavior for medieval knights

chlorofluorocarbon (CFC) a gaseous compound that is used in refrigerants, cleaning solvents, and aerosol propellants

Christianity the religion based on the teachings of Jesus

circle graph a graph that compares different parts of a whole by dividing a circle into wedges

citizen a person who owes allegiance to and is entitled to protection from a state

city-state an independently governed city that controlled surrounding areas of farmland

civil disobedience one's refusal to obey laws one considers unjust

civilization a complex society with an elaborate government

civil service a system of hiring and promotion in government employment based on competitive exams

clan a group of people descended from a common ancestor

climate the pattern of weather in a place over a long time

coalition government one in which two or more political parties form an alliance in order to rule

coastal plain a low, flat area along a coast

cold war an ongoing conflict between two countries or alliance systems that stops short of actual fighting

collectivization a government-forced change from many small private farms to larger collective farms, some of which were owned and operated by the government

comedy a humorous play that pokes fun at certain people or customs

command economy an economy in which key economic decisions are made by the government, and all major industries are under government control

Commercial Revolution a series of economic changes in Europe in the 1500s and 1600s, including the introduction of mercantilism and capitalism and shift in economic power from the Italian city-states to nations on the Atlantic Ocean

commune a rural community in which land is owned in common (or by the government) and work assignments and pay are handed out by managers

communism economic and political system whereby the economy and all other aspects of society are under the direct control of the government, which in turn, is controlled by the Communist party

Computer Revolution changes brought about by the widespread use of computers

Confucianism philosophy based on the ideas of Confucius, including duty to one's parents and society

containment a country's foreign policy that aims to prevent the expansion or influence of another country

continental climate a climate with cold winters and hot summers

contras Nicaraguan rebels who fought against the Sandinista regime in the 1980s

cottage industry an industry based in the home

cotton gin a machine that separates seeds from raw cotton

Counter-Reformation efforts of the Roman Catholic Church in the 16th century to combat Protestantism and reform itself

coup d'état a quick overthrow of a government by a small group

creole a person of European descent born in the West Indies and Spanish colonies

crucifixion the act of being nailed or bound to a cross

Crusades a series of military expeditions in the Middle Ages of Christian armies that sought to win control of the Holy Land in the Middle East

cultural diffusion the process by which ideas and practices spread from one area to another

culture all the customs, practices, and beliefs of a group of people

cuneiform a system of writing that used wedge-shaped characters to represent words and ideas

Cyrillic the alphabet that is the base for the modern Russian, Ukrainian, Serbian, and Bulgarian languages

death rate number of deaths per thousand people

decimal the numeral system based on tens

demilitarize to remove troops and armaments from an area

democracy a system of government by which people have a say (either directly or indirectly) in determining policies; also the protection of people's basic rights

democratic socialism an economic and political system in which free elections are held and some major industries are under government ownership

desertification the process by which land becomes so arid that it turns into a desert

détente policies aimed at reducing tensions between nations

developed nation a country that is highly industrialized and has a high standard of living

developing nation a country whose economy is more agricultural than industrial and whose standard of living is relatively low; underdeveloped nation

dharma a set of religious duties that each Hindu must exercise

diaspora the scattering or dispersion of people, especially of the Jews from Palestine

dictatorship a system of government by which a ruler has total (or nearly total) control over a nation's political system

Diet the Japanese legislature

direct democracy a democratic form of government in which all citizens can vote on pending laws

dissident one who criticizes official or established policies

divine right the idea that a monarch's authority comes directly from God
drug cartel an international organization of illegal drug traffickers
dynasty a succession of rulers from the same family

eclipse the obscuring of the sun or moon by the shadow of another celestial body
economic system the way that a society produces and distributes its goods and
services
embargo a ban on trade with a country or group of countries
enclosure movement the acquisition of lands formerly held by English farmers
in common
Enlightenment the era in European history (1700s) that emphasized rational
thinking and scientific advancements
ethnic cleansing a removal of an ethnic group from an area by force and terror
ethnocentrism a belief that one's culture is superior to all other cultures
excommunicate to expel someone from a church
existentialism a philosophy that states there is no absolute right or wrong
expansionism the addition of territories to a country, usually through warfare
extended family parents, children, grandparents, and other relatives all living
together
external slavery forced labor that involves transferring enslaved persons from
one world region to another
extraterritoriality an exemption from the jurisdiction of a country's laws and
courts

facsimile an exact copy
factory system the production of goods in a factory instead of in the homes of
workers
fallow left unplanted
fascism a system of government that demands total obedience to a dictator, uses
force and censorship to eliminate opposition, preaches an extreme form of
nationalism, and glorifies militarism
fasting refusing to eat
favorable balance of trade a situation whereby the value of a country's exports
exceeds the value of its imports
feudalism a political, economic, and social system involving protection
fief a feudal estate
Five Pillars of Wisdom basic religious practices of Muslims
five-year plan a government plan for production in a country's industries and
farms over a five-year period
free enterprise a situation whereby private businesses are free to operate for
profit in competition with one another and with little government interference
free trade zone an area with a general absence of tariffs and other restrictions
on international trade
fundamentalist, religious a person who adheres strictly to a set of religious
beliefs

gaucho a Spanish word for cowboy
general strike an agreement among various groups of workers not to go to work

genetic engineering the altering of genes of plants and animals

genocide the deliberate killing of many members of an ethnic, religious, or political group

geography the study of the earth's physical features and their effect on human cultures

geothermal energy heat from within the earth

ghetto a part of a city where Jews were forced to live

glasnost the policy of opening up Soviet society and political process by granting greater freedoms

global warming a theory that worldwide temperatures may increase gradually in the next century

glyph a symbolic figure or character in the Mayan writing system

golden age a time of unusually great artistic and scientific achievements in a culture

greenhouse effect the trapping of the sun's heat by gases in the atmosphere

Green Revolution increased production of food supplies resulting from scientific advances

grid pattern one in which intersecting straight lines form right angles

gross domestic product (GDP) a measure of a country's total wealth produced in one year

gross domestic product per capita a country's total wealth produced in one year divided by its population

guerrilla warfare small bands of fighters conducting hit-and-run attacks against larger forces

hacienda a Spanish word for a large estate

haiku a form of Japanese unrhymed poetry that usually had a set number of syllables

hemisphere a half of a globe

heresy a belief that is counter to official doctrines of a church

heretic one who dissents from accepted church doctrine

hieroglyphics a writing system that uses picture symbols

Hinduism a traditional religion of India

historic culture a culture of the past whose people left a written record

Holocaust the systematic killing of Jews by German authorities during World War II

horse collar a collar that allows a horse to be attached to a plow

humanism the idea that each individual is unique and has great worth

human right one of the several basic rights that belong to all people

icon a representation of a sacred Christian figure

ideology a system of beliefs

illiterate one who cannot read or write

illuminated manuscript a hand-copied book illustrated with gold, silver, or brilliant colors, with elaborate designs, or miniature pictures

imperialism a policy of strong countries aimed at gaining social, economic, and political control over weaker areas

impressionist an artist who uses dabs or strokes of color in order to convey qualities of light reflecting off a surface

indemnity a sum of money given in payment for damages suffered

Index a list of books that Roman Catholics were prohibited from reading

indirect democracy one in which citizens elect representatives who will pass laws

indulgence a pardon for sins granted by officials of the Roman Catholic Church

industrial age the time when most workers were employed in manufacturing jobs

Industrial Revolution the change from producing goods in home workshops with hand tools to mass-production in factories using complex machinery

infidel a nonbeliever in a particular religion

inflation major increases in prices

innovation any newly invented process

Inquisition a special tribunal (court) of the Roman Catholic Church whose chief purpose was to fight heresies

intensive farming methods methods (such as applying fertilizer and irrigating) used to cultivate the land to its maximum extent

interdependence the way that societies and nations depend upon one another for economic existence

interior plain a low, flat area in the interior of a continent

internal slavery forced labor in which the captive workers are held within their native region

Intifada an uprising among young Palestinians against Israeli rule

irrigation methods of bringing water to arid areas to aid farming

Islam the religion based on the teachings of Mohammed

joint-stock company a business organization that raises capital by the sale of shares of ownership

Judaism the religion of Jewish people that teaches belief in one God and the keeping of God's moral commandments

junta a group of persons who control a government after seizing power

karma the force generated by a person's actions that determines that person's next existence

khan a Mongol ruler

kibbutz an Israeli collective community, often an agricultural one

Knesset Israel's legislature

knight a medieval noble and soldier who had sworn allegiance to a greater lord

Koran the holy book of Islam

kulak a Russian farmer who was moderately well-off

laissez-faire a French phrase ("leave it alone") that describes a policy of noninterference by a government in its economy

land reform the breaking up of large estates in order to give small plots to landless peasants

leach to remove minerals from the soil by the action of water percolating

legion a unit of the Roman army

life expectancy the number of years that someone (usually a newly born infant) is expected to live

line graph a graph that shows various quantities of something (whatever can be measured, such as population or income) by means of dots and connecting lines

literacy rate the percentage of a group of people who can read and write

logic a set of rules for reasoning

magnetic compass a device with a needle that always points north, used in navigation

maize corn

malnutrition the condition of having not enough or the wrong kinds of food

mammography X-ray examination of the breasts

mandate a territory placed under the rule of a foreign power by the League of Nations

mandate of heaven the idea that a Chinese emperor had the right to rule

manor a large piece of land on which were located the lord's home, a church, and cottages for peasants and artisans

manorialism an economic, and social system involving a medieval lord and his estate and the peasants, artisans, and clergy who lived on it

Maori native person of New Zealand

map projection any one of a number of methods of showing the round surface of the earth on a flat surface

market economy an economy in which many businesses compete to sell their goods and services

Marxist one who believes in the socialist theories of Karl Marx

media forms of mass communication, including television, radio, recorded music, newspapers, books, and magazines

medieval of the Middle Ages, A.D. 500–1500

meditation the practice of focusing one's thoughts for a period of time

Mediterranean climate a climate characterized by hot, dry summers and mild, moist winters

mercantilism the theory that a country could enrich itself by obtaining minerals and other valuable raw materials from its overseas colonies and, in turn, by selling its manufactured goods to its colonists

Mercator projection a way of representing the earth on a map so that all lines of latitude have the same length as the equator, and all lines of longitude and latitude are parallel, straight lines

Mesopotamia an historic name for the area between the Tigris and Euphrates rivers

mestizo a person who has both European and Native American ancestors

militarism a nation's policy of building up its armed forces with the goal of having more military power than its rivals

mission a church and its agricultural lands in colonial Latin America

modernization the process of adopting new customs and technologies

Mollweide projection a way of representing the earth on a map so that the relative sizes of the continents are accurate, but not their shapes

monogamous the practice of having one spouse or one sexual partner at a time

monotheism the belief in a single God

monsoon changeable winds that in one season might bring heavy rains, while in other seasons may bring dry weather

mosaic any one of many patterns made from small tiles of glass, gold leaf, or marble

mosque a Muslim place of worship

movable type type in which each letter is set on a separate block

mulatto a person who has both European and African ancestors
multinational corporation large businesses that have operations in many countries
mummy a carefully preserved dead body
Muslim someone who follows the Islamic religion

nationalism loyalty to one's own country and/or cultural heritage; the belief that an ethnic group should have its own, independent nation
nationalize to take ownership, or control, by a government
nation-state a large area in which people share a common culture and language and are governed by a central government
Nazism the program of the German Nazi party, including totalitarian government, control over industries, and a dominant role for the Nordic race
neo-Nazi one who acts somewhat like the Nazis did and who admires the policies of the Nazis
nepotism the awarding of jobs to members of one's own family
nirvana in Buddhism, a state of spiritual bliss and release from worldly cares
nitrate a chemical compound, often used as a fertilizer
nomad a person who moves from place to place, usually to seek water and vegetation for grazing animals
nonalignment a policy whereby a country avoids all military alliances
notation the recording of musical notes on paper
nuclear family a household made up of two parents and their children

oasis a green area within a desert that has a source of water
one-crop economy an economy that relies heavily on the production and sale of just one crop
oral tradition the knowledge of the past that is transmitted by word of mouth
origami the Japanese art of folding paper to make figures, flowers, and other natural objects
outback the dry interior of Australia
overpopulation the condition of having too many people in an area
ozone shield layer of ozone gas in the upper atmosphere

padre a Spanish word for priest
Pampas vast, grassy plains in Argentina
Pan-Africanism a movement that seeks the unity and cooperation of all African peoples
papyrus a plant of the Nile Valley that was pressed and made into paper
Parliament the two-house legislature of Great Britain, Canada, or a number of other countries
partition to divide a country into two or more separate nations or as parts of other nations
pass laws South African laws that required blacks to carry a passbook that indicated where a person could live, work, or travel
patrician a member of the landowning class of the Roman Republic
peaceful coexistence a country's foreign policy of getting along with other nations
peasant a farmer with little or no land of his or her own
perestroika attempts at restructuring the Soviet economy under Gorbachev to allow free enterprise
permafrost permanently frozen soil

perspective an artistic technique that gives a feeling of depth to a two-dimensional scene

pesticide an agent (often chemical) used to kill pests (usually insects)

pharaoh a monarch of ancient Egypt

plateau an elevated plain

plebeian a citizen of the Roman Republic who was a farmer, artisan, or merchant

pogram organized attacks (often government sanctioned) against unarmed peoples, especially Jews

polar projection way of representing either the Northern or Southern Hemisphere on a map with the respective pole in the center of the map

polar region one of two regions located near the North and South poles, characterized by extremely low temperatures

political system the way in which people are governed

polygamy the practice whereby a man has two or more wives at a time

polytheism a belief in or worship of more than one god

population density the number of people per square mile or some other measure of how crowded an area is

porcelain a type of fine pottery

post-industrial revolution the change from a society in which most workers are employed in industries to one in which most workers are employed in service occupations

power loom a machine that made cloth using water power

precedent a court decision that influences later court cases

predestination the belief that a person's salvation is determined at birth

prehistoric culture a culture of the past whose people did not leave any written record

prime minister the chief executive in a parliamentary democracy

privatization the policy of selling government enterprises to private owners

proletariat a worker or the working class

protectionism government policies that attempt to limit foreign imports

Protestant Reformation the reform movement aimed at the Roman Catholic Church's practices and powers

provisional temporary

proxy war a war in which a power supports one side in a conflict but does not get involved itself

public transportation means of travel that move groups of people

public utility a company that provides essential services, such as electricity and water, to the public

racism the belief in the superiority of one racial group over others

radiation therapy a treatment of cancer using x-rays

radical extreme

radiocarbon dating the determination of the age of objects from the distant past by measuring the amount of radioactive carbon decay

rain forest a dense woodland that receives much rainfall

referendum a vote on a public issue

region any area of any size that is different in some way from neighboring areas

reincarnation the belief that one's soul reappears after one's death in another living form

Renaissance a period in European history known for the revival of classical Greek and Roman learning and achievements in the arts

reparations payments for war damages

republic a democratic form of government that has no monarch; a government whose officials are elected by the voters

revolution a violent overthrow of a political system; also any profound change in society

rotation of crops the growing of different crops in succession in one field

rural of the countryside

Russification the government policy to make the non-Russian peoples within the Russian empire into Russian speakers and members of the Russian Orthodox Church

samurai a Japanese warrior in feudal times

Sandinistas Nicaraguan leftists who overthrew a military dictatorship in 1979 and ruled until 1990

satellite a country politically and economically dominated or controlled by another, more powerful nation

savanna a tropical or subtropical grassland that has scattered trees

scapegoating the blaming of one group for problems caused by others or by society as a whole

scientific method a systematic method of making observations and experiments before drawing conclusions

Scientific Revolution dramatic advances in scientific knowledge made by Europeans in the 16th and 17th centuries

scorched earth policy the wartime destruction of one's homes, crops, factories, and other resources so they do not fall into the hands of an invading force

secular nonreligious, worldly

self-determination the goal of an ethnic or national group under the rule of others to win independence

sepoy an Indian who served as a soldier for a European power

serf a peasant who was tied to his or her lord's manor

service industry a business that specializes in providing a service

shah a Persian monarch

Shiite pertaining to one of two major groups within Islam—the Shi'a

Shintoism a traditional religion of Japan

shogun Japan's most powerful feudal lord, appointed by the emperor to govern the country

Sikhism a monotheistic religion of northern India that involves belief in reincarnation

silicon a chemical element

silicon chip a tiny square of silicon with electronic circuits printed on it

simony the buying and selling of Church positions

slash-and-burn technique the clearing of an area for farming by cutting down trees and brush and then burning them

socialism an economic system in which the means of production are publicly owned

socialist one who advocates socialism

socialist realism a Marxist idea to use art, literature, and music mainly to transform society

social mobility the degree to which people can move up and out of a lower social class

social revolution a revolution in which one social class tries to become or becomes the most powerful one

solar energy the heat from the sun's rays

solid waste garbage

sonnet a 14-line poem

soviet a Russian council or assembly

sphere of influence a geographical area in which a foreign nation had special and exclusive economic rights

spinning jenny a spinning machine that spun eight threads at one time from cotton fibers

steppe flat, arid land that is usually treeless

strait a narrow passage of water

subarctic zone the area just south of the Arctic Circle, characterized by cold winters, permafrost, and little vegetation

subcontinent a major subdivision of a continent

subregion an area that is part of a larger region but that is different in some way from the rest of this region

sub-Saharan Africa all of Africa that lies south of the Sahara Desert

subsidy money provided to a business by a government

subsistence farming farming that produces just enough food to feed one's family or village

sultan an Ottoman ruler

Sunni pertaining to one of two major branches of Islam—Sunnism

superpower an extremely powerful nation

surplus an amount of something that is more than needed for one's use

suspension bridge a bridge whose roadway is suspended from two or more cables

taiga subarctic forest land dominated by conifers

Taoism a traditional religion of China that emphasized learning from nature

tariff a tax that a government imposes on imported goods

technical assistance help in learning new technologies

technological innovation a change in the way things are made

technology a culture's methods and tools for making things

temperate zone one of two zones located north and south of the tropical zone, characterized by seasonal changes and moderate temperatures and amounts of rainfall

terraced farming farming on level strips of land dug into the steep slopes of mountainsides

terrorism use of violence or threat of violence to instill fear for political purposes

third world a former group of nations not aligned with either the Communist or the non-Communist blocs

three-field system a form of crop rotation in which in any given year two fields are planted and the third is left unplanted

tidal wave a high wave, usually caused by an earthquake

totalitarianism a political system by which the government has *total* control over all institutions in society, including the press and religions

total war a war in which civilian populations were often targets, as were military units, supply lines, and factories

toxic poisonous

tradition the observation of old customs

traditional economy an economy in which ways of producing goods are continued without change for generations

tragedy a play that portrays human conflicts from which there is no escape

trench warfare military conflict in which each side digs trenches facing the other

tributary a river that empties into a larger river

tribute a tax payment that implies submission to the payee

tropical zone an area near the equator characterized by high temperatures, heavy rainfall, and rain forests

tundra a treeless area that has permanently frozen subsoil

two-field system a method of farming whereby in a given year one field was planted and the other was left fallow so the latter could recover its fertility

typhoon a large system of winds that rotate around a center

ultimatum a list of final demands

underground literature illegal writings that criticize government policies; they are published (or copied) and passed around secretly

unfavorable balance of trade a situation whereby the value of a country's imports exceeds the value of its exports

unitary system of government a system in which power resides only in a central government

untouchable a member of the lowest caste in Hindu society

urbanization a shift in population from rural areas to cities

utopian socialist one who advocates that people form ideal communities in which all property and means of production are held in common

vassal a medieval lord who had received land from a greater lord in exchange for loyalty and protection

veto to refuse to approve something, thereby defeating it

viceroy an agent of the Spanish monarchy in a Spanish colony; he was the most powerful official in a colony

warlord a military leader who uses his command of an army to rule over a part of a country

warm-water port a port that is ice-free all year or nearly all year

welfare state a nation whose government assumes responsibility for providing for many of the economic needs of its citizens

Westernization the adoption of Western ideas and policies by non-Western peoples

zaibatsu powerful combination of Japanese banks and industries, each controlled by a wealthy family

zemstvo a local assembly in czarist Russia

Zionist a person who wished to establish a Jewish homeland in Palestine

INDEX

ACKNOWLEDGMENTS

Maps: Burmar Technical Corporation

Drawn art: Ed Malsberg and Neal Malsberg

Photographs and Prints: page 5, George Rodger, Magnum; page 13, American Museum of Natural History; page 16, M. Bryan Ginsberg; page 18, The Bettmann Archive; page 43, UN Photo by M. Grant; page 45, Reuters/Bettmann Newsphotos; page 51, George Holton/ Photo Researchers; page 56 (left), Arno Hammacher/Photo Researchers; page 56 (right), UPI/Bettmann; page 65, UPI/Bettmann; page 68, UN Photo; page 72, Reuters/Bettmann; page 75, Ray Ellis/Photo Researchers; page 78, Reuters/Bettmann; page 91, UPI/Bettmann; page 95, René Burri/Magnum; page 97, Louis Goldman/Photo Researchers; page 100, Arthur Glauberman/Photo Researchers; page 106, UN Photos; page 107 (left), The Bettmann Archive; page 107 (right), Library of Congress; page 113, UPI/Bettmann Newsphotos; page 114, Reuters/Bettmann Newsphotos; page 119, UPI/Bettmann; page 121, M. Granitsas/The Image Works; page 141, René Burri/Magnum Photos; page 145, Carl Frank/Photo Researchers; page 148, The Bettmann Archive; page 153, Steve Jantzen; page 158, The Bettmann Archive; page 165, The Bettmann Archive; page 169, Reuters/Bettmann; page 172, Carl Frank/Photo Researchers; page 177, Charles Trainor/Photo Researchers; page 180, Art Resource, NY/Frida Kahlo, "Self-portrait"/Private Collection; page 183, UPI/Bettmann Newsphotos; page 189, The Bettmann Archive; page 199, M. Bryan Ginsberg; page 206, The Bettmann Archive; page 207, The Bettmann Archive; page 209, Josephus Daniels/Photo Researchers; page 214, The Bettmann Archive; page 216, The Bettmann Archive; page 222, K. Bubriski/UN Photos; page 225, John Spragens, Jr./Photo Researchers; page 228, Reuters/Bettmann Newsphotos; page 245, Bruno Barbey/Magnum Photos; page 248, The Bettmann Archive; page 257, UPI/Bettmann Newsphotos; page 261, UPI/Bettmann Newsphotos; page 262, UPI/Bettmann Newsphotos; page 273, Robert A. Isaacs/ Photo Researchers; page 276, The Bettmann Archive; page 279, The Bettmann Archive; page 283, Paolo Koch/Photo Researchers; page 293, S. Smith/The Image Works; page 309, Henri Cartier-Bresson/ Magnum Photos; page 313, Greek National Tourist Organization; page 317, The Bettmann Archive; page 320, The Bettmann Archive;

page 329, Library of Congress; page 332, Brown Brothers; page 342, The Bettmann Archive; page 345, The Bettmann Archive; page 347, The Bettmann Archive; page 350, The Bettmann Archive; page 361, The Bettmann Archive; page 364, The Bettmann Archive; page 378, Library of Congress; page 381, The Bettmann Archive; page 384, Yutaka Nagata/UN Photo; page 391, Reuters/Bettman Newsphotos; page 409, Henri Cartier-Bresson/Magnum Photos; page 415, Cornell Capa/Magnum Photos; page 420, The Bettmann Archive; page 421, The Bettmann Archive; page 425, The Bettmann Archive; page 432, The Bettmann Archive; page 441, Library of Congress; page 450, UPI/Bettmann Newsphotos; page 457, Library of Congress; page 459, Perry Morse; page 461, S. Smith/The Image Works; page 464, Reuters/Bettmann Newsphotos; page 469, Sergio Penchansky/Photo Researchers; page 474, Wicks/Rothco Cartoons; page 493, Ulrike Welsch/Photo Researchers; page 499, Spencer Grant/Stock Boston; page 510, Reuters/Bettmann Newsphotos; page 512, Reuters/Bettmann Newsphotos; page 518, Spencer Grant/Stock Boston; page 522, Jon Burbank/The Image Works.